Two Minutes to Glory

CHURCHILL DOWNS

Two Minutes to Glory

THE OFFICIAL HISTORY OF THE KENTUCKY DERBY
IN COOPERATION WITH CHURCHILL DOWNS

CHURCHILL DOWNS

Pamela Brodowsky & Tom Philbin

Collins
An Imprint of HarperCollinsPublishers

We would like to thank the following people for their valuable contributions:

Churchill Downs Incorporated, for allowing us to use various parts of their historical information in the making of *Two Minutes to Glory,* as well as:

Charts 1875–1895 property of Churchill Downs Incorporated

All photos: Copyrighted Churchill Downs Incorporated/Kinetic Corporation

The Daily Racing Form Inc. for Charts 1896–1997, copyright 2006

Daily Racing Form, Inc. and Equibase Company for Charts 1998–2006, copyrighted 2006

Reprinted with permission of the copyright owner.

HarperCollins books may be purchased for educational, business, or sales promotional use. For information, please write: Special Markets Department, HarperCollins Publishers, 10 East 53rd Street, New York, NY 10022.

FIRST EDITION

Designed by Renato Stanisic

Printed on acid-free paper

Library of Congress Cataloging-in-Publication Data is available upon request.

ISBN: 978-0-06-123655-6

07 08 09 10 11   WBC/RRD   10 9 8 7 6 5 4 3 2 1

*For Carol Bloomgarden, a great reference librarian,
part detective, part nurse, who has been immensely helpful to me for many years.
Every author should be lucky enough to have access to someone like you.* —**TOM**

*For all of the people who feel that a great racehorse's life isn't over when
he stops racing, and for those who do everything in their power to provide these grand
animals with a happy, healthy, and safe retirement.* —**PAM**

Contents

Contents

Foreword
Pat Day

As a twenty-six-year veteran of Churchill Downs, I can honestly say you are in for the ride of your life. There is no denying it—America loves horse racing. We all hold a special place in our hearts for the celebrated races and the legendary horses that have provided us with breathtaking entertainment and golden memories, and there is no race that provides those memories and that pulse-pounding excitement more than the Kentucky Derby.

Pam Brodowsky and Tom Philbin have captured both memories and great excitement for us in *Two Minutes to Glory: The Official History of the Kentucky Derby*. Here you will experience all I have from horseback—and much, much, more.

This history of the greatest race of all is both historical and statistical; chock full of facts, factoids, and statistics but with the added punch of the stories behind the stories. In *Two Minutes to Glory* you will find out not only who crossed the finish line first but the amazing stories behind these great racehorses—and the humans behind them. Horse racing is a team effort, and with every team there comes another story, another dream to be realized or lost.

Brodowsky and Philbin have gone back 132 years in time, right to the first Derby, through countless records, stories, and clippings, to create for us this comprehensive history and collection of compelling race day stories. Every single race is described, and its backstory revealed.

I must say I was very impressed with the feeling that flows throughout this book. Most people aren't aware of the emotional highs and lows of horse racing, or what the jockeys, trainers, and owners go through. Brodowsky and Philbin get to the heart of the matter in more ways than one.

Having ridden racehorses for thirty-two years in little and big towns, on all kinds of tracks, in all kinds of weather and all kinds of situations, I thought I had seen, experienced, and heard just about everything related to horse racing. But I am happy to say this book taught me a few things and summoned up some wonderful memories. I hope you enjoy it. God Bless.

Pat Day spent thirty-two years as a jockey, retiring in 2005. In the Hall of Fame, he is the fourth leading rider in U.S. racing history, with 8,804 wins, and the all-time leader in career earnings, $297,941,912.

Introduction:
The Greatest Race of All

If one were to ask what the premiere horse racing event of the year is, nine out of ten times the answer would be, The Kentucky Derby. There is no other when it comes to prestige. Being the winner of the Kentucky Derby is as important to a horse's future as it is to the jockey and owner of the horse. It's the run for the roses, the crowning moment, in horse racing. Although some may argue that the Triple Crown is the most significant triumph, you have to consider the Triple Crown as being unobtainable if you have yet to capture the minds and hearts of the world and call yourself the winner of the Kentucky Derby.

People literally spend decades trying to win this race. Throughout its history there are many examples of people in their eighties, even nineties, whose dream of winning has been alive since they were young men and women. And some of them do finally win it.

And everyone—as everyone knows—has a chance. Indeed, many, many more non-favorites than favorites have won the race: you don't have to have Secretariat as your great-great-grandfather to win. Hall of Fame trainer Allen Jerkens, two of whose horses, Onion and Prove Out, actually beat Secretariat, expressed it perfectly. "What you know for certain," he said, "is that you don't know nothing for certain." In that moment before the gates clang open and the bell rings, you know that your horse, sired from nothing and out of nothing, can somehow be there at the end and cross the wire first.

Believe that.

This book, prepared in cooperation with some great folks at Churchill Downs, takes the most comprehensive and detailed look at the Kentucky Derby ever. It has two parts.

Part I is a capsule history of Churchill Downs and the Kentucky Derby. It tells the story of two incomparable people: Colonel M. Lewis Clark Jr., who dreamed and fought the Derby into existence, and Colonel Matthew Winn, who saved it when it was in the stretch run, tired, gasping for air, about to break down. But it also delves into all the wonderful traditions of the Derby—mint juleps, breathtaking hats, and how and why they drape a garland of roses over the winning horse. It is Kentucky Derby trivia heaven—and includes the three main human cogs in the team—jockey, trainer, and owner—who combine to go after that Derby win. Collectively—and individually—they are extraordinary people.

Part II, "Two Minutes to Glory, Race Day Stories, 1875–2006," is the heart of the book. It tells the story of each of the 132 races—not merely a description of who won the particular race and how. A variety of sidelights and/or backstories helps make each win more compelling, more real. Horse and rider are not just names and numbers on a page, but horses and men with hearts and souls.

The 1941 Derby, for example, brings us the story of Whirlaway, a horse his trainer characterized as not only psychotic but dumb, but who was worth training because he could outrun the wind.

There is the 1935 story of Omaha, a big horse with a nasty habit—if another horse brushed against him, he would stop running and attack the malefactor.

Other backstories will raise gooseflesh—and cause a few tears—as their protagonists triumph in ways that go far beyond winning a horse race.

In 1951, for example, Conn McCreary, as he sat on Count Turf at the post waiting for the race to start, knew he was not just riding for a victory in the Kentucky Derby—he was riding for his life.

There is the 1999 story of Chris Antley, sitting astride a 30–1 shot after climbing up out of an abyss of drink and drugs, looking down that straightaway, wondering if he could make the rest of his dream come true. And there is the 2005 story of 50–1 shot Giacomo, thundering to victory in the last seventy yards of a thrilling race, and his seventy-nine-year-old who raised him bursting into tears because Giacomo is so symbolic of life, having beaten another opponent called Death when he was a foal.

Throughout the book, charts set out just about every fact you could want to know about the Kentucky Derby, and of course photos galore bring to vivid life all these human and equine heroes.

Have a good ride!

—*Pam and Tom*

PART I

M. Lewis Clark

CHAPTER 1

The Kentucky Derby and Churchill Downs, a Capsule History

Central Kentucky and the area around Lexington has long been a breeding ground for great racehorses. There are a number of reasons. One is the porous nature of the subsoil; there's good drainage at all times. As Joe Estes of *Blood-Horse* magazine once said, "Hard feet and bone cannot be developed in horses walking around on marshy, soggy or ill-drained land."

Another is the fertility of the soil, which is laced with calcium and phosphorus, and nourishes a Kentucky strain of bluegrass called *Poa pratensis,* which grows particularly well in the area around Lexington, where hundreds of horse farms are clustered. Horses who eat this grass tend to have strong but light frames that can support their powerhouse musculature but not weigh them down when they gallop. Horses so raised are, in a sense, like Nature's version of light-framed race cars.

Another plus: the rolling nature of its topography. It is, quite simply, a great place for horses to run to their hearts' content—and strength.

Finally, central Kentucky has been good horse country because of the breed of people who have lived here—competitive, courageous people, warring with Indians, fighting with each other, people who needed, above all, action.

The horse race was the perfect vehicle, as it were, for this competitive mindset. In 1865, New York became the heartland of big-time racing, with a host of tracks available, including Saratoga. But in central Kentucky, there were not many places to race. During the preceding years many horse races took place directly on the streets of Louisville and private tracks situated on locally owned farms. Wherever, in a word, they could.

Into this situation came the perfect person, a tall, massive man with penetrating eyes and a high forehead—Colonel M. Lewis Clark, who, as someone said, "could look right through you, to the wall behind." But the qualities that made him so perfect were rock-ribbed integrity, and the heart of a wolverine. And he came with a dream—a dream of creating a place in central Kentucky where great races could be run by great racehorses, where the horses from the many breeding farms that dotted the area could find glory. He honed and clarified his ideas on an 1872 trip to England, where he carefully observed the Derby Stakes at Epsom. When he returned to America, he took some of what he had seen in England as his own vision, and he started to make the rounds, trying to convince people to share in his dream: to build a track and start hosting great stakes races featuring the marvelous horses bred in central Kentucky.

The first clubhouse at Churchill Downs

He was met, at first, with a negative reaction. In recent years Louisville, a city of 100,000 people, had not been in glowing fiscal health. It was hard to see how a racetrack could pay its way.

Clark had a kind of John Wayne persona, but he was not afraid to promote his ideas any way he could. The groups he talked to were different in many ways, but they were all Kentuckians, so he tried to appeal to their civic pride, their competitive instincts. New Orleans, he would say, had its Mardi Gras. Cincinnati, which Louisvillians loathed, had its music festival. And what did Louisville have? Nothing. They should, and this is just what they needed.

He persevered stubbornly—and finally some people started agreeing with him. It was worth a gamble.

On June 22, 1874, a small cadre of important Louisville businessmen and politicians met with Clark at Louisville's Galt House, a superelegant hotel, and approved the articles of incorporation of the Louisville Jockey Club, which would oversee the building of a track and run the operation. There would be 320 original members of the club, and each would contribute $100, for a basic stake of $32,000.

Clark leased eighty acres of land three miles from Louisville's southern limits from his uncles, John and Henry Churchill. The building of the track began.

One of Clark's qualities was perfectionism, and it showed when the one-mile oval track (still the same track used today) was finished. Local papers ballyhooed the track, saying that it was the safest in the country, with turns and stretches a quarter mile each—four 440-yard sections—and sixty to eighty feet wide, plenty of room to maneuver. The soil was light and designed for good drainage.

In fact, the newspapers were not exaggerating. It was a beautiful, highly functional track, as good as any in the country, a perfect reflection of Clark's personality. He wouldn't have it any other way.

But of course the Jockey Club didn't stop there. With the help of outside contributions, a grandstand that would hold two thousand spectators was built, as well as a small clubhouse next to it, and stables for horses.

Then, in early 1875, Clark set up the races to be run, drawing heavily on what he had learned in England. He scheduled three major stakes races, the Kentucky Derby, Kentucky Oaks, and Clark Handicap, following three premier races in England, the Epsom Derby, Epsom Oaks, and St. Leger Stakes, respectively. The logic was simple: they worked in England, and they'll work here. Indeed, each of these events has run continuously at Churchill Downs since their debut in 1875.

The track, originally known as the Louisville Jockey Club Course, started to be called Churchill Downs—which would eventually evolve into the corporate parent's name—beginning in 1886, when a newspaperman named Ben Ridgeley referred to it as that because of the name Churchill, after Clark's uncles, and the track's physical location on downs. It formally opened May 17, 1875, with four races scheduled. The winner of the first race was Bonaventure, but the winner of the day's featured race,

The grandstand circa 1922

the Kentucky Derby, was a three-year-old chestnut colt named Aristides. Owned by H. P. McGrath, Aristides was trained by and ridden by two black men, Ansel Williamson and Oliver Lewis, respectively. (See 1875 story, "The Best Laid Plans of Mice and Men" for details on how this race held some surprises.)

About ten thousand wildly cheering, highly competitive Kentuckians showed up, and it was a great success. From the outset, Clark set the standard for the races, always trying to attract the best horses, and that was one of the things at the heart of the race's appeal—and still is: *The best versus the best to see who is best!*

Despite the success of the first Derby, subsequent races were not turning up all roses for the Louisville Jockey Club. Revenues were not keeping pace with expenditures, and the buck usually stops at the top. On November 24, 1894, Clark was, in effect, replaced. (Aside from the fiscal difficulty, one reason was that along with his integrity he had a certain rigidity. One of the things he refused to do was shorten the length of the race; owners and breeders shied away from letting their young horses run in a one-and-a-half-mile race and risk damaging themselves or, as horsemen say, "breaking down."

Following Clark's replacement, the Louisville Jockey Club was incorporated. William F. Schulte was appointed president, and Clark was retained as "presiding judge," a job that involved essentially determining which horse won a race, often not a simple thing in these pre-photo-finish days, and required someone not only very experienced in horse racing but incorruptible.

Under Schulte, during the fall of 1894 and spring of 1895 a new grandstand was constructed—with the fiscal help of many bookmakers, who back then were regarded more as businessmen, not seedy characters—on the opposite side of the track, for a reported cost of $100,000. A young architect designed it with two spires crowning the grandstand roof, twin spires that would become the abiding symbol of the Kentucky Derby.

But Schulte and colleagues were no miracle men, for the Derby continued to have problems—all kinds of problems.

One big problem was the loss of quality racehorses. In 1886 millionaire owner and breeder James Ben Ali Haggin, a heavy bettor or "plunger," was miffed when he learned that bookmakers had been barred from the track, and he threatened to remove all his horses from the Downs stables if the bookmakers were not reinstated posthaste. Churchill Downs capitulated, but a remark by one official got back to Haggin, and he blew up, pulled all his horses, and went to New York. To make the situation even worse, owners from other areas refused to send their horses to the Derby in sympathy with Haggin. (See 1886 story, "Good-bye and _____ You!")

The track was also plagued by mismanagement, strikes, and internal dissension. By 1902, the Kentucky Derby was on its own kind of stretch run, gasping for air, tiring badly, about to break down. Churchill Downs needed a miracle. No one knew it but the miracle lived close by. His name was Matt Winn, and he came not from heaven—though sometimes it seemed that way—but from Louisville.

Winn had been a longtime horse and race lover. Born in Louisville June 1861, Winn attended the first running of the Derby in 1875. As a wide-eyed teenager, he watched the event from an infield seat on his father's grocery wagon. The race went through Winn like a tidal wave. He was hooked, and the hook went even deeper ten or so years later when he bought his first pari-mutuel ticket (*pari mutuel*, French for "mutual stake"—the machines were first used in Paris) in 1886 and won.

In 1902, Winn had nothing to do with the Derby. He was a charming, success- ful middle-aged, heavyset man with twinkling, highly observant eyes and a ready smile. Partner in a men's custom clothing store, he had developed a national cli- entele as a sales representative. His motto, and his life- long advice to others on how to succeed, he put in three words: "Always be polite."

After the 1902 spring meet, Charlie Price, Winn's friend and Churchill Downs secretary, knowing of Winn's skill, begged him to buy the operation so he could manage it. Without new management, the track was dead. While Winn was an astute man with great promo- tional skills, he, like Clark, had great courage, which he would need for what he decided to do. Devoted father to a large family, he took the biggest risk of his life. He sold his business and became vice president and general manager of Churchill Downs. And he had another Clark quality: purity. From the moment he was appointed vice president, he never placed another bet. The only thing

Matt Winn

that mattered to him was to have the Derby not only survive but thrive.

Winn plunged into the job of saving the Derby. He started to contact friends and acquaintances and, using a full measure of Irish charm and southern hospitality—and politeness—cajoled hotelman Louis Seelbach, Louisville mayor Charles Grainger, and others to form a new corporation. They also had one goal: to save the Derby.

By early 1903, Winn and his colleagues had sold two hundred new Jockey Club memberships at $100 each, and a $20,000 clubhouse was built with that money for the spring meet. Winn used his prodigious skills to promote the race, and it turned out to be that oddest of things for Churchill Downs: the race turned a profit, something that had not been done in the Derby's first twenty-eight years!

Turning a profit wasn't the end of Winn's problems, however. Indeed, for ten years, like a jockey on the stretch run, he struggled with and ultimately outplayed the Down's biggest rival, nearby Douglas Park. Another major problem he conquered was the 1908 proclamation of Louisville officials: bookmakers were barred from operating within the city limits. Winn cleverly resurrected the long-abandoned pari-mutuel machines for the track's bettors. He stayed legal, but the betting went on.

Another huge crisis—basically a knife poised over the heart of the Derby—was the pre–World War I "reform" movement that shut down tracks nationwide. Winn's solution: Open tracks in Mexico to keep racing alive. (One of the people he befriended was outlaw Pancho Villa. For more on this, read the 1917 story, "Pancho Villa Rides Again—On Your Horse!")

Over the years Winn constantly looked for situations advantageous to Churchill Downs, becoming involved in a variety of tracks, such as Washington Park, Illinois, Fairmont Park in East St. Louis, and Lincoln Fields in Crete, Illinois.

Winn promoted fun, goodwill, and fellowship, and the beneficiary was always Churchill Downs. One thing he did, for example, was to make Churchill Downs a community landmark, with concerts and fairs held in the Derby infield. But he used it in other ways as well. In 1945, for example, he allowed it to be used as a staging area for tanks, and before that, when he learned during World War II that potatoes were sorely needed, he converted the Derby infield into a potato farm. We have to wonder how that looked while great Derby Thoroughbreds powered around the track!

Perhaps above all, Winn loved the press, and they loved him. He would roll out the red carpet for writers like Red Smith and Grantland Rice when they came to Churchill Downs—and in turn they constantly spread the word about the great race called the Kentucky Derby.

The indefatigable Winn created several of the Kentucky Derby traditions that have become part and parcel of the Derby experience—the playing of "My Old Kentucky Home," the intricate garland of roses presented to the winner, and even Kentucky Derby glasses. For the Kentucky Derby's fiftieth anniversary, in 1924, he commissioned a unique gold cup to be presented to the winner. One just like it has been presented each year since that time.

Winn ate, drank, and slept the Derby twenty-four hours a day. Shortly after the 1934 Derby win of Cavalcade, for example, Winn told reporter Jim Henry of the *Louisville Herald-Post,* "My first love was the Kentucky Derby, and I saw to it that the owners of the three-year-olds with box office appeal flirted with no other stake but the Derby when Derby time came around. And we played one society queen against another until we steamrollered Louisville into a one-day capital of celebrities."

Matt Winn had a long and fulfilling life. He died October 6, 1949. But before he died he was presented with a special glass that read, "He saw them all!" And he did, every single race from 1875 to 1949. Indeed, he was the main reason why they could be run.

CHAPTER 2

Traditions

Tradition is an integral part of the Kentucky Derby and its history. A number of traditions have been going on for decades, and will likely go on for decades more.

No question about it, the tradition that is most likely to make spectators misty-eyed is the playing of Stephen Foster's song "My Old Kentucky Home," even if most of them are not from Kentucky. Perhaps because it reminds us that, as Dorothy once said, there "is no place like home"—and when you lose that, it hurts.

The lyrics go:

The sun shines bright on the old Kentucky home,
Tis summer, the people are gay;
The corn-top's ripe and the meadow's in the bloom
While the birds make music all the day.

The young folks roll on the little cabin floor
All merry, all happy and bright;
By'n by hard times comes a-knocking at the door
Then my old Kentucky home, Good-night!

Weep no more my lady. Oh! Weep no more today!
We will sing one song for my old Kentucky home
For the old Kentucky home, far away.

No one is certain when this particular tradition started. Some historians say 1921, the forty-seventh running of the classic, when the Kentucky-owned and -bred Behave Yourself triumphed. Famous scribe Damon Runyon pegged it as 1929, and a report in the *Philadelphia Public Ledger* has it in 1930. It is known for sure, though, that since 1936, with only a few exceptions, the song has been performed by the University of Louisville Marching Band. And, sadly, there is another fact. Songwriter Stephen Foster died in New York's Bowery district January 10, 1864, at the ripe old age of thirty-eight.

Churchill Downs, though, has not forgotten Foster. In 1982 the racecourse created the Stephen Foster Handicap, a race for three-year-olds and up. At one and one-eighth miles, it has grown in popularity and now serves as a Grade II event with a purse of $750,000, the richest stakes at the Downs outside of the Derby.

The Mint Julep

In 2006, for $1000 you could quaff the traditional Derby drink, the mint julep, and have the proceeds donated to charity. NBC broadcaster Bob Costas bought one and took an on-camera sip as if he expected it somehow to taste as if it was worth $1000. His expression, however, only seemed to say, "That's strong!"

The drink has been around a long time—about a hundred years. It can be purchased year-round at Churchill Downs, and during Derby week some 80,000 of these powerful concoctions are sold. If you can't make it to Kentucky, you can still enjoy a mint julep by making it yourself, though you should be warned that it's not exactly as easy as opening a can of beer. Here's the recipe:

Make a simple syrup by boiling 2 cups of sugar and 2 cups water for 5 minutes, without stirring. Fill a jar loosely with sprigs of fresh mint (uncrushed) and cover with the syrup when cooled. Cap and refrigerate 12–24 hours. Discard mint. Make one julep at a time.

Fill chilled julep cup with finely crushed ice; pour in half a tablespoon of the mint-flavored syrup and two ounces of Early Times Kentucky whiskey. Stick in a fresh sprig of mint and serve at once. You can get a head start by storing a batch, without mint, in the freezer until ready for use.

Kentucky Derby Glasses

If you like you can also buy your julep to sip out of a glass you keep. Kentucky Derby glasses have been sold since 1938, and are genuine collectibles.

The value of each glass, as with many other collectibles, is based on its rarity. From 1938 through 1952 fewer than 100,000 glasses were produced annually. In 1996 the production rose to 250,000 a year, with the number increasing to 400,000 for the hundredth running of the race in 1974. The production run hit 500,000 in 1985 and has since vaulted to approximately 700,000.

The mint julep glass started with the sixty-fourth Derby running in 1938. The first glasses were actually water glasses, but, as one official put it, they got very popular and started to "disappear." Officials had a bright idea. They tacked on a quarter to each meal, and let diners keep the glasses. Then, in 1939, the Libbey Glass Company was contracted to make glasses in color, and they were sold. Allowing patrons to keep their glasses tripled the sales of mint juleps.

In 1940 and 1941 a problem reared its head—or made a sharp point. Officials, having found broken glass on the racetrack grounds the previous two years, had started making mostly aluminum tumblers, though a limited number of glasses were still available, and distributed only on the backside area. During the war years 1942–44, however, aluminum was at a premium, so a ceramic tumbler of various colors was produced by Beetleware Company.

Libbey began producing the glasses again in 1945, and continues to do so. The glasses were sold exclusively at the track until the hundredth Derby in 1974, but of the nearly 700,000 officially licensed Kentucky Derby glasses that are now annually produced, more than two-thirds are sold off-track for private parties.

Over the years, there have been many different designs on the glasses, but generally the twin spires, the name "Kentucky Derby," and various racehorses have been featured. Since 1949 all previous Derby winners have been listed on the glasses, a tradition that has continued to today, with the exception of 1950, 1952, 1958, and 1969.

Silks

Between the Kentucky Derby program, the television monitors, the highly visible number on a horse's saddlecloth, and the track announcer's call, it is pretty easy for the average fan at the track to follow the progress of particular horses throughout a race. When horse racing debuted in the early eighteenth century, though, there were no such visual aids. When King Charles II first assembled race meets on the plains of Hempstead, the dukes and barons had trouble figuring out which horse was which. Thus, they adopted racing silks—or colors—so they could more easily distinguish their jockeys. At this time the silks were simple—red for one duke, black for another duke, orange for one earl, white for another earl, and so on.

The tradition of the silks, of course, remains today. Jockeys wear the colors of the owners, but since there are so many, the silks have become even more colorfully complex to identify various owners clearly. Probably the most famous silks of all time are the devil's red and blue of Calumet Farm, which dominated the Derby from the 1940s. The jockeys' room at Churchill Downs houses hundreds of silks, a conga line of colors lined up on pegs ready to be donned by jockeys on a particular day.

The Garland of Roses

Wreath, blanket, garland—the floral arrangement draped over the neck of the Kentucky Derby winner has been called all of these since it made its beautiful appearance. One story has it that the rose came into the Derby limelight following the 1883 running of the Derby. Roses were presented to all the ladies attending a Louisville party given by fashionable New York socialite and gamester E. Berry Wall. The roses created such a sensation with the ladies that track president M. Lewis Clark decided to feature the rose as the official flower for the 1884 Derby.

The first published account of roses draped on the winning horse came in 1896, when Ben Brush was presented with a collar of white and pink roses, fastened with white and magenta ribbon. However, it's not clear whether the Jockey Club sanctioned the rose garland in these early runnings or if indeed roses were always presented. One account has it that in 1898, the wife of J. W. Schorr, owner of Lieber Karl, the 1–3 favorite, purchased the most expensive floral design in Louisville for their big horse's victory. Plaudit, however, nipped Karl by a nose, and the roses went to waste. Another report states that the 1902 winner, Alan-a-Dale, was adorned with carnations and ferns.

Roses became the traditional way to honor the Derby winner during the early years of the twentieth century. Dating back to 1906, Churchill Downs has photos of the winner with the garland. In 1925 the late Bill Corum, a *New York Journal* sports columnist who later became the president of Churchill Downs, dubbed the Derby the "Run for the Roses."

The phrases and the roses were here to stay.

In 1931 Churchill Downs requested a standard pattern for the garland, and Louisville florist shop owner Mrs. Kingsley Walker designed and produced an intricate one using over five hundred of the darkest red roses and greenery stitched on a cloth-backed blanket. This design was first draped over the neck of 1932 Derby winner Burgoo King. Mrs. Walker retired in 1974, but her daughter, Betty Korfhage, continued the tradition.

Since 1987 the master floral designers from Kroger, the national grocery chain, have created and continued to enhance the garland of roses. The garland is ninety inches long and fourteen inches wide, and weighs approximately thirty-five pounds. Each of the 564 roses used are hand-selected "prime" roses. Since each bush only contains one prime rose, it takes 564 rosebushes for the task. The lining of the garland is made of green satin and features embroidery at each end. One end displays the twin-spires logo of Churchill Downs, and the other end is represented by the Great Seal of the Commonwealth of Kentucky. The center of the garland is made up of a "crown" of roses and features the same number of roses as horses competing in the Derby. A single rose in the crown's center is raised above the rest and symbolizes the struggle and heart displayed by the Derby winner.

Each individual rose that makes up the garland is inserted into its own water vial, and the roses are then hand-sewn to the garland with the vials hidden inside the lining. The outer edge is trimmed with a mix of fresh foliage such as coffee leaf, boxwood, and lemon leaf, in a combination that varies through the years.

The delicate operation of sewing the roses to the garland starts at exactly 4:00 p.m. on Friday, the day before the Derby. The entire operation is a public event, as the crew prepares the garland at the Kroger store for all to see and appreciate. The crew works approximately ten to twelve hours to finish the process, and then heads to the Kentucky Derby winner's circle to dress the area with a total of 2,100 roses that were not selected for the Derby garland. In addition a "Jockey's Bouquet" featuring sixty matching long-stemmed roses, wrapped with ten yards of red ribbon, is prepared to present to the winning rider.

The Derby Trophy

Presenting a gold trophy to the owner of the winning Derby horse has been a tradition since the fiftieth running of the Derby in 1924, when the almost mythic horse Black Gold won. President Matt Winn commissioned a standard design be developed for the golden anniversary of the Derby.

Outside of the jeweled embellishments that were added to note special Derby anniversaries in 1949 (seventy-fifth), 1974 (hundredth), and 1999 (hundred and twenty-fifth), only one change has been made to the original design. For the hundred and twenty-fifth Kentucky Derby in 1999, Churchill Downs acceded to racing lore and changed the direction of the decorative horseshoe displayed on the fourteen-karat gold trophy. The horseshoe, fashioned from eighteen-karat gold, had pointed downward on each of the trophies since 1924.

To commemorate Derby 125, the horseshoe was turned 180 degrees so that its ends pointed up. Racing superstition decrees that if a horseshoe is turned down, all the luck will run out.

Since 1975 the trophy has been created by New England Sterling, located in North Attleboro, Massachusetts. The trophy, which is topped by an eighteen-karat gold horse and rider and includes horseshoe-shaped handles, is twenty-two inches tall and weighs fifty-six ounces, excluding its jade base. The entire trophy is handcrafted with the exception of the horse and rider, which are both cast from a mold.

To complete the trophy by April, craftsmen begin the process during the fall of the previous year and work on it for hundreds of hours. The trophy is believed to be the only solid gold trophy annually awarded the winner of a major American sporting event. Horsemen ache for the trophy. In 1968, for example, though his horse Dancer's Image had been disqualified for drug use and Peter Fuller had lost a long court fight, he nevertheless tried desperately to retain the trophy. It is a powerful symbol of victory that he did not want to relinquish.

Sterling Silver Julep Cups

Silver julep cups were introduced by Downs president Bill Corum in 1951, fulfilling one of the many ideas that had flowed from the fecund mind of Colonel Matt Winn. Winn had discussed with Downs officials his feeling that there should be an official, useful souvenir of the Kentucky Derby.

The cups feature a small horseshoe on the side with a wreath of roses encircling the base. They hold 12 fluid ounces and weigh 5.5 troy ounces of sterling silver. The cups remained unchanged until 1984, when Leslie Combs II, the winning Oaks owner, expressed some concern that the horseshoe on the julep cups was pointing downward, which, superstition decrees, "makes the luck run out." Churchill Downs obligingly had the manufacturer turn the horseshoe 180 degrees, pointing upward. Tradition was the victim. Appropriately, Mr. Combs's Oaks winner that year was aptly named Lucky, Lucky, Lucky.

The julep cup also plays a part in Derby lore. Traditionally, the governor of Kentucky salutes the victorious Derby owner with a toast at the winner's party following the race. The julep cup used is then added to the complete set the track has—one for each of the Derby winners.

The Twin Spires

Though not a tradition, the spires on the grandstand have become a symbol of the Kentucky Derby. Described as towers in the original drawing, the hexagonal spires exemplify late-nineteenth-century architecture, in which symmetry and balance took precedence over function. Although the architect, Joseph D. Baldez, designed many

other structures in Louisville, the twin spires remain as an everlasting monument to the architect. Former Churchill Downs president Matt J. Winn is reported to have told Baldez, "Joe, when you die there's one monument that will never be taken down, the Twin Spires."

Baldez died in 1957, but a century after they were built, his twin spires continue to greet the winner of the Kentucky Derby and stand as a familiar beacon to horse racing enthusiasts everywhere.

The Winner's Circle

The much-coveted winner's circle has been a Derby tradition since Lawrin received his honors after winning in 1938. Prior to this there were various areas used for honoring the Derby winner. From 1875 through 1929 the winner would stand on the racetrack in a circled area drawn out in chalk dust, leading to the term *winner's circle*. In 1930 through 1937 track officials made the winner's presentation in an area that adjoined the clubhouse. Finally, for the sixty-fourth running in 1938, a presentation stand featuring a new electric odds board was constructed. Every Kentucky Derby winner since that time has been led to the infield presentation area to be honored. Since 1944, the winner's circle has included a landscaped horseshoe floral arrangement that the winning horse is led into for photographs. Over the years the presentation stand has undergone various changes, including the addition of terraced planters that were constructed adjoining the area when the turf course was developed in 1985. The odds board that helps make up the presentation stand was outfitted with an electronic message center display system in 1997 to replace the incandescent bulbs that previously announced odds and payoffs.

Although the winner's circle has been used mostly as an honored spot for the Kentucky Derby winner, a few lucky couples have used the site for weddings over the years. Also, though officials do not encourage the practice, the ashes of some horsemen have discreetly been spread on the hallowed ground. So have tears: many a winner has wept while standing here.

Millionaire's Row

Throughout its history celebrities have been attracted to and added luster to the Derby. One of the first celebrity sightings was in 1877, when famed Polish actress Helena Modjeska attended the third running of the Kentucky Derby. In Matt J. Winn's 1945 book *Down the Stretch*, it was noted that Modjeska was impressed by the Derby but even more charmed by the mint julep she was given by Colonel M. Lewis Clark following the race.

One of the more infamous celebrity attendees was Frank James, the brother of famed outlaw Jesse James and a leader in their outlaw gang. Frank was on hand at the fifteenth running in 1889 to watch Spokane beat favored Proctor Knott.

Celebrity Owners

Although most of the rich and famous who attend are guests of prominent ticket holders, the Derby has also attracted an impressive roster of celebrity horse owners. Since 1990, this group of celebrity owners has grown to include musician Hammer (Dance Floor, third in 1992); composer Burt Bacharach (Soul of the Matter, fifth in 1992, and Afternoon Deelites, eighth in 1994); music producer Berry Gordy (Powis Castle, eighth in 1994); film producer Albert Broccoli (Brocco, fourth in 1994); New York Yankees owner George Steinbrenner (Concerto, ninth in 1997); University of Louisville coach Rick Pitino (Hallory Hunter, fourth in 1998); and movie director Steven Spielberg (Atswhatimtalknbout, fourth in 2003).

Royalty

As a direct descendant of England's Epsom Derby, Churchill Downs has played host to British royalty for the running of the Kentucky Derby on three different occasions. In 1930, Edward George Villiers Stanley, the seventeenth Earl of Derby, from whose title the term *Derby* was derived, became the first English nobleman to attend. Prohibition was in effect at the time, and Lord Derby stated his disappointment at not being able to sample a mint julep. "You have a great many advantages I should like to copy for England," Derby said, "but Prohibition is not one of them." Derby was followed in 1951 by the Duke of Windsor, who had renounced the British throne in 1936 so he could wed the American divorcee Wallis Simpson. The hundredth running of the Kentucky Derby in 1974 brought Her Royal Highness, the Princess Margaret, and her husband, Lord Snowden. Princess Margaret, the sister of the queen of England, took part in the trophy presentation and awarded winning owner John Olin a specially crafted trophy for the milestone victory.

U.S. Presidents

Eight U.S. presidents have witnessed the Derby and marveled at the pageantry and spectacle of the famed event. Future president Harry S. Truman was reported as the first and was followed in 1952 by Lyndon Johnson, who attended as a Texas senator. In 2000, future president George W. Bush, who would win the election that same year, was on hand for the 126th running of the Derby with his father, former president George Bush. Of the eight, only Richard M. Nixon attended while serving in office. He had visited in 1968 as guest of Kentucky governor Louie B. Nunn and commented that if he was elected president, he would return to the 1969 Derby. That year also attracted two future presidents, Gerald R. Ford and Ronald Reagan. No other president has witnessed more Derbies than Ford. Beginning in 1977, Ford and his wife Betty attended almost every Derby for ten years as guests of longtime friend John Galbreath, a former Churchill chairman of the board. In 1983, for the 109th Derby, two past presidents and one future president were in attendance. Ford was joined by Jimmy Carter, the Democrat who had defeated him in 1976, and Vice President George Bush, who would win the 1988 election.

In 1999, Al Gore joined the list of vice presidents that have attended the Derby. The list includes: Charles Curtis, 1931; John Nance Garner, 1937; and Alben Barkley, 1958.

The Infield

Since the first running of the Kentucky Derby in 1875, the forty-acre Churchill Downs infield has been a gathering place to exercise the first rite of spring.

Attracting folks from all over the country, the infield at Churchill Downs regularly becomes home to 80,000 fans for Kentucky Oaks and Kentucky Derby days. For many, one visit to the infield is enough to last a lifetime (about all you may see of the races is a cloud of dust and a flash of silks); others come back year after year, graduating from the fun of their youthful college days to family picnics with the little ones. Whatever the activity, the infield revelry on Derby day ranks as one of America's great parties.

Steeplechase racing was periodically held in the infield during the early years of Churchill Downs. The first steeplechase event took place May 18, 1882, over a course of hurdles, stone walls, and water jumps.

Tunnels were constructed under the track in 1937 to provide better patron access to the infield. An additional tunnel, large enough to facilitate tractor-trailers, was added in 1985 when the turf course was built.

Over the years the infield has also served a variety of other purposes beyond racing. In 1910, the first recorded flight in Kentucky took place in the infield. Legendary aviator Glenn Curtiss, who founded Curtiss-Wright Aviation, shipped a plane to Louisville via freight train. After assembling the flying machine in the infield, Curtiss lifted off and flew around the track at a speed reported to be 60 mph.

During World War I, in the spring of 1918, with the country experiencing a potato shortage, a crop was planted in the Churchill infield. One thousand bushels were harvested and auctioned off, and the money was donated to the Red Cross. During the 1942 fall meet, soldiers from Fort Knox and Bowman Field were housed in the infield in tents. The area was named Camp Winn in honor of Churchill Downs president Matt J. Winn.

Today the infield continues to serve a variety of purposes but none as celebrated as the annual event held on the first Saturday of May.

CHAPTER 3

Historical Highlights

1911: Colonel Winn reduces minimum wager from $5 to $2 and installs two men in the betting booth—a ticket seller and a man to operate the clicker, which registers sales.

1913: Donerail becomes the longest shot to win the Derby, paying $184.90, $41.20, and $13.20, besides collecting $5,475 for the victory after Winn restructured the fees. (See 1913 story, "The Longest Shot of All.")

New charges are $25 to nominate, $100 to start, with the Downs adding $5,000 to the purse.

1914: Old Rosebud sets a track record of 2:03 2/5, winning the Derby by eight lengths. (See 1914 story, "More Like Greased Lightning.")

1915: Regret joins Donerail and Old Rosebud, wrapping up a three-year publicity splash by becoming the first filly to win the Derby. The three achievements help save the Derby, which was in trouble for various reasons. (See 1915 story, "A Lady Saves the Day.")

1922: A gold buffet service, valued at $7,000 and including a loving cup and candlesticks, is presented to the Kentucky Derby winner, the first Derby presentation of its kind.

1924: Black Gold wins the Golden Jubilee Derby. The trophy presented to the winner is the same style as used today. (See 1924 story, "The People's Horse.")

1925: First network radio broadcast of the Derby is aired on May 16, originating from Louisville station WHAS. The phrase "Run for the Roses" is coined by *New York Journal-American* writer Bill Corum, who will later become president of Churchill Downs (1950–58).

1930: The box starting mechanism is first used for the Kentucky Derby.

1931–33: First international broadcast of the Derby is carried on radio. Transmission is relayed from Louisville to Lawrenceville, New Jersey, and then to England's British Broadcasting Company.

1938: First tunnel under the track, extending from the grandstand to the infield. Admission to the infield is 50 cents. The infield presentation stand is built and first used for the Kentucky Derby winner.

1945: Government ban of all horse racing in January threatens to break the consecutive string of Derbies at seventy, but VE Day is followed by a May 8 announcement lifting the ban, and the 71st Derby is run June 9, about a month later than usual.

1949: Ponder, a 16–1 shot, wins the 75th Derby, telecast on a limited basis by local TV. (See 1949 story, "No More Chance Than a Shetland Pony.")

1952: First network television broadcast of a Derby, originating from CBS affiliate WHAS.

1968: First Derby winner disqualification sees the purse taken from first-place finisher Dancer's Image because postrace testing revealed an illegal medication. Second-place finisher Forward Pass is declared the winner. The disqualification fight took over five years, much of it in the courts. (See 1968 story, "Shocker.")

1973: Secretariat breaks the magic two-minute plateau for the Derby, winning the 99th Run for the Roses in 1:59 2/5. He goes on to become the first Triple Crown winner in twenty-five years. (See 1973 story, "Big Red.")

1974: An all-time record U.S. Thoroughbred racing crowd of 163,628 jams the Downs to see Cannonade top a field of twenty-three and win the 100th Derby. (See 1974 story, "A Country Boy Comes Home.")

1983: Pat Day finishes a brilliant year by burying old records with 169 winners in the spring meet and 54 in the fall meet. On five occasions he rides five winners in a single day.

1984: Warner L. Jones Jr. is named chairman and appoints Tom Meeker as president. Under this leadership, the track develops an aggressive marketing strategy headed by a five-year renovation program. First widespread simulcast of Kentucky Derby is a success, setting a North American record for wagering on a single race—$18,941,933 handled on-site and at twenty-four other tracks. Pat Day breaks a seventy-seven-year-old mark by riding seven winners in eight races on June 20. Track has its first Sunday racing on November 4, when a crowd of 8,971 braves showers and cool temperatures to wager $1,167,593.

Penny Tweedy Chenery, owner of Riva Ridge and Secretariat

1985: Track begins an ambitious multimillion-dollar capital improvement program in February, with a Phase I pre-Derby project. Phase II begins shortly before the end of the spring meet. On April 27, the new $7.5 million Kentucky Derby Museum is formally opened on the grounds with a black-tie fund-raising gala attended by 700. Twilight racing—a nine-race card beginning at 3:30 p.m. (EDT) on weekdays—is inaugurated May 7, with 9,343 present who wager $1,153,148.

1986: Completion of the paddock balcony and $2.6 million paddock/toteboard complex finalizes Phase III of President Tom Meeker's five-year capital improvement plan, with more than $13 million spent in the first two years. The track is formally placed on the register of National Historic Landmarks by the Department of the Interior at ceremonies dedicating the paddock/toteboard complex in the fall.

1987: Churchill Downs opens a private-membership Turf Club located in the area that was formerly Dining Room B. A million-dollar Pick Six pool, built up during

The 125th Kentucky Derby was won by longshot Charismatic (right)

the fall meet, ends on November 14 as three perfect tickets each return $396,958.60. That day, a crowd of 28,396 is in attendance, and more than 1,000 cars are ushered to the infield to alleviate the parking burden. On November 1, opening day of the fall meet, a larger-than-life-size statue of Aristides, winner of the first Kentucky Derby, is dedicated in the clubhouse garden.

1988: Churchill Downs establishes records in attendance and wagering for the spring and fall meets, to complete a string of nine consecutive record meets. Winning Colors (see 1988 story, "The Walk of a Hooker, the Look of a Queen") becomes only the third filly in racing history to capture the Kentucky Derby. The fall is highlighted by the $10 million Breeders' Cup Day races, witnessed by a record 71,237 fans on November 25. The fall meet also sees the advent of intertrack wagering (ITW), in which Churchill races are simulcast at in-state tracks.

1992: The Sports Spectrum, Churchill Downs's $15 million, state-of-the-art intertrack wagering and sports viewing facility, located on the site of the old Louisville Downs harness track, opens November 29. Warner L. Jones Jr., the seventy-six-year-old chairman of the board of Churchill Downs, announces in May that he will not seek reelection to the office. Jones had served on the track's board since 1941 and as chairman since 1984. William S. Farish succeeds Jones as chairman in June. The Derby is televised for the first time ever to Russia through the Russian State Television and Radio Company.

1995: For the first time in history, Kentucky Derby wagering is offered on race day to intertrack and OTB sources, with $1,618,608 betting reported. The Derby notches another first in its history as Ski Captain, who finished fourteenth, became the first Japanese-ridden and -trained contender. Derby Week at Churchill serves as the background for the filming of the ABC-TV movie *Derby,* which aired nationally on June 17. The Kentucky Derby purse is increased to $1 million guaranteed minimum gross and the Kentucky Oaks to $500,000 guaranteed, following a June 15 announcement by the board of directors. An agreement is reached to move the Kentucky Derby post position draw in 1996 from its traditional Thursday date to Wednesday in order to facilitate national television coverage on ESPN.

1996: Churchill enters the computer age as the track launches www.kentuckyderby .com on March 25. VISA-USA develops a commercial based on a Kentucky Derby theme at Churchill as part of their sponsorship agreement with the Triple Crown.

1997: For the first time in history, the infield is opened Thursday of Derby Week, with a record of 19,863 entering it. Kentucky Derby winner Silver Charm (See 1997 story, "Oh Lord, Don't Let It Happen Again!") trains the entire Triple Crown campaign at Churchill, highlighted by a public workout attended by nearly 2,500 on Tuesday, June 3. Silver Charm is later honored in a public appearance during the races on June 21.

1998: The Kentucky Derby post position draw is revised to allow owners and trainers the opportunity to select their post position following a random draw that determines the selection order. Wagering interests for the Kentucky Derby are expanded from 12 to 14. The first-ever Kentucky Derby Alumni Day is held with an all-star group of owners, trainers, and jockeys on hand for the June 13 event. African American Ansel Williamson, winning trainer in the first Kentucky Derby in 1875, is inducted into the Thoroughbred Racing Hall of Fame, located in Saratoga Springs, New York. The track serves as the location for the filming of the motion pictures *Nice Guys Sleep Alone* and *Simpatico*. The track announces its plans for a Derby Future Wager for 1999 to allow fans three separate opportunities (in February, March, and April) to bet on Derby contenders leading up to the race. Silver Charm makes his third appearance of the year at Churchill, as he wins the Clark Handicap to become the first Kentucky Derby winner to return and win at the Downs since Alysheba in the 1988 Breeders' Cup Classic.

1999: The 125th running of the Kentucky Oaks and Kentucky Derby highlights the year, and the end of the century. Oaks Day provides a record 101,034, the fifth consecutive record attendance for the event, and the Kentucky Derby draws the second largest crowd in history, 151,051. Charismatic, the eventual Derby winner, is listed as a field horse during each of the wagering sessions. Luke Kruytbosch is named the fifth announcer in the history of the track, replacing Kurt Becker. The Kentucky Lottery unveils a scratch-off game titled Derby 125—the $5-a-ticket game offers a top prize of $125,000 and features six scenes of the Derby, including a 125th Derby logo. As a tribute to Derby 125, a race car is developed with a Derby theme to race in NASCAR's California 500 the day after the Run for the Roses. Racing superstition finds its way into the design of the Kentucky Derby trophy; the decorative horseshoe is turned 180 degrees, the ends pointing up so the luck won't run out. NBC is made the network for the Derby and Triple Crown, it is announced on October 4, in a five-year agreement from 2001 to 2005.

2000: Fusao Sekiguchi becomes the first Japanese owner to win the Kentucky Derby when his Fusaichi Pegasus (named for the flying horse of myth) captures the historic

Kentucky Derby 2000 before a crowd of 153,204, the second largest crowd in race history. Jockey Marlon St. Julien becomes the first African American rider to compete in the Derby since Henry King rode Planet in 1921, finishing seventh aboard Curule. Jockey Pat Day scores his two thousandth Churchill Downs win on June 30. Churchill announces that the Derby will no longer offer betting on a mutuel field starting in 2001, and that the number of individual wagering interests may grow to as many as twenty. It is announced that the post time for the 2001 Derby will be moved from 5:30 to 6:00 p.m. to facilitate the National Derby telecast by NBC, which takes over ABC's network television rights to the Triple Crown.

2001: Growth of the Kentucky Derby continues on all fronts as the 127th running attracts a crowd of 154,210, the second largest attendance in Derby history. Overall Derby day wagering (all sources) rises to a record $107,598,904. For the first time in Derby pari-mutuel wagering history, all horses run uncoupled, with no entries or mutuel fields as betting interests. Monarchos (see 2001 story, "A Real Shot") wins the Derby in its second-fastest running ever, 1:59.97. The National Broadcasting Company's (NBC) first-ever television coverage of the Kentucky Derby attracts a national rating of 8.1, a 40 percent increase over ABC's 5.8 rating for the 2000 Derby. Jockey Pat Day scores the 8,000th win of his career on May 31, joining Laffite Pincay Jr. and Bill Shoemaker as the only North American riders to reach that plateau. An economic impact study commissioned by Churchill Downs is released in August and reports that the 2001 Kentucky Derby weekend (Thursday, Friday, and Saturday) provided nearly $218 million to the Kentucky economy. The 1990 Kentucky Derby winner, Unbridled, is euthanized on October 18 after suffering a severe bout of colic.

2002: City of Louisville officials and Churchill Downs seek special national security status for Kentucky Derby from Homeland Security Office, but are denied. Increased Oaks and Derby security measures are implemented, including magnetic wand searches of all persons entering the track; no coolers, backpacks, bottles, cans, or lotion containers; and an increase in the presence of uniformed security personnel. An eleventh race is added to the Derby day card, and the Derby is moved to the ninth event from its previous slot as the eighth race. For the first time in history, color-coded, standardized numbered saddlecloths are used for the Kentucky Derby. Derby attracts 145,033, the fifth largest crowd in history, and the Oaks draws 101,923, its third largest attendance. On May 7 Seattle Slew (see 2002 story, "A Case of Nerves"), the only remaining Triple Crown winner, dies on the twenty-fifth anniversary of his Derby win. Churchill Downs strengthens ties to the Derby Festival as official sponsor of the Great Steamboat Race. Two Japanese-breds are nominated for the Triple Crown, making a first for Japan. Employees cleaning a storage area find trainer

Woody Stephens's 1984 Derby trophy, which was mistakenly stored there for eighteen years, and the trophy is returned to Stephens's widow, Lucille.

2003: Churchill Downs Inc. launches the Pay Day online contest, which offers a $5 million prize to the player who picks the exact order of finish of the 129th Kentucky Derby. Funny Cide defeats heavily favored Empire Maker to become the first New York–bred to win the Kentucky Derby.

2004: For the second time a NASCAR stock car is created with a Kentucky Derby theme and is featured on Sterling Marlin's Coors Light Dodge–this follows the 1999 NASCAR stock car featuring the 125th Derby logo driven by Jeremy Mayfield. On

Thursday, just two days before the Derby, a federal judge rules that jockeys can wear advertising in the Kentucky Derby; on race day, the Kentucky Racing Authority broadened the ruling to include all jockeys racing in Kentucky. For the first time in over twenty years (since 1983), the Kentucky Derby winner, Smarty Jones (see 2004 story, "Just Great Good Luck"), is featured on the cover of *Sports Illustrated*. An international simulcast distribution agreement is made between CDI and Magna Entertainment Corp. to distribute race signals, including the Kentucky Oaks and Kentucky Derby, to Europe through Magna's Austrian subsidiary, MEC Sport and Entertainment, with outlets in Great Britain, Ireland, Austria, and Germany.

The 125th Kentucky Derby from left to right: Jockey Chris Antley, trainer D. Wayne Lukas, and Charismatic owners Robert & Beverly Lewis

2005: The Kentucky Derby purse doubles to a record $2 million guaranteed minimum gross, the first purse increase since 1996 Stakes purses rise to a record $10 million. NBC Sports, in its final year of a five-year agreement, renews to televise the Derby for an additional five years. Giacomo wins the Derby at 50–1, with the second biggest win payoff in Derby history ($102.60), in front of a crowd of 156,435, the second largest in race history. (See 2005 story, "Against Big Odds.") A May 7 stewards' ruling fines three jockeys for wearing unapproved advertising during the Derby. The original 1969 Kentucky Derby trophy is purchased by an individual in a public auction for $60,000, the first time a Derby trophy has been auctioned since 1951. Churchill's all-time leading rider, Pat Day, retires in August.

CHAPTER 4

The Man on the Horse—and Those Behind Him: Jockeys, Trainers, and Owners

Though it's probably not thought of this way often, running a Thoroughbred in a race like the Kentucky Derby is a team sport, and the major players in the team—other than the horse—are the jockeys, trainers, and owners. They are connected to and dependent on one another in an intimate way, a way as real and important as that depicted in the song that goes, "The head bone is connected to the neck bone; the neck bone is connected to the shoulder bone . . ."

Jockeys

The most obvious member of the team is the jockey: he's right there astride the horse as he gallops to victory—or defeat—though his partners (trainers and owners) are just as pivotal to success or failure, as shall be touched on later. The Kentucky Derby has always attracted the very best jockeys. When you think about it that makes sense: the jockeys will be riding the best horse they can find in the toughest race. Only the best need apply.

At the Derby's beginning, going back to the first race in 1875, black men dominated. Indeed, in the first race fourteen of fifteen jockeys were black.

Why black jockeys? It was all part of a logical progression. Men who owned horses employed—or had as slaves—black people as grooms and stable boys. Stable boys started riding when they were very young. As boys, of course, they were quite small—jockey size—but skilled on horseback, and owners started using them to race their Thoroughbreds. Some of them were quite young, too. For example, Alonzo "Lonnie"

Clayton won the Derby riding Azra in 1892 when he was just fifteen. And James "Soup" Perkins won the 1895 Derby aboard Halma when he was fifteen. William Walker, born into slavery, won in the 1877 Derby on Baden-Baden when he was seventeen—getting up there in years for a black jockey!

And most black jockeys were very good. Indeed, they won fifteen of the first twenty-eight Kentucky Derbies. And many people, looking back across the Derbies from the present to the distant past, feel that the best jockey who ever lived was Isaac Murphy, who was born Isaac Burns. Murphy was around in the midst of the Civil War. His father died as a Union soldier, and he went to live with his grandfather Green Murphy and adopted his last name.

Murphy's record is eye-opening. In later years superstar jockeys like Eddie Arcaro and Willie Shoemaker won in the low 20s percentile of all their races. Murphy's winning percentage was more than double that, 44 percent. And he was a man of character. In the early days of racing, cheating was commonplace, but Murphy had a reputation like Serpico: he was a bastion of integrity.

Jockey Pat Day aboard 1992 Kentucky Derby winner Lil E. Tee

By the beginning of the twentieth century, the black jockey became basically extinct. Why? Some pundits say that it's because white jockeys found out that it could be lucrative and forced black jockeys out. Others say that it was because young black jockeys got too big. What's the truth? No one seems to know.

Rough-and-Ready Riding

One characteristic of the early-twentieth-century white jockey was rough-and-ready riding. Some would try to win any way they could, anything from pulling their rival's saddlecloth to smacking opposing jockeys or interfering with the vision of or spooking or blocking their opponent's horse. And they'd get away with it—no films were taken of the races to prove they were cheating. Undoubtedly the most famous illustrations of this rough-and-ready style was the candid photo snapped of Herb Fisher riding Headplay and Don Meade on Brokers Tip in the 1933 Derby that shows them flailing at each other as they pounded down the stretch side by side. It's a wonder that no jockey was killed by another, fights so frequently broke out after such hair-raising, hotheaded races.

One of the roughest riders of all was Earl Sande, horse racing's version of boxer Mike Tyson or an enforcer for a pro hockey team. Nasty and ruthless, he was also a great jockey, on a par with Eddie Arcaro, Willie Shoemaker, and Bill Hartack.

In the 1930s one of the greatest jockeys who ever lived started riding: George Edward Arcaro, who weighed in at three pounds at his birth in Cincinnati but was raised across the river in Southgate, Kentucky. Eddie Arcaro, whose prominent nose eventually earned him the dubious nickname "Banana Nose," would ultimately win five Kentucky Derbies in twenty-one tries, but when he first started riding, he was as rough as they come. Said he: "I came into racing setting traps, grabbing saddlecloths, and leg locking." One of the stewards of the time said he was "the roughest kid with whom I ever had to deal." But Arcaro was given a wake-up call in the early 1940s in the form of a one-year suspension from riding.

There were other great jockeys in the 1940s and '50s, such as Conn McCreary and Johnny Longden, but the two names that stand out are Willie Shoemaker and Bill Hartack. Shoemaker, an articulate, funny man from Texas, won four Derbies; Hartack, who came out of poverty in a West Virginia mining town, was an angry man who loathed the press. But on a horse he had, as someone once said, "iced tea in his veins"; he never made the same mistake twice, and he exploited the bad habits of other jockeys to the fullest. It paid off. He has the best Derby winning percentage of all, winning an astonishing five Derbies in only nine tries.

In modern times names like Jerry Bailey, Gary Stevens, Kent Desmoreaux, and Angel Cordero Jr. resonate. All won multiple Derbies. Cordero is also famous—or infamous—for having been suspended from racing over two-hundred times for rough riding.

While some female jockeys have had mounts in the Derby—Diane Crump (1970), Patricia Cooksey (1984), Andrea Seefeldt (1991), Julie Krone (1992), and Rosemary Homeister (2003)—none of them has ever finished in the money.

Being a jockey has its hazards, of course. It would be hard to find one who never broke a bone, and many broke many bones and had multiple accidents, like Jose Santos, the winning jockey on Funny Cide. And you'd need a strong stomach to look at Angel Cordero naked. His body looked like he had met up with King Kong on a bad day.

Sometimes jockeys get killed, and sometimes their injuries can seem worse than death. For example, Ron Turcotte, the Canadian jockey who rode the incomparable Secretariat—"Big Red"—to victory in under two minutes in the 1973 Derby, was thrown by a horse named The Legend of Leyte and was turned into a paraplegic. In a classic decision, the courts decided against him in his suit against the track, saying that Turcotte was not entitled to any damages because when he rode the horse, he automatically consented to the normal hazards of his profession.

Controlling Weight

Keeping that weight down is another burden. Today, jockeys carry about 126 pounds, and they have to be on a perpetual diet to keep the weight off. Or—and this definitely happens—they can end up bulimic, eating and then throwing up. It's a practice that's been around for a long time. For example, Isaac Murphy was suspected of being bulimic when he rode, though the practice was then called "flipping"—for obvious reasons. Indeed, some people say it was a factor in the early deaths of a number of jockeys, including Murphy, who was a ripe old thirty-five when he took his last gallop.

What else does it take to be a great jockey?

Jockeys need the ability to make quick decisions. They have to evaluate and capitalize as if in a high-speed chess game, as horses move forward and into various positions—that call for a sometimes irrevocable decision in seconds—or milliseconds.

They must know the horse they're on, how he should be run—from off the pace or up front—and how he performs in mud. Then, too, the best ones have a certain something, an ability to speak to the horse so at that certain moment when it's needed, he can ask the horse to run all out, making what lots of jockeys describe as a clucking sound, rubbing his hands against the horse's neck, or even cracking his flank with a whip. Then the horse's afterburners go on, and what might have been an also-ran is now a Kentucky Derby winner. The agent of two-time Derby winner Chris Antley, Drew Mollica, has said that it also helps if you're "part horse."

Finally, there is that willingness to take life-or-death chances, like a high-wire walker. It may not have much to do with courage, though to other people it may look that way. It's not fear, it's necessity. To win—the point of the whole thing—they must do a Karl Wallenda act: Here's the three-eighth-inch cable stretched over Devil's Gorge; walk it so you can get to the other side.

Years ago, for example, Willie Shoemaker was asked if he was afraid—a necessary apposite to courage—when he powered his horse through an opening that was one horse wide, and one misstep could kill him.

Said Shoemaker: "You don't think about that when you do it."

Jockeys ride freelance, for a stable where they're under contract, or both. The good ones, like Eddie Arcaro, who was under contract to Calumet Farm, make a lot of money. One assumption people make: When a jockey wins a race, he/she gets all the purse money. Wrong. After he won the 2005 Derby, someone asked Arcaro what the greatest misconception is about jockeys. "That we get the entire purse. I wish it were true!" In fact, jockeys usually get 10 percent.

Quite a few times over Derby history jockeys have picked the wrong horse to ride, or the right one by mistake. For example, Eddie Arcaro didn't want to ride his first Derby winner, Lawrin, and Earl Sande tried to move heaven and earth to ride Quatrain in the 1925 Derby but ended up riding Flying Ebony by default—and won.

Trainers

In 1952, the great trainer Ben A. Jones and his son Jimmy were training Hill Gail, and he was acting up in the stable, being what Jimmy once characterized as "a well-authenticated bitch."

His father asked Jimmy to hold the horse's head steady and then punched Hill Gail right in the nose—and he calmed down.

Why did Jones do that? Anger, frustration—no question—but the answer behind it all was that he knew this could stop the horse, and he could do it and get away with it. Reason: Jones knew the horse inside and out.

Getting to know the horse he's training—which usually starts when the horse is a "yearling," a year old—is one of the main things trainers do. He does some basic things with the horse, such as "breaking" him (that is, letting a person straddle his back), teaching him how to break from a starting gate, and galloping him every day to keep him fit, but knowing the horse—bad habits and good—is crucial. Knowing the horse, the trainer can hand-tailor the horse's training regimen. If a trainer knows that the horse spooks easily, such as Whirlaway, who Jones characterized as "as nervous as a cat in a room full of rocking chairs," or if he knows that the horse tends to "lug"—drift to one side as he runs—he can take corrective actions, such as using blinkers or taking them off. If he knows the horse likes to come from behind, he can train him one way; if he knows the horse had great speed but limited endurance, he can try to build up that

Owner Warren Wright (left) with trainer Ben A. Jones (right)

endurance, or, failing that, enter him only in races where his speed will likely prevail.

Great trainers work very, very hard to get to know the horse they're training. Once a man saw Ben Jones standing by a fence at Calumet Farm, carefully observing a horse. The man went away but returned an hour or so later—and Jones was still there, watching the horse, which didn't appear to be doing much of anything.

"May I ask," the man said, "what are you doing?"

"Getting to know the horse."

Jones was the winningest trainer of all time. He had six Derby winners: Lawrin in

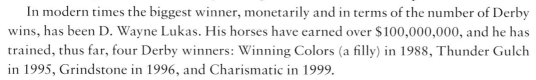

D. Wayne Lukas

1938, Whirlaway in 1941, Pensive in 1944, Citation in 1948, Ponder in 1949, and Hill Gail in 1952. H. J. "Derby Dick" Thompson trained four winners: Behave Yourself in 1921, Bubbling Over in 1926, Burgoo King in 1932, and Brokers Tip in 1933.

In modern times the biggest winner, monetarily and in terms of the number of Derby wins, has been D. Wayne Lukas. His horses have earned over $100,000,000, and he has trained, thus far, four Derby winners: Winning Colors (a filly) in 1988, Thunder Gulch in 1995, Grindstone in 1996, and Charismatic in 1999.

There have also been some great black trainers, the most famous being Dick "Brown Dick" Brown. He trained and sold Plaudit to owner John E. Madden, and the horse won the 1898 Derby.

Three trainers have won three Derbies apiece, and ten trainers have won a pair. Eleven women have trained Derby entrants. Though no female trainer has won, Shelley Riley came close with Casual Lies in the 1992 Derby when Lil E. Tee, Pat Day up, ran him down in the stretch for a one-length victory—the first Derby victory in nine tries for Day, the winningest jockey ever at Churchill Downs.

Today, trainers are mostly expected to produce a horse that will win the Derby and earn a lot of money. But there was a time, long ago, when trainers trained horses just to make a better horse. As "Sunny Jim" Fitzsimmons, who trained horses that won three Derbies—Gallant Fox in 1930, Omaha in 1935, and Johnstown in 1939—said: "Owners were sportsmen in the old days, interested in the horse for himself and not as a betting tool."

Of course, it should be noted that many owners care less about the money and more about winning the race. Many people have dreams, and dreams often don't involve money.

Just as jockeys have selected the wrong horses to ride, some trainers have trained a horse they didn't believe in that won the Derby and left them with huge amounts of egg on their faces. Two examples spring to mind. One was Assault, the "Clubfoot Comet," who the great trainer Max Hirsch didn't think much of. But Assault turned out to be that rarest of creatures, a Triple Crown winner in 1946, and is now generally regarded as one of the greatest racehorses that ever lived. How could a training whiz like Hirsch have missed Assault's greatness? Go figure.

The horse who gave trainer LeRoy Jolley an embarrassing moment was Genuine Risk (1980), only the second filly to win since Regret in 1915.

Jolley tried to convince the owners of Genuine Risk not to run her in the Derby, but they overruled him. Later, when sportscaster Jim McKay asked him why he didn't want to run her, all the embarrassed Jolley could say was, "Well, Jim, you have to keep an open mind about these things."

Jockeys, it seems, love and respect horses, but the same can't always be said for trainers—or owners. This was clearly evident in the treatment given Donau, the 1910 winner. As a tune-up for the Derby, most horses are run three or four times; some are not raced at all for months before the Derby. In the three months preceding the Derby, Donau was run *forty-one times*. It was a wonder he could stand, much less win the Derby!

A truly tragic case is that of Black Gold, the 1924 Derby winner, who captured the hearts of America as the people's horse. He was trained by an obese alcoholic named Hanley Webb who treated him badly, then returned him to racing when he was in poor condition, prompting his regular jockey to refuse to ride him. In the end, running in a race lame, he broke a leg and had to be put down. Webb denied that he knew the horse was lame, but this simply wasn't true.

Owners

For many years, as suggested earlier, Thoroughbred racing was considered to be strictly a sport: men would breed and develop horses just to be able to mount exciting competitions against one another. Then, around 1860, southern gentlemen started breeding horses not for sports but for the market. Sales heated up after the Civil War: it was a good way for southern gentlemen to survive.

Horsemen knew that the key to a horse's greatness as a racehorse was breeding. If you could buy a horse with the right pedigree, your chances of success were that much higher. Men became experts in breeding. For example, a yearling with, say, Man o' War as its father and the great filly Regret as its dam, or mother, and in good physical shape, would be considered very valuable, mainly because chances were that the blood of these two great champions would show up in their progeny. Indeed, Thoroughbred horseracing is all about bloodlines.

One of the most active and successful early breeding farms in Kentucky was the Woodburn Estate of Robert A. Alexander. Alexander happened to own the greatest sire who ever lived—Lexington, who lived from 1850 to 1875, and who William H. P. Robertson of the *Thoroughbred Record* called the "most successful stallion in history." Indeed, *fifty-two of the first sixty-one winners* of the Kentucky Derby had his blood, and all told he sired 600 fillies and colts, 260 of them being stakes race winners.

Another highly successful breeder—indeed, he did it as well as anyone who ever lived—was a handsome mustachioed Black Irish man named John E. Madden, who was born in 1856 and died in 1929. His recipe for success was to buy a horse for a low price, break and train it well, run it in a few stakes races where it could show its stuff, then wait for buyers to come calling. *Colonel E. R. Bradley*

Many owners, of course, would not train the horse but just put it up for sale; prospective buyers would examine the horse and its pedigree and go from there. Madden bred five Derby winners.

Another dominant owner was Colonel E. R. Bradley, a colorful gambler and horse

The Diamond Jubilee Derby, 1949

breeder, operator of the Idle Hour Stock Farm. He bred and trained four Derby winners himself: Behave Yourself in 1921, Bubbling Over in 1926, Burgoo King in 1932 and Brokers Tip in 1933. He liked all his horses' names to begin with the letter B—like his.

In the early 1940s, with Ben A. Jones as its head trainer, Calumet Farm started to win the Derby, starting with Whirlaway in 1941. Farms like Idle Hour and Calumet had the economic wherewithal to contract top-caliber riders—in the case of Calumet, Eddie Arcaro.

Today, many owners do not train their own horses, or even breed them. Mares are shipped to a breeding facility, where the foal is born and may be trained. This, for example, is what happened with Barbaro, who was born in one place, and trained in another, or actually two other places.

Most owners are not in racing for the money. They're in it for other reasons, reasons that mainly have to do with achieving an impossible dream. When their horse comes from far behind and crosses the finish line at the Derby first and they burst into tears, you can be just about sure it doesn't have a thing to do with money.

PART II

Two Minutes to Glory:
Race Day Stories, 1875–2006

Aristides
1st May 17, 1875

*Leamington	Faugh-a-Ballagh	Sir Hercules
		Guiccioli
	Mare by Pantaloon	Pantaloon
ARISTIDES		Daphne
Chestnut colt	Lexington	Boston
Sarong		Alice Carneal
	Greek Slave	*Glencoe
		Margaret Hunter

The Winner's Pedigree and Career Highlights

YEAR	AGE	STS.	1ST	2ND	3RD	EARNINGS
1874	2	9	3	3	0	$ 1,525
1875	3	9	4	2	1	$15,700
1876	4	2	2	0	0	$ 1,100
1878	6	1	0	0	0	$ -
TOTALS		**21**	**9**	**5**	**1**	**$18,325**

At 2 years	2ND	Thespian Stakes
	UNP	Saratoga Stakes
At 3 years	WON	Kentucky Derby, Withers Stakes, Jerome Stakes, Breckinridge Stakes
	2ND	Belmont Stakes, Ocean Hotel Stakes
	3RD	Travers Stakes

Race Day Statistics

HORSE	WT.	ST.	1/4	3/4	MILE	STR.	FIN.	JOCKEY	OWNER
Aristides	100	1	2	1	1	1	1²	O. Lewis	H. P. McGrath
Volcano	100	3	4	4	2	2	2¹/²	H. Williams	George H. Rice
Verdigris	100	4	5	5	4	3	3²	W. Chambers	C. A. Lewis
Bob Woolley	100	5	6	3	3	4	4¹/²	W. Walker	Robinson, Morgan & Co.
Ten Broeck	100	6	3	2	5	5	5⁶	M. Kelso	F. B. Harper
Grenoble	100	10	7	-	-	-	6	J. Carter	Allen Bashford
Bill Bruce	100	7	9	-	-	-	7	M. Jones	S. J. Salyer
Chesapeake	100	11	8	-	-	-	8	W. Henry	H. P. McGrath
Searcher	100	8	-	-	-	-	9	R. Colston	J. B. Rodes
Ascension	97	12	-	-	-	-	10	W. Lakeland	William Cottrill
Enlister	100	15	-	-	-	-	11	Halloway	Stringfield and Clay
McCreery	100	2	1	-	-	-	12	D. Jones	Gen. Abe Buford
Warsaw	100	14	-	-	-	-	13	Masterson	Stringfield and Clay
Vagabond	100	9	-	-	-	-	14	J. Houston	A. B. Lewis & Co.
Gold Mine	97	13	-	-	-	-	15	Stradford	J. A. Grinstead

Time: :26, :51, 1:17¹/², 1:45, 2:37³/⁴. Track fast.
Winner—Ch.c. by *Leamington-Sarong, by Lexington. Trained by Ansel Williamson; bred in Kentucky by H. P. McGrath.
Auction pools: McGrath entry (Aristides and Chesapeake) $105; Searcher $65; Ascension $55; Field $270.
$1,000 added. Net to winner $2,850; second $200.

42 nominations.

*Foreign bred

CHART ABBREVIATIONS DEFINITION KEY: **STS:** Starts **M:** Medication **Eq:** Equipment **Wt:** Weight **PP:** Post Position **ST:** Start **STR:** Stretch **FIN:** Finished

The Best Laid Plans of Mice and Men

H. PRICE MCGRATH, AN EXTRAVAGANT
gambler who won $105,000 (in 1872 when the
average blue-collar salary was $2 a day), moved
to Lexington, Kentucky to breed racehorses.
When the first Derby coalesced, he entered
two horses. One, Aristides, was a throwaway,
a small (15 hands) chestnut colt who was to be
the rabbit, tiring out the field. Then his other
powerhouse of a horse, Chesapeake, would
surge by everyone and win.

Riding Chesapeake, Aristides, and all of
the other horses in the race except one, ridden
by Billy Lakeland, who was white, were black
jockeys. Aboard Chesapeake was William
Henry, and astride Aristides was Oliver Lewis.

The weather was good, and the track—the
same track that is used today for the Derby,
except it was then one and a half miles rather
than one and a quarter—was fast. A string
was stretched across the track following a line
drawn in the dirt. The jockeys were instructed
to bring the horses to the line, which they did,
and when they were even, the starter, 125 yards
up the track thrust a red flag down, a drumroll
played, and the horses were off.

The horses immediately started to string
out, and Oliver Lewis, following McGrath's
instructions, brought Aristides into the lead.
Aristides wanted to go even faster than Lewis
wanted, so he had to pull back on the reins to
control his speed.

After about half a mile Verdigris, Enlister,
and Vagabond started to drop back—as did
Chesapeake. Indeed, the only horse keeping up
with Aristides, even at his reduced pace, was
Volcano.

McGrath's plan wasn't working out. Except
for Volcano, the other horses soon were strung
out, and if you wanted to see Chesapeake, you'd
have to borrow a telescope.

H. Price McGrath realized that the only
chance he had to win was Aristides, so he mo-
tioned to Lewis to go on—go for the win.

Lewis relaxed his burning arms and let
Aristides go, and he spurted forward. Volcano
came on like a mad dog, but he could not catch
Aristides.

The next day, the papers lauded McGrath
for his soaring genius for telling Lewis to "Go
on." But the plain fact is, he had no choice. It
was not genius, but necessity.

Oliver Lewis likely never rode again. Like
so many great black men of the time, he just
did a fade. In 1907 he reappeared, this time as
a spectator at the Derby. Where had he been,
what had he done? No one, sadly, would ever
know for sure.

Vagrant
2nd *May 15, 1876*

			*Glencoe
		Vandal	Mare by *Tranby
	Virgil		*Yorkshire
VAGRANT		Hymenia	Little Peggy
Brown gelding			Orlando
	Lazy	*Scythian	Scythia
		Lindora	Lexington
			Picayune

The Winner's Pedigree and Career Highlights

YEAR	AGE	STS.	1ST	2ND	3RD	EARNINGS
1875	2	6	5	0	1	$ 3,800
1876	3	4	3	1	0	$ 6,450
1877	4	0	0	0	0	$-
1878	5	12	0	0	4	$-
1879	6	14	3	2	2	$ 1,175
1880	7	23	7	3	3	$ 1,500
1881	8	21	2	5	2	$ 875
1882	9	7	0	1	0	$ 75
1883	10	1	0	0	0	$-
TOTALS		**88**	**20**	**12**	**12**	**$13,875**

At 2 years	WON	Alexander Stakes, Belle Meade Stakes, Sanford Stakes, Colt Stakes, and Colt and Filly Stakes
	3RD	Tennessee Stakes
At 3 years	WON	Kentucky Derby, Phoenix Hotel Stakes, Grand Exposition Stakes
	2ND	Clark Stakes

Race Day Statistics

HORSE	WT.	ST.	1/4	3/4	MILE	STR.	FIN.	JOCKEY	OWNER
Vagrant	97	4	4	1	1	1	1²	B. Swim	William Astor
Creedmore	100	3	3	3	2	2	2¹	D. Williams	Williams & Owings
Harry Hill	100	6	6	5	3	3	3¹	J. Miller	John Funk
Parole	97	1	1	4	5	4	4¹/²	P. Sparling	Pierre Lorillard
Germantown	100	5	5	6	4	5	5	W. Graham	(a) F. B. Harper
Lizzie Stone	97	-	-	-	-	6	6	W. James	(a) F. B. Harper
Marie Michon	97	-	-	-	-	-	7	Stradford	J. A. Grinstead
Bombay	100	-	-	-	-	-	8	W. Walker	Dan Swigert
Red Coat	100	-	-	-	-	-	9	L. Hughes	Green Clay
Leamingtonian	100	-	-	-	-	-	10	R. Colston	H. F. Vissman
Bullion	100	2	2	2	11	11	11	M. Kelso	A. Keene Richards

Time: :26, :51, 1:17¹/2, 1:45, 2:38¹/4. Track fast.
Coupled: (a) F. B. Harper entry.
Winner: Br. g. by Virgil–Lazy, by *Scythian. Trained by James Williams; bred in Kentucky by M. H. Sanford.
Auction pools: Vagrant, $525; Parole, $400; Creedmore, $275; Red Coat, $150; Field, $135.
$1,500 added. Net to winner $2,950; second $200.

34 nominations.

*Foreign bred

Son of "Lazy"

IT'S KIND OF HARD TO PREDICT A GREAT future for yourself as a racehorse when your mother's name is Lazy. But that was the name of the dam of the dark bay Vagrant, who won the second Derby. Vagrant, a gelding who cost $250 as a yearling, a piddling amount for a Thoroughbred even in 1876, still did quite well, undoubtedly because his daddy was Virgil, a horse that in addition to Vagrant sired two other Kentucky Derby winners, Hindoo (1881), who experts consider the best horse to win a Kentucky Derby in the nineteenth century, and Ben Ali (1886). Eventually Vagrant was purchased by millionaire William Astor for $7,000, a very large sum at the time.

The race itself was never in doubt. Vagrant kept in close contact with three or four horses who were leading, and halfway through the race his jockey Robert Swim stepped on the gas—which in those days meant using his spurs and whip and verbal urging—and Vagrant scampered home, winning by more than a length. Vagrant became the first of a number of geldings to win the Derby.

Every now and then, a heartbreak occurs in Thoroughbred horseracing, and Vagrant's fate was one. He raced nine seasons, and when he could race no more, could not turn a profit for his owners, he was sold. This Kentucky Derby winner spent the rest of his days pulling carts and other conveyances around the streets of Lexington.

Baden-Baden
3rd *May 22, 1877*

		West Australian	Melbourne
	*Australian		Mowerina
BADEN-BADEN		*Emilia	Young Emilius
Chestnut colt		Wagner	Persian
	Lavender		Sir Charles
		Alice Carneal	Maria West
			*Sarpedon
			Rowena

THE WINNER'S PEDIGREE AND CAREER HIGHLIGHTS

YEAR	AGE	STS.	1ST	2ND	3RD	EARNINGS
1876	3	4	1	3	0	$ 475
1877	4	6	3	0	1	$11,950
TOTALS		**10**	**4**	**3**	**1**	**$12,425**

At 2 years   WON   Young America Stakes
              2ND   Belle Meade Stakes, Sanford Stakes
At 3 years   WON   Kentucky Derby, Jersey Derby, Travers Stakes
              3RD   Belmont Stakes
              UNP   Clark Stakes, Kenner Stakes

RACE DAY STATISTICS

HORSE	WT.	ST.	1/4	3/4	MILE	STR.	FIN.	JOCKEY	OWNER
Baden-Baden	100	5	2	2	2	1	1^2	W. Walker	Daniel Swigert
Leonard	100	1	1	1	1	2	2^1	R. Swim	H. P. McGrath
King William	100	2	3	3	3	3	3^1	Bailey	Smallwood & Co.
Vera Cruz	97	11	9	7	6	5	4	I. Murphy	J. T. Williams
McWhirter	100	3	4	4	4	4	5	H. Moore	Gen. Abe Buford
Odd Fellow	100	8	6	-	-	6	6	D. Williams	J. J. Merrill
Malvern	100	4	5	-	-	-	7	S. Jones	George H. Rice
Early Light	97	7	-	-	-	-	8	W. James	F. B. Harper
Dan K.	97	10	-	-	-	-	9	McGrath	Johnson & Mills
Lisbon	100	6	-	-	-	-	10	Douglass	Daniel Swigert
Headlight	100	9	-	-	-	-	11	Shelton	L. B. Field

Time: :26^1/2, :52, 1:18, 1:44^3/4, 2:38. Track fast.
Winner: Ch. c. by *Australian-Lavender, by Wagner. Trained by Ed Brown; bred in Kentucky by A. J. Alexander.
Auction pools: Leonard, $150; Vera Cruz, $100; McWhirter, $50; Swigert, $50; Field (with Baden-Baden included) $45.
$1,500 added. Net to winner $3,300; second $200.

41 nominations.

*Foreign bred

"I Didn't Want to Tempt the Gods Twice"

BY THE THIRD RACE, THE DERBY WAS BLOS-soming in popularity both locally and across the country, getting a reputation as a race featuring high-quality horses and riders. This was partly reflected by a horde of reporters who came from the East and Midwest to cover the third race.

The Derby also had become a social event—and then some. It attracted all kinds of people, from men in fancy suits wearing high, shiny boots to women in colorful dresses and fancy hats who didn't know the difference between a racehorse and a rhino. Celebrities also came, such as Helena Modjeska, the star of Henrik Ibsen's play *The Dollhouse,* which was going to be put on in Louisville, and political luminaries such as Kentucky senator James Beck, Tennessee secretary of state Charles Gibbs, and the attorney general of Massachusetts, Joseph Ewalt. The Derby was already like an American version of the gala staging of a world championship boxing match, where the show outside the ring is as important as the one inside.

Certainly, the Derby promised to be exciting. Two of the best jockeys who ever lived, both black, had mounts in this race. On Baden-Baden was seventeen-year-old William Walker, who had been born into slavery in 1860 but by the advanced age of eleven was riding stakes winners! Three years earlier, when he was just thirteen, he had ridden Bombay to a fourth-place finish in the first Kentucky Derby. Astride Vera Cruz, one of the race favorites, was sixteen-year-old Isaac Murphy, a muscular young man with great riding skills who is considered by many racing savants to be the greatest jockey who ever lived.

Also in the race was Robert Swim, riding H. Price McGrath's Leonard; the year before, on Vagrant, Swim had beaten Walker on Bombay.

The day was bright and sunny, and the track, though dry, was not in the best shape. It had more than an occasional pockmark from an assault by recent rains. Delays occurred as they tried to line up the horses evenly, with various horses acting up, but when they were even, the flag plunged, the drumroll sounded, and the crowd bellowed: "They're off!!"

There was an immediate near disaster. Vera Cruz, the horse Murphy was on, reared, then stumbled, and it took all the young but master-

ful Murphy could do to right it. However, by the time he did, there was a lot of track between him and the other horses. It seemed obvious to the crowd that Murphy was out of the race. But not so fast.

Most of the horses, except for Vera Cruz and a couple of others, were bunched together in one of those scary, fast-moving clusters where everyone had to do the exact right thing or risk disaster. Then, gradually, the cluster started to break up, with horses dropping back or going ahead of the pack, and soon Robert Swim on Leonard broke into the lead.

Positions remained that way until the backstretch, when Baden-Baden, who had been in fourth place, started getting closer and closer to Leonard, the crowd noise rising in volume as he did. At the three-quarter-mile pole, the bobbing nose of Baden-Baden moved past Leonard just as they turned into the stretch, and they pounded down it together, Baden-Baden maintaining his lead.

Murphy was known for coming from way behind to win, and that was what he tried here. He had commenced his drive well before the stretch, and with the crowd cheering him on, he started to pass one horse after another until soon only Baden-Baden and Leonard were ahead of him, and he was closing. But on this day his mount didn't have enough, and he eventually finished fourth, with Baden-Baden grabbing the win and Leonard behind him. The time for the mile-and-a-half run was 2:38, quite unremarkable. Following the race, J. T. Williams, the owner of Vera Cruz, challenged Don Swigert, the owner of Baden-Baden, to a $2,500 match race.

He refused, saying: "I didn't want to tempt the gods twice."

Day Star
4th *May 21, 1878*

		Star Davis	*Glencoe	Sultan
				Trampoline
				Priam
	DAY STAR		Margaret Wood	Maria West
	Chestnut colt		Lexington	Boston
		Squeeze-'Em		Alice Carneal
			Skedaddle	*Yorkshire
				Magnolia

The Winner's Pedigree and Career Highlights

YEAR	AGE	STS.	1ST	2ND	3RD	EARNINGS
1877	2	2	0	1	0	$ 100
1878	3	6	2	1	1	$ 7,050
1879	4	8	0	1	0	$ 125
1880	5	9	3	1	2	$ 1,205
1881	6	10	5	3	1	$ 2,450
1882	7	7	1	0	1	$ 450
TOTALS		**42**	**11**	**7**	**5**	**$11,380**

At 2 years	2ND	Sanford Stakes
At 3 years	WON	Kentucky Derby, Blue Ribbon Stakes
	2ND	Clark Stakes
At 4 years	2ND	Merchants' Stakes

Race Day Statistics

HORSE	WT.	ST.	1/4	3/4	MILE	STR.	FIN.	JOCKEY	OWNER
Day Star	100	1	1	1	1	1	1^1	J. Carter	T. J. Nichols
Himyar	100	6	5	4	3	2	2^2	P. Robinson	B. G. Thomas
Leveler	100	7	6	5	5	3	3^{nk}	B. Swim	R. H. Owens
Solicitor	100	5	7	-	-	4	4$^{1/2}$	B. Edwards	L. P. Tarlton
McHenry	100	2	2	2	4	5	5^{hd}	W. James	Gen. Abe Buford
Respond	100	4	4	3	2	6	6	Ramey	Rodes & Carr
Burgundy	100	3	3	6	6	-	7	L. Jones	J. M. Wooding
Earl of Beaconsfield	100	8	8	-	-	-	8	Mahoney	A. Strauss & Co.
Charley Bush	100	9	9	-	-	-	9	J. Miller	Jennings & Hunt

Time: :25$^{1/2}$, :49$^{3/4}$, 1:16$^{1/2}$, 1:45$^{3/4}$, 2:37$^{1/4}$ (Derby record). Track dusty.
Winner: Ch.c. by Star Davis-Squeeze-'Em, by Lexington. Trained by Lee Paul; bred in Kentucky by J. M. Clay.
Auction pools: Himyar, $305; Field, $110. With Himyar out, Day Star, Burgundy, and Leveler sold about even.
Mutuel wagering in 1878, with four machines operating, but no prices available.
$5 minimum wager offered.

	Win	Place	Show
Day Star	$30.60		

No place or show tickets sold.

$1,500 added. Net to winner $4,050; second $200.

56 nominations.

*Foreign bred

A Threat in the Air

UNTIL WORLD WAR II, THE DERBY—AS were all horse races—was a rough-and-ready affair, and many jockeys would do anything they could get away with to win. Since the races weren't filmed, it was difficult for officials to prove misconduct. Jockeys could more or less do what they wanted, to exact revenge for some earlier race transgression, or just to win. Some jockeys could be bribed to do anything. Major Barak Thomas had heard rumors some people were bent on stopping his great horse Himyar in some way, so he took all precautions to protect the horse, including sleeping in his stable with him the night before the Derby.

Nine horses started. The track was said to be dusty—"two seconds slow," says writer John L. O'Connor in *History of the Kentucky Derby, 1875–1921*—but the weather was "spring-like," with a cooling breeze. There was a healthy crowd of 8,000 people watching, and many bet on Himyar, unaware of the possible danger he faced.

Himyar got off to a very bad start, and other horses were able to quickly get leads on him ranging from six to ten lengths. But he made up ground and soon only Day Star was ahead of him. But as he drove onward toward the finish, author Peter Chew wrote, "Jockey after jockey was heard to yell: 'Here he comes! Stop him! Stop him!'"

And they tried. Jockeys cut their horses in front of him, banged into him, and a couple of jockeys tried to grab his saddlecloth. Himyar's response was to do a broken field run through and around horses. In the end, though, the battering and extra effort took its toll, and Himyar was not able to catch Day Star, who won by two lengths. What that achieved for jockeys or others was never explained, but if someone investigated the episode today, their first investigative path would be to "follow the money."

The question lingered whether or not Himyar would have won without the interference. Carter rode a brilliant race on Day Star, chiefly by distancing his horse from the pack behind him, and at least one critic, race historian O'Connor, chalks Himyar's loss up to his jockey, P. Robinson, who, O'Connor maintains, rode him "miserably." Others say no, it was the blockade by other horses that did Himyar in.

Lord Murphy
5th *May 20, 1879*

			Boston
	Lexington		Alice Carneal
			American Eclipse
Pat Malloy	Gloriana		Trifle
+LORD MURPHY			Leviathan
Bay colt	Capt. Elgee		Reel
	Wenonah		
	Mare by *Albion	*Albion	
			Mare by Pacific

+Lord Murphy was originally named Patmus.

The Winner's Pedigree and Career Highlights

YEAR	AGE	STS.	1ST	2ND	3RD	EARNINGS
1878	2	4	1	2	0	$ 350
1879	3	8	5	3	0	$11,050
1880	4	1	0	0	0	$-
1881	5	1	0	0	0	$-
TOTALS		**14**	**6**	**5**	**0**	**$11,400**

At 2 years	2ND	Young America Stakes, Nashville Sweepstakes
	UNP	Flash Stakes
At 3 years	WON	Kentucky Derby, St. Leger Stakes, January Stakes, Belle Meade Stakes
	2ND	Dixie Stakes, Trial Stakes, Illinois Derby
At 4 years	UNP	Chatsworth Plate (England)
At 5 years	4TH	Newmarket Visitor's Plate (England)

Race Day Statistics

HORSE	WT.	ST.	1/4	3/4	MILE	STR.	FIN.	JOCKEY	OWNER
Lord Murphy	100	4	4	7	1	1	1^1	C. Shauer	Geo. W. Darden & Co.
Falsetto	100	8	7	5	3	2	2^1	I. Murphy	J. W. H. Reynolds
Strathmore	100	3	1	1	2	3	3^2	Hightower	George Cadwallader
Trinidad	100	2	3	3	4	4	4^1	A. Allen	Dan Swigert
One Dime	100	6	6	6	-	-	5	L. Jones	G. W. Bowen & Co.
General Pike	100	1	2	4	-	-	6	J. Stovall	Gen. Abe Buford
Ada Glenn	97	9	8	8	-	-	7	Ramey	G. D. Wilson
Buckner	100	7	5	2	5	-	8	D. Edwards	H. W. Farris
Wissahickon	97	5	9	9	-	-	9	L. Hawkins	H. P. McGrath

Time: :26, :52$^{1}/_{4}$, 1:17$^{1}/_{4}$, 1:45, 2:37 (Derby record). Track fast.
Winner:- B.c. by Pat Malloy-Wenonah, by Capt. Elgee. Trained by George Rice; bred in Tennessee by J. T. Carter.
Auction pools: Lord Murphy, $175; Strathmore and Falsetto, $60 each; Trinidad, $45; Ada Glenn, $25; Field, $30.
Mutuel tickets sold, but no payoff prices available.
$1,500 added. Net to winner $3,550; second $200.

46 nominations.

*Foreign bred

A Better Day

IT WAS SUBTLE, BUT SPECTATORS AT THE 1879 running of the Kentucky Derby seemed a little more upbeat than they had in previous years. It didn't take Freudian insight to determine why. Louisville had suffered a fiscal freefall in 1873, but had recovered by 1879. And if people had money to bet, this Derby offered a new way to do it. Bettors had a choice either to use pari-mutuel machines at the Louisville Oval, or use auction pools, a method of collective betting that most bettors favored.

Pride emanating from where colts were born and bred was always a factor in the Derby. There were Kentucky-breds—and everyone else. So, for example, owners would send horses born and bred in the East or California to compete, and this would energize races even more.

There were nine horses in the 1879 race, which would boil down to a contest between a Tennessee-bred bay colt named Lord Murphy, formerly called Patmos (why the name change, we don't know), and a Kentucky-bred colt (a colt is any male horse under five years of age) named Falsetto piloted by the great Isaac Murphy.

As the race started, Lord Murphy got bumped and went to his knees but with the help of his jockey maintained his balance and soon joined the others, who were together in a pack.

Dust always seemed to be part of these ancient Derbies, but this time it was particularly bad. Indeed, as the closely packed group of horses, a "hard-charging platoon of Cavalry," as one writer characterized them, were so tightly bunched that their collective dust-

pounding hooves raised a cloud that made them virtually invisible. Eventually, though, some riders emerged from the cloud, and colors and numbers could be read: General Pike and Trinidad were in the lead. As the race developed, however, Lord Murphy charged past them. At the mile, Isaac Murphy on Falsetto began one of his patented late charges from Nowheresville, passing many horses on his way to catching Lord Murphy. But though he was moving fastest of any of the horses at the end, he simply ran out of track, and Lord Murphy crossed the finish before he did.

Those defeated by Lord Murphy shouldn't have felt too bad. They might not have known it, but they were up against one of the progeny of Lexington, a sire whose blood would run in the veins of fifty-two Derby winners. And no, fifty-two is not a misprint.

Fonso
6th *May 18, 1880*

			King Tom
		*Phaeton	Merry Sunshine
	King Alfonso		Vandal
FONSO		Caoitola	Mare by
Chestnut colt			*Margrave
		Weatherbit	Sheet Anchor
		Mare by Birdcatcher	Miss Letty
	*Weatherwitch		Birdcatcher
			Colocynth

The Winner's Pedigree and Career Highlights

YEAR	AGE	STS.	1ST	2ND	3RD	EARNINGS
1879	2	9	3	2	2	$2,125
1880	3	3	2	1	0	$6,050
TOTALS		**12**	**5**	**3**	**2**	**$8,175**

At 2 years	WON	Maiden Stakes, Colt Stakes
	2ND	Tennessee Stakes
	3RD	Belle Meade Stakes, Colt and Filly Stakes
At 3 years	WON	Kentucky Derby, Phoenix Stakes
	2ND	Viley Stakes

Race Day Statistics

HORSE	WT.	ST.	1/4	3/4	MILE	STR.	FIN.	JOCKEY	OWNER
Fonso	105	1	1	1	1	1	1^1	G. Lewis	J. S. Shawhan
Kimball	105	2	2	2	2	2	2^3	W. Lakeland	William Cottrill
Bancroft	105	3	4	5	4	5	3$^{1/2}$	I. Murphy	Milton Young
Boulevard	105	4	3	3	5	4	4	A. Allen	W. C. McGavock & Co.
Quito	105	5	5	4	3	3	5	J. McLaughlin	Dwyer Bros.

Time: :25$^{1/2}$, :50$^{3/4}$, 1:17$^{3/4}$, 1:46$^{1/4}$, 2:37$^{1/2}$. Track very dusty.

Winner: Ch. c. by King Alfonso–*Weatherwitch, by Weatherbit. Trained by Tice Hutsell; bred in Kentucky by A. J. Alexander.

Auction pools: Kimball, $700; Quito, $362; Fonso, $222; Bancroft, $450; Boulevard was not sold because he was not announced as a starter until after the weighing-in bell was rung.

$5 minimum wager offered.

| | Win | Place | Show |
| Fonso | $15.70 | | |

No place or show tickets sold.

$1,500 added. Net to winner $3,800; second $200.

47 nominations.

*Foreign bred

"Dust Bowl"

The winning horse at this Derby, Fonso, a dark chestnut colt with a star on his head and two white feet, was the all-time Derby bargain. As horseman Howard Rowe points out, "Fonso was sold at the Woodburn yearling sales for $200. He raced only two seasons, yet piled up $8,175 in winnings."

In a way, it was a miracle that Woodburn existed. At the end of the Civil War marauding bands would raid stables and steal horses, and owner Robert Alexander had a lot of valuable horses, including Lexington. But the farm was able to survive because in 1862 Alexander met a horseman named Harry Belland and gave him thirty-four horses from the farm to do with as he pleased. Belland sold the horses wherever he could get a good price, raced them, and produced over $300,000 in earnings. Alexander said to Belland: "You have saved Woodburn!"

There were only five horses in the race this year, and it was so dusty that it made the 1879 Derby look absolutely pellucid. With the track blanketed with five inches of the stuff, it was nicknamed "the Dust Bowl." When Fonso, with black jockey George Garret Lewis aboard, broke into the lead at the outset, he disappeared in a cloud of dust. He stayed in the lead all the way, though he was challenged at one point by a horse named Kimball, piloted by Billy Lakeland.

It was no contest. Fonso went string to string and won.

But Lakeland tried to win another way. He became the first person ever to file a foul claim in the Derby, his contention being that he couldn't see Fonso because of the dust, so how could he compete? It was, of course, disallowed.

Fonso's jockey, George Garret Lewis, did not get to enjoy his great victory for long. About two months after the Derby, on June 8, he was involved in a spill during a mile race in St. Louis and died at his home in Hutchinson Station, Kentucky, on July 5. He was eighteen.

Hindoo

7th May 17, 1881

		Vandal	*Glencoe
			Alaric
	Virgil		*Yorkshire
HINDOO		Hymenia	Little Peggy
Bay colt		Lexington	Boston
	Florence		Alice Carneal
		*Weatherwitch	Weatherbit
			Mare by
			Birdcatcher

THE WINNER'S PEDIGREE AND CAREER HIGHLIGHTS

YEAR	AGE	STS.	1ST	2ND	3RD	EARNINGS
1880	2	9	7	1	1	$ 9,800
1881	3	20	18	1	1	$49,100
1882	4	6	5	1	0	$12,975
TOTALS		**35**	**30**	**3**	**2**	**$71,875**

At 2 years	WON	Colt and Filly Stakes, Alexander Stakes, Tennessee Stakes, Juvenile Stakes, Jockey Club Stakes, Criterion Stakes, Tremont Stakes
	2ND	Day Boat Line Stakes
	3RD	Windsor Hotel Stakes
At 3 years	WON	Blue Ribbon Stakes, Kentucky Derby, Clark Stakes, Tidal Stakes, Coney Stakes, Ocean Stakes, Lorillard Stakes, Monmouth Sweepstakes, Travers Stakes, Sequel Stakes, United States Hotel Stakes, Kenner Stakes, Champion Stakes, New Jersey St. Leger Stakes
	2ND	Brighton Beach Handicap
	3RD	September Handicap
At 4 years	WON	Louisville Cup, Merchants' Stakes, Turf Handicap, Coney Island Handicap, Coney Island Cup
	2ND	Dixiana Stakes

RACE DAY STATISTICS

HORSE	WT.	ST.	1/4	3/4	MILE	STR.	FIN.	JOCKEY	OWNER
Hindoo	105	2	1	1	1	1	1⁴	J. McLaughlin	Dwyer Bros.
Lelex	105	1	3	3	2	2	2ⁿᵏ	A. Allen	B. G. Thomas
Alfambra	105	6	6	6	4	3	3¹ᐟ²	G. Evans	G. W. Bowen & Co.
Sligo	105	4	5	5	5	5	4¹	B. Donohue	H. P. McGrath
Getaway	105	5	4	4	3	4	5	T. Fisher	Milton Young
Calycanthus	105	3	2	2	6	6	6	G. Smith	H. P. McGrath

Time: :25³/₄, :51¹/₄, 1:17³/₄, 1:47, 2:40. Track fast.
Winner: B. c. by Virgil–Florence, by Lexington. Trained by James Rowe Sr.; bred in Kentucky by Daniel Swigert.
Auction pools: Hindoo, $600; Lelax, $75; McGrath Entry (Sligo and Calycanthus), $70; Alfambra, $40; Getaway, $25.
$5 minimum wager offered.

	Win	Place	Show
Hindoo	$6.60		
Lelex		$12.70	

No show tickets sold.

$1,500 added. Net to winner $4,410; second $200.

62 nominations.

*Foreign bred

The Nineteenth Century's Greatest Horse

A MASS OF HUMANITY GATHERED AT Churchill Downs for this running. People were, figuratively and literally, hanging from the rafters. They were there to see the great Hindoo, regarded by many as the greatest horse of the century.

While there were plenty of people, there were only six horses. Small wonder! Hindoo was pegged as a 3–1 favorite. Why show up to lose?

If the word *gorgeous* could be applied to an animal, that was Hindoo. He was a sixteen-hand colt with a star on his forehead and a touch of gray hair highlighting his face; his right hind foot, bright white up to the pastern, gave him a somehow distinctive look, like a man with a long sock on. Besides being a naturally great horse, he was trained by James Rowe. But this was, of course, the Kentucky Derby, where unpredictability is de rigueur and the rule is, "Don't count your winnings before they're hatched"—or, to put it another way, as one writer did: "Betting on horses is an imprecise science."

When the race started, Hindoo, as expected, took the lead. Then, at the halfway pole, an unpleasant surprise occurred that scared the crowd, most of whom had bet on Hindoo: a horse named Lelex grabbed the lead. For Hindoo to lose the lead at this point in the race could be a harbinger of doom. He was going to lose!

Not yet. As the horses went into the turn, Hindoo regained the lead, and when he entered the stretch he was in total command—indeed, loafing. To wake him up, his jockey J. McLaughlin cracked him twice with the whip, which made his equine afterburners come on. He rocketed forward, and won by four lengths going away.

Hindoo's record is mind-boggling. As a two-year-old he won seven stakes races, at three, eighteen stakes races, and at four, five stakes races, plus a number of seconds and thirds. His last start was for the Coney Island Cup. Though he won easily, he broke down, his racing days finished. Consequently, his owners, the Dwyer brothers, two ex-butchers and a dominant force in racing for three decades, stopped entering their horses in long-distance races. This move by such a powerful pair was a significant factor in races in general being made shorter.

Apollo

8th *May 16, 1882*

	Lexington	*Boston*
	*Ashstead or Lever	*Alice Carneal*
APOLLO		**Trustee*
Chestnut gelding	*Levity*	*Mare by *Tranby*
	The Colonel	**Priam*
Rebecca T. Price		**My Lady*
	Mare by *Margrave	**Margrave*
		Rosalie Somers

THE WINNER'S PEDIGREE AND CAREER HIGHLIGHTS

YEAR	AGE	STS.	1ST	2ND	3RD	EARNINGS
1881	2	0	0	0	0	$-
1882	3	21	10	7	3	$14,030
1883	4	30	14	7	6	$ 7,600
1884	5	4	0	1	0	$ 50
TOTALS		**55**	**24**	**15**	**9**	**$21,680**

At 3 years	WON	Kentucky Derby, Cottrill Stakes, Coal Stakes, St. Leger Stakes, Drummers Stakes, Montgomery Stakes
	2ND	Kenner Stakes, United States Hotel Stakes, Glass Stakes, Pickwick Stakes
	3RD	Clark Stakes
At 4 years	WON	Merchants Stakes and thirteen other purses and handicap sweepstakes. Seven of the fourteen wins were consecutive in September.
	2ND	Cotton Stakes, Howard Cup
	3RD	Excelsior Stakes, Tennessee Club Post Stakes
	4TH	Champion Stakes
At 5 years	UNP	Wheeler Stakes

RACE DAY STATISTICS

HORSE	WT.	ST.	1/4	1/2	MILE	STR.	FIN.	JOCKEY	OWNER
Apollo	102	8	9	5	6	3	1^{1/2}	B. Hurd	Morris & Patton
Runnymede	105	5	5	4	3	2	2¹	J. McLaughlin	Dwyer Bros.
Bengal	105	6	-	-	8	6	3^{1/2}	T. Fisher	Bowen & Co.
Harry Gilmore	105	1	2	2	1	1⁴	4^{1/2}	Gibbs	William Cottrill
Babcock	102	2	1	3	2	5	5¹	M. Kelso	W. Lakeland
Monogram	103	7	-	-	-	6	6	B. Edwards	Milton Young
Highflyer	105	-	-	6	5	7	7	Brown	G. Kuhn & Co.
Wendover	105	9	-	-	-	-	8	Hovey	J. B. Sellers & Co.
+Pat Malloy colt	105	3	4	-	-	8	9	E. Henderson	P. C. Fox
Wallensee	107	-	-	-	-	-	10	L. Parker	Rodes & Carr
Newsboy	105	-	-	-	-	-	11	B. Quantrell	T. J. Megibben
Mistral	105	-	-	-	-	-	12	J. Stoval	L. P. Tarlton
Lost Cause	102	-	-	-	7	-	13	C. Taylor	Milton Young
Robert Bruce	105	4	3	1	4	-	14	L. Jones	A. Jackson

Time: 2:40¹/4. Track good.
Winner: Ch. g. by *Ashstead or Lever–Rebecca T. Price, by The Colonel. Trained by Green B. Morris; bred in Kentucky by Daniel Swigert.
(Three forms of betting in operation, bookmaking, odds being quoted for the first time.)
Auction pools: Runnymede, $250; Mistral, $50; Lost Cause, $40; Robert Bruce, $30; Bengal, $75; Field (with Apollo included), $75.
Bookmaking odds: Runnymede, 4 to 5, favorite; Apollo 10 to 1.
$5 minimum wager offered.

Program #		Win	Place	Show
	Apollo	$169.80		
	Runnymede		$8.50	
				No show tickets sold.

$1,500 added. Net to winner $4,560; second $200.

64 nominations.

*Foreign bred

+ The Pat Malloy colt was unnamed when racing in the Derby and is referred to by his sire's name, Pat Malloy.

Something Up His Sleeve

FOR THIS DERBY, TO BE RUN ON A TRACK pockmarked and softened by rain, Derby analysts put Apollo, a chestnut gelding, into the "can't win" category. Not that he wasn't a good horse. He was, but his black jockey, Babe Hurd, was up against some fierce competition, both horseflesh- and jockey-wise. Competitors included Erskine Henderson, a black jockey who would win the Derby a few years hence and was on a fine horse known as the "Pat Malloy colt," for his sire Pat Malloy, and M. Kelso, the jockey who had filed the foul against Fonso in the 1880 Derby, on a terrific horse named Babcock. And black owner Milton Young had entered the iron- ically named Lost Cause. And then there was the favorite, Runnymede, a superstar at eastern races. For his part, Apollo was a grandson of the astonishing sire Lexington. What's more, Hurd was gutsy, skilled, and had a trick or two up his white-and-purple silk sleeve.

After a few false starts, the horses broke cleanly. Hammering into the first turn, Bab- cock wrested the lead from Harry Gilmore, with Robert Bruce third. Runnymede was in a pocket in the back, but he worked free of it and pounded up to fifth, then third. Hurd had Apollo at sixth.

Apollo appeared to be finished. But Hurd had planned it: to hang way back, then make a final run for the cup. And he did. One writer described his equine broken field run: "Then the white and purple of Apollo wove in and out of the orange, the blue, the red, the green and the maroon silks." It was a dangerous maze. Indeed, the jockey on Lost Cause saw what Hurd was up to and started to follow him, but then gave it up: it was too treacherous a trail to follow.

With only a quarter mile left in the race, Runnymede had taken over the lead from Harry Gilmore by a head. But Apollo kept zigging and zagging, and with just an eighth of a mile left, he made what was described as a "cyclonic" charge that brought him even with Runnymede, then past him—to win by a half a length. It had worked out just the way Hurd had planned.

Apollo went on to win many more races— ten wins in twenty-one starts as a three-year- old and fourteen of thirty as a four-year-old, nine of those wins in a row.

In retrospect, analysts might have put him in another category: "can't lose"!

Leonatus
9th May 23, 1883

		*Leamington	Faugh-a-Ballagh
			Mare by
			Pantaloon
	Longfellow		Brawner's Eclipse
LEONATUS		Nantura	Queen Mary
Bay colt		*Phaeton	King Tom
	Semper Felix		Merry Sunshine
		Crucifix	Lexington
			Lightsome

THE WINNER'S PEDIGREE AND CAREER HIGHLIGHTS

YEAR	AGE	STS.	1ST	2ND	3RD	EARNINGS
1882	2	1	0	1	0	$ 100
1883	3	10	10	0	0	$21,335
TOTALS		**11**	**10**	**1**	**0**	**$21,435**

At 2 years   2ND   Maiden Stakes
At 3 years   WON   Kentucky Derby, Blue Ribbon Stakes, Tobacco Stakes,
                                  Woodburn Stakes, Hindoo Stakes, Ripple Stakes,
                                  Himyar Stakes, Dearborn Stakes, Green Stakes,
                                  Illinois Derby

RACE DAY STATISTICS

HORSE	WT.	ST.	1/4	3/4	MILE	STR.	FIN.	JOCKEY	OWNER
Leonatus	105	2	1	1	1	1	1^3	W. Donohue	Chinn & Morgan
Drake Carter	102	1	5	4	2	2	2	J. Spellman	Morris & Patton
Lord Raglan	105	3	3	3	3	3	3	B. Quantrell	Noah Armstrong
Ascender	102	4	6	5	4	4	4	J. Stoval	R. C. Pate
Standiford Kellar	105	5	4	6	5	5	5	H. Blaylock	J. R. Watts
Pike's Pride	102	7	7	7	6	6	6	G. Evans	Clipsiana Stable
Chatter	105	6	2	2	7	7	7	E. Henderson	W. C. McCurdy

Time: 2:43. Track heavy.
Winner: B. c. by Longfellow–Semper Felix, by *Phaeton. Trained by John McGinty; bred in Kentucky by John Henry Miller.
Auction pools: Leonatus, $800; Ascender, $500; Drake Carter, $450; Field, $500.
Bookmaking odds: Bookmakers operated, but prices not available.
$5 minimum wager offered.

	Win	Place	Show
Leonatus	(odds:1.96 to 1)		
	$14.80	No place or show tickets sold.	

$1,500 added. Net to winner $3,760; second $200.

50 nominations.

Foreign bred

Bet His Life Savings

Q. DID JOCKEY BILLY DONOHUE BELIEVE IN his Derby mount, Leonatus?

A. It was an open secret that Donohue bet his life savings on the horse!

Why did Donohue bet everything on Leonatus? It was a question of pure belief. In the Derby, Leonatus would be entering a grueling race—with what one would assume a very determined jockey on his back!—just six days after he had won the Blue Ribbon Stakes. He went off as a 9–5 favorite. But the crowd got at least one surprise. It had rained for three days prior to the Derby on Wednesday, and with the weather so unseasonably cool, the large crowd who showed up for the race wore rain gear and heavy coats—and were greeted by a lovely, sunny day, though the track condition was described as "heavy."

The horses broke cleanly, and the lead was taken by a horse named Drake Carter, but by the first quarter Billy Donohue—no doubt with visions of his life savings dancing in his head—took the lead by two lengths, and was never headed and, Lord be praised, won by three lengths. It was that simple, and that profound for Donohue. And how much did he win? Payoff amounts were not made available to the public back then. No odds were posted against the seven starters, with the exception of the winner.

Leonatus was undefeated as a three-year-old and won ten stakes races; counting the ten wins and one second, he won $21,435. In those days, horses were sturdier than their modern counterparts, but they were not made of steel. Not too long after the Derby, Leonatus broke down in training and never raced again.

Buchanan
10th *May 16, 1884*

			Newminster
		Buckden	Lord Clifden	The Slave
	BUCHANAN			Bay Middleton
	Chestnut colt		Consequence	Result
			Wagner	Sir Charles
				Maria West
	Mrs. Grigsby	Folly		*Yorkshire
				*Fury

THE WINNER'S PEDIGREE AND CAREER HIGHLIGHTS

YEAR	AGE	STS.	1ST	2ND	3RD	EARNINGS
1883	2	6	0	5	1	$ 500
1884	3	5	3	0	2	$ 9,385
1885	4	13	3	5	2	$ 2,100
1886	5	11	2	4	5	$ 1,125
TOTALS		35	8	14	10	**$13,110**

At 2 years	2ND	Maiden Stakes, Criterion Stakes, St. James Hotel Stakes, Alexander Stakes, Jackson Stakes
	3RD	Barrett Stakes, Belle Meade Stakes
At 3 years	WON	Kentucky Derby, Ripple Stakes, Clark Stakes
	3RD	Hindoo Stakes
At 4 years	2ND	Brewers' Stakes
At 5 years	3RD	Granite Mountain Stakes

RACE DAY STATISTICS

HORSE	WT.	ST.	1/4	3/4	MILE	STR.	FIN.	JOCKEY	OWNER
Buchanan	110	8	8	8	6	1	1¹	I. Murphy	Cottrill & Brown
Loftin	110	7	5	3	3	2	2¹	T. Sayers	R. A. Johnson & Co.
Audrain	110	3	3	5	4	4	3²	C. Fishburn	T. J. Megibben
Bob Miles	110	1	1	2	2	3	4¹ᐟ²	J. McLaughlin	J. T. Williams
Bob Cook	110	5	6	6	5	5	5	E. Gorham	R. M. McClelland
Boreas	110	9	9	9	9	7	6	O'Brien	R. M. McClelland
Admiral	110	4	4	1	1	6	7	C. Taylor	Clay & Woodford
Exploit	110	6	7	7	8	8	8	W. Conkling	Wooding & Puryear
Powhattan III	110	2	2	4	7	9	9	D. Williams	R. A. Johnson & Co.

Time: 2:40¹ᐟ₄. Track good.
Winner: Ch. c. by *Buckden–Mrs. Grigsby, by Wagner. Trained by William Bird; bred in Kentucky by Cottrill & Guest.
Auction pools: Audrain, $700; Bob Miles, $600; Buchanan, $530; Loftin (coupled with Powhattan III as R. A. Johnson & Co.'s entry), $270; Admiral, $125; Field, $90
Bookmaking odds: Buchanan, 3 to 1; Bob Miles, 3 to 1; Loftin, 7 to 2; Audrain, 4 to 1; Admiral, 5 to 1; Powhattan III, 8 to 1; Exploit, 12-1; Bob Cook and Boreas, 20 to 1.
$5 minimum wager offered.

	Win	Place	Show
Buchanan	$20.60		

No place or show tickets sold.

$1,500 added. Net to winner $3,990; second $200.

51 nominations.

*Foreign bred

Aboard: The Greatest Jockey of Them All

MORE THAN ONE HUNDRED YEARS AFTER HE hoisted his small, brown muscular body on a thousand pounds of racehorse, Isaac Murphy is, as mentioned before, regarded as arguably the greatest jockey of all time. It was noted that his winning race percentage was 44 percent—628 victories out of 1,412 races.

Isaac Murphy was born Isaac Burns on January 18, 1861, while the Civil War was busy decimating the country. And it was to decimate his family, as well. His father joined the Union army, but he was ultimately captured and taken to Camp Nelson, a little over twenty miles from Lexington, where he died—or was killed. As a result, Murphy and his siblings and their mother were uprooted and went to live with his grandfather, Green Murphy. Isaac eventually adopted the last name of the man who had served as a loving surrogate father.

In those days, life was, as it were, on the fast track very much more than today—people got married sooner, went to work sooner, and died sooner—and Murphy started riding professionally when he was fourteen. He quickly demonstrated his greatness, winning all kinds of stakes races.

Murphy was a different kind of jockey. Most jockeys would drive their spurs (which were no longer used after World War II) into a horse's flanks and beat on it—sometimes dementedly—with a whip as a race heated up, but not Murphy, not usually. He hunched down, his face close to the horse's neck, and spoke to it with his mouth and hands and with a heart that some people described as that of a lion.

Murphy was a patient rider; he had confidence in himself and the horse. Instead of propelling the horse to the front early, he would wait until the right moment and then, his horse still having a full or nearly full tank, drive from far back to win. He was, as someone from the time put it, "a great pacer."

In Murphy's time it was common to bribe jockeys and others, but not Murphy. He was a latter-day Serpico, a man who wouldn't take a dime. And he was a hero to both blacks and whites. In describing him, one old man who liked baseball and racing said; "He was Joe DiMaggio on horseback."

Despite Murphy's skills, for years he suffered the fate of many great jockeys—though trying a number of times, he could not get that garland of roses draped over his horse.

Then he intersected with a horse who he knew would give him a real a shot at the roses. The horse's name was Buchanan. Murphy knew he had only one problem: Buchanan was crazy. One aspect of his craziness was abruptly turning himself into a thirty-five-to-forty-mile-an-hour trampoline midway through a race and catapulting his jockey off, not a healthy occurrence in the middle of a race. Many jockeys would simply not ride him for a simple reason: they wanted to live.

But Murphy decided to give the horse a shot—his speed was worth it. He figured he could get him under control by Derby day, but he was wrong: he could not break the horse of his psychotic ways. Reluctantly, he informed Derby officials that he was withdrawing as Buchanan's jockey. And they reluctantly informed him that if he didn't race, he would be suspended from riding indefinitely.

Backed into a corner, Murphy got back up on Buchanan.

Murphy wasn't psychotic either, and he had no intention of becoming part of Buchanan's trampoline act. He had a plan for controlling him. When the race started, he pulled back on the reins, sending a message—with the bit jammed hard in Buchanan's mouth—that Murphy was in control by controlling Buchanan's head movement. The cost to Murphy was the stress on his small, powerful arms as he held that head steady. It seemed to work: Buchanan was moving at a good clip toward the front, giving no indication that he was going to send Murphy aloft.

Down the backstretch a horse named Admiral had led, setting a very fast pace. But now he paid for his sprint. At the three quarter-pole, as they say in racing, he "died."

Buchanan passed him, and set out for the few other horses ahead of him. But Murphy knew it was potential-trampoline time: there was no way to catch them without risking it all, releasing the pressure on the bit, relaxing and letting Buchanan go.

He relaxed his burning arms.

Buchanan drove on, his great head bobbing, sailing by horse after horse until he passed the best thing of all first—the finish line. With the runner-up two lengths behind him, Murphy, hallelujah, was still in the saddle. He had won his first Kentucky Derby—and lived to tell about it.

Joe Cotton
11th *May 14, 1885*

		Phaeton	King Tom
			Merry Sunshine
	King Alfonso		Vandal
JOE COTTON		Capitola	Mare by *Margrave
Chestnut colt		Macaroni	Sweetmeat
	*Inverness		Jocose
		Elfrida	Faugh-a-Ballagh
			Espoir

The Winner's Pedigree and career highlights

YEAR	AGE	STS.	1ST	2ND	3RD	EARNINGS
1884	2	12	2	3	1	$ 725
1885	3	11	8	0	1	$21,560
1886	4	8	3	0	2	$ 2,455
1887	5	11	3	2	3	$ 3,925
1888	6	10	1	0	0	$ 700
1889	7	2	0	1	0	$-
TOTALS		**54**	**17**	**6**	**7**	**$29,365**

At 2 years	2ND	Nursery Stakes, Post Stakes
	3RD	Hyde Park Stakes
	UNP	Walnut Hill Stakes, Optional Stakes, Kenwood Stakes
At 3 years	WON	Kentucky Derby, Great Western Handicap, Coney Island Derby, Tidal Stakes, Himyar Stakes, Louis and Gus Straus Stakes, Tennessee Derby, Cottrill Stakes
	3RD	Clark Stakes
	UNP	Travers Stakes, Oakwood Handicap
At 4 years	WON	Farewell Stakes
	3RD	Fourth of July Handicap
	UNP	Excelsior Handicap, Suburban Handicap
At 5 years	WON	Average Stakes, Twin City Handicap, Welter Stakes
At 6 years	UNP	Suburban Handicap

Race Day Statistics

HORSE	WT.	ST.	1/4	3/4	MILE	STR.	FIN.	JOCKEY	OWNER
Joe Cotton	110	8	7	7	5	1	1^{nk}	E. Henderson	J. T. Williams
Bersan	110	5	2	3	3	2	2$^{1/2}$	E. West	Morris & Patton
Ten Booker	110	10	10	4	4	3	3^{1}	J. Stoval	Milton Young
Favor	110	1	5	6	6	5	4^{2}	Thompkins	Morris & Patton
Irish Pat	110	3	4	2	2	4	5	I. Murphy	Ed Corrigan
Keokuk	110	2	1	1	1	6	6	C. Fishburn	W. P. Hunt
Clay Pate	110	7	9	9	9	9	7	T. Withers	R. C. Pate
Thistle	110	6	6	5	7	7	8	H. Blaylock	P. G. Speth
Playfair	107	9	8	8	8	8	9	W. Conkling	G. W. Darden & Co.
Lord Coleridge	107	4	3	10	10	10	10	L. Hughes	William Cottrill

Time: :25³/4, :51¹/2, 1:17¹/4, 1:44, 2:37¹/4. Track good.
Winner: Ch. c. by King Alfonso–*Inverness, by Macaroni. Trained by Abe Perry; bred in Kentucky by A. J. Alexander.
Auction pools: Joe Cotton, $500; Bersan and Favor, $215 (coupled as Morris & Patton entry); Ten Booker, $75; Irish Pat, $40; Playfair and Thistle, $35, each; Lord Coleridge, $25; Field $30.
Bookmaking odds: Joe Cotton, even money; Bersan, 2 to 1; Ten Booker, 10 to 1.
$5 minimum wager offered.

	Win	Place	Show
Joe Cotton	$9.30	$8.80	
Bersan		$7.40	

No show tickets sold.
$1,500 added. Net to winner $4,630; second $200.

69 nominations.

*Foreign bred

A Race to Remember

WOODBURN ESTATE, THE BREEDING FARM
that in the Civil War had been saved by Harry
Belland because of the infusion of $300,000
from horses that owner Robert Alexander had
given Belland to manage, had been returned
to full breeding prominence under Robert's
brother, A. J. Between 1877 and 1901 A. J. produced five Kentucky Derby winners (though he
never had a starter himself), one of whom was
Joe Cotton, whose sire was King Alfonso, who
also produced the 1880 winner Fonso.

Joe Cotton would be involved in one of the
most thrilling Derby runnings of all time.

He was piloted by a twenty-one-year-old
black jockey named Erskine "Babe" Henderson,
who had already ridden in two other Derbies.

The largest crowd ever had assembled in
the grandstand and other areas and flanked the
track ten deep for half a mile. It was a clear,
lovely day, the track fast. The horses started
cleanly, and by the half-mile mark a horse
named Bersan had taken the lead. Favor was in
second place, and Joe Cotton had moved easily
into third place. Henderson had to be very careful so he wasn't pocketed (trapped behind other
horses). It was, as it were, defensive driving
equine-style. Then, while the jockeys on Bersan
and Favor were busy themselves pocketing a
fast-moving horse named Thistle—bang! Henderson slipped Joe Cotton into the lead.

Henderson had to be super careful; keep Joe
Cotton moving without exhausting him. He did
this with his knees—not spurs—and his mouth,
talking to Joe, while the other two jockeys went
frantically to the whip.

Down the stretch they drove, and then another horse named Ten Booker entered the fray,
making a charge at Joe Cotton with everything
he had. Joe Cotton, frothing at the mouth, was
exhausted, and almost gave out—and then
Henderson went to the whip and spur.

But it was still not over. The crowd roared
anew as Bersan launched a final drive, passing
Ten Booker, and then was just a neck behind
Joe Cotton, himself reaching down into the
nothingness inside him, as great racehorses do,
to find a part of his heart that had not been
called on before, and he did—and won by a
neck.

Later, analysts said that Bersan would have
won if he had started his final drive sooner, and
his stablemate, Favor, who had run in front of
him at one point, had not interfered. Maybe—
and maybe not. But on that day Joe Cotton
looked invincible. When you can still run with
nothing left, you are very hard to beat.

Ben Ali
12th *May 14, 1886*

			*Glencoe
		Vandal	Alaric
	Virgil		*Yorkshire
BEN ALI		Hymenia	Little Peggy
Brown colt			Boston
	Ulrica	Lexington	Alice Carneal
			Young Emilius
	*Emilia	Persian	

THE WINNER'S PEDIGREE AND CAREER HIGHLIGHTS

YEAR	AGE	STS.	1ST	2ND	3RD	EARNINGS
1885	2	5	1	0	0	$ 3,340
1886	3	12	7	2	2	$18,550
1887	4	17	4	1	0	$ 2,850
1888	5	6	0	0	3	$ 350
TOTALS		**40**	**12**	**3**	**5**	**$25,090**

At 2 years	WON	Hopeful Stakes
	UNP	Flatbush Stakes, Autumn Stakes, Champion Stallion Stakes, Goodbye Stakes
At 3 years	WON	Kentucky Derby, Charles Green Stakes, St. Louis Derby, Ocean Stakes, Spirit of the Times Stakes, Winters Stakes
	2ND	First Special Sweepstakes, Champion Stakes
	3RD	Choice Stakes, Omnius Stakes
	UNP	American Derby
At 4 years	WON	Free Handicap, Fourth of July Handicap
	UNP	Woodlawn Handicap, Suburban Handicap
At 5 years	3RD	Westchester Handicap
	4TH	Equality Stakes

RACE DAY STATISTICS

HORSE	WT.	ST.	1/4	3/4	MILE	STR.	FIN.	JOCKEY	OWNER
Ben Ali	118	4	5	4	4	3	1$^{1/2}$	P. Duffy	J. B. Haggin
Blue Wing	118	10	9	8	8	2	2^2	E. Garrison	Melbourne Stable
Free Knight	118	5	7	5	2	1	3^1	W. Fitzpatrick	P. Corrigan
Lijero	118	8	6	9	10	7	4$^{1/2}$	I. Murphy	E. J. Baldwin
Jim Gray	118	2	4	7	6	6	5$^{1/4}$	T. Withers	Gray & Co.
Grimaldi	118	9	10	6	3	5	6	I. Lewis	J. & J. Swigert
Sir Joseph	118	1	3	3	5	4	7	W. Conkling	R. A. Swigert
Harrodsburg	118	6	2	2	1	8	8	J. Riley	Chinn & Morgan
Lafitte	118	7	8	10	9	9	9	J. Stovall	J. G. Greener & Co.
Masterpiece	118	3	1	1	7	10	10	E. West	S. S. Brown

Time: :24$^{3/4}$, :50, 1:16, 1:43, 2:36$^{1/2}$ (Derby record). Track fast.
Winner: Br.c. by Virgil-Ulrica, by Lexington. Trained by Jim Murphy; bred in Kentucky by Daniel Swigert.
Auction pools: Ben Ali, $500; Free Knight, $385; Blue Wing, $150; Jim Gray, $65; Lijero, $50; Field, $70.
Bookmaking odds: Bookmarkers did not operate because of failure to reach license agreement with management.
$5 minimum wager offered.

	Win	Place	Show
Ben Ali	$13.60	$12.00	
Blue Wing		$16.00	
			No show tickets sold.

$1,500 added. Net to winner $4,890; second $300; third $150.

107 nominations.

*Foreign bred

"Good-bye and _____ You!"

ONE OF THE WORST THINGS EVER TO HAP-
pen to the Kentucky Derby was perpetrated by
a Kentuckian named James Ben Ali Haggin.
Haggin, a pompous, egocentric kind of man,
became incensed when track officials decreed
the day before the 1886 Derby that people could
no longer place bets through bookies, a legal
activity at the time. Haggin was a well-known
"plunger," and his not being able to bet on
horses from his very large stable was not an op-
tion. He warned track officials to reverse their
position or he would remove all his horses from
the Derby stables and race elsewhere.

Officials buckled, but one of the Downs officials was overheard to say, "Who does he [Hag-
gin] think he is? To hell with him anyway."

The remark got back to Haggin, and he
moved his scores of horses to New York. New
York already had a better reputation for mounting quality races than Churchill Downs and
the Derby's image was further weakened when
other owners boycotted the Derby in sympathy
for Haggin.

But prior to this blowup he had a horse he
adored—Ben Ali, named after his son—in the
Derby.

Ben Ali was favored, and something new
had been added—literally—to this Derby. All
horses would now carry 118 pounds—instead
of 110—and fillies 113.

A horse named Masterpiece broke in the
lead, followed by Sir Joseph. Ben Ali was in
third. All were flying.

Near the half, Free Knight hammered into
the lead in front of Harrodsburg, Jim Gray a

head behind him. Close behind were Ben Ali,
Blue Wing, and Masterpiece. The pace continued to be fierce. At the three-quarter pole,
nearing the stretch, positions had changed: now
Free Knight was a half length in front of Ben
Ali, and Blue Wing was third. They changed
again at the furlong pole: driving head to head
were Ben Ali and Blue Wing, Free Knight a half
length behind.

Then, critics would say later, Blue Wing's
jockey made a fatal mistake. As they turned
into the stretch, he brought his horse outside,
losing some ground, so that Ben Ali went to
the rail and—just like that—gained a length
lead. They pounded down the stretch, and as
they did, Blue Wing gained inch after inch, but
it was not enough inches. Ben Ali crossed the
finish line a scant three-quarters of a length
ahead, and in the fastest time ever for a mile-
and-a-half Derby: 2:36 1/2.

Haggin the elder finally did return to
Churchill Downs with his stable—eleven years
after he left. "That man," one CD official said
in a masterpiece of understatement, "had a bad
temper."

Montrose
13th *May 11, 1887*

		Waverly	*Australian
	Duke of Montrose		Cicily Jopson
MONTROSE		Kelpie	*Bonnie Scotland
Bay colt			Mare by Sovereign
	Patti	*Billet	Voltigeur
			Calcutta
			Pat Malloy
	Dora		Etta Jr.

The Winner's Pedigree and Career Highlights

YEAR	AGE	STS.	1ST	2ND	3RD	EARNINGS
1886	2	13	2	2	2	$ 2,690
1887	3	10	3	2	4	$10,200
1888	4	12	5	3	0	$ 7,555
1889	5	16	4	4	3	$ 6,876
TOTALS		**51**	**14**	**11**	**9**	**$27,321**

At 2 years	WON	Free Handicap, Cotton Exchange Stakes
	2ND	Mechanics Stakes
	3RD	Prospect Stakes, Moet and Chandon Stakes
	UNP	Autumn Stakes, Optional Stakes, Camden Stakes, Red Bank Stakes, St. Louis Hotel Stakes
At 3 years	WON	Kentucky Derby, St. Leger Stakes, Blue Ribbon Stakes
	2ND	Sheridan Stakes, Phoenix Stakes
	3RD	Latonia Stakes
	UNP	American Derby
At 4 years	WON	Morrissey Stakes, Kearney Stakes, Great Western Handicap, Distillers' and Brewers' Stakes
	2ND	Grand Prize of Saratoga, Boulevard Stakes, Merchants Stakes
At 5 years	WON	Kearney Stakes, Cincinnati Hotel Handicap
	2ND	Boulevard Stakes, Kentucky Handicap
	3RD	Excelsior Handicap, Free Handicap, Distillers' and Brewers' Stakes
	UNP	Merchants' Stakes

Race Day Statistics

HORSE	WT.	ST.	1/4	3/4	MILE	STR.	FIN.	JOCKEY	OWNER
Montrose	118	3	1	1	1	1	1^2	I. Lewis	Labold Bros.
Jim Gore	118	4	4	5	2	2	2^1	W. Fitzpatrick	A. G. McCampbell
Jacobin	118	1	6	6	4	4	3^2	J. Stoval	Robert Lisle
Banburg	115	5	5	3	3	3	4no	H. Blaylock	J. D. Morrisey
Clarion	118	7	4	4	6	5	5	Arnold	Fleetwood Stable
Ban Yan	118	2	2	2	5	6	6	Godfrey	W. O. Scully
Pendennis	118	6	3	7	7	7	7	I. Murphy	Santa Anita Stable

Time: 2:39$^{1}/4$. Track fast.
Winner: B. c. by Duke of Montrose–Patti, by *Billet. Trained by John McGinty; bred in Kentucky by Milton Young.
Auction pools: 8 to 5 against Banburg; 2 to 1, Jim Gore; 4 to 1, Pendennis; 5 to 1, Jackobin; 6 to1, Ban Yan; 10 to 1, each, Montrose and Clarion.
Bookmaking odds: Montrose, 10 to 1; Jim Gore, 3 to 1; Jackobin, 6 to 1; Banburg, 7 to 5; Clarion, 10 to 1; Ban Yan, 5 to 1; Pendennis, 4 to 1.
$1,500 added. Net to winner $4,200; second $300; third $150.

86 nominations.

*Foreign bred

Sure Thing (Ho-Ho)

THE SKY, OVERCAST, SEEMED TO BE A PERfect physical symbol of what was going on in the Derby. With James Ben Ali Haggin now racing his horses elsewhere, there were fewer quality horses running. Still, a Kentucky Derby is a Kentucky Derby, and a large crowd showed up—perhaps another reason being that many of them wanted to win what looked like sure money on the long-striding Banburg, whom the *Louisville Courier-Journal* and others had marked as the overwhelming favorite. When the horse was led from the paddock and the crowd saw him, they gave him a thunderous ovation.

Not everyone thought Banburg a shoo-in. Some handicappers thought that Jim Gore would win the race if he did not break down. The horse that was hardly considered was Montrose, a bay colt with a blaze and white foot, a light body, and clean legs. Montrose's jockey

was a seventeen-year-old black man named Isaac Lewis, who would ride in four consecutive Derbies from 1886 to 1889. Also behind the string would be Isaac Murphy on Pendennis, making his seventh Derby appearance but still seeking his second Derby victory.

The race started well. Jacobin broke into the lead, Ban Yan was second, Banburg third, and the rest clustered behind.

Then, at the quarter pole, Montrose surged to the lead and, unbelievably, kept it. As they entered the stretch, he was ahead by a length. Jim Gore, who faltered at the half, rallied and was running behind Montrose—and that's the way they finished, Montrose winning by a length and a half in the snail's time of 2:39 1/2, Jacobin third, and the favorite, Banburg, whose day it obviously wasn't, fourth. Isaac Murphy came clip-clopping in a hundred yards down the track, in last place. It wasn't his day either.

Macbeth II
14th *May 14, 1888*

			Macaroni
		*Macaroon	Songstress
	Macduff		*King Ernest
	MACBETH II	Jersey Lass	Jersey Belle
	Brown gelding		Lexington
	Agnes	Gilroy	Magnolia
			Star Davis
		Laura Bruce	Alida

The Winner's Pedigree and Career Highlights

YEAR	AGE	STS.	1ST	2ND	3RD	EARNINGS
1887	2	8	1	1	0	$ 1,340
1888	3	25	7	5	5	$11,745
1889	4	16	3	1	2	$ 1,600
1890	5	35	10	9	5	$ 4,990
1891	6	9	3	3	1	$ 2,195
1892	7	1	0	0	0	$-
1893	8	12	1	2	1	$ 300
TOTALS		**106**	**25**	**21**	**14**	**$22,170**

At 2 years	WON	Kimball Stakes
	UNP	Maiden Stakes, Belle Meade Stakes, Blue Grass Stakes
At 3 years	WON	Kentucky Derby, Kansas City Derby, Gayoso Hotel Stakes, Peabody Hotel Stakes
	2ND	Phoenix Stakes, Distillers' Stakes, Merchants' Stakes, Cottrill Stakes
	UNP	Boulevard Stakes
At 4 years	3RD	Welter Handicap
At 5 years	WON	Green Stakes, Highweight Handicap
	UNP	Welter Stakes
At 6 years	WON	Clifton, N.J., New Year's Handicap

Race Day Statistics

HORSE	WT.	ST.	1/4	1/2	MILE	STR.	FIN.	JOCKEY	OWNER
Macbeth II	115	6	7	6	5	2	1^1	G. Covington	Chicago Stable
Gallifet	118	7	5	1	1	1	2^1	A. McCarthy	Melbourne Stable
White	118	4	3	4	6	4	3^2	T. Withers	W. O. Scully
Alexandria	118	5	2	2	3	5	4$^{1/2}$	L. Jones	Melbourne Stable
The Chevalier	118	1	4	3	2	3	5	I. Lewis	T. J. Clay
Autocrat	118	3	1	7	7	6	6	A. Hamilton	D. Gibson
Col. Zeb Ward	118	2	6	5	4	7	7	H. Blaylock	G. M. Rye

Time: 2:38^1/4. Track slow.
Winner: Br. g. by Macduff–Agnes, by Gilroy. Trained by John Campbell; bred in Kentucky by Rufus Lisle.
Bookmaking odds: Gallifet and Alexandria (Melbourne Stable entry), even money; The Chevalier, 3^1/2 to 1; White, 4 to 1; Macbeth II, 6 to 1; Col. Zeb Ward, 12 to 1; Autocrat, 12 to 1.
Mutuels: Pay-off prices not available.
Auction pools: Prices not available.
$2,500 added. Net to winner $4,740; second $500; third $200.

95 nominations.

*Foreign bred

Nasty Weather

THIS WAS THE YEAR THAT THE BLIZZARD of '88 occurred in New York City. Twenty-seven inches of snow fell on the city starting on March 12; many people died, and engineers learned that the best place for electric and phone wires was underground, not strung between poles. It was as if a faint reminder of that storm hit Louisville, because it was one of the worst weather days ever for the running of the Kentucky Derby. It was cloudy, cold, and raw, with a stiff breeze blowing directly across the track from the north. There was no rain, and as one observer described it, "the dust blew in blinding clouds." The only thing they didn't have was snow.

The track had been wetted down to help control the dust, and that helped, but it was still slow.

And with all this, how small was the crowd?

Not small at all. Fourteen thousand fans showed up on wagons, on horses, walking, and in mule-drawn streetcars. The show must go on.

As the race started, Chevalier jumped to the lead, followed by Gallifet and Autocrat. From that point until the halfway mark, Macbeth II, son of Macduff, a brown gelding who sported the orange-and-black silks of the Chicago Stable, with young George Covington up. Macbeth was running two lengths behind Gallifet as they turned into the homestretch, but he ran Gallifet down, and Macbeth crossed the finish line a length ahead.

One critic said that Gallifet was the best horse in the race, and though not in the best shape, "with a good jockey would have won." In any case, Macbeth was the third gelding to win the Derby, and no other was to win it until Old Rosebud in 1914. For his romp through the raw day, Macbeth II won $22,170 for his owner, G. Covington.

Spokane
15th *May 9, 1889*

			Faugh-a-Ballagh
		*Leamington	Mare by Pantaloon
	Hyder Ali		Lexington
	SPOKANE	Lady Duke	Magdalen
	Chestnut colt		Crater
	Interpose	*Intruder	Lady Bountiful
			Lightning
		Lilac	Dolly Carter

THE WINNER'S PEDIGREE AND CAREER HIGHLIGHTS

YEAR	AGE	STS.	1ST	2ND	3RD	EARNINGS
1888	2	5	2	0	0	$ 1,535
1889	3	8	3	2	1	$24,970
1890	4	4	0	2	1	$ 300
TOTALS		**17**	**5**	**4**	**2**	**$26,805**

At 2 years	WON	Maiden Stakes
	4TH	Hyde Park Stakes
At 3 years	WON	Kentucky Derby, American Derby, Clark Stakes
	2ND	Sheridan Stakes, Peabody Hotel Handicap
	3RD	Pelham Bay Handicap
	UNP	Twin City Handicap, Drexel Stakes

RACE DAY STATISTICS

HORSE	WT.	ST.	1/4	1/2	MILE	STR.	FIN.	JOCKEY	OWNER
Spokane	118	3	4	5	4	2	1no	T. Kiley	Noah Armstrong
Proctor Knott	115	4	1	1	1	1^1	2^2	S. Barnes	Scoggan & Bryant
Once Again	118	7	6	6	6	4	3^1	I. Murphy	Milton Young
Hindoocraft	118	1	2	3	3	3	4^1	Armstrong	Scoggan Bros.
Cassius	118	5	5	8	7	6	5$^{1/2}$	F. Taral	Beverwyck Stable
Sportsman	118	8	7	2	2	5	6	I. Lewis	J. K. Megibben & Co.
Outbound	118	6	8	7	5	7	7	Hollis	Fleetwood Stable
Bootmaker	118	2	3	4	7	8	8	Warwick	Wilson & Young

Time: :24$^{3/4}$, :48$^{1/2}$, 1:14$^{1/2}$, 1:41$^{1/2}$, 2:09$^{1/2}$; 2:34$^{1/2}$ (new Derby record). Track fast.
Winner: Ch. c. by Hyder Ali–Interpose, by *Intruder. Trained by John Rodegap; bred in Montana by Noah Armstrong.
Bookmaking odds: Proctor Knott, 1 to 2; Spokane, 6 to 1; Once Again and Bootmaker (Young Entry), 3 to 1; Hindoocraft, 10 to 1; Cassius, 15 to 1; Outbound, 15 to 1; Sportsman, 15 to 1.
$2 mutuel tickets sold for the first time this year.

	Win	Place	Show
Spokane	$34.80	$6.30	
Proctor Knott		$2.90	
		No show tickets sold.	

$2,500 added. Net to winner $4,880; second $300; third $150.

94 nominations.

*Foreign bred

Fastest Race Ever

EIGHT HORSES COMPETED IN THIS RACE ON a hot day and dusty track (what else?) but it turned out to be the fastest mile-and-a half Derby ever. It was also the most crowded ever. People came by the usual animal conveyances and by foot, but also by Louisville's first electric streetcar. People were there for one reason: it promised to be a particularly great race.

As the starter tried to get the race going, a huge, strong horse named Proctor Knott got into trouble right away. He false-started twice, almost throwing the ninety-pound boy who was his jockey over his head and each time running an eighth of a mile before he was stopped.

Finally, the eight horses went away evenly; Hindoocraft followed by Bootmaker and then Proctor Knott. They had not gone fifty yards when Proctor Knott dashed to the front and soon led by three lengths, and as they got to the backstretch the boy on his back urged him on, and he increased his lead to five lengths.

Proctor Knott held his lead at the quarter, but it had been reduced by three lengths by the half, with Sportsman second and Hindoocraft third.

Spokane moved up and took second place, and then it happened: as they neared the three-quarter pole S. Barnes, the boy jockey, was unable to control Proctor Knott and hold his head up. The horse bolted to the outside, an action that lost him three or four lengths. Before Barnes could straighten him out, Spokane was charging up next to the rail and took the lead. Inside the sixteenth pole, Proctor Knott charged again, and the two horses thundered virtually together to the wire, the huge crowd going wild: Spokane won by a short throat-latch. It was an amazing performance by Proctor Knott, but he was still the loser. Critics, of course, blamed his jockey. Indeed, it seemed that the criticism was valid; he was simply too small to manage such a beast. The time was 2:34 1/2.

Riley
16th *May 14, 1890*

		*Leamington	Faugh-a-Ballagh
	Longfellow		Mare by Pantaloon
+RILEY		Nantura	Brawner's Eclipse
Bay colt			Queen Mary
			Lexington
	Geneva	War Dance	Reel
			Uncle Vic
	La Gitana		Georgia Wood

+Riley was originally named Shortfellow.

THE WINNER'S PEDIGREE AND CAREER HIGHLIGHTS

YEAR	AGE	STS.	1ST	2ND	3RD	EARNINGS
1889	2	12	6	3	0	$ 4,505
1890	3	21	11	6	2	$21,065
1891	4	15	8	3	1	$14,360
1892	5	3	2	1	0	$ 1,050
1893	6	10	2	4	1	$ 2,150
1894	7	3	1	0	0	$ 300
TOTALS		**64**	**30**	**17**	**4**	**$43,430**

At 2 years	WON	Railway Stakes, Trial Stakes, Merchants' Stakes
	2ND	Kimball Stakes, Gaston Hotel Stakes
	UNP	Westside Stakes
At 3 years	WON	Kentucky Derby, Clark Stakes, Speculation Handicap, Fairview Lightweight Handicap, Pelham Bay Handicap
	2ND	St. Leger Stakes, Latonia Derby, Himyar Stakes
	3RD	Runnymede Handicap, Brookwood Handicap
At 4 years	WON	Monmouth Cup, Shrewsbury Handicap, Coney Island Cup, Bay Ridge Handicap, Free Handicap, Brooklyn Cup, Montgomery Stakes
	2ND	Monmouth Champion Stakes, Long Branch Handicap
	3RD	Distillers' Stakes
	UNP	Suburban, Metropolitan Handicap, Brooklyn Jockey Club Handicap
At 6 years	2ND	Boulevard Stakes

RACE DAY STATISTICS

HORSE	WT.	ST.	1/4	1/2	MILE	STR.	FIN.	JOCKEY	OWNER
Riley	118	5	6	2	1	1^2	$1^{1\text{-}3/4}$	I. Murphy	Ed Corrigan
Bill Letcher	118	1	5	5	2	2^2	2^2	A. Allen	W. R. Letcher
Robespierre	118	4	1	1	3	3	3^1	S. Francis	G. V. Hankins
Palisade	118	2	4	3	4	4	$4^{1/2}$	T. Britton	S. Williams
Outlook	118	6	3	6	5	5	5	Breckinridge	B. J. Treacy
Prince Fonso	118	3	2	4	6	6	6	A. Overton	J. C. Twymann & Co.

Time: 2:45. Track muddy. Start good.
Winner: B. c. by Longfellow–Geneva, by War Dance. Trained by Edward Corrigan; bred in Kentucky by C. H. Durkee.
Bookmaking odds: Robespierre, even money; Riley, 4 to 1; Bill Letcher, 5 to 1; Prince Fonso, 5 to 1; Palisade, 8 to 1; Outlook, 10 to 1.
No auction pools or mutuels sold at track after 1889 until 1908. However, auction pools sold in 1890, 1891 and for years thereafter in downtown Louisville, on night before, and morning of Derby.
$2,500 added. Net to winner $5,460; second $300; third $150.

115 nominations.

*Foreign bred

The End of Isaac Murphy?

IN 1887 SOMETHING STRANGE HAD happened to the wondrous Isaac Murphy in the Kentucky Derby: he finished last, on Pendennis. And more strangeness occurred in 1888, when he didn't have a Derby mount. People wondered what was going on, but many people thought that he was finished.

Not quite.

In 1889 he piloted Milton's Young Once to a third-place finish in the Derby, and the next year came to the post ready to pilot Riley, owned and trained by "Big Ed" Corrigan, a madman and drunk and gambler who would punch you in the jaw if he thought you were looking at him the wrong way—or with seemingly no provocation at all.

But that race, which Murphy won, hardly had a storybook finish, unless you like unhappy endings.

The weather god had been good to the Kentucky Derby, but not today. As the horses lined up to run, rain pounded down on the track, making it sloppy, slippery, a little dangerous, and supplying free mud baths to horses and jockeys.

When the race started, as he did with Buchanan, Murphy pulled the reins back to control Riley as he drove through the mud, but this time he didn't wait to make a move. At the backstretch he moved to the outside and took the lead, instantly panicking other jockeys to drive forward, fight to get the lead. But then Murphy pulled another one of his old tricks: he loosened the reins on Riley and the other horses, who seemed to be going at top speed, were left, as it were, standing still. Murphy and Riley went to the wire unchallenged. Isaac Murphy had won his second Derby.

But when Murphy marched Riley past the judge's stand, horse and man were a study in contrasts. Riley looked like he could run another half mile, and Murphy looked like he could not ride another inch.

Before the race, rumors had flown that Murphy was not giving himself regular nourishment. To control his weight he would gulp down a glass or two of champagne as a meal. And it's almost certain the rumors were right. Though medicine did not yet understand the enervating effects of yo-yo dieting, the effects could be clearly seen on Murphy: nine weeks before the Derby he weighed 133, but by race time he was down to 118 pounds, 15 pounds lighter, a substantial amount of weight for someone of Murphy's diminutive stature to lose so quickly. And then, of course, between races he regained the weight.

At any rate, a lot of people thought that he was through. What happened in the next Derby, in 1891, seemed to confirm it.

Kingman
17th May 13, 1891

			Windhound or Melbourne
		Thormanby	Alice Hawthorn
	*Glengarry		Rifleman
KINGMAN		Carbine	Troica
Bay colt			Lexington
	Patricia	Vauxhall	Verona
			Planet
		Minnie Mc	Edina

THE WINNER'S PEDIGREE AND CAREER HIGHLIGHTS

YEAR	AGE	STS.	1ST	2ND	3RD	EARNINGS
1890	2	16	4	6	2	$ 3,900
1891	3	12	6	0	4	$15,465
TOTALS		**28**	**10**	**6**	**6**	**$19,365**

At 2 years	2ND	Edgewater Handicap, Railway Stakes, Hyde Park Stakes
	3RD	Monmouth Free Handicap
At 3 years	WON	Kentucky Derby, Phoenix Stakes, Latonia Derby, St. Paul Free Handicap
	3RD	American Derby
	4TH	Sheridan Stakes

RACE DAY STATISTICS

HORSE	WT.	ST.	1/4	1/2	MILE	STR.	FIN.	JOCKEY	OWNER
Kingman	122	4	4	4	4	4	$1^{1/2}$	I. Murphy	Jacobin Stable
Balgowan	122	3	3	3	3	$1^{1/2}$	2^1	A. Overton	T. J. Clay
High Tariff	122	2	2	2	2	2nd	$3^{1/2}$	R. Williams	Eastin & Larabie
Hart Wallace	122	1	1	1	1	3^{nk}	4	T. Kiley	Bashford Manor

Time: $1:05^{1/2}$ (half), $1:35^{3/4}$ (six furlongs), 2:01 (mile), $2:52^{1/4}$. Track slow.
Winner: B. c. by *Glengarry–Patricia, by Vauxhall. Trained by Dud Allen; bred in Tennessee by A. C. Franklin.
Bookmaking odds: Kingman, 1 to 2; Balgowan, 3 to 1; High Tariff, 15 to 1; Hart Wallace, 7 to 2.
$2,500 added. Net to winner $4,550; second $300; third $150.

83 nominations.

*Foreign bred

"The Walking Derby"

ON AUGUST 26, 1890, AT MONMOUTH PARK, Isaac Murphy was the odds-on favorite on the filly Firenzi. What Murphy did—or didn't do—in that race was described in the *New York Times:* "Murphy's pitiful attempts to ride Firenzi culminated just after the mare passed the judges' stand last when he should have been first. He could not keep her tight, and she bolted over to the inner fence. . . . Murphy had strength enough left to prevent a collision. That was all. As soon as he had practically stopped her, what strength he had was gone and he fell out of the saddle in a heap on the track." And it resulted in Murphy being suspended from racing.

Just what was going on? Some people think it was a combination of drinking champagne as a meal, yo-yo dieting, and, worst of all, "flipping," the name given in those days to bulimia, where one eats and then vomits. But by the time the 1891 Derby came around, Murphy's suspension had been lifted, and he was astride a horse named Kingman in a race to be witnessed by 25,000 rabid fans.

When the race started, it immediately developed into what the *Louisville Courier-Journal* was to describe as a "funeral procession." The shocker was that none of these horses were in full gallop. It seemed that trainers told their jockeys not to make their moves until others did. Murphy seemed content to simply watch the three horses ahead of him.

Only in the stretch did Balgowan break from the pack, and Murphy took after him, caught him, and powered to a one-length victory.

The 1891 Derby was Isaac Murphy's true swan song to horseracing. Thereafter he returned to the depleted condition he was in and rode fewer and fewer mounts. On February 12, 1896, he died of a condition diagnosed as pneumonia. He was thirty-five years old.

Murphy was buried in an out-of-the-way cemetery, but somebody had the presence of mind to replace the wooden marker, which was rotting, with a concrete one. Many years later, in 1967, after a three-year search, his remains were found and he was buried next to Man o' War Memorial Park, indeed right next to the great horse, and a mile and half from Lexington. It is hard to think of a more fitting resting place: arguably the greatest jockey to ever live next to arguably the greatest horse. In 1967 Murphy was elected to the Racing Hall of Fame. Isaac Murphy will be remembered as long as horses race.

Azra
18th May 11, 1892

		*Leamington	Faugh-a-Ballagh
			Mare by Pantaloon
	Reform		The Knight of Kars
AZRA		*Stolen Kisses	Defamation
Bay colt			*Eclipse
	Albia	Alarm	*Maud
			Kentucky
		Elastic	Blue Ribbon

The Winner's Pedigree and Career Highlights

YEAR	AGE	STS.	1ST	2ND	3RD	EARNINGS
1891	2	13	2	2	3	$ 5,690
1892	3	10	3	1	4	$15,020
TOTALS		**23**	**5**	**3**	**7**	**$20,710**

At 2 years	WON	Champagne Stakes
	2ND	Essex Stakes
	3RD	Nursery Stakes, Dunmow Stakes, Partridge Stakes
	UNP	Select Stakes, Carteret Handicap, White Plains Handicap, Sapphire Stakes
At 3 years	WON	Kentucky Derby, Travers Stakes
	2ND	Choice Stakes
	3RD	Jerome Stakes, Bridge Handicap, Lorillard Stakes, Garfield Park Derby
	4TH	American Derby

Race Day Statistics

HORSE	WT.	ST.	1/4	1/2	MILE	STR.	FIN.	JOCKEY	OWNER
Azra	122	2	2	2	2	2	1no	A. Clayton	Bashford Manor
Huron	122	1	1	1	1	1	2^6	T. Britton	(a) Ed Corrigan
Phil Dwyer	122	3	3	3	3	3	3	A. Overton	(a) Ed Corrigan

Time: :25^1/4, :51^1/2, 1:17^3/4, 1:45^1/4, 2:41^1/2. Track heavy.
Coupled: (a) Huron and Phil Dwyer.
Winner: B. c. by Reform–Albia, by Alarm. Trained by John H. Morris; bred in Kentucky by George J. Long.
Bookmaking odds: Azra, 3 to 2; Huron and Phil Dwyer, 11 to 20.
$2,500 added. Net to winner $4,230; second $300; third $150.

68 nominations.

*Foreign bred

Surprise

THERE WAS NO QUESTION IN THE MIND OF many people that the eighteenth running of the Kentucky Derby was going to be a ho-hum affair. Three or four of the best horses had dropped out and the final lineup consisted of a grand total of three horses. What was more, the weather was cold and clammy.

The runners that day were Azra, piloted by Alonzo Clayton, Thomas Britton aboard Huron, and Monk Overton on Phil Dwyer. All of the jockeys were black.

But the race hardly turned out to be dull. Madman Ed Corrigan owned two of the entries, Huron and Phil Dwyer, and he had a simple strategy. Britton on Huron would be the rabbit, set a frenetic pace, and tire out Azra in the process. Then Overton on Phil Dwyer could coast past Azra to victory.

The race started out just that way. Huron

bolted ahead to a five-length lead over Azra, with Phil Dwyer a length and a half behind. As the horses approached the first turn, which would lead them all to mud, Huron and Phil Dwyer were taken outside to relatively dry track. But Clayton chose to take Azra though the mud—and take a three-length lead.

Huron kept driving and regained some of the lead, but Phil Dwyer was struggling.

Then as the horses rolled into the final turn, Azra drove hard, nibbling away at Huron's lead. Then Huron came back, and then Azra took over, nose to nose, first one horse ahead, then the other—all by a nose.

Then Azra was so close to the rail, Clayton couldn't use a whip. But Azra kept driving.

Down the stretch they drove, neck and neck, the crowd of 10,000 in full throat, the horses running inside the quiet eye of a tornado of sound, and just at the finish Azra nipped Huron by—what else—a nose.

Lookout
19th May 10, 1893

	Lisbon	*Phaeton
		*Lady Love
Troubadour		*Glenleg
LOOKOUT	Glenluine	Lute
Chestnut colt		*Phaeton
	King Alfonso	Capitola
Christina		Lexington
	Luileme	Rosette

THE WINNER'S PEDIGREE AND CAREER HIGHLIGHTS

YEAR	AGE	STS.	1ST	2ND	3RD	EARNINGS
1892	2	20	9	4	2	$ 5,585
1893	3	8	3	0	0	$ 8,730
1894	4	18	2	2	0	$ 1,000
1895	5	18	3	5	3	$ 1,910
1896	6	2	0	1	0	$ 125
TOTALS		**66**	**17**	**12**	**5**	**$17,350**

At 2 years	WON	Minneapolis Stakes
	2ND	Turf Exchange Stakes
	3RD	Merchants' Hotel Handicap
At 3 years	WON	Kentucky Derby, Gibson Stakes, Annual Stakes
	UNP	American Derby
At 5 years	WON	Coney Island Highweight Handicap
	3RD	Toronto Cup
	UNP	Royal Canadian Hurdle Handicap

RACE DAY STATISTICS

HORSE	WT.	ST.	1/4	1/2	MILE	STR.	FIN.	JOCKEY	OWNER
Lookout	122	2	1	1	1	1	1⁴	E. Kunze	(a) Cushing & Orth
Plutus	122	4	4	2	2	2	2²	A. Clayton	Bashford Manor
Boundless	122	6	6	6	4	4	3⁴	R. Williams	(a) Cushing & Orth
Buck McCann	122	5	5	5	3	3	4	C. Thorpe	Scoggan Bros.
Mirage	122	3	3	4	5	5	5	I. Murphy	James E. Pepper
Linger	122	1	2	3	6	6	6	E. Flynn	C. E. Railey

Time: :26, :51$\frac{1}{2}$, 1:17$\frac{1}{2}$, 1:45$\frac{1}{2}$, 2:39$\frac{1}{4}$. Track fast.
Coupled: (a) Lookout and Boundless.
Winner: Ch. c. by Troubadour–Christina, by King Alfonso. Trained by William McDaniel; bred in Kentucky by Scoggan Brothers.
Bookmaking odds: Cushing & Orth's entry of Lookout and Boundless, 7 to 10; Plutus, 9 to 2; Buck McCann, 4.
$3,000 added. Net to winner $3,840; second $400; third $150.

60 nominations.

*Foreign bred

"Kill 'Em!"

THERE WERE A COUPLE OF NEW THINGS at this Derby. One was that for the first time women were able to make their own bets. And for the first time the crowd broke 30,000.

The race seemed perfect for mudders. It had rained hard the day before and through the night, and though the sun broke through on Derby morning, the track was still designed, touts thought, for horses who like to run in mud.

Also according to the touts, of the six Derby starters, three good horses had shown an affinity for mud: Boundless, winner of the Arkansas Derby, Linger, who had captured the Distillers' Stakes at Lexington, and Lookout, who had won in Memphis. Two horses from the stable of Cushing and Orth, Lookout and Boundless, were favored.

William McDaniel, the trainer of Lookout, gave jockey Ed Kunze simple instructions: "Kill 'em." In other words, blast out at the beginning and stay there. When the race started, Kunze tried just that: he sprinted to the turn, grabbing a two-length lead rounding the turn, and never looked back, leading all the way and never really challenged. He won over Plutus by five lengths, and there was nary a dot of mud on his golden coat, which could hardly be said for the other finishers.

An also-ran in the Derby was Mirage, with the great three-time Derby winner Isaac Murphy aboard. Less than three years later, on February 12, 1896, Murphy would be gone.

Chant
20th *May 15, 1894*

		Enquirer	*Leamington
			Lida
	Falsetto		*Australian
CHANT		Farfaletta	Elkhorna
Bay colt			*Phaeton
	Addie C.	King Alfonso	Capitola
			Lexington
		Aerolite	Florine

The Winner's Pedigree and Career Highlights

YEAR	AGE	STS.	1ST	2ND	3RD	EARNINGS
1893	2	25	8	5	3	$ 3,900
1894	3	33	13	7	3	$13,835
1895	4	4	1	3	0	$ 545
1896	5	1	0	0	0	$ -
TOTALS		**63**	**22**	**15**	**6**	**$18,280**

At 2 years   UNP   Sensation Stakes, Harold Stakes
At 3 years   WON   Kentucky Derby, Clark Stakes, Phoenix Stakes
At 4 years   2ND   Country Club Stakes

Race Day Statistics

HORSE	WT.	ST.	1/4	1/2	MILE	STR.	FIN.	JOCKEY	OWNER
Chant	122	2	1	1	1	1^{10}	1^6	F. Goodale	Leigh & Rose
Pearl Song	122	4	3	2	2	2^{15}	2^{10}	R. Williams	C. H. Smith
Sigurd	122	1	2	3	3	3	3^{15}	A. Overton	Bashford Manor
Al Boyer	122	3	4	4	4	4	4	H. Ray	Anderson & Gooding
Tom Elmore	122	5	5	5	5	5	5	J. Irving	S. K. Hughes & Co.

Time: 2:41. Track fast.
Winner: B.c. by Falsetto–Addie C., by King Alfonso. Trained by Eugene Leigh; bred in Kentucky by A. J. Alexander.
Bookmaking odds: Chant, 1 to 2; Pearl Song, 3 to 1; Sigurd, 12 to 1.
$2,500 added. Net to winner $4,020; second $300; third $150; fourth 100.

55 nominations.

*Foreign bred

A New Home

1894 SAW $100,000 SPENT ON MASSIVE improvements at Churchill Downs, including a new grandstand featuring the now world-famous twin spires. Importantly, the architect, Joseph Baldez Jr., designed the grandstand so fans didn't have to look into the setting sun.

While there were still other problems with the Derby, as noted earlier in the book, the killer—sometimes literally—was still the length of the race. Owners were loath to run their young horses, with their relatively pliable bones, in a race that made more than a few break down, never to run again. As noted elsewhere, a horse turns three for race purposes on January 1 of his third year. A horse born later in the year can be awfully young to try and run with the weight of a man—albeit a small man—on his back over a mile and a half at top speed.

The 1894 race again suffered from a lack of quality horses. There were only five starters, and by the halfway mark a horse named Chant, who was a quality horse, was two lengths in the lead. He fairly loafed to the finish, the other four horses—who were not quality—strung out for forty lengths behind him. The time was 2:41 for the mile and a half, one of the slowest Derbies ever (the slowest was Riley's 2:47 in 1890).

The jockey who won the race, F. Goodale, did not have much time to enjoy his win. In a race two days later, his horse stumbled and fell, and Goodale was killed. It was a brutal reminder of just how dangerous Thoroughbred horse racing can be, and, as someone else once said, of "the brevity and precariousness of life itself."

Halma
21st May 6, 1895

				Virgil
			Hindoo	Florence
		Hanover		Bonnie Scotland
	HALMA		Bourbon Belle	Ella D.
	Black colt			*Leamington
			Longfellow	Nantura
		Julia L.		*Australian
			Christine	La Grande
				Duchesse

THE WINNER'S PEDIGREE AND CAREER HIGHLIGHTS

YEAR	AGE	STS.	1ST	2ND	3RD	EARNINGS
1894	2	9	2	1	2	$ 1,785
1895	3	5	4	1	0	$13,635
1896	4	0	0	0	0	$ -
1897	5	2	1	0	1	$ 465
TOTALS		**16**	**7**	**2**	**3**	**$15,885**

At 2 years	2ND	Nursery Stakes
	3RD	Dunmow Stakes
	UNP	White Plains Handicap, Matron Stakes, Seashore Stakes, Autumn Stakes
At 3 years	WON	Kentucky Derby, Latonia Derby, Clark Stakes, Phoenix Hotel Stakes
	2ND	Himyar Stakes

RACE DAY STATISTICS

HORSE	WT.	ST.	1/4	1/2	MILE	STR.	FIN.	JOCKEY	OWNER
Halma	122	1	1	1	1	1	1⁵	J. Perkins	Byron McClelland
Basso	122	4	4	4	4	2	2⁴	W. Martin	C. H. Smith
Laureate	122	2	2	2	2	3	3⁵	A. Clayton	Pastime Stable
Curator	122	3	3	3	3	4	4	A. Overton	Bashford Manor

Time: 2:37$^{1}/_{2}$. Track fast.
Winner: Blk. c. by Hanover–Julia L., by Longfellow. Trained by Byron McClelland; bred in Kentucky by Eastin & Larrabie.
Bookmaking odds: Halma, 1 to 3; Basso, 9 to 2; Laureate, 5 to 1; Curator, 20 to 1.
$2,500 added. Net to winner $2,970; second $300; third $150; fourth $100.

57 nominations.

*Foreign bred

The Youngest Jockey

THE SAYING GOES: "FALLING OFF A HORSE that is going forty miles an hour among other horses is no way to stay healthy."

In October of 1893 James "Soup" (as a jockey he probably favored it as food because of its low calorie content) Perkins, a black jockey, had a bad fall. As one of the reporters who witnessed it said, Perkins, "who rode with much success in the meeting here in Lexington, got a hard fall at Nashville last Tuesday, his mount Merry Eyes going down with him. Perkins was badly stunned and was unconscious for several hours. But the physician who attended him says that he is not injured. This is the first fall that Perkins ever had and it may have the effect of making him timid."

It didn't make him timid. What was far more dangerous to Perkins was "flipping," the same practice that Isaac Murphy almost surely used. He would eat and then purge himself, and it had a very negative effect. He died at the ripe old age of thirty-one.

In the 1895 Derby Perkins, who was just fifteen, was on a horse named Halma, wearing the green and orange silks of the owner, Byron McClelland, and he was a heavy favorite. There were only four horses in the race. As a three-year-old he had won the Phoenix Hotel Stakes at Lexington, the race directly before the Derby.

Perkins knew how good Halma was: at the start of the race he held the horse back so he

could pace him properly. Still, when the race started Halma quickly burst into the lead by a length. Perkins would say later, "I had an easy thing of it. I never let go of Halma's head. . . . I had to hold him clear to the finish. There was no place in the race when I could not have gone away from the field as I pleased, and I felt safe. He could have gone six miles further and beat such horses as those. . . ." When he crossed the finish three lengths to the good Perkins became the youngest jockey ever to win the Derby, a record that stood until 1978.

There was a change in this Derby. In the 1890s horses had been assigned 122 pounds, but after Halma's win the weight dropped again to 117 for most starters.

Ben Brush
22nd *May 6, 1896*

			Iago
		Bonnie Scotland	Queen Mary
	Bramble		*Australian
BEN BRUSH		Ivy Leaf	Bay Flower
Bay colt			*Leamington
	Roseville	Reform	Stolen Kisses
			Alarm
		Albia	Elastic

THE WINNER'S PEDIGREE AND CAREER HIGHLIGHTS

YEAR	AGE	STS.	1ST	2ND	3RD	EARNINGS
1895	2	16	13	1	1	$22,517
1896	3	8	4	1	1	$27,340
1897	4	16	8	3	3	$17,045
TOTALS		**40**	**25**	**5**	**5**	**$66,902**

At 2 years	WON	Champagne Stakes, Albany Stakes, Nursery Stakes, Heavy Handicap (all ages), Prospect Handicap, Holly Handicap, Diamond Stakes, Emerald Stakes, Harold Stakes
	2ND	Flatbush Stakes
	UNP	Great Eastern Handicap
At 3 years	WON	Kentucky Derby, Latonia Derby, Buckeye Stakes, Schulte Stakes
	2ND	National Derby
	3RD	Oakley Derby
	UNP	Fall Handicap
At 4 years	WON	Second Special, First Special, Omnium Handicap, The Citizens Handicap, Brighton Handicap, Suburban Handicap
	2ND	Oriental Handicap
	3RD	Brighton Cup, Midsummer Handicap
	UNP	Long Island Handicap, Sheepshead Bay Handicap

RACE DAY STATISTICS

HORSE	WT.	ST.	1/4	1/2	MILE	STR.	FIN.	JOCKEY	OWNER
Ben Brush	117	4	4	2	2	1^{hd}	1no	W. Simms	M. F. Dwyer
Ben Eder	117	1	7	4	4	2^{1}	2^{8}	J. Tabor	Hot Springs Stable
Semper Ego	117	2	3	3	3	4^{2}	3^{8}	A. Perkins	L. B. Ringgold
First Mate	117	5	1	1	1	3^{hd}	4	C. Thorpe	Eastin & Larabie
The Dragon	117	6	5	6	5	5	5	A. Overton	James E. Pepper
Parson	117	7	6	7	7	7	6	T. Britton	Himyar Stable
The Winner	117	3	2	5	6	6	7	W. Walker	William Wallace
Ulysses	117	8	8	8	8	8	8	R. Williams	Ed Brown

Time: :25, :49^{1}/$_{2}$, 1:15^{1}/$_{2}$, 1:42, 2:07^{3}/$_{4}$. Track very dusty. At post 20 minutes.
Winner: B. c. by Bramble–Roseville, by Reform. Trained by Hardy Campbell; bred in Kentucky by Clay & Woodford.
Bookmaking odds: Ben Brush, 1 to 2; Ben Eder, 2 to 1; Semper Ego, 9 to 1.
Value $6,000. Net to winner $4,850; second $700; third $300.

171 nominations.

*Foreign bred

Something He Didn't Want To Do

WHEN LONGTIME HORSEMAN HOWARD Rowe was asked who he thought was the greatest jockey who ever lived, the questioner had a few possibilities in mind: Eddie Arcaro? Willie Shoemaker? Bill Hartack? Isaac Murphy?

Rowe's answer was quick and definitive: "A black kid named Willie Simms."

Some might agree, some might disagree, but Simms was certainly up there with the very best. The bottom line is that Simms got the respect of white and black, and the general public, at a time when civil rights were abysmal, as reflected in 1896 by the U.S. Supreme Court ruling in *Plessey vs. Ferguson* that a black person could not sit where he wished on a public train.

In the Derby, Simms rode a horse named Ben Brush, who was named after a trainer. He won, but to win he had to do something that he didn't want to do: be brutal. There were seventeen starters in the race, and it was the first where the distance—to attract more contenders whose trainers would not subject their young horses to such a long race—was finally lowered from 1 1/2 to 1 1/4 miles. When the race started, just that quick, it was almost over for Simms. Ben Brush stumbled, and it took all of Simms's strength to pull him upright. By the time they hit the first turn, Ben Brush was fourth. As it happened, only one of the horses would pose a threat, Ben Eder, a horse who was at that moment running twelve lengths behind.

But as the race progressed and the lead horses fell out of contention, Ben Eder moved up . . . and up . . . until by the final furlong he had pulled even with Ben Brush. Simms was against using the whip, particularly at the end of a race, when, he said, a "horse at the end of the journey is tired . . . and all the support you can give him helps his chances."

But in the final yards, as Ben Eder surged by him, Simms cast his philosophy to the wind, whacked his spurs into the horse's heaving sides, used the whip, and spoke to the colt's innate courage by pushing his hands along his neck. Horse and man kept driving, and Ben Brush won in the final stride.

Simms's ride was certainly not pretty, but it worked.

Typhoon II
23rd *May 12, 1897*

		Sterling	Oxford
			Whisper
	*Top Gallant		Adventurer
TYPHOON II		Sea Mark	Sea Gull
Chestnut colt			Citadel
	Dolly Varden	*Glenleg	*Babta
			Virgil
		Nannie Black	Nannie Butler

The Winner's Pedigree and Career Highlights

YEAR	AGE	STS.	1ST	2ND	3RD	EARNINGS
1896	2	18	8	6	1	$ 7,565
1897	3	11	8	2	1	$12,420
1898	4	10	3	1	1	$ 2,340
TOTALS		**39**	**19**	**9**	**3**	**$22,325**

At 2 years	WON	Westchester Highweight Handicap, Golden Rod Stakes, Brewers' Stakes
	2ND	Nursery Stakes, Great Eastern Stakes, Two-Year-Old Champion Stakes
	3RD	Kindergarten Stakes
	UNP	White Plains Handicap, Rancocas Stakes, Champagne Stakes
At 3 years	WON	Kentucky Derby, St. Louis Club Members Handicap, Memorial Handicap, Peabody Hotel Handicap, Luehrmann Hotel Stakes, Chickasaw Club Handicap
	2ND	Tennessee Derby
	3RD	St. Louis Derby
At 4 years	WON	Highweight Handicap
	3RD	Coney Island Handicap
	UNP	Fall Handicap, Toboggan Handicap, Metropolitan Handicap

Race Day Statistics

HORSE	WT.	ST.	1/4	1/2	MILE	STR.	FIN.	JOCKEY	OWNER
Typhoon II	117	1	1	1	1	1[3]	1[nk]	F. Garner	J. C. Cahn
Ornament	117	4	5	2	2	2	2[20]	A. Clayton	C. T. Patterson & Co.
Dr. Catlett	117	6	6	4	4	4	3[4]	R. Williams	Turney Bros.
Dr. Shepard	117	5	4	3	3	3	4[30]	J. Hill	Foster Bros.
Goshen	117	2	2	6	5	5	5	W. Wilhite	John Rodegap
Ben Brown	117	3	3	5	6	6	6	S. Ballard	Chas. Fleischmann

Time: 2:12 1/2. Track heavy.
Winner: Ch. c. by *Top Gallant–Dolly Varden, by *Glenleg. Trained by J. C. Cahn; bred in Tennessee by John B. Ewing.
Bookmaking odds: Typhoon II, 3 to 1; Ornament, even; Dr. Catlett, 4 to 1.
Value $6,000. Net to winner $4,850; second $700; third $300.

159 nominations.

*Foreign bred

Down the Stretch

THE FAVORITE IN THE 1897 DERBY WAS Ornament, and many fans felt that he would win—that is, until it started to rain on Derby day. Many people knew that another horse, the Tennessee-bred Typhoon II, liked the mud more.

The rain didn't keep the crowd away. There were at least twenty thousand people on hand. Many were focused on Typhoon II because as the horses lined up for the race, he seemed very anxious, wheeling and plunging. Because of him, it took about six minutes to get the race under way.

The nervousness, or whatever it was that was making him antsy, also galvanized him into action when the race started. He immediately broke into the lead, and Ornament lit out after him. And from that moment on there was only one question: Would Ornament catch him? As E. L. Aroma, turf editor of the *Louisville Courier-Journal*, described it, "Around the far turn Clayton throws the whip into Ornament's side, and he runs out from under it marvelously. A full length is closed, but Clayton settled down to hand-riding again and no more of the gap is closed. Again, he does this as the finish of the first mile is passed. . . . And still Typhoon races in front."

Then they are in the homestretch, and "Boots" Garner, Typhoon's young rider, "swings Typhoon wide, landing him in the best and driest path. . . . [Alonzo] Clayton takes a chance. He hugs the rail and saves at least a length. . . . Ornament is closing on Typhoon.

"Clayton goes to the whip at the eighth pole and Ornament comes forward from under punishment. He is nearing Typhoon! What is this boy Garner going to do? Every ounce of Typhoon is out. . . ."

But Garner did nothing except look straight ahead. "He is climbing forward on the leader's withers coaxing him on, coaxing him always on. Typhoon is all out but done but Ornament is too, staggering a length back and the wire is overhead.

"Ornament is gaining, gaining, gaining at every jump, running from the whip, ready to go until he drops. But Typhoon, with that same steam-engine action with which he gained the lead, is holding it. The wire is reached. Garner is still climbing and coaxing, Ornament is still fighting. . . . Typhoon II is winner of the Kentucky Derby of 1897."

Plaudit
24th *May 4, 1898*

		Alarm	Eclipse
	Himyar		*Maud
PLAUDIT		Hira	Lexington
Brown colt			Hegira
	*Cinderella	Tomahawk or	Blue Mantle
		*Blue Ruin	Raffle
		Manna	Brown Bread
			Tartlet

THE WINNER'S PEDIGREE AND CAREER HIGHLIGHTS

YEAR	AGE	STS.	1ST	2ND	3RD	EARNINGS
1897	2	12	4	1	0	$ 8,345
1898	3	8	4	4	0	$23,720
TOTALS		**20**	**8**	**5**	**0**	**$32,065**

At 2 years	WON	Champagne Stakes, Nursery Stakes, Emerald Stakes
	2ND	Dash Stakes
	UNP	Great Plains Handicap, Futurity, Diamond Stakes
At 3 years	WON	Kentucky Derby, Buckeye Stakes, Oakley Derby, Clark Stakes
	2ND	Realization, St. Louis Derby, Latonia Derby

RACE DAY STATISTICS

HORSE	WT.	ST.	1/4	1/2	MILE	STR.	FIN.	JOCKEY	OWNER
Plaudit	117	3	2	2	2	2	1no	W. Simms	J. E. Madden
Lieber Karl	122	2	1	1	1	1	2^{20}	T. Burns	J. W. Schorr
Isabey	117	1	4	3	3	3	3	A. Knapp	Stanton & Tucker
Han d'Or	117	4	3	4	4	4	4	J. Conley	G. A. Singerly

Time: :25$1/2$, :50$1/4$, 1:16$1/2$, 1:43$1/4$, 2:09. Track good.
Winner: Br. c. by Himyar–*Cinderella, by Tomahawk. Trained by John E. Madden; bred in Kentucky by Dr. J. D. Neet.
Bookmaking odds: Plaudit, 3 to 1; Lieber Karl, 1 to 3; Isabey, 12 to 1; Han d'Or, 25 to 1.
Value $6,000. Net to winner $4,850; second $700; third $300.

179 nominations.

*Foreign bred

Nothing Left but Courage

WILLIE SIMMS HAD BEEN INVOLVED IN A brutal Derby in 1896. In 1898 history repeated itself.

Simms was on a horse named Plaudit. His chief competition and the favorite in the race was Lieber Karl, ridden by Tom Burns. The two jockeys disliked each other intensely, so much so that M. Lewis Clark, the head of Churchill Downs, warned them that they would be subject to a lengthy suspension if they engaged in unsportsmanlike conduct.

Most experts picked Lieber Karl to win, and when the race started the horse jumped into a lead of one and a half lengths. A couple of other horses, Han d'Or and Isabey, made a run at Lieber Karl, but they couldn't close the gap. The race soon became a race between Plaudit and Lieber Karl.

They stayed close to one another down the backstretch, and as they came around the final turn heading into the stretch, Simms started to press Plaudit to move faster. But it looked like it was going to be Lieber Karl's race. He was galloping along easily, while Plaudit was a little choppy, struggling.

As they hit the stretch, Plaudit was still trying, and though he started to "wobble," he had cut the gap between himself and Lieber Karl.

To win, though, Simms knew that he would have to ask Plaudit for everything he had. But he also knew this was a delicate operation. Simms was very aware that Plaudit was close to the point of no return, so although it was the stretch, Simms pulled back and gave the horse a breather. But then they were both at the eighth pole and there was no tomorrow. Both jockeys had to go all-out, and they did, stride for stride, both using the whip maniacally. As Simms would confirm later, during this final drive Plaudit had nothing left but his courage.

Plaudit won by a nose, earning Simms, at the time, the accolade of the "greatest jockey alive."

Manuel

25th May 4, 1899

	Bob Miles	Pat Malloy	Lexington
			Gloriana
		Dolly Morgan	Revenue
MANUEL			Sally Morgan
Bay colt		Alarm	*Eclipse
	Espanita		*Maud
		Outstep	Blue Eyes
			Etna

The Winner's Pedigree and Career Highlights

YEAR	AGE	STS.	1ST	2ND	3RD	EARNINGS
1898	2	17	3	4	4	$4,540
1899	3	4	1	1	0	$5,200
TOTALS		**21**	**4**	**5**	**4**	**$9,740**

At 2 years	WON	Prospect Stakes
	2ND	White Plains Handicap, Surf Stakes
	3RD	Champagne Stakes, Algeria Stakes, Wenonah Stakes
	UNP	Nursery Stakes, Great Eastern Stakes, Autumn Maiden Stakes, Flatbush Stakes
At 3 years	WON	Kentucky Derby
	2ND	Montgomery Handicap
	UNP	Twin City Handicap

Race Day Statistics

HORSE	WT.	ST.	1/4	1/2	MILE	STR.	FIN.	JOCKEY	OWNER
Manuel	117	1	3	1	1	1	1^2	F. Taral	A. H. & D. H. Morris
Corsini	122	5	5	3	2	2	$2^{1\text{-}1/2}$	T. Burns	Ed Corrigan
Mazo	117	4	4	4	3	3	3^6	J. Conley	J. E. Madden
His Lordship	110	2	1	2	4	4	4^3	N. Turner	J. D. Smith
Fontainebleu	117	3	2	5	5	5	5	A. Overton	J. M. Forsythe

Time: :25³/4, :51¹/4, 1:17³/4, 1:45¹/2, 2:12. Track fast. Start good.
Winner: B. c. by Bob Miles–Espanita, by Alarm. Trained by Robert J. Walden; bred in Kentucky by George J. Long.
Bookmaking odds: Manuel, 11 to 20; Corsini, 3 to 1; Mazo, 8 to 1.
Value $6,000. Net to winner $4,850; second $700; third $300.

151 nominations.

*Foreign bred

A Great Man Dies

THE TWENTY-FIFTH RUNNING OF THE KEN-tucky Derby was not one that writer/horseman John L. O'Connor loved. As he wrote in his *History of the Kentucky Derby, 1875–1921,* "The race was a poor one from the standpoint of time and would seem to indicate that with the single exception of 'Manuel' there was not a horse of Derby class" in the field. But perhaps O'Connor's eyes were elsewhere. Said he: "Although the race was by no means a sensational one, an immense crowd, estimated at 20,000 people, saw it. Of this number," noted the ever-watchful O'Connor, "probably one-third were ladies in their spring toilets and presenting a scene of beauty which is equaled at no other race in America."

There were five starters in the Derby. It was a warm, cloudy day, and the track was not in the best shape, covered with, guess what, dust. Still, the track was described as fast.

As soon as the red bunting dropped, Manuel sprang to the lead, but his jockey, Fred Taral, wanting to conserve the strength of the bay colt, as astute jockeys do, applied the brakes to some degree. He took up a position behind His Lordship and Fontainebleau and then at the half-mile point let Manuel go. He charged to the front and was never really threatened, winning by two lengths. His time, however, was nothing to neigh home about: 2:12.

The entire race, in a sense—despite the pretty women—had a pall over it. M. Lewis Clark, the innovative and great man who had gotten the Derby going down the track while president of Churchill Downs from 1875 to 1894, had, on April 22, just twelve days before the running of the Derby, used a pistol to kill himself in Memphis. It was said that he was very ill. But for the people who had known and loved this rigid but very straightforward man—a man whose integrity was the bedrock upon which Churchill Downs was built—a piece of themselves had died with him, and would never recover.

Lieut. Gibson
26th May 3, 1900

			*Leamington
		Iroquois	Maggie B. B.
	G. W. Johnson		*Bonnie Scotland
LIEUT. GIBSON		Brunette	Variella
Bay colt			Thormanby
	Sophia Hardy	*Glengarry	*Carbine
			Enquirer
		Unaka	Wampee

THE WINNER'S PEDIGREE AND CAREER HIGHLIGHTS

YEAR	AGE	STS.	1ST	2ND	3RD	EARNINGS
1899	2	18	7	4	2	$ 8,475
1900	3	6	3	1	1	$13,015
TOTALS		**24**	**10**	**5**	**3**	**$21,490**

At 2 years	WON	Kentucky Central Stakes, Kimball Stakes, Flatbush Stakes, Sensation Stakes
	2ND	Westchester Highweight Handicap
	3RD	Harold Stakes
At 3 years	WON	Kentucky Derby, Clark Stakes, Latonia Derby
	3RD	American Derby
	UNP	Great Western Handicap

RACE DAY STATISTICS

HORSE	WT.	ST.	1/4	1/2	MILE	STR.	FIN.	JOCKEY	OWNER
Lieut. Gibson	117	3	1	1	1	1	1^3	J. Boland	Charles H. Smith
Florizar	122	7	6	4	2	2	2^2	C. Van Dusen	(a) H. J. Scoggan
Thrive	122	5	4	6	5	5	3^1	J. Winkfield	J. C. Cahn
Highland Lad	122	6	5	2	3	4	4^3	Crowhurst	(a) H. J. Scoggan
His Excellency	122	1	3	3	4	3	5no	Gilmore	T. C. McDowell
Kentucky Farmer	117	2	2	5	6	6	6^8	W. Overton	Woodford & Buckner
Hindus	122	4	7	7	7	7	7	Vititoe	George J. Long

Time: :24³/4, :48, 1:13¹/2, 1:40¹/2, 2:06¹/4. Track fast (new Derby record).
Coupled: (a) Florizar and Highland Lad.
Winner: B. c. by G. W. Johnson–Sophia Hardy, by *Glengarry. Trained by Charles H. Hughes; bred in Kentucky by Baker & Gentry.
Bookmaking odds: Lieut. Gibson, 7 to 10; Florizar, 5 to 1; Thrive, 7 to 1.
Value $6,000. Net to winner $4,850; second $700; third $300.

131 nominations.

*Foreign bred

Maybe He Won't Make It

SOME EXPERTS CONSIDER ALL DERBY HORSES from 1899 to 1913 to be generally inferior, but it is hard to accept that when one considers the time of the winner of the twenty-sixth running: 2:06 1/4. This is not Man o' War at his best, but it is pretty fast, and faster than any Derby before it by 1 1/4 seconds.

There were seven starters in the race, and there was very little delay in getting the horses lined up and off. Immediately Lieut. Gibson, a very speedy bay colt, quickly charged to the lead, and he seemed clearly to be on his way to an easy victory.

Though many in the crowd cheered him on as a shoo-in, a number held back; he was setting such a fast pace that they worried he might peter out before the race was finished. As John L.

O'Connor says in his *History of the Kentucky Derby*, "The fourth eighth in: 12 1/4 carried him to the three-quarter pole in: 48, a heartbreaking clip of the first half mile of a mile and a quarter race."

Lieut. Gibson, carrying 117 pounds, did appear to be going too fast. Then, it was as if his jockey, J. Boland, could read the minds of the fearful in the stands. He pulled back on the horse, slowing him somewhat to make sure he had enough left for the final charge. As he came into the stretch—and before that, for many people—it was clear that he was going to win handily. He was struggling, but far less than the horses behind him.

When he crossed the line, Lieut. Gibson was four lengths ahead of Florizar, who had had no chance of catching him and therefore was not pushed during the final furlong or so.

His Eminence
27th *April 29, 1901*

		Enquirer	*Leamington
	Falsetto		Lida
HIS EMINENCE		Farfaletta	*Australian
Bay colt			Elkhorna
			Lexington
	Patroness	Pat Malloy	Gloriana
			Macaroni
	*Inverness		Elfrida

The Winner's Pedigree and Career Highlights

YEAR	AGE	STS.	1ST	2ND	3RD	EARNINGS
1900	2	17	6	1	2	$ 1,925
1901	3	7	2	1	1	$ 8,370
1902	4	12	2	2	0	$ 2,740
1903	5	12	1	1	3	$ 3,110
1904	6	5	0	2	2	$ 150
TOTALS		**53**	**11**	**7**	**8**	**$16,295**

At 2 years	3RD	Wenonah Stakes
At 3 years	WON	Kentucky Derby, Clark Stakes
	UNP	American Derby, Sheridan Stakes
At 4 years	2ND	Russet Handicap
At 5 years	2ND	Russet Handicap
	3RD	Twin City Handicap
	UNP	Turf Handicap, Advance Handicap, Sheepshead Bay Handicap, Suburban Handicap

Race Day Statistics

HORSE	WT.	ST.	1/4	1/4	MILE	STR.	FIN.	JOCKEY	OWNER
His Eminence	117	1	1	1	1	1	1$^{1-1/2}$	J. Winkfield	F. B. Van Meter
Sannazarro	117	5	5	4	2	2	2$^{2-1/2}$	D. O'Connor	William Hayes
Driscoll	110	3	4	5	5	3	3$^{1-1/2}$	J. Boland	Woodford Clay
Amur	110	4	3	3	4	4	4^{5}	J. Dupree	George J. Long
Alard Scheck	117	2	2	2	3	5	5	J. Woods	J. W. Schorr

Time: :25^{1}/2, :51, 1:16^{1}/4, 1:43, 2:07^{3}/4. Track fast.
Winner: B. c. by Falsetto–Patroness, by Pat Malloy. Trained by F. B. Van Meter; bred in Kentucky by O. H. Chenault.
Bookmaking odds: His Eminence, 3 to 1; Sannazarro, 4 to 1; Driscoll, 20 to 1; Amur, 25 to 1; Alard Scheck 7 to 10.
Value $6,000. Net to winner $4,850; second $700; third $300.

145 nominations.

*Foreign bred

An Easy Win

A SIGN THAT THE DERBY WAS IN TROUBLE was the scant number of starters in races, meaning that the event was still being shunned by the eastern tracks. Still, people loved the Derby, and over 20,000 rabid fans showed up for the 1901 running.

As usual, the horses went through a couple of false starts, but they were able to get under way within four minutes. As historian John L. O'Connor writes, "Then there was a flash of yellow and red, a long hoarse roar from the thousands packed in the stands and here they come, five good colts closely bunched with the black nose of Alard Scheck showing slightly in front."

But that lasted all of fifty yards. Great black jockey Jimmy Winkfield was in the race riding a horse named His Eminence, and he forged to the front. It was no contest.

As Winkfield, a gutsy, crafty rider, put it, "I got him away a little ahead, and after that I just breezed him around the track until I entered the stretch [and] I let him go just as easy. All the way I kept a good hold of his head and never moved on him. In the stretch I looked back and saw Sannazarro coming along. I shook up His Eminence some then and he came in easy. . . . I think I could have won in faster time if I had wanted to work him but he had it all his own way, anyhow, so what was the point?"

Alan-a-Dale
28th May 3, 1902

		Hanover	Hindoo
	Halma		Bourbon Belle
ALAN-A-DALE		Julia L.	Longfellow
Chestnut colt			Christine
	Sudie McNairy	Enquirer	*Leamington
			Lida
		Nannie McNairy	Jeff Davis
			Elizabeth
			McNairy

THE WINNER'S PEDIGREE AND CAREER HIGHLIGHTS

YEAR	AGE	STS.	1ST	2ND	3RD	EARNINGS
1901	2	4	3	0	0	$ 8,570
1902	3	1	1	0	0	$ 4,850
1903	4	9	5	3	0	$ 3,940
1904	5	10	5	3	0	$ 5,170
1905	6	13	3	1	1	$ 2,665
TOTALS		37	17	7	1	$25,195

At 2 years	WON	Brighton Junior Stakes
	UNP	Foxland Stakes
At 3 years	WON	Kentucky Derby
At 4 years	WON	Oakwood Handicap
	UNP	Harlem National Handicap
At 5 years	2ND	Fall Handicap, Ocean Handicap, Flight Handicap
At 6 years	UNP	Omnium Handicap, Ocean Handicap, Saratoga Handicap, Test Handicap

RACE DAY STATISTICS

HORSE	WT.	ST.	1/4	1/2	3/4	STR.	FIN.	JOCKEY	OWNER
Alan-a-Dale	117	3	1	1	1	1	1no	J. Winkfield	(a) T. C. McDowell
Inventor	117	2	4	4	3	3	2$^{1/2}$	R. Williams	T. W. Moore
The Rival	117	1	3	3	4	4	3no	N. Turner	(a) T. C. McDowell
Abe Frank	122	4	2	2	2	2	4	M. Coburn	G. C. Bennett & Co.

Time: :24, :48, 1:14, 1:40$^{3/4}$, 2:08$^{3/4}$. Track fast. Start good.
Coupled: (a) T.C. McDowell entry.
Winner: Ch.c. by Halma–Sudie McNairy, by Enquirer. Trained by T. C. McDowell; bred in Kentucky by T. C. McDowell.
Bookmaking odds: Alan-a-Dale (coupled with The Rival), 3 to 2; Inventor, 11 to 1; Abe Frank, 3 to 5.
Value $6,000. Net to winner $4,850; second $700; third $300.

112 nominations.

*Foreign bred

Sand Trap

JIMMY WINKFIELD, WHO HAD WON THE
1901 Derby on His Eminence, was looking for
his second Derby win in a row on a chestnut
colt named Alan-a-Dale. Alan-a-Dale was
noted for having bad legs that might give out at
any time, but if they held, the horse could run
like the wind. His sire was Halma. If Alan-
a-Dale won, he would be the first horse who
had been sired by a Derby winner.

Major Thomas C. McDowell owned both
Alan-a-Dale and The Rival, and he gave the
choice of riding either to a jockey named Nash
Turner, who he had under contract. Winkfield
was in charge of training the horses, and he
always held back Alan-a-Dale—who he knew
was naturally faster—so Rival would seem better. On average, Rival ran 2:09 for the Derby
distance. Winkfield held the bit tight when he
ran Alan-a-Dale, never letting the horse go
faster than 2:11. Turner, quite naturally, selected Rival for the Derby.

Winkfield showed the same craftiness as
a rider. He noticed that the groundskeepers
broomed the layer of sandy soil off near the rail,
pushing it to the outside to expose solid earth
for better footing. The outside was slow and
hazardous.

As the horses broke, jockey Nash Turner led
Rival past the stands. He was watching jockey
M. Coburn, on Abe Frank, and Coburn in turn
was watching Turner. "Nobody," Winkfield
said, "was paying much attention to me," so he
slipped into a three-length lead.

He still had the lead by the three-eighths
pole when he felt that Alan-a-Dale's legs were

doing a fade. "I was really holding him now,
trying to save him," and yearning for the finish
line.

But favorite Abe Frank was not to be denied.
Winkfield was running close to the rail, but
Abe Frank came up on the outside. Winkfield
reacted cleverly. "When the favorite come up
on my shoulder," he said, "I rode him into
that deep sand; it took a hold on him and he
stopped. The other two horses tried to duck
inside me but I ducked back on the rail; when
they tried to come around I took them outside
too, both at once. And that's all that saved me.
Alan-a-Dale got across the finish line by a nose,
and he pulled up lame."

His time was 2:08 3/4, not bad for a lame
horse who never did better than 2:11 in training! McDowell gave Winkfield $1,000, a
fortune around the turn of the century. Wonder
what he would have had to pay for the horse's
heart.

Judge Himes
29th *May 2, 1903*

		Claremont	Blair Athol
	*Esher		Coimbra
JUDGE HIMES		Una	Ellington or Dusk
Chestnut colt			*Conjecture
	Lullaby	Longfellow	*Leamington
			Nanura
		Lady Richards	War Dance
			Lucretia

The Winner's Pedigree and Career Highlights

YEAR	AGE	STS.	1ST	2ND	3RD	EARNINGS
1902	2	10	1	1	2	$ 400
1903	3	28	7	1	9	$19,865
1904	4	32	5	5	3	$ 3,500
1905	5	31	5	6	7	$ 4,155
1906	6	3	0	1	1	$ 75
TOTALS		**104**	**18**	**14**	**22**	**$27,995**

At 3 years	WON	Kentucky Derby, Hawthorne Handicap, Excelsior Handicap, Endurance Handicap, Oak Park Handicap
	3RD	Latonia Club Membership Handicap, Flyaway Handicap, Maywood Handicap, Blue Grass Stakes
	UNP	Tennessee Derby, Hotel Gayoso Stakes, Latonia Derby, American Derby
At 4 years	3RD	Elmridge Handicap, Superior Handicap, August Stakes
At 5 years	WON	Whirlpool Stakes
	2ND	Speculation Stakes, Park Hotel Stakes
	3RD	Eastman Hotel Stakes
	UNP	Country Club Handicap

Race Day Statistics

HORSE	WT.	PP	ST.	$^{1}/_{2}$	$^{3}/_{4}$	MILE	STR.	FIN.	JOCKEY	OWNER	ODDS TO $1
Judge Himes	117	4	3	$3^{1/2}$	$3^{1/2}$	4^3	2^2	$1^{3/4}$	H. Booker	Chas. R. Ellison	10.00
Early	117	2	4	4^6	4^6	$1^{1/2}$	$1^{1/2}$	2^6	J. Winkfield	M. H. Tichenor & Co.	.60
Bourbon	110	5	5	5^2	$5^{1-1/2}$	$5^{1/2}$	4^3	$3^{1/2}$	Crowhurst	T. C. McDowell	(f) 4.00
Bad News	114	1	2	$2^{1/2}$	2^{nk}	3^1	$3^{1/2}$	4^3	Davis	Woodford & Buckner	5.00
Woodlake	117	3	1	1^1	1^1	2^{nk}	5^1	5^5	G. Helgeson	T. C. McDowell	(f) 4.00
Treacy	110	6	6	6	6	6	6	6	Landry	T. H. Stevens	15.00

Time: :25$^{1}/_{2}$, :51, 1:16$^{1}/_{2}$, 1:42, 2:09. Went to post at 4:02. At post 4 minutes. Track fast. Start poor. Won driving; second easily. (f) Field.
Winner: Ch.c. by *Esher-Lullaby, by Longfellow. Trained by J. P. Mayberry; bred in Kentucky by Johnson N. Camden.
Value $6,000. Net to winner $4,850; second $700; third $300.

140 nominations.

*Foreign bred

A Great Jockey's Mistake

This Derby marked the first use of the web barrier to start a race. (The first mechanical gates did not appear until 1930.) Elastic webbing was stretched across the track and secured to metal poles. Once the horses were aligned, the starter hit a button, the webbing flew out of the way, and the horses were off. Sometimes they would power through the barrier, though, tearing it up, and the race would have to be restarted.

The odds were 10–1 against the sore-heeled Judge Himes, the winner of the Derby, a horse that raced five seasons and as an older horse won just a single minor stakes race in a whopping 104 tries. But the Derby was his moment. He was brought to the race by J. P. Mayberry, a very good trainer who prepared his horses very well, so much so that it was said that the training compensated for what his horses lacked in bloodlines.

And the second thing was good luck. Judge Himes owed his win not necessarily to his own jockey, but to the great James Winkfield, who had won the Derby two years in a row, first on His Eminence and then on Alan-a-Dale. But in this Derby Winkfield made a mistake.

The real race started in the backstretch, and when a bunch of horses went into the turn and straightened out, the highly recognizable and predictable canary silks of James Winkfield, mounted on the heavy favorite Early, were in the lead. Most of the crowd thought the race was over.

At the three-quarter pole Winkfield was in easy command, a length ahead of Woodlake, and the lead increased as he turned into the home stretch. Meanwhile Judge Himes and Bad News were in a neck-and-neck struggle for third, their noses at the flanks of Woodlake.

Then, as they swung into the stretch, Judge Himes's jockey, H. Booker, saw an opening. By the time the stretch had straightened out, Judge Himes had sneaked next to the rail. There he stayed, as the confident Winkfield pounded along, two lengths to the good.

Booker waited like a coiled snake, and at the eighth pole he struck. Suddenly the two lengths lead evaporated, and not until Judge Himes thundered down upon him was Winkfield aware of the colt. Instantly, he went to the whip and spur, but it was too little too late. Judge Himes won by a nose.

Later, Winkfield said overconfidence was his mistake. Once in the lead, he took the race for granted—and it cost him the Derby.

Elwood
30th *May 2, 1904*

		Ten Broeck	*Phaeton
	Free Knight		Fanny Holton
ELWOOD			Knighthood
Bay colt		Belle Knight	Kentucky Belle
		Alarm	*Eclipse
	Petticoat		*Maud
			*Leamington
	Lady Scarborough	*Lady Lumley

THE WINNER'S PEDIGREE AND CAREER HIGHLIGHTS

YEAR	AGE	STS.	1ST	2ND	3RD	EARNINGS
1903	2	17	1	2	1	$ 950
1904	3	23	6	4	3	$13,580
1905	4	12	1	1	1	$ 1,060
1906	5	3	0	0	0	$ -
1907	6	3	0	0	0	$ -
TOTALS		**58**	**8**	**7**	**5**	**$15,590**

At 2 years	2ND	Youngster Stakes, Competition Stakes
At 3 years	WON	Kentucky Derby, Latonia Derby
	2ND	California Derby
	3RD	St. Louis Derby
	UNP	American Derby, Clark Stakes

RACE DAY STATISTICS

HORSE	EQ.	WT.	PP	ST.	½	¾	MILE	STR.	FIN.	JOCKEY	OWNER	ODDS TO $1
Elwood	b	117	3	4	4^1	4^{hd}	4½	5½	1½	F. Prior	Mrs. Chas. Durnell	15.00
Ed Tierney		117	5	3	3^1	3$^{1-1/2}$	3^1	3^2	2^3	J. Dominick	Fay & Wehmhoff	1.10
Brancas		117	4	5	5	5	5	2½	3$^{2-1/2}$	L. Lyne	William Gerst	2.50
Prince Silverwings		117	1	2	2^2	1^1	1^1	1^{hd}	4^1	D. Austin	Talbot Bros.	7.00
Proceeds	b	122	2	1	1$^{1-1/2}$	2½	2nd	4½	5	G. Helgeson	S. S. Brown	1.00

Time: :25, :49½, 1:15¼, 1:42, 2:08½. Went to post at 4:15. At post 4 minutes. Track fast. Start good. Won driving; second easily.
Winner: B. c. by Free Knight–Petticoat, by Alarm. Trained by C. E. Durnell; bred in Missouri by Mrs. J. B. Prather.
Value $6,000. Net to winner $4,850; second $700; third $300.

140 nominations.
Equipment: b—blinkers

*Foreign bred

First Female Breeder—and Winner

THERE WERE A NUMBER OF REASONS WHY IT was clear that the homely Missouri-bred colt Elwood, trained by C. E. "Boots" Durnell, one of the slickest trainers in the business, had zero chances against the other four horses in the race. One was his breeding. As he lined up to take part in the race, his sire was busy doing what he did every day: pulling a plow on a farm.

Second, Elwood had done most of his racing in California, and his record as a two-year-old had been abysmal, with seventeen starts and only one win, two places, and one show.

Finally, his trainer had no faith in his ability to win the Derby; Durnell had not even wanted to ship him to Louisville.

But Elwood had two things going for him. Though he didn't even attend the race, Durnell had trained the colt to a fare-thee-well; and second, his breeder, Mrs. J. B. Prather, the first woman ever to breed a racehorse, believed in him absolutely. This was a slight problem considering that Durnell was her husband. They obviously "discussed" their difference of opinion, and then Mrs. Prather brought Elwood from Missouri, and Durnell stayed home.

Elwood went off at 15-to-1 odds. When the race started, he dropped back into a familiar place—last. And his jockey, Frankie Prior, kept him there for the first mile. Then, out of the blue, as they went into the stretch, Prior started to move him up on the outside. Suddenly he was not last anymore but fighting it out in the stretch with Brancas, Prince Silverwings, and Ed Tierney. Soon the race was between Elwood and Ed Tierney. The final fifty yards told the story of the 1904 Derby. Tierney tired, and Elwood didn't, winning by half a length in the time of 2:08 1/2 and making his breeder not only the first female breeder of a Kentucky Derby contender, but the first winner. One can only wonder what the ensuing conversation was between her and her husband, he of little faith!

Agile
31st *May 10, 1905*

		Billet	*Voltigeur*
	Sir Dixon		Calcutta
AGILE		Jaconet	*Leamington*
Bay colt			Maggie B. B.
	Alpena	King Alfonso	*Phaeton*
			Capitola
	Penumbra		Pat Malloy
			Penelope

THE WINNER'S PEDIGREE AND CAREER HIGHLIGHTS

YEAR	AGE	STS.	1ST	2ND	3RD	EARNINGS
1904	2	21	5	4	2	$ 4,530
1905	3	10	5	5	0	$32,835
1906	4	21	2	2	2	$ 1,485
1907	5	14	2	1	5	$ 950
TOTALS		**66**	**14**	**12**	**9**	**$39,800**

At 2 years	WON	Waldorf Stakes
	2ND	Southhold Handicap
	UNP	Nursery Handicap, Matron Stakes, Hopeful Stakes, Great Trial Stakes, Daisy Stakes
At 3 years	WON	Kentucky Derby, Advance Stakes, Phoenix Stakes, Tennessee Derby,
	2ND	Brighton Derby, Tidal Stakes, Broadway Stakes
At 4 years	UNP	Suburban Handicap, Edgemere Handicap, Election Day Handicap
At 5 years	UNP	Thanksgiving Handicap, Special

RACE DAY STATISTICS

HORSE	EQ.	WT.	PP	ST.	1/4	1/2	3/4	STR.	FIN.	JOCKEY	OWNER	ODDS TO $1
Agile		122	1	1	$1^{1\text{-}1/2}$	$1^{1\text{-}1/2}$	$1^{1\text{-}1/2}$	1^2	1^3	J. Martin	S. S. Brown	.33
Ram's Horn	s	117	2	2	2^5	2^{10}	2^{15}	2^{20}	2^{20}	L. Lyne	W. S. Williams & Co.	2.50
Layson		117	3	3	3	3	3	3	3	D. Austin	T. P. Hayes	16.00

Time: $:25^{1}/_{2}$, :50, 1:16, $1:42^3/_4$, $2:10^3/_4$. Went to post at 4:20. At post 1 minute. Track heavy. Won easily; second the same.
Winner: B. c. by Sir Dixon–Alpena, by King Alfonso. Trained by Robert Tucker; bred in Kentucky by E. F. Clay.
Value $6,000. Net to winner $4,850; second $700; third $300.

145 nominations.
Equipment: s—spurs

*Foreign bred

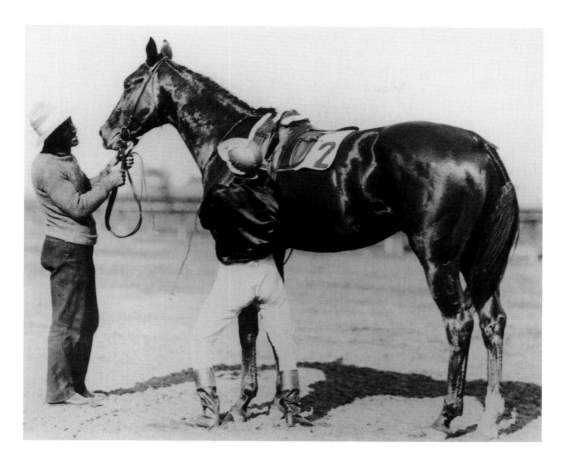

The Worst Derby Ever

THE ONLY FEATURE TO DISTINGUISH THIS Derby was that for the first time a bugle call was used to summon the horses from the paddock. And in this race all horses were in the money—there were only three entries, the smallest field since 1892, when Azra won.

Many experts consider 1905 the worst Derby ever. Still, the winner, Agile, had impressive winnings as a three-year-old, even though he only raced five times that season: $32,835, topped only by the celebrated Hindoo with over $49,000. The Derby only netted him $4,850 of that amount, however. Agile was favored, but was given the unbelievably short odds of 33 cents on a dollar.

The other two horses in the race were Ram's Horn and Layson.

When the web barrier lifted, the pretty-boy but tough and confident jockey Jack Martin got his horse going quickly on the heavy track, and, quite simply, the race was over. Agile stayed in front from start to finish. Later, he said that he would still have won if the track was bone dry, and L. Lyne, Ram's Horn's jockey, agreed. The third-place finisher, D. Austin on Layson, was twenty lengths off the pace. When people attempted to talk to him, he was so crushed by the experience that he remained mute.

Sir Huon
32nd *May 2, 1906*

			Leamington
		Enquirer	Lida
	Falsetto		*Australian
SIR HUON		Farfaletta	Elkhorna
Bay colt			Nutbourne
	Ignite	*Woodlands	Whiteface
			Alarm
		Luminous	*Lady Lumley

THE WINNER'S PEDIGREE AND CAREER HIGHLIGHTS

YEAR	AGE	STS.	1ST	2ND	3RD	EARNINGS
1905	2	9	4	2	0	$ 3,775
1906	3	7	5	1	0	$34,655
1907	4	1	0	0	0	$ -
1908	5	1	1	0	0	$ 550
TOTALS		**18**	**10**	**3**	**0**	**$38,980**

At 2 years	WON	Harold Stakes
	2ND	Cincinnati Trophy
	UNP	Golden Rod Stakes
At 3 years	WON	Kentucky Derby, Latonia Derby, Queen City Handicap, Commonwealth Stakes, Seagate Stakes
	2ND	Saratoga Cup
	UNP	The Advance Stakes

RACE DAY STATISTICS

HORSE	EQ.	WT.	PP	ST.	1/4	1/2	3/4	STR.	FIN.	JOCKEY	OWNER	ODDS TO $1
Sir Huon		117	4	3	2^2	2^2	1^{nk}	1^2	1^2	R. Troxler	Geo. J. Long	1.10
Lady Navarre		117	3	4	4^{hd}	3^{nk}	4^6	2^{nk}	2^3	T. Burns	C. R. Ellison	(a) 1.80
James Reddick	sb	117	5	1	5^2	4^3	3^{hd}	3^1	3^5	J. Dominick	C. R. Ellison	(a) 1.80
Hyperion II	sb	114	2	5	1^3	1^2	$2^{1-1/2}$	4^{hd}	4^{10}	D. Austin	J. S. Hawkins & Co.	8.00
Debar		117	1	6	6	$5^{1-1/2}$	5^6	5^{10}	5^3	D. Nicol	H. Shannon & Co.	3.50
Velours	sb	117	6	2	3^{nk}	6	6	6	6	E. Walsh	H. Franklin	40.00

Time: :24$^{3/4}$, :49$^{4/5}$, 1:15, 1:41$^{2/5}$, 2:08$^{4/5}$. Track fast. Went to post at 4:00. At post 2 minutes. Start good. Won driving; second and third the same.
Coupled: (a) Lady Navarre and James Reddick; no separate place or show betting.
Winner: B. c. by Falsetto–Ignite, by *Woodlands. Trained by Peter Coyne; bred in Kentucky by George J. Long.
Value $6,000. Net to winner $4,850; second $700; third $300.
Scratched: Creel.

110 nominations.
Equipment: s—spurs, b—blinkers

*Foreign bred

Previous Experience Not Required

SIR HUON, THE HORSE THAT WON THIS Derby, broke a tradition: he didn't have a single race leading up to the Derby. That had never been done before. As a two-year-old he had had four victories in nine starts, and his pedigree was significant: his sire was Falsetto, who had sired two other Derby winners, Chant (1894) and His Eminence (1901).

From time to time across the years, psychic phenomena have crept into the Derby. In this case, the day before the race a local paper carried a story about the Derby, and somehow the number 5 had worked its way into the photo.

Five just happened to be Sir Huon's number, and this created a surge of betting for him.

The race was not simple, though. Sir Huon, with Roscoe Troxler up, had stiff competition, particularly from a filly named Lady Navarre, who most people didn't believe could win because she was a filly. Lady Navarre put on a valiant fight, but could not close the gap in the stretch. "I felt confident of winning," said Roscoe Troxler. "I could feel the big colt was full of run under me."

Indeed, he said he felt Sir Huon was cantering at the end. He won by two lengths.

One thing is for sure. If he had been in the 1915 race against another filly, Regret, he wouldn't have been cantering at the end.

Pink Star
33rd May 6, 1907

		Leonatus	Longfellow
	Pink Coat		Semper Felix
			Hindoo
PINK STAR		Alice Brand	Lady of the Lake
Bay colt			Lexington
	Mary Malloy	Pat Malloy	Gloriana
			*King Ernest
		Favorite	Jersey Belle

THE WINNER'S PEDIGREE AND CAREER HIGHLIGHTS

YEAR	AGE	STS.	1ST	2ND	3RD	EARNINGS
1906	2	8	2	1	0	$ 825
1907	3	8	1	0	2	$4,925
TOTALS		**16**	**3**	**1**	**2**	**$5,750**

At 3 years   WON   Kentucky Derby
            UNP   Latonia Derby, Crescent City Derby, City Park Derby

RACE DAY STATISTICS

HORSE	EQ.	WT.	PP	ST.	¼	½	¾	STR.	FIN.	JOCKEY	OWNER	ODDS TO $1
Pink Star	b	117	6	6	6	6	4^{hd}	3^4	1^2	A. Minder	J. Hal Woodford	15.00
Zal		117	3	1	1$^{1/2}$	1^{hd}	1$^{1-1/2}$	1$^{1-1/2}$	2$^{1-1/2}$	J. Boland	William Gerst	8.00
Ovelando		117	1	2	3^{hd}	2^3	2^1	2^{hd}	3^2	D. Nicol	M. Doyle	3.00
Red Gauntlet		117	5	5	5^5	4^1	5^4	4^1	4^5	D. Austin	T. P. Hayes	1.50
Wool Sandals		117	4	4	2$^{1-1/2}$	3^{hd}	3^1	5^5	5^6	T. Koerner	W. E. Applegate	3.00
Orlandwick		110	2	3	4$^{1-1/2}$	5^2	6	6	6	J. Lee	A. S. Steele	10.00

Time: :24, :50, 1:17, 1:45, 2:12⅗. Track heavy. Start good. Won easily; second and third driving.
Winner: B. c. by Pink Coat–Mary Malloy, by Pat Malloy. Trained by W. H. Fizer; bred in Kentucky by J. Hal Woodford.
Value $6,000. Net to winner $4,850; second $700; third $300.
Scratched: Arcite, Boxara.

128 nominations.
Equipment: b—blinkers

*Foreign bred

O Ye of Little Faith

PINK STAR WAS THE GRANDSON OF THE
great Leonatus, the 1883 Derby winner, but the
crowd had little belief in the horse, nor did his
owner, Kentuckian Hal Woodford.

But one person did, and that was his trainer,
W. H. Fizer. Once he had looked at the other
horses, Zal, Orlandwick, Red Gauntlet, and
Wool Sandals, he bubbled with enthusiasm. "So
these," he said, "are the Derby horses. Well, if
they are Derby colts Pink Star will walk in."

Many people were disappointed because the
horse that was favored, Arcite, was scratched at
the last minute by his Louisville owner, George
J. Long, because the horse was not healthy
enough.

After passing the grandstand, the horses
cantered to the web barrier, up it went, and they
were off. Zal was leading, followed by Ovelando and then Wool Sandals. Quite recognizable by his jockey's pink jacket, Pink Star was
running last.

The horses shifted positions somewhat, but
Pink Star continued to be last until the three-
eighths pole, at which time he started to move
up. At the eighth pole, the race seem to have
come down to Ovelando and Zal, but as Pink
Star continued to come on, Ovelando started
to show signs of flagging. Pink Star pulled even
with Zal, and at the sixteenth pole he passed
him and started to pull away to win.

Stone Street
34th May 5, 1908

			*Leamington
	Longfellow		Nantura
	Long Street		*Glen Athol
STONE STREET	Semper Idem		Semper Vive
Bay colt			Blair Athol
	Stone Nellie	*Stonehenge	Coimbra
			*King Ernest
	Nell		Miss Nellie

THE WINNER'S PEDIGREE AND CAREER HIGHLIGHTS

YEAR	AGE	STS.	1ST	2ND	3RD	EARNINGS
1907	2	17	3	3	1	$ 1,450
1908	3	25	3	1	5	$ 5,828
1909	4	20	3	7	1	$ 1,250
1910	5	10	1	4	0	$ 617
1911	6	20	8	2	2	$ 3,667
TOTALS		92	18	17	9	$12,812

At 2 years UNP Juvenile Stakes
At 3 years WON Kentucky Derby

RACE DAY STATISTICS

HORSE	EQ.	WT.	PP	ST.	1/4	1/2	3/4	STR.	FIN.	JOCKEY	OWNER	ODDS TO $1
Stone Street	b	117	4	6	$2^{1\text{-}1/2}$	2^{hd}	1^{nk}	1^1	1^3	A. Pickens	C. E. & J. W. Hamilton	23.72
Sir Cleges		117	2	7	4^1	$3^{1\text{-}1/2}$	$2^{1/2}$	$3^{1/2}$	2nd	C. Koerner	Geo. J. Long	1.74
Dunvegan	b	114	1	5	3^{nk}	4^2	4^4	2^1	3^{hd}	P. Warren	J. N. Camden Jr.	(a) 7.37
Synchronized	sb	112	8	2	5^2	5^3	5^5	4^1	4^{hd}	F. Burton	D. Armstrong	68.92
Banridge	sb	110	5	3	$1^{1\text{-}1/2}$	1^2	3^1	5^5	5^6	V. Powers	B. Schreiber	3.24
Milford	b	117	3	1	6^1	6^4	6^6	6^1	6^{hd}	A. Minder	W. H. Fizer	3.64
Bill Herron	b	114	6	4	7^{10}	7^{20}	7^{15}	7^{20}	7^{20}	J. Lee	W. J. Young	(a) 7.37
Frank Bird	b	110	7	8	8	8	8	8	8	J. Williams	W. A. Hughes	22.43

Time: :25, :50^{1}/5, 1:17^{2}/5, 1:46, 2:15^{1}/5. Track heavy. Went to post at 4:20. At post 1 minute. Start good. Won easily; second and third driving.
Coupled: (a) Dunvegan and Bill Herron.
$5 minimum wager offered.

Program #		Win	Place	Show
7	Stone Street	$123.60	$37.90	$14.50
4	Sir Cleges		$11.10	$ 8.50
3	Dunvegan			$11.10

Winner: B. c. by Longstreet–Stone Nellie, by *Stonehenge. Trained by J. W. Hall; bred in Kentucky by J. B. Haggin.
Value $6,000. Net to winner $4,850; second $700; third $300.

114 nominations.
Equipment: b—blinkers; s—spurs

*Foreign bred

Condition Counts

OCCASIONALLY, A HORSE WHO DOES NOT have natural speed or even endurance will win a race just because it is in prime condition, a finely tuned equine machine ready to run the race of its life.

Such a horse was Stone Street, who as a two-year-old had done okay, with three wins, three places, and one show out of seventeen starts. His breeding was nothing to write home about. Still, when he arrived at the Derby he was what onlookers characterized as in prime condition.

The race started quickly, and Banridge broke to the front, with most of the crowd rooting for Sir Cleges, a Louisville hometown favorite. At the three-quarter pole, Stone Street went into the lead easily. Other horses, including Sir Cleges, who seemed to dislike the track, made a run at him but to no avail. The bay colt was able to hold off everyone until the end.

There was much more of a struggle for second and third, with Sir Cleges securing second place after a heroic run.

Wintergreen
35th *May 3, 1909*

		King Eric	*King Ernest
			*Cyclone
	Dick Welles		Hanover
WINTERGREEN		Tea's Over	Tea Rose
Bay colt			*Mortemer
	Winter	Exile	*Second Hand
			*Mr. Pickwick
		Wildflower	Woodflower

THE WINNER'S PEDIGREE AND CAREER HIGHLIGHTS

YEAR	AGE	STS.	1ST	2ND	3RD	EARNINGS
1908	2	10	5	1	3	$ 1,660
1909	3	8	1	4	0	$ 5,550
1910	4	5	1	3	1	$ 795
1911	5	5	3	0	1	$ 1,490
1912	6	22	6	4	0	$ 2,940
1913	7	11	0	2	3	$ 385
TOTALS		**61**	**16**	**14**	**8**	**$12,820**

At 2 years	3RD	Hurricane Stakes
At 3 years	WON	Kentucky Derby
	2ND	Saranac Handicap, Saratoga Cup
At 4 years	3RD	Brewers Exchange Stakes
At 5 years	3RD	Merchants' Stakes
	UNP	Frank Fehr Stakes

RACE DAY STATISTICS

HORSE	EQ.	WT.	PP	ST.	1/4	1/2	3/4	STR.	FIN.	JOCKEY	OWNER	ODDS TO $1
Wintergreen	b	117	6	1	$1^{1\text{-}1/2}$	1^2	$1^{1\text{-}1/2}$	1^1	1^4	V. Powers	J. B. Respess	1.96
Miami		117	1	8	$2^{1\text{-}1/2}$	2^2	$2^{1/2}$	2^{hd}	2^3	C. Shilling	J. N. Camden	2.90
Dr. Barkley		117	3	2	4^2	$4^{1/2}$	5^3	5^2	3^{hd}	S. Page	L. Smitha	41.34
Sir Catesby		110	9	9	$6^{1\text{-}1/2}$	5^2	4^2	$3^{1/2}$	4^4	Heidel	T. P. Hayes	33.58
Friend Harry	b	117	7	7	3^{hd}	3^{hd}	3^{hd}	4^2	5^3	P. Musgrave	E. Alvey	5.61
Direct	sb	117	5	3	7^2	7^6	6^3	6^2	6^3	A. Walsh	R. J. Mackenzie	(a) 10.01
Michael Angelo		117	8	4	9^3	8^5	8^{10}	7^2	7^3	G. Taplin	G. Hendrie	6.97
Warfield		117	10	6	$5^{1/2}$	$6^{1/2}$	7^4	8^2	8^8	D. Austin	J. H. Lesh	(a) 10.01
Campeon		110	2	5	8^2	$9^{1\text{-}1/2}$	9^{hd}	9^1	9^2	M. McGee	G. J. Long	51.25
Match Me	sb	107	4	10	10	10	10	10	10	J. Lee	A. J. Gorey	56.11

Time: :25, :49³/₅, 1:15⁴/₅, 1:42, 2:08¹/₅. Track slow. Went to post at 4:41. At post 3 minutes. Start good. Won easily; second and third driving.
Coupled: (a) Direct and Warfield.
Bookmaking odds: Wintergreen, 196 to 100 straight, 3 to 4 place, 72 to 100 show; Miami 83 to 100 place, 17 to 20 show; Dr. Barkley, 314 to 100 show.
$5 minimum wager offered.

Program #		Win	Place	Show
1	Wintergreen	$14.80	$8.75	$ 8.60
5	Miami		$9.15	$ 9.25
7	Dr. Barkley			$20.70

Winner: B. c. by Dick Welles–Winter, by Exile. Trained by Chas. Mack; bred in Ohio by J. B. Respess.
Value $6,000. Net to winner $4,850; second $700; third $300.

117 nominations.
Equipment: b—blinkers; s—spurs

*Foreign bred

Dream Come True

A HORSEMAN AND POLITICIAN NAMED
J. B. Rome Respess had ached for a Derby win
for a long time, and when the colt he called
Wintergreen was born, Rome made a predic-
tion: In three years this foal, born and bred in
Ohio, would be the Derby winner. And over the
next three years Respess spared no expense in
trying to make that dream come true.

As the race neared, there didn't seem to be
much reason to believe that Wintergreen would
win. He had run in five races in the run up to
the Derby, but only one of these was a Stakes
race, the Hurricane Stakes, and there he finished a measly third.

But Wintergreen had a couple of things
going for him. He had the blood of two great
horses—Dick Welles and Winter—coursing

through his veins. The other good thing was
his jockey, Vincent Powers, who led America's
jockey list in 1908. That would prove, in fact,
to be crucial.

It had rained the morning of the race, but
the track was still in good condition.

When the race started, Wintergreen got a
scare, being bumped by Dr. Barkley, but he
quickly recovered and took the lead. As he
strode along, it was evident to the crowd—and
to a giddy Respess—that Wintergreen was on
his way to winning the Derby. A powerful colt
named Miami had stayed with him, though,
and the crowd was stunned when they saw
Wintergreen falter around the eighth pole.

But here's where the jockey, Powers, came in.
He simply started using the whip, and Wintergreen spurted out of danger, winning by four
lengths. Respess's dream had come true.

Donau
36th *May 10, 1910*

			Voltigeur
	Tibthorpe	Little Agnes
*Woolsthorpe		Balfe
DONAU	Light of Other Days	Meteor
Bay colt		Albert Victor
	*Albert	Hawthorn Bloom
Al Lone		*Glengarry
	Fronie Louise	Rosa Clark

THE WINNER'S PEDIGREE AND CAREER HIGHLIGHTS

YEAR	AGE	STS.	1ST	2ND	3RD	EARNINGS
1909	2	41	15	6	14	$ 6,980
1910	3	10	4	0	1	$ 7,186
1911	4	30	6	3	8	$ 2,701
1912	5	30	5	9	7	$ 3,289
TOTALS		**111**	**30**	**18**	**30**	**$20,156**

At 2 years	WON	Wakefield Stakes
	2ND	San Gabriel Stakes
	3RD	Essex Handicap, Cincinnati Trophy, Bashford Manor Stakes
	UNP	Bell Stakes
At 3 years	WON	Kentucky Derby, Camden Handicap
	3RD	Latonia Derby
	UNP	Clark Stakes, Brewers Exchange Stakes, Independence Handicap
At 4 years	3RD	Brewers Selling Stakes

RACE DAY STATISTICS

HORSE	EQ.	WT.	PP	ST.	$1/4$	$1/2$	$3/4$	STR.	FIN.	JOCKEY	OWNER	ODDS TO $1
Donau		117	7	2	$1^{1-1/2}$	1^3	1^3	$1^{1/2}$	$1^{1/2}$	F. Herbert	William Gerst	2.65
Joe Morris	b	117	1	1	2^{hd}	2^2	$2^{1-1/2}$	2^{hd}	2^{hd}	V. Powers	R. H. Anderson	2.77
Fighting Bob	b	117	4	5	7	5^1	$3^{1-1/2}$	3^4	3no	S. Page	G. Reif	3.49
Boola Boola		117	3	3	6^{hd}	6^{nk}	5^2	4^6	4^{15}	T. Rice	J. N. Camden	17.95
Topland		114	5	7	3^{hd}	4^2	4^{hd}	5^1	5^2	D. Austin	C. C. Van Meter	25.10
John Furlong		107	2	6	$5^{1/2}$	3^{hd}	6^4	6^4	6^8	R. Scoville	J. C. Rogers	14.07
Gallant Pirate	b	117	6	4	4^1	7	7	7	7	B. Kennedy	J. R. Wainwright	37.59

Time: :24, :48$^{4/5}$, 1:14, 1:39$^{4/5}$, 2:06$^{2/5}$. Track fast. Went to post at 4:56. At post 1 minute. Start good. Won driving; second and third the same.
$5 minimum wager offered.

	Win	Place	Show
Donau	$13.25	$7.50	$7.50
Joe Morris		$7.50	$7.50
Fighting Bob			$8.50

Winner: B. c. by *Woolsthorpe–Al Lone, by *Albert. Trained by G. Ham; bred in Kentucky by Milton Young.
Value $6,000. Net to winner $4,850; second $700; third $300.
Scratched: Eye White.

117 nominations.
Equipment: b—blinkers

*Foreign bred

Thriller

A TRULY REMARKABLE—YET UNENVIABLE—
record was made by a horse named Donau.
Today, horses that are to run in the Derby
normally tune up with four or five races. As a
three-year-old prior to the Derby Donau went
to the post *forty-one times*, and managed
to win fifteen of those races. Despite all this
wear and tear—it would be like a major league
pitcher pitching fifty games a year—Donau
("Danube" in German) was the favorite in the
Derby. But this race was his most difficult of
all—and probably the most thrilling.

Forty thousand people were in the stands to
watch the race, the crowd swollen because ad-
mittance to the infield was free. The announcer
used a primitive microphone to announce the
race, but his voice fought a losing battle with
the crowd.

It had rained, but Derby day was warm and
sunny, and the track was dry.

When the race started, jockey Herbert immediately brought Donau to the lead by a half
length over Joe Morris. By the clubhouse turn
Donau led by three lengths, still followed by Joe
Morris and a gaggle of others.

As the race progressed, things tightened up.
And at the end of a mile Donau led by only half
a length over Joe Morris, who was ahead of
Fighting Bob and four lengths in front of Boola
Boola. As they blasted into the stretch, it was
anyone's race. As John O'Connor describes it
in his book *History of the Kentucky Derby,
1875–1921,* "Down the stretch they came, whips
whirling and resounding even above the roar

from the stands and the field, and those jockeys
rode desperately for the prize that hung at the
end of the tiring, heartbreaking journey now
less than a sixteenth of a mile away. On and
on they came to the black mark on the white
board that should proclaim the finish; flying,
yet struggling gamely and determinedly under
the punishment of the bending striving riders to
be first to that goal where hung fame, glory and
gold.

"Donau, though tiring fast, was still able
to hold the lead. Unshaken, his nose first passed
the finishing line with Joe Morris at his withers, Fighting Bob at Joe Morris's throatlatch,
and Boola Boola beaten only by a nose for
third money. . . . It was beyond question the
most thrilling finish ever seen in the Kentucky
Derby."

Meridian
37th May 13, 1911

		Ben Brush	Bramble
			Roseville
	Broomstick		Galliard
MERIDIAN		*Elf	*Sylvabelle
Bay colt			St. Simon
	Sue Smith	*Masetto	Lady Abbess
			*Whistle Jacket
		Ethel Lee	Marmora

THE WINNER'S PEDIGREE AND CAREER HIGHLIGHTS

YEAR	AGE	STS.	1ST	2ND	3RD	EARNINGS
1910	2	12	3	3	1	$ 2,395
1911	3	17	6	6	1	$11,655
1912	4	23	8	4	2	$ 7,186
1913	5	8	2	0	4	$ 3,780
1914	6	6	1	2	2	$ 1,475
TOTALS		66	20	15	10	$26,491

At 2 years	2ND	Double Event
	3RD	Foam Stakes
At 3 Years	WON	Kentucky Derby, National Handicap, Frontier Stakes
	2ND	Blue Grass Stakes, Hamilton Derby, Fourth of July Stakes, Kentucky Stakes
	3RD	Canadian Sportsmen's Handicap
At 4 years	WON	Washington's Birthday Handicap, Argyle Hotel Handicap, Kentucky Stakes
	2ND	Charleston Hotel Handicap, Latonia Inaugural
	3RD	Criterion Stakes, Juarez Stakes
At 5 years	WON	Excelsior Handicap
	3RD	Paumonok Handicap, Kings County Handicap
At 6 years	2ND	Queens County Handicap, Memorial Handicap
	3RD	Brookdale Handicap, Yonkers Handicap

RACE DAY STATISTICS

HORSE	WT.	PP	ST.	1/4	1/2	3/4	STR.	FIN.	JOCKEY	OWNER	ODDS TO $1
Meridian	117	5	1	1^4	1^3	1^2	1^2	$1^{3/4}$	G. Archibald	R. F. Carman	2.90
Governor Gray	119	7	3	6^1	4^1	3^1	2^{hd}	2^{15}	R. Troxler	R. N. Smith	1.00
Colston	110	1	7	3^4	$3^{1/2}$	4^2	4^4	3^2	J. Conley	Raleigh Colston	19.00
Mud Sill	107	2	6	$4^{1/2}$	6	6	6	4^{hd}	T. Koerner	Woodford-Buckner	17.00
Jack Denman	117	3	5	5^1	5	5	5	5^1	J. Wilson	F. J. Pons	21.00
Round the World	117	6	2	2^2	2^3	2^{hd}	3^2	6^{15}	M. McGee	W. G. Yanke	6.50
Col. Hogan	110	4	4	7	7	7	7	7	J. McIntyre	Henderson-Hogan	61.00

Time: :23$^{3/5}$, :47$^{4/5}$, 1:12$^{4/5}$, 1:39$^{1/5}$, 2:05 (Equals track record and is Derby record). Track fast. Went to post at 5:00. At post 2 minutes. Start good. Won driving; second and third the same.

Program #		Win	Place	Show
6	Meridian	$7.80	$2.70	$2.70
10	Governor Gray		$2.70	$2.60
1	Colston			$3.80

Winner: B. c. by Broomstick–Sue Smith, by *Masetto. Trained by Albert Ewing; bred in Kentucky by C. L. Harrison.
Value $6,000. Net to winner $4,850; second $700; third $300.
Scratched: Jabot, Ramazan, Captain Carmody.

117 nominations.

*Foreign bred

Something Rotten?

MERIDIAN, THE SON OF LESS THAN THE creatively named Broomstick, who had held the world record at one and a half miles and who was also the sire of Halma, the 1895 Derby winner, did not seem to have any problem at all winning the Derby. It was a nice day, the track was fast, and Meridian sped wire to wire to win in the quite rapid time of 2:05.

But something rotten had occurred in the race, at least from the point of view of one of the owners, Captain James T. Williams. He thought that his jockey, Roscoe Troxler, had run a very poor race on Williams's horse, Governor Gray, the favorite. In modern parlance, he thought Troxler had thrown the race.

One reason for his suspicion was that Troxler held back too far and for too long dur-ing the first part of the race. Governor Gray came on gamely at the end, but he had to come from too far back. The other reason was that Troxler was seen being handed some money by a bookmaker named Charley Ellis after the race. It looked very suspicious, but Troxler maintained that Ellis owed him money and was simply paying him off. Williams thought this the equivalent of what one calls oats and hay processed digestively by a horse, and he caught up with Troxler at the paddock and swung his cane, knocking off Troxler's cap.

Williams also filed charges, and Churchill Downs and Matt Winn, who protected CD like a momma lion protects her cubs, launched an investigation into the affair. The upshot was that Winn fined Troxler $100 for "improper behavior," but he was never declared the loser.

Worth
38th *May 11, 1912*

		Roseberry	Speculum
	*Knight of the Thistle		Ladylike
WORTH		The Empress Maud	Beauclerc
Brown colt			Stella
	Miss Hanover	Hanover	Hindoo
			Bourbon Belle
			Strathmore
	Miss Dawn		Dawn of Day

THE WINNER'S PEDIGREE AND CAREER HIGHLIGHTS

YEAR	AGE	STS.	1ST	2ND	3RD	EARNINGS
1911	2	13	10	1	0	$16,645
1912	3	18	5	6	3	$ 8,945
TOTALS		**31**	**15**	**7**	**3**	**$25,590**

At 2 years	WON	Raceland Stakes, Bashford Manor Stakes, Private Sweepstakes of $10,000
At 3 years	WON	Kentucky Derby, Chesapeake Stakes, Latonia Handicap
	2ND	Washington Handicap
	3RD	Latonia Derby

RACE DAY STATISTICS

HORSE	EQ.	WT.	PP	ST.	1/4	1/2	3/4	STR.	FIN.	JOCKEY	OWNER	ODDS TO $1
Worth		117	5	1	$1^{1\text{-}1/2}$	$1^{1\text{-}1/2}$	1^1	1^1	1^{nk}	C. Shilling	H. C. Hallenbeck	.80
Duval	b	117	7	4	4^3	$4^{1/2}$	2^1	2^2	2^5	J. Fain	Gallaher Bros.	20.00
Flamma	b	112	1	7	7	5^1	$3^{1\text{-}1/2}$	3^1	3^4	J. Loftus	E. F. Condran	17.00
Free Lance	b	117	4	6	2^1	$2^{1/2}$	$5^{1/2}$	$4^{1\text{-}1/2}$	4^1	C. Peak	G. Long	7.00
Guaranola	b	117	3	3	6^2	3^{hd}	4^2	5^4	5^6	F. Molesworth	Henderson & Hogan	80.00
Sonada	b	117	6	5	3^{hd}	7	6^8	6^{10}	6^{20}	T. Koerner	C. Woodford	12.50
Wheelwright	b	117	2	2	$5^{1/2}$	$6^{1/2}$	7	7	7	G. Byrne	J. N. Camden	4.20

Time: :24$^{3/5}$, :49$^{2/5}$, 1:16$^{1/5}$, 1:42$^{3/5}$, 2:09$^{2/5}$. Track muddy. Went to post at 4:39. At post 2 minutes. Start bad and slow. Won driving; second and third the same.

Program #		Win	Place	Show
6	Worth	$3.60	$ 3.90	$3.30
9	Duval		$14.00	$5.70
1	Flamma			$4.50

Winner: Br. c. by *Knight of the Thistle–Miss Hanover, by Hanover. Trained by F. M. Taylor; bred in Kentucky by R. H. McCarter Potter.
Value $6,000. Net to winner $4,850; second $700; third $300.
Scratched: The Manager, Patruche.

131 nominations.
Equipment: b—blinkers

*Foreign bred

A Day for Mudders—Or Not

MANY PEOPLE AT THE DERBY ON THIS DAY were using their field glasses not to bring the colorful parade of horses and riders on the track closer, but to examine the gathering mountains of dark clouds in the sky. The clouds were getting bigger and darker by the minute, and there seemed no way that the race could be completed before the heavens opened up.

The track was already muddy from previous rain, but a new, heavy rain would change it into a creek, and definitely have an impact on the horses. The same horse who would fly along on the track when it was dry would falter when it was muddy. So, too, the reverse was true: some horses took to mud like pigs.

People would have been foolish to think one horse or the other had the Derby sewed up. One horse by the name of Manager had already been scratched because he didn't run well in mud.

Worth, ridden by Carroll Shilling (a man), was the easy favorite in the race. Prior to the Derby he had racked up an impressive record. He had won nine of ten races and a private sweepstakes race of $10,000. As a two-year-old he won $16,645 altogether.

Worth started slowly when the race began, but he gradually picked up speed and went into the lead, though he was restrained by his jockey, who, of course, wanted to conserve his strength until the end of the race. The duel came near the finish, when a horse named

Duval came alongside Worth but could not pass him. Meanwhile, the only filly in the race, Flamma, also started to come on, but experts said that she started too late.

It would seem predictable that as Worth and Duval battled it out, Shilling would have gone to the whip, particularly after Duval had gained so much ground that he was at Worth's throat-latch. Worth celebrated the event by stumbling, and only some great jockeying by Shilling held the colt together. This day he beat Duval by a heartbeat.

Worth was exhausted by the race, which he ran in 2:09 2/5; this was quite rapid on a muddy track. At least the big rain never came.

Donerail
39th *May 10, 1913*

			Sir Hugo
		White Knight	Whitelock
	*McGee		Hermit
DONERAIL		Remorse	Vex
Bay colt			Hindoo
	Algie M.	Hanover	Bourbon Belle
			Bramble
		Johnson	Guildean

THE WINNER'S PEDIGREE AND CAREER HIGHLIGHTS

YEAR	AGE	STS.	1ST	2ND	3RD	EARNINGS
1912	2	10	2	0	3	$ 1,025
1913	3	15	3	3	2	$ 8,588
1914	4	28	5	5	5	$ 5,180
1916	6	8	0	3	0	$ 363
1918	8	1	0	0	0	$ -
TOTALS		62	10	11	10	$15,156

At 2 years	3RD	Golden Rod Stakes, Rosedale Stakes
At 3 years	WON	Kentucky Derby, Canadian Sportsmen's Handicap
	2ND	Windsor Special, Dominion Handicap, Blue Grass Stakes
At 4 years	WON	Hamilton Cup
	2ND	Latonia Autumn Inaugural, Independence Handicap, George Hendrie Memorial Handicap

RACE DAY STATISTICS

HORSE	EQ.	WT.	PP	ST.	1/4	1/2	3/4	STR.	FIN.	JOCKEY	OWNER	ODDS TO $1
Donerail		117	5	6^1	6^1	$6^{1-1/2}$	5^1	5^2	$1^{1/2}$	R. Goose	T. P. Hayes	91.45
Ten Point		117	4	1^1	1^2	1^3	1^2	$1^{1/2}$	$2^{1-1/2}$	M. Buxton	A. L. Astel	.20
Gowell		112	3	5^1	5^2	4^{hd}	$4^{1-1/2}$	4^1	3^{hd}	J. McCabe	J. T. Weaver	87.00
Foundation		117	8	2^1	2^1	$2^{1/2}$	2^{hd}	$3^{1/2}$	4^{nk}	J. Loftus	C. W. McKenna	2.30
Yankee Notions	b	117	6	3^1	$3^{1/2}$	3^{hd}	$3^{1/2}$	$2^{1/2}$	5^5	J. Glass	H. K. Knapp	4.90
Lord Marshall	b	117	1	7^1	7^1	7^1	6^2	6^1	6^8	T. Steele	J. O. & G. H. Keene	183.00
Jimmie Gill	b	110	2	8	8	8	8	7^{10}	7^{15}	C. Borel	Doerhoefer & West	36.00
Leochares		114	7	$4^{1/2}$	4^{hd}	$5^{1/2}$	7^{hd}	8	8	C. Peak	J. W. Schorr	14.00

Time: :23⁴/₅, :47⁴/₅, 1:12³/₅, 1:39³/₅, 2:04⁴/₅ (new track record). Track fast. Went to post at 4:51. At post 1 minute. Start good and slow. Won driving; second and third the same.

Program #		Win	Place	Show
9	Donerail	$184.90	$41.20	$13.20
8	Ten Point		$ 3.50	$ 3.30
5	Gowell			$14.10

Winner: B. c. by *McGee–Algie M., by Hanover. Trained by T. P. Hayes; bred in Kentucky by T. P. Hayes.
Value $5,000 added. Net to winner $5,475; second $700; third $300.
Scratched: Prince Hermis, Sam Hirsch, Flying Tom, Floral Park.

32 nominations.
Equipment: b—blinkers

*Foreign bred

The Longest Shot of All

OF ALL THE DERBIES OF ALL TIME, NONE produced a winner with greater odds against him than this one. His name was Donerail, and he was a 90–1 shot. In other words, if you laid $2 on the race, you would have gotten back $184.90, a large sum of money when you figure that $3 was a day's wages for a blue-collar worker.

The rider of this longest of all long shots had the unlikely moniker of Roscoe Goose, which sounds more like a cartoon character than a real-life jockey riding a Derby horse. But this man and this horse were no cartoon. Indeed, usually lost in his achievement was that Donerail's time of 2:04 4/5 was the fastest Derby ever.

The weather was good, the track fast, and the race went off without a hitch of any kind. As the race progressed, various horses captured the lead, and for a time it was Ten Point, Foundation in second, and Yankee Notions third. Roscoe Goose kept Donerail away from the pacesetters, but within striking distance.

As they so often do, the real race started as the horses churned into the stretch. Ten Point was still leading, but the supporters of Yankee Notions had high hopes: he was known to be quite good during the last part of a race.

Then Donerail struck. He pounded up from behind and, at high speed, quickly captured the lead. Other horses pursued him, but he did not yield, and they could not catch him. It was that

simple. And when he crossed the wire, he was half a body length ahead of Ten Point.

The jockey's purse for the Derby was over $500, but Goose spent it on a victory party, which he never suspected he would have to do. Before the race the jockeys had agreed that whoever won the race would fund a party, and Goose, knowing he didn't have a chance, had not objected.

Roscoe Goose stayed in racing for the rest of his long life as a trainer, and also proved that besides knowing how to win a big race on a long shot, he knew how to win at the money game. When he died at the age of eighty-one, he was a millionaire.

Old Rosebud
40th *May 9, 1914*

		Star Shoot	*Isinglass*
			Astrology
	Uncle		*Alarm*
	OLD ROSEBUD	*The Niece*	*Jaconet*
	Bay gelding		*Alarm*
	Ivory Bells	*Himyar*	*Hira*
			*Mr. Pickwick
		Ida Pickwick	*Ida K.*

THE WINNER'S PEDIGREE AND CAREER HIGHLIGHTS

YEAR	AGE	STS.	1ST	2ND	3RD	EARNINGS
1913	2	14	12	2	0	$19,057
1914	3	3	2	0	0	$ 9,575
1917	6	21	15	1	3	$31,720
1919	8	30	9	7	5	$12,182
1920	9	8	1	2	0	$ 1,295
1921	10	2	1	0	0	$ 700
1922	11	2	0	1	0	$ 200
TOTALS		**80**	**40**	**13**	**8**	**$74,729**

At 2 years	WON	Yucatan Stakes, Spring Trial Stakes, Harold Stakes, Flash Stakes, United States Hotel Stakes, Cincinnati Trophy
	2ND	Idle Hour Stakes, Bashford Manor Stakes
At 3 years	WON	Kentucky Derby
	UNP	Withers Stakes
At 6 years	WON	Clark Handicap, Queen City Handicap, Carter Handicap, Frontier Handicap, Bayview Handicap, Latonia Inaugural Handicap, Delaware Handicap
	3RD	Brooklyn Handicap
	UNP	Kentucky Handicap, Saratoga Handicap
At 8 years	2ND	Paumonok Handicap, Mt. Vernon Handicap
	3RD	Thanksgiving Handicap
	UNP	Yonkers Handicap, Arverne Handicap, Kingsbridge Handicap
At 9 years	UNP	Harford Handicap, Paumonok Handicap, Toboggan Handicap

RACE DAY STATISTICS

HORSE	EQ.	WT.	PP	ST.	1/4	1/2	3/4	STR.	FIN.	JOCKEY	OWNER	ODDS TO $1
Old Rosebud		114	6	1	1²	1¹⁻¹/²	1²	1⁶	1⁸	J. McCabe	H. C. Applegate	.85
Hodge		114	7	2	2²	2¹/²	2⁴	2⁴	2¹⁻¹/²	W. Taylor	K. Spence	5.40
Bronzewing	b	117	4	7	7	7	6¹/²	3²	3⁴	J. Hanover	A. P. Humphrey Jr.	13.50
John Gund	b	117	3	6	3¹/²	3¹/²	3¹/²	4²	4⁶	G. Byrne	A. Baker	10.00
Old Ben	b	114	1	3	6⁵	6³	5¹⁻¹/²	5¹	5²	C. Turner	W. G. Yanke	12.50
Surprising		117	5	4	5¹	4¹	4ʰᵈ	6⁵	6³	C. Peak	R. F. Carman	14.00
Watermelon	b	112	2	5	4¹⁻¹/²	5¹	7	7	7	W. French	J. E. Madden	15.00

Time: :23³/₅, :47⁴/₅, 1:13, 1:38⁴/₅, 2:03²/₅ (new track record). Track fast. Went to post at 5:03. At post 2 minutes. Start good and slow. Won easily; second and third driving.

Program #		Win	Place	Show
10	Old Rosebud	$3.70	$3.00	$2.80
11	Hodge		$3.60	$3.60
7	Bronzewing			$4.00

Winner: B. g. by Uncle—Ivory Bells, by Himyar. Trained by F. D. Weir, bred in Kentucky by J. E. Madden.
$10,000 added. Net to winner $9,125; second $2,000; third $1,000.
Scratched: Ivan Gardner, Brickley, Belloc, Constant.

47 nominations.
Equipment: b—blinkers

*Foreign bred

More Like Greased Lightning

OLD ROSEBUD SUFFERED THE FATE OF ALL geldings. He was unable to act as a sire, so the only thing available to him—and his owners—after he ran in the fortieth Derby was to race, and race he did, winning forty of eighty races despite suffering chronic lameness. Finally, still hammering around tracks at the age of eleven, he snapped a foreleg going to the front of a race and had to be destroyed.

But oh, could he run, as if he were involved in some heavenly barter: "You lose this but you gain this." "Truly," his trainer said, "he could keep pace with the wind." In the Derby he not only broke the record of Donerail but shattered it, crossing the wire in 2:03 2/5, more than a second faster than that most famous 1913 long shot. Old Rosebud was his name, but "Greased Lightning" would have been more accurate.

The race was run on a cloudy, gray day. It had rained all night and stopped in the morning, but the track was still splotched with water. Track superintendent Tom Young had an innovative idea. He ordered his men to buy up every sponge in Louisville and sop up as much water off the track as they could. They did, and vastly improved the surface.

The start of the race was uneventful, and Old Rosebud, with Johnny McCabe aboard, was not subtle about his intentions. He took the lead, and five of the other horses immediately started to fall back. Only Hodge stayed close. He had intentions too.

As the race progressed, Old Rosebud gradu-

ally increased his lead, and held it, but as the horses turned into the stretch, Hodge was still hounding him, and two lengths behind him was John Gund.

At the top of the stretch, his jockey asked for more, and Old Rosebud gave him much more. Onlookers were goggle-eyed as Old Rosebud turned on some sort of equine afterburner and raced away from the other horses. When he hit the wire, Old Rosebud was making it appear as if he were the only horse galloping.

Except for Hodge—he stayed close to Old Rosebud to the bitter end, and also broke the Derby speed record.

Old Rosebud's record would last seventeen years, until 1931, when Twenty Grand broke it.

Regret
41st *May 8, 1915*

			Bramble
		Ben Brush	Roseville
	Broomstick		Galliard
REGRET		*Elf	*Sylvabelle
Chestnut filly			Hanover
	Jersey	Hamburg	Lady Reel
	Lightning		Riley
		Daisy F.	Modesty

THE WINNER'S PEDIGREE AND CAREER HIGHLIGHTS

YEAR	AGE	STS.	1ST	2ND	3RD	EARNINGS
1914	2	3	3	0	0	$17,390
1915	3	2	2	0	0	$12,500
1916	4	2	1	0	0	$ 560
1917	5	4	3	1	0	$ 4,643
TOTALS		**11**	**9**	**1**	**0**	**$35,093**

At 2 years	WON	Saratoga Special, Sanford Memorial Handicap, Hopeful Stakes
At 3 years	WON	Kentucky Derby, Saranac Handicap
At 4 years	UNP	Saratoga Handicap
At 5 years	WON	Gazelle Handicap
	2ND	Brooklyn Handicap

RACE DAY STATISTICS

HORSE	EQ.	WT.	PP	ST.	1/4	1/2	3/4	STR.	FIN.	JOCKEY	OWNER	ODDS TO $1
Regret		112	2	1	$1^{1\text{-}1/2}$	$1^{1/2}$	$1^{1/2}$	$1^{1\text{-}1/2}$	1^2	J. Notter	H. P. Whitney	2.65
Pebbles	b	117	3	3	2^1	$2^{1\text{-}1/2}$	$2^{1\text{-}1/2}$	2^2	2^2	C. Borel	J. Butler	6.55
Sharpshooter	b	114	8	7	$3^{1/2}$	$3^{1/2}$	3^{hd}	3^1	3^1	J. Butwell	S. L. Parsons	9.60
Royal II	b	117	10	16	12^2	9^1	6^{nk}	5^{hd}	4^3	A. Neylon	J. Livingston	15.10
Emerson Cochran		117	5	2	$6^{1/2}$	4^1	$7^{1/2}$	$4^{1/2}$	$5^{1/2}$	W. Taylor	R. L. Baker	16.15
Leo Ray		117	11	13	10^{hd}	$8^{1\text{-}1/2}$	8^{hd}	7^{hd}	$6^{1\text{-}1/2}$	T. McTaggart	J. T. Looney	17.90
Double Eagle	sb	117	13	12	9^{hd}	$7^{1\text{-}1/2}$	$9^{1/2}$	6^2	7^4	C. Burlingame	J. F. Johnson	17.20
Dortch		110	1	11	7^1	$6^{1/2}$	$5^{1\text{-}1/2}$	$8^{1/2}$	8^5	A. Mott	W. W. Darden	(f) 5.40
For Fair	b	117	4	15	16	15	$10^{1/2}$	$9^{1/2}$	$9^{1/2}$	W. Warrington	G. M. Miller	(f) 5.40
Ed Crump	b	117	7	4	$4^{1\text{-}1/2}$	$5^{1/2}$	$4^{1/2}$	$10^{1/2}$	10^{hd}	R. Goose	J. W. Schorr	(a) 5.90
Little String		117	12	10	$11^{1\text{-}1/2}$	12^2	11^1	11^1	$11^{1\text{-}1/2}$	E. Pool	M. B. Gruber	(f) 5.40
Goldcrest Boy		114	6	8	$8^{1/2}$	$10^{1/2}$	13^1	12^1	12^2	J. Kederis	J. W. Schorr	(a) 5.90
Uncle Bryn	sb	117	16	14	14^1	14^1	$12^{1/2}$	13^1	13^2	J. McTaggart	Mrs. R. W. Walden	(f) 5.40
Tetan		117	15	6	13^2	13^2	14^6	14^6	14^2	J. Smyth	Johnson & Crosthwaite	(b,f) 5.40
Norse King	b	117	9	9	$5^{1/2}$	11^1	15^1	15	15^4	W. O' Brien	F. B. Lemaire	39.60
Booker Bill	b	117	14	5	15^1	16	16	16	16	W. Andress	M. C. Moore	(b, f) 5.40

Time: :23³/₅, :48³/₅, 1:13³/₅, 1:39²/₅, 2:05²/₅. Track fast. Went to post at 5:18. At post 4 minutes. Start good and slow. Won easily; second and third driving.
Coupled: (a) Ed Crump and Goldcrest Boy; (b) Tetan and Booker Bill.

Program #		Win	Place	Show
3	Regret	$7.30	$4.00	$3.60
5	Pebbles		$7.60	$4.80
11	Sharpshooter			$7.10

Winner: Ch. f. by Broomstick–Jersey Lightning by Hamburg. Trained by James Rowe Sr.; bred in New Jersey by H. P. Whitney.
$10,000 added. Net to winner $11,450; second $2,000; third $1,000; fourth $225.
Scratched: Kilkenny Boy, Phosphor, Commonada.

68 nominations.
Equipment: b—blinkers; s—spurs

*Foreign bred

A Lady Saves the Day

AS THE HORSES LINED UP BEHIND THE WEB barrier to start the running of the 1915 Kentucky Derby, many people knew that the Derby was teetering on the edge of oblivion. For years, it had suffered some serious image problems because of attracting so many low-quality horses. Also, Churchill Downs had been battered by internal dissension and various employee strikes. Another problem was the length of the race; many owners considered it too long to send their young horses to.

But on this day the Kentucky Derby would be saved, and mostly by a horse, a beautiful little filly named Regret. She had been entered into the forty-first running by two of racing's superstars. She was bred by Harry Payne Whitney, a famous and respected horseman of the time and the leading owner in 1914. More, her trainer, James Rowe, was one of the most respected trainers of the time, having produced thirty-four champions; as mentioned earlier in the book, he may stand as the greatest trainer of all time.

The odds were against Regret: no filly had ever won the Kentucky Derby.

One thing was for sure, though—she wasn't intimidated by her male opponents. When the race started, her highly skilled jockey, Joe Notter, took her immediately to the lead. That was it—all the other horses saw for the rest of the race was her beautiful backside.

And then came the miracle. Whitney, suffused with pride over Regret being the first filly to win the Derby and impressed by the overall experience of the Kentucky Derby itself, said to newspapermen, "I have seen much bigger crowds in the east and abroad, but I never saw a more enthusiastic one." And he went on to say what a great race it was.

Mind you, Whitney was not just anyone. He was Babe Ruth talking about baseball or Joe Louis talking about boxing or Steven Spielberg talking about movies: when he spoke, the world listened, and the brilliant Derby president and publicist Matt Winn took it from there. He wined and dined a bunch of influential journalists, who predictably started Derby stories that went from the pages in the back of their newspapers to the front pages, complete with splashy headlines.

In effect, Regret—and Winn—brought home a huge win for the Kentucky Derby, a championship if you will. This triumph is something that the Derby will likely hold on to for a long, long time.

George Smith
42nd *May 13, 1916*

		St. Simon
	Persimmon	Perdita II
*Out of Reach		Isonomy
GEORGE SMITH	*Sandfly	Sandiway
Black colt		Barcaldine
*Consuelo II	Bradwardine	Monte Rosa
		Pepper and Salt
	*Miss Pepper II	Great Dame

THE WINNER'S PEDIGREE AND CAREER HIGHLIGHTS

YEAR	AGE	STS.	1ST	2ND	3RD	EARNINGS
1915	2	12	9	0	0	$10,140
1916	3	4	1	2	0	$11,600
1917	4	7	3	1	1	$ 2,594
1918	5	8	4	2	2	$18,550
TOTALS		**31**	**17**	**5**	**3**	**$42,884**

At 2 years	WON	Aberdeen Stakes, Juvenile Stakes, Victoria Stakes, Spring Brewery Stakes, Annapolis Stakes
	UNP	Sanford Memorial Handicap, Eastern Shore Handicap, Erdenheim Handicap
At 3 years	WON	Kentucky Derby
	2ND	Latonia Derby
	UNP	Carter Handicap
At 4 years	WON	Warwick Handicap
	2ND	Long Beach Handicap
	3RD	Belmont Autumn Handicap
	UNP	Saratoga Handicap
At 5 years	WON	Excelsior Handicap, Edgemere Handicap, Yorktown Handicap, Bowie Handicap
	2ND	Bay View Handicap, October Handicap
	3RD	Brooklyn Handicap, Continental Handicap

RACE DAY STATISTICS

HORSE	EQ.	WT.	PP	ST.	1/4	1/2	3/4	STR.	FIN.	JOCKEY	OWNER	ODDS TO $1
George Smith		117	8	6	3^2	3^{hd}	1^1	1^2	1^{nk}	J. Loftus	John Sanford	4.15
Star Hawk		117	3	9	9	$7^{1/2}$	5^4	3^2	2^5	W. Lilley	A. K. Macomber	(c) 4.45
Franklin	b	117	1	2	2^2	$2^{1-1/2}$	2^1	2^{hd}	$3^{1/2}$	T. Rice	Weber & Ward	(a) 6.45
Dodge		117	4	1	5^1	$4^{1-1/2}$	$4^{1/2}$	4^2	4^6	F. Murphy	Weber & Ward	(a) 6.45
Thunderer		117	5	7	7^1	$5^{1/2}$	6^1	6^1	5^1	T. McTaggart	H. P. Whitney	(b) 1.05
The Cock	b	110	7	8	8^3	6^{hd}	7^2	7^2	6^5	M. Garner	A. K. Macomber	(c) 4.45
Dominant		117	2	3	1^3	$1^{1-1/2}$	$3^{1/2}$	5^1	7^5	J. Notter	H. P. Whitney	(b) 1.05
Kinney	b	117	9	5	$6^{1/2}$	8^6	8^6	8^{10}	8^{12}	L. Gentry	T. P. Hayes	32.55
Lena Misha		117	6	4	4^{hd}	9	9	9	9	E. Dugan	Beverwyck Stable	35.30

Time: :22^{2}/5, :46^{2}/5, 1:12^{1}/5, 1:38^{4}/5, 2:04. Track fast. Went to post at 5:15. At post 1 minute. Start good and slow. Won driving; second and third the same.
Coupled: (a) Star Hawk and The Cock; (b) Franklin and Dodge; (c) Thunderer and Dominant.

	Win	Place	Show
George Smith	$10.30	$4.80	$2.90
Star Hawk		$6.60	$4.40
Franklin			$3.50

Winner: Blk. c. by *Out of Reach–*Consuelo II, by Bradwardine. Trained by Hollie Hughes; bred in Kentucky by Chinn & Forsythe.
$10,000 added. Net to winner $9,750; second $2,000; third $1,000; fourth $225.
Scratched: St. Isidore, Bulse, Huffaker.

56 nominations.
Equipment: b—blinkers

*Foreign bred

His Time Was Better Than His Name

"WHAT A GREAT NAME FOR A HORSE," ONE trainer said sardonically. "'George Smith.' Exciting!" Perhaps. But it certainly didn't impede his ability to run fast. He won the Derby that day in 2:04, the second fastest time in twenty years, only bested by Old Rosebud, who covered the mile and a quarter in 2:03 2/5.

George Smith was not supposed to win. The great Harry Payne Whitney had two horses entered that day, Thunderer and Dominant, and the year before he had won with the great filly Regret, who had electrified Whitney and was to lead to his enthusiastic comments on the Derby, which helped save the race. George Smith entered the Derby with quite a good record as a two-year-old, though. He had started in twelve

races and finished first nine times, and second twice, earning $10,140. It was just that other horses were regarded as better.

The race was very close. Indeed, George Smith came close to losing it.

For the first three quarters of the race, jockey J. Loftus held George Smith back, but at the three-quarters he rushed into the lead. He seemed on his way to victory but a horse named Star Hawk, who had trailed for a half mile, suddenly started to run hard, and as George Smith galloped down the stretch, losing energy as he did, Star Hawk, urged by demented spurring and whipping by his jockey, W. Lilley, closed the gap. As he was just about to pass George Smith, his nose at the leader's shoulder, George's nose passed something else—the finish line.

*Omar Khayyam
43rd May 12, 1917

			Barcaldine	Solon
				Ballyroe
		Marco		Hermit
	*OMAR KHAYYAM		Novitiate	Retty
	Chestnut colt			St. Simon
		Lisma	Persimmon	Perdita II
				+Royal Hampton
			Luscious	Alveole

+ Harpenden or Royal Hampton.

THE WINNER'S PEDIGREE AND CAREER HIGHLIGHTS

YEAR	AGE	STS.	1ST	2ND	3RD	EARNINGS
1916	2	5	1	2	0	$ 3,465
1917	3	13	9	2	0	$49,070
1918	4	10	2	1	4	$ 4,475
1919	5	4	1	1	1	$ 1,426
TOTALS		**32**	**13**	**6**	**5**	**$58,436**

At 2 years	2ND	Hopeful Stakes, Piping Rock Invitational Handicap
At 3 years	WON	Kentucky Derby, Prospect Handicap, Brooklyn Derby, Kenner Stakes, Travers Stakes, Saratoga Cup, Lawrence Realization, Havre de Grace Handicap, Pimlico Autumn Handicap
	2ND	American Champion Stakes, Bowie Handicap
	UNP	Derby Trial, Brooklyn Handicap
At 4 years	WON	Marines' Liberty Bond Handicap
	2ND	Bowie Handicap
	3RD	Pimlico Spring Handicap, Dixie Handicap, Arlington Handicap, Monumental Handicap
	UNP	Metropolitan Handicap, Baltimore Handicap, Washington Handicap
At 5 years	WON	Rennert Handicap
	2ND	Merchants Handicap
	3RD	Pimlico Special Handicap
	UNP	Elmont Handicap

HORSE	EQ.	WT.	PP	ST.	1/4	1/2	3/4	STR.	FIN.	JOCKEY	OWNER	ODDS TO $1
*Omar Khayyam	b	117	8	11	10hd	10¹	6¹/²	2¹	1²	C. Borel	Billings & Johnson	12.80
Ticket	b	117	3	1	3hd	3¹⁻¹/²	4¹/²	1¹/²	2¹⁻¹/²	J. McTaggart	A. Miller	1.45
Midway	b	117	1	12	12¹	9¹	8¹/²	3hd	3⁴	C. Hunt	J. W. Parrish	14.65
Rickety		117	11	5	7¹/²	5¹	1hd	4¹/²	4¹	F. Robinson	H. P. Whitney	4.55
*War Star	b	110	9	6	5¹⁻¹/²	6¹	5¹/²	5hd	5hd	M. Buxton	A. K. Macomber	(a) 8.65
*Manister Toi	b	117	14	15	13¹/²	11¹/²	10¹	6¹/²	6hd	F. Keogh	E. Herz	(f) 15.45
Skeptic		117	4	14	6¹	4hd	9¹	7¹	7¹⁻¹/²	E. Martin	H. H. Hewitt	16.45
Guy Fortune	b	117	2	2	14¹	12¹	12¹	11¹	8¹/²	D. Connelly	Pastime Stable	(f) 15.45
Star Master	b	117	12	9	4¹/²	2hd	2hd	8¹¹	9hd	J. Loftus	A. K. Macomber	(a) 8.65
Stargazer	b	110	13	10	1¹/²	1¹/²	3hd	9¹/²	10²	W. Crump	A. K. Macomber	(a) 8.65
Cudgel	b	117	5	13	11¹	7¹	13¹	12¹/²	11⁵	F. Murphy	J. W. Schorr	23.00
Green Jones		117	7	3	9hd	13¹	11¹/²	13¹	12⁸	R. Goose	W. H. Baker	(f) 15.45
Top o'the Wave	b	117	10	4	15	14²	14¹	14¹	13⁴	J. Morys	Beverwyck Stable	(f) 15.45
Berline	b	117	6	7	2¹/²	8hd	7¹/²	10¹	14¹²	W. Andress	J. S. Ward	16.20
Acabado	b	114	15	8	8hd	15	15	15	15	A. Schuttinger	Wickliffe Stable	75.45

Time: :23³/₅, :47³/₅, 1:12⁴/₅, 1:38, 2:04³/₅. Track fast. Went to post at 4:53. At post 4 minutes. Start good and slow. Won easily; second and third driving.
Coupled: (a) War Star, Star Master, and Stargazer; (f) Field.

Program #		Win	Place	Show
10	*Omar Khayyam	$27.60	$10.90	$6.20
5	Ticket		$ 3.70	$2.80
2	Midway			$5.10

Winner: Ch. c. by Marco-Lisma, by Persimmon. Trained by C. T. Patterson; bred in England by Sir John Robinson.
Omar Khayyam was the first of four foreign-bred colts to win the Derby. Foaled in England, he was brought to this country as a yearling. Tomy Lee (1959) also was foaled in England. Northern Dancer (1964) was foaled in Canada, as was Sunny's Halo (1983). Omar Khayyam was brought to this country because of the wartime conditions in England.
$15,000 added. Net to winner $16,600; second $2,500; third $1,000; fourth $275. 76 nominations. Equipment: b—blinkers
*Foreign bred

Pancho Villa Rides Again—on Your Horse!

COLONEL MATT J. WINN MET A LOT OF famous people in his time, including the outlaw Pancho Villa, who showed up with his cohorts at the 1917 Derby. Villa liked racing and horses, and he had a string of them. The problem was that he didn't believe in paying for horses; stealing was far cheaper. So when he visited CD, Winn alerted his people to be on guard: watch their horses. When Villa was around, you could not only lose a race—but the horse. Trainer Ben Jones went one better to protect his best horse, Lemon Joe, against being stolen. He had the rear leg of the horse taped up so it looked as if the horse had broken down. Villa stole another horse, but not Lemon Joe.

In the race, Omar Khayyam—there was a famous poem around at that time by that name—went off as a 12–1 shot among the fifteen colts. At first, he traveled slowly, but as the race progressed he moved faster, gaining on the leaders so that by the far turn he was in a duel with Ticket. They drove down the stretch together, but Omar bested him at the end.

As a two-year-old Omar Khayyam had only won one race (second in another), but in his third year he won almost $50,000. He raced until he was five, fattening his earnings another $8 to $9,000 and then retiring to stud. Fortunately, Pancho Villa never returned for another visit to Churchill Downs or found out where Omar Khayyam had retired to.

Exterminator
44th *May 11, 1918*

			Sir Hugo
	White Knight	Whitelock
*McGee		Hermit
EXTERMINATOR	Remorse	Vex
Chestnut gelding		Hindoo
Fair Empress	Jim Gore	Katie
		*Pirate of Penzance
	Merry Thought	Raybelle

THE WINNER'S PEDIGREE AND CAREER HIGHLIGHTS

YEAR	AGE	STS.	1ST	2ND	3RD	EARNINGS
1917	2	4	2	0	0	$ 1,350
1918	3	15	7	4	3	$ 36,147
1919	4	21	9	6	3	$ 26,402
1920	5	17	10	3	2	$ 52,805
1921	6	16	8	2	5	$ 56,827
1922	7	17	10	1	1	$ 71,075
1923	8	3	1	1	1	$ 4,250
1924	9	7	3	0	2	$ 4,140
TOTALS		**100**	**50**	**17**	**17**	**$252,996**

At 3 years	WON	Kentucky Derby, Carrollton Handicap, Ellicott City Handicap, Pimlico Autumn Handicap, Latonia Cup, Thanksgiving Handicap
	2ND	Latonia Derby, Kenner Stakes, National Handicap
	3RD	Washington Handicap, Bowie Handicap, Cohoes Handicap
At 4 years	WON	Ben Ali Handicap, Camden Handicap, Galt House Handicap, Saratoga Cup, Pimlico Cup Handicap
	2ND	Champlain Handicap, Harford County Handicap, Havre de Grace Handicap, Annapolis Handicap, Latonia Cup
	3RD	Kentucky Handicap, Delaware Handicap, Merchants' and Citizens' Handicap
At 5 years	WON	Long Beach Handicap, Brookdale Handicap, Windsor Jockey Club Handicap, George Hendrie Memorial Handicap, Saratoga Cup, Autumn Gold Cup, Toronto Autumn Cup, Ontario Jockey Club Cup, Pimlico Cup
	2ND	Saratoga Handicap, Champlain Handicap
	3RD	Suburban Handicap, Frontier Handicap

RACE DAY STATISTICS

HORSE	EQ.	WT.	PP	ST.	1/4	1/2	3/4	STR.	FIN.	JOCKEY	OWNER	ODDS TO $1
Exterminator		114	5	5	5^1	$4^{1/2}$	1^{hd}	2^4	1^1	W. Knapp	W. S. Kilmer	29.60
Escoba	b	117	1	2	$3^{1-1/2}$	2^{hd}	2^1	1^{hd}	2^8	J. Notter	K. D. Alexander	4.25
Viva America		113	2	1	$1^{1-1/2}$	$1^{1-1/2}$	3^4	3^2	3^4	W. Warrington	C. T. Worthington	29.00
*War Cloud		117	4	7	4^{hd}	5^2	4^4	4^3	4^2	J. Loftus	A. K. Macomber	1.45
Lucky B		117	6	4	6^{hd}	7^8	$5^{1/2}$	5^6	5^6	J. McCabe	O. A. Bianchi	6.15
Jas. T. Clark	b	117	8	8	7^3	6^3	7^6	7^3	6^{12}	J. Morys	J. W. Schorr	8.90
Sewell Combs	b	117	3	3	2^{nk}	3^1	6^2	$6^{1/2}$	7^1	L. Gentry	Gallaher Bros.	8.75
American Eagle	sb	117	7	6	8	8	8	8	8	E. Sande	T. C. McDowell	19.25

Time: :24$^{1/5}$, :49$^{1/5}$, 1:16$^{1/5}$, 1:43$^{3/5}$, 2:10$^{4/5}$. Track muddy. Went to post at 5:19. At post 2 minutes. Start good and slow. Won handily; second and third driving.

Program #		Win	Place	Show
5	Exterminator	$61.20	$23.10	$12.40
1	Escoba		$ 4.90	$ 4.60
2	Viva America			$13.20

Winner: Ch. g. by *McGee–Fair Empress, by Jim Gore. Trained by Henry McDaniel; bred in Kentucky by F. D. Knight.
$15,000 added. Net to winner $14,700; second $2,500; third $1,000; fourth $275.

70 nominations.
Equipment: b—blinkers; s—spurs

*Foreign bred

One of the Best Ever

IN THIS YEAR, THE YEAR AFTER WORLD WAR I ended, the odds-on favorite to win the forty-fourth running of the Derby was a horse named Sun Briar. To tune him up a bit, the owner, W. S. Kilmer, decided to buy a horse who could run with him, help him work out. But a funny thing happened on the way to the Derby: Sun Briar did not train well, while the horse brought in to train him did, and Kilmer decided to send that horse instead of Sun Briar to the Derby. The horse, a chestnut gelding, was named Exterminator, and he would turn out to be one of the most exciting and popular racehorses ever.

Exterminator showed none of what he was to become prior to the Derby. As a two-year-old he had accomplished virtually nothing. The Derby was his first race as a three-year-old, and he was a 30–1 shot. Though there is no record

in print of his reaction, J. Cal Milan, the man who sold Exterminator to Kilmer, could not have felt any glee about his judgment when he found out what happened at the Derby.

The race was run on a muddy track before a crowd of 30,000. For the first three quarters W. Knapp, Exterminator's jockey, held the horse back, but then in the final quarter he slipped into the rail position and drove from there to the lead. A horse named Escoba tried to run him down, but "died" in the last eighth.

For Exterminator and fans, it was love at first sight that also lasted for years. Fans showed their affection by giving him a variety of nicknames such as "Old Hatrack," "Old Slim," and "Old Bones," based on the angularity of his body. Exterminator proved to be one of the greatest horses of all time, winning fifty of a hundred races and earning a whopping $252,996.

Sir Barton
45th May 10, 1919

			Isonomy
		Isinglass	Deadlock
	Star Shoot		Hermit
SIR BARTON		Astrology	Stella
Chestnut colt			Hindoo
	Lady Sterling	Hanover	Bourbon Belle
			Sterling
		*Aquila	Eagle

THE WINNER'S PEDIGREE AND CAREER HIGHLIGHTS

YEAR	AGE	STS.	1ST	2ND	3RD	EARNINGS
1918	2	6	0	1	0	$ 4,113
1919	3	13	8	3	2	$ 88,250
1920	4	12	5	2	3	$ 24,494
TOTALS		**31**	**13**	**6**	**5**	**$116,857**

At 2 years	2ND	Belmont Futurity
	UNP	Tremont Stakes, Flash Stakes, United States Hotel Stakes, Sanford Memorial Stakes, Hopeful Stakes
At 3 years	WON	Kentucky Derby, Preakness Stakes, Withers Stakes, Belmont Stakes, Potomac Handicap, Maryland Handicap, Pimlico Fall Serial No. 2, Pimlico Fall Serial No. 3
	2ND	Dwyer Stakes
	3RD	Havre de Grace Handicap, Pimlico Autumn Handicap
At 4 years	WON	Climax Handicap, Rennert Handicap, Saratoga Handicap, Dominion Handicap, Merchants' and Citizens' Handicap
	2ND	Kenilworth Park Gold Cup (match race with Man o'War), Pimlico Fall Serial No. 3
	3RD	Marathon Handicap, Laurel Stakes, Pimlico Fall Serial No. 2

RACE DAY STATISTICS

HORSE	EQ.	WT.	PP	ST.	1/4	1/2	3/4	STR.	FIN.	JOCKEY	OWNER	ODDS TO $1
Sir Barton	b	112$^{1/2}$	1	1	1^2	$1^{1/2}$	1^2	$1^{1/2}$	1^5	J. Loftus	J. K. L. Ross	(a) 2.60
Billy Kelly		119	11	8	$3^{1/2}$	3^4	2^3	2^4	2^1	E. Sande	J. K. L. Ross	(a) 2.60
*Under Fire		122	7	11	$9^{1/2}$	$9^{1/2}$	$6^{1/2}$	3^1	3^1	M. Garner	P. Dunne	19.15
Vulcanite		110	6	10	$10^{1/2}$	5^{hd}	$4^{1/2}$	4^1	4^6	C. Howard	W. F. Polson	70.00
Sennings Park	b	122	8	9	6^2	$4^{1/2}$	$5^{1/2}$	5^1	5^1	H. Lunsford	O. A. Bianchi	(f) 14.10
Be Frank		119	2	6	7^{hd}	$7^{1/2}$	$7^{1/2}$	$6^{1/2}$	$6^{1/2}$	J. Butwell	C. M. Garrison	27.45
Sailor	b	119	10	12	12	10^2	$10^{1/2}$	$8^{1/2}$	7^8	J. McIntyre	J. W. McClelland	(b) 2.10
St. Bernard		119	4	2	5^{hd}	6^1	9^1	7^2	8^2	E. Pool	B. J. Brannon	(f) 14.10
Regalo		117	9	7	8^2	$8^{1-1/2}$	8^1	9^2	9^4	F. Murphy	Gallaher Bros.	6.05
Eternal		122	5	3	$2^{1/2}$	$2^{1/2}$	$3^{1/2}$	10^5	10^{10}	A. Schuttinger	J. W. McClelland	(b) 2.10
Frogtown		119	12	4	11^2	$11^{1/2}$	11^2	11^{10}	11^{20}	J. Morys	W. S. Kilmer	22.45
Vindex		122	3	5	4^{nk}	12	12	12	12	W. Knapp	H. P. Whitney	8.15

Time: :24$^{1/5}$, :48$^{2/5}$, 1:14, 1:41$^{4/5}$, 2:09$^{4/5}$. Track heavy. Went to post at 5:10. At post 4 minutes. Start good and slow. Won easily; second and third driving.
Coupled: (a) Sir Barton and Billy Kelly; (b) Sailor and Eternal.

Program #		Win	Place	Show
1	Sir Barton	$7.20	$6.70	$ 6.00
13	Billy Kelly		$6.70	$ 6.00
8	Under Fire			$10.80

Winner: Ch. c. by *Star Shoot–Lady Sterling, by Hanover. Trained by H. G. Bedwell; bred in Kentucky by Madden and Gooch.
$20,000 added. Net to winner $20,825; second $2,500; third $1,000; fourth $275.

75 nominations.
Equipment: b—blinkers

*Foreign bred

Another Rabbit

IF SIR BARTON, A DARK, MUSCULAR COLT
built along the lines of a quarter horse, was in
a competition to measure disposition, he would
have finished last, or close to last—at least,
according to J. K. L. Ross, son of Sir Barton's
owner. In his book *Boots and Saddles,* Ross
wrote, "The horse was an irascible, exasper-
ating creature . . . downright evil. He had no interest in other horses and he completely ignored
and apparently despised all human beings. . . ."

In addition to his nasty temperament, columnist Red Smith characterized Sir Barton as "one
of the great hopheads of history, supposed to
have been coked to the eyes whenever he ran."

When he was a two-year-old, Sir Barton
did not win a single race, though he did come in
second in the final race of 1918, the Futurity
at Belmont Park. Nevertheless, his owner,
J. K. L. Ross, decided to enter him in the Derby
as a rabbit for another horse named Billy Kelly,
who Ross liked so much that he made a side
bet of either $20,000 or $50,000 with gambler
Arnold Rothstein.

But alas, as in the very first Derby, where
Aristides was supposed to be a rabbit, the best
laid plans of mice and men didn't quite work
out. For one thing, Sir Barton wasn't running
out of gas, and for another, his jockey, Johnny
Loftus, a good jockey who had won the 1916
Derby riding George Smith, and who was supposed to drop back when he spotted Billy Kelly,
said that he didn't do that because he didn't see
the horse. That statement was highly suspect:

all he had to do was turn around—Billy Kelly
was right behind him.

The real story is likely that Loftus knew
that he had a lot of horse left under him, so he
cracked Sir Barton once with the whip and took
off as if it were the beginning of the race. Loftus
might just as well have done it from nastiness;
he was just as churlish as Sir Barton.

Later, Billy Kelly closed on Sir Barton, who
responded by pulling away—and winning.

But Sir Barton didn't stop there. He went
on to win the Preakness by four lengths over
Eternal and then captured the Triple Crown by
winning the Belmont Stakes, which was then
1 3/8 miles.

Many years after the horse died in 1937, a
statue was erected of him in Douglas, Wyoming.
One trainer, who had also known Sir Barton,
said: "The statue doesn't need a nameplate. Just
look for a horse that looks pissed off."

Paul Jones
46th *May 8, 1920*

			St. Simon
		Persimmon	Perdita II
	*Sea King		Isonomy
PAUL JONES		Sea Air	Re-echo
Brown gelding			Hanover
	May Florence	Hamburg	Lady Reel
			*Goldfinch
		Fiesole	Firenze

THE WINNER'S PEDIGREE AND CAREER HIGHLIGHTS

YEAR	AGE	STS.	1ST	2ND	3RD	EARNINGS
1919	2	12	5	2	2	$ 6,404
1920	3	13	4	2	2	$44,636
1921	4	12	1	1	3	$ 2,708
1922	5	13	2	2	2	$ 5,432
1923	6	15	2	5	4	$ 4,991
TOTALS		**65**	**14**	**12**	**13**	**$64,171**

At 2 years	WON	Aberdeen Stakes, Boquet Stakes, Endurance
	3RD	Albany Handicap
At 3 years	WON	Kentucky Derby, Newark Handicap, Suburban Handicap
	2ND	Chesapeake Stakes, Oxford Handicap
	3RD	Whitehall Handicap, Pimlico Cup
At 4 years	WON	Susquehanna Handicap
	2ND	Pimlico Special Handicap
	3RD	Olambala Handicap, Lake George Handicap, Champlain Handicap
At 5 years	2ND	Calvert Handicap, Pimlico Cup Handicap
	3RD	Stafford Handicap
At 6 years	2ND	Philadelphia Handicap, Stafford Handicap
	3RD	Old Dominion Handicap, American Independence Handicap

HORSE	EQ.	WT.	PP	ST.	1/4	1/2	3/4	STR.	FIN.	JOCKEY	OWNER	ODDS TO $1
Paul Jones		126	2	1	$1^{1-1/2}$	$1^{1/2}$	1^2	1^{hd}	1^{hd}	T. Rice	Ral Parr	(a) 16.20
Upset		126	5	4	3^{hd}	3^{hd}	$2^{1/2}$	2^{hd}	2^4	J. Rodriguez	H. P. Whitney	(b) 1.65
On Watch	b	126	13	16	$13^{1/2}$	7^1	$3^{1/2}$	3^1	3^4	N. Barrett	G. W. Loft	(c) 4.30
Damask	b	126	8	9	7^{hd}	4^{hd}	4^1	4^1	4^2	E. Ambrose	H. P. Whitney	(b) 1.65
*Donnacona		126	7	10	6^{hd}	$6^{1/2}$	$5^{1/2}$	5^2	5^4	W. O'Brien	G. W. Loft	(c) 4.30
Blazes		126	15	7	$8^{1/2}$	5^1	$6^{1/2}$	6^1	$6^{1/2}$	C. Kummer	Ral Parr	(a) 16.20
By Golly		126	4	5	2^{hd}	8^1	$8^{1-1/2}$	8^1	7^{hd}	L. Lyke	E. R. Bradley	(f) 13.20
Wildair		126	14	8	$4^{1/2}$	2^{hd}	7^1	$7^{1/2}$	8^{hd}	L. Fator	H. P. Whitney	(b) 1.65
Bersagliere	b	126	9	3	$10^{1/2}$	$11^{1/2}$	9^1	9^1	$9^{1/2}$	T. Murray	G. A. Cochran	22.75
Patches	b	126	6	12	14^1	10^{hd}	10^2	10^{hd}	10^4	J. Hanover	F. C. Bain	(f) 13.20
Herron		126	1	6	9^{hd}	13^2	$11^{1-1/2}$	11^2	$11^{1/2}$	J. Butwell	E. Alvarez	(f) 13.20
Sandy Beal		126	10	14	15^2	14^2	12^1	12^1	$12^{1/2}$	J. Williams	W. S. Murray	12.50
Prince Pal		126	3	2	5^1	12^{hd}	13^2	13^2	13^2	A. Schuttinger	Simms & Oliver	18.90
David Harum	b	126	11	11	$11^{1/2}$	$9^{1/2}$	14^2	14^2	$14^{1-1/2}$	C. Fairbrother	W. R. Coe	(d) 35.20
Cleopatra	b	121	12	13	12^{nk}	15^4	15^5	15^1	15^5	L. McAtee	W. R. Coe	(d) 35.20
Peace Pennant	b	126	17	15	16^{10}	16^{20}	16^{20}	16^{20}	16^{20}	M. Garner	W. F. Polson	6.35
Sterling	b	126	16	17	17	17	17	17	17	J. Callahan	C. C. Van Meter	33.00

Time: :23⁴/5, :48¹/5, 1:14⁴/5, 1:42, 2:09. Track slow. Went to post at 5:08. At post 4 minutes. Start good and slow. Won driving; second and third the same.
Coupled: (a) Paul Jones and Blazes; (b) Upset, Damask, and Wildair; (c) On Watch and *Donnacona; (d) David Harum and Cleopatra; (f) Field.

Program #		Win	Place	Show
2	Paul Jones	$34.40	$12.30	$6.60
5	Upset		$ 3.20	$3.00
17	On Watch			$4.00

Winner: Br. g. by *Sea King–May Florence, by Hamburg. Trained by William Garth; bred in Kentucky by J. E. Madden.
$30,000 added. Net to winner $30,375; second $4,000; third $2,000; fourth $275. 104 nominations. Equipment: b–blinkers

*Foreign bred

The Derby That Man o' War Missed—Whew!

TWO THINGS WERE DISTINCTIVE ABOUT THE 1929 run for the roses, but undoubtedly the most notable was that Man o' War, generally regarded as the greatest racehorse who ever lived—or, as his groom, Will Herbert, put it, "the mostest hoss"—didn't run. His owner, Sam Riddle, felt that the 126 pounds he would have to carry—imposed this year for the first time—was too much too soon for the colt. He could get hurt.

The horse who was to win the Derby was developed by horseman John E. Madden, the "Wizard of the Turf," who bred five Derby winners and Triple Crown winner Sir Barton (1919). This was Paul Jones. He had actually run against Man o' War twice, and had lost by a combined distance of twenty-six and a half lengths. Jones was widely regarded as a so-so racehorse, but he had one quality that shone over all others: he had a nasty temperament and paid for it big-time. To improve his disposition his owners had his testicles cut off. It had something of a positive effect on him, but of course rendered him useless for stud service later.

Perhaps in part because of this, Paul Jones didn't have an affectionate or even respectful relationship with his jockeys. In his first five starts four different jockeys had ridden him, but in his sixth race Ted Rice climbed on his back, and horse and man hit it off well right away. He had not won a single race in the first six starts,

but with Rice piloting him, he won his first race, the Boquet Selling Stakes at Belmont Park.

As the Derby approached, Rice did fairly well with Paul Jones, winning some and losing some.

In the Derby, most prognosticators picked a horse named Blazes to win. Seventeen horses stood at the post, with Jones in position 2. Included was one horse named Upset who had achieved a rare distinction: he was the only horse in the group to have beaten Man o' War!

When the race started, Paul Jones burst into the lead, and he held it until near the end, when he appeared doomed. Upset was coming up on him fast, pulled even, and appeared to be the winner at the sixteenth pole, but tired just at the end, Paul Jones holding on for dear life to win.

Behave Yourself
47th *May 7, 1921*

			Bend Or
	Martagon		Tiger Lily
Marathon			St. Simon
BEHAVE YOURSELF	*Ondulee		Ornis
Bay colt			Hanover
	Miss Ringlets	Handball	Keepsake
			*The Ill-Used
	Bessie		Belle of Nantura

THE WINNER'S PEDIGREE AND CAREER HIGHLIGHTS

YEAR	AGE	STS.	1ST	2ND	3RD	EARNINGS
1920	2	7	3	0	1	$17,972
1921	3	11	1	2	0	$40,800
TOTALS		**18**	**4**	**2**	**1**	**$58,772**

At 2 years	WON	Queen City Handicap
	3RD	Kentucky Jockey Club Stakes
At 3 years	WON	Kentucky Derby
	2ND	Blue Grass Stakes, Latonia Derby
	UNP	Ben Ali Handicap, Kentucky Handicap, Proctor Knott Handicap, Saratoga Handicap, Greenwich Handicap, Latonia Handicap, Latonia Championship Stakes, Twin City Handicap

RACE DAY STATISTICS

HORSE	EQ.	WT.	PP	ST.	1/4	1/2	3/4	STR.	FIN.	JOCKEY	OWNER	ODDS TO $1
Behave Yourself		126	1	9	$8^{1/2}$	8^1	$6^{1/2}$	$1^{1/2}$	1^{hd}	C. Thompson	E. R. Bradley	(a) 8.65
Black Servant		126	7	2	1^1	1^{hd}	$1^{1/2}$	$2^{1/2}$	2^6	L. Lyke	E. R. Bradley	(a) 8.65
Prudery		121	2	4	$5^{1-1/2}$	$4^{1-1/2}$	3^{hd}	3^{hd}	$3^{1/2}$	C. Kummer	H. P. Whitney	(b) 1.10
Tryster		126	10	8	6^{hd}	$5^{1-1/2}$	5^{hd}	4^1	4^4	F. Coltiletti	H. P. Whitney	(b) 1.10
Careful		121	3	7	4^{hd}	3^{hd}	4^{hd}	5^2	5^4	F. Keogh	W. J. Salmon	13.60
Coyne		126	5	3	7^2	6^{hd}	7^2	7^1	6^1	M. Garner	Harned Bros.	11.20
Leonardo II		126	4	5	$3^{1/2}$	2^3	$2^{1/2}$	$6^{1/2}$	$7^{1/2}$	A. Schuttinger	Xalapa Farm Stable	(c) 4.30
Uncle Velo	s	126	12	1	11^1	10^2	$9^{1-1/2}$	8^2	8^2	E. Pool	G. F. Baker	65.30
Bon Homme	b	126	11	6	10^1	11^6	11^2	10^1	9^6	C. Robinson	Xalapa Farm Stable	(c) 4.30
Planet	b	126	6	12	12	12	12	$11^{1-1/2}$	10^5	H. King	H. P. Headley	81.30
Star Voter		126	8	11	9^1	7^1	8^{hd}	9^2	11^1	L. Ensor	J. K. L. Ross	8.55
Muskallonge	b	126	9	10	2^1	9^1	10^1	12	12	G. Carroll	H. C. Fisher	96.25

Time: :$23^{1/5}$, :$46^{4/5}$, 1:$11^{3/5}$, 1:$38^{3/5}$, 2:$04^{1/5}$. Track fast. Went to post at 4:50. At post 6 minutes. Start good and slow. Won driving; second and third the same.
Coupled: (a) Behave Yourself and Black Servant; (b) Prudery and Tryster; (c) Leonardo II and Bon Homme.

Program #		Win	Place	Show
1	Behave Yourself	$19.30	$13.00	$5.60
8	Black Servant		$13.00	$5.60
3	Prudery			$3.30

Winner: Br. c. by Marathon–Miss Ringlets by Handball. Trained by H. J. Thompson; bred in Kentucky by E. R. Bradley.
$50,000 added. Net to winner $38,450 and $5,000 gold cup; second $10,000; third $5,000; fourth $2,000.

109 nominations.
Equipment: b—blinkers; s—spurs

*Foreign bred

A Nasty Surprise

BY 1921, THE KENTUCKY DERBY WAS AN ES-tablished national event. In the 1921 race, for example, the race attracted over 70,000 spectators, including most of President Warren G. Harding's cabinet, and there there was no fence to keep them back. This might have been a factor, as it turned out, in who the winner would be.

The legendary Colonel Edward Riley Bradley, breeder, gambler, and man among men, who was to win four Derbies over the next twenty years until Calumet Farm started to dominate the race in the early 1940s, had two entries (he always liked to enter more than one horse) in the Derby. One was Black Servant, who a lot of people had bet on—including himself—and the other was Behave Yourself. A week earlier, Black Servant beat Behave Yourself and three other Derby entrants in the Blue Grass Stakes.

When the webbing whirred up to release the animals, Black Servant bettors rejoiced as their horse rocketed to the turn from post position 7, cut to the rail, and forged ahead, Now all he had to do was hold off whoever challenged him.

Down the backstretch jockey Lucien Lyke held Black Servant's position as speed horses came at him in a rush, and then dropped back, exhausted. And riding in the middle of a pack of horses clustered on the rail, was Behave Yourself, Charles Thompson up.

In the stands, Bradley's heart started to soar, as well as the many people who had bet on Black Servant. It was all working out just the way Bradley had planned.

But Behave Yourself had started to pursue Black Servant, blasting past one tired horse after the other. When he reached the one-eighth pole, his nose had reached Black Servant's throat, gaining on him not by inches but by millimeters.

Then it happened: a spectator skimmed his hat near Black Servant's head, and for just a heartbeat the colt pricked up his ears and lost stride. Thompson grabbed the moment and drove by Black Servant, and then was ahead by a couple of inches.

Black Servant's jockey, Lucien Lyke, knew that Thompson wanted to win the race, but he wasn't supposed to. He screamed above the thundering hoofbeats, "Take back, you son of a bitch."

Not today. Behave Yourself hung on by a nostril.

Later, Bradley, who was reputed to carry a derringer in his coat, looked for Thompson, clearly blaming him, not the hat, for the loss.

Fortunately, he didn't find him.

Morvich
48th *May 13, 1922*

			Friar's Balsam
	Voter	*Mavourneen*
Runnymede		*Domino*
MORVICH	*Running Stream*	*Dancing Water*
Brown colt		*Puryear D.*
Hymir	*Dr. Leggo*	*Sevens*
		Solitaire II
	Georgia Girl	*Georgia VI*

THE WINNER'S PEDIGREE AND CAREER HIGHLIGHTS

YEAR	AGE	STS.	1ST	2ND	3RD	EARNINGS
1921	2	11	11	0	0	$115,234
1922	3	5	1	2	1	$ 57,675
TOTALS		**16**	**12**	**2**	**1**	**$172,909**

At 2 years	WON	Suffolk Selling Stakes, Greenfield Selling Stakes, United States Hotel Stakes, Saratoga Special, Hopeful Stakes, Eastern Shore Handicap, Pimlico Futurity
At 3 years	WON	Kentucky Derby
	2ND	Carlton Stakes
	3RD	Kentucky Special
	UNP	Fall Highweight Handicap

RACE DAY STATISTICS

HORSE	EQ.	WT.	PP	ST.	1/4	1/2	3/4	STR.	FIN.	JOCKEY	OWNER	ODDS TO $1
Morvich		126	4	2	$1^{1-1/2}$	$1^{1/2}$	$1^{1-1/2}$	$1^{1-1/2}$	$1^{1-1/2}$	A. Johnson	Ben Block	1.20
Bet Mosie		126	7	8	$8^{1/2}$	6^3	$5^{1/2}$	4^1	2^{hd}	H. Burke	Idle Hour Stock Farm	(a) 2.90
John Finn	s	126	1	4	5^1	5^1	6^2	2^{hd}	3^1	E. Pool	G. F. Baker	22.60
Deadlock		126	6	6	4^1	$4^{1/2}$	$4^{1-1/2}$	3^{hd}	4^4	J. Mooney	R. H. Shannon	6.90
My Play		126	3	1	2^{hd}	2^{hd}	3^1	5^2	5^4	C. Robinson	Lexington Stable	19.05
Letterman		126	9	9	$7^{1/2}$	$7^{1/2}$	7^1	7^1	6^1	T. Rice	Greentree Stable	24.80
Surf Rider	b	126	8	7	6^1	8^1	$8^{1-1/2}$	8^1	$7^{1/2}$	E. Scobie	Montfort Jones	35.75
Startle		121	2	3	3^2	3^1	2^{hd}	$6^{1/2}$	8^{nk}	D. Connelly	H. H. Hewitt	13.90
By Gosh		126	10	10	9	9	9	9	9	E. Barnes	Idle Hour Stock Farm	(a) 2.90
Busy American	b	126	5	5	Broke Down					N. Barrett	Idle Hour Stock Farm	(a) 2.90

Time: :23$^{4/5}$, :47$^{3/5}$, 1:13, 1:39$^{1/5}$, 2:04$^{3/5}$. Track fast. Went to post at 4:50. At post 3 minutes. Start good and slow. Won easily; second and third driving.
Coupled: (a) Bet Mosie, By Gosh, and Busy American.

Program #		Win	Place	Show
4	Morvich	$4.40	$4.30	$3.50
7	Bet Mosie		$2.90	$2.70
3	John Finn			$6.60

Winner: Br. c. by Runnymede–Hymir by Dr. Leggo. Trained by Fred Burlew; bred in California by A. B. Spreckels.
$50,000 added, also $5,000 Gold Cup and $2,000 other gold trophies. Net to winner $53,775; second $6,000; third $3,000; fourth $1,000.

92 nominations.
Equipment: b—blinkers, s—spurs

*Foreign bred

He Sold the Wrong Horse

SMALL WONDER THAT IN 1922 THE FAVORITE in the Derby was Morvich, a brown colt that the perceptive trainer Max Hirsch, in one of those "Why did we trade the Bambino?" moments had sold to breeder Ben Block. Morvich had eleven races after that—and won them all.

Ten horses broke from the post, and Morvich immediately charged to the lead, which he just as quickly increased to one and a half lengths. But his jockey, Albert Johnson, was not ready to consider the race as finished. He knew that one of the horses, My Play, was a full brother to the amazing Man o' War, and Busy American, the favorite after Morvich, was a very good horse. He would have to be careful.

But then, Busy American broke down on the clubhouse turn and stopped.

In the backstretch, Man o' War's brother started to come at Morvich, but didn't have the firepower to overtake him. But the race was not over, not by any means. A horse called Bet Mosie came at Morvich with a fury, finally losing by only a head.

A couple of bizarre events also occurred. At one point in the race someone screamed as Morvich rounded the far turn that he "was finished," and a kind of hysteria swept through the crowd, as a result of which a soldier fell from his seat into the governor's box. The crazed owner of Morvich, Benjamin Block, almost fell off a chair as the race heated up.

At the time, Derby entrants were carrying 126 pounds, a heavy weight, and this was suspected to be a factor in why Morvich never won another race. He left his ability on the Derby track.

Zev
49th *May 19, 1923*

		Ogden	Kilwarlin
	The Finn		*Oriole
			*Star Shoot
ZEV		Livonia	Woodray
Brown colt			St. Simon
	Miss Kearney	*Planudes	Lonely
			*Sandringham
		Courtplaster	Set Fast

The Winner's Pedigree

Race Day Statistics

HORSE	EQ.	WT.	PP	ST.	$1/4$	$1/2$	$3/4$	STR.	FIN.	JOCKEY	OWNER	ODDS TO $1
Zev	b	126	10	5	1^2	1^2	$1^{1/2}$	1^2	$1^{1\text{-}1/2}$	E. Sande	Rancocas Stable	19.20
Martingale		126	19	12	2^2	$2^{1/2}$	2^{hd}	2^1	2^1	C. Kummer	J. S. Cosden	(a) 19.75
Vigil	b	126	5	14	$10^{1/2}$	8^1	$6^{1/2}$	5^1	3^1	B. Marinelli	W. J. Salmon	15.25
*Nassau		126	8	4	3^1	3^{hd}	$3^{1\text{-}1/2}$	3^1	4no	M. Garner	Fred Johnson	3.25
Chittagong	b	126	1	2	9^2	7^1	4^1	6^1	$5^{1\text{-}1/2}$	J. Heupel	Mrs. John Hertz	(f) 5.85
Enchantment	b	126	11	11	6^{hd}	4^1	$5^{1/2}$	$4^{1/2}$	6^2	L. McAtee	H. P. Whitney	(b) 2.30
Rialto		126	17	15	$12^{1/2}$	10^1	8^{hd}	$7^{1/2}$	7^2	F. Coltiletti	Greentree Stable	(b) 2.30
Aspiration	b	126	9	7	7^1	$5^{1/2}$	7^{nk}	9^1	$8^{1\text{-}1/2}$	B. Kennedy	Ben Block	(c) 29.20
Prince K.		126	4	1	4^1	$9^{1/2}$	9^{hd}	$11^{1/2}$	$9^{1/2}$	W. Kelsay	Marshall Bros.	(f) 5.85
Bright Tomorrow	b	126	7	3	14^{hd}	11^2	10^{nk}	8^1	$10^{1/2}$	C. Ponce	Idle Hour Stock Farm	28.05
In Memoriam		126	21	10	11^{hd}	$12^{1/2}$	$11^{1/2}$	16^1	$11^{1/2}$	J. Mooney	C. Weidemann	(f) 5.85
Bo McMillan		126	20	8	5^1	6^3	12^1	15^{hd}	12^1	D. Connelly	T. J. Pendergast	11.95
Better Luck		126	6	18	8^1	15^1	14^{hd}	$17^{1/2}$	13^1	A. Johnson	Ben Block	(c) 29.20
Wida		126	12	9	15^1	$13^{1/2}$	13^{hd}	14^{hd}	14^8	A. Yerrat	T. E. Mueller	(f) 5.85
Picketer		126	18	16	13^1	14^2	15^1	$10^{1/2}$	15^2	J. Corcoran	H. P. Whitney	(b) 2.30
General Thatcher		126	16	17	16^1	16^2	17^1	13^1	16^2	C. Robinson	Nevada Stock Farm	12.80
Calcutta	b	126	14	13	18^1	17^1	$16^{1/2}$	$19^{1/2}$	17^1	G. Yeargin	G. R. Allen	(f) 5.85
The Clown		126	2	21	$17^{1/2}$	19^2	19^1	$18^{1/2}$	18^4	H. Lunsford	Audley Farm	(f) 5.85
Golden Rule		126	15	6	19^1	$18^{1/2}$	18^{hd}	$12^{1/2}$	19^{10}	C. Lang	J. S. Cosden	(a) 19.75
Cherry Pie		126	3	20	21	21	20^1	20^4	20^2	L. Penman	Greentree Stable	(b) 2.30
Pravus	b	126	13	19	20^1	$20^{1/2}$	21	21	21	J. Owens	F. Wieland	(f) 5.85

Time: :23$^{2/5}$, :47$^{2/5}$, 1:12$^{2/5}$, 1:39, 2:05$^{2/5}$. Track fast. Went to post at 4:47. At post 6 minutes. Start good and slow. Won easily; second and third driving.
Coupled: (a) Golden Rule and Martingale; (b) Enchantment, Rialto, Picketer, and Cherry Pie; (c) Better Luck and Aspiration; (f) Field.

Program #		Win	Place	Show
11	Zev	$40.40	$30.60	$18.40
22	Martingale		$25.80	$16.60
5	Vigil			$12.30

Winner: Br. c. by The Finn–Miss. Kearney, by *Planudes. Trained by D. J. Leary; bred in Kentucky by J. E. Madden.
$50,000 added. Net to winner $53,600 and $5,000 Gold Cup; second $6,000; third $3,000; fourth $1,000.

145 nominations.
Equipment: b—blinkers

*Foreign Bred

CAREER HIGHLIGHTS

YEAR	AGE	STS.	1ST	2ND	3RD	EARNINGS
1922	2	12	5	4	2	$ 24,665
1923	3	14	12	1	0	$272,008
1924	4	17	6	3	3	$ 16,966
TOTALS		**43**	**23**	**8**	**5**	**$313,639**

At 2 years	WON	Grand Union Hotel Stakes, Albany Handicap
	2ND	Belmont Futurity
	3RD	Hopeful Stakes
	UNP	Hudson Stakes
At 3 years	WON	Kentucky Derby, Paumonok Handicap, Rainbow Handicap, Withers Stakes, Belmont Stakes, Queens County Handicap, Lawrence Realization, International Special No. 3, Autumn Championship Stakes, Pimlico Fall Serial No. 3, Match Race with In Memoriam ($25,000)
	2ND	Latonia Championship Stakes
	UNP	Preakness Stakes
At 4 years	WON	Kings County Handicap, Pimlico Serial No. 1
	2ND	Paumonok Handicap, Arverne Handicap, Interborough Handicap
	3RD	Excelsior Handicap, Continental Handicap, Pimlico Fall Serial No. 2

He Bet His Life Savings

ONE NIGHT A BOY IN PARIS, KENTUCKY, HAD a dream, and in it a horse named Zev won the Kentucky Derby. The boy believed with all his heart and soul that the horse would win, so on Derby day he traveled to Churchill Downs and bet his life savings—$200—on Zev.

As twenty-one horses—the largest field in the Derby's history—lined up in front of the webbing, it is unclear whether the boy knew that Zev's owner and trainer had lost his faith in the colt. A week before, Zev had finished twelfth in the Preakness, which was run first then. Zev's jockey, the great Earl Sande, believed in Zev, however, and had convinced the owner and the trainer to run him in the Derby.

Zev would have had a better chance, Sande knew, if the horse was running on a muddy track. But he wasn't. The track was fast.

When the race started, Zev and Sande had a surprise in store for the herd of horses in the race. Sande immediately charged Zev out into the lead, and held him there. In fact, other horses tried to catch him, but could not, and Zev opened up a two-and-a-half-length lead. One can only imagine what the boy was going through.

Near the end of the race, a horse named Martingale came at Zev with a fury but could only slice a length off his lead, and Zev won.

So, of course, did the boy. The $200 he bet on Zev turned into $3,800, with which he promised to buy his family a home and take a trip to the far-off country . . . Cincinnati!

The "O ye of little faith" owners were richly rewarded by Zev's performance in the Derby and in later races. In 1923 he won twelve of fourteen races and piled up $272,008 in winnings.

Black Gold
50th *May 17, 1924*

		Commando
	Peter Pan	**Cinderella*
	Black Toney	*Ben Brush*
BLACK GOLD	*Belgravia*	**Bonnie Gal*
Black colt		*Faustus*
	Useeit	*Bonnie Joe*
		Bonnie Rose
		Bowling Green
	Effie M.	*Alma Glyn*

The Winner's Pedigree and Career Highlights

YEAR	AGE	STS.	1ST	2ND	3RD	EARNINGS
1923	2	18	9	5	2	$ 19,163
1924	3	13	9	0	2	$ 91,340
1927	6	3	0	0	0	$ 50
1928	7	1	0	0	0	-
TOTALS		**35**	**18**	**5**	**4**	**$111,553**

At 2 years	WON	Bashford Manor Stakes
	2ND	Cincinnati Trophy, Tobacco Stakes
	3RD	Breeders' Futurity
At 3 years	WON	Kentucky Derby, Louisiana Derby, Derby Trial, Ohio State Derby, Chicago Derby
	3RD	Latonia Derby, Raceland Derby

Race Day Statistics

HORSE	EQ.	WT.	PP	ST.	1/4	1/2	3/4	STR.	FIN.	JOCKEY	OWNER	ODDS TO $1
Black Gold		126	1	3	5^{hd}	6^{hd}	3$^{1/2}$	3^2	1$^{1/2}$	J. Mooney	Mrs. R. M. Hoots	1.75
Chilhowee		126	13	6	4^1	3^{hd}	4$^{1-1/2}$	1^{hd}	2no	A. Johnson	Gallaher Brothers	15.25
Beau Butler	b	126	10	8	15^{hd}	11^{nk}	10^1	10^{hd}	3^{hd}	L. Lyke	Idle Hour Stock Farm	(a) 10.25
Altawood		126	7	19	19	14^1	7^4	5^2	4^{hd}	L. McDermott	C. B. Head	19.10
Bracadale	b	126	12	4	1$^{1/2}$	1^3	1^2	2$^{1/2}$	5^8	E. Sande	Rancocas Stable	(b) 3.40
Transmute		126	2	1	6^1	4^{hd}	2^2	4^3	6^{hd}	L. McAtee	H. P. Whitney	(c) 10.25
Revenue Agent		126	5	9	10$^{1/2}$	8^1	8^{hd}	7^1	7^{hd}	D. Hurn	G. A. Cochran	26.75
Thorndale	b	126	6	11	7^1	7$^{1-1/2}$	5^3	6$^{1/2}$	8^2	B. Marinelli	Ben Block	(f) 10.70
Klondyke		126	3	13	8^{hd}	10^{hd}	9^1	9^4	9^4	I. Parke	H. P. Whitney	(c) 10.25
Mad Play	b	126	9	14	11^{hd}	9$^{1/2}$	6$^{1/2}$	8^{hd}	10$^{1/2}$	L. Fator	Rancocas Stable	(b) 3.40
King Gorin II		126	4	12	12^2	17^2	12^1	13^1	11^2	M. Garner	Peter Coyne	36.60
Cannon Shot	b	126	8	18	18$^{1-1/2}$	19	11$^{1/2}$	12^1	12$^{1-1/2}$	G. Ellis	C. A. Hartwell	(f) 10.70
Modest	s	126	16	15	13^1	18^2	14^{hd}	11$^{1/2}$	13^1	J. Wallace	E. B. McLean	(f) 10.70
Diogenes		126	15	10	16^{hd}	15^1	13^1	14^1	14^2	C. Ponce	Mrs. W. M. Jeffords	(f) 10.70
Nautical		126	19	7	9^{hd}	16^{hd}	15^1	15^{hd}	15$^{1/2}$	C. Lang	J. S. Cosden	(f) 10.70
Mr. Mutt		126	17	17	17^1	13$^{1/2}$	17^1	16^1	16^2	J. Merimee	H. C. Fisher	35.00
Baffling	b	126	18	2	2$^{1/2}$	2$^{1/2}$	16$^{1/2}$	17^{hd}	17^1	G. Carroll	Idle Hour Stock Farm	(a) 10.25
Wild Aster		126	11	5	3^1	5^1	18^1	18^2	18^4	F. Coltiletti	Greentree Stable	(f) 10.70
(Bob Tail		126	14	16	14^1	12$^{1/2}$	19	19	19	E. Blind	Idle Hour Stock Farm	(a) 10.25

Time: :23^{2}/5, :47^{3}/5, 1:13, 1:39^{1}/5, 2:05^{1}/5. Track fast. Went to post at 4:43. At post 2 minutes. Start good and slow. Won driving; second and third the same.
Coupled: (a) Beau Butler, Baffling and Bob Tail; (b) Bracadale and Mad Play; (c) Transmute and Klondyke.
(f) Field.

Program #		Win	Place	Show
1	Black Gold	$5.50	$ 5.40	$4.40
13	Chilhowee		$12.30	$7.30
				$4.70
10	Beau Butler			

Winner: Blk. c. by Black Toney–Useeit, by Bonnie Joe. Trained by Hanly Webb; bred in Kentucky by Mrs. R. M. Hoots.
$50,000 added and $5,000 Gold Cup. Net to winner $52,775; second $6,000; third $3,000; fourth $1,000.
152 nominations.

Equipment: b—blinkers; s—spurs

* Foreign bred

The People's Horse

NO QUESTION ABOUT IT: PEOPLE CAN LOVE animals as much—and truth be known, sometimes more—than people.

So it was with a brown filly named Useeit—named after a brand of bottled water—and her owner Al Hoots, a cattleman and horse racer from Oklahoma. Hoots raced Useeit all over the Midwest and in Mexico, and it was in Juarez that he entered her in a claiming race where he obviously did not know the rules, and where the horse was claimed by a man named Tube Ramsey. A variety of stories are used to detail what happened next, but Hoots slipped out of Mexico in the middle of the night, his beloved mare in tow. (Some stories say he greeted those who came to take her with a shotgun.)

Through it all, though, Hoots had a dream: he would breed the mare to a Kentucky stallion and produce a foal who was a champion, a horse that would win the Kentucky Derby. Hoots died before his dream could come true, but the dream didn't die. He passed it on to his wife, Rosa, whose mother was full-blooded Osage Indian and had been around horses her whole life. The "spirit will always be with the foal of this mare," Hoots said; "The foal will be possessed of the wings of the tornado and the fire which is known only to the plains horses, which have so often proven their willingness to give their last tiny bit of strength to their riders. And I see this foal possessed of the undaunted spirit of the mother descended from horses which admitted defeat only in death. . . ."

After Hoots died, Rosa was approached a number of times to sell Useeit, but she would not do it.

And then one day an oil gusher came in on land where she was living in Oklahoma, and she became rich and was able to make Al's dream a reality. She had the wherewithal to mate Useeit with Black Toney, a stallion owned by Colonel Bradley, and on February 17, 1921 a pure black foal was born and given the name Black Gold, the name people gave to oil.

When he was old enough, Black Gold was given to a hard-driving trainer named Hanley Webb. Under Webb's harsh training—running endlessly—Black Gold won nine of his eighteen starts as a two-year-old. With the colorful background of his human parentage, the wild Irishman and the Indian woman, striking oil, his own physical beauty, and the big dreams of an ordinary person like Al Hoots, Black Gold became the horse of the people, a champion who would defeat the likes of Harry Payne Whitney's and Colonel Bradley's horses, eastern establishment horses, and all the rest. When Rosa Hoots entered him in the Derby, public interest and love for him increased exponentially.

And there, finally, he was, the people's horse, their champion, and no one could defeat him. He would carry their dreams as well.

By the time the Derby—in 1924—was ready to be run, over 80,000 people were watching as nineteen horses lined up behind the mesh, Black Gold in post position 1.

Black Gold was behind most of the way, but in the end it was decided in the last incredible forty yards, with Black Gold catching a horse named Chilhowee and beating him by a nose. The dream that Al Hoots had many years ago had been fulfilled, and the dreams of many ordinary people.

Black Gold continued to race, but it wasn't easy. He developed a crack in his hoof and was fitted with a bar shoe, but performed poorly in a number of races. His regular jockey, J. D. Mooney, disgusted and dispirited, quit riding him, and importuned Webb to stop running him.

Reluctantly, Hanley Webb retired him to stud, but Black Gold was unsuccessful. Then Webb—who was an obese alcoholic—did something he never should have done. Three years after his Derby win, he got Black Gold

back into racing, running in small-time races, tired and not in good physical condition. And then it happened. On January 18, 1928, in the Salome Purse, a race that was worth a mere $1,200, Black Gold ran his final race. With one-sixteenth of a mile to go, he snapped his foreleg just above the ankle. Though the jockey tried to stop him, he couldn't—it was said that Black Gold didn't know how to stop; he would run until he died. Indeed, he literally finished the race on three legs, and was destroyed. And in doing so he fulfilled the final dream of Al Hoots, who had said many years earlier, "I see this foal, possessed of undaunted spirit of a mother descended from horses which admitted defeat only in death."

Flying Ebony
51st May 16, 1925

			Kilwarlin
		*Ogden	*Oriole
	The Finn		*Star Shoot
	FLYING EBONY	Livonia	Woodray
	Black colt		*Wintercress
		Princess Mary Hessian	*Colonial
			Royal Hampton
		Royal Gun	*Spring Gun

THE WINNER'S PEDIGREE AND CAREER HIGHLIGHTS

YEAR	AGE	STS.	1ST	2ND	3RD	EARNINGS
1924	2	8	4	1	1	$ 5,320
1925	3	5	2	0	1	$ 57,100
TOTALS		**13**	**6**	**1**	**2**	**$ 62,420**

At 2 years	3RD	Saratoga Sales Stakes
	UNP	Cincinnati Trophy, United States Hotel Stakes
At 3 years	WON	Kentucky Derby, Initial Handicap
	3RD	Shevlin Stakes
	UNP	Toboggan Handicap, Latonia Derby

RACE DAY STATISTICS

HORSE	EQ.	WT.	PP	ST.	1/4	3/4	MILE	STR.	FIN.	JOCKEY	OWNER	ODDS TO $1
Flying Ebony	b	126	6	4	$1^{1/2}$	$2^{1/2}$	2^3	1^{hd}	$1^{1-1/2}$	E. Sande	G. A. Cochran	(f) 3.15
Captain Hal		126	11	5	$2^{1-1/2}$	$1^{1-1/2}$	1^{hd}	$2^{1/2}$	2no	J. Heupel	A. A. Kaiser	5.60
Son of John		126	12	8	3^{hd}	3^2	3^2	3^2	3^4	C. Turner	D. W. Scott	(a) 16.40
Single Foot		126	3	1	5^1	$5^{1-1/2}$	$4^{1/2}$	$4^{1/2}$	4^1	A. Johnson	J. E. Griffith	30.15
Step Along	sb	126	9	7	$6^{1/2}$	6^{hd}	6^{hd}	5^1	5^2	E. Pool	F. M. Grabner	(a) 16.40
Swope	b	126	4	9	8^{hd}	7^2	7^1	6^1	6no	E. Legere	H. C. Fisher	(f) 3.15
Prince of Bourbon	b	126	14	15	9^2	$10^{1/2}$	8^1	7^1	$7^{1/2}$	A. Schuttinger	Lexington Stable	(b) 3.15
Needle Gun	b	126	2	3	4^{hd}	$4^{1/2}$	$9^{1/2}$	9^1	8^5	C. Ponce	W. Ziegler, Jr.	(f) 3.15
Kentucky Cardinal		126	13	10	10^1	11^1	10^1	8^{hd}	9^{hd}	M. Garner	G. F. Croissant	7.50
Boon Companion		126	19	16	11^1	14^2	11^1	10^1	10^{hd}	E. Ambrose	S. A. Cowan	(f) 3.15
Broadway Jones		126	8	11	$12^{1/2}$	13^1	12^1	12^{hd}	11^{nk}	H. Meyer	Idle Hour Stock Farm	50.85
Quatrain	b	126	17	13	14^1	12^1	14^2	13^1	$12^{1/2}$	B. Breuning	Fred Johnson	1.95
Almadel	b	126	20	17	19^1	9^1	13^1	14^2	13^4	L. McDermott	H. P. Headley	26.45
Backbone		126	18	18	18^1	19^1	16^2	15^2	14^2	L. McAtee	H. P. Whitney	(c) 16.20
Sweeping Away		126	10	19	13^2	18^1	15^1	17^1	$15^{1-1/2}$	C. Robinson	Xalapa Farm Stable	(b) 3.15
Elector	b	126	7	20	20	20	20	$19^{1-1/2}$	16^2	J. D. Mooney	La Brae Stable	(f) 3.15
The Bat	b	126	1	6	15^1	15^{hd}	17^1	16^1	$17^{1-1/2}$	I. Parke	H. P. Whitney	(c) 16.20
Lee O. Cotner	b	126	15	12	7^1	$8^{1/2}$	$5^{1/2}$	11^4	18^6	W. Fronk	R. W. Collins	(f) 3.15
Voltaic		126	16	14	$16^{1/2}$	16^1	18^1	18^2	19^{20}	F. Coltiletti	R. L. Gerry	160.75
Chief Uncas		126	5	2	17^1	17^1	19^1	20	20	W. McCleary	A. A. Busch	(f) 3.15

Time: :23²/₅, :47³/₅, 1:12³/₅, 1:39³/₅, 2:07³/₅. Track sloppy. Went to post at 4:32. At post 4 minutes. Start good and slow. Won easily; second and third driving.
Coupled: (a) Son of John and Step Along; (b) Sweeping Away and Prince of Bourbon; (c) The Bat and Backbone; (f) field.

Program #		Win	Place	Show
6f	Flying Ebony	$8.30	$3.80	$2.80
12	Captain Hal		$5.50	$4.40
14	Son of John			$5.50

Winner: Blk. c. by The Finn–Princess Mary, by Hessian. Trained by W. B. Duke; bred in Kentucky by J. E. Madden.
$50,000 added and $5,000 Gold Cup. Net to winner $52,950; second $6,000; third $3,000; fourth $1,000.
Scratched: Reminder, Chantey, Reputation, King Nadi, Elsass.

139 nominations.
Equipment: b—blinkers; s—spurs

*Foreign bred

The Wrong Horse

ONE OF THE THEMES THAT RUNS THROUGH Derby races is that a jockey will pick one horse to ride, or have it thrust upon him, or have it come out of the blue, and as a result will be riding the wrong horse—or the right one—and lose or win as a result.

There are numerous instances of this occurring, and in the 1925 Derby it happened to Earl Sande, the Eddie Arcaro or Bill Hartack of his day.

For the 1925 Derby, Sande—a very aggressive rider; indeed, he was suspended a number of times for roughriding—was a man imbued with a white-hot desire to win, and that year he was very clear on who he wanted to ride. He desperately wanted to ride Quatrain, who was the favorite. Indeed, more than a favorite. Experts figured he was a shoo-in.

The jockey on Quatrain, B. Breuning, would not yield, so as a last resort Sande offered him $2,000 to switch mounts. Breuning would have none of it. He knew what kind of horse he would be astride.

Finally, Sande was forced to take whatever mount was available, and that year all he could get was a horse named Flying Ebony, which was owned by a man named Gifford A. Cochran. Originally, Cochran didn't want Sande, because he was so dirty, to ride Ebony, though Sande had won the 1923 Derby on the horse's brother Zev, but he finally gave in.

Flying Ebony would have been considered quite a long shot, but just before the race started it was as if some otherworldly power had placed

a bet on the horse; the rain that had been threatening came down and quickly turned the track into the kind of surface pigs frolic in. As it happened, Flying Ebony was a "mudder"—he just loved a sloppy track—while Quatrain was not.

When the race started, Sande immediately took Flying Ebony to the front—just as he had Zev in the 1923 Derby—and Quatrain's jockey immediately took his horse to the rear, as it were, and the rest of the horses spent the next two minutes trying to catch Flying Ebony.

For the first time the Derby went out over the radio, and six million listeners worldwide listened as "Credo" Harris, the director of WHAS radio in Louisville, announced the race. Flying Ebony—a horse that Sande was to ride just by chance—had made him a three-time Derby winner.

Bubbling Over
52nd May 15, 1926

		Sunstar		Sundridge
	*North Star III			Doris
		Angelic		St. Angelo
BUBBLING OVER				Fota
Chestnut colt				Ben Brush
	Beaming	Sweep		Pink Domino
	Beauty			Hippodrome
		Bellisario		Biturica

THE WINNER'S PEDIGREE AND CAREER HIGHLIGHTS

YEAR	AGE	STS.	1ST	2ND	3RD	EARNINGS
1925	2	10	7	2	1	$ 24,737
1926	3	3	3	0	0	$ 53,815
TOTALS		**13**	**10**	**2**	**1**	**$ 78,552**

At 2 years	WON	Champagne Stakes, Nursery Handicap
	2ND	Breeders' Futurity, Pimlico Futurity
	3RD	Grab Bag Handicap
At 3 years	WON	Kentucky Derby, Blue Grass Stakes

RACE DAY STATISTICS

HORSE	EQ.	WT.	PP	ST.	1/4	3/4	MILE	STR.	FIN.	JOCKEY	OWNER	ODDS TO $1
Bubbling Over		126	11	1	1^1	1^1	1^1	1^2	1^5	A. Johnson	Idle Hour Stock Farm	(a) 1.90
Bagenbaggage	b	126	3	3	7^{hd}	6^2	5^5	2^1	2^3	E. Blind	Idle Hour Stock Farm	(a) 1.90
Rock Man		126	2	2	3^{hd}	3^3	2^{hd}	3^4	3no	F. Coltiletti	Sagamore Stable	42.10
Rhinock		126	12	8	8^{hd}	10^{hd}	9^1	5^5	4^4	M. Garner	Parkview Stable	14.60
Pompey		126	9	5	2$^{1/2}$	2^{hd}	3^{hd}	4$^{1/2}$	5^2	L. Fator	W. R. Coe	2.10
Espino	b	126	6	6	9^1	5^{hd}	7^2	7^4	6^6	W. Smith	Wm. Ziegler Jr.	39.70
Light Carbine	b	126	1	4	6^{hd}	11^1	10^{hd}	8^1	7^5	S. Griffin	I. B. Humphreys	61.00
Canter		126	8	11	4^{hd}	4^{hd}	4^{hd}	6^2	8^2	C. Turner	J. E. Griffith	24.10
Blondin	sb	126	4	9	10^1	7$^{1/2}$	11^1	9^1	9^{hd}	L. McAtee	H. P. Whitney	9.30
Display	b	126	10	13	12^5	12^8	8^2	11^1	10^{hd}	J. Maiben	W. J. Salmon	16.20
Recollection	b	126	7	12	13	13	13	12^1	11^{hd}	J. Callahan	Kohn & Theisen	(f) 11.40
Champ de Mars		126	5	7	5^{hd}	8^1	6$^{1/2}$	10$^{1/2}$	12^1	E. Pool	Keeneland Stud Farm	(f) 11.40
Roycrofter		126	13	10	11^1	9^1	12^4	13	13	E. Scobie	G. F. Croissant	(f) 11.40

Time: :23, :47, 1:12$^{1/5}$ 1:38$^{1/2}$, 2:03$^{4/5}$. Track fast. Went to post at 5:05. At post 4 minutes. Start good and slow. Won easily; second and third driving.
Coupled: (a) Bubbling Over and Bagenbaggage; (f) Field.

Program #		Win	Place	Show
14	Bubbling Over	$5.80	$5.80	$ 4.60
4	Bagenbaggage		$5.80	$ 4.60
3	Rock Man			$30.00

Winner: Ch. c. by *North Star III—Beaming Beauty, by Sweep. Trained by H. J. Thompson; bred in Kentucky by Idle Hour Stock Farm.
$50,000 added and $5,000 Gold Cup. Net to winner $50,075; second $6,000; third $3,000; fourth $1,000.

164 nominations.
Equipment: b—blinkers, s—spurs

*Foreign bred

He Would Have Bet Everything He Owned

COLONEL E. R. BRADLEY, WHO, AS MEN-
tioned before, dominated Thoroughbred racing
from 1920 until 1945 (he was supplanted when
a psychotic horse from Calumet Farm named
Whirlaway beat the entries from his Idle Hour
Stock Farm). He liked to have more than one
horse in a race, and he also loved to gamble.
Two weeks before the 1926 Derby, he got a call
from a fellow gambler in New York named
Leonard Replogle telling him that there was
talk in New York of betting on the Derby,
particularly the horse Pompey. Bradley was incensed that no one had any faith in his colt Bubbling Over or his other horse, Bagenbaggage, so
Bradley challenged anyone in New York that he
would take any bet of any size that would equal
all his worldly possessions—including Idle
Hour Stock Farm—that Bubbling Over would
beat Pompey. That bet would be hundreds of
thousands and likely millions of dollars.

Replogle carried Bradley's message back to
New York, but was only able to get $15,000 in
action. Exactly how much he bet is not known,
but his belief in Bubbling Over is dramatically
indicated by what he was willing to bet.

Bradley was not just a gambler. He knew and
bred Thoroughbreds, and during his tenure Idle
Hour Stock Farm was involved in twenty-five
Derbies between 1920 and 1945. He usually, as
mentioned, had multiple entries in the race, and
a couple of times his horses finished one, two.
He won five Derbies—1921, 1924, 1926, 1932,
and 1933. It was said that he knew more about

horses than many of the trainers he hired but
never got in their way.

At any rate, Bradley's belief in Bubbling
Over was based on his observations as a
horseman.

Bubbling Over was hardly a shoo-in. He was
not perfect physically, and he had poor eyesight,
which meant he could become disoriented in
a race. Nevertheless, the crowd mostly bet on
Bubbling Over, and Bradley did everything in
his power to make sure they were winners. A
few days before the race, he told his jockey Albert Johnson that he would give him $10,000 if
he won, but $5,000 if he just beat Pompey.

It was no contest. For the first sixteenth of a
mile the field was bunched, but then Bubbling
Over burst ahead, and he stayed there all the
way to the finish line. Pompey finished fifth.

Whiskery
53rd *May 14, 1927*

Brown colt

		Broomstick	Ben Brush
	Whisk Broom II		*Elf
	WHISKERY		Sir Dixon
		Audience	Sallie McClelland
			Commando
	Prudery	Peter Pan	*Cinderella
			Burgomaster
		Polly Flinders	Slippers

THE WINNER'S PEDIGREE AND CAREER HIGHLIGHTS

YEAR	AGE	STS.	1ST	2ND	3RD	EARNINGS
1926	2	18	6	3	2	$ 13,115
1927	3	18	6	4	3	$ 94,950
1928	4	1	0	0	1	$ 500
1929	5	16	0	5	1	$ 1,196
1930	6	15	2	3	1	$ 3,250
1931	7	2	0	1	0	$ 200
TOTALS		**70**	**14**	**16**	**8**	**$122,211**

At 2 years	WON	Ardsley Handicap
	2ND	Endurance Handicap
	3RD	Pimlico Futurity
	UNP	Colorado Stakes, Youthful Stakes, Juvenile Stakes
At 3 years	WON	Kentucky Derby, Twin City Handicap, Stanley Produce Stakes, Chesapeake Stakes, Huron Handicap
	2ND	Fairmount Derby, Maryland Handicap, Potomac Handicap
	3RD	Preakness Stakes, Prince Georges Handicap
	UNP	American Derby, Latonia Championship, Manhattan Handicap, G. D. Bryan Memorial, Toronto Autumn Cup
At 4 years	3RD	Whitney Stakes
At 5 years	UNP	Covington Handicap
At 6 years	UNP	Grainger Memorial Handicap, Francis S. Peabody Memorial Handicap, Covington Handicap

HORSE	EQ.	WT.	PP	ST.	1/2	3/4	MILE	STR.	FIN.	JOCKEY	OWNER	ODDS TO $1
Whiskery	b	126	7	6	5^{hd}	3^{hd}	$3^{1-1/2}$	3^2	1^{hd}	L. McAtee	H. P. Whitney	(a) 2.40
Osmand		126	10	4	2^1	2^3	$2^{1/2}$	1^{hd}	$2^{1-1/2}$	E. Sande	J. E. Widener	(b) 6.90
Jock		126	1	3	1^5	1^5	$1^{1/2}$	$2^{1/2}$	3^1	C. Lang	E. B. McLean	(c) 37.80
Hydromel	sb	126	5	8	6^{hd}	7^1	4^{nk}	$4^{1/2}$	4^{hd}	W. Garner	J. N. Camden	16.00
Bostonian		126	12	11	9^2	$8^{1/2}$	$7^{1/2}$	6^4	5^4	A. Abel	H. P. Whitney	(a) 2.40
Buddy Bauer	b	126	4	10	10^{nk}	$9^{1-1/2}$	5^3	$5^{1-1/2}$	6^2	G. Johnson	Idle Hour Stock Farm	(d) 15.40
Royal Julian		126	2	1	$7^{1-1/2}$	5^{hd}	$6^{1/2}$	7^{nk}	7^4	W. Lilley	W. H. Whitehouse	(f) 14.70
Fred Jr.	b	126	13	15	15	14^2	9^1	9^3	8^6	N. Burger	S. W. Grant	18.30
Scapa Flow	b	126	15	7	3^{hd}	$4^{1/2}$	8^2	$8^{1/2}$	9^2	F. Coltiletti	W. M. Jeffords	7.00
Black Panther	b	126	6	5	8^{hd}	10^1	10^1	10^1	10^8	L. Schaefer	W. J. Salmon	(f) 14.70
Kiev	b	126	8	14	11^{hd}	11^2	12^2	12^2	11^2	M. Garner	J. E. Widener	(b) 6.90
Rolled Stocking	b	126	3	2	$4^{1-1/2}$	6^{hd}	$11^{1/2}$	11^2	12^3	W. Pool	J. W. Parrish	4.70
Rip Rap	b	126	11	13	12^1	12^1	13^4	14^4	13^4	S. O'Donnell	Sage Stable	11.60
Bewithus	b	126	9	9	$13^{1/2}$	15	14^2	13^1	14^5	A. Johnson	Idle Hour Stock Farm	(d) 15.40
War Eagle	b	126	14	12	$14^{1-1/2}$	13^2	15	15	15	E. Ambrose	E. B. McLean	(c) 37.80

Time: :23$^{1/5}$, :47$^{1/5}$, 1:12$^{2/5}$, 1:38$^{4/5}$, 2:06. Track slow. Went to post at 5:09. At post 2 minutes. Start good and slow. Won driving; second and third the same.
Coupled: (a) Bostonian and Whiskery; (b) Kiev and Osmand; (c) Jock and War Eagle; (d) Buddy Bauer and Bewithus; (f) Field.

Program #		Win	Place	Show
9	Whiskery	$6.80	$3.80	$3.40
12	Osmand		$6.40	$5.80
1	Jock			$14.20

Winner: Br. c. by Whisk Broom II–Prudery, by Peter Pan. Trained by F. Hopkins; bred in Kentucky by H. P. Whitney.
$50,000 added and $5,000 Gold Cup. Net to winner $51,000; second $6,000; third $3,000; fourth $1,000.

162 nominations.
Equipment: b—blinkers; s—spurs

*Foreign bred

As If Aware of What Was Happening . . .

THE MORNING OF THE 1927 KENTUCKY Derby a groom saved Whiskery, a long-necked brown colt who would win the Derby, from not even being in the race. As the horse exited his stall, he almost got his leg caught between the door and the frame and could have easily damaged it. Ironically, as it turned out, Whiskery and his jockey L. McAtee had to endure some man-made damage to win.

Whiskery was owned by Harry Payne Whitney, the man whose praise of the 1915 Derby after his great filly Regret won had helped save the Derby. Whitney had been waiting a long, long time for another Derby victor—in fact, since 1915.

The track was muddy, in abysmal shape, as the race started, and a horse named Jock, with Chick Lang up, burst to the front, quickly assuming a lead of five lengths over Osmand. Osmand was piloted by Earl Sande, who was as dirty a rider as there was, and would prove it once again before the race ended.

Whiskery, wearing blinkers, and McAtee, wearing Whitney's pale blue and coffee-brown silks, both spattered with mud, gradually moved up to third. Then, in the stretch, McAtee started to drive Whiskery, but Sande got in stride with him, leg-locked McAtee, and grabbed his stirrup about seventy yards from the finish. It looked like McAtee was going to fall off. But McAtee managed to release himself and drive Whiskery to victory. In the jocks' room he said to Sande: "It's a good thing I won or I'd kill you sure as hell."

The Whitneys were euphoric, but nothing expressed the joy, the significance, of the victory better than what C. V., Whitney's son, saw in the stable area the night of the Derby triumph.

"I saw a bonfire," he said, "on top of the hill, and there were about five hundred blacks gathered around singing spirituals." He walked toward the hill and saw a horse silhouetted in the light. He asked one of the men, an old man, "What's going on?"

"Why Mister Sonny," the old man said, "that's Regret." He explained that the workers had taken her out of her stall—this was the horse whose run in 1915 had saved the Derby—and were singing to her as a way of showing their joy for Whiskery's victory. Whitney was entranced, and drew even closer. "I just stood there and watched as the music of the old spirituals filled the night air, and Regret stood like a statue, as if aware of what was happening."

Reigh Count
54th *May 19, 1928*

		Sundridge	Amphion
	*Sunreigh		Sierra
REIGH COUNT		*Sweet Briar II	St. Frusquin
Chestnut colt			Presentation
	*Contessina	Count Schomberg	Aughrim
			Cloavarn
		Pitti	St. Frusquin
			Florence

THE WINNER'S PEDIGREE

RACE DAY STATISTICS

HORSE	EQ.	WT.	PP	ST.	1/2	3/4	MILE	STR.	FIN.	JOCKEY	OWNER	ODDS TO $1
Reigh Count		126	4	3	5^{hd}	5^{hd}	2$^{1\text{-}1/2}$	1^{hd}	1^3	C. Lang	Mrs. John D. Hertz	(a) 2.06
Misstep		126	1	1	1^1	1^1	1$^{1\text{-}1/2}$	2^4	2^2	W. Garner	Le Mar Stock Farm	10.20
Toro		126	7	6	6^{hd}	6^{hd}	3$^{1/2}$	3$^{1/2}$	3^4	E. Ambrose	E. B. McLean	4.75
Jack Higgins		126	8	7	8^2	7^2	4^{hd}	4^6	4$^{1\text{-}1/2}$	C. Allen	W. J. Curran	(f) 4.42
Reigh Olga		126	5	4	7$^{1/2}$	8$^{1/2}$	7$^{1/2}$	5$^{1/2}$	5^2	E. Pool	Otto Lehmann	(a) 2.06
Lawley		126	9	15	16^1	16$^{1/2}$	9$^{1/2}$	6^5	6^2	H. Thurber	Viking Stable	(f) 4.42
Don Q.		126	2	20	20^1	20^1	22	7^1	7^2	P. Walls	Sagamore Stable	(f) 4.42
Bobashela		126	20	11	11^1	11^1	5^{hd}	11^1	8^2	H. Fisher	Audley Farm	(b) 12.08
Blackwood	b	126	10	2	2$^{1\text{-}1/2}$	2$^{1\text{-}1/2}$	8$^{1/2}$	8^1	9$^{1/2}$	F. Chiavetta	Bloomfield Stable	(f) 4.42
Martie Flynn	b	126	6	5	3^1	3$^{1\text{-}1/2}$	6^2	16^1	10^{hd}	W. Fronk	Syl Peabody	14.18
Sun Beau	b	126	18	16	18^1	18^1	14^1	10^1	11^{hd}	J. Craigmyle	W. S. Kilmer	38.42
Bar None	b	126	13	19	21^1	21^1	12^1	9^2	12$^{1/2}$	J. Kederis	Longridge Stable	(f) 4.42
Distraction	b	126	19	21	22	22	19^1	17$^{1/2}$	13^1	D. McAuliffe	Wheatley Stable	11.51
Petee-Wrack	b	126	15	17	14^1	14^1	10^1	18^1	14^3	A. Johnson	J. R. Macomber	(f) 4.42
Typhoon	b	126	17	22	19$^{1/2}$	19^2	18^1	12^2	15^1	E. Barnes	Kenton Farm Stable	41.21
Replevin	b	126	11	9	12^{hd}	12^{hd}	16^1	13^1	16^1	V. Peterson	Fred Johnson	(f) 4.42
Cartago	b	126	3	10	9^1	9^1	15^1	19^2	17^{hd}	K. Horvath	R. E. Leichleiter	(f) 4.42
Bonivan		126	21	8	4^{hd}	4^{hd}	20^4	15^2	18^2	C. Landolt	A. A. Kaiser	(f) 4.42
Charmarten	b	126	22	18	17$^{1/2}$	17^1	13$^{1/2}$	14$^{1/2}$	19^2	J. Butwell	Wild Rose Farm Stable	(f) 4.42
Vito		126	12	13	10$^{1/2}$	10$^{1/2}$	11^1	20^1	20^2	C. Kummer	A. H. Cosden	(c) 39.04
Sortie	b	126	14	12	15^1	15^1	17$^{1/2}$	21^8	21^{12}	F. Weiner	A. C. Schwartz	(c) 39.04
Strolling Player		126	16	14	13^{hd}	13^{hd}	21^{hd}	22	22	G. Fields	Salubria Stable	(b) 12.08

Time: :24$^{1/5}$, :49$^{3/5}$, 1:15$^{4/5}$, 1:43$^{2/5}$, 2:10$^{2/5}$. Track heavy. Went to post at 5:05. At post 6 minutes. Start good and slow. Won easily; second and third driving.
Coupled: (a) Reigh Count and Reigh Olga; (b) Bobashela and Strolling Player; (c) Vito and Sortie; (f) Field.

Program #		Win	Place	Show
4	Reigh Count	$6.12	$5.78	$3.98
1	Misstep		$8.28	$5.90
7	Toro			$3.76

Winner: Ch. c. by *Sunreigh–*Contessina, by Count Schomberg. Trained by B. S. Michell; bred in Virginia by Willis Sharpe Kilmer.
$50,000 added and $5,000 Gold Cup. Net to winner $55,375; second $6,000; third $3,000; fourth $1,000.

196 nominations.
Equipment: b—blinkers

*Foreign bred

CAREER HIGHLIGHTS

YEAR	AGE	STS.	1ST	2ND	3RD	EARNINGS
1927	2	14	4	3	0	$ 56,030
1928	3	8	7	0	0	$112,640
1929	4	5	1	1	0	$ 12,125
TOTALS		**27**	**12**	**4**	**0**	**$180,795**

+ includes winnings in England

At 2 years	WON	Walden Handicap, Kentucky Jockey Club Stakes
	2ND	Eastern Shore Handicap, Belmont Futurity
At 3 years	WON	Kentucky Derby, Miller Stakes, Huron Handicap, Saratoga Cup, Lawrence Realization, Jockey Club Gold Cup
At 4 years	WON	Coronation Cup
(in England)	2ND	Ascot Gold Cup
	UNP	Great Jubilee Handicap, Newbury Spring Cup Handicap, Lingfield Handicap

Killer Instinct

ONE DAY AN AUSTRIAN IMMIGRANT NAMED John D. Hertz, an ex-fighter and an astute man who founded the Yellow Cab Company and then Hertz Rent-a-Car, was watching a race, and he couldn't help but see one of the contenders, Reigh Count, bite another horse. To most people, that would be a negative quality. Not to Hertz. He thought it reflected a killer instinct, and wanted him.

Killer instinct or not, it was his seventh race before he broke his maiden. But once he got under Hertz's tutelage—or more particularly his wife's—and the watchful eye of trainer Barney Mitchell, he started to win. Indeed, at two years he won a number of important races, including the Walden Handicap and the Kentucky Jockey Club Stakes. But then Miller opted for an unusual plan to get Reigh Count ready for the Derby. Instead of having him run his way into condition in races, he merely worked him out.

But as Miller watched as Reigh Count, Chick Lang up, stood among the huge field about to charge down a track that was characterized as "heavy," he felt the horse was ready.

When the race started, jockey Chick Lang raced into the lead after the first half mile, then Lang really started to pound the track, forcing the pace as much as he could on the heavy track, and just kept leading, losing horses as he pounded up the backstretch. When he turned for home, Lang had him leading by a head. At the finish line he was three lengths ahead.

After he retired to stud, Reigh Count was a successful sire for the Hertzes, but none of his offspring was a Derby winner. Then, Hertz, ever the innovator, had an idea: Instead of breeding Reigh Count to famous, high-priced mares, he bred him to a tired old horse named, ironically, Quickly. The joining was successful, but when the foal was born, people were slightly horrified and hoped that looks did not equate with speed. The foal was downright ugly.

They didn't need to worry. The ugly little foal grew up to be Count Fleet, who in 1943 won the Triple Crown, and later, at stud, sired a foal who didn't do as well. His name was Count Turf, and he only succeeded in winning the Kentucky Derby in 1951.

Clyde Van Dusen
55th *May 18, 1929*

			Hastings
	Fair Play	*Fairy Gold
Man o' War		*Rock Sand
CLYDE VAN DUSEN	Mahubah	*Merry Token
Chestnut gelding		*Star Shoot
Uncle's Lassie	Uncle	The Niece
		*Planudes
	Planutess	Wanda

THE WINNER'S PEDIGREE AND CAREER HIGHLIGHTS

YEAR	AGE	STS.	1ST	2ND	3RD	EARNINGS
1928	2	17	8	3	2	$ 55,768
1929	3	10	3	3	2	$ 65,319
1930	4	5	1	0	1	$ 1,025
1933	7	10	0	1	3	$ 290
TOTALS		**42**	**12**	**7**	**8**	**$122,402**

At 2 years	WON	Kentucky Jockey Club Stakes, Orphanage Stakes, Valley Stakes, Idle Hour Stakes
	2ND	American National Futurity
	3RD	Breeders' Futurity
At 3 years	WON	Kentucky Derby
	2ND	Latonia Derby
	3RD	Classic Stakes, Grainger Memorial Handicap

HORSE	EQ.	WT.	PP	ST.	1/2	3/4	MILE	STR.	FIN.	JOCKEY	OWNER	ODDS TO $1
Clyde Van Dusen	b	126	20	7	$1^{1/2}$	1^3	1^2	1^3	1^2	L. McAtee	H. P. Gardner	3.00
Naishapur	b	126	4	2	$12^{1/2}$	12^2	8^3	$5^{1/2}$	2^3	C. Allen	Wilshire Stable	5.57
Panchio	b	126	13	1	4^2	3^3	2^{hd}	$2^{1/2}$	3no	F. Coltiletti	Three D's Stock Farm	(a, f) 8.44
Blue Larkspur		126	21	4	$3^{1/2}$	$4^{1/2}$	$5^{1/2}$	3^{hd}	$4^{1-1/2}$	M. Garner	E. R. Bradley	(b) 1.71
Windy City		126	19	9	$8^{1/2}$	8^1	7^3	$8^{1-1/2}$	5^{hd}	E. Pool	F. M. Grabner	22.84
Voltear	b	126	1	8	$5^{1/2}$	5^2	6^{hd}	7^{hd}	6^{hd}	S. O'Donnell	Dixiana	18.42
The Nut	b	126	18	3	17^1	10^1	4^{hd}	6^1	7^1	A. Robertson	Warm Stable	40.62
Folking	b	126	14	18	2^3	$2^{1-1/2}$	$3^{1-1/2}$	4^3	8^1	A. Pascuma	H. T. Archibald	(f) 8.44
Karl Eitel	b	126	10	16	7^1	$7^{1/2}$	9^{hd}	9^{hd}	9^4	R. Jones	J. J. Coughlin	28.80
Upset Lad		126	5	13	$10^{1/2}$	17^1	14^1	13^1	10^6	F. Chiavetta	Bell Isle Stable	(f) 8.44
Calf Roper	b	126	9	15	16^1	15^1	10^3	10^3	11^{hd}	L. Hardy	Three D's Stock Farm	(a, f) 8.44
Minotaur	b	126	7	14	10^1	9^2	11^2	$11^{1/2}$	12^{hd}	F. Halbert	J. R. Thompson	30.80
Bay Beauty	b	126	15	10	11^1	$11^{1-1/2}$	12^{hd}	17^1	13^4	K. Horvath	E. R. Bradley	(b) 1.71
Chicatie	b	126	3	12	14^1	14^{hd}	13^1	13^1	$14^{1/2}$	W. Garner	Fair Stable	87.09
Paul Bunyan	b	126	12	17	19^2	19^1	18^2	15^1	$15^{1/2}$	O. Clelland	L. M. Severson	(f) 8.44
Essare	b	126	6	5	$6^{1/2}$	6^1	15^{hd}	14^1	16^3	D. Connelly	Jacques Stable	(f) 8.44
Lord Braedalbane	b	126	8	11	13^1	13^1	16^1	16^2	17^2	W. Crump	Desha Breckinridge	(f) 8.44
Ben Machree	b	121	16	21	20^3	18^{hd}	17^1	18^1	18^1	A. Abel	C. C. & G. Y. Hieatt	(f) 8.44
Chip	b	126	11	20	21	20^3	19^3	19^3	19^6	J. Heupel	Mrs. E. L. Swikard	(f) 8.44
Prince Pat	b	126	17	19	18^{hd}	21	21	20^4	20^4	O. Laidley	Three D's Stock Farm	(a, f) 8.44
Paraphrase	b	126	2	6	$9^{1/2}$	16^{hd}	20^1	21	21	W. Fronk	H. P. Headley	(f) 8.44

Time: :24, :49, 1:15²/5, 1:42⁴/5, 2:10⁴/5. Track muddy. Went to post 4:58. At post 13 minutes. Start good and slow. Won easily; second and third driving.
Coupled: (a) Panchio, Calf Roper, and Prince Pat; (b) Blue Larkspur and Bay Beauty; (f) Field.

Program #		Win	Place	Show
25	Clyde Van Dusen	$8.00	$3.70	$3.06
5	Naishapur		$4.72	$3.26
16	Panchio			$3.50

Winner: Ch. g. by Man o' War–Uncle's Lassie, by Uncle. Trained by Clyde Van Dusen; bred in Kentucky by H. P. Gardner.
$50,000 added and $5,000 Gold Cup. Net to winner $53,950; second $6,000; third $3,000; fourth $1,000.

159 nominations.
Equipment: b—blinkers

*Foreign bred

"A Mud Runnin' Fool"

CLYDE VAN DUSEN, DESPITE BEING A SON OF Man o' War, was not supposed to win the 1929 Derby because he was up against Blue Larkspur, a horse that had won five of his first eight starts and had already beaten Van Dusen by a neck in a Derby prep race.

The horse—named after his trainer, "Keys" Van Dusen—was small, weighing around 900 pounds, but he did not lack speed, and he was very good at running on a sloppy track. The day before the Derby, the black workers at the stable Van Dusen was from prayed for rain, and when Derby day dawned, their prayers had been answered. It didn't dawn—the sky was gray and cloudy, and it rained, and rained, and rained some more. When it finally stopped, 1.19 inches had fallen, and the track was a shallow creek masquerading as a racetrack, in such poor condition that it was suggested that horses be shod with "mud caulks," a special shoe for better footing. Every horse was except for Blue Larkspur, this decreed by a substitute trainer! It mattered greatly.

There were twenty-one horses in the race, and the start was difficult—ultimately, it seems, to the benefit of L. McAtee, the jockey astride Clyde Van Dusen.

This would be the last time the horses would be lined up behind webbing, which had been used since 1903. It took thirteen minutes before starter Bill Hamilton let this herd of horses be released, and in the interim Van Dusen, who was out in the hinterlands in post position 20, gradually moved to a better position, films show, that was close to the middle of the pack, a far more advantageous spot.

His jockey saw Van Dusen for the first time on Derby day. What he saw, of course, was a small horse that he admitted later made him "a little scared," but he knew, when they went into the first turn, "that I had a good horse under me." Much later he would comment that Van Dusen not only could run, but was "a mud runnin' fool."

Meanwhile, Blue Larkspur was doing his version of slipping and sliding behind him. Clyde Van Dusen stayed ahead, swimming to victory, as it were, by five lengths over Blue Larkspur.

Later, writer Jim Bolus was to say in *Derby Magic,* "Meanwhile, back at Few Acres Farm, the farm help was jubilant. John Dishman, a groom at the farm, walked over to Clyde Van Dusen's mother, Uncle's Lassie, and said, 'Come here honey, you're famous now. Let me tell you what your little son did this afternoon.'"

And he did.

Gallant Fox
56th May 17, 1930

	*Teddy	Ajax
*Sir Gallahad III		Rondeau
GALLANT FOX	Plucky Liege	Spearmint
Bay colt		Concertina
	Celt	Command
Marguerite		Maid of Erin
		Radium
	*Fairy Ray	Seraph

The Winner's Pedigree and Career Highlights

YEAR	AGE	STS.	1ST	2ND	3RD	EARNINGS
1929	2	7	2	2	2	$ 19,890
1930	3	10	9	1	0	$308,275
TOTALS		**17**	**11**	**3**	**2**	**$328,165**

At 2 years	WON	Flash Stakes, Junior Champion Stakes
	2ND	United States Hotel Stakes
	3RD	Belmont Futurity
	UNP	Tremont Stakes
At 3 years	WON	Kentucky Derby, Wood Memorial Stakes, Preakness Stakes, Belmont Stakes, Dwyer Stakes, Classic Stakes, Saratoga Cup, Lawrence Realization, Jockey Club Gold Cup
	2ND	Travers Stakes

Race Day Statistics

HORSE	EQ.	WT.	PP	ST.	1/2	3/4	MILE	STR.	FIN.	JOCKEY	OWNER	ODDS TO $1
Gallant Fox	b	126	7	8	4^1	1^1	1^2	1^2	1^2	E. Sande	Belair Stud	1.19
Gallant Knight	b	126	8	7	7^1	$6^{1/2}$	3^3	$2^{1\text{-}1/2}$	2^2	H. Schutte	Audley Farm	22.73
Ned O.		126	3	3	$12^{1\text{-}1/2}$	13^{hd}	$9^{1\text{-}1/2}$	4^{hd}	3^1	J. Mooney	G. W. Foreman	25.79
Gone Away	b	126	10	14	$14^{1\text{-}1/2}$	$11^{1\text{-}1/2}$	$7^{1/2}$	5^2	4^4	M. Garner	Wm. Ziegler Jr.	52.92
Crack Brigade	s	126	6	13	6^1	4^{nk}	2^{hd}	3^{hd}	$5^{1/2}$	G. Ellis	T. M. Cassidy	16.62
Longus	b	126	1	15	15	14^4	10^{hd}	7^1	6^2	R. O'Brien	R. C. Stable	(f) 18.12
Uncle Luther		126	2	12	$8^{1\text{-}1/2}$	8^{hd}	$6^{1\text{-}1/2}$	6^1	7^2	R. Creese	L. Stivers	(f) 18.12
Tannery		126	12	2	3^1	3^1	5^{hd}	$8^{1\text{-}1/2}$	8^{hd}	W. Garner	E. F. Prichard	3.12
Broadway Limited	b	126	14	11	$10^{1/2}$	$12^{1\text{-}1/2}$	12^2	10^2	$9^{1\text{-}1/2}$	P. Walls	Three D's Stock Farm	(a) 50.43
Alcibiades		121	4	4	1^2	$2^{1/2}$	4^{hd}	9^{hd}	10^{hd}	L. Jones	H. P. Headley	(f) 18.12
Kilkerry		126	9	9	$11^{1\text{-}1/2}$	10^{hd}	$11^{1/2}$	11^4	11^6	T. May	Three D's Stock Farm	(a) 50.43
Breezing Thru	b	126	13	6	13^1	9^2	14^{hd}	13^1	12^5	J. Smith	E. R. Bradley	(b) 8.75
Buckeye Poet	b	126	15	5	2^{hd}	$5^{1\text{-}1/2}$	$8^{1/2}$	12^2	13^1	E. Legere	E. R. Bradley	(b) 8.75
High Foot		126	5	1	5^{hd}	7^1	$13^{1/2}$	14^8	14^8	C. Meyer	Valley Lake Stable	22.88
Dick O'Hara		126	11	10	9^2	15	15	15	15	N. Barrett	P. H. Joyce	(f) 18.12

Time: $:23^{3/5}$, $:47^{4/5}$, $1:14$, $1:40^{4/5}$, $2:07^{3/5}$. Track good. Went to post 5:00. At post $2^{1/2}$ minutes. Start good out of machine. Won easily; second and third driving.
Coupled: (a) Broadway Limited and Kilkerry; (b) Breezing Thru and Buckeye Poet; (f) Field.

Program #		Win	Place	Show
7	Gallant Fox	$4.38	$ 3.76	$ 3.42
8	Gallant Knight		$14.60	$ 8.78
3	Ned O.			$10.14

Winner: B. c. by *Sir Gallahad III–Marguerite, by Celt. Trained by James Fitzsimmons; bred in Kentucky by Belair Stud.
$50,000 added and $5,000 Gold Cup. Net to winner $50,725; second $6,000; third $3,000; fourth $1,000.

150 nominations.
Equipment: b—blinkers; s—spurs

*Foreign bred

Not Much of a Race

THE 1930 DERBY, RUN IN THE BOWELS OF the Depression, was the first time the race was announced over a PA system to the crowd. And it was the first time a stall machine, known appropriately as a Waite device, replaced the web barrier that had been used for years.

What this Derby was not notable for was the race. Many of the fifteen starters who lined up in the newfangled machine belonged in another race, say, the Palookaville Memorial.

For example, Dick O'Hara, who was last in the Derby, had achieved seven more last-place finishes in an additional seven starts. Another horse, Broadway Limited (apparently very limited), failed to earn anything in nine races. He was a son of Man o' War, who, author Jim Bolus said, "would have disowned him."

Still, the Derby was not a cakewalk, and it took all the skill of jockey Earl Sande, who would win three Derbies in all, to bring Gallant Fox home a winner. In those days riders played rough and dirty, and many of them would do just about anything to win.

One rider, Willie Garner, knew that Gallant Fox was the horse to beat—any way he could. When the race started, Garner was focused not on the faraway finish, but on Gallant Fox. As soon as the race started he guided his horse, Tannery, toward Gallant Fox, hoping to box him in and harass him.

But Sande was not just dirty. He was no fool. He immediately let Gallant Fox drop back, so Tannery couldn't box him in.

Then, as the race progressed—and the track

was in good shape, despite an all-day drizzle— he let the horse go. When they turned for home, Gallant Fox pulled into the clear and moved ahead. He was briefly challenged by a horse named Gallant Knight, but came home to win by two lengths.

Interestingly, it was normal for Gallant Fox to win by a small margin; he never had what trainers call the "killer instinct." He never won a race by more than four lengths, and won all his races by a total of nineteen and a half lengths. Some horses win single races by that amount, and more. But size, as it were, didn't matter, at least to supertrainer Sunny Jim Fitzsimmons. Indeed, Fitzsimmons, who trained some of the greatest horses of the twentieth century, said Gallant Fox was the best horse he ever had . . . and that accolade, coming from Fitzsimmons, is huge.

Twenty Grand
57th *May 16, 1931*

	Swynford	*John O' Gaunt*
		Canterbury Pilgrim
St. Germans		*Torpoint*
TWENTY GRAND	*Hamoaze*	*Maid of the Mist*
Bay colt		*Persimmon*
	Bonus	*All Gold*	*Dame d'Or*
		Hamburg
	Remembrance	*Forget*

THE WINNER'S PEDIGREE AND CAREER HIGHLIGHTS

YEAR	AGE	STS.	1ST	2ND	3RD	EARNINGS
1930	2	8	4	2	1	$ 41,380
1931	3	10	8	1	1	$218,545
1932	4	2	1	1	0	$ 915
1935	7	5	1	0	1	$ 950
TOTALS		**25**	**14**	**4**	**3**	**$261,790**

At 2 years	WON	Kentucky Jockey Club Stakes, Junior Champion Stakes
	2ND	Pimlico Futurity
	3RD	Walden Handicap
	UNP	Babylon Handicap
At 3 years	WON	Kentucky Derby, Wood Memorial Stakes, Belmont Stakes, Dwyer Stakes, Travers Stakes, Saratoga Cup, Lawrence Realization, Jockey Club Gold Cup
	2ND	Preakness Stakes
	3RD	Classic Stakes
At 7 years	UNP	Santa Anita Handicap, Queen Anne Stakes (England)

RACE DAY STATISTICS

HORSE	EQ.	WT.	PP	ST.	1/2	3/4	MILE	STR.	FIN.	JOCKEY	OWNER	ODDS TO $1
Twenty Grand		126	5	9	$10^{1\text{-}1/2}$	6^1	2^2	1^1	1^4	C. Kurtsinger	Greentree Stable	(a) .88
Sweep All	b	126	1	10	4^1	$3^{1\text{-}1/2}$	$1^{1/2}$	2^3	2^3	F. Coltiletti	Dixiana	26.96
Mate		126	10	11	7^{hd}	4^{hd}	3^{hd}	3^4	3^4	G. Ellis	A. C. Bostwick	2.83
Spanish Play		126	6	4	$8^{1\text{-}1/2}$	8^1	$6^{1\text{-}1/2}$	5^2	$4^{1\text{-}1/2}$	C. Allen	Knebelkamp & Morris	45.09
Boys Howdy		126	7	3	2^1	5^1	5^1	4^{hd}	5^6	G. Riley	H. C. Hatch	23.26
Insco	b	126	12	6	9^{hd}	11^1	8^3	6^3	6^1	S. O'Donnell	Griffin Watkins	(f) 22.91
Pittsburgher		126	9	7	11^3	10^1	$9^{1/2}$	8^{hd}	7^{hd}	C. Corbett	Shady Brook Farm Stable	8.49
The Mongol		126	3	1	5^{hd}	9^{hd}	11^1	$9^{1/2}$	8^1	J. McCoy	Hamburg Place	(f) 22.91
Ladder	b	126	4	2	$3^{1/2}$	$1^{1/2}$	4^3	7^1	9^{hd}	L. Schaefer	W. J. Salmon	26.00
Anchors Aweigh	b	126	2	12	12	12	$10^{1\text{-}1/2}$	10^6	10^2	E. Steffen	Greentree Stable	(a) .88
Surf Board		126	8	8	6^{hd}	7^1	$7^{1/2}$	$11^{1/2}$	11^8	E. Watters	Greentree Stable	(a) .88
Prince d' Amour	b	126	11	5	1^{hd}	$2^{1/2}$	12	12	12	E. James	Joseph Leiter	76.23

Time: :23$^{1/5}$, :47$^{2/5}$, 1:12, 1:37$^{2/5}$, 2:01$^{4/5}$ (new track record). Track fast. Went to post 5:02. At post 1$^1/2$ minutes. Start good out of machine. Won easily; second and third driving.
Coupled: (a) Twenty Grand, Anchors Aweigh, and Surf Board; (f) Field.

Program #		Win	Place	Show
8	Twenty Grand	$3.76	$ 3.00	$2.60
1	Sweep All		$15.58	$7.16
3	Mate			$3.62

Winner: B. c. by *St. Germans–Bonus, by *All Gold. Trained by James Rowe Jr.; bred in Kentucky by Greentree Stable.
$50,000 added and $5,000 Gold Cup. Net to winner $48,725; second $6,000; third $3,000; fourth $1,000.

130 nominations.
Equipment: b—blinkers

*Foreign bred

With Speed to Spare

THE WHITNEYS, HARRY PAYNE AND HIS wife, Helen Hay, dubbed "the First Lady of the Turf" by the press, had four winners in the Derby out of fifty-nine tries: Regret in 1915; Whiskery in 1927; Twenty Grand in 1931; and Shut Out in 1942. Their name—and their watermelon-colored silks with black stripes—became well known.

The 1931 winner, Twenty Grand, was lucky. A horse named Equipoise, who had had a thrilling, nose-to-nose duel with Twenty Grand in a race the year before, had withdrawn from the race because of an injury. Twenty Grand's jockey, Charley Kurtsinger, still had to contend with a dozen other horses, though.

The track was fast and the stands packed. People had come from far and wide to see the race, even by fledgling airplanes, including

private two-seaters and thirty-passenger Fokker transports for the daring, which had landed at Bowman Field. One would never know that 1931 was the midst of the Depression. This was a great race. Poverty was tomorrow!

Twenty Grand was the favorite, and supposed to be the best, but he didn't show that when the race started. He came out of the blocks slowly, and was still lengths off the pace by the half mile.

But then he started to close the gap between himself and the leaders, and by the three-quarter-mile marker he was only six lengths off. By the mile he was two lengths behind.

His main competition was Sweep All, but not for long. Twenty Grand wore him down and swept even farther ahead down the stretch. He hit the wire four lengths to the good and obviously with speed to spare.

Burgoo King
58th *May 7, 1932*

	North Star III	*Sunstar*
		Angelic
Bubbling Over		*Sweep*
BURGOO KING	*Beaming Beauty*	*Bellisario*
Chestnut colt		*Cupbearer*
Minawand	*Lonawand*	*St. Flora*
		Minting
	Mintless	*Gorseberry*

THE WINNER'S PEDIGREE AND CAREER HIGHLIGHTS

YEAR	AGE	STS.	1ST	2ND	3RD	EARNINGS
1931	2	12	4	0	1	$ 6,000
1932	3	4	2	1	0	$102,825
1934	5	5	2	1	2	$ 2,115
TOTALS		21	8	2	3	**$110,940**

At 2 years	3RD	Pimlico Futurity
	UNP	Spalding Lowe Jenkins Handicap, Sanford Stakes, Hopeful Stakes, Champagne Stakes, Futurity Stakes, Richard Johnson Stakes
At 3 years	WON	Kentucky Derby, Preakness Stakes
	UNP	Withers Stakes

RACE DAY STATISTICS

HORSE	EQ.	WT.	PP	ST.	1/2	3/4	MILE	STR.	FIN.	JOCKEY	OWNER	ODDS TO $1
Burgoo King		126	13	4	3^1	3^2	2^3	1^4	1^5	E. James	E. R. Bradley	(a) 5.62
Economic	b	126	10	2	1^2	$1^{1-1/2}$	1^{hd}	$2^{1-1/2}$	2^{hd}	F. Horn	J. H. Louchheim	16.92
Stepenfetchit	b	126	4	12	$9^{1/2}$	5^1	$4^{1-1/2}$	4^1	$3^{1/2}$	L. Ensor	Mrs. J. H. Whitney	(b) 3.23
Brandon Mint	b	126	11	3	$2^{1/2}$	2^{hd}	3^1	3^{hd}	4no	G. Ellis	Brandon Stable	(f) 6.68
Over Time	b	126	5	13	13^{hd}	8^2	6^3	5^{hd}	5no	E. Sande	Mrs. J. H. Whitney	(b) 3.23
Tick On	b	126	6	14	12^1	10^2	5^2	6^6	6^4	P. Walls	Loma Stable	1.84
Our Fancy	b	126	3	1	4^{hd}	$7^{1/2}$	8^2	7^{hd}	7^1	C. Allen	J. B. Respess	(f) 6.68
Gallant Sir	b	126	19	18	$11^{1/2}$	6^{hd}	7^3	8^2	8^2	G. Woolf	Northway Stable	(f) 6.68
Hoops	b	126	8	9	14^2	11^2	10^4	9^1	$9^{1/2}$	R. Fischer	W. F. Knebelkamp	28.62
Cold Check	b	126	12	5	$7^{1/2}$	4^{hd}	9^1	10^2	$10^{1-1/2}$	W. Garner	J. W. Parrish	45.88
Adobe Post	b	126	7	20	$16^{1/2}$	15^{hd}	16^{hd}	13^1	11^3	C. Landolt	Knebelkamp & Morris	28.52
Crystal Prince		126	1	8	20	14^1	12^{hd}	$12^{1/2}$	12^3	C. Corbett	P. C. Thompson	(f) 6.68
Oscillation		121	2	7	6^1	9^{hd}	11^1	11^{hd}	13^2	E. Neal	Longridge Stable	(f) 6.68
Prince Hotspur	b	126	17	16	18^1	16^1	17^2	16^2	$14^{1-1/2}$	A. Anderson	Joseph Leiter Estate	78.37
Cee Tee		126	14	11	15^1	18^2	15^{hd}	15^1	15^4	C. McCrossen	Dixiana	(f) 6.68
Cathop		126	20	19	19^1	$17^{1-1/2}$	18^8	17^2	$16^{1/2}$	L. Pichon	R. M. Eastman	(f) 6.68
Lucky Tom	b	126	16	17	8^{hd}	13^2	14^1	14^1	17^8	A. Pascuma	J. J. Robinson	10.64
Thistle Ace	b	126	9	10	$10^{1/2}$	19	19	19	18^8	G. Elston	G. Collins	(f) 6.68
Brother Joe		126	18	6	5^{hd}	12^{hd}	13^1	18^{hd}	19	L. Fator	E. R. Bradley	(a) 5.62
Liberty Limited	b	126	15	15	17^{hd}	Broke	Down			M. Garner	Three D's Stock Farm	(f) 6.68

Time: :24 1/5, :48 1/5, 1:13, 1:38 4/5, 2:05 1/5. Track fast. Went to post 5:04. At post 15 1/2 minutes. Start good out of machine. Won easily; second and third driving.
Coupled: (a) Burgoo King and Brother Joe; (b) Stepenfetchit and Over Time; (f) Field.

Program #		Win	Place	Show
13	Burgoo King	$13.24	$ 5.08	$4.00
10	Economic		$15.62	$8.54
4	Stepenfetchit			$3.52

Winner: Ch. c. by Bubbling Over–Minawand, by Lonawand. Trained by H. J. Thompson; bred in Kentucky by H. N. Davis and Idle Hour Stock Farm.
$50,000 added and $5,000 Gold Cup. Net to winner $52,350; second $6,000; third $3,000; fourth $1,000.

115 nominations.
Equipment: b—blinkers

*Foreign bred

Haunted

CERTAINLY HOLLYWOOD WOULD NEVER come calling to do a movie about the 1932 Kentucky Derby. But it might certainly show interest in a movie about what happened after the Derby.

For one thing, there was already a certain pall or negative energy in the air on Derby day.

Of course, 1932 was the middle of the Depression, and this was surely reflected at the Derby. People didn't have a lot of money—if any—to spend, and betting for the seven races on Derby day was $850,809, the lowest since 1919. The crowd was variously estimated to be between 35,000 and 50,000; 5,000 of these had disregarded mounted cops and other security and swarmed into the infield and grandstand without paying to get in. What's more, a number of leading horses were scratched before the race.

Burgoo (a Kentucky dish prepared for outdoor gatherings) King went off as a 5–1 underdog in a race that had not a single star among its twenty starters. Finally, it was uncomfortably hot.

Just getting the race going was difficult. Five or six horses acted up, and it took the starter, William Hamilton, more than fifteen minutes to get them away cleanly.

The race could hardly be described as exciting. Burgoo King stayed with the pacesetters, and at the top of the stretch caught Economic, a 16–1 shot who finished second behind Burgoo King.

The shocker about this Derby was that five of the jockeys riding horses in it died tragic deaths. The lineup:

Eugene James, who rode Burgoo King to victory in the Derby, drowned in Lake Michigan on June 11, 1933, though there was some specu-

lation that he had been killed by the Mafia. He was nineteen years old.

Laverne Fator, who rode Brother Joe and, some believed, was the greatest jockey who ever lived, plunged to his death from a hospital window, where he had been hospitalized for an infected appendix; blood poisoning had made him delirious.

Pete Walls, who rode a favored horse named Tick On and finished sixth, died of injuries incurred in a baseball game in Saratoga Springs, New York.

Labelle "Buddy" Ensor, who rode Stepenfetchit, died penniless in Queens General Hospital in 1947.

Earl Sande, who rode Over Time and would actually go on to win three Derbies, died in 1968 in an Oregon nursing home.

What were the odds of five jockeys dying like this? "It goes," said one man who had seen the race, "off the scale." Small wonder that some people characterized it as the "Depression Derby"—in more ways than one.

Brokers Tip
59th *May 6, 1933*

	Peter Pan	*Commando*
		*Cinderella
Black Toney	*Belgravia*	*Ben Brush*
BROKERS TIP		**Bonnie Gal*
Brown colt		*Prestige*
*Forteresse	*Sardanapale*	*Gemma*
		Ossian
	Guerriere	*Amazone III*

THE WINNER'S PEDIGREE AND CAREER HIGHLIGHTS

YEAR	AGE	STS.	1ST	2ND	3RD	EARNINGS
1932	2	4	0	1	1	$ 600
1933	3	5	1	1	0	$49,000
1936	6	5	0		0	$ 0
TOTALS		14	1	2	1	**$49,600**

At 2 years   3RD   Cincinnati Trophy
At 3 years   WON   Kentucky Derby
            UNP   Preakness Stakes, Maryland Handicap

RACE DAY STATISTICS

HORSE	EQ.	WT.	PP	ST.	1/2	3/4	MILE	STR.	FIN.	JOCKEY	OWNER	ODDS TO $1
Brokers Tip	b	126	11	11	11^1	$8^{1/2}$	4^2	$2^{1-1/2}$	1no	D. Meade	E. R. Bradley	8.93
Head Play		126	7	5	$3^{1/2}$	$1^{1/2}$	1^1	1^{hd}	2^4	H. Fisher	Mrs. S. B. Mason	5.64
Charley O.	b	126	1	6	7^{hd}	6^1	$2^{1-1/2}$	3^4	$3^{1-1/2}$	C. Corbett	R. M. Eastman Estate	6.02
Ladysman	b	126	4	7	$5^{1/2}$	7^3	$5^{1-1/2}$	$5^{1-1/2}$	4no	R. Workman	W. R. Coe	(a) 1.43
Pomponius		126	12	12	$10^{1/2}$	$9^{1-1/2}$	$6^{1/2}$	6^3	5^3	J. Bejshak	W. R. Coe	(a) 1.43
Spicson	b	126	9	13	13	12^3	$10^{1-1/2}$	7^1	$6^{1-1/2}$	R. Fischer	L. M. Severson	(f) 25.85
Kerry Patch	b	126	5	1	$6^{1-1/2}$	$5^{1/2}$	3^{hd}	4^{hd}	7^2	L. Schaefer	Lee Rosenberg	26.89
Mr. Khayyam		126	13	9	9^1	11^3	9^{hd}	9^2	$8^{1/2}$	P. Walls	Catawba Stable	(b) 4.09
Inlander	b	126	6	8	8^2	10^2	8^1	8^2	$9^{1-1/2}$	D. Bellizzi	Brookmeade Stable	44.27
Strideaway	b	126	8	4	$12^{1/2}$	13	12^3	10^3	10^5	A. Beck	Three D's Stock Farm Stable	(f) 25.85
Dark Winter	b	126	3	10	4^2	4^{hd}	7^2	11^8	11^{12}	R. Jones	W. S. Kilmer	(f) 25.85
Isaiah	b	126	10	2	$2^{1-1/2}$	$3^{1/2}$	11^2	12^8	12	C. McCrossen	J. W. Parrish	66.86
Good Advice	b	126	2	3	1^{hd}	2^{hd}	13	13	Pulled up	E. Legere	Catawba Stable	(b) 4.09

Time: :$23^{1/5}$, :$47^{1/5}$, 1:$12^{4/5}$, 1:$40^{2/5}$, 2:$06^{4/5}$. Track good. Went to post 5:10. At post 8 minutes. Start good out of machine. Won driving; second and third the same.
Coupled: (a) Ladysman and Pomponius; (b) Mr. Khayyam and Good Advice; (f) Field.

Program #		Win	Place	Show
16	Brokers Tip	$19.86	$6.28	$4.54
9	Head Play		$5.52	$4.08
2	Charley O.			$3.84

Winner: Br. c. by Black Toney–*Forteresse, by Sardanapale. Trained by H. J. Thompson; bred in Kentucky by Idle Hour Stock Farm.
$50,000 added and $5,000 Gold Cup. Net to winner $48,925; second $6,000; third $3,000; fourth $1,000.

118 nominations.
Equipment: b—blinkers

*Foreign bred

Fight to the Finish

THE 1933 KENTUCKY DERBY WAS distinguished—or undistinguished—by a highly visible physical fight between two jockeys as their mounts sprinted side by side to the wire.

The happening was perhaps foreshadowed by the suspension of one of the jockeys involved in the brawl, eighteen-year-old Don Meade, who would be wearing the green-and-white colors of Colonel Bradley on Brokers Tip, who had performed fairly well in racing leading up to the Derby, but who had yet to "break his maiden"—register a first-place finish. But happily for Meade the suspension applied only to run-of-the mill races, not a stakes race like the Kentucky Derby.

Riding Head Play—a name some might say would be more accurately applied to the jockey—was Canadian American Herb Fisher, but he was favored to win.

When the race started, various horses vied, as usual, for position, most particularly a sprinter named Isaiah. Down the backstretch, though, Head Play took the lead. Though Brokers Tip was gaining ground on him, it seemed that only a horse named Charley O. had a shot at the leader, but Brokers Tip passed him at the mile mark, and gradually moved up some more. As they turned onto the stretch, Meade was only a length behind Fisher and Head Play. Then Meade found some daylight near the rail and burst through, passing Charley O. and coming abreast of Head Play, and they drove for the finish, Siamese twins moving at around forty miles an hour.

What happened next was debatable, but for

the last three-sixteenths of a mile, the jockeys started to lash out at one another, with Fisher holding on to Head Play's right rein as he grabbed Brokers Tip's saddlecloth, and Meade lashing back at him with his right arm. After they crossed the line, Fisher hit Meade with his whip.

Brokers Tip, who had never won a race before or after, was judged the winner.

Who started it? There is no way to know, but neither jockey could deny that they both participated. A photographer lying near the finish (lying, it is said, because he was drunk on mint juleps) snapped a famous photo showing both men attacking each other.

The stewards suspended both jockeys for thirty days, but gave Fisher an extra five because when he got back to the jockey quarters, he assaulted Meade. The men didn't talk for years, but finally, fifty years after the fight, they posed together, both smiling.

Cavalcade
60th *May 5, 1934*

		John o' Gaunt
	Swynford	Canterbury Pilgrim
*Lancegaye		Spearmint
CAVALCADE	Flying Spear	Gallop-Along
Brown colt		Marcovil
*Hastily	Hurry On	Tout Suite
		Junior
	Henley	Helenora

THE WINNER'S PEDIGREE AND CAREER HIGHLIGHTS

YEAR	AGE	STS.	1ST	2ND	3RD	EARNINGS
1933	2	11	2	3	3	$ 15,730
1934	3	7	6	1	0	$111,235
1935	4	2	0	1	0	$ 200
1936	5	2	0	0	0	$ 0
TOTALS		**22**	**8**	**5**	**3**	**$127,165**

At 2 years	WON	Hyde Park Stakes
	2ND	Spalding Lowe Jenkins Handicap, Eastern Shore Handicap, Sanford Stakes
	3RD	Saratoga Sales Stakes, Walden Handicap
	UNP	Richard Johnson Stakes, United States Hotel Stakes
At 3 years	WON	Kentucky Derby, Chesapeake Stakes, American Derby, Detroit Derby, Classic Stakes
	2ND	Preakness Stakes
At 4 years	UNP	Suburban Handicap

RACE DAY STATISTICS

HORSE	EQ.	WT.	PP	ST.	1/2	3/4	MILE	STR.	FIN.	JOCKEY	OWNER	ODDS TO $1
Cavalcade		126	8	11	7^1	$5^{1/2}$	3^1	2^3	$1^{2-1/2}$	M. Garner	Brookmeade Stable	(a) 1.50
Discovery	b	126	6	4	3^2	$3^{1-1/2}$	1^2	1^{nk}	2^4	J. Bejshak	A. G. Vanderbilt	12.10
Agrarian		126	9	7	$10^{1-1/2}$	$8^{1/2}$	8^1	5^{hd}	3no	C. Kurtsinger	Mrs. F. J. Heller	14.90
Mata Hari	b	121	3	1	1^{hd}	1^{hd}	2^{hd}	3^4	4no	J. Gilbert	Dixiana	6.30
Peace Chance		126	2	12	$12^{1-1/2}$	10^{hd}	$9^{1-1/2}$	6^1	$5^{1-1/2}$	W. Wright	J. E. Widener	9.70
Spy Hill		126	11	10	9^1	$7^{1-1/2}$	7^{hd}	7^2	6^4	S. Coucci	Greentree Stable	33.30
Time Clock	b	126	1	13	13	11^6	11^8	12^{10}	7^{hd}	D. Bellizzi	Brookmeade Stable	(a) 1.50
Singing Wood		126	7	5	$4^{1/2}$	$4^{1/2}$	$4^{1/2}$	$4^{1/2}$	8^{hd}	R. Jones	Mrs. J. H. Whitney	24.10
Bazaar		121	12	9	6^1	$6^{1-1/2}$	$6^{1/2}$	8^2	9^6	D. Meade	E. R. Bradley	5.10
Speedmore		126	5	2	8^{hd}	$9^{1-1/2}$	$10^{1/2}$	$10^{1/2}$	$10^{1-1/2}$	F. Horn	J. H. Louchheim	(f) 10.40
Sgt. Byrne	b	126	10	6	2^3	2^2	$5^{1-1/2}$	9^4	11^3	S. Renick	J. Simonetti	(f) 10.40
Sir Thomas	b	126	4	8	$11^{1-1/2}$	13	12^4	11^2	12^{10}	A. Pascuma	A. B. Gordon	36.20
Quasimodo	b	126	13	3	5^1	$12^{1/2}$	13	13	13	J. Burke	Mrs. B. Franzheim	(f) 10.40

Time: :23, :47$^{1/5}$, 1:12$^{1/5}$, 1:37$^{2/5}$, 2:04. Track fast. Went to post 5:13. At post 8$^{1/2}$ minutes. Start good and slow. Won handily; second and third driving.
Coupled: (a) Cavalcade and Time Clock; (f) Field.

Program #		Win	Place	Show
11	Cavalcade	$5.00	$4.00	$3.20
7	Discovery		$9.20	$5.80
12	Agrarian			$5.00

Winner: Br. c. by *Lancegaye–*Hastily, by Hurry On. Trained by R. A. Smith; bred in New Jersey by F. W. Armstrong.
$30,000 added and $5,000 Gold Cup. Net to winner $28,175; second $5,000; third $2,500; fourth $1,000.

124 nominations.
Equipment: b—blinkers

*Foreign bred

This Time, They Won

THIRTEEN TIMES JOCKEY WILLIE GARNER had been astride a horse in the Kentucky Derby, but he had never won, coming closest with a second-place finish aboard a horse named Misstep in 1928.

Trainer R. A. Smith also had never had a big winner, though he could have, if it weren't for a wrong decision he made when he was a boy. He loved horses so much that in 1887 he bought one for $210 at Sheepshead Bay, Brooklyn. It was a runt of a colt, but when he was ridiculed for the horse's appearance, he sold it. It grew up to be Tenny, a great match race runner.

In the 1934 Derby, Mack Garner would be astride a colt named Cavalcade, a horse that was conceived in England but born in America, and bought for a measly $1,200 by Isabel Dodge Sloan, the so-called Mistress of Brook-

meade (stables), who had inherited $7 million from her father, John F. Dodge, automobile baron. Mrs. Sloan loved horses and first was involved with steeplechase races, and then those on the flat.

Thirteen horses went to the post, and when the race started, Mata Hari got the lead and held it for the first mile.

Cavalcade had gotten a slow start and was blocked in for the first half mile, but he started to move up on the backstretch at the half-mile mark. He picked his way between horses, and powered after Discovery, who he caught and went by fairly easily. Discovery made a final rush at him, but it was too little, too late.

Mrs. Sloan, a usually staid person, was said to have gone semi-berserk as she watched her colt pound to victory, but for sure she wasn't happier than Mack Garner or the horse's trainer, R. A. Smith.

Omaha
61st *May 4, 1935*

			*Teddy
		*Sir Gallahad III	Plucky Liege
	Gallant Fox		Celt
OMAHA		Marguerite	*Fairy Ray
Chestnut colt			Robert le Diable
Flambino	*Wrack		Samphire
		*Durbar II	
	*Flambette	*La Flambee	

The Winner's Pedigree and Career Highlights

YEAR	AGE	STS.	1ST	2ND	3RD	EARNINGS
1934	2	9	1	4	0	$ 3,850
1935	3	9	6	1	2	$142,255
1936	4	4	2	2	0	$ +8,600
TOTALS		**22**	**9**	**7**	**2**	**$154,705**

+Includes winnings in England.

At 2 years	2ND	Sanford Stakes, Champagne Stakes, Junior Champion Stakes
	UNP	Saratoga Special, United States Hotel Stakes, Hopeful Stakes, Futurity Stakes
At 3 years	WON	Kentucky Derby, Preakness Stakes, Belmont Stakes, Dwyer Stakes, Classic Stakes
	2ND	Withers Stakes
	3RD	Wood Memorial Stakes, Brooklyn Handicap
At 4 years	WON	Victor Wild Stakes, Queen's Plate
(in England)	2ND	Ascot Gold Cup, Princess of Wales Stakes

HORSE	EQ.	WT.	PP	ST.	1/2	3/4	MILE	STR.	FIN.	JOCKEY	OWNER	ODDS TO $1
Omaha	b	126	10	12	9$^{1/2}$	5^1	1^2	1$^{1-1/2}$	1$^{1-1/2}$	W. Saunders	Belair Stud	4.00
Roman Soldier	b	126	3	10	11^1	8$^{1-1/2}$	4^{hd}	2^2	2^4	L. Balaski	Sachsenmaier & Reuter	6.20
Whiskolo		126	8	15	12$^{1/2}$	10$^{1-1/2}$	2^1	3^2	3$^{1-1/2}$	W. Wright	Milky Way Farm	(f) 8.40
Nellie Flag		121	9	1	8$^{1-1/2}$	7$^{1/2}$	5^3	4^3	4^{hd}	E. Arcaro	Calumet Farm	3.80
Blackbirder	b	126	13	14	14^1	11^1	11^2	5^1	5^2	W. Garner	Mrs. C. Hainsworth	(f) 8.40
Psychic Bid	b	126	7	11	4^{hd}	4^1	7^1	6^3	6^4	R. Jones	Brookmeade Stable	49.20
Morpluck	sb	126	11	16	16^1	13^2	12^2	7^{hd}	7^{hd}	M. Garner	J. H. Louchheim	(f) 8.40
Plat Eye		126	15	4	1$^{1/2}$	1$^{1/2}$	3^1	8^1	8^1	S. Coucci	Greentree Stable	16.40
McCarthy	b	126	4	18	18	15^1	14^4	14^1	9^3	R. Finnerty	Morrison & Keating	(f) 8.40
Commonwealth	b	126	17	17	17^4	12^1	9^{hd}	10^2	10^2	G. Woolf	Mrs. W. M. Jeffords	9.50
Sun Fairplay	b	126	5	3	10^1	9$^{1-1/2}$	13^3	11^1	11^3	J. Renick	Fair Fields Stable	52.30
Today	b	126	16	6	6^1	6$^{1/2}$	8^1	9^2	12^6	R. Workman	C. V. Whitney	8.40
Whopper	sb	126	2	9	5$^{1/2}$	3$^{1/2}$	6$^{1/2}$	12^1	13$^{1-1/2}$	C. Landolt	H. P. Headley	(f) 8.40
Bluebeard	b	126	6	2	7^1	14$^{1-1/2}$	15^1	15^1	14$^{1-1/2}$	H. Schutte	Mrs. R. B. Fairbanks	(f) 8.40
Tutticurio	b	126	18	13	13^{hd}	16^4	16^3	16^4	15^1	C. Corbett	Brandon Stable	(f) 8.40
Boxthorn	b	126	12	8	3$^{1-1/2}$	2^1	10^{hd}	13^1	16^2	D. Meade	E. R. Bradley	5.00
St. Bernard		126	1	5	2^{hd}	18	18	18	17$^{1/2}$	P. Keester	E. G. Shaffer	(f) 8.40
Weston	b	126	14	7	15^{hd}	17^1	17^1	17^1	18	S. Young	Braedalbane Stable	(f) 8.40

Time: :23, :47^3/5, 1:13^2/5, 1:38^3/5, 2:05. Track good. Went to post at 5:13. At post 2^1/2 minutes. Start good and slow. Won easily; second and third driving. (f) Field.

Program #		Win	Place	Show
11	Omaha	$10.00	$5.00	$3.80
3	Roman Soldier		$6.40	$4.20
9f	Whiskolo			$3.40

Winner: Ch. c. by Gallant Fox–Flambino, by Wrack. Trained by J. Fitzsimmons; bred in Kentucky by Belair Stud. $40,000 added and $5,000 Gold Cup. Net to winner $39,525; second $6,000; third $3,000; fourth $1,000.

110 nominations.
Equipment: b—blinkers; s—spurs

*Foreign bred

I've Got a Secret

OMAHA, ONE OF THE FAVORITES IN THE
1935 run for the roses, had a secret, and his
owner, William Woodward, his jockey, Willie
"Smokey" Saunders, and his exercise rider were
terrified that others would find out. If they did,
it could result in the big horse being lured into a
trap that would eliminate him from the race.

Saunders had discovered the problem during
a workout.

"They used to work two horses with him,"
Saunders said; "they'd work a horse the first
half mile, and then they'd bring another horse
in with him, and they broke this horse off the
outside fence to hook in with him and didn't get
him straightened out fast enough and brushed
Omaha when he come in."

And what does Omaha do? He stops and
fights the other horse. And he could do that
again, so all someone would have to do was
bring another horse in there to bump Omaha
and get him fighting—not running. "Naturally," Saunders said, "I was very cautious.
That's why I always had to take him around
horses, rather than take a chance on a horse
hitting him."

The owner, jockey, and exercise boy—
anyone who knew—worried about such an
encounter right up to the Derby. But then it was
upon them, and to heighten their worry, the
weather had turned drizzly.

Despite the weather, over 53,000 people
showed up for the Derby—and so did the
National Guard and heavy wire barriers. As
it happened, each year hordes of young men
would break through from the cheap seats to
the expensive seats, and the Louisville police

department found itself unable to cope. But
when the crowd saw the guards lined up at key
points and armed with heavy sticks and baseball bats, they backed off.

Omaha was a big (sixteen hands plus) horse
with impeccable lineage: his father was Gallant
Fox, the 1930 Derby winner, who always won
by very small margins but nevertheless had won
the Triple Crown.

Slightly favored in the race was a filly from
the emerging Calumet Farm, but as he waited
for the bell to sound, Smokey Saunders worried
and wondered about one horse—Omaha. What
would he do if brushed? But nothing happened.
There were eighteen horses in the field, and the
expected crowding in the beginning, but Saunders was able to avoid any collisions and sailed
smoothly.

Omaha went on to win both the Preakness
and Belmont Stakes, just as his sire, Gallant
Fox, did in 1930. No other horses within the
same family have duplicated that feat.

Bold Venture
62nd May 2, 1936

	Swynford	John o' Gaunt
		Canterbury Pilgrim
*St. Germans		Torpoint
BOLD VENTURE	Hamoaze	Maid of the Mist
Chestnut colt		Commando
Possible	Ultimus	*Running Stream
		*Royal Flush III
	Lida Flush	Lida H.

The Winner's Pedigree and Career Highlights

YEAR	AGE	STS.	1ST	2ND	3RD	EARNINGS
1935	2	8	3	2	0	$ 2,500
1936	3	3	3	0	0	$ 65,800
TOTALS		11	6	2	0	$ 68,300

At 2 years   UNP   Arlington Futurity, Hopeful Stakes
At 3 years   WON   Kentucky Derby, Preakness Stakes

Race Day Statistics

HORSE	EQ.	WT.	PP	ST.	1/2	3/4	MILE	STR.	FIN.	JOCKEY	OWNER	ODDS TO $1
Bold Venture		126	5	13	8[1-1/2]	1[1]	1[1-1/2]	1[1]	1[hd]	I. Hanford	M. L. Schwartz	20.50
Brevity	b	126	10	10	9[1-1/2]	6[1-1/2]	3[1]	2[2]	2[6]	W. Wright	J. E. Widener	.80
Indian Broom	b	126	2	7	6[hd]	3[2]	2[1-1/2]	3[5]	3[3]	G. Burns	A. C. T. Stock Farm Stable	5.10
Coldstream		126	13	6	2[hd]	4[1]	5[3]	5[3]	4[5]	N. Wall	Coldstream Stud Stable	15.20
Bien Joli	b	126	6	2	4[hd]	7[1]	6[3]	6[2]	5[hd]	L. Balaski	E. R. Bradley	14.90
Holl Image	b	126	14	12	12[1]	11[1]	11[1-1/2]	7[3]	6[4]	H. Fisher	Superior Stable	(f) 43.40
He Did	sb	126	3	1	1[2]	2[1/2]	4[4]	4[hd]	7[hd]	C. Kurtsinger	Mrs. S. B. Mason	33.80
Teufel	b	126	8	9	11[1/2]	10[1]	8[hd]	8[1]	8[hd]	E. Litzenberger	Wheatley Stable	(a) 10.60
Gold Seeker	b	121	12	14	13	12[2]	10[1/2]	10[4]	9[4]	M. Peters	Foxcatcher Farms Stable	(f) 43.40
Merry Pete	b	126	1	8	7[1-1/2]	8[3]	7[1]	9[hd]	10[6]	T. Malley	Belair Stud Stable	(a) 10.60
The Fighter		126	7	3	5[hd]	9[hd]	12[6]	11[4]	11[5]	A. Robertson	Milky Way Farm	(b) 16.50
Grand Slam	b	126	9	5	3[2]	5[hd]	9[2]	12[8]	12[10]	R. Workman	Bomar Stable	19.10
Sangreal	b	126	11	11	10[2]	13	13	13	13	M. Garner	Milky Way Farm	(b) 16.50
Granville	b	126	4	4	Lost rider					J. Stout	Belair Stud Stable	(a) 10.60

Time: :23³/₅, :47⁴/₅, 1:12³/₅, 1:37⁴/₅, 2:03³/₅. Track fast. Went to post at 4:41. At post 4½ minutes. Start good and slow. Won driving; second and third the same.
Coupled: (a) Teufel, Merry Pete, and Granville; (b) The Fighter and Sangreal; (f) Field.

Program #		Win	Place	Show
6	Bold Venture	$43.00	$11.80	$6.60
12	Brevity		$ 5.00	$4.00
3	Indian Broom			$3.80

Winner: Ch. c. by *St. Germans–Possible, by Ultimus. Trained by Max Hirsch; bred in Kentucky by M. L. Schwartz.
$40,000 added and $5,000 Gold Cup. Net to winner $37,725; second $6,000; third $3,000; fourth $1,000.

102 nominations.
Equipment: b—blinkers; s—spurs

*Foreign bred

A Race You Don't Forget

FOR SURE, A DERBY WIN LINGERS IN MEMory for a long, long time. This was quite evident when a few years ago an ex-jockey and trainer named Ira "Babe" Hanford, eighty-seven, recalled the 1936 Derby and his run on Bold Venture sixty-nine years after it had been run. And it was a heck of a race from start to finish.

"It was a pretty rough start. In those days there weren't any doors at the front of the starting gates, and there wasn't a handler for every horse either. So the start of a race could be sort of wild, and that's how it was for the Derby.

"The horse to the right of me, Bien Joli, bore into me, we bumped Granville, who went to his knees and he lost his rider. Then everybody was just trying to straighten their horses up and go on running."

Fourteen horses had broken from the doorless starting gate, and Hanford soon found himself locked in behind a line of seven to eight posteriors. But Hanford was not rattled because Bold Venture was running "real easy," unaffected by the rough-and-tumble start. At one point in the backstretch he guided the colt to the outside, and as they turned into the stretch, he was in the lead.

But the race wasn't over. The favorite in the race, Brevity, ridden by Wayne Wright, lit out after Bold Venture and cut into his lead with every stride. The race would be decided in the final quarter mile.

"We're both riding our horses pretty hard, both of us going to the whip, then right at the wire my horse dug down one more time and we won by a head. That's when it hit me that I'd just won the Kentucky Derby."

Looking back, Hanford also remembers Mary Hirsch—the daughter of famous trainer Max Hirsch, and the first female horse trainer in the country to get a license—for her kindness, how when he was only eighteen she gave him a shot to ride a horse in competition at Hialeah Park in the winter of 1935.

Hanford had not a hint from that race that he would ever be a Thoroughbred race jockey. When he got off the horse, he was "weak kneed." But eventually, as they say, he got the hang of it—and roses hanging off Bold Venture's neck.

War Admiral
63rd *May 8, 1937*

			Hastings
	Fair Play		*Fairy Gold
Man o' War			*Rock Sand
WAR ADMIRAL	Mahubah		*Merry Token
Brown colt			Ben Brush
Brushup	Sweep		Pink Domino
			Harry of Hereford
	Annette K.		*Bathing Girl

The Winner's Pedigree and Career Highlights

YEAR	AGE	STS.	1ST	2ND	3RD	EARNINGS
1936	2	6	3	2	1	$ 14,800
1937	3	8	8	0	0	$ 166,500
1938	4	11	9	1	0	$ 90,840
1939	5	1	1	0	0	$ 1,100
TOTALS		**26**	**21**	**3**	**1**	**$ 273,240**

At 2 years   WON   Eastern Shore Handicap
             2ND   Great American Stakes, Richard Johnson Stakes
             3RD   National Stallion Stakes
At 3 years   WON   Kentucky Derby, Preakness, Belmont Stakes,
                              Chesapeake Stakes, Pimlico Special, Washington
                              Handicap
At 4 years   WON   Widener Handicap, Whitney Stakes, Jockey Club Gold
                              Cup, Saratoga Cup, Wilson Stakes, Queens County
                              Handicap, Rhode Island Handicap, Saratoga Handicap
             2ND   Pimlico Special
             UNP   Massachusetts Handicap

HORSE	EQ.	WT.	PP	ST.	1/2	3/4	MILE	STR.	FIN.	JOCKEY	OWNER	ODDS TO $1
War Admiral		126	1	2	$1^{1\text{-}1/2}$	1^1	$1^{1\text{-}1/2}$	1^3	$1^{1\text{-}3/4}$	C. Kurtsinger	Glen Riddle Farms	1.60
Pompoon		126	14	6	5^2	4^1	2^2	2^5	2^8	H. Richards	J. H. Louchheim	8.00
Reaping Reward	b	126	17	7	$8^{1/2}$	$6^{1/2}$	8^3	5^3	3^3	A. Robertson	Milky Way Farm	(a) 4.60
Melodist		126	3	10	6^{hd}	5^1	5^{hd}	4^{hd}	4^1	J. Longden	Wheatley Stable	15.10
Sceneshifter	b	126	12	13	$10^{1/2}$	$12^{1/2}$	11^{hd}	$7^{1\text{-}1/2}$	5^2	J. Stout	Maxwell Howard	(b) 11.20
Heelfly		126	10	1	$3^{1\text{-}1/2}$	$2^{1/2}$	3^3	$3^{1/2}$	6^{hd}	W. Wright	Three D's Stock Farm	16.20
Dellor	b	126	2	4	$7^{1\text{-}1/2}$	$9^{1/2}$	$6^{1/2}$	$6^{1/2}$	$7^{1/2}$	B. James	J. W. Parrish	13.70
Burning Star	b	126	15	15	14^1	13^1	13^1	10^1	8^{hd}	C. Parke	Shandon Farm	(f) 9.30
Court Scandal	b	126	6	11	$12^{1/2}$	8^{hd}	9^3	12^1	9^1	E. Steffen	T. B. Martin	(f) 9.30
Clodion	b	126	13	14	13^2	$14^{1/2}$	12^2	9^{hd}	10^1	I. Anderson	W. A. Carter	(f) 9.30
Fairy Hill	b	126	4	3	$2^{1\text{-}1/2}$	3^3	$4^{1/2}$	$8^{1\text{-}1/2}$	$11^{1\text{-}1/2}$	M. Peters	Foxcatcher Farms	44.60
Merry Maker	b	126	7	19	17^2	11^1	$10^{1/2}$	$11^{1/2}$	$12^{1/2}$	H. Dabson	Miss E. G. Rand	(f) 9.30
No Sir	b	126	19	17	16^{hd}	17^1	$17^{1/2}$	$13^{1\text{-}1/2}$	13^{hd}	H. Le Blanc	Miss M. Hirsch	(f) 9.30
Grey Gold	b	126	11	18	19^2	$19^{1\text{-}1/2}$	19^1	$14^{1/2}$	14^1	J. Rosen	E. W. Duffy	(f) 9.30
Military	sb	126	5	9	$15^{1\text{-}1/2}$	15^1	15^1	15^1	$15^{1/2}$	C. Corbett	Milky Way Farm	(a) 4.60
Sunset Trail II	b	126	18	20	20	20	20	$16^{1\text{-}1/2}$	16^2	R. Dotter	Raoul Walsh	(f) 9.30
Fencing	sb	126	8	12	$9^{1/2}$	$10^{1/2}$	16^{hd}	17^2	17^5	J. Westrope	Maxwell Howard	(b) 11.20
Bernard F.		126	16	16	18^5	18^3	$19^{1/2}$	18^3	18^1	L. Hardy	I. J. Collins	(f) 9.30
Sir Damion	b	126	20	8	$11^{1\text{-}1/2}$	16^{hd}	14^3	19^4	19^{12}	E. Yager	Marshall Field	(f) 9.30
Billionaire	b	126	9	5	4^{hd}	$7^{1/2}$	7^2	20	20	G. Woolf	E. R. Bradley	16.50

Time: :23$^{1/5}$, :46$^{4/5}$, 1:12$^{2/5}$, 1:37$^{2/5}$, 2:03$^{1/5}$. Track fast. Went to post at 4:42. At post 8$^{1/2}$ minutes. Start good and slow. Won easily; second and third driving.
Coupled: (a) Reaping Reward and Military; (b) Sceneshifter and Fencing; (f) Field.

Program #		Win	Place	Show
1	War Admiral	$5.20	$4.20	$3.40
14	Pompoon		$9.40	$6.00
7	Reaping Reward			$3.80

Winner: Br. c. by Man o' War–Brushup, by Sweep. Trained by George Conway; bred in Kentucky by S. D. Riddle.
$50,000 added and $5,000 Gold Cup. Net to winner $52,050; second $6,000; third $3,000; fourth $1,000.

103 nominations.
Equipment: b— blinkers; s—spurs

*Foreign bred

Not Far from the Tree

SAM RIDDLE, THE OWNER AND BREEDER OF Man o' War, arguably the greatest racehorse who ever lived, prevented the horse from entering the Derby because he wasn't feeling that good. What's more, he felt that a mile and a quarter was a little too long a race for a three-year-old colt.

But that was not the case with one of Man o' War's sons, War Admiral. Riddle decided to run him in the 1937 Derby, and, predictably, War Admiral proceeded to make history. He was another instance of the apple, as they say, not falling too far from the tree.

War Admiral first showed his promise in 1936, when he won three of six races, plus was second in two and a third in the other. As a race-

horse, War Admiral had only one problem. He didn't like the starting gate, and was fractious and nervous as his handlers tried to load him in on Derby day. It took eight and a half minutes before they succeeded, but he surely liked leaving the starting gate rapidly, and went rapidly all the way. The closest horse to him was a two-year-old champion, Pompoon, but when War Admiral crossed the wire he was three lengths ahead and had never been pressed, and his time of 2:03 1/5 was one of the fastest times ever in the Derby.

In the Preakness, War Admiral had a neck-and-neck run against Pompoon, which he succeeded in winning by a nose. Shortly thereafter, his jockey, Charles Kurtsinger, nicknamed "The Flying Dutchman," took him to an easy victory in the Belmont Stakes—and he'd won the Triple Crown.

Lawrin
64th *May 7, 1938*

		*Sir Gallahad III	*Teddy
			Plucky Liege
	Insco		SunStar
LAWRIN		*Starflight	Angelic
Brown colt			*Rock Sand
	Margaret	*Vulcain	Lady of the Vale
	Lawrence		
			*Wagner
		Bohemia	Mattie T.

THE WINNER'S PEDIGREE AND CAREER HIGHLIGHTS

YEAR	AGE	STS.	1ST	2ND	3RD	EARNINGS
1937	2	15	3	6	0	$ 3,060
1938	3	11	6	2	2	$123,215
TOTALS		**26**	**9**	**8**	**2**	**$126,275**

At 2 years	2ND	Finished second in six consecutive allowance races at six different race tracks
At 3 years	WON	Kentucky Derby, Hialeah Stakes, Flamingo Stakes, Hollywood Trial Stakes, American Invitational
	2ND	Derby Trial

RACE DAY STATISTICS

HORSE	EQ.	WT.	PP	ST.	1/2	3/4	MILE	STR.	FIN.	JOCKEY	OWNER	ODDS TO $1
Lawrin		126	1	5	5^{hd}	$5^{1/2}$	2^{hd}	1^3	1^1	E. Arcaro	Woolford Farm	8.60
Dauber	b	126	3	10	$9^{1/2}$	$8^{1/2}$	6^4	3^1	2^5	M. Peters	Foxcatcher Farms	9.70
Can't Wait	b	126	7	4	4^1	$3^{1-1/2}$	3^3	4^4	3no	L. Balaski	Myron Selznick	24.20
Menow	b	126	10	7	1^2	$1^{1-1/2}$	$1^{1-1/2}$	2^2	4^{nk}	R. Workman	H. P. Headley	8.50
The Chief		126	9	8	$6^{1/2}$	6^1	5^{hd}	5^4	5^6	J. Westrope	Maxwell Howard	12.00
Fighting Fox		126	5	6	2^3	2^{hd}	$4^{1/2}$	6^3	6^3	J. Stout	Belair Stud	1.40
Co-Sport	b	126	2	9	$8^{1-1/2}$	9^2	9^5	7^2	7^2	G. Woolf	B. Friend	89.50
Bull Lea	b	126	6	1	7^4	$7^{1/2}$	8^3	8^1	8^{hd}	I. Anderson	Calumet Farm	2.90
Elooto	b	126	4	2	10	10	10	10	9^2	F. Faust	Blue Ridge Farm	122.30
Mountain Ridge		126	8	3	$3^{1-1/2}$	4^1	7^2	$9^{1-1/2}$	10	A. Robertson	Milky Way Farm	105.20

Time: :23^1/5, :47^2/5, 1:12^2/5, 1:38^1/5, 2:04^4/5. Track fast. Went to post at 4:32. At post 4^1/2 minutes. Start good and slow. Won driving; second and third the same.

Program #		Win	Place	Show
1	Lawrin	$19.20	$ 8.80	$4.80
3	Dauber		$12.00	$6.00
7	Can't Wait			$8.20

Winner: Br. c. by Insco—Margaret Lawrence, by *Vulcain. Trained by B. A. Jones; bred in Kansas by H. M. Woolf.
$50,000 added and $5,000 Gold Cup. Net to winner $47,050; second $6,000; third $3,000; fourth $1,000.

103 nominations.
Equipment: b—blinkers

*Foreign bred

A Horse He Didn't Want to Ride

THE GREAT EDDIE ARCARO WAS JUST AT THE beginning of his career in 1938, but he knew enough to not want to ride Lawrin, a brown colt who was owned by a Kansas City clothier named Herbert M. Woolf. The colt had won only six of twenty-three races prior to the Derby, he had a cracked rib, and his damaged left forefoot required him to wear bar shoes, which were heavy—like putting snow tires on wheels—and slowed the colt down a bit. There was also a question of whether he had peaked too early.

However, a positive sign was when he finished just a head behind a horse called The Chief, who won the Derby trial in track record time.

Too, Arcaro had no other mount, it was a payday, and the trainer who asked him to ride Lawrin was the great Ben Jones. And then two days before the Derby, Stagehand, the heavy favorite, was scratched. And Jones decided to risk Lawrin going lame, taking his heavy shoes off.

If Arcaro didn't believe in Lawrin, Woolf, the owner of the Kansas-bred colt, surely did: he bet heavily on his horse. If he won, Woolf would walk away with over $100,000 in Derby winnings—not a poke in the eye with a sharp stick in 1938! (Or even now.)

Jones had one word of caution for Arcaro: Stay away from the inside of the track. He had checked it out and found that there were holes here and there.

When the race started, the worst thing, in light of the track condition, happened. Said

Arcaro, "I had the post position, got knocked around coming out of the gate, and never did get away from that rail. I had horses outside of me nearly all the way."

But despite the holes—none of which Lawrin stepped in—and the risk of going lame, Lawrin didn't set a foot wrong and by the top of the stretch he was three lengths ahead. Then, with an eighth of a mile to go, he started to die inside, as horses do, drifting to the center of the track. Coming up fast on him with every stride was a horse named Dauber. Lawrin's body was gone; the only thing left inside was his Thoroughbred's heart—and he hit the wire just before Dauber pulled even with him.

In the stands, his owner, Herbert Woolf, was going wild. As it turned out, he did not win $100,000—it was estimated to be closer to $150,000!

Johnstown
65th *May 6, 1939*

		St. James	*Ambassador IV
			*Bobolink II
	Jamestown		Fair Play
JOHNSTOWN		Mille. Dazie	Toggery
Bay colt			*Teddy
	La France	Sir Gallahad III	Plucky Liege
			*Dunbar II
	*Flambette		*La Flambee

THE WINNER'S PEDIGREE AND CAREER HIGHLIGHTS

YEAR	AGE	STS.	1ST	2ND	3RD	EARNINGS
1938	2	12	7	0	2	$ 31,420
1939	3	9	7	0	1	$137,895
TOTALS		**21**	**14**	**0**	**3**	**$169,315**

At 2 years	WON	Babylon Stakes, Richard Johnson Stakes, Remsen Handicap, Breeders' Futurity
	3RD	Hopeful Stakes, Junior Champion Stakes
	UNP	Flash Stakes, Belmont Futurity
At 3 years	WON	Kentucky Derby, Wood Memorial, Paumonok Handicap, Withers Stakes, Belmont Stakes, Dwyer Stakes
	3RD	Classic Stakes
	UNP	Preakness Stakes

RACE DAY STATISTICS

HORSE	EQ	WT.	PP	ST.	$\frac{1}{2}$	$\frac{3}{4}$	MILE	STR.	FIN.	JOCKEY	OWNER	ODDS TO $1
Johnstown	b	126	5	2	1^2	1^4	1^4	1^5	1^8	J. Stout	Belair Stud	.60
Challedon		126	7	5	7^5	$5^{1/2}$	4^6	3^1	2^1	G. Seabo	W. L. Brann	6.60
Heather Broom		126	2	6	$4^{1/2}$	6^1	3^{hd}	4^6	$3^{1/2}$	B. James	J. H. Whitney	12.00
Viscounty	b	126	3	8	6^1	4^1	2^1	2^{hd}	4^6	C. Bierman	Valdina Farm	52.20
Technician	b	126	6	4	5^1	7^8	$5^{1-1/2}$	5^5	5^8	J. Adams	Woolford Farm	5.80
El Chico		126	1	1	$2^{1/2}$	$2^{1/2}$	6^4	6^3	6^3	N. Wall	Wm. Ziegler Jr.	8.20
T. M. Dorsett	b	126	8	3	3^3	3^1	7^{12}	7^{15}	7	L. Haas	Joe W. Brown	64.90
On Location	b	126	4	7	8	8	8	8	Pulled up	A. Robertson	Milky Way Farm	97.70

Time: :23^2/5, :47^2/5, 1:12^4/5, 1:38, 2:03^2/5. Track fast. Went to post 4:29. At post ^{1}/2 minute. Start bad and slow. Won easily; second and third driving.

Program #		Win	Place	Show
6	Johnstown	$3.20	$3.00	$2.80
9	Challedon		$3.60	$3.20
3	Heather Broom			$3.00

Winner: B. c. by Jamestown–La France, by *Sir Gallahad III. Trained by James Fitzsimmons; bred in Kentucky by A. B. Hancock.
$50,000 added and $5,000 Gold Cup. Net to winner $46,350; second $6,000; third $3,000; fourth $1,000.

115 nominations.
Equipment: b—blinkers

*Foreign bred

Good Thing He Didn't Use the Whip

WILLIAM WOODWARD AND "SUNNY JIM" Fitzsimmons were from the same school when it came to horsemen—the old school. Said Fitzsimmons in 1939, speaking for both of them, "We were horsemen interested in his horse for himself and not as a betting tool." But dedication to their sport paid off. Over ten or so years in the 1930s, the pair won three Derbies in just six tries: Gallant Fox in 1930; Omaha in 1935; and in 1939 their horse Johnstown triumphed.

For some undetermined reason, Johnstown was known as the "Old Man of the Mountains." He hardly ran like an old man. He had four stakes wins as a two-year-old, and when he was three, he set a track record at Jamaica Park. His jockey, James Stout, had an embarrassment to rectify. In the 1936 Derby, on a horse named Granville, he was unseated at the post.

Johnstown was the overwhelming favorite, and he showed why. He quickly surged ahead of the other seven horses in the field and stayed there, blasting past everyone, winner by eight lengths. It was, of course, Sunny Jim's third Kentucky Derby win.

One of the competing jockeys, Nick Wall, was grateful for something: "All I'm thankful for is that Stout didn't whack Johnstown across the rear end once during the whole race because if he had, Johnstown would have won by a half-mile."

Gallahadion
66th *May 4, 1940*

		Ajax
	*Teddy	Rondeau
*Sir Gallahad II		Spearmint
GALLAHADION	Plucky Liege	Concertina
Bay colt		*Sunreigh
	Reigh Count	*Contessina
Countless		Dark Ronald
Time	*Breathing Spell	*Romagne

THE WINNER'S PEDIGREE AND CAREER HIGHLIGHTS

YEAR	AGE	STS.	1ST	2ND	3RD	EARNINGS
1939	2	5	0	1	0	$ 180
1940	3	17	5	4	1	$89,590
1941	4	14	1	1	3	$ 2,850
TOTALS		36	6	6	4	$92,620

At 3 years	WON	Kentucky Derby, San Vicente Handicap
	2ND	Derby Trial, Classic Stakes
	3RD	Preakness Stakes
	UNP	Santa Anita Derby, San Juan Capistrano Handicap, Belmont Stakes, Kent Handicap, American Derby, Lawrence Realization
At 4 years	3RD	Clark Handicap, Stars and Stripes Handicap
	UNP	Ben Ali Handicap, Churchill Downs Handicap, Dixie Handicap, Equipoise Mile

RACE DAY STATISTICS

HORSE	EQ.	WT.	PP	ST.	1/2	3/4	MILE	STR.	FIN.	JOCKEY	OWNER	ODDS TO $1
Gallahadion	b	126	1	4	3^{hd}	2^{hd}	4^1	3^2	1$^{1-1/2}$	C. Bierman	Milky Way Farm	35.20
Bimelech		126	2	1	2$^{1/2}$	3^{hd}	1^{hd}	1$^{1/2}$	2no	F. Smith	E. R. Bradley	.40
Dit	b	126	6	5	4^1	4^1	3^3	2$^{1/2}$	3^1	L. Haas	W. A. Hanger	6.70
Mioland	b	126	3	3	5^2	5$^{1/2}$	5^2	4^1	4^2	L. Balaski	C. S. Howard	6.40
Sirocco	b	126	5	6	6^1	6^3	6^5	6^6	5^2	J. Longden	Dixiana	42.70
Roman	b	126	4	2	1$^{1-1/2}$	1$^{1-1/2}$	2^{hd}	5^{hd}	6^6	K. McCombs	J. E. Widener	24.20
Royal Man	b	126	7	7	7^2	7^{hd}	7$^{1/2}$	7^3	7^3	J. Gilbert	Tower Stable	61.20
Pictor		126	8	8	8	8	8	8	8	G. Woolf	W. L. Brann	18.00

Time: :23$^{2/5}$, :48, 1:12$^{4/5}$, 1:38$^{3/5}$, 2:05. Track fast. Went to post at 4:48. At post 2 minutes. Start good and slow. Won driving; second and third the same.

Program #		Win	Place	Show
1	Gallahadion	$72.40	$13.80	$4.80
2	Bimelech		$ 3.20	$2.40
7	Dit			$2.80

Winner: B. c. by *Sir Gallahad III-Countess Time, by Reigh Count. Trained by Roy Waldron; bred in Kentucky by R. A. Fairbairn.
$75,000 added and $5,000 Gold Cup. Net to winner $60,150; second $8,000; third $3,000; fourth $1,000.
Trainer awards: first $3,000; second $2,000; third $1,000. Breeder awards: first $2,000; second $1,000; third $500.

127 nominations.
Equipment: b—blinkers

*Foreign bred

He Looked Delicious

WHEN HE SAW THE BAY COLT GALLAHADION coming out of the paddock on his way to the running of the 1940 Derby, one of the spectators commented about him, "He looks delicious." And why wouldn't he? Gallahadion and his jockey, Carroll Bierman, were clad in the rich, happy colors—bright orange, chocolate, and bright white—that reflected the business of owner Ethel V. Mars, who had used part of her husband's candy fortune to create a top racing stable called Stars of the Milky Way.

Today Gallahadion would have his work cut out for him. He was a long shot who had won a grand total of $180 as a two-year-old, and he was up against Bimelech, who was regarded as the greatest horse in America and had trounced him in the Derby Trials a short while earlier, after also winning the Blue Grass Stakes.

There was another potential problem. Gallahadion's jockey would be riding him for the first time, and Bierman himself happened

to think that Bimelech was the greatest horse in America.

When the race started, both Bimelech and Gallahadion were running together, but nearing the final quarter Bimelech went into the lead. At the final eighth Gallahadion made a move, and Bimelech could not hold him off. He paid $72.40 for every $2 bet.

Postrace analysis focused on mistakes Bimelech's new trainer had made. His regular trainer, "Derby Dick" Thompson, had passed away, and a new trainer named Bill Hurley was hired. Hurley, it was said, didn't train Bimelech hard enough, only starting to train him in the early spring before the Derby, and then he ran him in two races that were very close to the Derby, the Blue Grass Stakes and the Derby Trials two days later. Bimelech trounced the other horses, but analysts say that it tired him terribly. The final assessment was that he had left what could have been a winning Derby run on the tracks of those pre-Derby races.

Whirlaway
67th *May 3, 1941*

	Blandford	Swynford
		Blanche
*Blenheim II		Charles O' Mally
WHIRLAWAY	Malva	Wild Arum
Chestnut colt		Ben Brush
Dustwhirl	Sweep	Pink Domino
		Superman
	Ormonda	Princess Ormonde

THE WINNER'S PEDIGREE AND CAREER HIGHLIGHTS

YEAR	AGE	STS.	1ST	2ND	3RD	EARNINGS
1940	2	16	7	2	4	$ 77,275
1941	3	20	13	5	2	$272,386
1942	4	22	12	8	2	$211,250
1943	5	2	0	0	1	$ 250
TOTALS		**60**	**32**	**15**	**9**	**$561,161**

At 2 years	WON	Saratoga Special, Hopeful Stakes, Breeders' Futurity, Walden Stakes
	2ND	United States Hotel Stakes, Grand Union Hotel Stakes
	3RD	Arlington Futurity, Belmont Futurity, Pimlico Futurity
	UNP	Hyde Park Stakes, Nedayr Stakes
At 3 years	WON	Kentucky Derby, Preakness Stakes, Belmont Stakes, Saranac Handicap, Travers Stakes, American Derby, Lawrence Realization, Dwyer Stakes
	2ND	Jockey Club Gold Cup, Blue Grass Stakes, Derby Trial, Classic Stakes, Narragansett Special
At 4 years	WON	Clark Handicap, Dixie Handicap, Brooklyn Handicap, Massachusetts Handicap, Trenton Handicap, Narragansett Special, Jockey Club Gold Cup, Washington Handicap, Governor Bowie Handicap, Louisiana Handicap
	2ND	Phoenix Handicap, Suburban Handicap, Butler Handicap, Arlington Handicap, match race with Alsab, Manhattan Handicap, Riggs Handicap
	3RD	Carter Handicap, New York Handicap
At 5 years	UNP	Equipoise Mile

RACE DAY STATISTICS

HORSE	EQ.	WT.	PP	ST.	1/2	3/4	MILE	STR.	FIN.	JOCKEY	OWNER	ODDS TO $1
Whirlaway	b	126	4	6	8^1	$6^{1-1/2}$	4^1	1^3	1^8	E. Arcaro	Calumet Farm	2.90
Staretor		126	2	1	7^2	$4^{1-1/2}$	5^3	$2^{1/2}$	2^{nk}	G. Woolf	H. S. Nesbitt	36.00
Market Wise	b	126	7	5	6^2	8^4	6^3	5^3	3^2	I. Anderson	Louis Tufano	19.10
Porter's Cap	b	126	9	4	2^{hd}	3^5	$2^{1-1/2}$	3^{hd}	4^1	L. Haas	C. S. Howard	3.30
Little Beans	b	126	5	10	10^{12}	9^5	8^5	7^2	5^1	G. Moore	Mrs. Louise Palladino	12.10
Dispose		126	11	2	1^2	1^2	1^{hd}	4^{hd}	$6^{1-1/2}$	C. Bierman	King Ranch	7.20
Blue Pair	b	126	3	3	3^5	2^{hd}	$3^{1/2}$	$6^{1/2}$	$7^{1/2}$	B. James	Mrs. V. S. Bragg	20.60
Our Boots		126	10	9	4^3	$5^{1/2}$	7^2	8^5	8^3	C. McCreary	Woodvale Farm	3.90
Robert Morris		126	8	8	$5^{1-1/2}$	7^1	9^6	9^8	9^{12}	H. Richards	J. F. Byers	13.90
Valdina Paul	b	126	6	7	9^3	10^{15}	10^{15}	10^{15}	10^{12}	H. Lemmons	Valdina Farm	(f) 24.30
Swain	b	126	1	11	11	11	11	11	11	J. Adams	Cleveland Putnam	(f) 24.30

Time: :23²/₅, :46³/₅, 1:11³/₅, 1:37²/₅, 2:01²/₅ (new track record). Track fast. Went to post at 5:53. At post 1½ minutes. Start good and slow. Won easily; second and third driving. (f) Field.

Program #		Win	Place	Show
4	Whirlaway	$7.80	$ 5.00	$ 4.40
2	Staretor		$35.20	$17.00
7	Market Wise			$10.80

Winner: Ch. c. by *Blenheim II–Dustwhirl, by Sweep. Trained by B. A. Jones; bred in Kentucky by Calumet Farm.
$75,000 added and $5,000 Gold Cup. Net to winner $61,275; second $8,000; third $3,000; fourth $1,000.
Trainer awards: first $3,000; second $2,000; third $1,000. Breeder awards: first $2,000; second $1,000; third $500.

112 nominations.
Equipment: b—blinkers

*Foreign bred

"As Nervous as a Cat in a Room Full of Rocking Chairs"

IF WHIRLAWAY WAS HUMAN, HE MIGHT HAVE been summarily institutionalized in a psychiatric facility. But he was a small horse (fifteen hands high), and he, his owner, and racing fans all over the world got lucky: he intersected with trainer Ben A. Jones, the head of trainers at the superpower Calumet Farm.

Jones said that in addition to being highstrung and unpredictable, Whirlaway was dumb, "the dumbest horse I ever trained, you could teach him, but you couldn't teach him much." But Whirlaway could run like the wind, the fastest juvenile colt and far and away the best prospect Jones had for the 1941 Kentucky Derby.

When Whirlaway's problems on the track showed up, they could be scary and entertaining at the same time, and fans loved him. One tendency was sometimes not to run in a straight line. A race would start, and he would carry a terrified jockey on a diagonal line toward the outer rail, flipping the jockey head over heels into the crowd. Or in the middle of a race he might just stop dead, also launching the jockey forward.

Whirlaway also had a strange "motor," as one trainer commented. Once that motor started to rev into high gear, you better leave it alone because once it slowed down, it couldn't get back up to its former speed, a decidedly annoying habit if you were astride him in the middle of a race and he slowed, say, because another horse galloped across and into his path. Whirlaway could be trained, one trainer

observed, but it was "like controlling mercury poured into the palm of your hand."

But if anyone could control that mercury, it was Ben A. Jones, generally regarded as one of the greatest trainers who ever lived. Because of his great ability, Jones spent many hours studying Whirlaway, trying to determine why he did the things he did, and one day he thought he had it figured out. For one thing, he determined that the horse would run to the right rail because it was most obvious to him as a guide of where to run. Once he reached it, he would run next to it for the duration of the race—and sometimes win!

Jones figured that he had to block that rail, so he started fitting Whirlaway with blinkers that were solid on the right—Whirlaway couldn't see that siren-like right rail—but open on the left, so he could see the inside rail and use it as a guide.

Another Jones innovation was to let Whirlaway's tail grow. Most horses had their tails trimmed to just above the hocks, but Jones, ever fearful of his horse being spooked by other horses, let his tail grow almost to the point where it could be used to sweep the track. When Whirlaway was in full, blazing gallop, the tail stood out, moving, pointing—saying, Stay the hell away from me, to other horses.

But the biggest idea of all was finding a jockey with the skill and strength to ride Whirlaway, and also with what Woody Allen once said was the most important human quality, "courage."

Jones interviewed a number of jockeys to ride Whirlaway in the Derby, but all said no. Indeed, one jockey, a previous Derby winner, told Jones that he couldn't for one main reason: "I have a family!"

But Jones got lucky. He found a jockey from a rival stable who, by some fluke, had no Derby mount and also had all the qualities he needed. Indeed, he happened to be one of the greatest jockeys who ever lived. His name was Eddie Arcaro.

Arcaro started to ride Whirlaway, and developed a method, as he said in his book *I Ride to Win,* to control the horse. "You had to take a long hold on him and freeze with it. Although I might look like a coachman, it was the old way to handle him."

When the race started, Whirlaway soon settled into sixth in the field of eleven, around nine lengths from the leader, but blocked a bit.

So far, Arcaro had not had to contend with any of Whirlaway's antics, and by the mile marker he was in fourth, but starting to make a big move. And then, as they turned into the stretch, he drove Whirlaway between two horses, Staretor, a long shot from California, and Market Wise. Then Whirlaway showed why Jones tolerated all kinds of craziness and difficulty with him. He roared to the front, and, tail flying, he was poetry in very fast motion, driving down the stretch, a horse possessed. Behind him, daylight expanded between him and the other horses with every stride, and he rocketed across the wire in a record time of 2:01 2/5, a record that would stand for twenty-one years.

But he didn't stop at the Derby. He went on to win the Triple Crown, and became Horse of the Year. Crazy, slow-witted. But fast . . . very, very, very fast.

Shut Out

68th *May 2, 1942*

		Pennant	Peter Pan
			*Royal Rose
	Equipoise		Broomstick
SHUT OUT		Swinging	*Balancoire II
Chestnut colt			Spearmint
	Goose Egg		Lady Hamburg II
		*Chicle	Fair Play
			Olympia
		Oval	

THE WINNER'S PEDIGREE AND CAREER HIGHLIGHTS

YEAR	AGE	STS.	1ST	2ND	3RD	EARNINGS
1941	2	9	3	2	1	$ 17,210
1942	3	12	8	2	0	$238,972
1943	4	17	5	2	2	$ 60,925
1944	5	2	0	0	1	$ 400
TOTALS		**40**	**16**	**6**	**4**	**$317,507**

At 2 years	WON	Grand Union Hotel Stakes
	2ND	Hopeful Stakes, Saratoga Special
	3RD	Ardsley Handicap
At 3 years	WON	Kentucky Derby, Blue Grass Stakes, Belmont Stakes, Yankee Handicap, Classic Stakes, Travers Stakes
	2ND	Dwyer Stakes
	UNP	Preakness Stakes, Gallant Fox Handicap
At 4 years	WON	Wilson Stakes, Laurel Stakes, Pimlico Special
	2ND	Edgemere Handicap, Riggs Handicap
	3RD	Washington Handicap, Saratoga Handicap

RACE DAY STATISTICS

HORSE	EQ.	WT.	PP	ST.	1/2	3/4	MILE	STR.	FIN.	JOCKEY	OWNER	ODDS TO $1
Shut Out		126	3	1	4²	3¹⁻¹/²	3ʰᵈ	1¹/²	1²⁻¹/⁴	W. Wright	Greentree Stable	(a) 1.90
Alsab	b	126	7	5	10¹	8¹	4¹/²	4²	2ʰᵈ	B. James	Mrs. Al Sabath	5.10
Valdina Orphan	b	126	14	10	2ʰᵈ	2¹/²	2²	2ʰᵈ	3¹⁻¹/²	C. Bierman	Valdina Farm	(b) 9.90
With Regards		126	15	4	1²	1¹	1¹/²	3²	4¹/²	J. Longden	Mr. & Mrs. T. D. Grimes	5.40
First Fiddle	b	126	2	11	11¹/²	10ʰᵈ	9ʰᵈ	6³	5³	C. McCreary	Mrs. E. Mulrenan	(f) 9.20
Devil Diver	b	126	5	2	5¹⁻¹/²	5¹⁻¹/²	5¹⁻¹/²	5²	6¹⁻¹/²	E. Arcaro	Greentree Stable	(a) 1.90
Fair Call	b	126	1	7	6¹	6¹⁻¹/²	6¹	7¹	7ⁿᵏ	H. Lindberg	Mill River Stable	(f) 9.20
Dogpatch	b	126	10	3	3ʰᵈ	4¹/²	7ʰᵈ	8¹/²	8ʰᵈ	J. Skelly	Milky Way Farm	59.70
*Hollywood		126	6	14	14⁵	13¹	12³	10¹	9¹	G. Woolf	Valdina Farms	(b) 9.90
Sweep Swinger	b	126	4	15	15	14⁵	13³	11²	10¹/²	A. Shelhamer	T. D. Buhl	(f) 9.20
Apache		126	13	6	7¹	7¹/²	8¹/²	9¹	11¹	J. Stout	Belair Stud	16.90
Sir War	b	126	8	8	9¹⁻¹/²	11¹/²	11²	12⁴	12⁴	J. Adams	Circle M Ranch	(f) 9.20
Fairy Manah	b	126	9	13	12¹	9ʰᵈ	10¹	13²	13⁶	J. Gilbert	Foxcatcher Farm	39.90
Requested		126	12	9	8¹⁻¹/²	12¹/²	14⁶	14⁵	14⁵	L. Haas	B. F. Whitaker	5.10
Boot and Spur	b	126	11	12	13¹/²	15	15	15	15	A. Craig	E. C. A. Berger	(f) 9.20

Time: :23³/₅, :47²/₅, 1:12³/₅, 1:39, 2:04²/₅. Track fast. In gate 5:31. Off at 5:33 CWT. Start good from stall gate. Won ridden out; second and third driving.
Coupled: (a) Shut Out and Devil Diver; (b) Hollywood and Valdina Orphan; (f) Field.

Program #		Win	Place	Show
3	Shut Out	$5.80	$3.40	$3.00
7	Alsab		$6.20	$4.80
16	Valdina Orphan			$5.20

Winner: Ch. c. by Equipoise–Goose Egg, by *Chicle. Trained by J. M. Gaver; bred in Kentucky by Greentree Stable.
$75,000 added and $5,000 Gold Cup. Net to winner $64,225; second $8,000; third $3,000; fourth $1,000.
Trainer awards: first $3,000; second $2,000; third $1,000. Breeder awards: first $2,000; second $1,000; third $500.

150 nominations.
Equipment: b—blinkers

*Foreign bred

A Special Audience

IN 1942, THE GRANDSTAND AND OTHER viewing areas of the Derby were flying their own colors, the khaki, blue, gray, and white of men and women in the U.S. Armed Forces. They weren't about to let a little thing like World War II get in the way of viewing the classic race.

This year the race was to see one of those curious—and really, illogical—occurrences that sometimes defy explanation. Instead of the great Eddie Arcaro being on the back of Shut Out as a top rider, he instead was astride Shut Out's stablemate at Greentree Stable, Devil Diver.

Additionally, it was not as if Shut Out came to the fray without impressive parents. Indeed, he was the last son of Equipoise, a great horse who won just about everything he was in and was a clear favorite in the Kentucky Derby, and

probably didn't win that for only one reason: he didn't run. Just before the Derby, he came up lame.

On Derby day Shut Out's jockey was a tough little rider from Idaho, Wayne Wright, who was on the comeback trail. Shut Out was given a good ride by Wright and ran steadily and strongly for most of the race, though not in the lead. Then, approaching the last eighth, Wright let him go, and he hammered past the other colts and won by two lengths with Alsab and Valdina Orphan behind him.

Arcaro was sixth on Devil Diver, yet in the Preakness he chose Devil Diver again—and again was beaten by Shut Out. Finally, the proverbial lightbulb went on above his head, and he rode Shut Out in the Belmont Stakes—and won.

The race marked a first. Mrs. Payne Whitney, owner of Shut Out, became the first woman to own two Derby winners, the first being Twenty Grand in 1931.

Count Fleet
69th *May 1, 1943*

			Sundridge
	*Sunreigh		*Sweet Briar II
Reigh Count			Count Schomberg
COUNT FLEET	*Contessina		Pitti
Brown colt			*Maintenant
Quickly	Haste		Miss Malaprop
			*Stefan the Great
Stepanie			Malachite

THE WINNER'S PEDIGREE AND CAREER HIGHLIGHTS

YEAR	AGE	STS.	1ST	2ND	3RD	EARNINGS
1942	2	15	10	4	1	$ 76,245
1943	3	6	6	0	0	$174,055
TOTALS		**21**	**16**	**4**	**1**	**$250,300**

At 2 years	WON	Champagne Stakes, Pimlico Futurity, Walden Stakes, Wakefield Stakes
	2ND	East View Stakes, Washington Park Futurity
	3RD	Belmont Futurity
At 3 years	WON	Kentucky Derby, Wood Memorial, Preakness Stakes, Withers Stakes, Belmont Stakes

RACE DAY STATISTICS

HORSE	EQ.	WT.	PP	ST.	1/2	3/4	MILE	STR.	FIN.	JOCKEY	OWNER	ODDS TO $1
Count Fleet	b	126	5	1	1^{hd}	1^2	1^2	1^2	1^3	J. Longden	Mrs. John D. Hertz	.40
Blue Swords	b	126	1	2	4$^{1/2}$	4$^{1-1/2}$	2$^{1-1/2}$	2^2	2^6	J. Adams	A. T. Simmons	9.00
Slide Rule	b	126	2	6	6$^{1/2}$	3^{hd}	4$^{1-1/2}$	3^3	3^6	C. McCreary	W. E. Boeing	10.80
Amber Light	b	126	7	5	5$^{1-1/2}$	5^3	3$^{1/2}$	4^2	4$^{1/2}$	A. Robertson	Dixiana	17.50
Bankrupt		126	6	9	9^3	9^1	7$^{1/2}$	6$^{1/2}$	5$^{1-1/2}$	F. Zufelt	T. B. Martin	(f) 21.90
No Wrinkles		126	10	7	8^3	7$^{1/2}$	6^1	7^{hd}	6^{hd}	R. Adair	Milky Way Farm	34.60
Dove Pie	b	126	4	10	10	10	8^2	8^1	7^3	W. Eads	J. W. Rodgers	86.50
Gold Shower		126	9	4	2^4	2^1	5^3	5$^{1/2}$	8^{10}	T. Atkinson	V. S. Bragg	12.10
Modest Lad	b	126	3	8	7^{hd}	6^{hd}	9^4	9^4	9^8	C. Swain	Mrs. H. Finch	71.20
Burnt Cork	b	126	8	3	3^1	8$^{1-1/2}$	10	10	10	M. Gonzalez	Eddie Anderson	(f) 21.90

Time: :23$^{1/5}$, :46$^{3/5}$, 1:12$^{3/5}$, 1:37$^{3/5}$, 2:04. Track fast. In gate 5:30$^{1/2}$. Off at 5:31$^{1/2}$ CWT. Start good from stall gate. Won handily; second and third driving.
(f) Field.

Program #		Win	Place	Show
5	Count Fleet	$2.80	$2.40	$2.20
1	Blue Swords		$3.40	$3.00
2	Slide Rule			$3.20

Winner: Br. c. by Reigh Count–Quickly, by Haste. Trained by G. D. Cameron; bred in Kentucky by Mrs. J. Hertz.
$75,000 added and $5,000 Gold Cup. Net to winner $60,725; second $8,000; third $3,000; fourth $1,000.
Trainer awards: first $3,000; second $2,000; third $1,000. Breeder awards: first $2,000; second $1,000; third $500.
Scratched- Twoses, Ocean Wave.

110 nominations.
Equipment: b—blinkers

*Foreign bred

Ugly Duckling

COUNT FLEET WAS A VERY PROUD HORSE when he went on to stud, said Charles Kenney, farm manager of Stoner Creek Stud in Paris, Kentucky. "Wouldn't come over for sugar or to be petted. He knew he was royalty." The "Count of Stoner Creek" was his nickname on the farm. But even counts can be afraid, and Count Fleet, like a little boy, was afraid of the dark!

The reason he got to be royalty was the Triple Crown. He won it, and in one case by an astonishing margin.

As related earlier in the book, as a foal Count Fleet was the classic ugly duckling, but his daddy was Reigh Count, winner of the 1928 Derby. His owner was John D. Hertz, and he didn't like the horse, perhaps in part because he did have a roguish personality. Hertz wanted to sell him, but jockey Johnny Longden saw something that he liked, and implored him not

to do this. Longden had his way, and Hertz also asked him to ride Count Fleet.

Count Fleet did not suddenly become a super-horse. As a yearling, he did well but then lost the futurity race at Belmont, where he stayed behind a filly named Askmenow. No matter what Longden did, he couldn't break Count Fleet free. "For the last three-eighths he laid on Askmenow and I couldn't drag him off." But the race was significant in another way. It was a turning point, the last loss of the horse's career.

The Derby was a slam dunk. He got out in the lead early, and led all the way, winning by three lengths. In the Preakness he won by eight lengths, and in the Belmont he foreshadowed Secretariat, winning by twenty-five lengths.

At stud, Count Fleet sired 1951 Derby champion Count Turf, which meant—since his sire Count Reigh was also a Derby winner—that for the first time, three successive generations of horses had won the Derby.

Pensive
70th *May 6, 1944*

			Bayardo
	Gainsborough	*Rosedrop
Hyperion		Chaucer
PENSIVE	Selene	Sernissima
Chestnut colt		Sunstar
*Penicuik II	Buchan	Hamoaze
		Hurry On
Pennycomequick	Plymstock

The Winner's Pedigree and Career Highlights

YEAR	AGE	STS.	1ST	2ND	3RD	EARNINGS
1943	2	5	2	0	2	$ 5,490
1944	3	17	5	5	2	$162,225
TOTALS		**22**	**7**	**5**	**4**	**$167,715**

At 2 years	3RD	Champagne Stakes, Oden Bowie Stakes
	UNP	Belmont Futurity
At 3 years	WON	Kentucky Derby, Rowe Memorial Handicap, Preakness Stakes
	2ND	Bowie Handicap, Chesapeake Stakes, Belmont Stakes
	3RD	Classic Stakes
	UNP	Stars and Stripes Handicap, Skokie Handicap, Dick Welles Handicap, American Derby, Washington Park Handicap

Race Day Statistics

HORSE	EQ.	WT.	PP	ST.	½	¾	MILE	STR.	FIN.	JOCKEY	OWNER	ODDS TO $1
Pensive		126	4	4	13^1	10^{hd}	$5^{1\text{-}1/2}$	$3^{1\text{-}1/2}$	$1^{4\text{-}1/2}$	C. McCreary	Calumet Farm	7.10
Broadcloth	b	126	9	7	$3^{1/2}$	3^2	$1^{1/2}$	1^{hd}	2^1	G. Woolf	Mrs. Geo. Poulsen	7.40
Stir Up	b	126	5	5	$4^{1\text{-}1/2}$	4^1	2^2	2^{hd}	3^{hd}	E. Arcaro	Greentree Stable	1.40
Shut Up	b	126	10	12	14^3	$13^{1\text{-}1/2}$	$7^{1\text{-}1/2}$	5^2	4^{hd}	R. Eccard	Erlanger Stable	(f) 7.70
Brief Sigh	b	126	13	3	$9^{1/2}$	$8^{1\text{-}1/2}$	$3^{1\text{-}1/2}$	$4^{1\text{-}1/2}$	$5^{3/4}$	V. Nodarse	River Divide Farm	(f) 7.70
Gay Bit		126	7	16	16	16	16	$6^{1\text{-}1/2}$	6^1	J. Westrope	Bobanet Stable	25.80
Bell-Buzzer	b	126	3	15	15^1	15^3	13^2	9^2	$7^{1\text{-}1/2}$	B. Thompson	David Ferguson	(f) 7.70
Gramps Image	b	126	14	10	11^1	$12^{1/2}$	9^2	8^{hd}	8^4	D. Grohs	Mrs. A. J. Abel	20.00
Skytracer	b	126	2	1	$7^{1/2}$	6^{hd}	$6^{1/2}$	$7^{1/2}$	9^2	M. Caffarella	M. B. Goff	8.40
Challenge Me	b	126	1	2	$6^{1\text{-}1/2}$	$7^{1/2}$	10^3	10^5	$10^{1/2}$	W. Garner	Brolite Farm	8.90
Alorter	b	126	6	6	5^{hd}	5^{hd}	11^2	11^4	11^5	J. Adams	A. C. Ernst	19.50
Comenow	b	126	16	11	2^1	$2^{1\text{-}1/2}$	$4^{1/2}$	$12^{1\text{-}1/2}$	12^2	J. Layton	Philip Godfrey	(f) 7.70
Valley Flares	b	126	11	14	$8^{1/2}$	$11^{1\text{-}1/2}$	12^1	13^2	13^2	G. Burns	B. R. Paton	(f) 7.70
Diavolaw	b	126	12	9	1^1	$1^{1/2}$	$8^{1/2}$	$14^{1\text{-}1/2}$	14^1	J. Molbert	W. C. Hobson	(f) 7.70
Rockwood Boy	b	126	8	8	10^1	9^{hd}	$14^{1\text{-}1/2}$	$15^{1\text{-}1/2}$	15^5	W. Bailey	W. C. Davis	(f) 7.70
American Eagle	b	126	15	13	12^2	14^2	15^4	16	16	J. Higley	J. V. Maggio	

Time: :23³/5, :47¹/5, 1:12²/5, 1:38¹/5, 2:04¹/5. Track good. In gate 5:17. Off at 5:19 CWT. Start good from stall gate. Won ridden out; second and third driving.
(f) Field.

Program #		Win	Place	Show
5	Pensive	$16.20	$7.20	$4.60
3	Broadcloth		$6.80	$4.60
6	Stir Up			$3.00

Winner: Ch. c. by Hyperion–*Penicuik II, by Buchan. Trained by B. A. Jones; bred in Kentucky by Calumet Farm.
$75,000 added and $5,000 Gold Cup. Net to winner $64,675; second $8,000; third $3,000; fourth $1,000.
Trainer awards: first $3,000; second $2,000; third $1,000. Breeder awards: first $2,000; second $1,000; third $500.

148 nominations.
Equipment: b—blinkers

*Foreign bred

Calumet Gets Rolling

ON MAY 6, 1944, CALUMET FARM, WHICH was to dominate Thoroughbred horse racing like no other stable before or since, had its second Derby winner with jockey Conn McCreary wearing the red-and-blue silks and riding Pensive. Before Calumet Farm was finished, it would have racked up six more Derby wins.

Pensive faced stiff competition in the Derby. The favorite was Greentree Stable's Stir Up, with the great Eddie Arcaro aboard. But Pensive had solid parentage.

Like Cavalcade, the 1934 Derby winner, Pensive was out of English horses. In 1940, England's Lord Astor had a mare named Penicuik II to sell, and he said he'd sell her to an American named Warren Wright—Calumet's owner—on the condition that he breed the mare to Hyperion, the English Derby winner. Wright agreed, and the resulting chestnut colt out of Penicuik II was named Pensive.

When the gates clanged open, Pensive quickly fell back, but this by design—McCreary's design. He was known for holding his mounts back, then coming from far back to win. Indeed, it was a technique that an owner would be drawn to seven years later, in the 1951 Derby, when McCreary was down and out as a jockey and the owner gave him one final chance to lift himself up.

In this race, McCreary dropped all the way back to thirteen in the field of sixteen.

As he approached the mile marker, he started to move up to fifth on the inside. And then, boom, he started to really run, powering along next to the rail. Horses fell behind as he went past.

The plain fact was that no one could keep him off, and he drove to the lead against Broadcloth and Stir Up and kept driving until he crossed the wire some four and a half lengths ahead of Broadcloth. It was McCreary's fourth attempt to win a Derby, and the third Derby win for Calumet Farm trainer, Ben Jones.

Hoop Jr.
71st June 9, 1945

			Ajax
		*Teddy	Rondeau
	*Sir Gallahad III		Spearmint
HOOP JR.		Plucky Liege	Concertina
Bay colt			Prestige
	One Hour	*Snob II	May Dora
			*Star Shoot
	Daylight Saving	Tea Enough

THE WINNER'S PEDIGREE AND CAREER HIGHLIGHTS

YEAR	AGE	STS.	1ST	2ND	3RD	EARNINGS
1944	2	5	2	3	0	$ 5,300
1945	3	4	2	1	0	$93,990
TOTALS		**9**	**4**	**4**	**0**	**$99,290**

At 2 years	2ND	Bowie Kindergarten Stakes, Aberdeen Stakes, Pimlico Nursery Stakes
At 3 years	WON	Kentucky Derby, Wood Memorial Stakes
	2ND	Preakness Stakes

RACE DAY STATISTICS

HORSE	EQ.	WT.	PP	ST.	1/2	3/4	MILE	STR.	FIN.	JOCKEY	OWNER	ODDS TO $1
Hoop Jr.		126	12	2	1^1	1^1	1^1	1^6	1^6	E. Arcaro	F. W. Hooper	3.70
Pot O' Luck		126	7	15	$14^{1-1/2}$	$10^{1/2}$	8^2	5^2	$2^{3/4}$	D. Dodson	Calumet Farm	3.30
Darby Dieppe	b	126	9	16	12^{hd}	9^1	$6^{1-1/2}$	$3^{1/2}$	3^{nk}	M. Calvert	Mrs. W. G. Lewis	5.60
Air Sailor		126	5	5	$5^{1-1/2}$	5^2	3^4	4^2	4^4	L. Haas	T. D. Buhl	20.90
Jeep	b	126	3	6	$7^{1/2}$	$7^{1/2}$	5^{hd}	6^4	5^3	A. Kirkland	C. V. Whitney	6.80
Bymeabond	b	126	10	1	$2^{1/2}$	2^3	$2^{1-1/2}$	2^{hd}	6^3	F. Smith	J. K. Houssels	(f) 6.80
Sea Swallow	b	126	2	3	$6^{1-1/2}$	$8^{1-1/2}$	10^3	$7^{1-1/2}$	$7^{1-1/2}$	G. Woolf	Mrs. C. S. Howard	(f) 6.80
Fighting Step		126	13	11	4^2	4^1	4^1	8^1	$8^{1-1/2}$	G. South	Murlogg Farm	19.80
Burning Dream		126	6	7	$10^{1-1/2}$	$11^{1/2}$	11^4	9^4	9^2	A. Snider	E. R. Bradley	15.80
Alexis		126	11	4	$3^{1/2}$	$3^{1-1/2}$	$7^{1/2}$	11^6	$10^{1/2}$	K. Scawthorn	Christiana Stables	12.20
Foreign Agent	b	126	4	9	9^1	6^{hd}	$9^{1/2}$	$10^{1/2}$	11^5	K. Knott	Lookout Stock Farm	25.90
Misweet	b	121	1	8	8^{hd}	13^1	13^1	13^4	12^5	A. Craig	Arthur Rose	(f) 6.80
Tiger Rebel		126	8	10	11^1	12^4	12^5	12^{hd}	$13^{1-1/2}$	J. Layton	Brent & Talbot	(f) 6.80
Bert G.	b	126	14	14	15^4	15^{15}	15^{20}	14^1	14^{10}	R. Summers	T. L. Graham	(a,f) 6.80
Jacobe	b	126	15	12	$13^{1-1/2}$	14^4	14^4	15^{20}	15^8	H. Lindberg	A. R. Wright	(f) 6.80
Kenilworth Lad	b	126	16	13	16	16	16	16	16	F. Wiedaman	T. L. Graham	(a,f) 6.80

Time: :23^{1}/5, :48, 1:14, 1:41, 2:07. Track Muddy. Went to post 5:17. Off at 5:22 CWT. Start good from stall gate. Won easily; second and third driving.
Coupled: (a) Bert G. and Kenilworth Lad; (f) Field.

Program #		Win	Place	Show
2	Hoop Jr.	$9.40	$5.20	$4.00
7	Pot O' Luck		$4.80	$3.60
9	Darby Dieppe			$4.00

Winner: B. c. by *Sir Gallahad III–One Hour, by *Snob II. Trained by I. H. Parke; bred in Kentucky by R. A. Fairbairn.
$75,000 added and $5,000 Gold Cup. Net to winner $64,850; second $8,000; third $3,000; fourth $1,000.
Trainer awards: first $3,000; second $2,000; third $1,000. Breeder awards: first $2,000; second $1,000; third $500.

155 nominations.
Equipment: b—blinkers

*Foreign bred

One Lucky Day

MANY HORSEMEN SPEND THEIR ENTIRE lives trying to win the Kentucky Derby, and in the end they don't. But other horsemen do, and some of them do it very quickly. "Their stars," said one horseman, "are in alignment."

So it was in 1945, as World War II was coming to a close, that Freddy Hooper, a man who owned a horse farm in Montgomery, Alabama, went to the Keeneland yearling sale in August of 1943. He had never bought or even owned a Thoroughbred. But he bought (for $10,200) a yearling he liked the looks of and named it Hoop Jr., after his son, and trained him at his farm.

Finally, at the start of 1945, when he was officially three, he raced in New York, and though he didn't do well, he met a jockey who agreed to ride him. His name was Eddie Arcaro.

Hoop Jr's. next start was the Wood Memorial, and Arcaro was up.

As he did with most of the races where his colts ran, Hooper bet on Hoop Jr., this time $10,000—which was a lot of belief. Hoop Jr. won by two and two-third lengths.

The colt was primed for the Derby, but he and the other colts and everyone else had to wait—for World War II. It was just ending, but because of travel restrictions under wartime conditions, the Derby was rescheduled for June 9, instead of the first Saturday in May.

Hoop Jr. was the favorite in Hooper's mind, but not on the tote board. Ben Jones was running the favorite, Pot O' Luck.

One thing was for sure: whoever won would

have to be a good mudder. It rained hard, and by race time the track was a river. Still, there were 80,000 people who attended the race.

Hoop Jr., breaking from the 12 hole, ran well. By the first quarter he was leading, and as the race progressed he increased his lead, and won going away by eight lengths. Pot O' Luck finished second after a big charge from way back.

Hooper commented after the race, "I never thought I'd make it this quick."

Years later, after failing to win the Derby with Olympia (sixth) in 1949 and Crozier (second) in 1961 and Admirals' Voyage (ninth) in 1962, he understood Eddie Arcaro's comment after he won in 1945: "That's the most expensive race you'll ever win," Arcaro said.

"Why?" Hooper asked.

"You'll spend the rest of your life trying to win it again."

He never did win again, dying when he was ninety-six.

Assault
72nd *May 4, 1946*

The Winner's Pedigree

	St. Germans	*Swynford*
		Hamoaze
Bold Venture		*Ultimus*
ASSAULT	*Possible*	*Lida Flush*
Chestnut colt		*Pennant*
Igual	*Equipoise*	*Swinging*
		Chicle
	Incandescent	*Masda*

Race Day Statistics

HORSE	EQ.	WT.	PP	ST.	1/2	3/4	MILE	STR.	FIN.	JOCKEY	OWNER	ODDS TO $1
Assault	b	126	2	3	$5^{1/2}$	4^{hd}	$3^{1/2}$	$1^{2-1/2}$	1^8	W. Mehrtens	King Ranch	8.20
Spy Song		126	6	2	1^2	$1^{1/2}$	$1^{1/2}$	2^2	2^{hd}	J. Longden	Dixiana	7.80
Hampden	b	126	17	14	6^1	5^{hd}	$4^{2-1/2}$	5^2	3^1	J. Jessop	Foxcatcher Farm	5.80
Lord Boswell		126	3	1	$9^{1/2}$	$7^{1/2}$	$9^{1-1/2}$	$3^{1/2}$	$4^{1-1/2}$	E. Arcaro	Maine Chance Farm	(a) 1.10
Knockdown		126	11	4	$2^{1/2}$	$2^{1/2}$	$2^{1-1/2}$	$4^{1/2}$	5^4	R Permane	Maine Chance Farm	(a) 1.10
Alamond	b	126	7	8	$11^{1/2}$	$8^{1/2}$	11^2	6^1	6^1	A. Kirkland	A. C. Ernst	65.30
Bob Murphy	b	126	13	16	$13^{1/2}$	$11^{1/2}$	6^2	$7^{1/2}$	$7^{1/2}$	A. Bodiou	David Ferguson	(f) 31.80
Pellicle	b	126	8	11	12^2	$9^{1/2}$	8^{hd}	8^{hd}	$8^{1-1/2}$	G. Hettinger	H. P. Headley	16.10
Perfect Bahram		126	5	12	15^3	13^2	$10^{1/2}$	$11^{1/2}$	$9^{1/2}$	T. Atkinson	Maine Chance Farm	(a) 1.10
Rippey		126	14	7	4^{hd}	6^1	5^{hd}	9^1	10^1	F. Zufelt	William Helis	10.20
Jobar		126	16	17	17	17	16^4	16^4	$11^{1-1/2}$	J. Layton	H. W. Fielding	(f) 31.80
Dark Jungle	b	126	12	6	$3^{1-1/2}$	3^{hd}	$7^{1/2}$	$10^{1/2}$	12^2	A. LoTurco	Lucas B. Combs	60.70
Alworth	b	126	4	10	10^1	12^1	13^{hd}	13^3	$13^{1/2}$	O. Scurlock	Mrs. R. D. Patterson	(f) 31.80
With Pleasure	b	126	10	9	$7^{1/2}$	10^1	14^2	14^2	$14^{1-1/2}$	C. Wahler	Brolite Farm	48.30
Marine Victory	b	126	15	15	14^1	14^3	15^3	$15^{1/2}$	15^1	D. Padgett	Bobanet Stable	45.00
Wee Admiral	b	126	9	5	$8^{1-1/2}$	16^1	$12^{1/2}$	2^2	16^3	R. Watson	R. S. McLaughlin	59.40
Kendor	b	126	1	13	16^6	15^1	17	17	17	W. Johnson	Mrs. D. Hollingsworth	(f) 31.80

Time: :23²/₅, :48, 1:14¹/₅, 1:40⁴/₅, 2:06³/₅. Track slow. Went to post 5:17. Off at 5:20 CDT. Start good from stall gate. Won driving; second and third the same.
Coupled: (a) Lord Boswell, Knockdown and Perfect Bahram; (f) Field.

Program #		Win	Place	Show
3	Assault	$18.40	$9.60	$6.80
5	Spy Song		$9.00	$6.60
11	Hampden			$5.20

Winner: Ch. c. by Bold Venture–Igual, by Equipoise. Trained by M. Hirsch; bred in Texas by King Ranch.
$100,000 added and $5,000 Gold Cup. Net to winner $96,400; second $10,000; third $5,000; fourth $2,500.
Trainer awards: first $3,000; second $2,000; third $1,000. Breeder awards: first $2,000; second $1,000; third $500.

149 nominations.
Equipment: b—blinkers

*Foreign bred

The Clubfoot Comet

1946 WAS A HAPPY AND HEADY TIME FOR America. The guns of war were stilled. Men and women returned from places that had changed them forever. It was peacetime, and lots of people turned out to drink mint juleps, relax, laugh, dream, and see something that would clutch at their hearts in a different way, because no one would likely die. They came out to watch a great horse race.

And did they ever turn out! There to see it were 105,000 spectators, including many women who seemed to have chosen this year to start their own mini wars, wearing fancy, fanciful, and sometimes outrageous hats, most

CAREER HIGHLIGHTS

YEAR	AGE	STS.	1ST	2ND	3RD	EARNINGS
1945	2	9	2	2	1	$ 17,250
1946	3	15	8	2	3	$424,195
1947	4	7	5	1	1	$181,925
1948	5	2	1	0	0	$ 3,250
1949	6	6	1	1	1	$ 45,900
1950	7	3	1	0	1	$ 2,950
TOTALS		**42**	**18**	**6**	**7**	**$675,470**

At 2 years	WON	Flash Stakes
	3RD	Babylon Handicap
At 3 years	WON	Kentucky Derby, Experimental Free Handicap, Wood Memorial Stakes, Preakness Stakes, Belmont Stakes, Dwyer Stakes, Pimlico Special, Westchester Handicap
	2ND	Jersey Handicap, Roamer Handicap
	3RD	Discovery Handicap, Manhattan Handicap, Gallant Fox Handicap
	UNP	Derby Trial, Arlington Classic
At 4 years	WON	Grey Lag Handicap, Dixie Handicap, Suburban Handicap, Brooklyn Handicap, Butler Handicap
	2ND	Belmont Special
	3RD	Belmont Gold Cup
At 6 years	WON	Brooklyn Handicap
	3RD	Edgemere Handicap

of which shared a common characteristic: you couldn't see through them, and you would need a ladder to see over.

Assault, the horse who was to win the Derby that day, didn't seem to have much chance. While his sire was Bold Venture, 1936 Derby winner, his mare was Igaul, who was so sickly as a foal that veterinarians were a heartbeat away from putting her down. But they didn't, of course, and though she was never good enough to run, one day out of her body would come a horse for the ages.

Assault was foaled on the King Ranch of Robert Kleberg. He was not highly regarded, in part because when he was very young he stepped on some sharp object—it was never determined what—and it gave him a funny gait when he walked.

When trainer Max Hirsch first saw Assault in early April of his three-year-old season, Hirsch was not impressed. Prior to the 1946 Derby the horse had twelve starts and had never

been favored. He had won just one stakes victory, the five-and-a-half-furlong Flash, where he went off at 70–1.

Seventeen horses broke from the 1946 Derby starting gate, and everyone was in for a big surprise. Said Assault's jockey, Warren Mehrtens, "After the first quarter I knew he was full of run and wanted to run. We were fourth, then third down the backside, slipped through along the rail to take the lead, and then to keep his mind on his work I slashed him a couple of times."

He won by eight lengths.

As writer Tommy Fitzgerald wrote in the *Louisville Courier-Journal*, "It wasn't assault in the Kentucky Derby yesterday. It was murder!"

Assault went on to win the Triple Crown with Mehrtens aboard, and he lived many years. He is regarded as one of the greatest horses ever, and because of his gait became known as "the Clubfoot Comet."

Jet Pilot
73rd May 3, 1947

			Swynford
		Blandford	Blanche
	*Blenheim II		Charles O'Malley
JET PILOT		Malva	Wild Arum
Chestnut colt			*Teddy
	Black Wave	*Sir Gallahad III	Plucky Liege
			Friar Rock
		Black Curl	*Frizeur

THE WINNER'S PEDIGREE AND CAREER HIGHLIGHTS

YEAR	AGE	STS.	1ST	2ND	3RD	EARNINGS
1946	2	12	5	3	2	$ 87,830
1947	3	5	2	0	0	$110,910
TOTALS		**17**	**7**	**3**	**2**	**$198,740**

At 2 years	WON	Pimlico Nursery Stakes, National Stallion Stakes, Tremont Stakes, Pimlico Futurity
	2ND	Arlington Futurity, Commonwealth Stakes
	3RD	Futurity Stakes, Champagne Stakes
At 3 years	WON	Kentucky Derby, Jamaica Handicap
	UNP	Preakness Stakes, Withers Stakes, San Felipe Stakes

RACE DAY STATISTICS

HORSE	EQ.	WT.	PP	ST.	1/2	3/4	MILE	STR.	FIN.	JOCKEY	OWNER	ODDS TO $1
Jet Pilot		126	13	1	$1^{1\text{-}1/2}$	1^1	$1^{1\text{-}1/2}$	$1^{1\text{-}1/2}$	1^{hd}	E. Guerin	Maine Chance Farm	5.40
Phalanx	b	126	8	13	13	10^2	$5^{1\text{-}1/2}$	$5^{1/2}$	2^{hd}	E. Arcaro	C. V. Whitney	2.00
Faultless		126	3	2	$6^{2\text{-}1/2}$	$6^{1\text{-}1/2}$	$4^{1/2}$	3^{hd}	3^1	D. Dodson	Calumet Farm	6.30
On Trust	b	126	9	5	2^{hd}	2^1	3^1	2^{hd}	$4^{2\text{-}1/4}$	J. Longden	E. O. Stice & Sons	4.90
Cosmic Bomb	b	126	1	4	$3^{1/2}$	$3^{1\text{-}1/2}$	$6^{2\text{-}1/2}$	$6^{1/2}$	5^2	S. Clark	William Helis	31.90
Star Reward		126	5	3	5^1	4^{hd}	2^{hd}	4^1	6^1	S. Brooks	Dixiana	11.20
Bullet Proof		126	4	6	9^{hd}	$7^{1/2}$	7^3	7^5	7^5	W. Wright	Mrs. M. E. Whitney	13.10
W L Sickle	b	126	7	11	8^2	$8^{1/2}$	8^{hd}	$8^{1/2}$	8^{hd}	R. Campbell	W-L Ranch	(a) 16.50
Stepfather	b	126	6	9	12^1	9^1	9^3	9^2	9^6	J. Westrope	W-L Ranch	(a) 16.50
Liberty Road	b	126	12	10	10^1	11^1	11^5	10^1	$10^{1/2}$	J. Jessop	Brookmeade Stable	45.20
Riskolater	b	126	10	12	11^1	$12^{1/2}$	10^5	11^6	11^6	W. Balzaretti	Circle M Farm	15.00
Double Jay	b	126	2	7	4^3	$5^{1/2}$	12^6	12^6	12^{15}	J. Gilbert	Ridgewood Stable	47.30
Jett-Jett		126	11	8	7^{hd}	13	13	13	13	W. Hanka	W. M. Peavey	49.40

Time: :24, :49, 1:14$^{2/5}$, 1:40$^{2/5}$, 2:06$^{4/5}$. Track slow. Went to post 4:47^{1}/2. Off at 4:50^{1}/2 CDT. Start good from stall gate. Won driving; second and third the same.
Coupled: (a) W L Sickle and Stepfather.

Program #		Win	Place	Show
11	Jet Pilot	$12.80	$5.20	$4.00
8	Phalanx		$4.00	$3.00
5	Faultless			$4.60

Winner: Ch. c. by *Blenheim II–Black Wave, by *Sir Gallahad III. Trained by Tom Smith; bred in Kentucky by A. B. Hancock & Mrs. R. A. Van Clief.
$109,660 gross value and $5,000 Gold Cup. Net to winner $92,160; second $10,000; third $5,000; fourth $2,500.
Trainer awards: first $3,000; second $2,000; third $1,000. Breeder awards: first $2,000; second $1,000; third $500.
Scratched: Balheim.

135 nominations.
Equipment: b—blinkers

*Foreign bred

A Ride for Revenge

ELIZABETH GRAHAM ARDEN, COSMETICS queen, was known for being hard to work for, particularly if you were a trainer. Said one trainer proudly to another who asked him how long he had worked for Arden, "Eight and a half days!"

"Wow, a longtimer, huh?"

As hard as she was with the help, she was impeccable when it came to running her Maine Chance horse farm. She was a pro, not a neophyte. She poured a lot of money into it, and always treated the horses—whom she may well have liked more than people—extremely well. Indeed, she used to ship bottles and tubes of lotion for grooms to rub all over their horses and painted stalls frequently, even spraying the stalls with perfume—the latter operation seeming to be an uphill fight!

She regularly sent horses to the post, but in the 1947 running of the Derby she didn't seem to have a horse who could win. Phalanx, a Calumet Farm colt—and Calumet was in its prime around this time—with the great Eddie Arcaro up, was favored. She sent Jet Pilot.

But what Arcaro—indeed no one—knew was that there was one rider, on a horse named Faultless, looking for revenge against Arcaro. As it happened, the year before in the Preakness Arcaro had accidentally blocked a jockey named Doug Dodson, so he lost by a neck. He was infuriated.

For most of the race, Dodson was ahead of Arcaro, on Phalanx, and Jet Pilot, with Eric

Guerin aboard, a shade back. Dodson and Arcaro seemed to be more concerned with each other than the race. Meanwhile, Guerin kept Jet Pilot close and in position, and at the right moment let him go, passing both Phalanx and Faultless and streaking for the finish.

Arcaro went after him, but this meant getting around Dodson, who blocked him, and by the time he got free—with Faultless then in pursuit of him and both gaining on Jet Pilot—he was too late. Jet Pilot won by a neck.

Jet Pilot faded, but the legend of Elizabeth Graham Arden continued. In 1966, when she died, someone said of her: "At least she didn't go through husbands like employees. She was only married three times."

Citation
74th *May 1, 1948*

		Bull Dog	*Teddy
			Plucky Liege
	Bull Lea		Ballot
	CITATION	Rose Leaves	*Colonial
	Bay colt		Gainsborough
	*Hydroplane II	Hyperion	Selene
			Hurry On
		Toboggan	Glacier

THE WINNER'S PEDIGREE AND CAREER HIGHLIGHTS

YEAR	AGE	STS.	1ST	2ND	3RD	EARNINGS
1947	2	9	8	1	0	$ 155,680
1948	3	20	19	1	0	$ 709,470
1950	5	9	2	7	0	$ 73,480
1951	6	7	3	1	2	$ 147,130
TOTALS		**45**	**32**	**10**	**2**	**$1,085,760**

At 2 years   WON   Elementary Stakes, Belmont Futurity, Pimlico Futurity
          2ND   Washington Park Futurity
At 3 years   WON   Kentucky Derby, Derby Trial, Seminole Handicap, Everglades Handicap, Flamingo Stakes, Chesapeake Stakes, Preakness Stakes, Jersey Stakes, Belmont Stakes, Stars and Stripes Handicap
          2ND   Chesapeake Trial Stakes
At 5 years   WON   Golden Gate Handicap
          2ND   San Antonio Handicap, Santa Anita Handicap, San Juan Capistrano Handicap, Forty Niners Handicap, Golden Gate Handicap
At 6 years   WON   American Handicap, Hollywood Gold Cup
          2ND   Argonaut Handicap
          UNP   Hollywood Premier Handicap (only time in career out of money)

RACE DAY STATISTICS

HORSE	EQ.	WT.	PP	ST.	1/2	3/4	MILE	STR.	FIN.	JOCKEY	OWNER	ODDS TO $1
Citation		126	1	2	2^{hd}	2^3	2^5	1^2	$1^{3-1/2}$	E. Arcaro	Calumet Farm	(a) .40
Coaltown	b	126	2	1	1^6	$1^{3-1/2}$	$1^{1/2}$	2^4	2^3	N. Pierson	Calumet Farm	(a) .40
My Request		126	6	3	4^{hd}	4^3	$3^{1-1/2}$	3^1	$3^{1-1/2}$	D. Dodson	B. F. Whitaker	3.80
Billings		126	5	6	$5^{1/2}$	$3^{1/2}$	4^8	4^{15}	4^{20}	M. Peterson	Walmac Stable	14.70
Grandpere		126	4	4	3^2	6	6	$5^{1/2}$	5^{nk}	J. Gilbert	Mrs. J. P. Adams	17.80
Escadru	b	126	3	5	6	5^6	$5^{1-1/2}$	6	6	A. Kirkland	W. L. Brann	7.10

Time: :23²/5, :46³/5, 1:11²/5, 1:38, 2:05²/5. Track sloppy. Went to post 4:32. Off at 4:32½ CDT. Start good from stall gate. Won handily; second and third driving.
Coupled: (a) Citation and Coaltown.

Program #		Win	Place	Show
1	Citation	$2.80		

No place or show betting

Winner: B. c. by Bull Lea–*Hydroplane II, by Hyperion. Trained by B. A. Jones; bred in Kentucky by Calumet Farm.
$111,450 gross value and $5,000 Gold Cup. Net to winner $83,400; second $10,000; third $5,000; fourth $2,500.
Trainer awards: first $3,000; second $2,000; third $1,000. Breeder awards: first $2,000; second $1,000; third $500.

109 nominations.
Equipment: b—blinkers

*Foreign bred

"He Was So Fast He Scared Me"

THE SEVENTY-FOURTH RUNNING OF THE Kentucky Derby was a relatively small race, with only six horses competing. The reason was simple. Not many trainers felt they had any sort of a chance against the two speedy brothers from Calumet Farm, Coaltown and Citation. In fact, it was felt that the only chance either of them had to be beaten was by each other. Prior to the Derby, Citation as a two-year-old had built up an impressive résumé of victories, winning eight of nine races. He continued his winning ways as a three-year-old, knocking off a group of older horses on Groundhog Day in Florida on February 2, and impressing a world-class trainer, Sunny Jim Fitzsimmons, who said of him, "Up to this point Citation's done more than any horse I ever saw—and I saw Man o' War."

But stablemate Coaltown was a star in his own right, and if anyone could beat Citation, it was he. He had not unveiled his prowess as a two-year-old because of a chronic throat infection, but when he finally started to run, he was quite impressive. And just prior to the Derby Coaltown won the Blue Grass Stakes, going the mile and an eighth in 1:49 1/5.

Some of the Louisville pundits indeed saw Coaltown as the favorite. Said one to Citation's trainer Jimmy Jones, who had come up to Louisville with the horse, "What are you doin' here?" "I come over to win the Derby," Jones said. "You won't see anything," one of the reporters said, "but a big brown heinie. That's all you'll see."

As the race neared, even Hall of Famer Eddie Arcaro, who was to ride Citation, had his doubts about whether Citation could beat Coaltown, which would have N. L. Pierson aboard. Jimmy Jones's father, Ben, who had trained the horse even longer than his son, reassured him. "Jimmy," he said, "you can sleep well tonight, and you can take this as gospel: any horse Citation can see, he can catch. And he's got perfect eyesight."

The stage was set for a memorable race, and both horses would go off at 2–5.

The track, though, was not the best. It had rained torrentially during the night, and only started clearing up around dawn. By the time the race started, the track could be characterized as "sloppy." What effect it would have on the horses was not known. Despite the weather, fans were figuratively hanging from the rafters.

When the gates opened, Citation, contrary to plan, broke in the lead, but then Arcaro reined him and Coaltown took the lead—a big lead. Before too long he was six lengths ahead, with Citation second, with a slight lead over Grandpere, and two lengths back, Billings and Escadru.

Coaltown hammered through the slop, manufacturing most of his lead down the backstretch, doing five furlongs at :59 1/5. But as they whacked through the slop into the turn for home, Eddie Arcaro released Citation, and he steadily gained ground on Coaltown, the crowd going wild.

The air was pure electricity as they went stride for stride down the stretch, brother against brother, twin emblems of the glory days of a great stable, but then Citation edged ahead. And then he was gone—just gone, all alone, whacking across the wire three and a half lengths ahead of his brother.

Citation, in a sense, ran right into history. He was the Triple Crown winner, and over four years of his racing life he won thirty-two of forty-five starts, finished second ten times, and was third twice. Only in the twilight of his ca-reer did he finish out of the money. He became the first horse to earn over a million dollars.

There is only one way many horsemen could think about him, and that was in full gallop. He just never stopped. Perhaps the great Eddie Arcaro put it best. Of the thousands of horses he rode, he said, "Citation was the best. He was so fast he scared me."

Ponder
75th May 7, 1949

		Hyperion	Gainsborough
			Selene
	Pensive		Buchan
PONDER		*Penicuik II	Pennycomequick
Dark bay colt			Blandford
	Miss Rushin	*Blenheim II	Malva
			*Sir Gallahad III
		Lady Erne	*Erne

THE WINNER'S PEDIGREE AND CAREER HIGHLIGHTS

YEAR	AGE	STS.	1ST	2ND	3RD	EARNINGS
1948	2	4	0	1	0	$ 400
1949	3	21	9	5	2	$321,825
1950	4	14	5	1	2	$218,850
1951	5	1	0	0	0	-
TOTALS		**40**	**14**	**7**	**4**	**$541,075**

At 3 years WON Kentucky Derby, Peter Pan Handicap, Arlington
                 Classic, American Derby, Lawrence Realization, Jockey
                 Club Gold Cup
            2ND Derby Trial, Belmont Stakes, Whirlaway Stakes
            3RD Narragansett Special Handicap
            UNP Preakness Stakes
At 4 years WON Santa Anita Maturity, San Antonio Handicap,
                 Marchbank Handicap, Tanforan Handicap, Arlington
                 Handicap
            2ND Thanksgiving Handicap
            3RD San Pasqual Handicap, Manhattan Handicap

RACE DAY STATISTICS

HORSE	EQ.	WT.	PP	ST.	$1/2$	$3/4$	MILE	STR.	FIN.	JOCKEY	OWNER	ODDS TO $1
Ponder		126	2	14	14	12^2	6^1	3^1	1^3	S. Brooks	Calumet Farm	16.00
Capot	b	126	9	5	2^2	2^1	2^1	1^3	$2^{4-1/2}$	T. Atkinson	Greentree Stable	(a) 13.10
Palestinian	b	126	13	9	7^1	3^{hd}	3^2	$2^{1/2}$	3^2	H. Woodhouse	Isidore Bieber	8.30
Old Rockport	b	126	15	13	9^1	6^1	4^3	5^5	$4^{4-1/2}$	G. Glisson	Clifford Mooers	4.90
Halt	b	126	10	12	11^{hd}	13^{10}	9^3	7^2	$5^{1/2}$	C. McCreary	Woodvale Farm	14.20
Olympia		126	4	1	$1^{1-1/2}$	1^1	1^1	$4^{1/2}$	$6^{4-1/2}$	E. Arcaro	F. W. Hooper	.80
Model Cadet		126	6	8	8^2	$4^{1/2}$	$5^{2-1/2}$	$6^{1/2}$	$7^{1/2}$	O. Scurlock	Mrs. Ada L. Rice	66.00
Duplicator	b	126	14	11	12^3	10^1	$8^{1/2}$	8^4	8^5	B. James	Mr. & Mrs. J. H. Seley	146.30
Johns Joy	b	126	7	3	$5^{1-1/2}$	5^1	7^{hd}	9^6	9^7	J. Adams	J. A. Kinard Jr.	15.50
Ky. Colonel	b	126	3	4	10^2	11^{hd}	12^1	10^8	10^{nk}	M. Peterson	J. A. Goodwin	41.60
Lextown		126	11	6	3^{hd}	9^1	$11^{1/2}$	11^1	$11^{1-3/4}$	J. Richard	Lexbrook Stable	(f) 97.30
Jacks Town	b	126	1	2	$6^{1/2}$	8^{hd}	10^2	12^4	12^5	W. Taylor	Afton Villa Farm	90.20
Wine List	b	126	12	7	$4^{1/2}$	7^1	13^8	13	13	D. Dodson	Greentree Stable	(a) 13.10
Senecas Coin	b	126	8	10	13^1	14	14	Pulled up		J. Duff	Mrs. Albert Roth	(f) 97.30

Time: :22$^{2/5}$, :46$^{2/5}$, 1:12$^{3/5}$, 1:38$^{3/5}$, 2:04$^{1/5}$. Track fast. Went to post 4:31. Off at 4:32$^{1/2}$ CDT. Start good from stall gate. Won driving; second and third the same.
Coupled: (a) Capot and Wine List; (f) Field.

Program #		Win	Place	Show
3	Ponder	$34.00	$11.60	$6.20
1	Capot		$ 9.60	$5.80
10	Palestinian			$4.80

Winner: Dk. b. c. by Pensive–Miss Rushin, by *Blenheim II. Trained by B. A. Jones; bred in Kentucky by Calumet Farm.
$119,650 gross value and $10,000 Gold Cup. Net to winner $91,600; second $10,000; third $5,000; fourth $2,500.
Trainer awards: first $3,000; second $2,000; third $1,000. Breeder awards: first $2,000; second $1,000; third $500.

113 nominations.
Equipment: b—blinkers

*Foreign bred

"No More Chance Than a Shetland Pony"

TRAINER BEN A. JONES ALWAYS DOWN-
played the chances his horses had in big races.
With Ponder, a Calumet Farm entry, Jones was
particularly downbeat. (Newspapermen, by the
way, disregarded Jones's downplaying of his
chances.) He told newspapermen that Ponder
had no more chance of winning the Derby than
a "Shetland pony."

Racing writer Bill Corum, who was to
succeed Matt Winn as president of Churchill
Downs, heard what Jones had said and wrote
a column in which he said, "I'm going to bet
on Ponder if only because a Ben Jones–trained
entry should be held at 15 to 1 (even) if Ben
were running an old brown billy goat off a
garbage heap." Indeed, a statement from Jones's
own mouth at one point showed exactly how
he felt about all of the horses he entered in the
Kentucky Derby: "I don't want to run any horse
in the Kentucky Derby and take second money.
Isn't worth it. This is a tough horse race, one
of the toughest in the world. These horses are
only three years old and this is early in the year
at a mile and a quarter. You can ruin a good
colt running in the Derby and unless you win
it really isn't worth it. When I run a horse in
the Derby I expect to win it." This statement
seemed to be reinforced by what happened in
the Derby Trials a week before the Derby. Ponder won it—against many of the same horses he
would be running against in the Derby.

There were fourteen horses at the post, and
when the race started, a horse named Olympia,

owned by Fred Hooper, and with Eddie Arcaro
up, bolted to the front, followed by Capot and
Palestinian. But Ponder, after a late start, was
right there, and at the far turn he was sixth and
driving past horses as he came closer and closer
to the leaders.

Then, observers must have thought they
saw the true Ponder in the stretch, because he
started to slow, dropping back to fourth. But
then he got what might be called a second wind.
He started to move fast, so fast that none of the
other horses could stay with him, and he hit the
wire the winner by three lengths.

The horse paid $34 for a $2 bet, and when
Ben Jones was in the winner's circle, he seemed
surprised to be there. Then again, this was not
Jones's final race. The show, as it were, must go
on.

Middleground
76th May 6, 1950

	*St. Germans	Swynford
		Hamoaze
Bold Venture		Ultimus
MIDDLEGROUND	Possible	Lida Flush
Chestnut colt		*Chicle
	Chicaro	Wendy
Verguenza		Bubbling Over
	Blushing Sister	Lace

The Winner's Pedigree and Career Highlights

YEAR	AGE	STS.	1ST	2ND	3RD	EARNINGS
1949	2	5	4	0	1	$ 54,225
1950	3	10	2	6	1	$181,250
TOTALS		**15**	**6**	**6**	**2**	**$235,475**

At 2 years	WON	Hopeful Stakes	
	3RD	Arlington Futurity	
At 3 years	WON	Kentucky Derby, Belmont Stakes	
	2ND	Derby Trial, Wood Memorial, Withers Stakes, Preakness Stakes	
	3RD	Leonard Richards Stakes	

Race Day Statistics

HORSE	EQ.	WT.	PP	ST.	1/2	3/4	MILE	STR.	FIN.	JOCKEY	OWNER	ODDS TO $1
Middleground		126	14	7	$5^{1/2}$	$3^{1/2}$	2^1	$1^{1/2}$	$1^{1\text{-}1/4}$	W. Boland	King Ranch	(a) 7.90
Hill Prince	b	126	5	9	$8^{1\text{-}1/2}$	$6^{1/2}$	5^2	$3^{1\text{-}1/2}$	$2^{1/2}$	E. Arcaro	C. T. Chenery	2.50
Mr. Trouble		126	2	5	3^1	$1^{1/2}$	3^{hd}	2^1	$3^{2\text{-}3/4}$	D. Dodson	C. V. Whitney	(c) 6.20
Sunglow	b	126	8	3	$9^{1/2}$	$8^{1/2}$	$7^{1/2}$	$4^{1/2}$	4^5	J. Robertson	Brookmeade Stable	27.20
Oil Captial (dh)	b	126	6	1	6^3	5^1	4^1	6^1	5	K. Church	Tom Gray	8.70
Hawley (dh)	b	126	13	6	4^{hd}	4^{hd}	9^1	7^{hd}	$5^{3/4}$	G. Glisson	Clifford Mooers	82.80
Lotowhite	b	126	9	4	11^3	9^1	10^1	9^2	$7^{1\text{-}1/2}$	O. Scurlock	H. P. Headley	37.20
On The Mark	b	126	11	12	$10^{1\text{-}1/2}$	10^5	$8^{1/2}$	$8^{1/2}$	$8^{1\text{-}1/2}$	E. Guerin	King Ranch	(a) 7.90
Your Host		126	1	2	1^2	$2^{1\text{-}1/2}$	$1^{1/2}$	$5^{1/2}$	9^4	J. Longden	W. M. Goetz	1.60
Hallieboy		126	7	13	12^1	$13^{1/2}$	13^1	13^1	$10^{1\text{-}1/2}$	G. Atkins	W. T. Fugate	69.20
Dooly		126	3	8	14	12^2	$12^{1/2}$	11^{hd}	11no	S. Brooks	C. V. Whitney	(c) 6.20
Trumpet King	b	126	4	10	7^{hd}	$11^{1/2}$	11^{hd}	$10^{1/2}$	12^2	H. Woodhouse	Willorene Farm	106.40
Stranded	b	126	10	14	$13^{1/2}$	14	14	12^1	$13^{1\text{-}1/2}$	R. Baird	Abercrombie & Smith	120.90
Black George	b	126	12	11	2^3	$7^{1/2}$	6^1	14	14	E. Nelson	W. H. Veeneman	27.00

Time: :22^4/5, :46^3/5, 1:11^2/5, 1:36^4/5, 2:01^3/5. Track fast. Went to post 4:31. Off at 4:32^1/2 CDT. Start good from stall gate. Won driving; second and third the same.
Coupled: (a) Middleground and On The Mark; (c) Mr. Trouble and Dooly.
(dh) Old Capitol and Hawley dead-heated for fifth.

Program #		Win	Place	Show
1a	Middleground	$17.80	$5.40	$3.80
6	Hill Prince		$3.80	$3.20
2	Mr. Trouble			$3.60

Winner: Ch. c. by Bold Venture–Verguenza, by Chicaro. Trained by Max Hirsch; bred in Texas by King Ranch.
$120,700 gross value and $5,000 Gold Cup. Net to winner $92,650; second $10,000; third $5,000; fourth $2,500.
Trainer awards: first $3,000; second $2,000; third $1,000. Breeder awards: first $2,000; second $1,000; third $500.

134 nominations.
Equipment: b—blinkers

*Foreign bred

The Right Horse on the Right Day

AS THE 1950 DERBY APPROACHED, IT became clear to trainer Max Hirsch that Eddie Arcaro, by then a superstar jockey who was contracted to ride Hirsch's horse in the run for the roses, did not want to. He made it clear that he wanted to ride Hill Prince. Hirsch took a big gamble and allowed Arcaro to walk away from his horse, Middleground, and gave the mount to his young apprentice Billy Boland. If Boland did poorly, Hirsch was going to have, as it were, mint julep all over his face and a lot of explaining to do.

Though a gamble, it was not without calculation. The Texas-born Hirsch was one of the most astute trainers around. In 1936 his long shot Bold Venture won the Derby, and in 1946 Assault—one of the greatest horses of the century, and sired by Bold Venture—had also sired Middleground.

Fourteen horses broke from the starting gates as the bell sounded, and the favorite, Your Host, with the great Johnny Longden up, took the lead on the fast track. Billy Boland immediately steered Middleground until he was behind but close to Your Host. As the horses turned toward home, Your Host started to fade—and fade badly. But Middleground had plenty of gas in the tank.

The race was not over, though. Eddie Arcaro, who had gotten himself and Hill Prince locked behind a group of horses, took a while to move out from behind them. Then in the stretch, charging toward Middleground, gaining, he had to swerve—and consequently lose some time—to get around a tiring Your Host. The great Arcaro continued to close the gap on Middleground, but he ultimately faced one unassailable problem: there was not enough track left, and the son of Bold Venture went across the finish line first. Middleground was no flash in the Derby pan. He went on to lose the Preakness to Hill Prince with Arcaro aboard but won the Belmont Stakes.

As for Hirsch, he said he got more satisfaction out of Middleground's Derby win than any other race he was involved in—because he won it when he wasn't supposed to.

Count Turf
77th *May 5, 1951*

	Reigh Count	*Sunreigh
Count Fleet		*Contessina
COUNT TURF	*Quickly*	Haste
Bay colt		Stephanie
		*Sun Briar
Delmarie	*Pompey*	Cleopatra
		*Polymelian
Charming Note		*Alburn

THE WINNER'S PEDIGREE AND CAREER HIGHLIGHTS

YEAR	AGE	STS.	1ST	2ND	3RD	EARNINGS
1950	2	10	3	2	1	$ 22,200
1951	3	14	3	0	2	$107,350
1952	4	10	1	1	0	$ 6,300
1953	5	11	1	1	3	$ 30,525
TOTALS		**45**	**8**	**4**	**6**	**$166,375**

At 2 years	WON	Dover Stakes
	2ND	Youthful Stakes, Christiana Stakes
At 3 years	WON	Kentucky Derby
	UNP	Flamingo, Belmont Stakes, Wood Memorial, Everglades, Experimental No.1, Experimental No. 2, Palos Verdes Handicap
At 4 years	UNP	In six stakes
At 5 years	WON	Questionnaire Handicap
	3RD	Queens County Handicap, Massachusetts Handicap, Valley Forge Handicap

HORSE	EQ.	WT.	PP	ST.	1/2	3/4	MILE	STR.	FIN.	JOCKEY	OWNER	ODDS TO $1
Count Turf	b	126	9	18	11^3	$6^{1-1/2}$	4^1	$1^{2-1/2}$	1^4	C. McCreary	J. J. Amiel	(f) 14.60
Royal Mustang	b	126	16	4	4^1	$4^{1/2}$	$6^{1/2}$	5^2	2nd	P. Bailey	S. E. Wilson Jr.	(a) 53.00
Ruhe	b	126	10	12	7^{hd}	$10^{1/2}$	7^{hd}	$6^{1-1/2}$	$3^{2-1/2}$	J. Jessop	Mrs. E. Denemark	10.80
Phil D		126	18	5	1^{hd}	$1^{1/2}$	2^1	$3^{1/2}$	4^{hd}	R. York	W. C. Martin	(f) 14.60
Fanfare		126	5	1	$5^{1/2}$	$7^{1/2}$	5^2	$4^{1/2}$	$5^{3/4}$	S. Brooks	Calumet Farm	6.30
Battle Morn	b	126	11	14	18^1	15^{hd}	$10^{1/2}$	10^2	$6^{1-1/2}$	E. Arcaro	Cain Hoy Stable	2.80
Anyoldtime		126	1	2	10^{hd}	9^2	$9^{1/2}$	$8^{1/2}$	7^{nk}	R. L. Baird	W. M. Peavey	(c) 68.90
Pur Sang		126	20	8	$12^{1/2}$	$11^{1-1/2}$	$11^{1-1/2}$	$9^{1/2}$	$8^{1-1/2}$	J. Adams	Springbrook Farm	(f) 14.60
Hall of Fame	b	126	17	6	2^2	$2^{1-1/2}$	3^1	7^3	$9^{1/2}$	T. Atkinson	Greentree Stable	(b) 8.70
Timely Reward		126	3	11	$14^{1/2}$	14^{hd}	15^1	$13^{1-1/2}$	10^1	J. Stout	Mrs. Wallace Gilroy	8.60
Counterpoint		126	2	7	8^{hd}	5^{hd}	12^1	$11^{1/2}$	11^2	D. Gorman	C. V. Whitney	(x) 5.90
Repertoire	b	126	19	20	$3^{2-1/2}$	3^{hd}	1^1	2^1	12^{nk}	P. McLean	Mr. & Mrs. S. C. Mikell	8.40
King Clover	b	126	12	9	$9^{1/2}$	8^1	8^3	14^2	$13^{1/2}$	F. Bone	C. C. Boshamer	(f) 14.60
Sonic		126	6	3	$6^{1/2}$	$12^{1/2}$	$14^{1/2}$	$15^{1/2}$	$14^{1/2}$	W. Boland	King Ranch	8.30
Sir Bee Bum		126	13	15	17^6	18^4	17^2	16^3	15no	D. Madden	W. M. Peavey	(c) 68.90
Snuzzle		126	14	17	15^{hd}	17^2	13^2	17^3	16^4	G. Porch	Brown Hotel Stable	120.70
Fighting Back	b	126	8	10	13^1	$13^{1/2}$	16^1	12^{hd}	$17^{2-1/2}$	W. Johnson	Murlogg Farm	(f) 14.60
Big Stretch	b	126	15	19	$16^{1/2}$	16^{hd}	18^5	18^{15}	18^{10}	D. Dodson	Greentree Stable	(b) 8.70
Golden Birch	b	126	4	13	19^8	19^{10}	19^4	19^5	19^5	C. Swain	S. E. Wilson Jr.	(a) 53.00
Mameluke	b	126	7	16	20	20	20	20	20	R. Adair	C. V. Whitney	(x) 5.90

Time: :23²/5, :47²/5, 1:12²/5, 1:37, 2:02³/5. Track fast. Went to post 4:38. Off at 4:39¹/2 CDT. Start good from stall gate. Won driving; second and third the same.
Coupled: (a) Royal Mustang and Golden Burch; (b) Hall of Fame and Big Stretch; (c) Anyoldtime and Sir Bee Bum; (x) Counterpoint and Mameluke; (f) Field.

Program #		Win	Place	Show
14f	Count Turf	$31.20	$14.00	$ 6.60
4a	Royal Mustang	$53.00	$24.80	
9	Ruhe			$ 7.80

Winner: B. c. by Count Fleet–Delmarie, by Pompey. Trained by Sol Rutchick; bred in Kentucky by Dr. and Mrs. F. P. Miller.
$126,100 gross value and $5,000 Gold Cup. Net to winner $98,050; second $10,000; third $5,000; fourth $2,500.
Trainer awards: first $3,000; second $2,000; third $1,000. Breeder awards: first $2,000; second $1,000; third $500.

122 nominations.
Equipment: b—blinkers

*Foreign bred

A Ride for His Life

IN 1944 JOCKEY CONN MCCREARY WAS ON top of the world. He had won the Kentucky Derby on Pensive and was in great demand as a rider. But by 1951 that had all changed. As writer Peter Chew said, "Somewhere along the line, McCreary had lost his magic." Late rushes that he was famous for died in midstretch; he lost on horses that were supposed to win. Indeed, since January 1951 he had only had four winners, an abysmal record for a jockey of McCreary's caliber. And perhaps worst of all, around the track it was commonly assumed that he was washed up. Just to keep himself, his wife, and his four kids going, he had taken all kinds of jobs, including acting as training rider for various owners.

Unknown to McCreary, at the time there was a horse that was being regarded with the same lack of respect. The horse, Count Turf, was going to be entered in the Derby, but of the seventy-six sportswriters polled by the Associated Press, not a single one had picked Count Turf to win, place, or show in the Derby.

But Jack Amiel, an oversize man who owned Count Turf—who he had bought for a song a few years earlier—had observed his colt in various races, and he liked what he saw. When he saw him run in the Wood Memorial, he became convinced that he could win the Derby. "He was stopped dead in the stretch," Amiel said, "another horse come over on him. Still, he made another run." And he finished fast and strong, something he had also done in two other races. Amiel believed that with the

right jockey, Count Turf could win the Derby coming from behind. But he needed a jockey who would have the cool and the heart and the experience in coming from behind. One day he said to Sol Rutchick, his trainer, "Take me to the jock's room."

Rutchick asked, "Why?" and Amiel said, "I want Conn McCreary to ride Count Turf in the Kentucky Derby."

"Everyone," Rutchick protested, "knows he's finished."

"If you won't go," Amiel said angrily, "I'll ask McCreary myself."

When McCreary was asked, he said to Amiel. "I'm poison. You know that."

But Amiel said that he had heard that but didn't believe it, and that he would only be sending Count Turf to the post if McCreary rode him.

McCreary said yes, and the trainer, in protest, dropped out. Amiel had to get an older substitute trainer, a man named George "Slim" Sully, and he and that man trained Count Turf for the Derby.

As he sat quietly in the jockey's room on Derby day, knowing that this was a chance to reclaim his life, maybe his last chance, Mc-Creary overheard many of the jockeys lay out their strategy for the day; many of them planned to hang back until the stretch and then make a run. There were twenty horses in the field, and McCreary could see himself getting lost in a crowd. Right then, right there, he formulated a strategy: he would get in among the leaders, the first five or six horses, and then make his bid—if Count Turf still had gas in the tank—from there. Amiel had told him, in effect, do what you got to do.

The track was fast and dusty and McCreary, breaking from the 9 hole, managed to get among the leaders as they drove around the first turn. As the horses thundered past the stands, he was eighth. And as they neared the final turn into the stretch, Repertoire, Phil D, and Hall of Fame were still in contention—and so was Count Turf.

And then they turned into the stretch, and somehow it was 1944 again and Conn Mc-

Creary found what he had lost: he was riding a powerful, nimble horse, picking his way through horses as he had done on Pensive, doing it with his hands, his heart, his mouth, clucking and speaking to his horse to take him home, to bring him back . . . all the way back. And it did. It was another two minutes to glory, and the other horses couldn't catch him and he went across the finish line, the winner of the ride of his life—powered, really, by one man's belief in him—by four lengths.

Hill Gail
78th May 3, 1952

			*Teddy
		*Bull Dog	Plucky Liege
	Bull Lea		Ballot
HILL GAIL		Rose Leaves	*Colonial
Dark bay colt			Blandford
	Jane Gail	*Blenheim II	Malva
			Ladkin
		Lady Higloss	Hi Gloss

THE WINNER'S PEDIGREE AND CAREER HIGHLIGHTS

YEAR	AGE	STS.	1ST	2ND	3RD	EARNINGS
1951	2	7	4	1	0	$ 79,790
1952	3	8	5	1	1	$226,725
1953	4	8	2	1	1	$ 21,710
1954	5	9	0	2	1	$ 7,400
TOTALS		**32**	**11**	**5**	**3**	**$335,625**

At 2 years	WON	Arlington Futurity
	2ND	Washington Park Futurity
At 3 years	WON	Kentucky Derby, Derby Trial, San Vicente Stakes,
		Santa Anita Derby, Phoenix Handicap
	3RD	San Gabriel Stakes
At 4 years	3RD	Equipoise Mile
At 5 years	2ND	San Carlos Handicap
	3RD	Palm Springs Handicap

RACE DAY STATISTICS

HORSE	EQ.	WT.	PP	ST.	1/2	3/4	MILE	STR.	FIN.	JOCKEY	OWNER	ODDS TO $1
Hill Gail		126	1	1	$2^{1/2}$	$1^{1/2}$	1^5	1^3	1^2	E. Arcaro	Calumet Farm	1.10
Sub Fleet		126	9	8	$6^{1/2}$	$5^{1/2}$	$3^{1/2}$	2^6	$2^{8-3/4}$	S. Brooks	Dixiana	22.90
Blue Man		126	14	16	13^2	$12^{1/2}$	6^1	6^2	$3^{1/2}$	C. McCreary	White Oak Stable	4.40
Master Fiddle	b	126	13	14	$10^{1/2}$	$9^{1/2}$	5^2	$4^{1/2}$	$4^{1-1/4}$	D. Gorman	Myhelyn Stable	(c) 9.30
Count Flame	b	126	4	10	14^4	14^3	13^1	8^3	$5^{1/2}$	W. Shoemaker	J. J. Amiel	(c) 9.30
Arroz		126	16	13	11^{hd}	10^{hd}	10^2	7^3	$6^{1-1/4}$	R. York	Mrs. G. Guiberson	31.70
Happy Go Lucky	b	126	12	7	$3^{1/2}$	3^{hd}	4^2	3^{hd}	$7^{2-1/2}$	A. Ferraiuolo	H. G. Bockman	54.60
Hannibal	b	126	15	3	1^2	2^3	$2^{1-1/2}$	$5^{1/2}$	8^3	W. Passmore	Bayard Sharp	76.80
Cold Command		126	11	6	15^2	16	11^2	$11^{1/2}$	$9^{3/4}$	G. Porch	C. V. Whitney	8.50
Smoke Screen		126	10	15	16	15^1	12^2	12^4	10^{nk}	J. Adams	Reverie Knoll Farm	103.70
Gushing Oil	b	126	7	11	$12^{1/2}$	13^2	$8^{1/2}$	$9^{1/2}$	11^{nk}	T. Atkinson	S. E. Wilson Jr.	6.70
Pintor		126	6	9	$8^{1/2}$	7^2	7^1	10^1	$12^{4-1/4}$	H. Mora	Montpelier Stable	42.50
Shag Tails	b	126	5	4	4^3	4^2	$9^{1/2}$	13^3	13^2	J. Nazareth	Milton Shagrin	(f) 18.80
Eternal Moon	b	126	8	12	9^6	$11^{1/2}$	14^5	14^3	$14^{1-1/2}$	J. Layton	Emerald Hill	(f) 18.80
Brown Rambler	b	126	3	2	5^2	6^3	16	15^{10}	15^{18}	D. Dodson	Mildred F. Underwood	(f) 18.80
Swoop		126	2	5	7^2	$8^{1/2}$	15^2	16	16	K. Church	High Tide Stable	(f) 18.80

Time: :23³/5, :46⁴/5, 1:11, 1:35²/5, 2:01³/5. Track fast. In gate 4:37 CDT. Off at 4:38 CDT. Start good from stall gate. Won ridden out; second and third driving.
Coupled: (c) Master Fiddle and Count Flame; (f) Field.

Program #		Win	Place	Show
1	Hill Gail	$4.20	$ 4.00	$3.20
5	Sub Fleet		$14.60	$7.80
9	Blue Man			$3.60

Winner: Dk. b. c. by Bull Lea–Jane Gail, by *Blenheim II. Trained by B. A. Jones; bred in Kentucky by Calumet Farm.
$124,350 gross value and $10,000 Gold Cup. Net to winner $96,300; second $10,000; third $5,000; fourth $2,500.
Trainer awards: first $3,000; second $1,000; third $500. Breeder awards: first $2,000; second $1,000; third $500.

167 nominations.
Equipment: b—blinkers

*Foreign bred

"Son of a Well-Authenticated Bitch"

JUST AS A HORSE CAN INHERIT THE RACing abilities of his sire and dam, he (or she) can inherit their personalities. So it was that Calumet Farm's Hill Gail, a contender in the seventy-eighth run for the roses, inherited a crazy, obstinate streak from Blenheim II, the sire of his dam, Jane Gail, herself described by trainer Jimmy Jones, son of the great Ben A. Jones and a great trainer in his own right, as a "well-authenticated bitch."

The day of the race, Hill Gail, a dark bay colt, was doing what came naturally—or unnaturally—acting up in the paddock. Ben Jones, sophisticated trainer that he was, asked his groom to straighten the horse's head—and then punched him in the nose, an act that had the desired effect: he stopped acting up.

Still, the horse was unpredictable—as he was to demonstrate during the race. Fortunately, though, the great Eddie Arcaro was on his back when he did. The weather was good and the track fast, and when the gates clanged open, sixteen horses made for the turn like they always do—possessed. Hill Gail, the favorite in the race, though, swerved, crowded Swoop and Brown Rambler, and was able to bust out into the lead, only Hannibal trying to stay with him.

At the five-eighths pole, Hill Gail took command of the race, and all was going well. Then, as he pounded into the backstretch, Eddie Arcaro sensed that Hill Gail was starting to drift, and the feeling continued along the backstretch

and then got strong: Hill Gail, he thought, was going to forget the race, cut off the track, and make a beeline for the stable area—he had done that before.

Arcaro made an instant decision. He cracked the horse with his whip, which refocused him, and he spurted ahead to take a six-length lead.

But though the race was over for most of the horses, and Hill Gail was clearly on his way to winning, it was not over for a horse called Sub Fleet. He came on like gangbusters, driving, but Hill Gail had enough to make it to the wire first.

His time was 2:01 3/5, just 1/5 of a second off the record eleven years earlier of his crazy uncle, a horse named Whirlaway.

Dark Star
79th *May 2, 1953*

Brown colt

		Dastur
	Dhoti	Tricky Aunt
*Royal Gem II		Beau Fils
DARK STAR	French Gem	Fission
		*Teddy
Isolde	*Bull Dog	Plucky Liege
		Bostonian
	Fiji	O Girl

The Winner's Pedigree and Career Highlights

YEAR	AGE	STS.	1ST	2ND	3RD	EARNINGS
1952	2	6	3	0	2	$ 24,087
1953	3	7	3	2	0	$ 107,250
TOTALS		**13**	**6**	**2**	**2**	**$ 131,337**

At 2 years	WON	Hialeah Juvenile Stakes
	3RD	Belmont Juvenile Stakes, Belmont Futurity
	UNP	Champagne Stakes
At 3 years	WON	Kentucky Derby, Derby Trial Stakes
	UNP	Preakness Stakes, Florida Derby

Race Day Statistics

HORSE	EQ	WT.	PP	ST.	1/2	3/4	MILE	STR.	FIN.	JOCKEY	OWNER	ODDS TO $1
Dark Star		126	10	3	1$^{1\text{-}1/2}$	1$^{1/2}$	1$^{1\text{-}1/2}$	1$^{1\text{-}1/2}$	1^{hd}	H. Moreno	Cain Hoy Stable	24.90
Native Dancer		126	6	6	8^3	4$^{1/2}$	4^2	2^1	2^5	E. Guerin	A. G. Vanderbilt	(a) .70
Invigorator		126	4	5	7$^{1/2}$	6$^{1/2}$	6^1	4^1	3^2	W. Shoemaker	Saxon Stable	40.90
Royal Bay Gem		126	11	11	11	8^2	7$^{1\text{-}1/2}$	7$^{1\text{-}1/2}$	4$^{1\text{-}1/2}$	J. Combest	E. Constantin Jr.	6.80
Correspondent		126	2	2	2^2	2^1	2$^{1/2}$	3^1	5$^{1\text{-}3/4}$	E. Arcaro	Mrs. G. Guiberson	3.00
Straight Face	b	126	9	7	4^3	3^1	3$^{1/2}$	5^{hd}	6^{nk}	T. Atkinson	Greentree Stable	10.40
Social Outcast		126	8	10	10$^{1/2}$	10$^{1\text{-}1/2}$	8^2	8^2	7^2	J. Adams	A. G. Vanderbilt	(a) .70
Money Broker	b	126	7	9	5$^{1/2}$	5$^{1/2}$	5^{hd}	6^3	8$^{2\text{-}3/4}$	A. Popara	G. & G. Stable	45.80
Ram O' War	b	126	3	8	9$^{1/2}$	11	10^1	9^1	9^{nk}	D. Dodson	B. S. Campbell	85.10
Curragh King	b	126	5	4	6^2	9^1	11	11	10^{hd}	D. Erb	E. M. Goemans	99.10
Ace Destroyer	b	126	1	1	3$^{1/2}$	7^2	9^3	10^1	11	J. Jessop	Mr. & Mrs. T. M. Daniel	91.80

Time: :23$^{4/5}$, :47$^{4/5}$, 1:12$^{1/5}$, 1:36$^{3/5}$, 2:02. Track fast. Reached post at 4:42. Off at 4:32$^{1/2}$. Start good from stall gate. Won driving; second and third the same.
Coupled: (a) Native Dancer and Social Outcast.

Program #		Win	Place	Show
10	Dark Star	$51.80	$13.60	$7.00
1	Native Dancer		$ 3.20	$2.80
5	Invigorator			$9.40

Winner: Br. c. by *Royal Gem II–Isolde, by *Bull Dog. Trained by Eddie Hayward; bred in Kentucky by W. L. Jones Jr.
$118,100—gross value and $5,000 Gold Cup. Net to winner $90,050; second $10,000; third $5,000; fourth $2,500.
Trainer awards: first $3,000; second $2,000; third $1,000. Breeder awards: first $2,000; second $1,000; third $500.
Scratched: Spy Defense.

137 nominations.
Equipment: b—blinkers

*Foreign bred

In the Bag

THE WINNER OF THE SEVENTY-NINTH KENtucky Derby was Native Dancer. The only thing that had to be done was for the race to occur to confirm it.

There was no question that Native Dancer, a light gray locomotive of a horse with the nickname "Gray Ghost"—probably because he would get ahead in a race and disappear from view—would win. As a two-year-old he had won every race he had entered, and experts characterized him as not just one of the best horses of 1953, but one of the best racehorses ever.

And the world knew about him. In the early 1950s, television was making its presence known in America's living rooms, and stations were more than happy to tell the world about this wondrous horse. He became famous.

But the problem with the Derby is that it's always unpredictable, and no one told a brown colt named Dark Star how it was impossible to win.

When the race started, H. Moreno, Dark Star's jockey, immediately took the colt to the front. Native Dancer, with Eric Guerin aboard, was roughed up on the first turn by Money Broker, which probably cost him dearly—some experts say he would have won if he wasn't roughed up—and was eased back to secure racing room, but at the stretch he made a run for Dark Star and gained with every stride. Moreno, in a panic as Native Dancer closed, went to the whip, but it could not stop the inexorable drive of the Gray Ghost. He gained and gained and gained, and when they crossed the finish line Native Dancer's nose was even with Dark Star's cheek, and he was gaining. Time was 2:02, and, of course, Dark Star won.

Dark Star was a great horse, but many people do think he got lucky that day when Native Dancer was roughed up in the beginning. From that Derby on, Native Dancer was in twenty-two races, and he won twenty-one. In fact, the only time he ever lost was in the Kentucky Derby.

Determine
80th *May 1, 1954*

		Hyperion	Gainsborough
	*Alibhai		Selene
DETERMINE		Tersina	Tracery
Gray colt			Blue Tie
	Koubis	*Mahmoud	*Blenheim II
			Mah Mahal
		Brown Biscuit	Sir Andrew
			Swing On

THE WINNER'S PEDIGREE AND CAREER HIGHLIGHTS

YEAR	AGE	STS.	1ST	2ND	3RD	EARNINGS
1953	2	14	4	1	5	$ 26,435
1954	3	15	10	3	2	$328,700
1955	4	15	4	3	2	$218,360
TOTALS		**44**	**18**	**7**	**9**	**$573,495**

At 2 years	WON	San Francisco Handicap, Robert O'Brien Handicap
	3RD	Salinas Handicap
At 3 years	WON	Kentucky Derby, San Gabriel Stakes, San Felipe Handicap, Santa Anita Derby, San Jose Handicap, Peter Clark Handicap, Bay Meadows Derby, Oakland Handicap, Golden Gate Handicap, Debonaire Stakes
	2ND	Derby Trial, San Vicente Stakes, Californian Stakes
	3RD	Westerner Stakes
At 4 years	WON	Inglewood Handicap, Golden Gate Mile, Malibu Sequet Stakes, Santa Anita Maturity (through disqualification)
	2ND	Californian Stakes, Golden Gate Handicap, San Juan Capistrano Handicap
	3RD	Hollywood Gold Cup

HORSE	EQ.	WT.	PP	ST.	1/2	3/4	MILE	STR.	FIN.	JOCKEY	OWNER	ODDS TO $1
Determine	b	126	7	5	3^3	$3^{1/2}$	$2^{1/2}$	$1^{1/2}$	$1^{1-1/2}$	R. York	A. J. Crevolin	(c) 4.30
Hasty Road	b	126	1	1	$1^{1-1/2}$	1^2	1^2	$2^{2-1/2}$	$2^{2-1/2}$	J. Adams	Hasty House Farm	(a) 5.30
Hasseyampa	b	126	12	12	$12^{1-1/2}$	8^3	$5^{1/2}$	3^{hd}	$3^{2-1/2}$	A. Kirkland	Walmac Farm	25.60
Goyamo	b	126	5	16	16^6	15^1	$10^{1-1/2}$	$6^{1/2}$	4^{nk}	E. Arcaro	Woodvale Farm	4.90
Admiral Porter	b	126	8	3	$4^{1-1/2}$	$4^{1-1/2}$	4^{hd}	4^2	5^1	P. Bailey	Sunny Blue Farm	54.10
Correlation	b	126	4	15	$15^{1-1/2}$	16^{10}	9^1	5^1	$6^{3-1/4}$	W. Shoemaker	R. S. Lytle	3.00
Fisherman		126	16	7	6^1	$6^{1/2}$	$6^{1/2}$	7^2	$7^{2-1/2}$	H. Woodhouse	C. V. Whitney	6.30
James Session		126	10	8	8^{hd}	$13^{1/2}$	13^1	13^1	8no	L. Risley	Mr. & Mrs. Harry James	71.10
Allied	b	126	3	10	10^1	7^{hd}	$8^{1/}$	9^1	9^{hd}	S. Brooks	A. J. Crevolin	(c) 4.30
Gov. Browning	b	126	2	14	14^6	14^2	$11^{1/2}$	$10^{1/2}$	10^1	D. Erb	Martin-McKinney	(f) 16.20
Super Devil		126	9	11	$11^{1/2}$	9^1	$12^{1/2}$	11^{hd}	11^{nk}	R. Baird	Rebel Stable	(f) 16.20
Red Hannigan	b	126	13	13	13^2	12^2	$14^{1-1/2}$	14^3	12^{nk}	W. Boland	Woodley Lane Farm	(f) 16.20
Black Metal	b	126	15	6	$5^{1/2}$	5^{hd}	$7^{1-1/2}$	12^{hd}	13^2	A. DeSpirito	Maine Chance Farm	13.20
Timely Tip		126	14	2	2^3	2^3	3^1	8^2	$14^{2-1/2}$	H. Craig	A. L. Birch	53.70
Sea O Erin	b	126	6	4	7^3	$11^{1/2}$	$15^{1-1/2}$	$15^{1/2}$	15^3	C. McCreary	Hasty House Farm	(a) 5.30
King Phalanx		126	11	17	17	17	$16^{1/2}$	$16^{1/2}$	16^1	D. Dodson	S. E. Wilson Jr.	32.30
Mel Leavitt	b	126	17	9	9^1	10^2	17	17	17	R. McLaughlin	J. W. Brown	(f) 16.20

Time: :$23^{3/5}$, :$47^{3/5}$, 1:12, 1:37, 2:03. Track fast. In gate 4:34 CDT. Off at 4:35 CDT. Start Good. Won driving; second and third the same.
Coupled: (a) Hasty Road and Sea O Erin; (c) Determine and Allied; (f) Field.

Program #		Win	Place	Show
2c	Determine	$10.60	$5.60	$ 4.80
1	Hasty Road		$6.80	$ 5.60
8	Hasseyampa			$12.00

Winner: Gr. c. by *Alibhai–Koubis, by *Mahmoud. Trained by Willie Molter; bred in Kentucky by Dr. Eslie Asbury.
$124,100 gross value and $5,000 Gold Cup. Net to winner $102,050; second $10,000; third $5,000; fourth $2,500.

137 nominations.
Equipment: b—blinkers

*Foreign bred

Carrying His Own Bag

WHEN EDDIE ARCARO CAME OUT OF THE jockeys' room showered and dressed and with a suitcase in his hand following the 1954 running of the Kentucky Derby, he stopped when a fan approached for an autograph. He put down the bag and said with a chuckle, "Ah, this fickle world. Whenever I've won the Derby, there have always been four or five guys trying to carry my bag for me. I lose and I carry it myself."

The man who would have had his bag carried that day was twenty-two-year-old jockey Ray York, who piloted a small—the smallest colt in the race at fifteen hands, and weighing only 845 pounds, as opposed to heaviest colt in the race, Hasty Road, who weighed 1,140—tough gray colt named Determine to victory.

Not many trainers believed in him. But one did. Drawled Missouri-born Ben Jones, who had trained six Derby winners: "I've seen that little gray before. It won't hurt him none."

But as he left the gate, he got in a jam and, as one observer put it, was knocked almost bow-legged. Hasty Road, running from the number 1 post position, had blasted out so he couldn't get trapped by a herd of horses, and the number 14 position horse, Timely Tip, veered toward the inside, forming a funnel that drove another horse, James Session, owned by bandleader Harry James and his wife, World War II pinup Betty Grable, into Determine.

But, as Jones had said, he was a tough little horse. He didn't go down, and York, riding like a clone of Eddie Arcaro, who was on Goyamo,

pulled back on the reins, slowing the little horse so he was able to avoid disaster. Then he steered him around other horses into an opening and strode along, waiting.

Hasty Road, who had of course beaten Determine in the Derby trial, took over the lead just as he had in the trial. The race was being run just as it had in the trial, only this time it was different. Instead of waiting for a long time, York made his move at the top of the stretch, and this time Hasty Road could not hold him off. He not only won, but won going away.

Sometime after the race York provided some levity when he was asked if he had placed a bet on Determine. York's face screwed up: "Do you think I'm crazy? I have more sense than to waste my money on horse races."

Swaps
81st May 7, 1955

			Gainsborough
	Hyperion	Selene
Khaled		Ethnarch
SWAPS	*Éclair*	Black Ray
Chestnut colt		Son-in-Law
Iron Reward	*Beau Pere*	Cinna
		War Admiral
	Iron Maiden	Betty Derr

THE WINNER'S PEDIGREE AND CAREER HIGHLIGHTS

YEAR	AGE	STS.	1ST	2ND	3RD	EARNINGS
1954	2	6	3	0	2	$ 20,950
1955	3	9	8	1	0	$418,550
1956	4	10	8	1	0	$409,400
TOTALS		**25**	**19**	**2**	**2**	**$848,900**

At 2 years	WON	June Juvenile Stakes
	3RD	Westchester Stakes, Haggin Stakes
At 3 years	WON	Kentucky Derby, San Vicente Stakes, Santa Anita Derby, Will Rogers Stakes, Californian Stakes, Westerner Stakes, American Derby
	2ND	Match race with Nashua
At 4 years	WON	Argonaut, American, Inglewood, Hollywood Gold Cup, Sunset, Washington Handicap
	2ND	Californian Stakes

RACE DAY STATISTICS

HORSE	EQ.	WT.	PP	ST.	1/2	3/4	MILE	STR.	FIN.	JOCKEY	OWNER	ODDS TO $1
Swaps		126	8	4	1^1	1^1	$1^{1/2}$	$1^{1/2}$	$1^{1\text{-}1/2}$	W. Shoemaker	R. C. Ellsworth	2.80
Nashua		126	5	1	3^1	3^1	2^1	2^4	$2^{6\text{-}1/2}$	E. Arcaro	Belair Stud	1.30
Summer Tan	b	126	10	6	4^6	4^5	3^4	3^2	3^4	E. Guerin	Mrs. J. W. Galbreath	4.90
Racing Fool		126	7	5	5^1	5^1	5^1	4^3	$4^{1/2}$	H. Moreno	Cain Hoy Stable	(a) 5.70
Jean's Joe	b	126	9	9	10	8^3	$6^{1/2}$	5^2	$5^{1\text{-}1/2}$	S. Brooks	Murcain Stable	16.20
Flying Fury		126	2	10	8^3	9^1	9^2	$6^{1/2}$	$6^{3/4}$	C. McCreary	Cain Hoy Stable	(a) 5.70
Honeys Alibi		126	4	2	6^3	6^3	7^1	$7^{1\text{-}1/2}$	$7^{3\text{-}1/2}$	W. Harmatz	W.-L. Ranch Co.	55.60
Blue Lem	b	126	1	7	$9^{1/2}$	10	10	9^4	$8^{1\text{-}1/2}$	C. Rogers	H. C. Fruehauf	23.30
Nabesna	b	126	3	8	7^3	$7^{1\text{-}1/2}$	8^1	8^1	9^{10}	J. Adams	Clifford Mooers	52.80
Trim Destiny		126	6	3	$2^{2\text{-}1/2}$	2^{hd}	4^{hd}	10	10	L. C. Cook	G. R. White	50.90

Time: :23$^{3/5}$, :47$^{2/5}$, 1:12$^{2/5}$, 1:37, 2:01$^{4/5}$. Track fast. In gate 4:31 CDT. Off at 4:31$^{1/2}$ CDT. Start good. Won driving; second and third the same.
Coupled: (a) Racing Fool and Flying Fury.

Program #		Win	Place	Show
7	Swaps	$7.60	$3.40	$2.60
5	Nashua		$3.00	$2.40
9	Summer Tan			$3.00

Winner: C.h. c. by *Khaled–Iron Reward, by *Beau Pere. Trained by M. A. Tenney; bred in California by R. C. Ellsworth.
$152,500 gross value and $5,000 Gold Cup. Net to winner $108,400; second $25,000; third $12,500; fourth $5,000.

125 nominations.
Equipment: b—blinkers

*Foreign bred

Fate Intersected

AS DERBY DAY APPROACHED, WILLIE SHOE-maker figured he had it made. In April he was winning races at Golden Gate Fields in San Francisco, and when that first Saturday in May came to pass, he would be astride a very good horse, Swaps—and he would win.

Then, at an ordinary race at Golden Gate, he hurt himself, and at the hospital, he and his agent, Harry Wilbert, got the terrible news from the doctor: "Mr. Wilbert, this young man will be in no condition to ride for at least three, maybe four weeks." The Derby would have passed.

But maybe, just maybe, Wilbert told Shoe-maker, you can be fixed up enough so you can at least try to ride. Shoemaker was all for that, but then another call came to Wilbert, and this was a dagger in the heart. Swaps's owners wanted Willie to ride in the Derby tune-up in Louisville, the Jefferson Purse, in a few days.

So how do you get from California to Louis-ville, repair your leg in a few days, and ride?

No one knew. Wilbert said, "We got to go. Mesh [Swaps's trainer] isn't going to like having another boy on the horse one day and another on him for the Derby." So they decided to go, even though, in a way, they didn't know where they were headed. In the dead of night, in a scene straight out of a Hollywood movie, Wilbert picked up his 110-pound jockey—he couldn't walk well—out of his hospital bed, carried him into a waiting car, and then to the airport, where Shoemaker was hoisted into a propeller-driven plane that took off and landed in Louisville a torturous ten hours later.

One look at Shoemaker's knee showed the effect of the trip: it looked like a Virginia ham, having swollen to three times its normal size.

Maybe, Wilbert thought, a whirlpool would help. They found a health club, went there, and immersed Willie's pain-racked swollen knee into warming, swirling waters.

It didn't help at all.

But when Willie got out of the whirlpool, a man who had gone there for a rubdown identi-fied himself to Willie and Wilbert as the trainer for the University of Louisville football team. If Willie wanted to try, maybe he could help him by letting him use the university's equipment.

Willie and Wilbert wanted to try. Willie got into the university whirlpool, which was more sophisticated than the health club's apparatus, hoping against hope it would work. And while he was in it, a young man introduced himself to Shoemaker. He was tall and wiry with crew-cut blond hair, and said he was a quarterback at the University of Louisville. His name, he said, was Johnny Unitas—arguably the greatest quarterback who ever lived. Later, Willie would see it as a good luck omen.

The treatment lowered the swelling in Shoe-maker's leg, and when the Jefferson Purse was run, Willie Shoemaker was on the back of Swaps, who blasted to a nine-length victory.

And a few days later the kid who was sup-posed not to be able to ride for three weeks or a month was on Swaps when the Derby gates opened, and he took the lead early. When he turned for home he was still leading slightly, but the great Nashua, with Eddie Arcaro aboard, was driving at him, and Shoemaker said he "clucked to Swaps and whacked him with the whip and the afterburners came on." He won by a length and a half going away.

Needles
82nd *May 5, 1956*

			Hyperion
		Pensive	*Penicuik II
	Ponder		*Blenheim
NEEDLES		Miss Rushin	Lady Erne
Bay colt			John P. Grier
	Noodle Soup	Jack High	Priscilla
			Supremus
		Supromene	*Melpomene

THE WINNER'S PEDIGREE AND CAREER HIGHLIGHTS

YEAR	AGE	STS.	1ST	2ND	3RD	EARNINGS
1955	2	10	6	0	2	$129,805
1956	3	8	4	2	0	$440,850
1957	4	3	1	1	1	$ 29,700
TOTALS		**21**	**11**	**3**	**3**	**$600,355**

At 2 years	WON	Sapling Stakes, Hopeful Stakes
	3RD	World's Playground Stakes, Garden State
At 3 years	WON	Kentucky Derby, Flamingo Stakes, Florida Derby, Belmont Stakes
	2ND	Preakness Stakes
At 4 years	WON	Fort Lauderdale Handicap
	2ND	Iron Mask Handicap
	3RD	Gulfstream Park Handicap

RACE DAY STATISTICS

HORSE	EQ.	WT.	PP	ST.	1/2	3/4	MILE	STR.	FIN.	JOCKEY	OWNER	ODDS TO $1
Needles		126	1	12	16^3	16^6	$7^{1/2}$	$2^{1/2}$	$1^{3/4}$	D. Erb	D & H Stable	1.60
Fabius	b	126	12	2	3^2	$2^{1-1/2}$	$1^{1/2}$	1^{hd}	$2^{1-1/2}$	W. Hartack	Calumet Farm	(c) 4.00
Come on Red		126	10	14	14^1	10^1	$4^{1/2}$	$3^{1-1/2}$	$3^{3/4}$	A. Popara	Helen W. Kellogg	(f) 29.00
Count Chic	b	126	5	15	11^2	12^2	9^3	$4^{1/2}$	$4^{1/2}$	S. Brooks	Mr. & Mrs. D. Lozzi	8.00
Pintor Lea	b	126	3	11	$12^{1/2}$	$11^{1/2}$	$6^{1-1/2}$	5^1	$5^{1-1/2}$	R. Baird	Calumet Farm	(c) 4.00
Career Boy	b	126	2	13	15^3	$13^{1/2}$	10^2	$8^{1-1/2}$	$6^{2-1/2}$	E. Guerin	C. V. Whitney	(a) 4.90
No Regrets	b	126	7	6	5^1	4^{hd}	2^{hd}	$7^{1/2}$	$7^{1-1/4}$	D. Dodson	W. E. Britt	52.80
Head Man	b	126	4	4	4^{hd}	3^{hd}	5^1	6^1	$8^{3/4}$	E. Arcaro	C. V. Whitney	(a) 4.90
King O'Swords	b	126	16	9	$7^{1/2}$	6^1	8^1	9^1	9^1	R. Borgemenke	Reverie Knoll Farm	(f) 29.00
High King		126	6	17	17	17	17	12^4	10^{nk}	W. Cook	Joseph Gavegnano	79.50
Jean Baptiste	b	126	14	16	$13^{1-1/2}$	$15^{1/2}$	$12^{1/2}$	$11^{1/2}$	11no	J. Nichols	Mrs. L. P. Tate	(f) 29.00
Terrang	b	126	11	1	$2^{2-1/2}$	$1^{1/2}$	3^1	10^2	12^5	W. Shoemaker	Rex C. Ellsworth	8.30
Black Emperor	b	126	13	10	10^2	14^2	11^3	13^3	13^5	J. Adams	Hasty House Farm	26.40
Besomer	b	126	9	8	$8^{1-1/2}$	$8^{1-1/2}$	14^{hd}	14^2	$14^{1-1/2}$	N. Shuk	Companas Stable	71.20
Invalidate	b	126	15	3	6^2	7^1	16^3	15^4	15^2	L. Gilligan	T. A. Grissom	(f) 29.00
Ben A. Jones	b	126	8	5	1^{hd}	5^3	13^2	17	16^1	P. Bailey	G & M Stable	53.80
Countermand	b	126	17	7	9^4	9^{hd}	$15^{1/2}$	16^2	17	A. Kirkland	Brandywine Stable	12.00

Time: :23⁴/₅, :47¹/₅, 1:11³/₅, 1:36⁴/₅, 2:03²/₅. Track fast. In gate 4:33 CDT. Off at 4:33¹/₂ CDT. Start good. Won driving; second and third the same.
Coupled: (a) Career Boy and Head Man; (c) Fabius and Pintor Lea; (f) Field.

Program #		Win	Place	Show
3	Needles	$5.20	$3.60	$3.40
2c	Fabius		$3.80	$3.60
12f	Come on Red			$6.60

Winner: B. c. by Ponder–Noodle Soup, by Jack High. Trained by H. L. Fontaine; bred in Florida by W. E. Leach.
$167,550 gross value and $5,000 Gold Cup. Net to winner $123,450; second $25,000; third $12,500; fourth $5,000.

169 nominations.
Equipment: b—blinkers

*Foreign bred

"Beware of Needles!"

THE WINNER OF THE 1956 DERBY, THE FIRST Florida-bred colt ever to win the race, had a name that, unfortunately, had been given to describe the many treatments that vets had given him to cure a wide variety of ailments he suffered as a foal: Needles.

As it turned out, Needles, who was the son of Ponder, the 1949 Derby winner, grew up to be strong and healthy—those needles worked—and he was fast, very fast. As a two-year-old he won the Sapling Stakes as well as the Hopeful Stakes.

There was a major question on how he would perform in the Derby. For one thing, he had not run in a major stakes race for six weeks prior to the Derby, or even had a good workout.

There was also the question of his style of running. The bridle, as it were, doesn't fall far from the tree. Like his father, Ponder (his mother's glorious name was Noodle Soup), he loved to come from behind—way behind. To com-plicate the life of the horse, trainer, jockey, and owners, Needles drew post position 1, right on the rail. This might be fine for most horses, but not desirable for a stretch runner, who would have a more difficult time working his way into position to make that run. Hugh Fontaine, Needles's trainer, could only joke about it. "I love it," he said, "I might as well love it because it's the only one I'm going to get."

When the race started, concerns that Needles might get too far behind to win seemed to come true. He was an astonishing twenty-seven lengths behind, with three-quarters of the race gone. He then started to move quicker, but as he turned into the top of the stretch, he was still fifteen lengths behind.

Not to worry. Said his jockey, Dave Erb, "When I asked him for it he just went 'boom.' We found an opening about the three-eighths pole, went outside, and then in." Threading his way, as it were, in and around other horses, Needles eventually wore Fabius down and won.

Iron Liege
83rd *May 4, 1957*

			*Teddy
		*Bull Dog	Plucky Liege
	Bull Lea		Ballot
IRON LIEGE		Rose Leaves	*Colonial
Bay colt			Man o' War
	Iron Maiden	War Admiral	Brushup
			*Sir Gallahad III
		Betty Derr	Uncle's Lassie

THE WINNER'S PEDIGREE AND CAREER HIGHLIGHTS

YEAR	AGE	STS.	1ST	2ND	3RD	EARNINGS
1956	2	8	2	1	1	$ 10,705
1957	3	17	8	5	3	$310,625
1958	4	8	1	3	1	$ 80,839
TOTALS		**33**	**11**	**9**	**5**	**$402,169**

At 2 years	UNP	Belmont Futurity, Garden State
At 3 years	WON	Kentucky Derby, Jersey Stakes, Laurance Armour Memorial Stakes, Sheridan Handicap
	2ND	Fountain of Youth, Preakness, Arlington Classic, Clang Handicap, American Derby
	3RD	Everglades, Flamingo, Florida Derby
	UNP	Derby Trial
At 4 years	WON	McLennan Handicap
	2ND	Widener Handicap, Royal Palm Handicap, Royal Poinciana Handicap
	3RD	Camden Handicap

RACE DAY STATISTICS

HORSE	EQ.	WT.	PP	1/4	1/2	3/4	MILE	STR.	FIN.	JOCKEY	OWNER	ODDS TO $1
Iron Liege		126	6	4	3^3	$2^{1-1/2}$	$2^{1-1/2}$	$1^{1/2}$	1no	W. Hartack	Calumet Farm	8.40
*Gallant Man		126	4	6	7^2	7^1	$5^{1/2}$	$3^{1/2}$	$2^{2-3/4}$	W. Shoemaker	Ralph Lowe	3.70
Round Table	b	126	3	5	4^3	4^3	4^2	4^{hd}	3^3	R. Neves	Kerr Stable	3.60
Bold Ruler		126	7	3	2^{hd}	$3^{1-1/2}$	$3^{1/2}$	5^3	$4^{1-1/4}$	E. Arcaro	Wheatley Stable	1.20
Federal Hill	b	126	2	1	$1^{1-1/2}$	$1^{1/2}$	1^{hd}	2^{hd}	$5^{3/4}$	W. Carstens	Clifford Lussky	7.90
Indian Creek	b	126	5	7	$6^{2-1/2}$	$6^{1/2}$	7^3	7^3	6^1	G. Taniguchi	Mrs. A. L. Rice	73.10
Mister Jive	b	126	1	2	5^3	$5^{2-1/2}$	$6^{1/2}$	$6^{1/2}$	$7^{3-1/2}$	H. Woodhouse	J. L. Applebaum	55.90
Better Bee		126	9	9	9	9	8^3	8^6	8^{10}	J. Adams	W. S. Miller	42.40
Shan Pac	b	126	8	8	$8^{1/2}$	$8^{1/2}$	9	9	9	J. R. Adams	T. A. Grissom	46.50

Time: :23$^{3/5}$, :47, 1:11$^{2/5}$, 1:36$^{4/5}$, 2:02$^{1/5}$. Track fast. In gate 4:32 CDT. Off at 4:32 CDT. Start good. Won driving; second and third the same.

Program #		Win	Place	Show
1a	Iron Liege	$18.80	$9.40	$6.20
5	*Gallant Man		$5.00	$4.00
4	Round Table			$4.00

Winner: B. c. by Bull Lea–Iron Maiden, by War Admiral. Trained by H. A. Jones; bred in Kentucky by Calumet Farm.
$152,050 gross value and $5,000 Gold Cup. Net to winner $107,950; second $25,000; third $12,500; fourth $5,000.

133 nominations.
Equipment: b—blinkers

*Foreign bred

Nightmare

A FEW NIGHTS BEFORE THE KENTUCKY Derby, Texas oil man Ralph Lowe, who had entered a very fast horse named Gallant Man in the Derby, had a nightmare. In it, he dreamed that during a race his horse would be leading when, stupefyingly, the jockey would suddenly pull the horse to a stop and another horse surged by him for the win.

Lowe was nervous but knew it couldn't happen because his jockey was Willie Shoemaker, easily one of the greatest jockeys who ever lived.

The bell went off, and speedy Federal Hill charged to the front with Bold Ruler and Iron Liege, with Bill Hartack up, close behind. Down the backstretch Iron Liege surged in front of Wheatley Stables's Bold Ruler, but then the front-running Federal Hill ran out of gas and forced Bill Hartack to take Iron Liege to the outside, a move that, his trainer estimated, lost him a good hunk of real estate.

But Iron Liege was all heart, and this was the race of his life. He drove past the fading Federal Hill at the top of the stretch, and hammered on toward victory in the Derby.

The race wasn't over yet, though; coming up the outside was Gallant Man, this very little Texas tough guy named Willie Shoemaker aboard. Down the stretch they drove, neck and neck, each horse guided by world-class jockeys, men who would ultimately win multiple Derbies, a tornado of sound around them.

Gallant Man gained inches with every stride, and as he watched, Gallant Man's trainer, Johnny Nerd, was euphoric, and yelled to Ralph Lowe, "Go down to the winner's circle and get your roses and take 'em back to Texas!"

But then, as the horses hammered past the sixteenth pole, Willie Shoemaker made Ralph Lowe's nightmare come true. Shoemaker, who later would explain that he misjudged the finish line, stood up in the saddle for a few milliseconds—and immediately, realizing his mistake, sat back down and resumed riding. But Gallant Man was apparently thrown off his stride, and Shoemaker could not catch Iron Liege, who beat him by a nose.

Later, the infuriated Johnny Nerd waited for Shoemaker to explain what had happened, and he said that if Shoemaker blamed what happened on the horse, he was going to "hit him with the fucking [field] glasses." But Shoemaker didn't. As he exited the jockey quarters, he spotted Nerd waiting for him, went over, and said: "I'm sorry, John, I made a mistake."

All Nerd could say was "Okay," and that they would meet again.

Tim Tam
84th *May 3, 1958*

			Pharamond II
	Menow	Alcibiades
	Tom Fool		*Bull Dog*
TIM TAM		Gaga	Alpoise
Dark bay colt			*Bull Dog*
	Two Lea	Bull Lea	Rose Leaves
			The Porter
		Two Bob	Blessings

THE WINNER'S PEDIGREE AND CAREER HIGHLIGHTS

YEAR	AGE	STS.	1ST	2ND	3RD	EARNINGS
1957	2	1	0	0	0	$ 275
1958	3	13	10	1	2	$467,200
TOTALS		**14**	**10**	**1**	**2**	**$467,475**

At 3 years WON Kentucky Derby, Derby Trial, Preakness Stakes, Everglades Stakes, Flamingo Stakes, Fountain of Youth Handicap, Florida Derby
2ND Belmont Stakes
3RD Bahamas Stakes

RACE DAY STATISTICS

HORSE	EQ.	WT.	PP	ST.	1/2	3/4	MILE	STR.	FIN.	JOCKEY	OWNER	ODDS TO $1
Tim Tam		126	2	8²	8¹	5¹	4ʰᵈ	2³	1¹ᐟ²	I. Valenzuela	Calumet Farm	2.10
Lincoln Road	b	126	7	1ʰᵈ	1²	1²	1¹⁻¹ᐟ²	1²	2¹ᐟ²	C. Rogers	Sunny Blue Farm	46.90
Noureddin	b	126	11	11³	12⁴	12³	8¹ᐟ²	3²	3⁶	J. Combest	Crabgrass Stable	15.40
Jewel's Reward		126	3	6²	6¹⁻¹ᐟ²	6ʰᵈ	5¹	4ʰᵈ	4ⁿᵒ	E. Arcaro	Maine Chance Farm	(a) 2.00
Martins Rullah	b	126	5	12²	13¹¹	13¹⁰	10³	9³	5³	C. McCreary	Mr. & Mrs. Geo. Lewis	43.10
Chance It Tony		126	10	13¹⁰	11¹⁻¹ᐟ²	9ʰᵈ	11²	8²	6¹⁻³ᐟ⁴	L. Batchellor	Mrs. Anthony Cannuli	245.00
A Dragon Killer		126	9	9²	9²	10ʰᵈ	7²	7¹ᐟ²	7ʰᵈ	L. Hansman	Mrs. S. H. Sadacca	294.40
Gone Fishin'		126	4	5²	4¹⁻¹ᐟ²	2¹ᐟ²	2ʰᵈ	5¹ᐟ²	8¹	R. Neves	Llangollen Farm	20.10
Benedicto		126	14	10²	10²	8¹ᐟ²	6ʰᵈ	6³	9²	R. Dever	Bellardi & Harkins	(f) 59.30
Ebony Pearl		126	13	4ʰᵈ	3¹ᐟ²	3¹⁻¹ᐟ²	3⁴	10³	10²⁻¹ᐟ²	M. Ycaza	Maine Chance Farm	(a) 2.00
Red Hot Pistol		126	8	3ʰᵈ	5³	4ʰᵈ	13	12²	11²⁻¹ᐟ²	D. Dodson	Mrs. S. E. Wilson Jr.	(f) 59.30
Silky Sullivan		126	12	14	14	14	12²	11¹	12¹⁻¹ᐟ²	W. Shoemaker	Ross & Klipstein	2.10
Flamingo	b	126	6	7¹⁻¹ᐟ²	7¹ᐟ²	11³	9³	13	13	G. Glisson	C. V. Whitney	49.50
Warren G	b	126	1	2²	2²	7¹	Eased			K. Church	W. G. Reynolds	122.30

Time: :23¹/5, :47³/5, 1:13¹/5, 1:38²/5, 2:05. Track muddy. In gate 4:32 CDT. Off at 4:32 CDT. Start good. Won driving.
Coupled: (a) Jewel's Reward and Ebony Pearl; (f) Field.

Program #		Win	Place	Show
3	Tim Tam	$6.20	$ 3.80	$ 3.00
7	Lincoln Road		$26.80	$11.40
10	Noureddin			$ 5.60

Winner: Dk. b. c. by Tom Fool–Two Lea, by Bull Lea. Trained by H. A. Jones; bred in Kentucky by Calumet Farm.
$160,500 gross value and $5,000 Gold Cup. Net to winner $116,400; second $25,000; third $12,500; fourth $5,000.

140 nominations.
Equipment: b—blinkers

*Foreign bred

Silky Sullivan

IN THIS RACE, THE HORSES WERE UP AGAINST a miracle horse named Silky Sullivan, a three-year-old out of Mentone, California. In 1957 Silky went to the post seven times, won four races, and earned only $21,750. In 1958 he raced seven times, winning three races, and earned $103,900.

But it was the way he won that captured the public's imagination—by a long, improbable drive from far, far back. For example, in the Santa Anita Derby he was loping along some twenty-eight and one-half lengths behind, and then put on the afterburners and came from behind to win. Newspapers across America carried the picture progression of "Silky," as he came to be known, gaining on the leaders and winning. And he won other races as well, all in his come-from-behind style. By the time Derby day rolled around, America was in a frenzy of adulation for the horse, and many put their money where their mouth was. Silky was their horse. As one newspaper put it, Silky had "captured the fancy of the American public much as had Babe Ruth in his baseball heyday."

On Derby day, Silky had generated so much interest that CBS, who broadcast the Derby, used a split-screen technique; the main part of the screen followed the race itself, while an inset picture followed Silky, who, it was assumed, would be running his usual multi-length-behind race and come on near the end to win, or almost win.

Silky was installed as one of the favorites in

the race, along with Tim Tam, who had won a host of races prior to the Derby, and Jewel's Reward and Ebony Pearl.

When the race, on a muddy track, started, Silky Sullivan was exactly where his many admirers in the crowd of 70,451—who had wagered $369,726 on him in the Derby, which included a record number of $2 tickets—knew he would be: in last place, this time thirty-two lengths behind the leader.

Then Silky started to move, and the crowd roared: "Here comes Silky!"

Silky passed one horse—and that was about it. His patented come-from-behind finish was not to be, and he went from people's hero to unprintable within two minutes. Silky's time was 2:09 2/5, while the ultimate winner, Tim Tam, ran in 2:05.

*Tomy Lee
85th May 2, 1959

		Owen Tudor	Hyperion
			Mary Tudor
	*Tudor Minstrel		Sansovino
*TOMY LEE		Sansonnet	Lady Juror
Bay colt			Blandford
	Auld Alliance	Brantome	Vitamine
			Hyperion
		Iona	Jiffy

THE WINNER'S PEDIGREE AND CAREER HIGHLIGHTS

YEAR	AGE	STS.	1ST	2ND	3RD	EARNINGS
1958	2	8	6	1	1	$213,460
1959	3	7	4	2	0	$163,657
1960	4	2	0	0	0	$ 5,000
1962	6	1	1	0	0	$ 4,125
1963	7	13	3	1	2	$ 18,772
TOTALS		**31**	**14**	**4**	**3**	**$405,014**

At 2 years	WON	Haggin Stakes, C.S. Howard Stakes, Starlet Stakes, Del Mar Futurity
	2ND	+Champagne Stakes, Garden State Stakes
At 3 years	WON	Kentucky Derby, Blue Grass Stakes
	2ND	San Vicente Stakes, San Felipe Handicap
At 4 years	UNP	Santa Anita Maturity

+ disqualified and placed third

RACE DAY STATISTICS

HORSE	EQ.	WT.	PP	ST.	1/2	3/4	MILE	STR.	FIN.	JOCKEY	OWNER	ODDS TO $1
*Tomy Lee		126	9	2^2	$2^{1-1/2}$	1^{hd}	$2^{1-1/2}$	2^2	1no	W. Shoemaker	Mr. & Mrs. F. Turner Jr.	3.70
Sword Dancer	b	126	14	$4^{1/2}$	$4^{1/2}$	4^2	$1^{1/2}$	1^{hd}	$2^{2-1/4}$	W. Boland	Brookemeade Stable	8.80
First Landing	b	126	3	7^1	$8^{1/2}$	5^{hd}	$4^{1/2}$	$4^{1-1/2}$	3^1	E. Arcaro	Meadow Stable	3.60
Royal Orbit	b	126	17	$10^{1-1/2}$	12^3	11^3	8^2	6^{hd}	4^{hd}	W. Harmatz	J. Braunstein Est.	46.60
Silver Spoon		121	4	9^1	9^2	$6^{1/2}$	3^2	3^{hd}	$5^{2-1/2}$	R. York	C. V. Whitney	10.80
Finnegan	b	126	8	6^2	6^1	$7^{1/2}$	$5^{1-1/2}$	7^2	$6^{3/4}$	J. Longden	Neil McCarthy	10.60
Dunce	b	126	7	$14^{1/2}$	13^2	12^3	$11^{1/2}$	8^1	$7^{1-3/4}$	S. Brooks	Claiborne Farm	(f) 7.30
Open View	b	126	13	5^2	5^4	8^2	6^2	$5^{1/2}$	8^3	K. Korte	Elkcam Stable	(a) 17.20
Atoll		126	5	$3^{1/2}$	3^{hd}	$3^{1/2}$	7^1	$9^{1-1/2}$	9no	S. Boulmetis	Elkcam & Chesler	(a) 17.20
Rico Tesio	b	126	2	17	17	17	13^2	11^1	$10^{1-1/2}$	M. Ycaza	Briardale Farm	48.10
Festival King		126	15	$8^{1/2}$	7^{hd}	9^2	9^2	10^{hd}	$11^{3/4}$	W. Carstens	C. B. Fischbach	(f) 7.30
John Bruce		126	11	$16^{1/2}$	$16^{1-1/2}$	$15^{1/2}$	14^3	14^1	12no	K. Church	K. G. Marshall	34.50
Easy Spur		126	6	13^3	10^{hd}	10^1	$10^{1-1/2}$	$13^{1/2}$	13^{hd}	W. Hartack	Spring Hill Farm	7.90
The Chosen One		126	16	11^1	14^4	14^4	$12^{1/2}$	$12^{1/2}$	$14^{4-1/2}$	J. Combest	Mrs. S. H. Sadacca	(f) 7.30
Our Dad	b	126	1	$12^{1/2}$	$11^{1/2}$	13^2	15^2	15^4	15^1	P. Anderson	Patrice Jacobs	8.00
*Die Hard		126	12	15^2	$15^{1/2}$	$16^{1/2}$	16^3	16^8	16^6	J. Sellers	Jacnot Stable	(f) 7.30
Troilus	b	126	10	$1^{1/2}$	$1^{1-1/2}$	$2^{1/2}$	17	17	17	C. Rogers	Bayard Sharp	(f) 7.30

Time: :24^1/5, :47^3/5, 1:11^3/5, 1:36, 2:02^1/5. Track fast. In gate 4:37 CDT. Off at 4:37^1/2 CDT. Start good. Won driving.
Coupled: (a) Open View and Atoll; (f) Field.

Program #		Win	Place	Show
8	*Tomy Lee	$9.40	$4.80	$3.80
10	Sword Dancer		$9.00	$6.20
4	First Landing			$4.00

Winner: B. c. by *Tudor Minstrel*Auld Alliance, by Brantome. Trained by Frank Childs; bred in England by D. H. Wills.
$163,750 gross value and $5,000 Gold Cup. Net to winner $119,650; second $25,000; third $12,500; fourth $5,000.

130 nominations.
Equipment: b—blinkers

*Foreign bred

Riding on the Wrong Horse

WILLIE SHOEMAKER WAS AN HONEST MAN, and when the 1959 Derby came around, he predicted that Sword Dancer would be the winner. There was only one problem. He would be astride another horse, Tomy Lee.

In fact, he had his choice of riding either horse. He had ridden Tomy Lee in the Garden State Stakes in late 1958, and finished second with him behind a great horse named First Landing. Tomy Lee's trainer was a nice man named Frank Childs and a good friend of Shoemaker's manager, Harry Wilbert, and after the race he asked Harry if Willie would ride Tomy Lee in the Derby. He said fine, but there was a problem. Shoemaker had received a call from a trainer named Elliott Burch, who asked him if he would ride Sword Dancer. Shoemaker, who had ridden and won on Sword Dancer, agreed.

When Harry found out, he said: "I gave Frank Childs my word that you would ride his colt in the Derby." The statement angered Shoemaker. He said to his agent: "Okay, but let me tell you, Harry, Sword Dancer is going to win the Derby." Elliot Burch was upset when he found out, but he gave Bill Boland, who had won the 1950 Derby, Sword Dancer to ride.

Shoemaker recalls that as he waited in the post for the race to start he knew he was on the wrong horse, and it would lead to him saying something during the race that would be the difference, he thought, between winning and losing. Both Sword Dancer and Tomy Lee were in contention, head to head, as they rounded the turn into the stretch, and Shoemaker, seeing

that Sword Dancer had plenty of gas left, yelled across to Boland:

"Good luck, Bill, go ahead. You got it won."

But Boland thought the comment was some sort of trick. When Tomy Lee accidentally made contact with Sword Dancer, this confirmed a conspiracy to Boland. Instead of focusing on driving his colt to the wire, he bumped Sword Dancer against Tomy Lee. Shoemaker, who was trying desperately to change Tomy Lee from his left to a right lead without success, instantly made Tomy Lee switch. The horse was dying inside, but he had just enough left to win by a nose.

Boland complained of foul, but film revealed that both riders had bumped each other, and the standoff resulted in Shoemaker being declared the victor. After the bumping incident, Shoemaker said, "If he'd given Sword Dancer the whip and gone on, he'd have won it."

Venetian Way
86th May 7, 1960

			Pilate
		Eight Thirty	Dinner Time
	Royal Coinage		*Bull Dog
VENETIAN WAY		Canina	Coronium
Chestnut colt			Balladier
	Firefly	Papa Redbird	Taj Bibi
			*Royal Minstrel
		Minstrelette	Bannerette

THE WINNER'S PEDIGREE AND CAREER HIGHLIGHTS

YEAR	AGE	STS.	1ST	2ND	3RD	EARNINGS
1959	2	9	4	1	2	$141,902
1960	3	11	3	3	1	$217,520
TOTALS		**20**	**7**	**4**	**3**	**$359,422**

At 2 years	WON	Prairie State Stakes, Washington Park Futurity
At 3 years	WON	Kentucky Derby, Warren Wright Memorial Stakes
	2ND	Florida Derby, Belmont Stakes
	3RD	Arlington Classic
	UNP	Preakness, Jersey Derby, Bahamas, Everglades

RACE DAY STATISTICS

HORSE	EQ.	WT.	PP	1/4	1/2	3/4	MILE	STR.	FIN.	JOCKEY	OWNER	ODDS TO $1
Venetian Way		126	9	4^2	$4^{2-1/2}$	2^2	2^5	1^2	$1^{3-1/2}$	W. Hartack	Sunny Blue Farm	6.30
Bally Ache	b	126	3	1^{hd}	$1^{1-1/2}$	1^2	1^1	2^6	$2^{7-1/2}$	R. Ussery	Edgehill Farm	1.70
Victoria Park	b	126	11	9^4	8^3	8^3	5^3	4^3	$3^{2-1/4}$	M. Ycaza	Windfields Farm	16.60
Tompion	b	126	13	$3^{1-1/2}$	3^{hd}	3^2	3^2	3^{hd}	4no	W. Shoemaker	C. V. Whitney	1.10
Bourbon Prince	b	126	10	$12^{1-1/2}$	12^5	10^3	8^5	5^1	$5^{5-1/2}$	C. Roger	Mrs. A. L. Rand	77.00
Cuvier Relic		126	4	5^{hd}	5^{hd}	$6^{1/2}$	7^1	6^3	6^5	J. Sellers	S. I. Crew	22.90
Tony Graff	b	126	6	13	13	13	13	10^5	$7^{1-1/2}$	W. Chambers	Anthony Graffagnini	67.90
Spring Broker	b	126	1	8^{hd}	9^2	9^2	9^6	9^3	$8^{1-1/2}$	J. L. Rotz	M. H. Van Berg	(f) 40.60
Divine Comedy	b	126	12	6^3	6^2	4^1	4^1	7^{hd}	$9^{1-1/4}$	I. Valenzuela	Llangollen Farm	61.60
Fighting Hodge		126	7	7^{hd}	$7^{1/2}$	7^1	6^{hd}	8^2	10^7	D. Pierce	Mrs. C. S. Hodge	(f) 40.60
Yomolka	b	126	2	10^{hd}	10^{hd}	11^{hd}	11^1	11^1	$11^{4-1/4}$	P. I. Grimm	Valley Farms	137.60
Lurullah	b	126	5	11^3	11^3	12^9	12^1	12^6	12^{16}	S. Brooks	T. A. Grissom	74.20
Henrijan	b	126	8	$2^{1/2}$	2^2	5^{hd}	10^2	13	13	A. Valenzuela	Mr. & Mrs. S. H. Elmore	(f) 40.60

Time: :23^2/5, :46^4/5, 1:11, 1:36^3/5, 2:02^2/5. Track good. In gate 4:31 CDT. Off at 4:31 CDT. Start good. Won ridden out.
(f) Field.

Program #		Win	Place	Show
7	Venetian Way	$14.60	$4.60	$3.40
2	Bally Ache		$3.00	$3.00
9	Victoria Park			$5.00

Winner: Ch. c. by Royal Coinage–Firefly, by Papa Redbird. Trained by V. J. Sovinski; bred in Kentucky by J. W. Greathouse.
$158,950 gross value and $5,000 Gold Cup. Net to winner $114,850; second $25,000; third $12,500; fourth $5,000.

142 nominations.
Equipment: b—blinkers

*Foreign bred

Fastest Ever on a Wet Track

THOUGH THE TRACK ON THIS DAY WAS officially characterized as good, it wasn't that good. It was damp. As writer Red Smith colorfully described it, about the consistency of "used chewing tobacco."

There was a crowd of 75,000 on hand for the 1960 Derby running, and most of the money was on a horse named Tompion, who had won the Blue Grass Stakes and the Santa Anita Derby. A good number of bets were also placed on Bally Ache. The third favorite in the race was Venetian Way, ridden by Bill Hartack, who had one Derby win under his belt. He did not appear likely to win, however, because Bally Ache had beaten him in three of their four encounters.

The owner of Venetian Way, Isaac Blumberg, and trainer Vic Sovinski were hungering for a Derby win. In 1958 they figured they had a good chance with Lincoln Road, but Tim Tam beat them there and elsewhere. Sovinski said that he would rather "win the Kentucky Derby than any other race in the world, and I don't care if I win another race."

Hartack rode his usual fine race on Venetian Way. Hartack held the horse back, but then, nearing the stretch, he came up on the outside and passed the leader, Bally Ache. Then Hartack put the pedal to the metal, and Venetian Way galloped home with no one able to run him down. Small wonder: Venetian Way's 2:02 2/5 was the fastest ever recorded on an "off" track. It was also the second of what was to be Bill Hartack's five Derby wins.

Carry Back
87th May 6, 1961

		Swing and Sway	Equipoise
	Saggy		Nedana
CARRY BACK		*Chantress	Hyperion
Brown colt			Surbine
	Joppy	Star Bien	*Blenheim II
			*Starweed
			Teddy Beau
	Miss Fairfax	Bellicent	

THE WINNER'S PEDIGREE

HORSE	EQ.	WT.	PP	1/4	1/2	3/4	MILE	STR.	FIN.	JOCKEY	OWNER	ODDS TO $1
Carry Back		126	14	11²	11¹⁻¹/²	11¹/²	6¹⁻¹/²	4³	1³/⁴	J. Sellers	Mrs. Katherine Price	2.50
Crozier	b	126	11	3²	2ʰᵈ	3⁶	3⁶	1¹/²	2²	B. Baeza	F. W. Hooper	3.50
Bass Clef		126	9	15	15	15	9¹	5¹/²	3²⁻¹/⁴	R. Baldwin	Mrs. V. E. Smith	(f) 16.50
Dr. Miller	b	126	15	12¹/²	14³	14¹	14³	7³	4¹	W. Shoemaker	Mrs. E. D. Jacobs	8.60
Sherluck		126	3	9²	7¹/²	6²	4²	6²	5¹⁻¹/⁴	E. Arcaro	Jacob Sher	5.70
Globemaster		126	8	1¹⁻¹/²	1³	1¹/²	2³	3³	6³/⁴	J. L. Rotz	L. P. Sasso	8.70
Four-and-Twenty	b	126	4	2¹	3⁵	2²	1ʰᵈ	2¹	7¹/²	J. Longden	Albert Ranches Ltd.	(a) 5.30
Flutterby	b	126	13	10¹/²	10²⁻¹/²	10¹/²	10ʰᵈ	9¹/²	8¹	H. Moreno	Albert Ranches Ltd.	(a) 5.30
Loyal Son	b	126	5	13ʰᵈ	12¹/²	12¹/²	11¹/²	10³	9ʰᵈ	L. Hansman	Eastwood Stable	71.40
On His Metal		126	2	14¹/²	13³	13²	12¹	8¹	10⁵	D. Dodson	J. Graham Brown	53.60
Light Talk		126	12	5²	4ʰᵈ	5³	5²	11¹	11¹⁻¹/²	R. Nono	Jacnot Stable	64.90
Ambiopoise	b	126	10	8²	8²	8²	8²	12²	12²⁻¹/⁴	R. Ussery	Robert Lehman	16.20
Ronnie's Ace	b	126	6	6²	9²	7¹	13³	13¹	13¹⁻¹/⁴	A. Maese	Clark-Radkovich	(f) 16.50
Dearborn	b	126	1	4ʰᵈ	5²	4ʰᵈ	7ʰᵈ	14³	14¹/²	B. Phelps	E. A. Dust	82.40
Jay Fox	b	126	7	7ʰᵈ	6ʰᵈ	9ʰᵈ	15	15	15	L. Gilligan	Brae Burn Farm	(f) 16.50

Time: :23⁴/₅, :47³/₅, 1:11²/₅, 1:36¹/₅, 2:04. Track good. In gate 4:31 CDT. Off at 4:31¹/₂ CDT. Start good. Won driving.
Coupled: (a) Four-and-Twenty and Flutterby; (f) Field.

Program #		Win	Place	Show
10	Carry Back	$7.00	$4.20	$3.20
8	Crozier		$4.60	$4.20
14f	Bass Clef			$5.60

Winner: Br. c. by Saggy–Joppy, by Star Blen. Trained by J. A. Price; bred in Florida by J. A. Price.
$163,000 gross value and $5,000 Gold Cup. Net to winner $120,500; second $25,000; third $12,500; fourth $5,000.

155 nominations.
Equipment: b—blinkers

*Foreign bred

Career Highlights

YEAR	AGE	STS.	1ST	2ND	3RD	EARNINGS
1960	2	21	5	4	4	$ 286,299
1961	3	16	9	1	3	$ 565,349
1962	4	19	5	5	3	$ 319,177
1963	5	6	2	1	1	$ 70,340
TOTALS		**62**	**21**	**11**	**11**	**$1,241,165**

At 2 years	WON	Cowdin Stakes, Garden State Stakes, Remsen Stakes
	2ND	Florida Breeders' Stakes, Christiana Stakes, Dover Stakes
	3RD	Tyro Stakes, Great American Stakes, Sapling Stakes
	UNP	Cherry Hill Stakes, Seashore Stakes, World's Playground Stakes, Champagne Stakes
At 3 years	WON	Kentucky Derby, Flamingo Stakes, Everglades Stakes, Florida Derby, Preakness Stakes, Jerome Handicap, Trenton Handicap
	2ND	Wood Memorial Stakes
	3RD	Fountain of Youth Stakes, Woodward Stakes, Lawrence Realization
	UNP	Belmont Stakes, Bahamas Stakes, United Nations Handicap
At 4 years	WON	Metropolitan Handicap, Monmouth Handicap, Whitney Stakes
	2ND	Seminole Handicap, Widener Handicap, Grey Lag Handicap, Trenton Handicap, Palm Beach Handicap
	3RD	New Orleans Handicap, Gulfstream Park Handicap, Washington D.C. International Stakes
	UNP	Aqueduct Stakes, Prix de l'arc de Triomphe, Suburban Handicap
At 5 years	WON	Trenton Handicap
	2ND	Buckeye Handicap
	3RD	United Nations Handicap
	UNP	Woodward Stakes

A Little Miscalculation

As author Jim Bolus said in his book *Run for the Roses: 100 Years at the Kentucky Derby*, one of the contenders, Carry Back, was not a classically bred racehorse. He was "by Saggy out of Joppy, which didn't figure to produce anything faster than a jalopy." But it was this jalopy who was to mount one of the greatest comebacks in Derby history. Indeed, someone said, "He didn't start his drive to the wire at Churchill Downs. He was further back, like in Columbus, Ohio."

While Saggy was a sprinter—he had once even beaten Citation at six furlongs—Joppy had won nothing, and a breeder named Jack Price bought her, for some unknown reason,

for $300, and then bred her to Saggy for a stud fee of $400. The foal that resulted was named Carry Back.

Price was not impressed with Carry Back, so, he said, "I decided to race him early and often to get as much out of him as I could before he faded." But, like the rabbit with the batteries that never go dead, Carry Back just kept racing and winning, and by the time the 1961 Derby rolled around, he had brought in earnings of $492,368.

Prior to the race, jockey Johnny Sellers and Price went over their strategy. Sellers would stay about ten lengths off the pace, then make his move at around the half-mile pole. But the plan was to go quite awry.

Sellers held back—way back. Just before entering the stretch, Carry Back was thirteen lengths behind.

But behind whom? The horses ahead were fading as Carry Back blasted by them.

And then there was one, just inside the eighth pole: Crozier, though it didn't look like Carry Back could catch him. But Carry Back kept running hard. Soon they were neck and neck, and then it was "See ya!" and Sellers brought him across the wire in a three-quarter-length victory.

Then came the shocker. Johnny Sellers had misread the number of lengths he was behind in the backstretch. He was not ten, but twenty lengths behind. The horse had to make up at least double the amount of ground than Sellers thought.

Price, who won $120,500 in purse money, still insisted that that was all that mattered. The Derby? Ho-hum. "I almost went to sleep two hours before the race," Price said, "and had to take a pep-up pill."

Decidedly
88th *May 5, 1962*

		Alibhai	Hyperion
			Teresina
	Determine		*Mahmoud*
DECIDEDLY		Koubis	Brown Biscuit
Gray colt			Man o' War
	Gloire Fille	War Glory	Annette K.
			Beau Pere
		Belle Femme	French Vamp

THE WINNER'S PEDIGREE AND CAREER HIGHLIGHTS

YEAR	AGE	STS.	1ST	2ND	3RD	EARNINGS
1961	2	8	2	1	1	$ 7,550
1962	3	12	2	4	1	$144,330
1963	4	13	5	1	2	$150,309
1964	5	10	2	3	0	$ 16,800
TOTALS		**43**	**11**	**9**	**4**	**$318,989**

At 2 years	UNP	Garden State Stakes
At 3 years	WON	Kentucky Derby
	2ND	Everglades Stakes, Blue Grass Stakes
	UNP	Preakness, Belmont, Jerome Handicap, Discovery Handicap, Long Island Handicap
At 4 years	WON	Monmouth Handicap, Dominion Day Handicap, Ben Ali Handicap
	2ND	Michigan Mile and One-Sixteenth Handicap
	3RD	Grey Lag Handicap
	UNP	Aqueduct Stakes, Metropolitan Handicap, Santa Anita Handicap, Strub Stakes
At 5 years	UNP	Bernard Baruch, Stymie, Manhattan Handicap

HORSE	EQ.	WT.	PP	1/4	1/2	3/4	MILE	STR.	FIN.	JOCKEY	OWNER	ODDS TO $1
Decidedly	b	126	4	10^2	$9^{1/2}$	8^1	$5^{1-1/2}$	$3^{1/2}$	$1^{2-1/4}$	W. Hartack	El Peco Ranch	8.70
Roman Line	b	126	14	$7^{1/2}$	6^2	6^2	$4^{1-1/2}$	1^{hd}	2^{nk}	J. Combest	T. A. Grissom	26.30
Ridan		126	13	5^1	2^{hd}	2^1	3^2	2^{hd}	3^{nk}	M. Ycaza	Jolley-Woods-Greer	1.10
*Sir Ribot		126	5	2^1	$8^{1-1/2}$	7^2	6^2	5^2	$4^{1-1/2}$	R. York	Mr. & Mrs. F. Turner Jr.	13.00
Sunrise Country	b	126	2	4^2	$3^{1-1/2}$	1^{hd}	$2^{1/2}$	4^2	5^2	W. Shoemaker	T. B. Martin	2.80
*Crimson Satan	b	126	11	$14^{1/2}$	14^{hd}	12^1	10^3	6^2	$6^{1-3/4}$	B. Phelps	Crimson King Farm	21.50
Green Hornet		126	6	$11^{1/2}$	13^4	13^4	$12^{1-1/2}$	9^3	$7^{3/4}$	J. Longden	Mrs. J. W. Brown	49.50
Good Fight		126	12	$9^{1-1/2}$	10^2	10^{hd}	$9^{1-1/2}$	$10^{1-1/2}$	8^{hd}	R. Broussard	F and B Farms	(f) 28.70
Admiral's Voyage		126	3	3^1	4^2	3^1	1^{hd}	7^3	$9^{4-1/2}$	B. Baeza	F. W. Hopper	12.10
Royal Attack	b	126	8	$8^{1/2}$	5^{hd}	$5^{1/2}$	8^2	8^2	10^5	E. Burns	N. S. McCarthy	81.30
Touch Bar	b	126	10	15	15	15	15	14	$11^{2-1/2}$	J. J. Rivera	Estopinal-Arnaud	(f) 28.70
Lee Town	b	126	7	1^2	$1^{1-1/2}$	$4^{1-1/2}$	$7^{1/2}$	12^8	12^8	W. Carstens	J. V. P. Stables	(f) 28.70
Mister Pitt	b	126	9	13^1	11^2	11^2	11^2	11^3	13^7	W. Harmatz	Golden Triangle Stables	123.30
Sharp Count	b	126	1	6^{hd}	$7^{1/2}$	$9^{1-1/2}$	13^1	13^1	14	E. Curry	Reverie Knoll Farm	(f) 28.70
Prego	b	126	15	12^3	12^{hd}	14^1	14^2	Pulled up		L. Adams	Robert Lehman	28.90

Time: :22 3/5, :45 4/5, 1:10 1/5, 1:35 1/5, 2:00 2/5 (new track record). Track fast. In gate 4:33 1/2 EST. Off at 4:34 EST. Start good. Won driving.
(f) Field.

Program #		Win	Place	Show
3	Decidedly	$19.40	$ 8.20	$4.20
10	Roman Line		$19.20	$7.60
9	Ridan			$3.00

Winner: Gr. c. by Determine–Gloire Fille, by War Glory. Trained by H. A. Luro; bred in California by G. A. Pope Jr.
$162,150 gross value and $5,000 Gold Cup. Net to winner $119,650; second $25,000; third $12,500; fourth $5,000.
Scratched: Sir Gaylord, Donut King, Cicada.

139 nominations.
Equipment: b—blinkers

*Foreign bred

"The Madder I Get, the Better I Ride"

The 1962 Kentucky Derby was a barn burner, one of the most exciting Derbies in history—and the fastest to date. The winner was clocked in 2:00 2/5.

As is the case with so many Derby winners, the winner, Decidedly, a gray colt, gave little indication that he had a Derby-winning race inside himself, particularly one so fast. In 1961, when he was a two-year-old, he won one race and $7,550. But he had one great thing going for him. His father, Determine, was another gray who had won the Derby, in 1954.

And, he had some great horsemen behind him. Astride him would be Bill Hartack, a small man with a big anger inside him who once stated, "Hatred is necessary for my work. The madder I get, the better I ride." And Hartack rode very well, having already notched two Derby wins.

Decidedly's trainer was Argentinean Horatio Luro, who was a bon vivant, a very laid-back man. For example, he once told reporters, "I like sunlight"—which meant he began to train his horses not in the early-morning hours but starting at eight-thirty or nine. Still, Luro was a thoroughgoing professional; he paid attention to detail, watching his horses carefully to detect any shift in their mood that might signify illness, and was very careful about matching horse and rider.

Fifteen horses started in the race, and in the beginning Hartack and the gray colt were behind a number of horses, Hartack actually holding Decidedly back. Then, as the race progressed, it turned into the barn burner. First Lee Town was leading, then Sunrise Country, then Admiral's Voyage, and then Roman Line. Finally, Decidedly broke through on the outside at the eighth pole, and Hartack, riding with all the rage he could muster, hit the wire two and a quarter lengths ahead of Roman Line. Thus far only two grays had won the Derby—Decidedly and his father, Determine. Hartack would go on to win five Derbies—in nine attempts. Eddie Arcaro also won five, but it took him twenty-one tries.

Chateaugay
89th *May 4, 1963*

		Swaps	*Khaled*	*Hyperion*
				Éclair
		Swaps		*Beau Pere*
		CHATEAUGAY	Iron Reward	*Iron Maiden*
		Chestnut colt		*Unbreakable*
		Banquet Bell	Polynesian	*Black Polly*
				*Pot au Feu
			Dinner Horn	*Tophorn*

THE WINNER'S PEDIGREE AND CAREER HIGHLIGHTS

YEAR	AGE	STS.	1ST	2ND	3RD	EARNINGS
1962	2	5	2	2	0	$ 12,587
1963	3	12	7	1	2	$332,585
1964	4	3	1	1	0	$ 11,325
1965	5	4	1	0	0	$ 4,225
TOTALS		**24**	**11**	**4**	**2**	**$360,722**

At 2 years	UNP	Pimlico Futurity
At 3 years	WON	Kentucky Derby, Blue Grass Stakes, Jerome Handicap, Belmont Stakes
	2ND	Preakness Stakes
	3RD	Travers Stakes, Dwyer Handicap
	UNP	Lawrence Realization, Yankee Handicap
At 4 years	2ND	Roseben Handicap
	UNP	Carter Handicap
At 5 years	UNP	Widener Handicap, Seminole Handicap, Royal Palm Handicap

RACE DAY STATISTICS

HORSE	EQ.	WT.	PP	1/4	1/2	3/4	MILE	STR.	FIN.	JOCKEY	OWNER	ODDS TO $1
Chateaugay		126	1	6^1	6^{hd}	6^3	4^2	1^1	$1^{1\text{-}1/4}$	B. Baeza	Darby Dan Farm	9.40
Never Bend		126	6	$1^{1/2}$	1^1	1^1	1^1	2^2	2^{nk}	M. Ycaza	Cain Hoy Stable	3.10
Candy Spots	b	126	9	3^2	$3^{2\text{-}1/2}$	3^3	3^{hd}	3^2	$3^{4\text{-}3/4}$	W. Shoemaker	R. C. Ellsworth	1.50
On My Honor	b	126	8	9	9	9	7^3	6^2	$4^{1\text{-}1/4}$	P. Frey	Ambush Stable	30.80
No Robbery	b	126	7	2^3	2^2	2^2	2^2	4^2	$5^{1\text{-}1/4}$	J. L. Rotz	Greentree Stable	2.70
Bonjour	b	126	3	5^2	$4^{1/2}$	4^2	6^7	$5^{1\text{-}1/2}$	6^3	I. Valenzuela	Patrice Jacobs	9.30
Gray Pet	b	126	5	4^1	5^4	5^2	5^{hd}	7^6	7^6	A. Gomez	Walnut Hill Farm	40.00
Investor	b	126	2	8^1	$8^{1/2}$	$8^{1/2}$	9	8^2	$8^{3\text{-}1/2}$	F. Callico	J. J. Cherock	37.40
Royal Tower	b	126	4	7^3	7^5	7^3	8^2	9	9	G. Hernandez	B. J. Ridder	138.70

Time: :23, :46$^{2/5}$, 1:10, 1:35$^{2/5}$, 2:01$^{4/5}$. Track Fast. In gate 4:29$^{1/2}$ EST. Off at 4:30 EST. Start good. Won driving.

Program #		Win	Place	Show
1	Chateaugay	$20.80	$7.00	$3.60
6	Never Bend		$5.00	$3.40
9	Candy Spots			$2.80

Winner: Ch. c. by Swaps–Banquet Bell, by Polynesian. Trained by J. P. Conway; bred in Kentucky by J. W. Galbreath.
$151,400 gross value and $5,000 Gold Cup. Net to winner $108,900; second $25,000; third $12,500; fourth $5,000.

129 nominations.
Equipment: b—blinkers

*Foreign bred

Two Chicken Bones and a Prayer

YOU MIGHT EXPECT RACEHORSE OWNERS to be hardheaded realists. After all, they're all basically rich (the bumper sticker that reads "Poverty Is Owning a Horse" wasn't invented for nothing), and you would expect that their decisions would be based on facts, not feelings.

But that would not be true. The annals of the Derby are filled with instances of owners following hunches based on nothing but their gut, or regarding dreams as reality (such as when the owner of Gallant Man dreamed that his jockey, Willie Shoemaker, was going to pull his mount to a stop before the finish line). So as hardheaded businessman John W. Galbreath saddled his horse, Chateaugay, prior to the running of the 1963 Derby, he was also very careful to attach two wishbones to the horse that his cook had sent over for luck.

Ironically, eight years earlier, the rider of Chateaugay's father, Swaps, who won the 1955 Derby, also invoked some hocus-pocus. The rider of Swaps, Willie Shoemaker, was in the whirlpool in the training room at the University of Louisville, trying desperately to reduce the swelling in his damaged knee, when a square-shouldered young man with a blond crew cut introduced himself to Shoemaker, saying he was a football player at the university. His name was Johnny Unitas. Shoemaker had always regarded meeting Unitas as a good omen—he was a winner.

A further irony was that in today's race Shoemaker was on a horse named Candy Spots, while Braulio Baeza was on Swaps's son, Cha-

teaugay. Chateaugay had looked good winning the Blue Grass Stakes, but bettors more or less avoided him and instead plunked their money down on two other horses in the race who had been undefeated.

Baeza, a Panamanian, knew exactly how to handle Chateaugay. For the first six furlongs he held the colt back, then eased to the extreme outside soon after leaving the backstretch. Then he moved with a rush to wear down the leader, Never Bend, and prevailed in a long drive. Time was 2:01 4/5.

Baeza did well, Chateaugay did well, and the trainer did well. But you just know that someone was giving part of the real credit for the victory to the wishbones on the saddle.

Northern Dancer
90th May 2, 1964

	Nearco	Pharos
		Nogara
Nearctic		Hyperion
NORTHERN DANCER	*Lady Angela	Sister Sarah
Bay colt		Polynesian
Natalma	Native Dancer	Geisha
		*Mahmoud
	Almahmoud	Arbitrator

THE WINNER'S PEDIGREE AND CAREER HIGHLIGHTS

YEAR	AGE	STS.	1ST	2ND	3RD	EARNINGS
1963	2	9	7	2	0	$ 90,635
1964	3	9	7	0	2	$490,012
TOTALS		**18**	**14**	**2**	**2**	**$580,647**

At 2 years	WON	Summer Stakes, Coronation Futurity, Carleton Stakes, Remsen Stakes
	2ND	Vandal Stakes, Cup and Saucer Stakes
At 3 years	WON	Kentucky Derby, Flamingo Stakes, Florida Derby, Blue Grass Stakes, Preakness, Queen's Plate
	3RD	Belmont Stakes

RACE DAY STATISTICS

HORSE	EQ.	WT.	PP	$\frac{1}{4}$	$\frac{1}{2}$	$\frac{3}{4}$	MILE	STR.	FIN.	JOCKEY	OWNER	ODDS TO $1
Northern Dancer	b	126	7	7$^{2-1/2}$	6^{hd}	6^{2}	1^{hd}	1^{2}	1^{nk}	W. Hartack	Windfields Farm	3.40
Hill Rise		126	11	6$^{1-1/2}$	7$^{2-1/2}$	8^{hd}	4^{hd}	2$^{1-1/2}$	2$^{3-1/4}$	W. Shoemaker	El Peco Ranch	1.40
The Scoundrel	b	126	6	3$^{1/2}$	4^{hd}	3^{1}	2^{1}	3^{2}	3no	M. Ycaza	R. C. Ellsworth	6.00
Roman Brother		126	12	9^{2}	9$^{1/2}$	9^{2}	6^{2}	4$^{1/2}$	4^{nk}	W. Chambers	Harbor View Farm	30.60
Quadrangle	b	126	2	5^{1}	5$^{1-1/2}$	4^{hd}	5$^{1-1/2}$	5^{1}	5^{3}	R. Ussery	Rokeby Stables	5.30
Mr. Brick		126	1	2^{3}	1$^{1/2}$	1$^{1/2}$	3^{1}	6^{3}	6$^{3/4}$	I. Valenzuela	Roy Sturgis	15.80
Mr. Moonlight		126	5	8^{2}	8^{1}	7^{hd}	7^{3}	7^{4}	7^{5}	J. Combest	Mrs. Magruder Dent	54.40
Dandy K.		126	9	12	12	12	8^{hd}	8$^{1-1/2}$	8$^{2-1/4}$	M. Solomone	Cecil Carmine	17.40
Ishkoodah	b	126	8	11^{2}	11^{2}	11^{2}	9^{2}	9^{3}	9^{4}	R. Baldwin	Tumblewood Stable	29.20
Wil Rad		126	3	4^{hd}	3$^{1/2}$	5^{hd}	11$^{1/2}$	11^{7}	10no	J. Vasquez	Clark-Radkovich	57.70
Extra Swell	b	126	4	10$^{1/2}$	10^{hd}	10$^{1/2}$	12	10^{hd}	11^{14}	M. Volzke	Mr. & Mrs. Earle Davis	152.20
Royal Shuck	b	126	10	1^{hd}	2^{2}	2^{hd}	10^{hd}	12	12	H. Bolin	E. A. Dust	179.40

Time: :22^{2}/5, :46, 1:10^{3}/5, 1:36, 2:00 (new track record). Track fast. In gate 4:31 EST. Off at 4:31 EST. Start good. Won driving.

Program #		Win	Place	Show
7	Northern Dancer	$8.80	$3.60	$3.00
11	Hill Rise		$3.00	$2.60
6	The Scoundrel			$3.20

Winner: B. c. by Nearctic–Natalma, by Native Dancer. Trained by H. A. Luro; bred in Canada by E. P. Taylor.
$156,800 gross value and $5,000 Gold Cup. Net to winner $114,300; second $25,000; third $12,500; fourth $5,000.

138 nominations.
Equipment: b—blinkers

*Foreign bred

The Fastest Final Quarter Ever

TWO GREAT JOCKEYS WERE ABOARD GREAT horses when the gates opened on the 1964 Derby. On Hill Rise was Willie Shoemaker, and on Canadian-bred Northern Dancer was the great and irascible Bill Hartack. Both had tons of experience, and both were multiple Derby winners. The overflow crowd suspected that the race was going to be a good one. They were not disappointed. The winner would win in the fastest time yet recorded for a Kentucky Derby.

The track was fast. As the horses broke from the starting gate, Northern Dancer went into the lead, staying close to the inside, with Hill Rise, the favorite, behind him. Then the horses were even, behind a wall of horses—and abruptly Hartack dropped the hammer. The move caught Hill Rise, as it were, flat-footed. As *Blood-Horse* magazine stated, Hartack "moved decisively with Northern Dancer at the five-furlong pole, taking Shoemaker and Hill Rise by surprise. The two horses had been running side by side behind a wall of three horses. Hartack eased his horse away from the rail and Northern Dancer spurted in front of Hill Rise and to the outside."

And was just about gone.

Said Shoemaker, he "could not get his bigger horse moving to prevent Northern Dancer's nimble escape."

But the race wasn't over. Hill Rise mounted a charge down the last quarter in 23 3/5 seconds, matching Whirlaway's final quarter in 1941, the fastest quarter in Derby history.

But though Hill Rise closed ground, the charge was not quite enough. Northern Dancer, who ran the last quarter in 24 seconds, won by a long neck.

One trainer was heard to exclaim, "You could describe the last quarter in a single word . . . zip."

Lucky Debonair
91st *May 1, 1965*

	The Rhymer	**St. Germans*
		Rhythmic
Vertex		*Case Ace*
LUCKY DEBONAIR	*Kanace*	*Kanlast*
Bay colt		*Reigh Count*
	Fresh as Fresh	*Count Fleet*	*Quickly*
		Bull Lea
	Airy	*Proud One*

THE WINNER'S PEDIGREE AND CAREER HIGHLIGHTS

YEAR	AGE	STS.	1ST	2ND	3RD	EARNINGS
1964	2	1	0	0	0	$-
1965	3	10	6	3	0	$257,210
1966	4	5	3	0	0	$113,750
TOTALS		**16**	**9**	**3**	**0**	**$370,960**

At 3 years	WON	Kentucky Derby, Stakes, San Vicente Handicap, Santa Anita Derby, Blue Grass Stakes
	2ND	San Felipe Handicap
	UNP	Preakness
At 4 years	WON	Santa Anita Handicap
	UNP	Malibu Stakes

RACE DAY STATISTICS

HORSE	EQ.	WT.	PP	1/4	1/2	3/4	MILE	STR.	FIN.	JOCKEY	OWNER	ODDS TO $1
Lucky Debonair		126	8	3^{hd}	$2^{2-1/2}$	$2^{1/2}$	2^2	1^3	1^{nk}	W. Shoemaker	Mrs. Ada L. Rice	4.30
Dapper Dan	b	126	1	11	11	11	7^1	$5^{1/2}$	2^2	I. Valenzuela	Ogden Phipps	30.00
Tom Rolfe		126	9	7^2	5^1	$3^{1-1/2}$	$4^{1-1/2}$	3^{hd}	3^1	R. Turcotte	Powhatan	5.60
Native Charger	b	126	4	4^3	$4^{1-1/2}$	$4^{1/2}$	$3^{1/2}$	4^1	4^{nk}	J. L. Rotz	Warner Stable	6.40
Hail to All		126	7	9^2	10^2	$9^{1-1/2}$	8^{hd}	$6^{1-1/2}$	$5^{2-1/4}$	M. Ycaza	Mrs. Ben Cohen	3.80
Mr. Pak		126	10	8^2	$8^{2-1/2}$	7^2	$6^{1/2}$	8^4	6^{hd}	J. Nichols	Mrs. Mary Keim	53.80
Swift Ruler		126	11	10^{hd}	$9^{1/2}$	$8^{1/2}$	10^2	$7^{1/2}$	7^3	L. Spraker	Earl Allen	34.90
Flag Raiser	b	126	5	1^2	1^{hd}	1^{hd}	1^{hd}	2^{hd}	$8^{2-1/2}$	R. Ussery	Isidor Bieber	17.90
Carpenter's Rule	b	126	6	$6^{1-1/2}$	7^2	10^3	11	9^1	$9^{1/2}$	W. Harmatz	P. L. Grissom	78.70
Bold Lad	b	126	3	5^{hd}	$6^{1-1/2}$	$6^{1/2}$	5^{hd}	$10^{1/2}$	10^2	W. Hartack	Wheatley Stable	2.00
Narushua		126	2	2^{hd}	3^{hd}	5^2	$9^{1/2}$	11	11	T. Dunlavy	J. W. Mecom	92.00

Time: :23$^{1/5}$, :47$^{1/5}$, 1:11$^{4/5}$, 1:37, 2:01$^{1/5}$. Track fast. In gate 5:00 EDT. Off at 5:00 EDT. Start good. Won driving.

Program #		Win	Place	Show
8	Lucky Debonair	$10.60	$ 5.40	$ 4.20
1	Dapper Dan		$26.00	$12.60
9	Tom Rolfe			$ 4.80

Winner: B. c. by Vertex–Fresh as Fresh, by Count Fleet. Trained by Frank Catrone; bred in Kentucky by Danada Farm.
$154,500 gross value and $5,000 Gold Cup. Net to winner $112,000; second $25,000; third $12,500; fourth $5,000.

130 nominations.
Equipment: b—blinkers

*Foreign bred

Close Call

AS THE 1965 DERBY DEVELOPED, IT SEEMED that the most exciting moment was what happened before the race. There was a fire in the upper grandstand near the first turn, but the 90,000-plus people attending did not panic, and firemen quickly extinguished it. But the finish was something else.

When the race started, Flag Raiser broke into the lead, followed by Willie Shoemaker, trying for his third Derby win on Lucky Debonair, and, close up, the favorite, Bold Lad, piloted by Bill Hartack and trained by Bill Winfrey. Winfrey had suffered a terrible loss— he was expected to win—in 1953 with Native Dancer. He also had another horse in the race, a 30–1 long shot named Dapper Dan who Winfrey didn't think much of. At a Derby party during the week, Winfrey said, "Dapper Dan will run a mile and a quarter. It's just a matter of how long it'll take him."

By the time the horses turned for home, Flag Raiser, who was more a sprinter than a horse who could keep up the pace in a mile-and-a-quarter race, was kaput. Shoemaker took Lucky Debonair into the lead, and as they drove down the stretch the lead grew to three lengths. It was at this point that a race once again proved that anyone can win the Kentucky Derby. Dapper Dan, the horse that his trainer had joked disparagingly about, started an electrifying kick from last place at the last quarter, getting closer and closer as the wire

approached. Shoemaker tried to fight him off, urging Lucky Debonair on.

The only thing that saved Lucky Debonair was the wire. Dapper Dan blasted the last quarter in a blistering 23 1/5, two-fifths of a second faster than Whirlaway had gone the distance in 1941 or Hill Rise in 1964, and a track record. The long shot had lost by just a neck because Dapper Dan's jockey had started his kick a heartbeat or so too late and simply ran out of real estate. No one was more aware of how close the race was than Willie Shoemaker. In the stretch run he remembered the 1959 race on Gallant Man, where he slowed down close to the wire, allowing Iron Liege to win. "I didn't let up on him," he joked, "until we were a six-teenth of a mile past the finish line. This time I wanted to be sure."

Kauai King
92nd May 7, 1966

		Unbreakable
	Polynesian	Black Polly
Native Dancer		Discovery
KAUAI KING	Geisha	Miyako
Dark bay/ brown colt		Blandford
Sweep In	*Blenheim II	Malva
		Sweep
	Swepesta	Celesta

THE WINNER'S PEDIGREE AND CAREER HIGHLIGHTS

YEAR	AGE	STS.	1ST	2ND	3RD	EARNINGS
1965	2	4	1	1	1	$ 6,120
1966	3	12	8	1	0	$375,277
TOTALS		**16**	**9**	**2**	**1**	**$381,397**

At 2 years   3RD   Joliet Stakes
At 3 years   WON   Kentucky Derby, Preakness Stakes, Governor's Gold
                        Cup, Prince George's Stakes, Fountain of Youth Stakes
            2ND   Hutcheson Stakes
            UNP   Belmont Stakes, Florida Derby

RACE DAY STATISTICS

HORSE	EQ.	WT.	PP	1/4	1/2	3/4	MILE	STR.	FIN.	JOCKEY	OWNER	ODDS TO $1
Kauai King	b	126	12	1^1	1^3	1^2	1^1	$1^{1\text{-}1/2}$	$1^{1/2}$	D. Brumfield	Ford Stable	2.40
Advocator	b	126	5	6^{hd}	5^2	3^2	2^1	3^1	2no	J. Sellers	Mrs. Ada L. Rice	16.90
Blue Skyer	b	126	2	11^2	8^1	8^2	3^1	$4^{1\text{-}1/2}$	$3^{3/4}$	E. Fires	Padgett-Grant	(f) 17.00
Stupendous	b	126	3	9^2	6^{hd}	4^{hd}	4^1	$2^{1/2}$	4^{nk}	B. Baeza	Wheatley Stable	5.40
Abe's Hope	b	126	13	10^{hd}	$12^{1\text{-}1/2}$	9^{hd}	$5^{1/2}$	5^2	5^1	W. Shoemaker	Grand Prix Stable	3.20
Rehabilitate	b	126	4	14^3	$11^{1/2}$	13^{hd}	12^3	6^2	$6^{1\text{-}1/4}$	R. Turcotte	Robert Lehman	(f) 17.00
Amberoid		126	1	15	15	12^2	$8^{1\text{-}1/2}$	7^3	7^8	W. Boland	R. N. Webster	6.10
Fleet Shoe	b	126	7	$13^{1/2}$	14^2	14^{hd}	11^3	8^3	8^6	L. Gilligan	George Putnam	33.50
Exhibitionist	b	126	8	5^{hd}	7^2	$7^{1/2}$	9^{hd}	10^2	$9^{1\text{-}1/2}$	E. Belmonte	Mrs. E. D. Jacobs	20.10
Sky Guy	b	126	10	4^2	4^1	5^2	$7^{1/2}$	11^1	10^{nk}	L. Adams	W. G. Helis, Jr.	68.40
Williamston Kid		126	15	12^1	$13^{1\text{-}1/2}$	11^1	10^1	12^4	$11^{2\text{-}1/2}$	R. Stevenson	Ternes-Bartlett	19.00
Quinta	b	126	14	$2^{1\text{-}1/2}$	2^4	2^3	$6^{1\text{-}1/2}$	9^1	$12^{3\text{-}1/2}$	P. Kallai	Bokum II-Scott II	63.70
Tragniew		126	11	8^2	10^{hd}	10^1	13^1	13^2	13^3	D. Pierce	B. J. Richards	11.80
Beau Sub		126	9	$7^{1/2}$	$9^{1/2}$	15	14^5	14^6	14^{14}	R. Parrott	Clear Springs Stable	(f) 17.00
Dominar	b	126	6	3^2	3^1	6^{hd}	15	15	15	W. Harmatz	Flying M Stable	(f) 17.00

Time: :22$^{4/5}$, :46$^{1/5}$, 1:10$^{3/5}$, 1:35$^{3/5}$, 2:02. Track fast. In gate 4:32 EST. Off at 4:32 EST. Start good. Won driving.
(f) Field

Program #		Win	Place	Show
8	Kauai King	$6.80	$ 4.20	$3.60
3	Advocator		$13.00	$8.60
12f	Blue Skyer			$5.40

Winner: Dk. b. or br. c. by Native Dancer–Sweep In, by Blenheim II. Trained by Henry Forrest; bred in Maryland by Pine Brook Farm.
$163,000 gross value and $5,000 Gold Cup. Net to winner $120,500; second $25,000; third $12,500; fourth $5,000.

150 nominations.
Equipment: b—blinkers

*Foreign bred

"Help Me, Lord, 'Cause I Need You Now"

FRONT-RUNNING IN THE KENTUCKY DERBY has been a disaster for many horses. But some horses have done it successfully. and one of these was Kauai King, the son of Native Dancer, the "Gray Ghost" who lost the 1953 Derby to Dark Star though Dancer's victory, before the race, was considered a fait accompli. In fact, following his Derby loss Dancer won all twenty-one of his remaining races.

Aboard Kauai King that warm day on a fast track in front of over 100,000 people was Donald Brumfield, who was quite good at racing over the Churchill Downs track. He had raced there hundreds of times. Brumfield's plan was simple: Grab the lead at the beginning and go wire to wire.

And grab the lead he did, blasting out of the chute and hammering to first by the time the horses hit the first turn, fourteen horses pursuing him but not catching him, not yet: he burned the first quarter in 22 4/5. Brumfield took the horse past the halfway mark at 1:35, prompting some people to wonder whether Kauai King might not die before the race was over.

But he kept chugging along, the crowd noise building as he did, and then here came the other horses, with Johnny Sellers on Advocator almost catching him at the quarter pole and Abe's Hope, with Willie Shoemaker up, mounting a blistering run but dying at the top of the stretch. Other horses came at him too, and as he drove down the stretch on this son of the great Native Dancer, his heart cried out, "Help me, Lord, 'cause I need you now."

He didn't seem to need the help, and that was help itself. He hit the wire, alone, in 2:02. Everyone in the Kauai King camp was euphoric, but perhaps groom James L. "Popeye" Brooks said it best. A smile wreathing his face as he led the roses-draped Kauai King from the winner's circle, he said, "This the biggest day of my life!"

Proud Clarion
93rd *May 6, 1967*

			*Royal Charger
		*Turn-To	*Source Sucree
	Hail to Reason		Blue Swords
PROUD CLARION		Nothirdchance	Galla Colors
Bay colt			Djebel
	Breath O'Morn	*Djeddah	Djezima
			*Blenheim II
		Darby Dunedin	Ethel Dear

The Winner's Pedigree and Career Highlights

YEAR	AGE	STS.	1ST	2ND	3RD	EARNINGS
1966	2	3	0	0	1	$ 805
1967	3	13	6	2	1	$210,525
1968	4	9	0	2	0	$ 7,400
TOTALS		25	6	4	2	**$218,730**

At 3 years	WON	Kentucky Derby, Roamer Handicap
	2ND	Blue Grass Stakes, Queens County Handicap
	3RD	Preakness
	UNP	Belmont Stakes, Gallant Fox Handicap
At 4 years	UNP	Widener Handicap

Race Day Statistics

HORSE	EQ.	WT.	PP	1/4	1/2	3/4	MILE	STR.	FIN.	JOCKEY	OWNER	ODDS TO $1
Proud Clarion	b	126	7	9^5	9^3	8^1	5^{hd}	2^2	1^1	R. Ussery	Darby Dan Farm	30.10
Barbs Delight	b	126	5	1^1	$1^{1-1/2}$	1^2	1^1	1^{hd}	2^3	K. Knapp	Huguelet Jr.– Spalding-Steele Jr.	15.70
Damascus		126	2	6^{hd}	4^1	4^1	4^2	3^4	$3^{1-1/4}$	W. Shoemaker	Mrs. E. W. Bancroft	1.70
Reason to Hail	b	126	13	8^2	8^2	$6^{1/2}$	6^2	5^2	$4^{1/2}$	W. Blum	Patrice Jacobs	20.70
Ask the Fare	b	126	14	5^{hd}	$7^{1/2}$	9^1	8^3	4^{hd}	$5^{2-1/4}$	D. Holmes	Holiday Stable	66.40
Successor	b	126	6	10^2	$10^{1-1/2}$	12^1	12^3	6^1	6^1	B. Baeza	Wheatley Stables O. M. Phipps	4.60
Gentleman James	b	126	10	13^4	12^2	7^2	$7^{1-1/2}$	7^1	$7^{1-1/2}$	R. Campbell	M. G. Phipps	37.10
Ruken	b	126	1	12^{hd}	13^6	$10^{1/2}$	9^2	9^2	8^{hd}	F. Alvarez	Louis Rowan	4.80
Diplomat Way	b	126	4	$3^{1/2}$	3^2	3^4	$2^{1/2}$	8^{hd}	9no	J. Sellers	Harvey Peltier	7.10
Second Encounter	b	126	12	14	14	14	14	13^5	10^2	B. Phelps	Harris-Pierce Jr.	(f) 17.30
Dawn Glory	b	126	8	2^2	$2^{1/2}$	2^{hd}	3^{hd}	10^2	11^1	E. Fires	Establo Eden	(f) 17.30
Dr. Isby		126	3	11^2	11^1	11^1	$11^{1/2}$	11^2	12^{nk}	W. Hartack	P. L. Grissom	11.00
Field Master		126	9	$4^{1-1/2}$	5^1	13^{15}	13^{10}	12^6	13^7	A. Pineda	Mr. & Mrs. J. H. Seley	(f) 17.30
Lightning Orphan		126	11	7^2	$6^{1-1/2}$	$5^{1/2}$	10^1	14	14	D. Brumfield	Reverie Knoll Farm	78.20

Time: :22$^{1/5}$, :46$^{3/5}$, 1:10$^{4/5}$, 1:36, 2:00$^{3/5}$. Track fast. In gate 4:31 EST. Off at 4:31$^{1/2}$ EST. Start good. Won driving.
(f) Field.

Program #		Win	Place	Show
7	Proud Clarion	$62.20	$27.80	$12.00
5	Barbs Delight		$16.00	$ 7.60
2	Damascus			$ 3.40

Winner: B. c. by Hail to Reason–Breath O'Morn, by *Djeddah. Trained by Loyd Gentry; bred in Kentucky by J. W. Galbreath.
$162,200 gross value and $5,000 Gold Cup. Net to winner $119,700; second $25,000; third $12,500; fourth $5,000.

162 nominations.
Equipment: b—blinkers

*Foreign bred

Go Figure

The great Hall of Fame trainer Allen Jerkens, who trained two horses—Onion and Prove Out—that beat the great Secretariat, once said, "What you know for certain is that you don't know nothing for certain."

The trainer was mainly talking about why so many horses who win the Derby could never logically expect to win. Such a horse was Proud Clarion, who in 1967 had won just $805 and was a 30–1 shot in the Derby, ridden by a jockey, Bobby Ussery, who not only lost his own Derby mount but was the second choice of Proud Clarion's owner, who regarded the colt as the lesser of two he was running in the Derby, the superior horse being Damascus. Ussery was supposed to ride Reflected Glory for another stable. But after a winter without problems, the colt came up lame before the Derby and was scratched.

Ussery may not have had a chance to ride Proud Clarion if Braulio Baeza's contract with the Galbreaths' Darby Dan Farm had not expired about a week before the Derby, and Baeza had been interested in piloting Successor for breeder O. M. Phipps.

Ussery's selection as the jockey on Proud Clarion started with Galbreath remembering the terrific job that Ussery had done riding Galbreath's Bramalea in the Coaching Club Oaks five years earlier, in 1962. He asked Ussery if he wanted to ride Proud Clarion, and Ussery agreed. He had a feeling that after failed attempts at winning the Derby, this was going to be his year.

Also hoping was Galbreath's trainer, Lloyd "Boo" Gentry, who had had bad luck. A very good horse he trained named Graustark, who would have been favored in the Derby, hurt himself permanently while running on a muddy track in the Blue Grass Stakes.

When the race started, it didn't look like Proud Clarion was going to be trouble to anyone. As the thundering horses passed the grandstand for the first time, he was well back, in ninth, while Damascus, with the great Willie Shoemaker aboard, had his mount under control, waiting to explode. Meanwhile, a horse named Barbs Delight, a sprinter, was in the lead.

At the half-mile mark the positions were about the same, with Shoemaker still waiting to strike. At the stretch, Shoemaker went after Barbs Delight . . . and coming up to challenge on the outside was Bobby Ussery and the 30–1 shot, Proud Clarion. The pace was frenetic, but Proud Clarion proved Ussery's hunch right as he blasted across the finish line first. It was one of the most exciting Derbies ever and, as mentioned, one of the fastest—at 2:00 3/5, the third fastest in Derby history.

Like Jerkens might say: Go figure.

Forward Pass
94th *May 4, 1968*

			Nearco
		Nasrullah	Mumtaz Begum
	On-and-On		Bull Lea
	FORWARD PASS	Two Lea	Two Bob
	Bay colt		Hyperion
	Princess Turia	*Heliopolis*	Drift
			Blue Larkspur
		Blue Delight	Chicleight

THE WINNER'S PEDIGREE AND CAREER HIGHLIGHTS

YEAR	AGE	STS.	1ST	2ND	3RD	EARNINGS
1967	2	10	3	2	2	$ 33,957
1968	3	13	7	2	0	$546,674
TOTALS		**23**	**10**	**4**	**2**	**$580,631**

At 2 years	WON	Flash Stakes
	3RD	Sanford Stakes
	UNP	Tyro Stakes, Saratoga Special, Hopeful
At 3 years	WON	Kentucky Derby, Hibiscus, Everglades, Florida Derby, Blue Grass Stakes, Preakness, American Derby
	2ND	Belmont Stakes, Travers
	UNP	Bahamas, Flamingo (Disqualified and placed fourth in Fountain of Youth)

RACE DAY STATISTICS

HORSE	EQ.	WT.	PP	1/4	1/2	3/4	MILE	STR.	FIN.	JOCKEY	OWNER	ODDS TO $1
Dancer's Image		126	12	14	14	$10^{1/2}$	8^{hd}	1^1	$1^{1-1/2}$	R. Ussery	Peter Fuller	3.60
Forward Pass	b	126	13	3^2	4^4	3^4	2^2	$2^{1/2}$	2^{nk}	I. Valenzuela	Calumet Farm	2.20
Francie's Hat		126	10	11^3	11^2	7^2	7^2	4^2	$3^{2-1/2}$	E. Fires	Saddle Rock Farm	32.50
T.V. Commercial	b	126	2	$9^{1/2}$	8^1	9^1	$6^{1/2}$	5^{hd}	4^1	H. Grant	Bwamazon Farm	24.00
Kentucky Sherry		126	4	$1^{1/2}$	1^2	1^2	1^{hd}	3^2	5^1	J. Combest	Mrs. J. W. Brown	(f) 14.70
Jig Time	b	126	3	$7^{1-1/2}$	$6^{1/2}$	$6^{1/2}$	4^{hd}	6^{hd}	$6^{1/2}$	R. Broussard	Cragwood Stable	36.30
Don B		126	7	5^2	5^2	5^1	$5^{1-1/2}$	7^4	7^5	D. Pierce	D. B. Wood	35.50
Trouble Brewing		126	5	$12^{1/2}$	9^1	11^2	13^4	12^4	8^{nk}	B. Thornburg	Coventry Rock Farm	(f) 14.70
Proper Proof		126	11	13^3	12^1	12^2	11^2	$8^{1-1/2}$	9^4	J. Sellers	Mr. M. R. Fisher	9.90
Te Vega	b	126	6	8^{hd}	13^{hd}	13^1	12^2	9^2	$10^{3/4}$	M. Manganello	Brunswick Farm	(f) 14.70
Captain's Gig		126	9	2^{hd}	2^{hd}	2^1	3^2	10^2	$11^{1-1/2}$	M. Ycaza	Cain Hoy Stable	6.10
Iron Ruler		126	1	$10^{1/2}$	$7^{1/2}$	$8^{1/2}$	9^{hd}	11^1	12^3	B. Baeza	October House Farm	5.70
Verbatim	b	126	8	6^{hd}	10^{hd}	14	14	14	13no	A. Cordero Jr.	Elmendorf	37.40
Gleaming Sword	b	126	14	$4^{1/2}$	$3^{1/2}$	4^{hd}	10^2	13^1	14	E. Belmonte	C. V. Whitney	31.20

Time: :22$^{1/5}$, :45$^{4/5}$, 1:09$^{4/5}$, 1:36$^{1/5}$, 2:02$^{1/5}$. Track fast. In gate 4:40 EDT. Off at 4:40$^{1/2}$ EDT. Start good. Won driving.
(f) Field.

Program #		Win	Place	Show
9	Dancer's Image	$9.20	$4.40	$4.00
10	Forward Pass		$4.20	$3.20
7	Francie's Hat			$6.40

Winner: Gr. c. by Native Dancer–Noors Image, by Noor. Trained by L. C. Cavalaris; bred in Maryland by Peter Fuller.
$165,100 gross value and $5,000 Gold Cup. Net to winner $122,600; second $25,000; third $12,500; fourth $5,000.

191 nominations.
Equipment: b—blinkers

*Foreign Bred

Shocker

THE 1968 DERBY HAD A COUPLE OF UN-usual features. One was that five of the four-teen horses were colored gray, which led to the race being characterized as "The Gray Horse Derby." But the most unusual aspect of this Derby was the contest after the Derby was over, a contest that was to take five years—mainly in the courts—before being decided.

The favorite in the race was Forward Pass, jockeyed by Ishmael "Milo" Valenzuela. The horse was looked on as a stepping-stone for its owner, Calumet Farm, to regain its former greatness. The race attracted its usually large crowd—over 92,000.

One of the contenders was Dancer's Image, a horse noted for sore ankles and the ability to drive from far back to win. In this case, he was piloted by Bobby Ussery, who took him all the way from last place to contention as the stretch run began.

Ussery, a great jockey, saw a hole and drove the gray colt through, and at the three-sixteenths pole he was in the lead, at which point Usserry dropped his whip, but it didn't matter. Dancer's Image was flying, and Ussery took him home, followed by Forward Pass, who was able to hold off the hard-charging Francie's Hat.

The ecstatic owner of Dancer's Image, Bostonian Peter Fuller, leaped onto the track to lead his colt and jockey to the winner's circle, accompanied by Lou Cavalaris, the trainer, who was heard to comment, "It's the top of the world, training the horse that just won the world's champion race."

But his feelings were to change.

That evening routine tests for the presence of illegal medications were run, and one of the technicians noticed that one of the samples changed color, indicating something illegal. The technician didn't know who the sample, la-beled 3956U, belonged to. The illegal substance was phenylbutazone, a painkiller known in the horse world as "bute."

Soon, the name of the horse was announced: Dancer's Image.

Investigation showed that the drug had been put in Dancer's Image's feed, but it was never determined by whom. Over a five-year period, Peter Fuller—an amateur boxer with a never-say-die personality—pursued a complicated odyssey, suing in court and winning and then having that win upset.

In the end Fuller—who spent over $200,000 in legal fees, more than the purse, which was $122,600—and Dancer's Image lost everything, including the Derby trophy, which was awarded to Forward Pass.

Majestic Prince
95th *May 3, 1969*

		Polynesian
	Native Dancer	Geisha
Raise a Native		Case Ace
MAJESTIC PRINCE	Raise You	Lady Glory
Chestnut colt		Nearco
Gay Hostess	*Royal Charger	Sun Princess
		Alibhai
	Your Hostess	Boudoir II

The Winner's Pedigree and Career Highlights

YEAR	AGE	STS.	1ST	2ND	3RD	EARNINGS
1968	2	2	2	0	0	$ 5,500
1969	3	8	7	1	0	$408,700
TOTALS		**10**	**9**	**1**	**0**	**$414,200**

At 2 years   WON Maiden on 1st attempt
At 3 years   WON Kentucky Derby, Los Feliz Stakes, San Vicente Stakes, San Jacinto Stakes, Santa Anita Derby, Preakness
              2ND Belmont Stakes

Race Day Statistics

HORSE	EQ.	WT.	PP	1/4	1/2	3/4	MILE	STR.	FIN.	JOCKEY	OWNER	ODDS TO $1
Majestic Prince		126	8	4^{hd}	$3^{1/2}$	$3^{1/2}$	2^3	$1^{1/2}$	1^{nk}	W. Hartack	Frank McMahon	1.40
Arts and Letters		126	3	2^{hd}	4^3	4^4	$1^{1/2}$	2^2	$2^{1/2}$	B. Baeza	Rokeby Stable	4.40
Dike		126	7	7^8	6^{hd}	5^4	3^2	3^7	3^{10}	J. Velasquez	Claiborne Farm	4.20
Traffic Mark		126	2	8	8	8	6^4	$4^{1-1/2}$	$4^{1-3/4}$	P. Grimm	Mr. & Mrs. R. F. Roberts	45.20
Top Knight	b	126	1	3^{hd}	2^{hd}	1^1	4^5	5^8	5^{13}	M. Ycaza	S. B. Wilson Estate	2.30
Ocean Roar		126	6	1^4	1^2	$2^{1/2}$	5^{hd}	6^4	6^9	R. Stewart	Leo Miller	28.00
Fleet Allied	b	126	5	6^5	7^7	6^2	7^8	7^{10}	7^8	D. Hall	Mr. & Mrs. V. Kanowsky	57.00
Rae Jet	b	126	4	5^1	5^1	$7^{1/2}$	8	8	8	R. Howard	R. E. Harris	70.90

Time: :23³/5, :48, 1:12²/5, 1:37³/5, 2:01⁴/5. Track fast. In gate 5:39 EDT. Off at 5:39¹/2 EDT. Start good. Won driving.

Program #		Win	Place	Show
8	Majestic Prince	$4.80	$3.40	$2.60
3	Arts and Letters		$4.20	$3.00
7	Dike			$2.80

Winner: Ch. c. by Raise a Native–Gay Hostess, by *Royal Charger. Trained by John Longden; bred in Kentucky by Leslie Combs II.
$155,700 gross value and $5,000 Gold Cup. Net to winner $113,200; second $25,000; third $12,500; fourth $5,000.

187 nominations.
Equipment: b—blinkers

*Foreign bred

Bill "Don't Call Me Willie" Hartack

ON A THOROUGHBRED, BILL "DON'T CALL Me Willie" Hartack (he really loathed being called Willie, among other loathings) was a study in efficiency, a master of racing a horse. When he hit the wire, his entire game was behind him on the track. Nothing was left in the locker room.

And it was said of him that he never made the same mistake with a horse. In his first Derby, for example, the 1956 Derby, he started his mount Fabius's drive to the finish from too far out, and was beaten by a horse named Needles by a length. No, his problem was never on a horse—but off it he was churlish and short-tempered, and he had a scalding honesty that earned him a lot of enemies.

For years, it didn't seem to matter to those who hired him to ride their horses, but after his great 1964 ride on Northern Dancer, his phone stopped ringing. People just did not want to work with him anymore.

But not everyone. Johnny Longden, an ex-rider and Derby winner himself, didn't care that Bill Hartack wasn't Mr. Warmth. What he cared about was Hartack's ability to bring a horse from point A to point B in the shortest amount of time. Longden contracted with Hartack to ride Majestic Prince, a celebrated horse who had been bought for $250,000, a huge amount of money in 1969. Hartack promptly showed how great he was as a rider. Under him, Majestic Prince won six straight races.

On Derby day, Majestic Prince was a 7–5

favorite, but it was a great field, with both Eddie Arcaro and Willie Shoemaker in the mix.

The field broke from the gate, and a 28–1 shot named Ocean Roar set the pace. Then on the far turn, positions changed, and Arts and Letters, Braulio Baeza up, was ahead, with Majestic Prince on his tail. With three furlongs to go, turning into the stretch, Hartack spoke to his horse: it is time to lay it down. And Majestic Prince did, spurting ahead of Arts and Letters. Braulio Baeza urged his colt forward, challenging Majestic Prince, who had gained a half-length lead on Arts and Letters at the furlong pole, and though Arts and Letters kept coming, when they crossed the wire he was still a neck behind. Bill Hartack had won Derby number five, and Johnny Longden had become the only man to both ride (Count Fleet) and train (Majestic Prince) a Derby winner ever.

Dust Commander
96th *May 2, 1970*

	Bold Ruler	*Nasrullah
	Bold Commander	Miss Disco
DUST COMMANDER	High Voltage	*Ambiorix
Chestnut colt		Dynamo
Dust Storm	*Windy City II	Wyndham
		Staunton
	Challure	Challedon
		Capitivation

THE WINNER'S PEDIGREE AND CAREER HIGHLIGHTS

YEAR	AGE	STS.	1ST	2ND	3RD	EARNINGS
1969	2	14	4	1	2	$ 25,245
1970	3	23	4	4	2	$187,331
1971	4	5	0	0	0	$ 2,436
TOTALS		42	8	5	4	**$215,012**

At 2 years   WON   Maiden on 5th Attempt, City of Miami Beach Handicap
At 3 years   WON   Kentucky Derby, Blue Grass Stakes
             2ND   *Fayette Handicap
             3RD   Clark Handicap, Monmouth Invitational
             UNP   Preakness, Fountain of Youth, Hutcheson, Boardwalk, Ventnor
At 4 years   UNP   Oaklawn Handicap, Razorback Handicap, Southland Handicap
             *Placed second through disqualification after finishing third

HORSE	EQ.	WT.	PP	1/4	1/2	3/4	MILE	STR.	FIN.	JOCKEY	OWNER	ODDS TO $1
Dust Commander	b	126	2	9²	6¹ᐟ²	5²	7¹	1¹⁻¹ᐟ²	1⁵	M. Manganello	R. E. Lehman	15.30
My Dad George	b	126	12	16³	14²	14¹	5ʰᵈ	3³	2¹ᐟ²	R. Broussard	R. M. Curtis	2.80
High Echelon	b	126	11	17	17	17	15²	5²	3ʰᵈ	L. Adams	Ethel D. Jacobs	(a) 4.90
Naskra	b	126	14	10²	10²	10²⁻¹ᐟ²	8²	4ʰᵈ	4¹	B. Baeza	Her-Jac Stable	15.90
Silent Screen		126	6	6³	3ʰᵈ	3¹	1¹	2¹	5²⁻¹ᐟ²	J. Rotz	Elberon Farm	5.70
Admiral's Shield		126	15	14²	16⁵	16²	16	7³	6ʰᵈ	J. Nichols	W. C. Robinson Jr.	29.70
Corn off the Cob		126	17	5ʰ	5²	6¹⁻¹ᐟ²	3¹⁻¹ᐟ²	6³	7³	A. Cordero Jr.	Fence Post Farm	13.10
Personality	b	126	16	7ʰᵈ	9¹⁻¹ᐟ²	11¹⁻¹ᐟ²	9ʰᵈ	8ʰᵈ	8²⁻¹ᐟ²	E. Belmonte	Ethel D. Jacobs	(a) 4.90
Native Royalty	b	126	8	8¹⁻¹ᐟ²	8¹	8¹	4¹ᐟ²	9²	9²⁻¹ᐟ⁴	I. Valenzuela	Happy Valley Farm	(f) 10.10
Robin's Bug	b	126	7	3ʰᵈ	4²	4ʰᵈ	10¹⁻¹ᐟ²	10³	10¹ᐟ²	L. Moyers	W. J. Hickey– R. F. Kuhn	(f) 10.10
Terlago		126	13	4¹⁻¹ᐟ²	7¹⁻¹ᐟ²	7ʰᵈ	11²	11²	11¹⁻¹ᐟ⁴	W. Shoemaker	S. J. Agnew	7.40
Dr. Behrman	b	126	3	11²	11¹	12¹	14¹ᐟ²	12²	12²	C. Baltazar	Lin-Drake Farm	(f) 10.10
Action Getter		126	9	15¹⁻¹ᐟ²	15ʰᵈ	15¹ᐟ²	13²	13¹	13²⁻¹ᐟ²	M. Venezia	E. V. Benjamin– J. Jones Jr.	(f) 10.10
George Lewis		126	1	2¹⁻¹ᐟ²	2⁴	2¹⁻¹ᐟ²	2¹ᐟ²	14¹	14ʰᵈ	W. Hartack	Mr. & Mrs. A. Magerman	9.40
Fathom	b	126	10	12¹ᐟ²	13³	9¹	12³	15³	15³⁻¹ᐟ²	D. Crump	W. L. L. Brown	(f) 10.10
Rancho Lejos	b	126	5	1³	1³	1¹	6²	16	16	H. Campas	S. Carson-I. Apple	(f) 10.10
Holy Land	b	126	4	13⁴	12¹ᐟ²	13¹ᐟ²	Fell			H. Pilar	Mrs. J. S. Dean Jr.	15.90

Time: :23¹/₅, :46⁴/₅, 1:12, 1:37²/₅, 2:03²/₅. Track good. In gate 5:42 EDT. Off at 5:42½ EDT. Start good. Won ridden out.
Coupled: (a) High Echelon and Personality; (f) Field.

Program #		Win	Place	Show
3	Dust Commander	$32.60	$12.60	$7.00
7	My Dad George		$ 5.00	$3.20
1	High Echelon			$4.40

Winner: Ch. c. by Bold Commander–Dust Storm, by *Windy City II. Trained by Don Combs; bred in Illinois by Pullen Bros. $168,300 gross value and $5,000 Gold Cup. Net to winner $127,800; second $25,000; third $12,500; fourth $5,000.
Scratched: Protanto.

193 nominations.
Equipment: b—blinkers

*Foreign bred

Not a Chance

THE 1970 DERBY WAS MARKED BY A NUM-
ber of unusual incidents, one being that no one
thought of the ultimate winner, Dust Commander, as a horse who could win the Derby.
The odds against him were 35–1. Perhaps this
was because he was not imposing, weighing just
nine hundred pounds, a hundred less than most
colts, and being only fifteen hands high. Or
maybe it was his jockey, Mike Manganello. He
rode in the Midwest, and was not regarded as
anyone special, just a journeyman jockey.

Still there was very clear evidence by Derby
day that he was a threat. He won the Blue Grass
Stakes in 2:03 1/5 on a sloppy track. As Jim Bolus, writing for the *Louisville Courier-Journal*,
noted, "The trim little colt, after pulling away
from his Blue Grass score, worked an additional
furlong in a sparkling time to complete the
Derby distance in 2:03 4/5—on a sloppy track."

Another incident was that Dust Commander
was blessed by a Catholic bishop, Emanuel
Milango of Zambia. As it happened, the bishop
had had his education underwritten by Dust
Commander's owner, Mr. Robert E. Lehman,
through an organization called the Society for
the Propagation of the Faith. Milango had been
in America and had dropped by for a visit with
the Lehmans and blessed the horse.

But a more ominous note was a sense the
bishop had that something was going to go terribly wrong in the Derby. Mrs. Lehman asked

him what was wrong, and the bishop answered,
"A dark cloud hangs over the Derby."

"How?" Mrs. Lehman asked.

The bishop didn't know. All he knew was
that it "involved the number 4 horse."

When the race began, there were no problems. Manganello got Dust Commander a good
spot on the rail and was riding along when the
crowd gasped and grew silent. Up ahead, on the
far turn, a horse had gone down, and the jockey
lay motionless on the track.

Manganello went wide and was able to avoid
a collision and get in position, ultimately winning by five lengths.

The horse that had gone down, it chillingly turned out, was Holy Land, the number 4
horse . . . just as the bishop had predicted.

Canonero II
97th May 1, 1971

	Doutelle	Prince Chevalier
		Above Board
*Pretender		Verso II
CANONERO II	Limicola	Uccello
Bay colt		*Nasrullah
	Nantallah	Shimmer
Dixieland II		Johnstown
	Ragtime Band	Marial Air

THE WINNER'S PEDIGREE AND CAREER HIGHLIGHTS

YEAR	AGE	STS.	1ST	2ND	3RD	EARNINGS
1970	2	4	2	0	1	$ 12,851
1971	3	11	6	0	3	$312,159
1972	4	8	1	3	0	$ 35,970
TOTALS		23	9	3	4	**$360,980**

At 2 years	WON	Maiden on 1st attempt, Two allowance races in Venezuela
	UNP	Del Mar Futurity
At 3 years	WON	Kentucky Derby, Preakness Stakes (won 4 races in Venezuela)
	UNP	Belmont Stakes
At 4 years	WON	Stymie Handicap
	2ND	Carter Handicap
	UNP	Metropolitan, Title

HORSE	EQ.	WT.	PP	1/4	1/2	3/4	MILE	STR.	FIN.	JOCKEY	OWNER	ODDS TO $1
Canonero II		126	12	16^1	18^5	15^3	4$^{1/2}$	1^3	1$^{3-3/4}$	G. Avila	Edgar Caibett	(f) 8.70
Jim French	b	126	10	10^{hd}	11^2	10^2	7^2	5$^{1/2}$	2^2	A. Cordero Jr.	F. J. Caldwell	4.80
Bold Reason	b	126	14	18^6	16$^{1/2}$	12^2	9^2	6^2	3^{nk}	J. Cruguet	W. A. Levin	18.30
Eastern Fleet	b	126	17	6^2	3^{hd}	2$^{1-1/2}$	2$^{1-1/2}$	2^{hd}	4^{hd}	E. Maple	Calumet Farm	(a) 3.80
Unconscious		126	8	7^2	6^2	5^1	5^{hd}	4$^{1/2}$	5$^{1-3/4}$	L. Pincay Jr.	A. A. Seeligson Jr.	2.80
Vegas Vic	b	126	7	13^3	13^3	13^1	13$^{1/2}$	7^1	6^{nk}	H. Grant	Betty Sechrest & C. Fritz	19.30
Tribal Line	b	126	15	15^2	14^{hd}	17^6	8$^{1-1/2}$	8^2	7no	D. Whited	J. E. & T. A. Grissom	80.80
Bold and Able	b	126	1	1^{hd}	1^2	1$^{1-1/2}$	1^{hd}	3^{hd}	8^3	J. Velasquez	Calumet Farm	(a) 3.80
List	b	126	18	17^{hd}	17$^{1/2}$	14^2	14$^{1-1/2}$	9^2	9^3	J. Nichols	Mrs. J. W. Brown	8.60
Twist the Axe		126	11	9$^{1/2}$	10^1	7^1	6$^{1-1/2}$	10^2	10$^{1-1/2}$	G. Patterson	Pastorale Stable	(x) 5.10
Going Straight		126	2	11^2	8^{hd}	6^{hd}	10^3	12^2	11^{hd}	O. Torres	Donamire Farm	45.60
Royal Leverage		126	5	19^8	15^2	16^1	18^5	11^{hd}	12^2	M. Fromin	Phil Teinowitz	(c) 41.60
Impetuosity		126	20	8$^{1-1/2}$	9^2	8^2	15^1	13^{hd}	13$^{1-1/2}$	E. Guerin	W. P. Rosso	(x) 5.10
Helio Rise		126	16	12$^{1/2}$	12^1	9^{hd}	11^1	14^1	14^3	K. Knapp	R. W. & R. T. Wilson Jr.	58.20
On the Money		126	9	20	20	20	17$^{1/2}$	15$^{1-1/2}$	15^1	M. Solomone	Teinowitz-Schmidt	(c) 41.60
Barbizon Streak		126	6	2^{hd}	5^1	11^1	12^1	16^6	16^{18}	D. Brumfield	Mrs. H. J. Udouj	(f) 8.70
Knight Counter	b	126	13	4^2	4$^{1-1/2}$	3^1	3^1	17^6	17^{11}	M. Manganello	Robert Huffman	(f) 8.70
Jr's Arrowhead	b	126	4	3^{hd}	2^1	4^1	16$^{1-1/2}$	18^2	18^6	A. Rini	Walnut Hill Farm	(f) 8.70
Fourulla		126	19	5^{hd}	7$^{1/2}$	18^3	19^4	19^4	19^{14}	D. MacBeth	A. H. Sullivan	(f) 8.70
Saigon Warrior		127	3	14^3	19^9	19^5	20	20	20	R. Parrot	C. M. Day	(f) 8.70

Time: :23, :46$^{4/5}$, 1:11$^{3/5}$, 1:36$^{1/5}$, 2:03$^{1/5}$. Track fast. In gate 5:42 EDT. Off at 5:42$^{1/2}$ EDT. Start good. Won ridden out.
Coupled: (a) Eastern Fleet and Bold and Brave; (c) Royal Leverage and On the Money; (x) Twist the Axe and Impetuosity; (f) Field.

Program #		Win	Place	Show
15f	Canonero II	$19.40	$8.00	$ 4.20
7	Jim French		$6.20	$ 4.40
8	Bold Reason			$12.60

Winner: B. c. by *Pretender–Dixieland II, by Nantallah. Trained by Juan Arias; bred in Kentucky by E. B. Benjamin.
$188,000 gross value and $5,000 Gold Cup. Net to winner $145,500; second $25,000; third $12,500; fourth $5,000.

220 nominations.
Equipment: b—blinkers

*Foreign bred

"Who the Hell Is That?"

"THEY ALL SEEMED THREE QUARTS LOW," said one observer in describing the bay colt Canonero II and his contingent, who had traveled from Venezuela for the ninety-seventh running of the Kentucky Derby. Another observer characterized the horse and his entourage as a "farce"; another, as a "running joke."

One reason was the way the horse wore his forelock, the hair between the ears on the forehead. Most horses wear it loose. His was cut in bangs. "He looked," someone said, "like Moe of the Three Stooges."

There was also the horrific condition he was in when he arrived in Lexington: he was incredibly emaciated and could barely walk, much less run. This was because of what he had endured on the way to America. Two planes he was in developed mechanical trouble, and finally he was transported from South America to the United States in a cargo plane with ducks and chickens as companions. When he arrived in Miami, he didn't have the proper papers and stood twelve sweltering hours before being unloaded, and four days in quarantine. Then, he went 1200 miles to Lexington from Miami in a truck because his owner had not given his trainer, Juan Arias, enough money for a flight. Overall he lost seventy pounds, and his ribs stuck out prominently.

Then there were the training techniques of Arias. Arias, a black man always dressed in a suit and tie even in the stable, approached his horse not as a horse but as his son. And he was a loving, indulgent father. He petted him, hugged him, kissed him—and acted on what the horse said. That is, he would ask Canonero (he was named Canonero II because there was already another Canonero), say, if he felt like working out today, then place his ear on the horse and listen for the answer. If the horse said no, that was it. He did not train. Or eat, or whatever the horse told him.

Arias was also not averse to running his horse slowly. "Most of the American trainers train for speed," he explained. "I train Canonero to be a star, a horse of depth who is versatile and can be ridden in front or from behind. They say I train my horse too slow. Let's see if he runs that slow on Saturday." But Arias's methods didn't seem to be working. The first time Canonero ran in Lexington, for example, he covered a half mile in a turtle-like 53 3/5.

Then, of course, feeding into the three-quarts-low feeling about the Venezuelans there was *why* he was running. Pedro Baptista,* who had actually purchased Canonero in America but raced him in South America, entered him in the Kentucky Derby because his deceased mother told him to do so in a dream.

Perhaps adding to this running joke was that not many people knew the horse or how fast he could run. His image, to those who saw him prior to the Derby, was simply that of a slow-moving horse who was also a patient in a madhouse. In fact, he had run well—very well—in South America.

One thing was for sure. Canonero wouldn't have a beginner on his back when the gates opened to release the large field of twenty horses. To ride him, Baptista had engaged top South American jockey Gustavo Avila, nicknamed "El Monstruo"—"The Monster"—who had ridden Canonero three times and won twice.

Like a loving father, Arias had total faith in Canonero. And a few hours before the race, between drags on his omnipresent cigarette, he said, "Nobody knows my horse. But after today the world will know him."

Perhaps, or maybe he was a person who needed a dream to come true, needed the world to wrap their arms around his horse, and maybe him. He was a man who knew all about love or the lack of it, who had grown up in the slums of Caracas, where his father had deserted the family when he was a little boy, and who had spent his life with horses—what he called "the beautiful world of horses"—as far from the heartache of his childhood as possible.

The track was fast. The sun was out, the sky powder blue. A clang and a bell and the gates opened—and a pack of mad dogs posing as race-horses thundered down the track.

Almost immediately, Canonero seemed to confirm what most people assumed: that he couldn't run fast. He dropped back—way back—into eighteenth place, only two horses behind him.

But Arias, watching from the rail, still believed. And as he watched, the Monster moved Canonero into fifteenth place, without a single stroke of the whip. Love wouldn't allow the whip. He would win with his hands and his skill, or he would not win.

Then, with three-quarters of the race gone, just a half mile to go, the race changed as Derbies do. Many of the jockeys started to smell the wire and move their mounts more quickly, positioning themselves for a final run down the stretch, "Heartbreak Lane," where most races are won or lost.

And so did Canonero. Stooge forelock flying back, he started to move faster and faster. And as he did, Arias and the rest of the Venezuelan team screamed "Canonero! Canonero!" It was as if the horse heard them. He went into overdrive, and his brown coat, coupled with Avila's brown silks and cap, looked, collectively, like what one spectator described as a "brown blur." He caught and started to pass other horses as if they were statues—and, *kaboom!*, suddenly there were no more horses to pass: he was in the lead and pulling away, and no one was going to catch him. Arias burst into tears, and up in the stands many of the spectators, including a man named Chick Lang, who was on the nominating committee of the Derby and other races asked the same question: *"Who the hell is that?"*

And then Lang remembered and almost swallowed his tongue. A few weeks earlier, in a hotel in Miami, he had received a phone call from a man with a Spanish accent who said his name was Pedro Baptista. He wanted to get his horse nominated, and Lang had written the name on a cocktail napkin. At first he thought it was a joke. But he checked it out and found that Canonero II was a legitimate horse. And that horse with his name on that cocktail napkin—which Lang almost discarded—roared across the wire the winner of the Kentucky Derby by three and three-quarter lengths.

Within minutes, someone was screaming into the long-distance phone to Pedro Baptista, whose business had forced him to stay in Caracas, that Canonero had won the Kentucky Derby and Venezuelans started to crowd the streets and go wild with pride and joy. Baptista and his son drove to a cemetery and knelt down by his mother's grave and thanked her.

Canonero, who the media started calling "the Caracas Cannonball," was to go on to win the Preakness. Experts say he would have become a Triple Crown winner, except he was sick when the Belmont Stakes was run, and came in fourth.

For as long as people remember the Kentucky Derby, one of its greatest moments will always be trying to identify the brown blur who came from eighteen lengths off the pace and the crazy people who weren't so crazy after all.

---

*Edgar Canonero was owned by Pedro Baptista, but ran under his son-in-law's name (Caibett) because of superstitions.

Riva Ridge
98th *May 6, 1972*

	*Turn-to	*Royal Charger
First Landing		*Source Sucree
RIVA RIDGE	Hildene	Bubbling Over
Bay colt		Fancy Racket
Iberia	*Heliopolis	Hyperion
		Drift
		*Easton
	War East	Warrior Lass

THE WINNER'S PEDIGREE AND CAREER HIGHLIGHTS

YEAR	AGE	STS.	1ST	2ND	3RD	EARNINGS
1971	2	9	7	0	0	$ 503,263
1972	3	12	5	1	1	$ 395,632
1973	4	9	5	2	0	$ 212,452
TOTALS		**30**	**17**	**3**	**1**	**$1,111,347**

At 2 years	WON	Maiden on 2nd attempt, Flash, Futurity, Champagne, Pimlico-Laurel Futurity, Garden State
	UNP	Great American
At 3 years	WON	Kentucky Derby, Belmont Stakes, Blue Grass, Hibiscus, Hollywood Derby
	2ND	Stymie Handicap
	3RD	Jockey Club Gold Cup
	UNP	Everglades, Preakness, Monmouth Invitational, Woodward, D. C. International
At 4 years	WON	Massachusetts Handicap, Brooklyn Handicap, Stuyvesant
	2ND	Marlboro Cup
	UNP	Jockey Club Gold Cup, Metropolitan

HORSE	EQ.	WT.	PP	1/4	1/2	3/4	MILE	STR.	FIN.	JOCKEY	OWNER	ODDS TO $1
Riva Ridge	b	126	9	$1^{1/2}$	$1^{1-1/2}$	$1^{1-1/2}$	$1^{1-1/2}$	1^3	$1^{3-1/4}$	R. Turcotte	Meadow Stud	1.50
No Le Hace	b	126	16	6^2	6^5	5^3	3^3	3^5	$2^{3-1/2}$	P. Rubbicco	J. R. Straus	4.50
Hold Your Peace	b	126	3	$3^{1-1/2}$	$2^{1/2}$	2^5	2^8	2^3	$3^{3-1/2}$	C. Marquez	Maribel G. Blum	3.90
Introductivo	b	126	4	8^2	7^2	7^{hd}	8^1	4^3	4^2	R. Breen	Mr. & Mrs. C. J. Robertson Sr.	52.90
Sensitive Music	b	126	2	10^2	9^3	9^5	4^1	$5^{1-1/2}$	$5^{3/4}$	J. L. Rotz	F. H. Lindsay	31.00
Freetex	b	126	1	11^3	11^4	6^{hd}	7^{hd}	6^2	6^1	C. Baltazar	Middletown Stable	15.90
Big Spruce		126	15	$12^{1/2}$	13^2	11^1	13^2	7^2	$7^{1-1/2}$	L. Adams	Elmendorf	(f) 8.90
Head of the River		126	14	9^{hd}	10^{hd}	10^4	9^3	8^6	8^5	M. Hole	Rokeby Stable	19.00
Big Brown Bear		126	7	14^{hd}	12^1	14^5	12^{hd}	10^2	$9^{1-3/4}$	R. Broussard	Mr. & Mrs. A. E. Reinhold	27.80
Kentuckian	b	126	8	15^4	14^1	12^2	11^5	11^3	$10^{3/4}$	D. Brumfield	P. W. Madden	16.70
Hassi's Image	b	126	11	5^3	$4^{1/2}$	3^2	6^2	$9^{1-1/2}$	11^2	H. Gustines	Hassi Shina	31.00
Majestic Needle	b	126	12	$2^{1/2}$	3^2	4^2	5^2	$12^{1/2}$	12no	M. Manganello	R. E. Lehmann	(f) 8.90
Our Trade Winds		126	6	16	16	16	15^2	$13^{1/2}$	$13^{1/2}$	J. Nichols	Robert Mitchell	(f) 8.90
Napoise	b	126	13	$13^{1-1/2}$	15^7	15^2	16	14^5	$14^{4-1/2}$	R. Kotenko	R. E. Lehmann	(f) 8.90
Dr. Neale		126	5	4^{hd}	5^3	8^1	$10^{1-1/2}$	16	15^{nk}	W. Leeling	C. H. Nicholas	(f) 8.90
Pacallo	b	126	10	7^1	8^1	13^2	14^3	15^1	16	G. Avila	Walnut Hill Farm	54.50

Time: :23$^{4/5}$, :47$^{3/5}$, 1:11$^{4/5}$, 1:36, 2:01$^{4/5}$. Track fast. In gate 5:34 EDT. Off at 5:34 EDT. Start good. Won handily.
(f) Field.

Program #		Win	Place	Show
7	Riva Ridge	$5.00	$3.80	$3.00
2	No Le Hace		$4.40	$3.40
3	Hold Your Peace			$3.60

Winner: B. c. by First Landing–Iberia, by *Heliopolis. Trained by Lucien Laurin; bred in Kentucky by Meadow Stud, Inc.
$182,800 gross value and $5,000 Gold Cup. Net to winner $140,300; second $25,000; third $12,500; fourth $5,000.

258 nominations.
Equipment: b—blinkers

*Foreign bred

Of Special Stuff

JOCKEYS AND HORSES AND TRAINERS WHO win Kentucky Derbies usually have to be made of special stuff, but so, too, many times, do the owners. One of these very special people was Helen "Penny" Tweedy, a pretty, well-dressed, soft-looking woman who had a cast-iron stomach. She took over Meadow Stud in Doswell, Virginia, when her elderly father, Chris Chenery, partially paralyzed by a series of circulatory problems, could no longer run it. To add to the unhappiness, Meadow Stud was in deep fiscal difficulty, this more than amply shown the first year of her tenure, when the company lost $85,000. The advice of friends and experts: sell. She could get $1,000,000 for the Thoroughbreds she owned alone. But there were a number of problems that complicated that obvious solution: she loved horses, she loved her father, and she wanted to keep it going for him. And then there was that cast-iron stomach. She simply had to keep the royal blue-and-white silks of Meadow Stud flying.

She would not do it. The doors would stay open, and stay open they did, because, as it happened, two horses were born there that were as important as any that ever lived. They saved Meadow Stud.

One was Secretariat, who would go on to be one of the most honored, loved, and respected horses who had ever raced. But Riva Ridge, a light bay colt described by writer Red Smith as the color of expensive luggage, was at that moment even more important: Without the money

he won as a two-year-old, Meadow Stud would have been no more.

Early on, Riva Ridge was picked out by his trainer Lucien Laurin as a special horse. He had thin legs like a deer, but that was not a negative—they were the kind of legs that great Thoroughbreds have. But there was also that look in his eye, an aristocratic look that showed he knew his place in the world. Indeed, looks-wise, he was perfect—except for his floppy ears.

Ron Turcotte, the great Canadian jockey, who had been Riva Ridge's rider since he was a two-year-old, was chosen to ride him in the Derby. The day was clear and sunny, and at first glance the track was rated "fast." But just to be on the safe side Turcotte rode in the fourth race to check it out for himself. He was surprised to see that near the rail the track was cupped and tiring to run on. He knew that he would have to keep Riva Ridge five or six feet from the rail.

When the sixteen horses were at the post, there were 130,564 spectators in the stands and on the infield. At 5:34 the gates clanged open.

Turcotte planned to run fourth, not lead. But when he glanced to his left, he saw the two lead horses, Hold Your Peace and No Le Hace, were not going to take the lead. Turcotte changed plans in a heartbeat. To the astonishment of many people, including experts, he gunned Riva Ridge to the front and stayed there. Other horses tried to catch him, but each time they came close, Turcotte would press on the gas a little and pull away.

And in the stands, Penny Tweedy thought that her father, who was now in the hospital and could not attend the Derby, had told her to always be "ready for heartbreaking disappointment in racing." But not today. Her heart soared as Riva Ridge went wire to wire to win, one of only thirteen horses in Derby history to do that, and flashed across the finish in 2:01 4/5, the seventh fastest time in Derby history.

At the hospital, the TV broadcasting the Derby had been turned on in Chris Chenery's room, but it was reported that he did not seem to be able to see. But somehow, when the camera came close to Penny, she held the gold cup toward the camera, and then his nurse enthused, "Mr. Chenery, Mr. Chenery, you have just won the Kentucky Derby."

He heard her. The tears running down the sides of his face proved it.

Secretariat
99th *May 5, 1973*

		Nasrullah	Nearco
			Mumtaz Begum
	Bold Ruler		Discovery
SECRETARIAT		Miss Disco	Outdone
Chestnut colt			Prince Rose
	Somethingroyal	*Princequillo	Cosquilla
			Caruso
		Imperatrice	Cinquepace

The Winner's Pedigree and Career Highlights

YEAR	AGE	STS.	1ST	2ND	3RD	EARNINGS
1972	2	9	7	1	0	$ 456,404
1973	3	12	9	2	1	$ 860,404
TOTALS		**21**	**16**	**3**	**1**	**$1,316,808**

At 2 years	WON	Maiden on 2nd attempt, Sanford, Hopeful, Belmont Futurity, Laurel Futurity, Garden State
	2ND	Champagne (1st, disqualified and placed 2nd)
At 3 years	WON	Kentucky Derby, Preakness, Belmont Stakes, Bay Shore, Gotham, Arlington Invitational, Marlboro Cup, Man o' War, Canadian International
	2ND	Woodward, Whitney
	3RD	Wood Memorial

Race Day Statistics

HORSE	EQ.	WT.	PP	1/4	1/2	3/4	MILE	STR.	FIN.	JOCKEY	OWNER	ODDS TO $1
Secretariat	b	126	10	11^{hd}	$6^{1/2}$	5^1	$2^{1-1/2}$	$1^{1/2}$	$1^{2-1/2}$	R. Turcotte	Meadow Stud	(a) 1.50
Sham	b	126	4	5^1	3^2	2^1	$1^{1/2}$	2^6	2^8	L. Pincay Jr.	Sigmund Sommer	2.50
Our Native	b	126	7	$6^{1/2}$	$8^{1-1/2}$	8^1	5^{hd}	3^{hd}	$3^{1/2}$	D. Brumfield	Pritchard, Thomas, & Resseguet Jr.	10.60
Forego		126	9	$9^{1-1/2}$	$9^{1/2}$	$6^{1/2}$	6^2	$4^{1/2}$	$4^{2-1/2}$	P. Anderson	Lazy F Ranch	28.60
Restless Jet		126	1	$7^{1-1/2}$	7^{hd}	$10^{1-1/2}$	$7^{1-1/2}$	$6^{1-1/2}$	$5^{2-1/4}$	M. Hole	Elkwood Farm	28.50
Shecky Greene	b	126	11	$1^{1-1/2}$	1^3	$1^{1-1/2}$	3^3	5^1	$6^{1-1/2}$	L. Adams	Joe Kellman	(c) 5.70
Navajo	b	126	5	$10^{1-1/2}$	10^1	11^4	$8^{1-1/2}$	8^2	7no	W. Soirez	J. Stevenson & R. Stump	52.30
Royal and Regal		126	8	3^1	4^3	4^3	4^1	$7^{1-1/2}$	$8^{3-1/2}$	W. Blum	Aisco Stable	28.30
My Gallant	b	126	12	8^{hd}	$11^{1-1/2}$	12^3	11^2	$10^{1/2}$	9^{hd}	B. Baeza	A. I. Appleton	(c) 5.70
Angle Light		126	2	4^{hd}	$5^{1-1/2}$	7^1	$10^{1-1/2}$	$9^{1-1/2}$	$10^{1-3/4}$	J. LeBlanc	Edwin Whittaker	(a) 1.50
Gold Bag	b	126	13	2^{hd}	2^{hd}	$3^{1/2}$	9^1	11^1	11no	E. Fires	R. Sechrest-Gottdank	68.30
Twice a Prince	b	126	6	13	13	13	13	12^2	$12^{1-1/2}$	A. Santiago	Elmendorf	62.50
Warbucks		126	3	12^1	12^3	9^{hd}	$12^{1-1/2}$	13	13	W. Hartack	E. E. Elzemeyer	7.20

Time: :23$^{2/5}$, :47$^{2/5}$, 1:11$^{4/5}$, 1:36$^{1/5}$, 1:59$^{2/5}$ (new track record). Track fast. In gate 5:37 EDT. Off at 5:37 EDT. Start good. Won handily.
Coupled: (a) Secretariat and Angle Light; (c) Shecky Greene and My Gallant.

Program #		Win	Place	Show
1a	Secretariat	$5.00	$3.20	$3.00
5	Sham		$3.20	$3.00
8	Our Native			$4.20

Winner: Ch. c. by Bold Ruler–Somethingroyal, by *Princequillo. Trained by Lucien Laurin. Bred in Virginia by Meadow Stud, Inc.
$198,800 gross value and $5,000 Gold Cup. Net to winner $155,050; second $25,000; third $12,500; fourth $6,250.

218 nominations.
Equipment: b—blinkers

*Foreign bred

Big Red

IN THE CONTINUOUSLY BRAIN-DEFYING world of Thoroughbred horse racing, there was a special breeding arrangement between Penny Tweedy of Meadow Stud and horse breeder Ogden Phipps. Which foal each would get out of the mare Somethingroyal would be decided by coin toss. Whoever won the coin toss would get the first foal; the loser would get the second.

Phipps won the toss and won a filly named The Bride, who in 1971 in four races never finished higher than sixth. The loser of the coin toss, Penny Tweedy, got the second foal, a chestnut colt. His name was Secretariat.

Secretariat's nickname was "Big Red," but some called him "the Locomotive." Indeed, his power was evident when he was standing stock-still. And he showed it on the track. As a two-year-old he triumphed in a bunch of stakes races at Belmont, Laurel, Saratoga, and Garden State and generated unparalleled excitement in horse-racing circles. Small wonder that as a two-year-old he was named "Horse of the Year." And in early 1973 he was syndicated for the highest price in history, $6,080,000. At the time, one writer, William Nack, said that at that price, "Secretariat was literally worth three times his weight in gold."

As Derby day, May 5, approached, trainer Lucien Laurin was under great pressure to have Secretariat win. His jockey would be Ron Turcotte, who had ridden Riva Ridge to victory in the Derby the year before. Laurin—as with Riva Ridge—only entered Secretariat in three races prior to the Derby. The first was in March in the seven-furlong Bayshore Stakes, followed by a resounding victory in the mile-long Gotham Stakes. Then came a shock: In the Wood Memorial, the last tune-up race prior to the Derby, Secretariat finished third.

Speculation as to why raged. Most focused on the idea that something was wrong with him, including an abscess on the inside of his mouth the size of a silver dollar—but others just said that he could not run a long distance. One thing was for sure: on Derby day, everyone would find out.

On Derby day the track was fast, the weather good, and there were thirteen horses in the race. The starting gate opened, and the horses thundered up the stretch for the first time. And many bettors were keenly aware that Secretariat was running last.

But it wasn't for long. Secretariat made a move, and by the far turn he was in fifth place. Around the turn and then onto the backstretch the race turned into a duel between Sham, ridden by the great Lafitte Pincay Jr., and a determined horse named Shecky Greene.

But as the horses turned into the stretch, Secretariat made another move. He lost ground by swinging outside, but he passed Shecky Greene, and then it was a two-horse race, Sham and Secretariat to the wire. But Secretariat was not to be denied. He crushed the last quarter mile in 23 seconds—a time that still stands as the fastest quarter ever—and hit the wire two and one half lengths ahead of Sham. He broke the equivalent of horse racing's four-minute mile, covering the mile and a quarter in under two minutes—1.59 2/5, still the fastest time ever recorded on the Derby track. "It was weird," said one trainer, "horses are supposed to slow down at the end of a race. He was going faster than he had during the rest of the race."

If that wasn't enough to prove his mettle, Secretariat, with Turcotte still aboard, went on to win the Preakness, and then became the first Triple Crown winner in twenty-five years (he won the Belmont Stakes by thirty-one lengths, or one-third of a football field).

Secretariat was to retire to stud and live in pleasant, bucolic surroundings. Ron Turcotte was to enter into agony. On July 13, 1978, at Belmont Park, he went down on a horse named Flag of Leyte Gulf, breaking his back and putting him into a wheelchair for the rest of his painful life. And it is said that all he has left is the memory of riding Secretariat to victory in that long-ago Derby. "I dream of him sometimes," Turcotte once said. "Not long ago I dreamed that he had come back to racing and that I could walk and that I rode him again. It was a tremendous sensation. In a dream like that you hear and see everything. He had a big neck, a long neck, and I remember riding him and looking between his ears. It was like the Kentucky Derby. I came from behind and won."

Cannonade
100th *May 4, 1974*

		Bold Ruler	*Nosrullah
	Bold Bidder		Miss Disco
	CANNONADE	High Bid	To Market
	Bay colt		Stepping Stone
		*Ribot	Tenerani
	Queen Sucree		Romanella
		Cosmah	Cosmic Bomb
			Almahmoud

THE WINNER'S PEDIGREE AND CAREER HIGHLIGHTS

YEAR	AGE	STS.	1ST	2ND	3RD	EARNINGS
1973	2	17	5	2	4	$141,870
1974	3	8	2	1	2	$359,294
TOTALS		**25**	**7**	**3**	**6**	**$501,164**

At 2 years	WON	Maiden on 3rd attempt, Great American, Kentucky Jockey Club, Aqueduct Handicap
	3RD	Champagne, Heritage Stakes
At 3 years	WON	Kentucky Derby
	2ND	Florida Derby
	3RD	Preakness, Belmont Stakes
	UNP	Flamingo, Dwyer, Fountain of Youth

RACE DAY STATISTICS

HORSE	EQ.	WT.	PP	1/4	1/2	3/4	MILE	STR.	FIN.	JOCKEY	OWNER	ODDS TO $1
Cannonade	b	126	2	12^2	$11^{1/2}$	5^{hd}	1^2	1^4	$1^{2-1/4}$	A. Cordero Jr.	J. M. Olin	(a) 1.50
Hudson County		126	18	2^2	2^2	2^{hd}	3^{hd}	2^2	$2^{3-1/4}$	M. Miceli	R. B. Cohen	(f) 5.20
Agitate		126	1	$10^{1-1/2}$	$9^{1/2}$	$7^{1-1/2}$	$5^{1-1/2}$	3^1	$3^{3/4}$	W. Shoemaker	Meeken Stable	3.40
J. R.'s Pet	b	126	8	14^1	16^1	$9^{1-1/2}$	7^1	5^2	4^{nk}	D. McHargue	W. C. Partee	16.50
Little Current		126	10	23	$21^{1-1/2}$	20^1	$17^{1-1/2}$	$7^{1-1/2}$	$5^{1/2}$	R. Ussery	Darby Dan Farm	22.60
Destroyer		126	15	4^2	4^1	4^1	$2^{1/2}$	4^2	$6^{3/4}$	I. Valenzuela	Kenneth Opstein	35.30
Buck's Bid	b	126	23	7^1	7^2	$8^{1/2}$	6^2	6^2	7^{nk}	D. MacBeth	Bright View Farm	75.20
Judger	b	126	22	22^4	22^2	21^7	12^1	8^2	$8^{2-1/2}$	L. Pincay Jr.	S. W. Hancock	(a) 1.50
Pat McGroder		126	13	19^1	19^1	$19^{1/2}$	15^5	10^1	$9^{3/4}$	T. Barrow	Oxford Stable	(f) 5.20
Rube the Great		126	12	13^2	$12^{1/2}$	$11^{1/2}$	10^1	9^1	10^{nk}	M. A. Rivera	Sigmund Sommer	(b) 5.10
*Sir Tristram	b	126	20	3^{hd}	3^1	6^1	$8^{1/2}$	11^2	$11^{2-1/2}$	W. Hartack	Powhatan	25.80
Confederate Yankee	b	126	16	$17^{1/2}$	15^1	13^4	14^{hd}	$12^{1-1/2}$	$12^{1/2}$	H. Grant	M. H. Boyce	(f) 5.20
Sharp Gary	b	126	7	18^2	$17^{1/2}$	$18^{1/2}$	13^2	13^3	$13^{3-1/2}$	E. Fires	E. R. Scharps	(f) 5.20
Ga Hai		126	14	11^1	10^1	$12^{1-1/2}$	16^{hd}	14^2	$14^{3/4}$	M. Manganello	Laguna Seca Ranch	47.10
Crimson Ruler	b	126	11	$9^{1-1/2}$	8^1	$10^{1/2}$	9^{hd}	15^4	15^3	K. LeBlanc	Lee Matherne	(f) 5.20
Set n' Go		126	19	6^2	$5^{1-1/2}$	3^2	$11^{1/2}$	$16^{1/2}$	16^{nk}	W. Gavidia	A. J. Isturiz	(f) 5.20
Triple Crown	b	126	17	1^{hd}	$1^{1/2}$	$1^{1/2}$	4^{hd}	19^5	17^2	B. Baeza	Samuel Lehrmann	53.90
Accipiter	b	126	4	5^{hd}	6^{hd}	$14^{1/2}$	19^{hd}	17^2	18no	A. Santiago	Sigmund Sommer	(b) 5.10
Gold and Myrrh	b	126	21	16^1	14^1	$16^{1/2}$	18^1	18^3	19^9	D. Brumfield	W. F. & J. P. Wilmot	(f) 5.20
Consiglieri	b	126	6	8^1	13^2	15^1	21^{15}	20^4	20^4	D. Brown	Mrs. W. C. Jacobs	(f) 5.20
Bold Clarion	b	126	9	$21^{1-1/2}$	20^2	17^{hd}	20^{hd}	21^5	21^1	W. Chambers	Mrs. Roger Braugh	(f) 5.20
Lexico	b	126	3	$15^{1-1/2}$	18^2	22	22	22	22	G. Avila	Mrs. V. DeBaptista	(f) 5.20
Flip Sal	b	126	5	$20^{1-1/2}$	23	Lame				E. Maple	B. Cohen-S. Tufano	58.80

Time: :$22^4/5$, :$46^3/5$, 1:$11^4/5$, 1:$38^3/5$, 2:04. Track fast. Off at 5:$38^1/2$ EDT. Start good. Won ridden out.
Coupled: (a) Cannonade and Judger; (b) Rube the Great and Accipiter; (f) Field.

Program #		Win	Place	Show
1	Cannonade	$5.00	$3.00	$2.40
19f	Hudson County		$4.40	$2.60
3	Agitate			$2.80

Winner: B. c. by Bold Bidder–Queen Sucree, by *Ribot. Trained by W. C. Stephens; bred in Kentucky by J. M. Olin.
$326,500 gross value and $16,000 Gold Cup. Net to winner $274,000; second $30,000; third $15,000; fourth $7,500.

290 nominations.
Equipment: b—blinkers

*Foreign bred

A Country Boy Comes Home

CANNONADE, A BAY COLT, WAS ONLY ONE OF the entries trained by Woody Stephens for the hundredth running of the Kentucky Derby. He was a trainer known for his expertise as well as his integrity, and different owners were more than happy to have him train their colts. As well as Cannonade, who was owned by John M. Olin, and Judger, owned by Seth Hancock, two other horses, Accipiter, and Rube the Great, both owned by Sigmund Sommer, had once also been trained by Stephens.

It was "a funny feeling," he said; as it happened, he had trained the first four horses that came out onto the track on Derby day.

The favorite in the race was Judger, ridden by Lafitte Pincay Jr. Cannonade, ridden by Angel Cordero Jr., was not expected to have much chance.

It was a festive day, and the crowd had shattered the attendance record by 30,000. Princess Margaret was there from England to give out a special diamond-studded cup, and after playing "God Save the Queen," "The Stars and Stripes Forever," and "My Old Kentucky Home," the horses were released onto a fast track. But the track should not only have been fast but wider: there were twenty-three entries—the largest field ever—and Judger had drawn the terrible post position number 22. As someone said, "Half of the horses shouldn't even have been in the race."

There was the usual wild rush to the first turn—seemingly wilder because there were so many animals—and Judger, the great Lafitte Pincay Jr. aboard, having to come from so far

outside and with a wall of horseflesh ahead of him, got trapped. As it worked out, he never got out of it. Cannonade was roughed up at the start, but he was able to get outside and move along well. The front runner was Hudson County, and in the end the race evolved into a long stretch drive between him and Cannonade. Cannonade triumphed by four lengths, with Hudson County taking place money.

The time was 2:05, hardly fast, but it didn't matter to Stephens. In a long career that included training eleven champions, someone asked Stephens later, "What was your bigger thrill—ever?" he said, "The five Belmonts are beautiful, but I can never forget the one back home, the hundredth Derby. I won it in front of the home folks. That was a mighty big afternoon. Princess Margaret handed me that trophy and I walked back headed to the press box and I said, 'This country boy came a *long* way.' "

Foolish Pleasure
101st *May 3, 1975*

		Bold Ruler	*Nasrullah
	What a Pleasure		Miss Disco
FOOLISH PLEASURE		Gray Flight	*Mahmoud
Bay colt			Planetold
			Menow
	Fool-Me-Not	Tom Fool	Gaga
			Tourbillon
		Cuadrilla	Bouillabaisse

The Winner's Pedigree and Career Highlights

YEAR	AGE	STS.	1ST	2ND	3RD	EARNINGS
1974	2	7	7	0	0	$ 284,595
1975	3	11	5	4	1	$ 716,278
1976	4	8	4	0	2	$ 215,832
TOTALS		**26**	**16**	**4**	**3**	**$1,216,705**

At 2 years	WON	Maiden on 1st attempt, Dover, Tremont, Sapling, Hopeful, Cowdin, Champagne
At 3 years	WON	Kentucky Derby, Flamingo, Wood Memorial, Match race with Ruffian ($225,000)
	2ND	Preakness, Belmont Stakes, Governor
	3RD	Florida Derby
	UNP	Marlboro Cup
At 4 years	WON	Suburban Handicap, Donn Handicap, Arlington Golden Invitational
	3RD	Bel Air Handicap, Brooklyn Handicap
	UNP	Canadian Turf, Hollywood Gold Cup

Race Day Statistics

HORSE	EQ.	WT.	PP	1/4	1/2	3/4	MILE	STR.	FIN.	JOCKEY	OWNER	ODDS TO $1
Foolish Pleasure		126	3	11^6	8^{hd}	6^{hd}	4^1	$2^{1/2}$	$1^{1-3/4}$	J. Vasquez	John L. Greer	1.90
Avatar	b	126	10	4^4	2^{hd}	2^{hd}	2^2	$1^{1/2}$	$2^{2-1/2}$	W. Shoemaker	A. A. Seeligson Jr.	11.40
Diabolo	b	126	13	$6^{1/2}$	6^4	4^2	1^{hd}	3^2	$3^{2-1/2}$	L. Pincay Jr.	Frank McMahon	6.20
Master Derby		126	5	$9^{1/2}$	7^{hd}	$8^{1-1/2}$	$3^{1-1/2}$	4^4	$4^{2-1/4}$	D. McHargue	Golden Chance Farm Inc.	5.20
Media	b	126	1	12^{hd}	$11^{1/2}$	10^{hd}	7^{hd}	5^2	$5^{3-1/4}$	J. Cruguet	Elmendorf	23.90
Prince Thou Art		126	8	15	15	15	9^2	$6^{1-1/2}$	6^{hd}	B. Baeza	Darby Dan Farm	(a) 2.90
Promised City		126	15	14^2	14^1	$14^{1/2}$	8^{hd}	7^3	$7^{4-1/2}$	D. Whited	Big I Farm	42.70
Bold Chapeau		126	7	13^4	13^4	12^1	11^1	9^3	$8^{2-1/2}$	C. Alleman	T. A. Isbell, et al	77.20
Sylvan Place	b	126	14	$5^{1-1/2}$	$5^{1/2}$	7^2	5^3	8^2	$9^{1-1/4}$	A. Cordero Jr.	Darby Dan Farm	(a) 2.90
Fashion Sale	b	126	6	3^{hd}	4^2	5^1	10^2	11^3	$10^{3/4}$	W. Gavidia	Clarence Benjamin	(f) 27.10
Round Stake		126	12	$8^{1-1/2}$	$9^{1-1/2}$	9^1	$13^{1-1/2}$	10^2	$11^{3-1/4}$	M. Hole	Hobeau Farm	55.10
Gatch	b	126	9	$10^{1/2}$	12^3	13^2	14^4	$12^{1-1/2}$	12^4	J. C. Espinoza	P. A. Diaz	(f) 27.10
Honey Mark		126	2	7^{hd}	10^4	11^3	12^1	13^2	13^2	E. Delahoussaye	Mr. & Mrs. R. F. Roberts	24.30
Rushing Man		126	4	2^1	3^2	3^{hd}	15	14^2	14^3	J. McKnight	J. W. Mecom	(f) 27.10
Bombay Duck	b	126	11	1^1	1^3	$1^{1/2}$	6^{hd}	15	15	M. Aristone	Ronald Aristone Sr.	27.90

Time: :22, :45²/5, 1:10³/5, 1:36, 2:02. Track fast. Off at 5:40¹/2 EDT. Start good. Won ridden out.
Coupled: (a) Prince Thou Art and Sylvan Place; (f) Field.

Program #		Win	Place	Show
4	Foolish Pleasure	$5.80	$4.40	$3.60
7	Avatar		$9.20	$5.60
10	Diabolo			$4.40

Winner: B. c. by What a Pleasure–Fool-Me-Not, by Tom Fool. Trained by LeRoy Jolley; bred in Florida by Waldemar Farms, Inc.
$262,100 gross value and $15,000 Gold Cup. Net to winner $209,600; second $30,000; third $15,000; fourth $7,500.

246 nominations.
Equipment: b—blinkers

*Foreign bred

He Got No Respect

OF COURSE, THE KENTUCKY DERBY generates a lot of excitement. In 1975 it overwhelmed announcer Chick Anderson, who in describing the race said that Prince Thou Art had beaten Foolish Pleasure, after a long stretch duel. This was news to a lot of people, but mainly to Jacinto Vasquez, who crossed the finish line first, and it was particularly good news to Braulio Baeza, who was on Prince Thou Art and, far from dueling with Foolish Pleasure, was in fact sixth.

Some people doubted Foolish Pleasure's ability, and one wonders why. As a two-year-old he won all seven races he started, and garnered $284,595 in winnings. Maybe they just didn't think that a horse with the name Foolish Pleasure could be that good.

Jacinto Vasquez ran a very smart race. When the gates opened, he held Foolish Pleasure back and kept him at steady pace until Bombay Duck faded on the far turn, and Avatar and Master Derby moved into the lead. The horses

were racing side by side as they went to the head of the stretch, and Foolish Pleasure seized the moment: he galloped up between the two horses and was suddenly in the lead. Moments later, there was a collision as Diabolo smacked into Avatar, almost knocking him sideways, but he kept his feet and tried to catch Foolish Pleasure, which was a lost cause.

One of the most shocking moments in all sports was to occur three months after the Derby was done. A match race was arranged between Foolish Pleasure and Ruffian, a speedy black filly, Horse of the Year, and a fan favorite. Millions tuned in to watch it on television.

At first, Foolish Pleasure led, but by the time they got into the backstretch Ruffian had gained the lead. The two horses were flying, and then just like that, Ruffian snapped her front ankle. She ran on, determined to finish the race, for a few strides and stopped. There was nothing anyone could do. She was put down and buried in the infield of Belmont Park. People who saw it happen never forgot it, and likely never will.

Bold Forbes
102nd *May 1, 1976*

		Nasrullah
	Bold Ruler	Miss Disco
Irish Castle		Tulyar
BOLD FORBES	Castle Forbes	Longford
Dark bay/brown colt		Bull Lea
Comely Nell	Commodore M.	Early Autumn
		*Blenheim II
	Nellie L.	Nellie Flag

THE WINNER'S PEDIGREE AND CAREER HIGHLIGHTS

YEAR	AGE	STS.	1ST	2ND	3RD	EARNINGS
1975	2	8	7	0	1	$ 62,749
1976	3	10	6	1	3	$460,286
TOTALS		**18**	**13**	**1**	**4**	**$523,035**

At 2 years	WON	Maiden on 1st attempt, Tremont, Saratoga Special, Dia Padras
At 3 years	WON	Kentucky Derby, Wood Memorial, San Jacinto, Bay Shore, Belmont Stakes
	2ND	San Miguel
	3RD	San Vicente, Preakness, Vosburgh

RACE DAY STATISTICS

HORSE	EQ.	WT.	PP	1/4	1/2	3/4	MILE	STR.	FIN.	JOCKEY	OWNER	ODDS TO $1
Bold Forbes	b	126	2	1^1	1^5	1^3	$1^{1/2}$	$1^{1/2}$	1^1	A. Cordero Jr.	E. R. Tizol	3.00
Honest Pleasure		126	5	$2^{2\text{-}1/2}$	2^3	2^2	2^2	2^4	$2^{3\text{-}1/4}$	B. Baeza	B. R. Firestone	.40
Elocutionist		126	3	4^2	$4^{1/2}$	$4^{1/2}$	4^3	3^2	$3^{1\text{-}1/4}$	J. Lively	E. C. Cashman	10.30
Amano	b	126	6	3^1	$3^{1\text{-}1/2}$	3^{hd}	$3^{1\text{-}1/2}$	4^2	$4^{1\text{-}1/2}$	L. Melancon	J. C. Irvin	55.40
On the Sly		126	1	9	9	7^{hd}	7^1	$5^{1\text{-}1/2}$	$5^{1\text{-}1/4}$	G. McCarron	Balmak Stable	24.50
Cojak	b	126	7	5^1	6^3	$6^{1\text{-}1/2}$	6^2	$6^{1/2}$	$6^{3/4}$	C. McCarron	Entremont Stable	38.60
Inca Roca	b	126	9	8^7	8^3	9	8^4	7^2	$7^{1\text{-}3/4}$	W. Nemeti	C. R. Jarrell	67.60
Play the Red	b	126	8	$7^{1\text{-}1/2}$	$5^{1/2}$	5^2	$5^{1/2}$	8^8	8^6	J. Velasquez	Elmendorf	15.10
Bidson		126	4	6^{hd}	7^{hd}	8^1	9	9	9	D. MacBeth	Sacred Racing Stable	72.70

Time: :22$^{2/5}$, :45$^{4/5}$, 1:10$^{2/5}$, 1:35$^{3/5}$, 2:01$^{3/5}$. Track fast. Off at 5:39 EDT. Start good. Won driving.

Program #		Win	Place	Show
2	Bold Forbes	$8.00	$2.40	$2.60
5	Honest Pleasure		$2.40	$2.20
3	Elocutionist			$2.60

Winner: Dk. b. or br. c. by Irish Castle–Comely Nell, by Commodore M. Trained by L. S. Barrera; bred in Kentucky by Eaton Farms and Red Bull Stable. $217,700 gross value and $15,000 Gold Cup. Net to winner $165,200; second $30,000; third $15,000; fourth $7,500.

252 nominations.
Equipment: b—blinkers

*Foreign bred

Dr. Jekyll and Mr. Hyde Rides Again

ONE OF THE CANDIDATES FOR THE 1976 Derby was Bold Forbes, a States-bred colt whose sire was Irish Castle and his dam Comely Nell. He was owned by a Puerto Rican sportsman named Enrique Rodriguez Tizol, and had literally run out of competition in Puerto Rico. As a two-year-old he had won seven races. Tizol decided to ship him to the United States to run, but when he arrived, he was not held in high regard by American horsemen, who looked on Puerto Rican racing as bush league.

The question, though, was who would ride him in America. Tizol was able to get Angel Cordero Jr., to ride him.

Cordero, who was born in Santurce, Puerto Rico, is a Hispanic version of Dr. Jekyll and Mr. Hyde. Meet him on the street, and you'd love him. He seems to never stop smiling, flashing a big white smile, singing Spanish songs, and always has time to exchange some conversation—and quips—with his fans. He is also kind, visiting sick children in the hospital.

But meet him on the track, and you'd probably want to shoot him. He rode one way, and with white-hot intensity: to win any way he could. And win he did. As the 1976 Derby approached, Cordero had 6,000 winners—and 200 suspensions for roughriding.

As he waited in the number 2 post position for the race to start, Cordero knew he was on a horse that could fly. But he knew also that the favorite, Honest Pleasure, could sprint. But sprinting wasn't Cordero's plan, nor trainer L. S. Barrera's intention. As fast as he was, Bold Forbes also had endurance problems, and

Barrera had galloped him long and hard to try to build him up. As mad-dog intense as he was on a horse, Cordero was also clever. All he wanted to do was get the lead as quickly as he could, and control the horse's pace after that. And that's just what he did. He sprinted to the front, piling up a lead of five lengths before Braulio Baeza, on Honest Pleasure, could gather his wits and react.

Then, though, Baeza tried, cutting into Cordero's lead with every stride. But he couldn't catch him. Cordero managed the strength and stamina of the horse like a cook adding measured ingredients to a recipe, and Baeza was only able to close four of those lengths. Cordero won by one length—and wasn't suspended!

Seattle Slew
103rd May 7, 1977

		Boldnesian	Bold Ruler
	Bold Reasoning		Alanesian
	SEATTLE SLEW	Reason to Earn	Hail to Reason
	Dark bay colt		Sailing Home
	May Charmer	Poker	Round Table
			Glamour
			Jet Action
		Fair Charmer	Mytle Charm

Boldnesian — Bold Ruler / Alanesian
Bold Reasoning
SEATTLE SLEW — Reason to Earn — Hail to Reason / Sailing Home
Dark bay colt
May Charmer — Poker — Round Table / Glamour
— Fair Charmer — Jet Action / Mytle Charm

THE WINNER'S PEDIGREE AND CAREER HIGHLIGHTS

YEAR	AGE	STS.	1ST	2ND	3RD	EARNINGS
1976	2	3	3	0	0	$ 94,350
1977	3	7	6	0	0	$ 641,370
1978	4	7	5	2	0	$ 473,006
TOTALS		**17**	**14**	**2**	**0**	**$1,208,726**

At 2 years	WON	Maiden on 1st attempt, Champagne
At 3 years	WON	Kentucky Derby, Flamingo, Wood Memorial, Preakness, Belmont Stakes
	UNP	Swaps
At 4 years	WON	Marlboro Cup, Woodward, Stuyvesant
	2ND	Patterson, Jockey Club Gold Cup

RACE DAY STATISTICS

HORSE	EQ.	WT.	PP	1/4	1/2	3/4	MILE	STR.	FIN.	JOCKEY	OWNER	ODDS TO $1
Seattle Slew		126	4	2^1	2^4	2^4	1^{hd}	1^3	$1^{1-3/4}$	J. Cruguet	Karen L. Taylor	.50
Run Dusty Run		126	8	$4^{1/2}$	4^3	4^1	3^1	2^3	2^{nk}	D. McHargue	Golden Chance Farm	(a) 5.50
Sanhedrin	b	126	1	$12^{1-1/2}$	10^1	12^2	8^2	$4^{1-1/2}$	$3^{3-1/4}$	J. Velasquez	Darby Dan Farm	14.60
Get the Axe		126	5	9^2	$9^{1-1/2}$	9^{hd}	9^{hd}	7^2	4no	W. Shoemaker	Bwamazon Farm	27.90
Steve's Friend	b	126	11	$7^{1-1/2}$	$7^{1-1/2}$	$5^{1-1/2}$	4^2	$5^{1/2}$	5no	R. Hernandez	Kinship Stable	29.20
Papelote	b	126	14	$5^{1-1/2}$	6^2	$8^{1-1/2}$	$7^{1-1/2}$	6^2	$6^{2-1/4}$	M. Rivera	Marvin L. Warner	(f) 42.80
Giboulee	b	126	13	11^2	$8^{1/2}$	10^{hd}	$13^{1-1/2}$	$9^{1-1/2}$	7^{hd}	J. Fell	J. L. Levesque	40.20
For the Moment	b	126	10	$1^{1/2}$	1^{hd}	1^1	2^3	$3^{1/2}$	$8^{3/4}$	A. Cordero Jr.	Gerald Robins	7.00
Affiliate	b	126	7	$10^{1/2}$	12^2	11^{hd}	$6^{1/2}$	$8^{1/2}$	$9^{1-3/4}$	L. Pincay Jr.	Harbor View Farm	38.20
Flag Officer		126	6	15	$11^{1/2}$	$13^{1/2}$	10^1	$10^{1-1/2}$	$10^{1/2}$	L. Ahrens	Nasty Stable	46.90
Bob's Dusty		126	3	3^3	3^5	3^2	5^2	12^2	11^{nk}	J. Espinoza	R. N. Lehmann	(a) 5.90
Sir Sir		126	2	$6^{1/2}$	5^1	6^2	12^2	11^{hd}	12^2	J. Rodriguez	La Luna Stable	(f) 42.80
Nostalgia	b	126	15	$13^{1-1/2}$	$14^{1/2}$	14^1	14^3	13^6	13^3	L. Snyder	W. S. Farish III	40.00
Western Wind		126	9	$14^{1-1/2}$	15	15	15	14^7	14^{10}	R. Turcotte	J. M. Roebling	31.10
Best Person	b	126	12	8^3	$13^{1/2}$	7^1	11^1	15	15	G. Patterson	W. C. Partee	(f) 42.80

Time: :23, :45$^{4/5}$, 1:10$^{3/5}$, 1:36, 2:02$^{1/5}$. Track fast. Off at 5:41 EDT. Start good. Won ridden out.
Coupled: (a) Run Dusty Run and Bob's Dusty; (f) Field.

Program #		Win	Place	Show
3	Seattle Slew	$3.00	$2.80	$2.80
1a	Run Dusty Run		$3.40	$3.20
2	Sanhedrin			$4.60

Winner: Dk. b. or br. c. by Bold Reasoning–My Charmer, by Poker. Trained by William H. Turner, Jr.; bred in Kentucky by Ben S. Castleman.
$267,200 gross value and $15,000 Gold Cup. Net to winner $214,700; second $30,000; third $15,000; fourth $7,500.

297 nominations.
Equipment: b—blinkers

A Case of Nerves

AN HOUR BEFORE THE 1977 DERBY the favorite, Seattle Slew, was asleep. "With all the fanfare, excitement, and crowd, we try to keep him as relaxed as possible," said Billy Turner, the colt's trainer. "This is just like a heavy-weight fighter before a championship fight." Later, Seattle Slew was led to the paddock, and hearing the crowd cheering, his ears pricked up and he started bouncing. "This is the moment," Turner said, "when we lead the horse into the paddock, we know we've made it to the Derby."

Once there, though, there used to be a problem. From 1924 to 1986 the paddock was a close, cramped structure, and many times horses became upset in the crowded conditions, as eager spectators crowded in to shake hands with the owners, jockeys, and so on. Even though the accommodations had been remodeled and were much better in 1977, this happened to Seattle Slew. He became nervous and kicked a hind leg against a paddock stall, and was nervous when he paraded toward the post. He was sweating, moving skittishly. A horse in this condition could be scratched.

Whether or not the hullabaloo upset him is debatable, but there is no question that a disaster almost occurred when the horses broke from the gate. Seattle Slew, breaking from the number 4 position, swerved to his right into a horse named Get the Axe and immediately was behind a wall of horses. Atop Slew, jockey Jan Cruguet was jarred and rocked in his saddle.

Slew's fans in shock, Cruguet immediately got his wits about him and focused on control-ling the horse and catching the pack. And he moved at such a high rate of speed that by the time he passed the wire for the first time, he was back in the race with a vengeance and neck and neck with the leader, For the Moment.

It was a two-horse battle all the way, and when they turned into the stretch, Seattle Slew was all alone. By the eighth pole, with Cruguet using the whip, Seattle Slew had opened up a three-length lead. Nervous or not, there was no catching him that day, though Run Dusty Run and Sanhedrin reduced the gap to one and three-quarters lengths at the wire. For the Moment finished eighth.

The time was 2:02 1/5, one of the fastest Derbies ever. The race Seattle Slew had run had impressed a lot of people, but they were even more impressed when he went on to win the Preakness and the Belmont Stakes—and became a member of that rarest of clubs, Triple Crown winners.

Affirmed
104th *May 6, 1978*

			Native Dancer
	Raise a Native	Raise You
	Exclusive Native		Shut Out
AFFIRMED		Exclusive	Good Example
Chestnut colt			Fighting Fox
	Won't Tell You	Crafty Admiral	Admiral's Lady
			Volcanic
	Scarlet Ribbon	Native Valor

THE WINNER'S PEDIGREE AND CAREER HIGHLIGHTS

YEAR	AGE	STS.	1ST	2ND	3RD	EARNINGS
1977	2	9	7	2	0	$ 343,477
1978	3	11	8	2	1	$ 901,541
1979	4	9	7	1	1	$1,148,800
TOTALS		**29**	**22**	**5**	**1**	**$2,393,818**

At 2 years	WON	Maiden on 1st attempt, Youthful Stakes, Hollywood Juvenile, Hopeful, Sanford, Futurity, Laurel Futurity
	2ND	Great American, Champagne
At 3 years	WON	Kentucky Derby, Preakness Stakes, Belmont Stakes, Santa Anita Derby, Hollywood Derby, San Felipe, Jim Dandy
	2ND	Marlboro Cup, Travers (1st, disqualified and placed second)
	UNP	Jockey Club Gold Cup
At 4 years	WON	Jockey Club Gold Cup, Hollywood Gold Cup, Santa Anita Handicap, Charles H. Strub Stakes, Californian, Woodward
	2ND	San Fernando
	3RD	Malibu

RACE DAY STATISTICS

HORSE	EQ.	WT.	PP	1/4	1/2	3/4	MILE	STR.	FIN.	JOCKEY	OWNER	ODDS TO $1
Affirmed		126	2	2^{hd}	$3^{2-1/2}$	$3^{1-1/2}$	2^3	1^2	$1^{1-1/2}$	S. Cauthen	Harbor View Farm	1.80
Alydar	b	126	10	9^{hd}	9^5	8^{hd}	4^{hd}	3^3	$2^{1-1/4}$	J. Velasquez	Calumet Farm	1.20
Believe It		126	9	$4^{1/2}$	$4^{1/2}$	5^3	1^{hd}	2^2	$3^{4-1/4}$	E. Maple	Hickory Tree Stable	7.40
Darby Creek Road	b	126	7	$7^{1/2}$	7^2	7^2	$5^{1/2}$	4^2	$4^{2-1/4}$	D. Brumfield	Mr. & Mrs. J. W. Phillips	33.00
Esops Foibles	b	126	3	$5^{1-1/2}$	5^4	4^1	6^3	5^3	$5^{5-1/4}$	C. McCarron	Jerry Frankel	49.70
Sensitive Prince	b	126	11	$3^{2-1/2}$	$1^{1-1/2}$	1^3	$3^{1-1/2}$	6^3	$6^{1/2}$	M. Solomone	Top the Marc Stable	4.50
Dr. Valeri	b	126	8	11	11	10^4	10^5	$7^{1-1/2}$	$7^{3-1/4}$	R. Riera Jr.	V. & R. Renzi	96.10
Hoist the Silver		126	5	8^2	$8^{1/2}$	9^5	7^3	8^5	8^7	R. DePass	Washington Stud	123.70
Chief of Dixieland	b	126	6	6^3	6^2	$6^{1/2}$	9^1	9^1	9^1	A. Rini	Dixie-Jake Inc.	121.70
Raymond Earl		126	1	1^2	2^4	2^2	8^1	10^2	10^2	R. Baird	R. H. Lehmann	117.10
Special Honor	b	126	4	10^3	$10^{1/2}$	11	11	11	11	P. Nicolo	Gaston-Haynes	177.10

Time: :22³/₅, :45³/₅, 1:10⁴/₅, 1:35⁴/₅, 2:01¹/₅. Track fast. Off at 5:41 EDT. Start good for all but Special Honor. Won driving.

Program #		Win	Place	Show
2	Affirmed	$5.60	$2.80	$2.60
10	Alydar		$2.60	$2.40
9	Believe It			$2.80

Winner: Ch. c. by Exclusive Native–Won't Tell You, by Crafty Admiral. Trained by Lazaro Barrera; bred in Florida by Harbor View Farm.
$239,400 gross value and $15,000 Gold Cup. Net to winner $186,900; second $30,000; third $15,000; fourth $7,500.

319 nominations.
Equipment: b—blinkers

Rumble in the Bluegrass

THE 104TH RUNNING OF THE KENTUCKY Derby in 1978 was as close as the race would ever get to being the emotional equivalent of a world championship heavyweight bout. The crowd was huge, fans bet like drunken sailors, and though the horses had faced each other a half dozen times, the burning question persisted, and was freely debated: Who was better?

In one corner was Affirmed, a Florida-bred chestnut colt whose great-grandfather was the great Native Dancer, his father Exclusive Native. So dominant was his father that Thoroughbred insiders felt that Exclusive Native would be as good, but an injury ended his career and he went on to stud duty.

Affirmed's opponent, Alydar, also a chestnut colt, was a product of Calumet Farm, which had been in decline. Once the greatest stable in the world, producing eight Kentucky Derby winners between 1941 and 1968, starting with Triple Crown winner Whirlaway, it was now coming back under new owners and trainer John Vetch. And Alydar was also a son of Raise a Native.

From the beginning, the careers of both horses had been watched by experts. They were something special—clearly superior to most of the horses they raced against. Out of the half dozen times they had raced against each other, Affirmed had won four times, once beating Alydar by a neck in the Belmont Futurity.

Complicating the issue was that the horses had faced each other when very young. The thing was that no one could be really sure who was better; as is shown time and time again, a

horse that is two years old is hardly the same horse at three. Horses can change dramatically; yesterday's also-ran can become today's Secretariat.

As the race got closer, the debate over who was better got more and more vigorous, and the media exploited the rivalry just as they would before a heavyweight title bout.

As the eleven horses were loaded into the gates, bettors had Alydar as a 6–5 favorite and Affirmed at 9–5, reputedly because longtime racegoers had a special feeling for Calumet Farm and its owners, Admiral and Mrs. Markey, who were trying to bring the stable back to its former glory. Astride Affirmed was the wunderkind Steve Cauthen, while Jorge Velasquez was piloting Alydar. A crowd of 131,000-plus was there to watch this fight to the finish.

When the race started, it appeared to be over before it began. A couple of speed horses, Sensitive Prince and 117–1 shot Raymond Earl, jumped out to the lead. Affirmed was right there in third place, moving along about five lengths behind the leaders. And where was Alydar? He had dropped back a whopping seventeen lengths behind the leaders, and Velasquez would say later that the horse, at this point, did not seem to have any interest in running.

The race stayed more or less like that; according to Steve Cauthen, though he did not see Alydar he still feared him, and he moved Affirmed along at a steady pace. Then, at the top of the stretch, he moved on the leader, Believe It.

But Cauthen was right to be wary of Alydar. This was no nag from Palookaville. He finally had started to move, and as he did, he flashed past other horses and made a huge run at Affirmed, the crowd, as one writer described it, "going berserk." Gradually the lead dissipated, and he came on and on . . . but he had that one big problem that rears its ugly head over and over: he ran out of track. Though he had gained two and a half lengths on Affirmed in the final eighth of a mile, he lost by a length and a quarter.

Of course, as in a heavyweight champion-ship fight, the debate on who was better was not settled that day; it had been a decision rather than a knockout.

In subsequent races, though, such as the Belmont, Alydar got even closer than in the Derby, but he never could beat Affirmed. Perhaps Affirmed's trainer, Laz Barrera, put it best: "They can go one mile, they go five miles, and it makes no difference. Affirmed is just waiting for a horse that can make him run."

Spectacular Bid
105th *May 5, 1979*

		Bold Ruler	*Nasrullah
	Bold Bidder		Miss Disco
	SPECTACULAR BID		To Market
Gray colt		High Bid	Stepping Stone
	Spectacular		Palestinian
		Promised Land	Mahmoudess
			To Market
		Stop On Red	Danger Ahead

THE WINNER'S PEDIGREE AND CAREER HIGHLIGHTS

YEAR	AGE	STS.	1ST	2ND	3RD	EARNINGS
1978	2	9	7	1	0	$ 384,484
1979	3	12	10	1	1	$1,279,183
1980	4	9	9	0	0	$1,117,790
TOTALS		**30**	**26**	**2**	**1**	**$2,781,457**

At 2 years	WON	Maiden on 1st attempt, World's Playground, Champagne, Young America, Laurel Futurity, Heritage
	2ND	Dover Stakes
	UNP	Tyro
At 3 years	WON	Kentucky Derby, Preakness Stakes, Flamingo, Blue Grass, Florida Derby, Hutcheson, Fountain of Youth, Marlboro Cup, Meadowlands Cup
	2ND	Jockey Club Gold Cup
	3RD	Belmont Stakes
At 4 years	WON	Malibu, San Fernando, Charles H. Strub, Santa Anita Handicap, Mervyn Leroy Handicap, California Stakes, Washington Park Stakes, Amory Haskell, *Woodward Stakes

*Walkover

RACE DAY STATISTICS

HORSE	EQ.	WT.	PP	1/4	1/2	3/4	MILE	STR.	FIN	JOCKEY	OWNER	ODDS TO $1
Spectacular Bid		126	3	7^2	6^{hd}	$4^{1/2}$	$2^{1-1/2}$	$1^{1-1/2}$	$1^{2-3/4}$	R. Franklin	Hawksworth Farm	.60
General Assembly		126	6	1^{hd}	2^5	2^{hd}	1^{hd}	2^5	2^3	L. Pincay Jr.	B. R. Firestone	(a) 11.10
Golden Act		126	1	$8^{1-1/2}$	9^{hd}	8^{hd}	7^4	3^{hd}	$3^{1-3/4}$	S. Hawley	W. Oldknow–R. Phipps	19.20
King Celebrity	b	126	7	$6^{1-1/2}$	7^4	$5^{1/2}$	5^3	$4^{1/2}$	$4^{2-1/2}$	C. Asmussen	Che-Bar Stable	112.40
Flying Paster	b	126	9	3^{hd}	4^{hd}	3^{hd}	3^1	5^4	$5^{3-1/2}$	D. Pierce	B. J. Ridder	2.20
Screen King		126	5	10	8^1	7^4	6^{hd}	$6^{1/2}$	$6^{3-1/4}$	A. Cordero Jr.	Flying Zee Stable	9.80
Sir Ivor Again		126	8	9^{hd}	10	9^5	9^{15}	8^3	$7^{1-1/4}$	D. MacBeth	Mrs. T. Christopher	(a) 11.10
Shamgo		126	4	2^{hd}	$1^{1/2}$	1^{hd}	4^{hd}	7^5	$8^{4-1/4}$	F. Olivares	Rogers Red Top Inc.	102.20
Lot o' Gold		126	10	4^3	$3^{1-1/2}$	$6^{1/2}$	8^{hd}	9^{20}	9^{25}	D. Brumfield	F. E. Lehmann	50.90
Great Redeemer	b	126	2	$5^{1-1/2}$	5^3	10	10	10	10	R. DePass	Mr. & Mrs. J. Mohamed	78.70

Time: :24$^{1/5}$, :47$^{2/5}$, 1:12$^{2/5}$, 1:37$^{3/5}$, 2:02$^{2/5}$. Track fast. Off at 5:39 EDT. Start good. Won driving.
Coupled: (a) General Assembly and Sir Ivor Again.

Program #		Win	Place	Show
4	Spectacular Bid	$3.20	$3.00	$2.80
1	General Assembly		$5.80	$3.40
2	Golden Act			$4.20

Winner: Gr. c. by Bold Bidder–Spectacular, by Promised Land. Trained by G. G. (Bud) Delp; bred in Kentucky by Mrs. William Jason and Mrs. William Gilmore. $317,400 gross value and $18,000 Gold Cup. Net to winner $228,650; second $50,000; third $25,000; fourth $13,750.

299 nominations.
Equipment: b—blinkers

*Foreign bred

Just Call Him Spectacular

IT WOULD REALLY HAVE BEEN MORE AC-
curate to have dropped the "Bid" part of the
steel-gray colt Spectacular Bid's name and just
called him Spectacular. It more precisely described his achievements as a racehorse. To wit:
of thirty races he started, he won twenty-six,
finished lower than third just once, and won
$2,781,607, which was a record.

When Spectacular Bid went to the 1979
Derby post, he was undefeated in all ten previous races, and if he won people would likely not
be impressed: he was the favorite, therefore it
was no big deal. But it was a big deal: from that
race on it would be twenty years before another
Derby favorite won the race.

There was no lack of confidence that he
would win in his camp. His trainer, Grover
"Buddy" Delp, told people that "he was the
greatest horse that ever looked through a bridle.
The only two horses that would have given him
a run were Citation and Secretariat." And as he
walked the horse to the paddock on Derby day,
he hollered encouragingly to fans: "Go bet! Go
bet!" And many did.

The track was fast, and as the relatively
small field of ten horses hammered into the
turn, Ronnie Franklin, the teenager piloting
Spectacular Bid, moved the horse slightly
outside to stay clear of the pack. At the five-
eighths pole, still staying wide to be clear, he
passed General Assembly with Flying Paster
inside him. As they turned into the stretch, he

was slightly bumped by Flying Paster, who had
been ricocheted toward him because General
Assembly had moved to the outside. But then he
moved steadily forward, breaking clear of everyone at the eighth pole and driving to victory
over General Assembly, who ran gamely—but
not fast enough.

Specatcular Bid was to go on to win the
Preakness, but a bizarre event, it was said, kept
him from becoming a Triple Crown winner. On
the morning of the race he stepped on a pin in
his stall, and examination showed an infection
that was actually life-threatening. The hoof
was drilled clean, and he appeared okay for
the race, but the pin was blamed when he lost.
Others blamed his jockey, Franklin, who took
him out very fast and, it was said, did not leave
him enough gas left to win. From that race on,
Franklin no longer rode him.

Genuine Risk
106th *May 3, 1980*

		Native Dancer
	Raise a Native	*Raise You*
Exclusive Native		*Shut Out*
GENUINE RISK	*Exclusive*	*Good Example*
Chestnut filly		**Migoli*
Virtuous	**Gallant Man*	**Majideh*
		Zucchero
	Due Respect II	*Auld Alliance*

THE WINNER'S PEDIGREE AND CAREER HIGHLIGHTS

YEAR	AGE	STS.	1ST	2ND	3RD	EARNINGS
1979	2	4	4	0	0	$100,245
1980	3	8	4	3	1	$503,742
1981	4	3	2	0	1	$ 42,600
TOTALS		**15**	**10**	**3**	**2**	**$646,587**

At 2 years	WON	Maiden on 1st attempt, Tempted, Demoiselle
At 3 years	WON	Kentucky Derby, Ruffian
	2ND	Preakness, Belmont Stakes, Maskette
	3RD	Wood Memorial
At 4 years	WON	2 allowances
	3RD	1 allowance (no stakes)

RACE DAY STATISTICS

HORSE	EQ.	WT.	PP	1/4	1/2	3/4	MILE	STR.	FIN.	JOCKEY	OWNER	ODDS TO $1
Genuine Risk		121	10	$7^{1\text{-}1/2}$	7^3	4^{hd}	$1^{1\text{-}1/2}$	1^2	1^1	J. Vasquez	Mrs. B. R. Firestone	13.30
Rumbo		126	9	13	$12^{1\text{-}1/2}$	11^3	$5^{1/2}$	3^3	2^1	L. Pincay Jr.	Gayno Stable & Bell Bloodstock Co.	4.00
Jaklin Klugman		126	2	$8^{1/2}$	8^{hd}	$8^{1/2}$	$4^{2\text{-}1/2}$	$2^{1\text{-}1/2}$	3^4	D. McHargue	Klugman-Dominguez	7.10
Super Moment		126	3	$10^{1\text{-}1/2}$	$9^{1\text{-}1/2}$	$9^{1\text{-}1/2}$	9^3	$5^{1/2}$	4no	D. Pierce	Elmendorf	8.60
Rockhill Native		126	6	2^{hd}	$1^{1\text{-}1/2}$	2^{hd}	$2^{1/2}$	$4^{1\text{-}1/2}$	5^{nk}	J. Oldham	Harry A. Oak	2.10
Bold 'n Rulling	b	126	1	$6^{1\text{-}1/2}$	2^{hd}	1^{hd}	$6^{1\text{-}1/2}$	7^3	6^2	P. Valenzuela	Hughes Brothers	68.70
Plugged Nickle		126	11	1^{hd}	$3^{1\text{-}1/2}$	$3^{1\text{-}1/2}$	$3^{1\text{-}1/2}$	6^{hd}	$7^{3\text{-}1/4}$	B. Thornburg	John M. Schiff	2.60
Degenerate Jon	b	126	4	$9^{2\text{-}1/2}$	6^{hd}	5^{hd}	8^3	$8^{1\text{-}1/2}$	$8^{1\text{-}1/4}$	R. Hernandez	Barry K. Schwartz	61.70
Withholding		126	12	$4^{1/2}$	10^1	10^1	11^2	9^2	9^2	M. Morgan	Russell Michael Jr.	64.10
Tonka Wakhan	b	126	5	12^{hd}	13	$12^{1/2}$	12^3	10^2	$10^{2\text{-}1/4}$	M. Holland	Glenn Bromagen	(f) 58.90
Execution's Reason		126	13	$3^{1\text{-}1/2}$	$5^{1/2}$	$7^{2\text{-}1/2}$	10^1	11^3	11^3	R. Romero	Howard B. Noonan	111.80
Gold Stage		126	7	5^{hd}	$4^{1/2}$	6^{hd}	$7^{1/2}$	$12^{1\text{-}1/2}$	12no	A. Cordero Jr.	Mrs. Philip B. Hofmann	41.50
Hazard Duke	b	126	8	11^3	$11^{1/2}$	13	13	13	13	D. Brumfield	Andrew Adams	(f) 58.90

Time: :24, :48, $1:12^{4}/_5$, $1:37^{3}/_5$, 2:02. Track fast. Off at 5:39 EDT. Start good. Won driving.
(f) Field.

Program #		Win	Place	Show
8	Genuine Risk	$28.60	$10.60	$4.80
7	Rumbo		$ 5.20	$3.40
3	Jaklin Klugman			$4.40

Winner: Ch. f. by Exclusive Native–Virtuous by *Gallant Man. Trained by LeRoy Jolley; bred in Kentucky by Mrs. G. Watts Humphrey Jr.
$339,300 gross value and $45,000 Gold Cup. Net to winner $250,550; second $50,000; third $25,000; fourth $13,750.

293 nominations.
Equipment: b—blinkers

*Foreign bred

One Helluva Woman

WOMEN ARE USUALLY SMALLER THAN MEN, and not as physically strong, and the same holds true in horse racing. Occasionally, though, that pattern is broken. Such a filly was Genuine Risk, the 1980 Derby winner, who also captured second in both the Preakness and Belmont, performing best of the three fillies—Regret (1915) and Winning Colors (1988)—who won the Derby in its 132-year history.

In the race, Genuine Risk ran a different way than Regret and Winning Colors. In their races, they led from wire to wire, but Genuine Risk stayed back—jockey Jacinto Vasquez had her seventh in the backstretch. But then she made a big move in the upper stretch and ran the final quarter in 24 2/5, faster than the three previous Derby winners, Seattle Slew in 1977, Affirmed in 1978, and Spectacular Bid in 1979. The horse, Rumbo, who chased Genuine Risk down the stretch, went 24 4/5, and the race had an overall time of 2:02. There were no gentlemen on the track that day!

Genuine Risk almost didn't run in the Derby. Her trainer, LeRoy Jolley, had suggested that he wasn't going to send Genuine Risk to the Derby because she had only finished third in the Wood Memorial. But the owners, Bert Firestone and his wife, Diana, felt that the filly deserved a shot, and overruled Jolley. Later, after her victory, ABC sports commentator Jim McKay asked Jolley why she had run after he said she wouldn't. Jolley, smiling through the spattered egg on his face, said, "Well, Jim, you have to keep an open mind about these things."

Genuine Risk retired after fifteen starts, winning ten times and with three seconds and two thirds. Then she was put out to breeding, and encountered difficulties that would probably have killed anyone but a champion like her. She was bred to Secretariat first, then to many other horses, and didn't give birth to a living foal until she was sixteen years old.

"She was," one of her grooms once said, "a champion in more ways than one."

Pleasant Colony
107th *May 2, 1981*

	Ribot	Tenerani
		Romanella
His Majesty	Flower Bowl	*Alibhai*
PLEASANT COLONY		Flower Bed
Dark bay or brown colt	Sunrise Flight	Double Jay
Sun Colony		Misty Morn
	Colonia	Cockrullah
		Naiga

THE WINNER'S PEDIGREE

RACE DAY STATISTICS

HORSE	EQ.	WT.	PP	$1/4$	$1/2$	$3/4$	MILE	STR.	FIN.	JOCKEY	OWNER	ODDS TO $1
Pleasant Colony		126	7	17^1	16^{hd}	$15^{1/2}$	4^{hd}	$1^{1-1/2}$	$1^{3/4}$	J. Velasquez	Buckland Farm	3.50
Woodchopper		126	11	$20^{1/2}$	19^2	$19^{1-1/2}$	$11^{1/2}$	5^{hd}	2^3	E. Delahoussaye	Greentree Stable	34.20
Partez	b	126	3	12^1	12^1	10^1	2^2	2^1	$3^{2-1/4}$	S. Hawley	Greene-Davis	(f) 7.90
Classic Go Go		126	13	$19^{1/2}$	$18^{2-1/2}$	17^{hd}	9^2	7^{hd}	4no	A. Black	V. H. Winchell	(f) 7.90
Television Studio	b	126	18	21	20^{hd}	$20^{1/2}$	10^2	8^1	$5^{1-1/4}$	D. Whited	Bwamazon Farm	(f) 7.90
Pass the Tab		126	8	11^1	10^1	$7^{1/2}$	3^1	$6^{1/2}$	6^{nk}	L. Pincay Jr.	L. Villareal	31.10
Splendid Spruce	b	126	1	10^1	$9^{1/2}$	$9^{1/2}$	$5^{1/2}$	4^{hd}	7^{nk}	D. McHargue	Surf & Turf Stable	13.60
Flying Nashua	b	126	21	18^{hd}	15^3	16^{hd}	15^{hd}	9^3	$8^{2-3/4}$	A. Cordero Jr.	Jensen, Digiulio, Holman, Ronca	48.00
Noble Nashua		126	9	14^2	13^{hd}	$13^{1-1/2}$	13^1	$10^{2-1/2}$	9no	C. Asmussen	Flying Zee Stable	71.70
Bold Ego		126	15	2^1	2^{hd}	2^{hd}	1^{hd}	3^1	$10^{2-3/4}$	J. Lively	Double B Ranch-Kidd	9.90
Double Sonic		126	4	16^1	21	21	17^1	11^1	$11^{2-3/4}$	B. Thornburg	Fred & Louis Elias	(f) 7.90
Hoedown's Day		126	10	$6^{1-1/2}$	7^1	$11^{1-1/2}$	$12^{1-1/2}$	$12^{1/2}$	12^{nk}	T. Chapman	Dominguez, Freidel, Thatcher	(f) 7.90
Beau Rit	b	126	17	15^{hd}	$17^{1-1/2}$	18^1	$18^{1/2}$	13^{hd}	13^{nk}	P. Rubbicco	Carol Roussel	(f)7.90
Tap Shoes		126	19	13^1	14^3	$14^{1-1/2}$	$14^{1/2}$	14^6	14^7	R. Hernandez	Hancock III–Peters et al.	7.60
Cure the Blues	b	126	16	$8^{1-1/2}$	6^{hd}	8^{hd}	$16^{1/2}$	15^2	15^2	W. Shoemaker	B. R. Firestone	4.70
Well Decorated		126	12	$4^{1/2}$	4^{hd}	4^{hd}	$6^{1/2}$	$16^{1/2}$	$16^{1/2}$	D. MacBeth	Herbert Allen	65.10
Mythical Ruler	b	126	20	5^1	$5^{1-1/2}$	5^{hd}	$7^{1/2}$	17^2	$17^{2-1/2}$	K. Wirth	Risen Jr.–Price	(f) 7.90
Proud Appeal		126	5	$3^{1/2}$	$3^{1-1/2}$	3^2	$8^{1/2}$	18^3	18^2	J. Fell	Winfield et al	(a) 2.30
Top Avenger		126	14	1^{hd}	1^1	1^{hd}	19^1	19^3	$19^{4-1/2}$	L. Snyder	W. P. Bishop	(f) 7.90
Habano		126	6	9^{hd}	11^1	12^2	$20^{1-1/2}$	20^4	20^5	B. Feliciano	M. A. Coello	(f) 7.90
Golden Derby		126	2	$7^{1/2}$	$8^{2-1/2}$	$6^{2-1/2}$	21	21	21	J. Espinoza	Lehmann-Gaines	(a) 2.30

Time: :21 4/5, :45 1/5, 1:10 1/5, 1:36, 2:02. Track fast. Off at 5:41 EDT. Start good. Won ridden out.
Coupled: (a) Proud Appeal & Golden Derby; (f) Field.

Program #		Win	Place	Show
4	Pleasant Colony	$9.00	$ 5.60	$ 4.40
6	Woodchopper		$23.40	$13.00
12f	Partez			$ 4.00

Winner: Dk. b. or Br. c. by His Majesty–Sun Colony, by Sunrise Flight. Trained by John P. Campo; bred in Virginia by Thomas M. Evans.
$413,450 gross value and $44,000 Gold Cup. Net to winner $317,200; second $55,000; third $27,500; fourth $13,750.

432 nominations.
Equipment: b—blinkers

*Foreign bred

CAREER HIGHLIGHTS

YEAR	AGE	STS.	1ST	2ND	3RD	EARNINGS
1980	2	5	2	1	0	$ 87,968
1981	3	9	4	2	1	$877,415
TOTALS		14	6	3	1	**$965,383**

At 2 years	WON	Maiden on 2nd attempt, Remsen (placed first through disqualification)
	2ND	Pilgrim
	UNP	Maryland Nursery
At 3 years	WON	Kentucky Derby, Wood Memorial, Preakness, Woodward
	2ND	Fountain of Youth, Travers
	3RD	Belmont Stakes
	UNP	Florida Derby, Marlboro Cup

The Fat Man Rides to Victory

THE STORY OF THE 1981 DERBY IS DOMInated by the personality of John Campo, the trainer of Pleasant Colony, known by his nickname "the Fat Man." (He was about five-seven and weighed 250 pounds.) As actor Jack Klugman described him, "He's by Damon Runyon out of a Don Rickles mare."

All during the weeks preceding the Derby, Campo was telling everyone who would listen that his colt, Pleasant Colony, would win the Derby, and disparaging other horses. Campo, using verbiage not designed to make friends and influence people, said of Pleasant Colony's opponents, "These ain't good horses. They're just a cut above sprinters."

Campo, though, was the main reason why Pleasant Colony turned into such a great horse.

Campo had started his career under trainer Neloy, but then he began training on his own, and his colt Jim French finished second in the Derby and the Belmont Stakes. Then, in March of 1981, Thomas Mellon Edwards, owner of Buckland Farm of Virginia, became unhappy with the progress that his trainer Odie Lee was making with a promising colt named Pleasant Colony. Campo had been training horses for

Edwards, and the owner liked what he saw, so he turned the training of Colony over to Campo. Under Campo's training, the colt won the 1981 Wood Memorial. Then in the Derby, he came from far, far back to win.

As writer Red Smith described the race: "In the biggest Derby ever run, sixteen of his twenty rivals beat the Fat Man's horse in the first quarter mile, fifteen had him beaten after the half mile, fourteen were still in front of him after six furlongs and seven led him at the mile. But at a mile and a quarter Pleasant Colony was in front with three-quarters of a length to spare over the hard-closing Woodchopper." After the race, a reporter asked Campo if Pleasant Colony had encountered any problems in the race because there were twenty-one horses in it. "My only problem," Campo said, "was they were in the way."

Pleasant Colony won the Preakness, but not the Belmont.

Despite his blunt ways, many people liked Campo, and beneath his aggressiveness he certainly was a man with a heart. He loved his family, and he loved horses. He died in 2005 at the age of sixty-seven.

Gato Del Sol
108th *May 1, 1982*

		Tehran
	Tale of Two Cities	Menda II
*Cougar II		Madara
GATO DEL SOL	Cindy Lou II	Maria Bonita
Gray colt		Bold Ruler
	Jacinto	Cascade II
Peacefully		Hail to Reason
	Morning Calm	Yellow Mist

THE WINNER'S PEDIGREE

RACE DAY STATISTICS

HORSE	EQ.	WT.	PP	1/4	1/2	3/4	MILE	STR.	FIN.	JOCKEY	OWNER	ODDS TO $1
Gato Del Sol		126	18	18^{hd}	19	$10^{1/2}$	$5^{1/2}$	$1^{1/2}$	$1^{2-1/2}$	E. Delahoussaye	Hancock & Peters	21.20
Laser Light		126	8	19	17^{hd}	$18^{1/2}$	10^1	9^{hd}	2^{nk}	E. Maple	Live Oak Plantation	18.20
Reinvested		126	10	$16^{1-1/2}$	$16^{1/2}$	14^1	7^1	$2^{1/2}$	$3^{2-1/2}$	D. MacBeth	Harbor View Farm	(f) 8.90
Water Bank		126	13	$14^{1-1/2}$	$12^{1-1/2}$	$16^{1-1/2}$	8^2	5^{hd}	$4^{3/4}$	M. Castaneda	Elmendorf	(a) 12.60
Muttering		126	11	4^{hd}	$5^{1/2}$	$4^{1/2}$	4^{hd}	4^{hd}	5^3	L. Pincay Jr.	Tartan Stable	4.20
Rockwall	b	126	14	12^1	9^1	$5^{1-1/2}$	6^1	$7^{1-1/2}$	$6^{3/4}$	H. Valdivieso	Nelson B. Hunt	47.80
Air Forbes Won		126	7	3^{hd}	3^3	3^2	3^3	3^{hd}	$7^{1-1/4}$	A. Cordero Jr.	Edward Anchel	2.70
Star Gallant		126	16	6^1	$7^{1/2}$	9^{hd}	9^1	10^1	8no	W. Shoemaker	Buckram Oak Farm	15.70
Majesty's Prince		126	19	13^{hd}	$13^{1/2}$	17^1	14^2	$11^{1/2}$	9^{hd}	R. Hernandez	John D. Marsh	(f) 8.90
Cupecoy's Joy		121	1	$1^{1-1/2}$	$1^{3-1/2}$	1^4	$1^{1/2}$	8^{hd}	$10^{1/2}$	A. Santiago	Ri-Ma-Ro Stable	(f) 8.90
El Baba		126	4	$2^{1/2}$	2^3	2^2	2^{hd}	6^{hd}	11^1	D. Brumfield	Mrs. Joe W. Brown	3.30
Wavering Monarch		126	6	11^2	10^{hd}	11^{hd}	$11^{1/2}$	12^2	$12^{1-1/4}$	R. Romero	Greathouse Family	39.50
Cassaleria		126	17	15^{hd}	15^{hd}	15^{hd}	$13^{1/2}$	$13^{1/2}$	13^{nk}	D. McHargue	20/20 Stable	(a) 12.60
Royal Roberto		126	5	17^1	$18^{1/2}$	19	$17^{1/2}$	$14^{1/2}$	$14^{1/2}$	M. Rivera	Key West Stable	9.30
Music Leader	b	126	9	$8^{1-1/2}$	$8^{1/2}$	8^{hd}	$12^{1-1/2}$	15^{hd}	$15^{2-1/2}$	P. Day	Glaser-Ellett et al.	(f) 8.90
Bold Style	b	126	2	7^2	4^{hd}	7^{hd}	$15^{1/2}$	$16^{1/2}$	16^{nk}	J. Fell	Len Mayer	29.30
Wolfie's Rascal		126	15	$5^{1/2}$	6^{hd}	$6^{1/2}$	16^2	17^3	$17^{1-1/2}$	J. Velasquez	Cohen-Cohen-Kumble	(f) 8.90
New Discovery		126	3	$10^{1/2}$	11^{hd}	13^{hd}	$18^{1-1/2}$	18^4	18^6	J. Bailey	Herbery Allen	(f) 8.90
Real Dare		126	12	9^1	14^1	$12^{1-1/2}$	19	19	19	R. Guidry	J. E. Jumonville Sr.	(f) 8.90

Time: :23, :46$^{1/5}$, 1:10$^{4/5}$, 1:37$^{1/5}$, 2:02$^{2/5}$. Track fast. Off at 5:40 EDT. Start good. Won driving.
Coupled: (a) Water Bank and Cassaleria; (f) Field.

Program #		Win	Place	Show
11	Gato Del Sol	$44.40	$19.00	$9.40
7	Laser Light		$17.00	$9.20
15f	Reinvested			$4.40

Winner: Gr. c. by *Cougar II–Peacefully, by Jacinto. Trained by Edwin Gregson; bred in Kentucky by Hancock III & Peters.
$550,100—gross value and $40,000 Gold Cup. Net to winner $428,850; second $60,000; third $30,000; fourth $15,000.

388 nominations.
Equipment: b—blinkers

*Foreign bred

CAREER HIGHLIGHTS

YEAR	AGE	STS.	1ST	2ND	3RD	EARNINGS
1981	2	8	2	1	3	$ 220,828
1982	3	9	2	3	1	$ 588,779
1983	4	10	2	2	0	$ 109,900
1984	5	10	0	2	3	$ 367,000
1985	6	2	1	1	0	$ 53,600
TOTALS		**39**	**7**	**9**	**7**	**$1,340,107**

At 2 years	WON	Maiden on 3rd attempt, Del Mar Futurity
	2ND	Hollywood Prevue
	3RD	Balboa Stakes, Norfolk
	UNP	Hollywood Futurity
At 3 years	WON	Kentucky Derby
	2ND	San Felipe, Blue Grass Stakes, Belmont
	UNP	Santa Anita Derby, Travers, Suburban Hanidcap
At 4 years	WON	Cabrillo
	2ND	Del Mar Handicap
	UNP	Caballero, Marlboro Cup, Sunset, American Handicap
		Carlton F. Burke, Auld Lang Syne

Cat of the Sun

ONE DAY EDDIE GREGSON, AN EX–Hollywood actor turned horse trader, noticed a beautiful gray cat lying in the sun. It inspired the name for a gray colt that Gregson was training; he called it Cat of the Sun, only using the Spanish translation Gato Del Sol, because the colt's sire was Cougar II and he was from Chile. He would win the Derby, becoming one of four gray colts to do that, along with Determine, Decidedly, and Spectacular Bid, up to this point.

Not many people expected Gato Del Sol to win; his odds were 21–1 as he stood at the post. But his trainer and his owner, Arthur Hancock III, son of Bull Hancock, wanted the win not only for himself, but for his father, who had spent his life trying to win the Derby but never had. The closest he came was with Dike in the 1969 Derby, who finished second to Bill Hartack on Majestic Prince.

To the causal observer, it didn't look as if Gato Del Sol was going to win anything.

He was literally running last at the beginning of the race, trailing by nineteen lengths. But Gregson and Hancock knew that didn't mean much. Gato Del Sol was primed for this distance.

In the backstretch, his jockey, Louisiana-born Eddie Delahoussaye, started to move Gato up. Slowly, inexorably, he started to pass horses until he passed the leaders, Air Forbes Won, El Baba, and finally, the filly who had led all the way, Cupecoy's Joy. He hit the wire two and half lengths to the good, and got there in a white-hot 2:00 2/5. More, his payout was $44.40 on a $2 ticket, the biggest payoff since Proud Clarion in 1967.

The win was ironic. When Bull Hancock died, his executors left his horse farm, Claiborne, to his brother Seth. Arthur, though, had founded his own farm, Stoner, and it was from this farm that Gato Del Sol came. Nevertheless, when Arthur received the gold cup, he said, "I'd like to dedicate this trophy to my dad. He taught me everything I know—and how to get it."

Sunny's Halo
109th *May 7, 1983*

	Hail to Reason	*Turn-to
Halo		Nothirdchance
SUNNY'S HALO	Cosman	Cosmic Bomb
Chestnut colt		Almahmoud
Mostly Sunny	Sunny	*Princequillo
		Sunshine Well
	Dolly	Daumier
		Lecount

THE WINNER'S PEDIGREE

RACE DAY STATISTICS

HORSE	EQ.	WT.	PP	1/4	1/2	3/4	MILE	STR.	FIN.	JOCKEY	OWNER	ODDS TO $1
Sunny's Halo		126	10	2^{hd}	$2^{1/2}$	$1^{1/2}$	1^{hd}	$1^{1/2}$	1^2	E. Delahoussaye	D. J. Foster Racing Stable	2.50
Desert Wine		126	5	$3^{1-1/2}$	3^3	3^{hd}	2nd	$2^{2-1/2}$	2^{nk}	C. McCarron	T90 Ranch-Cardiff Stud Farm	15.90
Caveat	b	126	20	$16^{2-1/2}$	$17^{1-1/2}$	15^1	11^{hd}	$7^{1-1/2}$	3^1	L. Pincay Jr.	August Belmont IV, et al	(b) 6.70
Slew O' Gold		126	1	$7^{1/2}$	7^2	6^2	7^{hd}	3^{hd}	4^{nk}	A. Cordero Jr.	Equusequity Stable	10.10
Marfa	b	126	18	$13^{1/2}$	14^2	$14^{1-1/2}$	8^1	$4^{1-1/2}$	5^1	J. Velasquez	French-Beal-Lukas	(a) 2.40
Play Fellow	b	126	2	11^2	10^{hd}	$10^{1/2}$	6^1	$5^{1/2}$	6^2	J. Cruguet	Vanier-Lauer-Victor	10.90
Pax In Bello		126	14	8^{hd}	$9^{1-1/2}$	$8^{1/2}$	$9^{1-1/2}$	6^{hd}	7^{hd}	J. Fell	Mr. & Mrs. A. A. Willcox	24.40
Country Pine		126	7	12^1	$12^{1-1/2}$	$11^{1-1/2}$	$10^{1/2}$	$9^{2-1/2}$	$8^{2-1/2}$	M. Venezia	Daniel M. Galbreath	47.40
Balboa Native	b	126	3	$19^{1/2}$	16^{hd}	18^1	$18^{1-1/2}$	14^{hd}	9^{nk}	S. Hawley	Robert H. Spreen	(a) 2.40
Paris Prince	b	126	16	$9^{1-1/2}$	8^{hd}	7^1	5^1	$8^{1-1/2}$	10^2	T. Lipham	Dolly Green	(f) 10.90
Current Hope		126	12	$18^{1/2}$	20	19^{hd}	17^1	$10^{1-1/2}$	11^{nk}	A. Solis	R. Baker & H. Kaskel	18.30
Chumming		126	4	20	18^1	20	19^1	13^2	12^{nk}	E. Maple	Hickory Tree Stable	(b) 6.70
Freezing Rain		126	8	17^2	$19^{1/2}$	17^1	$16^{1-1/2}$	$12^{1/2}$	13^{hd}	W. Gavidia	Bwamazon Farm	(c) 23.50
My Mac	b	126	15	14^{hd}	15^3	16^1	15^{hd}	$11^{1/2}$	14^4	D. MacBeth	Aronow Stable	(f) 10.90
Explosive Wagon		126	11	10^{hd}	$11^{1-1/2}$	12^1	14^2	15^2	15^1	C. Mueller	Peggy McReynolds	(f) 10.90
Parfaitement		126	13	$6^{1-1/2}$	6^1	$5^{1/2}$	$4^{1/2}$	$16^{2-1/2}$	16^2	H. McCauley	Mrs. Bernard Daney	41.20
Highland Park	b	126	19	5^{hd}	5^2	$4^{1-1/2}$	$3^{1-1/2}$	17^1	17^{hd}	D. Brumfield	Bwamazon Farm	(c) 23.50
Luv a Libra		126	17	4^{hd}	4^{hd}	9^1	12^1	19^6	18^2	J. Espinoza	V. DeCosta & S. Yagoda	(f) 10.90
Law Talk		126	6	15^2	13^{hd}	13^1	13^1	$18^{1-1/2}$	19^{15}	C. Marquez	Buckram Oak Farm	(f) 10.90
Total Departure		126	9	$1^{1/2}$	$1^{1-1/2}$	2^1	20	20	20	P. Valenzuela	Rebalot Stable	(a) 2.40

Time: :23^4/5, :47^1/5, 1:11^4/5, 1:36^4/5, 2:02^1/5. Track fast. Off at 5:40 EDT. Start good. Won driving.
Coupled: (a) Marfa, Balboa Native, and Total Departure; (b) Caveat and Chumming; (c) Freezing Rain and Highland Park; (f) Field.

Program #		Win	Place	Show
8	Sunny's Halo	$7.00	$ 4.80	$4.00
6	Desert Wine		$12.20	$9.80
2b	Caveat			$5.20

Winner: Ch. c. by Halo—Mostly Sunny, by Sunny. Trained by David C. Cross Jr.; bred in Canada by David J. Foster.
$531,000—gross value and $42,000 Gold Cup. Net to winner $426,000; second $60,000; third $30,000; fourth $15,000.

405 nominations.
Equipment: b—blinkers

*Foreign bred

CAREER HIGHLIGHTS

YEAR	AGE	STS.	1ST	2ND	3RD	EARNINGS
1982	2	11	5	2	1	$ 235,829
1983	3	9	4	1	1	$1,011,962
TOTALS		**20**	**9**	**3**	**2**	**$1,247,791**

At 2 years	WON	Maiden on 1st attempt, Colin, Swynford, Grey, Coronation Futurity
	2ND	Victoria, Clarendon
	3RD	Tremont
	UNP	Laurel Futurity, Young America, Sanford
At 3 years	WON	Kentucky Derby, Arkansas Derby, Rebel, Super Derby
	2ND	Volante
	3RD	Whitney
	UNP	Preakness, Jerome, Arlington Classic

"I Knew How Good He Could Be"

SIX MONTHS BEFORE THE 1983 DERBY, no one thought much of Sunny's Halo, the Canadian-bred colt. At the time, the horse was soundly beaten in the Laurel Futurity and the Young America as a two-year-old and virtually everyone had given up on the colt as a good running prospect, except his trainer, David Cross. "I knew how good he could be," Cross said, "and I had to follow my belief."

Then came the moment when Cross was ready to see if his belief in the colt—his high-stakes judgment—had been justified. He raced Sunny's Halo in the Arkansas Derby, where the colt ran the most impressive race of the year by a three-year-old, beating Caveat by four lengths. There was no question: Sunny's Halo was ready to see just how far he could take Cross's belief. He was entered into the Kentucky Derby.

There was a huge crowd on hand, 134,444, a long way from the 10,000 that attended the first Derby.

Sunny's Halo surged to the lead after six furlongs, but it was hardly a finished race. Indeed, Desert Wine, ridden by Chris McCarron, surged by Sunny's Halo and was a head in front of them as they turned for home.

Delahoussaye had not gone to the whip. He just leaned down into the horse's mane and spoke to him, urging him forward. Sunny's Halo heard him. He found more inside himself and hammered to the front, suddenly up by half a length with a furlong, 200 yards or so, left to go. And then he went, and was alone at the wire.

David Cross's belief had been evident long ago, when he had bet $500 on Sunny's Halo in the winter books at a 500–1 shot and won $50,000. But it started even before that, as he remembered Sunny Halo's dam, Mostly Sunny, whose life pointed to what was inside Sunny's Halo. She was the "sorest and gamest" runner he ever trained. "She'd win one day and then go lie down in her stall three days. She had a heart that must have weighed 122 pounds."

The first time Mostly Sunny was bred, she aborted the foal; the next died soon after birth. Sunny's Halo was her first foal to live—and did he ever.

Swale
110th May 5, 1984

THE WINNER'S PEDIGREE

		Bold Reasoning	Boldnesian
			Reason to Earn
	Seattle Slew		Poker
SWALE		My Charmer	Fair Charmer
Dark bay	brown colt		Aristophanes
	Tuerta	*Forli	Trevisa
			Double Jay
		Continue	Courtesy

RACE DAY STATISTICS

HORSE	EQ.	WT.	PP	1/4	1/2	3/4	MILE	STR.	FIN.	JOCKEY	OWNER	ODDS TO $1
Swale		126	15	$3^{1-1/2}$	3^1	2^1	1^2	1^5	$1^{3-1/4}$	L. Pincay Jr.	Claiborne Farm	3.40
Coax Me Chad		126	19	17^3	$17^{1-1/2}$	$14^{1-1/2}$	7^{hd}	2^{hd}	2^2	H. McCauley	E. E. Miller	(f) 9.90
At the Threshold		126	14	$11^{1/2}$	$9^{1-1/2}$	$6^{1/2}$	$4^{1-1/2}$	$3^{1/2}$	3^{nk}	E. Maple	W. C. Partee	37.70
(D)Gate Dancer	b	126	20	$19^{1/2}$	18^3	15^1	$9^{1-1/2}$	6^1	$4^{3/4}$	E. Delahoussaye	K. Opstein	18.90
Fali Time	b	126	7	$7^{1/2}$	$7^{1/2}$	$7^{1-1/2}$	$6^{1/2}$	5^{hd}	5^1	S. Hawley	Mamakos & Stubrin	18.70
Pine Circle		126	18	$14^{1/2}$	14^4	$11^{1/2}$	$12^{1/2}$	$7^{1/2}$	$6^{3/4}$	M. Smith	Loblolly Stable	(b) 6.00
Fight Over		126	6	6^{hd}	5^1	3^1	$2^{1-1/2}$	4^1	7^{hd}	O. Vergara	Bwamazon Farm– T. Sabarese	78.90
Life's Magic		121	5	$13^{1-1/2}$	13^1	$9^{1/2}$	8^1	8^3	8^1	D. Brumfield	Mel Hatley Racing Stable	(a) 2.80
Silent King		126	11	20	20	20	19	11^2	9^3	W. Shoemaker	Hawksworth Farm	4.80
Rexson's Hope	b	126	9	$18^{1-1/2}$	19^4	19^3	$18^{1/2}$	$10^{1/2}$	10^{nk}	R. Gaffglione	Elsie A. Rose Stable, Inc.	(f) 9.90
So Vague		126	4	$15^{1/2}$	$15^{1-1/2}$	18^3	$16^{1/2}$	$12^{1/2}$	11^2	P. Cooksey	Hyperion Thoroughbreds	(f) 9.90
Biloxi Indian	b	126	17	$5^{1-1/2}$	4^{hd}	4^{hd}	3^{hd}	$9^{1-1/2}$	$12^{1-1/4}$	G. Patterson	Sundance Stable	(f) 9.90
Taylor's Special		126	10	9^1	8^{hd}	8^{hd}	10^2	13^2	13^3	S. Maple	W. F. Lucas	6.80
Raja's Shark	b	126	2	$8^{2-1/2}$	$11^{1-1/2}$	12^1	14^{hd}	14^{hd}	14^{hd}	R. Wilson	I. Feiner	59.10
Bedouin		126	8	$16^{1-1/2}$	16^1	$17^{1/2}$	$17^{1/2}$	16^2	15^{nk}	R. Sibille	Elmendorf	(f) 9.90
Vanlandingham		126	12	$4^{1/2}$	6^{hd}	$10^{1-1/2}$	$11^{1/2}$	$15^{1/2}$	16^2	P. Day	Loblolly Stable	(b) 6.00
Secret Prince		126	13	$10^{1/2}$	$12^{1/2}$	$13^{1/2}$	$13^{1/2}$	$17^{1/2}$	$17^{2-1/4}$	C. Perret	Elaine M. Brodsky	(f) 9.90
Bear Hunt	b	126	3	$2^{1/2}$	$2^{1/2}$	5^1	$15^{1-1/2}$	$18^{1-1/2}$	$18^{7-1/2}$	D. MacBeth	Taylor's Purchase Farm	57.40
Althea		121	1	$1^{1/2}$	1^1	1^{hd}	$5^{1/2}$	19	19	C. McCarron	Alexander-Aykroyd- Groves	(a) 2.80
Majestic Shore		126	16	12^5	10^{hd}	$16^{1/2}$	Eased	-	-	J. Lively	Oldknow & Phipps	(f) 9.90

Time: :23$^{2/5}$, :47$^{2/5}$, 1:11$^{4/5}$, 1:36$^{3/5}$, 2:02$^{2/5}$. Track fast. Off at 5:40 EDT. Start good for all but Gate Dancer. Won driving.
Coupled: (a) Life's Magic and Althea; (b) Pine Circle and Vanlandingham. (D) Gate Dancer disqualified and placed fifth. (f) Field.

Program #		Win	Place	Show
10	Swale	$8.80	$4.80	$ 3.40
18f	Coax Me Chad		$8.00	$ 4.00
9	At the Threshold			$13.80

Winner: Dk. b. or br. c. by Seattle Slew–Tuerta, by *Forli. Trained by W. C. Stephens; bred in Kentucky by Claiborne Farm.
$712,600—gross value and $40,000 Gold Cup. Net to winner $537,400; second $100,000; third $50,00; fourth $25,000.

312 nominations.
Equipment: b—blinkers

*Foreign bred

CAREER HIGHLIGHTS

YEAR	AGE	STS.	1ST	2ND	3RD	EARNINGS
1983	2	7	5	1	1	$ 491,951
1984	3	7	4	1	1	$1,091,710
TOTALS		14	9	2	2	**$1,583,661**

At 2 years	WON	Maiden on 2nd attempt, Saratoga Special, Futurity, Young America, Breeders Futurity
	3RD	Hopeful
At 3 years	WON	Kentucky Derby, Belmont Stakes, Florida Derby, Hutcheson
	2ND	Lexington
	3RD	Fountain of Youth
	UNP	Preakness

A Big Decision

BEFORE THE 1984 DERBY, TRAINER WOODY Stephens had a decision to make, and he was hardly in the best physical condition to do it. He had been hospitalized in Louisville for twelve days with emphysema and other problems.

The decision was whether to run a horse named Devil's Bag or nothing in the Derby. Devil's Bag had been very, very good. As a two-year-old he won all five starts, including a six-length triumph in the one-mile Champagne Stakes in a white-hot 1:34 1/5.

After twelve days in the hospital, four days before the Derby, Stephens made the decision. He announced that Devil's Bag wouldn't be running in the Derby. But Stephens had another horse, a dark bay who was ready to go. His name was Swale. Indeed, his father was the 1977 Triple Crown champion Seattle Slew, but Swale himself was not sporting a glittering recent racing résumé. The overwhelming favorite in the Lexington Stakes at Keeneland, he came in eight lengths behind a horse named He Is a Great Deal on a muddy track. Stephens chose to focus on how well Swale did by winning in

the Florida Derby. All Stevens had to do was get that kind of race out of him.

Two days before the Derby started, he checked himself out of the hospital and viewed the race from the directors' room at Churchill Downs.

There were twenty starters, but that didn't bother Swale. He immediately jumped out hard and took off after Althea from the outside. As they turned into the backstretch, he was in the lead.

For Stephens, the big question was answered. Says Stephens, "He's going to win by five."

Swale only won by three and a half lengths, but it was said that if his jockey, Lafitte Pincay Jr., had pushed him, he could have made it five.

Swale's life ended bizarrely. He lost the Preakness but won the Belmont Stakes. Eight days after this, he was outside his barn being bathed, and he suddenly reared up and fell back dead. Efforts to revive him failed. An autopsy was performed, and a heart attack speculated—which Stephens didn't believe—but the definitive cause of this three-year-old horse's death was never established.

Spend a Buck
111th *May 4, 1985*

		Buckpasser	Tom Fool
	Buckaroo		Busanda
			No Robbery
SPEND A BUCK		Stepping High	*Behop II
Bay colt			Prince John
	Belle de Jour	Speak John	Nuit de Folies
			Jaipur
		Battle Dress	Armorial

The Winner's Pedigree and Career Highlights

YEAR	AGE	STS.	1ST	2ND	3RD	EARNINGS
1984	2	8	5	2	1	$ 667,985
1985	3	7	5	1	1	$3,552,704*
TOTALS		**15**	**10**	**3**	**2**	**$ 4,220,689***

(*Includes $2 million Garden State Bonus)

At 2 years	WON	Maiden on 1st attempt, Cradle, Arlington-Washington Futurity
	2ND	Criterium, Young America
	3RD	Breeders' Cup Juvenile
At 3 years	WON	Kentucky Derby, Cherry Hill, Garden State, Monmouth Handicap, Jersey Derby
	2ND	Haskell Invitational
	3RD	Bay Shore

Race Day Statistics

HORSE	EQ.	WT.	PP	1/4	1/2	3/4	MILE	STR.	FIN.	JOCKEY	OWNER	ODDS TO $1
Spend a Buck		126	10	$1^{1\text{-}1/2}$	1^6	1^6	1^6	1^5	$1^{5\text{-}1/4}$	A. Cordero Jr.	Hunter Farm	4.10
Stephan's Odyssey		126	6	13	13	$10^{1/2}$	5^1	3^{hd}	$2^{1/2}$	L. Pincay Jr.	H. deKwiatkowski	13.40
Chief's Crown		126	2	$2^{1/2}$	$2^{1\text{-}1/2}$	2^{hd}	$2^{2\text{-}1/2}$	2^1	3^{nk}	D. MacBeth	Star Crown Stable	1.20
Fast Account	b	126	13	11^1	$10^{1/2}$	8^1	4^1	4^4	4^2	C. McCarron	W. R. Hawn	92.80
Proud Truth		126	11	12^1	$12^{1/2}$	11^1	$9^{1/2}$	$5^{1\text{-}1/2}$	5^3	J. Velasquez	Darby Dan Farm	4.90
Skywalker		126	12	$6^{1/2}$	7^{hd}	$9^{1\text{-}1/2}$	8^{hd}	7^1	6no	E. Delahoussaye	Oak Cliff Stable	17.70
Tank's Prospect	b	126	4	7^1	$8^{1\text{-}1/2}$	$3^{1/2}$	$3^{1/2}$	$6^{1/2}$	7^2	G. Stevens	Mr. & Mrs. E. Klein	11.30
Floating Reserve		126	9	$8^{1/2}$	$9^{1/2}$	12^2	11^5	8^5	$8^{6\text{-}1/2}$	S. Hawley	Robert Hibbert	134.80
Rhoman Rule		126	3	$9^{1\text{-}1/2}$	$6^{1/2}$	6^1	$10^{1/2}$	10^3	$9^{3/4}$	J. Vasquez	Brownell Combs II	(a) 7.50
Encolure		126	7	3^{hd}	4^{hd}	5^{hd}	$7^{1/2}$	9^1	10^4	R. Ardoin	Fred Porter Estate	103.50
Irish Fighter		126	1	$4^{1/2}$	3^{hd}	$4^{1\text{-}1/2}$	6^{hd}	$11^{1\text{-}1/2}$	$11^{3/4}$	P. Day	Izzie Proler	40.90
Eternal Prince	b	126	5	5^1	$5^{1\text{-}1/2}$	$7^{1/2}$	$12^{1/2}$	12^2	$12^{3\text{-}1/2}$	R. Migliore	Hurst, Steinbrenner, Post & Spendthrift Farm	(a) 7.50
I Am the Game	b	126	8	$10^{1/2}$	11^3	13	13	13	13	D. McHargue	Leatherbury & Mandjuris	101.30

Time: :23, :45^4/5, 1:09^3/5, 1:34^4/5, 2:00^1/5. Track fast. Off at 5:39 EDT. Start good. Won driving.
Coupled: (a) Rhoman Rule and Eternal Prince.

Program #		Win	Place	Show	$2 Exacta (9-5)
9	Spend a Buck	$10.20	$ 5.40	$3.40	$118.20
5	Stephan's Odyssey		$10.20	$5.00	
3	Chief's Crown			$2.80	

Winner: B. c. by Buckaroo–Belle de Jour, by Speak John. Trained by Cam Gambolati; bred in Kentucky by Harper Roe.
$581,800—gross value and $40,000 Gold Cup. Net to winner $406,800; second $100,000; third $50,00; fourth $25,000.

359 nominations.
Equipment: b—blinkers

*Foreign bred

Speed Demon

SPEND A BUCK, WHO WON THE 1985 DERBY under Angel Cordero Jr., had more trouble with his name than he did in winning the Derby. His owner, Dennis Diaz, says that Spend a Buck was his sixth choice for a name, the Jockey Club having rejected five others— Money Talks, Pass the Buck, Pass the Hat, Raise a Buck, and Turn a Buck had all been used before.

The race was supposed to be a duel between Spend a Buck and Eternal Prince, but when it started, Eternal Prince broke badly—his jockey says he was distracted by the crowd—and Spend a Buck moved into an unchallenged lead. Still, it would be hard to imagine many horses beating Spend a Buck this day. He ran the third fastest Derby ever. He immediately went into the lead when the gates opened, and from then on it was a game of catch-up—fast catch-up. His first quarter was 23 seconds flat, and then

he ran the fastest three-quarter mile in Derby history and the fastest mile. He ran the latter in 1:34 4/5, one-fifth of a second faster than the 1:35 of Bold Forbes in 1976.

Eternal Prince was never in the race. One horse, Chief's Crown, did have a shot catching Spend a Buck. This horse had won nine of its last ten starts, but there was a problem: he was forced to go after Spend a Buck earlier than he wanted. Unable to cut into the lead by more than a length, he was cut down by Stephan's Odyssey in the final strides and knocked back to third.

For Angel Cordero, it was his third Derby: he also won with Cannonade in 1974 and Bold Forbes in 1976.

Spend a Buck's winning time was 2:00 1/5, only 1/5 of a second slower than Northern Dancer's time in 1964, and 4/5 of a second slower than Secretariat. Said his trainer, in a masterpiece of understatement: "He was moving."

Ferdinand
112th May 3, 1986

			Nearctic
		Northern Dancer	Natalma
	Nijinsky II		Bull Page
FERDINAND		Flaming Page	Flaring Top
Chestnut colt			Balladier
	Banja Luka	Double Jay	Broomshot
			Dark Star
		Legato	Vulcania

THE WINNER'S PEDIGREE AND CAREER HIGHLIGHTS

RACE DAY STATISTICS

HORSE	EQ.	WT.	PP	$1/4$	$1/2$	$3/4$	MILE	STR.	FIN.	JOCKEY	OWNER	ODDS TO $1
Ferdinand		126	3	15^{hd}	16	$11^{1\text{-}1/2}$	$5^{1/2}$	1^1	$1^{2\text{-}1/4}$	W. Shoemaker	Mrs. Elizabeth A. Keck	17.70
*Bold Arrangement		126	4	14^{hd}	$11^{1/2}$	$7^{1/2}$	$2^{1/2}$	$3^{1/2}$	$2^{3/4}$	C. McCarron	A. & R. Richards	9.10
Broad Brush	B	126	9	$7^{1\text{-}1/2}$	$6^{1/2}$	$6^{1\text{-}1/2}$	1^{hd}	2^{hd}	3^{nk}	V. Bracciale Jr.	Robert E. Meyerhoff	14.40
Rampage	BL	126	8	$11^{1\text{-}1/2}$	$10^{1\text{-}1/2}$	9^1	7^2	6^3	$4^{1\text{-}1/2}$	P. Day	Nancy & H. John Reed	9.00
Badger Land	Bb	126	10	$9^{1/2}$	$9^{1/2}$	8^1	$3^{1/2}$	4^3	5^4	J. Velasquez	Lukas, Hartley & Lukas	2.60
Wheatly Hall	BL	126	11	$8^{1/2}$	$7^{1/2}$	$5^{1\text{-}1/2}$	6^1	5^{hd}	$6^{1\text{-}1/2}$	G. Stevens	John McKinnon	47.70
Fobby Forbes	B	126	16	12^{hd}	$12^{1/2}$	14^{hd}	$10^{1\text{-}1/2}$	$7^{1/2}$	$7^{3\text{-}1/4}$	R. Romero	Due Process Stable	(f) 16.00
Icy Groom	B	126	5	10^{hd}	$13^{1\text{-}1/2}$	12^1	$9^{1/2}$	8^3	8^2	E. Maple	William J. Fleming	(f) 16.00
Wise Times	BLb	126	3	$13^{1/2}$	$15^{1/2}$	$15^{1\text{-}1/2}$	$11^{1\text{-}1/2}$	10^{hd}	9^{nk}	K. Allen	R. L. Reineman Stable	(f) 16.00
Mogambo	B	126	2	16	$14^{1/2}$	16	14^5	$11^{2\text{-}1/2}$	$10^{3\text{-}3/4}$	J. Vasquez	Peter M. Brant & Calumet Farm	8.80
Snow Chief	Bb	126	12	5^4	4^6	3^{hd}	4^1	9^{hd}	11^{nk}	A. Solis	Grinstead & Rochelle	2.10
Zabaleta	Bb	126	15	2^1	$2^{1\text{-}1/2}$	$2^{1\text{-}1/2}$	$8^{1/2}$	$12^{3\text{-}1/2}$	12^3	D. McHargue	Michael Riordan	(f) 16.00
Southern Appeal	Lb	126	6	$6^{1/2}$	$5^{5\text{-}1/2}$	10^{hd}	$13^{1/2}$	13^2	$13^{8\text{-}1/2}$	J. Davidson	Howard M. Bender	(f) 16.00
Bachelor Beau	Bb	126	13	3^1	$3^{1/2}$	4^2	12^{hd}	14^6	14^{11}	L. Melancon	Waterfield & Tafel	60.00
Vernon Castle	B	126	7	5^{hd}	8^3	13^{hd}	16	15^2	$15^{7\text{-}1/2}$	E. Delahoussaye	North Ridge, A. Paulson (lessee)	12.20
Groovy	BL	126	14	1^1	1^1	1^{hd}	15^2	16	16	L. Pincay Jr.	Ballis & Kruckel	57.30

Time: :22^1/5, :45^1/5, 1:10^1/5, 1:37, 2:04^4/5. Track fast. Off at 5:40 EDT. Start good. Won driving.
(f) Field.

Program #		Win	Place	Show	$2 Exacta (1-3)
1	Ferdinand	$37.40	$16.00	$8.60	$385.00
3	Bold Arrangement		$ 9.40	$6.80	
6	Broad Brush			$9.20	

Winner: Ch. c. by Nijinsky II–Banja Luka, by Double Jay. Trained by Charles Whittingham; bred in Kentucky by Howard B. Keck.
$784,400—gross value and $40,000 Gold Cup. Net to winner $609,400; second $100,000; third $50,00; fourth $25,000.

452 nominations.
Medication: B—bute; L—Lasix
Equipment: b—blinkers

*Foreign bred

CAREER HIGHLIGHTS

YEAR	AGE	STS.	1ST	2ND	3RD	EARNINGS
1985	2	5	1	1	2	$ 178,650
1986	3	8	3	3	2	$ 981,678
1987	4	10	4	2	1	$2,185,150
1988	5	6	0	3	1	$ 432,500
TOTALS		**29**	**8**	**9**	**6**	**$3,777,978**

At 2 years	WON	Maiden on 4th attempt
	3RD	Hollywood Futurity
At 3 years	WON	Kentucky Derby, Santa Catalina, Malibu
	2ND	Preakness, San Rafael, Los Feliz
	3RD	Santa Anita Derby, Belmont Stakes
At 4 years	WON	Breeders' Cup Classic, Goodwood, Cabrillo, Hollywood Gold Cup
	2ND	Strub, Santa Anita Handicap
	3RD	John Henry
	UNP	San Fernando, San Luis Rey, Californian
At 5 years	2ND	San Antonio, Santa Anita, San Bernardino
	3RD	Hollywood Gold Cup
	UNP	Californian, Goodwood

To Find the Magic One More Time

HE HAD BEEN ONE OF THE GREATEST JOCKEYS who ever lived, but Willie Shoemaker was near the end. He was fifty-four years old, a time when most jockeys were taking their grandchildren to amusement parks, not hunched down on a galloping thousand-pound horse, where any misstep could put them in the hospital or the morgue.

As the 1986 Derby approached, a number of observers wondered if the great "Shoe" still had it.

But one of them, Ferdinand's trainer, Charles Wittingham, whose nickname was "the Bald Eagle," was not one of them. He had great faith in Shoemaker. Still, Shoemaker knew that he was near the end: "I'm in the twilight of my career," he said.

The horse he was on, Ferdinand, was not the greatest. But Wittingham believed in the horse, in particular his power in the final quarter mile. He knew that Ferdinand would have a great chance, particularly if Shoemaker could reach down inside himself and find the magic one more time.

The race started. As they passed the finish line for the first time, Ferdinand was last.

But then, down the backstretch, Shoemaker brought him along, getting closer, and at the half-mile pole he started to move even more. By the quarter pole, he was in a contending position.

And then came the moment, in the upper stretch, when Willie Shoemaker would answer all questions. As the horses thundered along, an opening appeared between two horses ahead of him. Should he try to go through?

He continued to drive to victory by two and a quarter lengths over an English horse, Bold Arrangement.

Later someone asked him if taking Ferdinand through the "hole between the horses" wasn't dangerous. "You don't think about that in the Kentucky Derby," Shoemaker said. No, you don't if you're Willie Shoemaker.

For Shoemaker, it was the best Derby of the four he had won. He loved winning it for Charles Wittingham, and he loved that he had won it for himself. Shoemaker was to say later, "I had a few tears in my eyes coming back to the winner's circle." And he thought, "Well, old Jack Nicklaus did it, and I did it too."

Alysheba
113th *May 2, 1987*

	Alydar	Raise a Native	Native Dancer
			Raise You
ALYSHEBA		Sweet Tooth	On-and-On
Bay colt			Plum Cake
	Bel Sheba	Lt. Stevens	Nantallah
			Rough Shod II
		Belthazar	War Admiral
			Blinking Owl

THE WINNER'S PEDIGREE

RACE DAY STATISTICS

HORSE	EQ.	WT.	PP	1/4	1/2	3/4	MILE	STR.	FIN.	JOCKEY	OWNER	ODDS TO $1
Alysheba	BLb	126	3	14^2	$13^{2-1/2}$	$7^{1/2}$	3^1	$2^{1-1/2}$	$1^{3/4}$	C. McCarron	Dorothy & Pamela Scharbauer	8.40
Bet Twice		126	14	$5^{1/2}$	6^1	4^1	1^{hd}	1^1	$2^{2-1/4}$	C. Perret	B. P. Levy & Cisley Stable	10.10
Avies Copy	b	126	16	10^{hd}	10^2	$8^{1/2}$	4^{hd}	3^1	3^{nk}	M. Solomone	T. Brown Badgett	(f) 24.50
Cryptoclearance		126	1	$16^{1-1/2}$	$15^{1-1/2}$	$14^{1/2}$	$7^{1/2}$	4^1	$4^{1/2}$	J. Santos	Philip Teinowitz	6.50
Templar Hill	Bb	126	4	9^{hd}	$11^{1-1/2}$	9^2	$9^{1/2}$	$6^{1/2}$	$5^{1/2}$	G. Hutton	Ervin J. Kowitz	(f) 24.50
Gulch	B	126	6	$15^{1-1/2}$	16^{hd}	$15^{1/2}$	12^1	7^3	$6^{1/2}$	W. Shoemaker	Peter M. Brant	(b) 4.90
Leo Castelli	Bb	126	8	7^{hd}	$4^{1/2}$	5^1	6^1	$5^{1-1/2}$	7^5	J. Vasquez	Peter M. Brant	(b) 4.90
Candi's Gold		126	12	$3^{1/2}$	3^{hd}	$6^{1-1/2}$	8^{hd}	$8^{2-1/2}$	$8^{2-1/4}$	S. Hawley	Royal Lines (Lessee)	48.50
Conquistarose	Bb	126	15	17	17	16	16	13^4	9^2	J. Bailey	H. deKwiatkowski	52.80
On the Line	Bb	126	9	$1^{1/2}$	$2^{2-1/2}$	$1^{1/2}$	$2^{1-1/2}$	$9^{1/2}$	10^2	G. Stevens	Eugene V. Klein	(a) 6.30
Shawklit Won	Bb	126	13	$11^{1/2}$	$9^{1/2}$	11^1	$11^{1/2}$	$12^{1/2}$	11^{nk}	R. Migliore	Edward Anchel	50.20
Masterful Advocate	BL	126	7	6^{hd}	$7^{1/2}$	$10^{1/2}$	$13^{1/2}$	$11^{1/2}$	12no	L. Pincay Jr.	H. J. Belles & D. A. Leveton	6.20
War	Bb	126	2	$8^{1-1/2}$	$5^{1/2}$	$3^{1/2}$	$5^{1/2}$	10^1	13^7	W. McCauley	Tom Gentry	(a) 6.30
Momentus	Bb	126	11	$12^{1-1/2}$	12^1	13^2	15^3	14^3	$14^{2-1/2}$	D. Brumfield	Chillingworth & Duckett et al	(f) 24.50
No More Flowers	B	126	17	$4^{1-1/2}$	$8^{1/2}$	12^2	14^2	$15^{1-1/2}$	15	W. Guerra	Arthur I. Appleton	55.30
Capote	B	126	5	$2^{2-1/2}$	$1^{1-1/2}$	2^{hd}	10^1	16	Eased	A. Cordero Jr.	Klein-French-Beal	(a) 6.30
Demons Begone	B	126	10	13^1	$14^{1-1/2}$	Pulled up— bled				P. Day	Loblolly Stables	2.20

Time: :22⁴/₅, :46²/₅, 1:11, 1:36⁴/₅, 2:03²/₅. Track fast. Off at 5:35 EDT. Start good. Won driving.
Coupled: (a) Capote, On the Line, and War; (b) Gulch and Leo Castelli; (f) Field.

Program #		Win	Place	Show	$2 Exacta (4-9)
4	Alysheba	$18.80	$ 8.00	$6.20	$109.60
9	Bet Twice		$10.00	$7.20	
14f	Avies Copy			$6.80	

Winner: B. c. by Alydar–Bel Sheba, by Lt. Stevens. Trained by Jack C. Van Berg; bred in Kentucky by Preston Madden.
$793,600—gross value and $40,000 Gold Cup. Net to winner $618,600; second $100,000; third $50,00; fourth $25,000.

422 nominations.
Medication: B—bute; L—Lasix
Equipment: b—blinkers

CAREER HIGHLIGHTS

YEAR	AGE	STS.	1ST	2ND	3RD	EARNINGS
1986	2	7	1	4	1	$ 359,486
1987	3	10	3	3	1	$2,511,156
1988	4	9	7	1	0	$3,808,600
TOTALS		26	11	8	2	$6,679,242

At 2 years	WON	Maiden on 3rd attempt
	2ND	In Memoriam, Breeders' Futurity, Hollywood Futurity
	3RD	Breeders' Cup Juvenile
At 3 years	WON	Kentucky Derby, Preakness, Super Derby
	2ND	San Felipe Hdcp., Haskell Invitational, Breeders' Cup Classic
	3RD	Blue Grass (won, disqualified to 3rd)
	UNP	Belmont, Travers
At 4 years	WON	Breeders' Cup Classic, Charles Strub, Santa Anita, San Bernardino, Iselin, Woodward, Meadowlands Cup
	2ND	Hollywood Gold Cup
	UNP	Pimlico Special

"C'mon Wire!"

IN THIS YEAR'S DERBY, THERE WAS STILL A fundamental question in the air about the favorite, Alysheba. Just how good was he?

Why? One explanation was that he sometimes got lazy, or it could be the physical condition in his throat that was corrected with a new procedure just before the Derby.

When the gates opened on the race, Alysheba, with Chris McCarron up, would answer all questions.

Most Derbies are controlled chaos. But most of the time, at one point, the horses get to run to the wire, mano a mano, and that is when the race is decided.

The 113th running turned out to be one of the roughest, most dangerous races in Derby history, with horses banging into the rail, crowded together in a mad dash to get position, and a shocker: the favorite, Demons Begone, had to pull up when it was discovered that he was bleeding profusely from the nose.

Alysheba, who was bumped coming out of the gate, was fourteenth at the turn, but in the backstretch he started to move up, passing a dozen horses on his way. By the seven-sixteenths

pole he was one of the four leaders, all thundering along together: On the Line on the rail, Bet Twice beside him, and Avie's Copy running next to him.

They turned into the stretch, and it was the same story: the place, usually, where dreams are won or lost. On the Line faded, Chris McCarron and Alysheba moved strongly on the outside, and Bet Twice moved ahead at the quarter pole and held his lead inside the eighth pole. It seemed clear he was going to win.

And then it happened: the final nail in Alysheba's coffin. Running behind Bet Twice, the stretch almost gone, Alysheba clipped Bet Twice's heels and started to go down, his head almost to the ground. Jockey Chris McCarron said later, "I thought I was gone."

But he wasn't. Somehow he stayed in stride and straightened up with three-sixteenths of a mile to go, six or seven seconds, Alysheba in full bore, a madman known as McCarron astride him, 131,000 fans going berserk, and McCarron's heart screaming, "C'mon wire!" And the wire came to him first. Alysheba had won.

Yes, it was one of the roughest, most dangerous races in Derby history, but it was also one of the best ever for showing the heart that can make a Thoroughbred racehorse so great.

Winning Colors
114th *May 7, 1988*

		Fortino	Gray Soverign
	Caro (Ire)		Ranavalo
WINNING COLORS		Chambord	Chamossaire
Roan filly			Life Hill
	All Rainbows	Bold Hour	Bold Ruler
			Seven Thirty
		Miss Carmie	T. V. Lark
			Twice Over

THE WINNER'S PEDIGREE

RACE DAY STATISTICS

HORSE	EQ.	WT.	PP	1/4	1/2	3/4	MILE	STR.	FIN.	JOCKEY	OWNER	ODDS TO $1
Winning Colors	B	121	11	1^1	$1^{3-1/2}$	1^4	1^3	$1^{3-1/2}$	1^{nk}	G. Stevens	Eugene V. Klein	3.40
Forty Niner	B	126	17	$2^{1-1/2}$	3^1	$4^{1/2}$	$5^{1-1/2}$	$3^{1-1/2}$	2^3	P. Day	Claiborne Farm	(a) 4.90
Risen Star	B	126	1	13^3	$13^{1-1/2}$	13^1	$9^{1/2}$	$6^{1-1/2}$	$3^{1/2}$	E. Delahoussaye	L. Roussel III & Lamarque Stable	5.50
Proper Reality		126	12	10^{hd}	$5^{1/2}$	3^1	2^2	$2^{1/2}$	4^{hd}	J. Bailey	Mrs. James Winn	27.20
Regal Classic	L	126	3	12^5	10^{hd}	9^{hd}	6^{hd}	$5^{1/2}$	$5^{1/2}$	L. Pincay Jr.	Sam-Son Farm & Windfields Farm	(f) 17.40
Brian's Time		126	5	17	17	17	$15^{1-1/2}$	10^2	$6^{3/4}$	A. Cordero Jr.	Mr. & Mrs. James Phillips	8.30
Seeking the Gold		126	8	$6^{1-1/2}$	2^1	2^1	$3^{1-1/2}$	$4^{1-1/2}$	$7^{3/4}$	R. Romero	Ogden Phipps	15.90
Cefis	b	126	2	16^3	16^5	16^4	11^1	$8^{1/2}$	$8^{1/2}$	E. Maple	J. Ryan & R. Kirkham	(a) 4.90
Private Terms		126	16	$7^{1/2}$	7^{hd}	6^2	$4^{1/2}$	7^{hd}	9^{nk}	C. Antley	Locust Hill Farm	3.40
Jim's Orbit	L	126	13	$8^{1/2}$	$11^{1-1/2}$	$10^{1/2}$	7^{hd}	9^{hd}	$10^{2-1/2}$	S. Romero	James Cottrell	64.60
Granacus	BL	126	6	$15^{1/2}$	$14^{1/2}$	14^3	$16^{1/2}$	$13^{1/2}$	11^{nk}	J. Vasquez	S. A. Stavro	21.70
Lively One	BL	126	15	9^1	9^{hd}	11^2	10^2	12^{hd}	12no	W. Shoemaker	Thomas J. Curnes (Lessee)	(b) 18.60
Din's Dancer	B	126	9	3^{hd}	4^{hd}	5^{hd}	$8^{1/2}$	11^2	13^{hd}	J. Lively	K. Opstein—W. & G. Theisen	(f) 17.40
Kingpost	BL	126	4	11^{hd}	$12^{3-1/2}$	$12^{2-1/2}$	$12^{1/2}$	$14^{1-1/2}$	$14^{2-1/2}$	J. Velasquez	Mark Warner	16.50
Intensive Command	B	126	7	14^1	$15^{2-1/2}$	15^1	$14^{1/2}$	15^5	15^9	J. Pezua	Thomas J. Curnes (Lessee)	(b) 18.60
Purdue King	BL	126	14	$5^{1/2}$	8^2	8^{hd}	17	$16^{1-1/2}$	16^3	K. Desormeaux	Bob Starnes	(f) 17.40
Sea Trek	B	126	10	4^{hd}	6^1	7^{hd}	13^{hd}	17	17	P. Johnson	Diana Stables	(f) 17.40

Time: :23, :46⁴/5, 1:11²/5, 1:36, 2:02¹/5. Track fast. Off at 5:35 EDT. Start good. Won driving.
Coupled: (a) Forty Niner and Cefis; (b) Lively One and Intensive Command; (f) Field.

Program #		Win	Place	Show	$2 Exacta (8-1)
8	Winning Colors	$8.80	$5.20	$4.60	$63.40
1a	Forty Niner		$5.20	$4.60	
3	Risen Star			$5.40	

Winner: Ro. f: by Caro (Ire)—All Rainbows, by Bold Hour. Trained by D. Wayne Lukas; bred in Kentucky by Echo Valley Horse Farm Inc.
$786,200—gross value and $40,000 Gold Cup. Net to winner $611,200; second $100,000; third $50,00; fourth $25,000.

401 nominations.
Medication: B—bute, L—Lasix
Equipment: b—blinkers

CAREER HIGHLIGHTS

YEAR	AGE	STS.	1ST	2ND	3RD	EARNINGS
1987	2	2	2	0	0	$ 31,400
1988	3	10	4	3	1	$1,347,746
1989	4	7	2	0	0	$ 147,691
TOTALS		**19**	**8**	**3**	**1**	**$1,526,837**

At 2 years	WON	Maiden on 1st attempt
At 3 years	WON	Kentucky Derby, Santa Anita Oaks, Santa Anita Derby, La Centinel
	2ND	Breeders' Cup Distaff, Las Virgenes, Maskette
	3RD	Preakness
	UNP	Belmont, Spinster
At 4 years	WON	Turfway Budweiser Breeders' Cup
	UNP	Breeders' Cup Distaff, A Gleam Handicap, Shuvee Handicap, Maskette, Aqueduct Budweiser Breeders' Cup

"The Walk of a Hooker and the Look of a Queen"

WHEN IT CAME TO FILLY RACEHORSES, legendary trainer D. Wayne Lukas applied the following evaluation. He liked the horse to have "the walk of a hooker and the look of a queen." Arrogant and, as it were, cocksure, but beautiful in form and substance.

He apparently had seen that in a filly named Winning Colors, and thought she had a chance in the Derby. He asked Gary Stevens to test her.

In a race Stevens rode, the filly won, and he was impressed by her speed, power, and toughness. She was a lady, but a huge lady at over seventeen hands, and seemed to be able to intimidate the colts who ran with her.

One of the major assets of Winning Colors was that she would start a race as if touched with a cattle prod, getting out in front and, if her racing history was any indicator, staying there. Hence, when she was given post position 11, in the middle of the field, Lukas and Stevens were not worried. Bettors liked Winning Colors, but many experts, Stevens said, doubted that she could go full-bore in a mile and a quarter race; they believed that at the end quality

horses like Private Terms and Forty Niner, with the great Pat Day aboard, would run her down. Now Stevens was about to find out.

As instructed by Lukas, he held her back until the final three-eighths pole, and then asked her to bring all of herself to the track. She did. She was going to win.

But not so fast—Stevens saw that Forty Niner was gaining ground, Pat Day flailing wildly with the whip. And the big filly was tiring.

Then, Forty Niner still closing, Stevens was at the last fifty yards, and he could feel the horse not only badly tiring but "lugging," pulling to the rail, where the soft ground would slow her.

This was the moment for a great jockey to be a great jockey. Stevens guided her back off the rail, and for almost the last five strides he was alone, but he was not alone in the final stride. It was Siamese time: Forty Niner was with them, but it was a neck too late. Then Gary Stevens felt a special electricity, the thrill of having finally won the Kentucky Derby, and on the broad back of only the third filly in history to have done it!

Sunday Silence
115th *May 6, 1989*

		Hail to reason	Me. Prospector
	Halo		Killaloe
SUNDAY SILENCE		Cosmah	Dr. Fager
Dark bay/brown colt			Quiet Charm
	Wishing Well	Understanding	In Reality
			Breakfast Bell
		Mountain Flower	Raise a Native
			Gay Hostess

THE WINNER'S PEDIGREE AND CAREER HIGHLIGHTS

YEAR	AGE	STS.	1ST	2ND	3RD	EARNINGS
1988	2	3	1	2	0	$ 21,700
1989	3	9	7	2	0	$4,578,454
1990	4	2	1	1	0	$ 368,400
TOTALS		**14**	**9**	**5**	**0**	**$4,968,554**

At 2 years	WON	Maiden on 2nd attempt
At 3 years	WON	Kentucky Derby, Preakness, San Felipe, Santa Anita
		Derby Super Derby, Breeders' Cup Classic
	2ND	Belmont, Swaps
At 4 years	WON	Californian
	2ND	Hollywood Gold Cup

RACE DAY STATISTICS

HORSE	EQ.	WT.	PP	1/4	1/2	3/4	MILE	STR.	FIN.	JOCKEY	OWNER	ODDS TO $1
Sunday Silence		126	10	$4^{1/2}$	$4^{1-1/2}$	4^1	$3^{1-1/2}$	$1^{1-1/2}$	$1^{2-1/2}$	P. Valenzuela	Hancock III, Gaillard & Whittingham	3.10
Easy Goer	B	126	13	6^2	5^{hd}	6^2	5^{hd}	6^3	2^{hd}	P. Day	Ogden Phipps	(b) .80
Awe Inspiring	B	126	12	10^{hd}	$11^{1/2}$	$8^{1/2}$	6^3	5^{hd}	$3^{3/4}$	C. Perret	Ogden Mills Phipps	(b) .80
Dansil	B	126	7	5^{hd}	$6^{1-1/2}$	$5^{1/2}$	4^{hd}	4^1	4no	L. Snyder	John Franks	27.00
Hawkster	BL	126	4	$14^{1/2}$	15	13^{hd}	$10^{1/2}$	7^{hd}	$5^{1/2}$	M. Castaneda	Mr. & Mrs. J. S. Meredith	67.20
Northern Wolf	BLb	126	15	3^1	$3^{3-1/2}$	$3^{2-1/2}$	$2^{1/2}$	$2^{1/2}$	$6^{1/2}$	C. Ladner III	Deep Silver Stable	(f) 47.90
Irish Actor	B	126	11	8^1	9^{hd}	$12^{1-1/2}$	11^1	$8^{1/2}$	$7^{1-1/4}$	D. Howard	Tiffany Farms	46.10
Houston	B	126	6	1^{hd}	$1^{1-1/2}$	1^1	$1^{1/2}$	$3^{1/2}$	8^{nk}	L. Pincay Jr.	Beal, French, Jr. & Lukas	(a) 5.50
Triple Buck	B	126	9	$12^{1/2}$	$10^{1-1/2}$	$10^{1-1/2}$	7^{hd}	$9^{1-1/2}$	9^2	J. Santos	Gary Marano	65.80
Shy Tom	B	126	5	11^{hd}	12^{hd}	11^{hd}	13^4	$11^{1/2}$	$10^{3/4}$	C. Antley	Overbrook Farm	(a) 5.50
Wind Splitter	BLb	126	14	$9^{1/2}$	$8^{1-1/2}$	$9^{1/2}$	$9^{1-1/2}$	10^1	11^1	D. Miller Jr.	Randall Williams Jr.	(f) 47.90
Flying Continental	BL	126	2	7^1	$7^{1/2}$	7^1	12^1	12^2	12^6	C. Black	Jack Kent Cooke	84.30
Clever Trevor	BL	126	1	$2^{2-1/2}$	$2^{1-1/2}$	$2^{1-1/2}$	8^{hd}	13^9	13^7	D. Pettinger	Cheri & Don McNeill	52.60
Faultless Ensign	B	126	8	$13^{1/2}$	13^{hd}	15	15	14^{hd}	14^{nk}	C. DeCarlo	Anthony Tornetta, et al	74.90
Western Playboy	BL	126	3	15	$14^{1/2}$	14^{hd}	$14^{1/2}$	15	15	R. Romero	Nancy Vanier & Raymond Roncari	9.50

Time: :23, :46³/₅, 1:11²/₅, 1:37⁴/₅, 2:05. Track muddy. Off at 5:42 EDT. Start good. Won driving.

Program #		Win	Place	Show	$2 Exacta (10-2)
10	Sunday Silence	$8.20	$3.00	$3.60	$15.20
2b	Easy Goer		$2.60	$3.40	
2	Awe Inspiring			$3.40	

Winner: Dk. b. or br. c. by Halo–Wishing Well, by Understanding. Trained by Charlie Whittingham; bred in Kentucky by Oak Cliff Thoroughbreds, Ltd.
$749,200—gross value and $40,000 Gold Cup. Net to winner $574,200; second $100,000; third $50,000; fourth $25,000.
Scratched: Notation.

394 nominations.
Medication: B—bute; L—Lasix
Equipment: b—blinkers

Lucky to Be There

SUNDAY SILENCE, IN A WAY, IS TYPICAL OF many Derby winners. He started out unwanted, but after he started to run—and won the Derby—he ended up being very wanted, with people willing to pay millions of dollars. So, that was some luck. But he also had some luck before that. He did not die.

At the time, his owner, a man named Arthur Hancock III, who owned Stoner Farm, was having him transported in a van to be sold as a two-year-old in a sale in California. The driver had a heart attack and the van flipped over, but Sunday Silence was not harmed. But one of the people who owned him regarded it as a bad omen and sold him—to the legendary trainer/ owner Charlie Whittingham, "the Bald Eagle," who had won the Derby in 1986. Sunday Silence joined Whittingham's stable in Santa Anita, California, and enjoyed a good life.

Under Whittingham's tutelage, the colt started to win for the first time, and each of his races indicated that he was getting stronger and stronger. For his part, Whittingham thought him a fabulous colt. When the time came for him to enter the Derby, though Easy Goer had been established as the favorite, Whittingham totally believed that Sunday Silence would win.

The only negative thing that Whittingham noticed was not about the horse but about the jockey, Pat Valenzuela. He and others had noticed that Valenzuela whipped Sunday Silence eleven times in the stretch in the Santa Anita Derby, despite the fact that he was a runaway winner. "He hit him a lot more than I wanted to see. I think he must have heard the announcer say that some other horse was making a move. After the race I told him, 'Your head's on a swivel, you know. Use it.' Pat's a good rider, but he's no Rhodes Scholar."

Hancock, a superstitious owner, searched out and found a four-leaf clover on the day of the race, for luck. But Sunday Silence didn't need luck. He hung back in fourth for most of the race, and went down the stretch well in the lead, but the cacophonous noise scared the horse. He sashayed from left to right as he ran, Valenzuela now having to use the whip to correct him so he'd go straight.

After the Derby Sunday Silence would go on to win the Preakness, but he could not conquer that old devil Belmont.

Unbridled
116th *May 5, 1990*

		Raise a Native
	Mr. Prospector	*Gold Digger*
Fappiano		*Dr. Fager*
UNBRIDLED	*Killaloe*	*Grand Splendor*
Bay colt		*Wild Risk*
Gana Facil	**Le Fabuleux*	*Anguar*
		In Reality
	Charedi	*Magic*

THE WINNER'S PEDIGREE AND CAREER HIGHLIGHTS

YEAR	AGE	STS.	1ST	2ND	3RD	EARNINGS
1989	2	6	2	2	2	$ 174,546
1990	3	11	4	3	2	$3,718,149
1991	4	7	2	1	2	$ 596,780
TOTALS		**24**	**8**	**6**	**6**	**$4,489,475**

At 2 years	WON	Maiden on 1st attempt, What a Pleasure Stakes
	2ND	Florida Stallion, Canterbury Juvenile,
	3RD	Arch Ward, Waukegan
At 3 years	WON	Kentucky Derby, Breeders' Cup Classic, Florida Derby
	2ND	Preakness, Secretariat, Super Derby
	3RD	Fountain of Youth, Blue Grass
	UNP	Belmont, Tropical Park Derby
At 4 years	WON	Deputy Minister
	2ND	Fayette Handicap
	3RD	Pacific Classic, Breeders' Cup Classic
	UNP	Oaklawn Handicap, Pimlico Special

HORSE	EQ.	WT.	PP	1/4	1/2	3/4	MILE	STR.	FIN.	JOCKEY	OWNER	ODDS TO $1
Unbridled	BL	126	8	11^{hd}	12^3	6$^{1/2}$	2^2	1^1	1$^{3-1/2}$	C. Perret	Frances A. Genter Stable, Inc.	10.80
Summer Squall	L	126	13	6^{hd}	6^1	4^{hd}	1$^{1/2}$	2^5	2^6	P. Day	Dogwood Stable	2.10
Pleasant Tap	Bb	126	9	12$^{2-1/2}$	11$^{1/2}$	5^2	4^{hd}	3$^{2-1/2}$	3^3	K. Desormeaux	Buckland Farm	40.70
Video Ranger	B	126	4	14^2	14^4	14^7	7$^{1/2}$	5^2	4$^{1-1/4}$	R. Hansen	Myung Kwon Cho	(f) 65.80
Silver Ending	BL	126	10	10^2	9^1	7$^{1/2}$	5$^{1/2}$	4$^{1/2}$	5$^{1-1/2}$	C. McCarron	A. Costanza & Deborah McAnally	6.40
Killer Diller	Bb	126	2	13^1	13^5	11$^{1/2}$	11^4	7^2	6^1	J. Bruin	Barry Schwartz	60.90
Land Rush	BL	126	14	8^2	8$^{1-1/2}$	8^1	8^{hd}	6$^{1/2}$	7^3	A. Cordero Jr.	D.W. Lukas & Overbrook Farm	(b) 14.00
Mister Frisky	B	126	5	4^{hd}	2$^{1-1/2}$	2^2	3$^{1-1/2}$	8^4	8^3	G. Stevens	Solymar Stud	1.90
Thirty Six Red	B	126	11	5^5	3$^{1/2}$	3^2	10$^{1/2}$	9$^{1/2}$	9^{nk}	M. Smith	B. Giles Brophy	5.80
Power Lunch	B	126	15	15	15	15	13^5	12^2	10$^{2-1/2}$	R. Romero	Calumet Farm	(b) 14.00
Real Cash	Bb	126	6	2$^{1/2}$	1^{hd}	1^{hd}	6$^{1-1/2}$	10^3	11$^{3/4}$	A. Solis	D.W. Lukas & Overbrook Farm	(b) 14.00
Dr. Bobby A.	BL	126	1	7$^{1-1/2}$	7^{hd}	9^{hd}	9^{hd}	11$^{1/2}$	12$^{2-1/2}$	N. Santagata	Sue Kat Stable	(f) 99.30
Pendleton Ridge	B	126	3	9^{hd}	10$^{1/2}$	10$^{1-1/2}$	12$^{1/2}$	13^3	13^{15}	L. Pincay Jr.	Bruce McNall	(a) 33.80
Burnt Hills	B	126	12	3^{hd}	5^6	13^2	14^{10}	14^4	14^6	P. Valenzuela	Edmund A Gann	(a) 33.80
Fighting Fantasy	B	126	7	1$^{1/2}$	4^1	12$^{1/2}$	15	15	15	S. Sellers	Raymond Cottrell Sr.	111.30

Time: :22^{3}/5, :46, 1:11, 1:37^{3}/5, 2:02. Track good. Off at 5:34 EDT.
Coupled: (a) Pendleton Ridge and Burnt Hills; (b) Land Rush, Power Lunch and Real Cash; (f) Field.

Program #		Win	Place	Show	
7	Unbridled	$23.60	$7.80	$ 5.80	$65.80
11	Summer Squall		$3.80	$ 3.80	
8	Pleasant Tap			$12.00	

$2 Exacta (7-11)

Winner: B. c. by Fappiano—Gana Facil, by *Le Fabuleux. Trained by Carl A. Nafzger; bred in Florida by Tartan Farms Corp.
$756,000—gross value and $40,000 Gold Cup.
Net to winner $581,000; second $100,000; third $50,000; fourth $25,000.

348 nominations.
Medication: B—bute, L—Lasix
Equipment: b—blinkers

*Foreign bred

"You've Just Won The Kentucky Derby, Mrs. Genter. I Love You"

ONE OF THE MOST MOVING AND DRAMATIC Derby moments ever came during and after the 1990 Derby. Since 1941, ninety-two-year-old Mrs. Frances Genter had been involved in racing with her husband, most particularly after 1990, when Florida became a major racing center in the United States. But she had never won the Kentucky Derby, and this, as it happened, would be her last chance. Indeed, she passed on before the next Derby.

For this one, though, since her eyes and her hearing were so diminished, she sat in a wheelchair near the railing, and her horse's trainer, Carl Nafzger, announced the race for her.

Nafzger figured that Unbridled, her horse, had a great chance. He was a come-from-behind type horse, and a number of the better horses in the race were speed horses.

As predicted, Unbridled came from off the pace, moving up in the backstretch, but by the quarter pole Summer Squall was in the lead, with Unbridled coming up fast.

Unbridled's jockey, Craig Perret, said he wasn't sure he could catch Summer Squall, but by the quarter pole, he said, "I had loped up on him pretty easy and I saw Pat when he hit his horse left-handed. He was still there right next to me, and I said, 'You're in trouble.' I think I got a little more energy at that point, too."

Unbridled roared down the stretch, and Nafzger—who, remember, was not only the race announcer for Mrs. Genter but Unbridled's

trainer—yelled out each of the horse's moves until finally he yelled, "He's taking the lead! He's gonna win! He's gonna win! He's a winner, Mrs. Genter. You've won the Kentucky Derby, Mrs. Genter. I love you."

Indeed, Unbridled was clocked at 2:02, the fastest time ever on a track characterized as not fast but good.

Later, Pat Day said that his horse had become distracted because of the roar of the crowd as he turned for home, though he also said that he was not making excuses. Then he saw the television replay of the old lady sitting in her wheelchair as Nafzger announced the race. Day got tears in his eyes. "She's been in the business a long time and I congratulate her. I couldn't understand why I lost until I seen Mrs. Genter win. Maybe it just wasn't meant for us to win today."

Strike the Gold
117th *May 4, 1991*

		Native Dancer
	Raise a Native	Raise You
Alydar		On-and-On
STRIKE THE GOLD	Sweet Tooth	Plum Cake
Chestnut colt		The Axe II
Majestic Gold	Hatchet Man	Bebopper
		Pappa Fourway
	Majestic Gold	Secret Session

THE WINNER'S PEDIGREE

RACE DAY STATISTICS

HORSE	EQ.	WT.	PP	1/4	1/2	3/4	MILE	STR.	FIN.	JOCKEY	OWNER	ODDS TO $1
Strike the Gold	B	126	5	$12^{1-1/2}$	$12^{1/2}$	10^2	$6^{1/2}$	$2^{1/2}$	$1^{1-3/4}$	C. Antley	Brophy, Condren, Cornacchia	4.80
Best Pal	BL	126	15	$10^{1/2}$	8^{hd}	8^1	7^2	5^2	$2^{1-3/4}$	G. Stevens	Golden Eagle Farm	5.20
Mane Minister	BLb	126	10	$8^{1-1/2}$	10^3	5^{hd}	$4^{1/2}$	$3^{1-1/2}$	3^{hd}	A. Solis	T. McCaffery & J. Toffan	86.90
Green Alligator	Bb	126	8	16	16	15^1	13^1	9^2	$4^{3/4}$	C. Nakatani	Anderson Fowler	(f) 16.30
Fly So Free	B	126	1	$4^{1/2}$	$4^{1/2}$	3^{hd}	3^1	$4^{1/2}$	$5^{1-3/4}$	J. Santos	Thomas Valando	3.30
Quintana	BL	126	16	9^{hd}	13^5	$12^{1-1/2}$	8^{hd}	$8^{1-1/2}$	$6^{1/2}$	A. Cordero Jr.	Gary Garber	28.50
Paulrus	BL	126	11	14^2	14^3	14^{hd}	14^1	$11^{2-1/2}$	7^{hd}	S. Sellers	Hermitage Farms	(f) 16.30
Sea Cadet	BL	126	4	1^{hd}	$1^{1/2}$	1^{hd}	$1^{1/2}$	1^{hd}	8^2	C. McCarron	V H W Stable, Inc. Lessee	15.90
Corporate Report	B	126	12	3^{hd}	3^{hd}	4^1	2^{hd}	6^{hd}	9^2	P. Day	Overbrook Farm & D. W. Lukas	8.70
Hansel	BL	126	6	$5^{1/2}$	6^3	$7^{1-1/2}$	5^{hd}	7^{hd}	10^{hd}	J. Bailey	Lazy Lane Farms	2.50
Happy Jazz Band	B	126	14	13^1	11^{hd}	$13^{1/2}$	$12^{1/2}$	12^1	$11^{1/2}$	C. Asmussen	Straus-Medina Ranch	107.80
Lost Mountain	Bb	126	9	11^5	$7^{1/2}$	$9^{1-1/2}$	$9^{1-1/2}$	10^3	$12^{8-1/2}$	W. McCauley	Loblolly Stable	72.60
Another Review		126	13	7^{hd}	$9^{1/2}$	$11^{1-1/2}$	10^{hd}	13^{hd}	13^{nk}	A. Madrid Jr.	Buckland Farm, Inc.	(f) 16.30
Alydavid	BL	126	2	$6^{1/2}$	5^1	$6^{1/2}$	11^1	14^2	$14^{1-1/2}$	C. Black	David's Farm	17.80
Wilder Than Ever	B	126	3	15^{hd}	15^{hd}	16	15^1	15^8	15^{16}	J. Deegan	Raymond Cottrell Sr.	(f) 16.30
Forty Something	BLb	126	7	2^1	$2^{1-1/2}$	2^2	16	16	16	A. Seefeldt	Sam Morrell	(f) 16.30

Time: :23.26, :46.58, 1:11.35, 1:37.51, 2:03.08. Track fast. Off at 5:36 EDT.
(f) Field.

Program #		Win	Place	Show	$2 Exacta (4-10)
4	Strike the Gold	$11.60	$6.20	$ 5.40	$73.40
10	Best Pal		$6.40	$ 5.40	
7	Mane Minister			$25.60	

Winner: Ch. C. by Alydar–Majestic Gold, by Hatchet Man. Trained by Nicholas P. Zito. Bred in Kentucky by Calumet Farm.
$905,800—gross value and $40,000 Gold Cup. Net to winner $655,800; second $145,000; third $70,000; fourth $35,000.

407 nominations.
Medication: B—bute; L—Lasix
Equipment: b—blinkers

CAREER HIGHLIGHTS

YEAR	AGE	STS.	1ST	2ND	3RD	EARNINGS
1990	2	3	1	0	0	$ 17,400
1991	3	12	2	3	3	$1,443,850
1992	4	13	2	5	1	$1,820,176
1993	5	3	1	0	1	$ 75,600
TOTALS		31	6	8	5	$3,457,026

At 2 Years	WON	Maiden on 3rd attempt
At 3 Years	WON	Kentucky Derby, Blue Grass
	2ND	Florida Derby, Belmont
	3RD	Jim Dandy, Jockey Club Gold Cup
At 4 years	WON	Pimlico Special, Nassau County
	2ND	Gulfstream Park, Thirty Six Red, Suburban, Jockey Club Gold Cup
	3RD	Broward
At 5 years	3RD	Nassau County

Run to Daylight

BY THE TIME HE RETIRED IN 1993, THE rough-and-ready jockey Angel Cordero Jr. had a body that looked like it had met up with King Kong on a bad day. Over a career of 7,057 victories he had broken innumerable body parts: both ankles, both knees, both elbows, nine fingers, his collarbone and ribs on one side of his body. He had a sweet smile that belied a white-hot competitiveness.

For Chris Antley, a great rider in his own right, Angel Cordero was his idol, mentor, and rival—Antley called him "Poppy"—and when it came to taking chances, Antley was not afraid.

On this muggy Saturday, May 4, both of these great riders, great friends, and great rivals would be at the post, Antley in sky blue silks with a pink star on his chest on Strike the Gold, and Cordero, nearing the end of his career, dressed in silks with purple, white, and blue colors, on Quintana.

The race would be like most Derby races, and like many would involve strategy, speed, perhaps almost fouling—both riders were very

skilled about bumping each other and other horses without getting suspended.

The race started. By the five-eighths pole Antley and Cordero were so close they could touch each other. Ahead, there was an opening between two horses, but only room for one of them.

If he didn't do it, he would be trapped, so Antley ran to daylight, driving into the slot, which was so far outside that no horse was in his way. And Cordero got boxed in and Antley had left him far back in the field and Strike the Gold started to really run, passing horses. But he was on the outside. Antley knew he had to get Strike the Gold closer to the rail; there was no winning the Derby if he had to close from far outside the turn.

He started whipping the horse on the left side and pulling his right rein to get Strike the Gold to angle back toward the rail, but the horse refused to shift to his right lead; indeed, the colt was drifting out. But Antley got him under control, and from there it was no contest. "I think I was already grinning at the time coming to the quarter pole." Antley sensed that the roses were his.

And they were.

Lil E. Tee
118th *May 2, 1992*

		Norcliffe	Buckpasser
			Drama School
	At the Threshold		Vertex
LIL E. TEE		Winver	Windsor Lady
Bay colt			What a Pleasure
	Eileen's	For the Moment	Tularia
	Moment		
			*Hawaii
	Sailaway		Quick Wit

THE WINNER'S PEDIGREE

RACE DAY STATISTICS

HORSE	EQ.	WT.	PP	$1/4$	$1/2$	$3/4$	MILE	STR.	FIN.	JOCKEY	OWNER	ODDS TO $1
Lil E. Tee	B	126	10	12^{hd}	10^2	$7^{1/2}$	5^3	2^1	1^1	P. Day	W. Cal Partee	16.80
Casual Lies	BL	126	4	3^{hd}	$6^{1/2}$	3^1	2^{hd}	1^{hd}	$2^{3-1/4}$	G. Stevens*	Shelley L. Riley	29.90
Dance Floor	BL	126	16	$5^{1/2}$	$1^{1/2}$	1^1	$1^{1-1/2}$	3^2	3^2	C. Antley	Oaktown Stable	(a) 33.30
Conte Di Savoya	Bb	126	8	$11^{1/2}$	$9^{1/2}$	$10^{1-1/2}$	6^2	6^2	4^1	G. Stevens*	Jaime S. Carrion	21.30
Pine Bluff	B	126	12	4^{hd}	$3^{1/2}$	$2^{1/2}$	4^{hd}	5^{hd}	$5^{3/4}$	C. Perret	Loblolly Stable	10.50
Al Sabin	B	126	1	$6^{1-1/2}$	5^1	5^{hd}	7^3	$7^{1-1/2}$	6^{hd}	C. Nakatani	Calumet Farm	(a) 33.30
Dr Devious (IRE)	B	126	15	15^{hd}	16^{hd}	17^7	$10^{1/2}$	$8^{1-1/2}$	7^{hd}	C. McCarron	Sidney H. Craig	20.80
Arazi	B	126	17	$17^{2-1/2}$	17^{hd}	$8^{1/2}$	3^2	4^{hd}	8^2	P. Valenzuela	A. Paulson & Sheikh Mohammed	.90
My Luck Runs North	B	126	14	18	15^3	18	17^1	9^3	$9^{2-1/4}$	R. Lopez	Melvin A. Benitez	(f) 12.80
Technology	B	126	2	$9^{1-1/2}$	$8^{1-1/2}$	$6^{1/2}$	$9^{1-1/2}$	10^2	10^2	J. Bailey	Scott Savin	4.20
West by West	BLb	126	11	$14^{2-1/2}$	$12^{1/2}$	$12^{1-1/2}$	8^{hd}	$11^{1/2}$	11no	J. Samyn	John Peace	(f) 12.80
Devil His Due		126	6	$2^{1/2}$	4^1	11^{hd}	12^1	12^5	12^6	M. Smith	Lion Crest Stable	21.60
Thyer	b	126	5	$10^{1/2}$	13^{hd}	13^{hd}	$15^{1/2}$	15^4	$13^{3/4}$	C. Roche	Maktoum al Maktoum	(f) 12.80
Ecstatic Ride	Bb	126	13	13^1	$14^{1/2}$	$15^{1-1/2}$	$13^{1/2}$	$14^{1/2}$	14^{nk}	J. Krone	DanDar Farm & Joan Rich	(f) 12.80
Sir Pinder LBb		126	9	16^1	18	14^{hd}	$14^{1-1/2}$	13^{hd}	$15^{3-1/2}$	R. Romero	James Lewis Jr.	(f) 12.80
Pistols and Roses	BL	126	7	8^{hd}	7^{hd}	$9^{1/2}$	11^{hd}	16^2	$16^{1-1/2}$	J. Vasquez	Willis Family Stables	13.40
Snappy Landing	Bb	126	3	1^1	$2^{1-1/2}$	$4^{1/2}$	$16^{1/2}$	$17^{1-1/2}$	$17^{2-3/4}$	J. Velasquez	Frederick McNeary	(f) 12.80
Disposal	BL	126	18	7^{hd}	$11^{1/2}$	$16^{1/2}$	18	18	18	A. Solis	Bramble Farm	(f) 12.80

Time: :23.44, :47.90, 1:12.37, 1:37.72, 2:03.04. Track fast. Off at 5:34 EDT.
Coupled: (a) Dance Floor and Al Sabin. (f) Field.

Program #		Win	Place	Show	$2 Exacta (7-3)
7	Lil E. Tee	$35.60	$12.20	$ 7.60	$854.40
3	Casual Lies		$22.20	$11.60	
1a	Dance Floor			$12.60	

Winner: B. c. by At the Threshold–Eileen's Moment, by For the Moment. Trained by Lynn S. Whiting. Bred in Pennsylvania by Larry Littman.
$974,800—gross value and $40,000 Gold Cup. Net to winner $724,800; second $145,000; third $70,000; fourth $35,000.
Scratched—A.P. Indy was scratched Saturday morning. All wagers on A.P. Indy were ordered refunded.

407 nominations.
Medication: B—bute; L—Lasix
Equipment: b—blinkers

*Foreign Bred

And a Horse That Should Have Died

"THE THING ABOUT THE KENTUCKY DERBY," someone once said, "is that it allows dreams to come true. Very few events can do that—particularly in two minutes."

There were many dreamers among the 130,000 or so spectators at Churchill Downs as they waited for the gates to open on the 118th Kentucky Derby and release a torrent of high-powered horseflesh. In Box 318 with family and friends was a dreamer named Cal Partee who,

CAREER HIGHLIGHTS

YEAR	AGE	STS.	1ST	2ND	3RD	EARNINGS
1991	2	4	2	2	0	$ 29,106
1992	3	6	3	1	1	$1,148,000
1993	4	3	2	1	0	$ 260,400
TOTALS		13	7	4	1	**$1,437,506**

At 2 years	WON	Maiden on 2nd attempt
At 3 years	WON	Kentucky Derby, Jim Beam
	2ND	Arkansas Derby
	3RD	Southwest
	UNP	Preakness
At 4 years	WON	Razorback Handicap
	2ND	Oaklawn Handicap

at eighty-two, was in the twilight of his life, a Thoroughbred horse owner for thirty-seven years and a Thoroughbred race enthusiast all his life. His horses had won many big races, but never the Derby. Now, he knew, every day he woke up was a gift, and he was more than aware than anyone that this might be his last run for the roses.

Also in the box was Lynn Whiting, fifty-one,

his trainer, a highly respected pro who also had won many big races, but never the Derby. Today, he felt, he had a shot.

And astride the horse who would carry their dreams that humid, gray afternoon, dressed in bright orange-and-white silks, was Pat Day, a drug-and-drink survivor, a born-again Christian, a jockey who had won every important race in sight and then some and who was already, at the age of thirty-eight, in the Racing Hall of Fame. But nine times he had tried to win the Kentucky Derby, and nine times he had failed, once losing by just a nose.

It was his dream to win too. He believed he had a legitimate shot with the horse Lil E. Tee (so named because when he was a foal and was hungry he made a cute sound like the little alien in the movie *E. T.*). The horse was fast, tough, and headstrong—sometimes too headstrong, running the way he wanted when he wanted— but if anyone could handle him, it was Day. He was soft and knew how to communicate with a horse, but he was also a hundred-pound piece of gristle. And he had already won a couple of Derby prep races with E.T., including the Jim Beam Sweepstakes.

The odds against E.T. as he waited for the gate to open were big. In betting parlors across America he was 56–1, and the Derby tote board had him 17–1. Plus he and the other sixteen horses were lined up against Arazi, a multimillion-dollar stallion who was being touted as the next Secretariat.

But Lil E. Tee had been up against big odds before.

He was born at four in the morning on March 29, 1989, and unlike most foals after birth, he did not get up on spindly, rickety legs,

fall down, and get up again. He just lay on the stable floor, motionless. A vet was called, and the diagnosis was dire: E.T. suffered from an immune disorder, a condition that put him at great risk of contracting a variety of lethal maladies. But the vet fought hard, medicating him and doing a variety of other procedures that saved him.

Later, when he was grown, he developed a colic condition that required a big operation that the vet would later jokingly describe as "rerouting his plumbing" but that many horses, at the time, did not survive. He survived.

E.T. was also from the wrong side of the tracks, Thoroughbred-wise. He was born and bred in Pennsylvania, hardly a place famed for breeding Kentucky Derby winners, and his own bloodline simply was not there. As proof, his mother, Eileen's Moment, and father, At the Threshold, had produced over a hundred foals, but not a single one of them had become a champion of any consequence. Why should E.T.?

His original path as a racehorse was an odyssey to nowhere, small races in small towns and then good-bye. Larry Littmann, his owner and breeder at Pin Oak Lane Farm, put him up for sale at the age of two for a whopping $3,000. But one highly astute horse trainer, Chuck Wienike, who made his living taking horses off the scrap heap and turning them into salable merchandise, saw something he liked. To Wienike he was like a big, rawboned teenager. He figured if he could fill him out, the colt could well be worth something. Maybe he could get $20,000 for him.

Months later he had filled out, and Wienike got $25,000. One of the bidders, Bill McGreevy, who had lost out on the sale to a man named

Al Jevromovic, was very upset because he had seen in E. Tee's eyes something old-time horse breeders call "the look of eagles"—knowing, confident, fierce. The look of a winner. And later McGreevy learned he was just one $1,000 bid away from getting him.

Jevromovic started to run E.T., and he started to win—and his value rose until finally Jevromovic put him up for sale for $200,000, and Lynn Whiting urged Cal Partee to buy him, which he did. And Pat Day agreed to ride him in the Derby.

"And what," a breeder was to say later, "were the odds of an astute guy like Chuck Wienike intersecting with the horse? That horse had a lot of luck."

At 5:43 the gates opened.

Lynn Whiting watched through binoculars, and immediately his stomach dropped. E.T. was in trouble. He was jammed in behind a pack of ten horses heading for the far turn. Whiting saw no easy way out. He moaned, and others in the box heard him.

"What?" everyone cried, "what?"

"He got pinched back pretty well," Whiting said. "That's probably enough to get us beat right there."

But it wasn't. Pat Day didn't get to the Hall of Fame because he didn't know how to handle a Thoroughbred in a crowd. He just backed E.T. off a little to avoid a collision, and stayed there as the race continued at a relatively slow pace.

Arazi, Day knew, was in the pack behind him, and he wondered when he would make a move. Then, suddenly, he knew. Arazi, coming from outside, went by him in a flash and past the pack ahead, knocking off horses like ten pins. And Day wondered if on this afternoon he would be just running for "second money." But then, nearing the top of the stretch, Pat Day spoke to E.T. It was time, Day said, for him to run, run with all his heart and soul.

Ahead, Arazi had passed everyone except Casual Lies, and as they turned into the stretch, they dueled briefly. But Day noticed something; Arazi was tiring. And then he got proof: Arazi could not pass Casual Lies, who suddenly was all alone, on his way to victory in the Derby . . . except for one lone horse, the horse who should have died and who came from the wrong side of the tracks, coming up on the outside, Pat Day now uncharacteristically using the whip. At the sixteenth pole E.T. and Casual Lies were neck and neck, and then Lynn Whiting, binoculars still glued to his head, saw that only one of the two horses had any gas left—E.T. The dream was going to come true. He screamed above the hysteria of the crowd, "Do you believe this? Do you believe this son of a bitch is going to win!"

And then E.T. did, roaring alone across the wire, winner by a length, and Pat Day stood up in the saddle and pumped his fist to the gray sky.

"Hallelujah," he shouted. "Thank you, Jesus!"

And in Box 318 Cal Partee's son Wilbur grabbed his father by the shoulders.

"Cal! You just won the Kentucky Derby!"

The old man's answer were the tears that started to stream down his face.

Sea Hero
119th *May 1, 1993*

			Danzing	Northern Dancer
	Polish Navy			Pas de Nom
SEA HERO		Navsup		Tatan
Bay colt				Busanda
				*Ribot
	Growing	Graustark		Flower Bowl
	Tribute			Hail to Reason
		Admiring		Searching

THE WINNER'S PEDIGREE AND CAREER HIGHLIGHTS

YEAR	AGE	STS.	1ST	2ND	3RD	EARNINGS
1992	2	7	3	1	0	$ 339,720
1993	3	9	2	0	2	$2,484,190
1994	4	8	1	2	2	$ 105,959
TOTALS		**24**	**6**	**3**	**4**	**$2,929,869**

At 2 years	WON	Maiden on 4th attempt, Champagne
	UNP	Breeders' Cup Juvenile
At 3 years	WON	Kentucky Derby, Travers
	3RD	Molson Million
	UNP	Preakness, Belmont, Blue Grass, Jim Dandy
At 4 years	2ND	Bowling Green
	3RD	Brooklyn Handicap
	UNP	Fayette, Belmont Budweiser Breeders' Cup, Sword Dancer Inv.

RACE DAY STATISTICS

HORSE	EQ.	WT.	PP	1/4	1/2	3/4	MILE	STR.	FIN.	JOCKEY	OWNER	ODDS TO $1
Sea Hero	L	126	6	$13^{1-1/2}$	$12^{1-1/2}$	$10^{1/2}$	$7^{1-1/2}$	1^1	$1^{2-1/2}$	J. Bailey	Rokeby Stable	12.90
Prairie Bayou		126	5	$16^{1/2}$	$16^{1/2}$	16^{hd}	$9^{1/2}$	6^3	2^{hd}	M. Smith	Loblolly Stable	4.40
Wild Gale		126	13	12^{hd}	13^{hd}	$11^{2-1/2}$	6^{hd}	$3^{1/2}$	3^{nk}	S. Sellers	Little Fish Stable	(f) 8.50
Personal Hope		126	7	$2^{1-1/2}$	2^1	$2^{1-1/2}$	$1^{1/2}$	$2^{1-1/2}$	4^3	G. Stevens	Debi & Lee Lewis	8.20
Diazo	Lb	126	18	11^2	$11^{1/2}$	$9^{1/2}$	$4^{1/2}$	4^{hd}	5^{hd}	K. Desormeaux	Allen Paulson	(a)17.40
Corby	L	126	17	$4^{1/2}$	$5^{1-1/2}$	3^{hd}	2^{hd}	$5^{1/2}$	$6^{3/4}$	C. McCarron	Allen Paulson	(a) 17.40
Kissin Kris	b	126	2	18^{hd}	19	19	$18^{1/2}$	9^{hd}	7^2	J. Santos	John Franks	16.30
Silver of Silver	L	126	9	14^{hd}	15^2	15^2	11^{hd}	8^{hd}	8no	J. Vasquez	Chevalier Stable	(f) 8.50
Ragtime Rebel		126	14	19	17^{hd}	18^2	$16^{1/2}$	$10^{1/2}$	9^2	R. Lester	Alexander Schmidt	(f) 8.50
Bull In the Heather	L	126	10	8^{hd}	$9^{1-1/2}$	7^{hd}	8^{hd}	$12^{1/2}$	11no	W. Ramos	Arthur Klein	5.20
Dixieland Heat	L	126	15	7^{hd}	$8^{1/2}$	8^{hd}	$12^{1/2}$	$13^{1/2}$	12^{nk}	R. Romero	Leland Cook	20.80
Wallenda		126	16	$15^{2-1/2}$	$14^{1/2}$	$14^{1/2}$	$15^{1/2}$	$14^{1-1/2}$	13^2	P. Day	Dogwood Stable	12.50
Mi Cielo		126	12	$10^{1/2}$	10^2	$13^{1-1/2}$	14^{hd}	$15^{1/2}$	$14^{1-1/4}$	A. Gryder	Thomas Carey	(f) 8.50
Union City	L	126	4	$6^{1/2}$	$6^{1/2}$	4^1	3^1	$7^{1/2}$	$15^{1-1/4}$	P. Valenuela	Overbrook Farm	5.90
Storm Tower		126	1	$1^{1/2}$	$1^{1/2}$	$1^{1/2}$	5^1	17^5	16no	R. Wilson	Char-Mari Stable	9.00
Rockamundo	L	126	8	3^{hd}	3^{hd}	5^1	10^2	16^1	17^8	C. Borel	Gary & Mary West	10.20
El Bakan		126	19	$9^{1-1/2}$	7^1	$12^{1/2}$	19	19	$18^{1-1/2}$	C. Perret	Robert Perez	(f) 8.50
Tossofthecoin		126	11	$5^{1-1/2}$	$4^{1/2}$	6^1	$13^{1/2}$	18^2	19	L. Pincay Jr.	Sidney Craig	(f) 8.50

Time: :22.80, :46.63, 1:11.22, 1:36.96, 2:02.42. Track fast. Off at 5:34 EDT.
Coupled: (a) Diazo and Corby. (f) Field.

Program #		Win	Place	Show	$2 Exacta (6-5)
6	Sea Hero	$27.80	$12.80	$8.00	$190.60
5	Prairie Bayou		$7.20	$4.80	
16	Wild Gale			$4.20	

Winner: B. c. by Polish Navy–Glowing Tribute, by Graustark. Trained by MacKenzie Miller, Bred in Virginia by Paul Mellon.
$985,900—gross value and $40,000 Gold Cup. Net to winner $735,900; second $145,000; third $70,000; fourth $35,000.

367 nominations.
Medication: L—Lasix
Equipment: b—blinkers

*Foreign bred

Once More, for the Roses

IN 1992, AFTER FIVE LOSING DERBY RIDES, jockey Jerry Bailey was excited when he rode Sea Hero, owned by Paul Mellon, to victory in the Champagne Stakes. Bailey said that he finally felt that he had a legitimate contender for a Derby win, and that he himself, after a long torturous bout with alcoholism and years of experience riding, would be on that horse.

Then, in the often inscrutable, mysterious ways of horse racing, Sea Hero started running poorly. He ran in the Breeders' Cup Juvenile at Gulf Stream Park in Florida at the end of October and finished seventh and did poorly in other races.

Bailey decided not to ride him. It was not an easy choice for Bailey. Paul Mellon was eighty-five and had never won a Derby, and neither had his trainer. All wanted to win. Then, for whatever reason, he decided to ride Sea Hero one more time before the Derby in the Blue Grass Stakes, and though the horse came in fourth, Bailey liked his performance. He had seen a pattern in the horse that he analyzed over and over again, and came to realize that the horse was very reluctant to drive through holes between other horses. Bailey made a suggestion to the trainer: Take off Sea Hero's blinkers, so he could see the whole track.

Mack agreed, Mellon agreed. Bailey would test it at the Kentucky Derby.

Bailey is a very patient rider, and it didn't bother him that when the race started he was

twelfth of eighteen horses. His horse was a closer. It was just up to him to get him a position so he could have a clear run to the wire.

And Bailey found that this time, sans blinkers, when a hole opened between horses and Bailey asked Sea Hero to go between them, he went. As the race progressed, Sea Hero moved steadily toward the horses in the front.

Then, it was just one horse, Personal Hope, ahead of him, with Gary Stevens aboard. Just as they turned into the stretch, Bailey rapped Sea Hero three times, and they were past Personal Hope and driving to the finish. The race favorite, Prairie Bayou, drove at them as they approached, but it was too little too late. Sea Hero—seeing it all—drove to victory by two and half lengths.

Go for Gin
120th *May 7, 1994*

			Ribot
		His Majesty	Flower Bowl
	Cormorant		Tudor Bowl
GO FOR GIN		Song Sparrow	Swoon's Tune
Bay colt			Prince John
	Never Knock	Stage Door Johnny	Peroxide Blonde
			Never Bend
		Never Hula	Hula Hula

THE WINNER'S PEDIGREE

RACE DAY STATISTICS

HORSE	EQ.	WT.	PP	1/4	1/2	3/4	MILE	STR.	FIN.	JOCKEY	OWNER	ODDS TO $1
Go for Gin		126	8	$2^{1/2}$	$1^{1/2}$	$1^{1-1/2}$	$1^{1-1/2}$	1^4	1^2	C. McCarron	W. J. Condren & J. M. Cornacchia	9.10
Strodes Creek	Lb	126	7	$7^{1/2}$	8^{hd}	9^1	7^{hd}	2nd	$2^{2-1/2}$	E. Delahoussaye	Hancock, Rose Hill Stb, Whittingham	7.90
Blumin Affair	L	126	13	$10^{1/2}$	11^3	$8^{1/2}$	6^1	$5^{1/2}$	$3^{3/4}$	J. Bailey	Leroy Bowman & Arthur Vogel	14.90
Brocco	L	126	10	$9^{1-1/2}$	6^1	$7^{1/2}$	$4^{1/2}$	$3^{1/2}$	$4^{1-1/4}$	G. Stevens	Albert & Dana Broccoli	4.30
Soul of the Matter	L	126	1	12^5	$10^{1/2}$	$10^{2-1/2}$	8^2	6^1	$5^{2-1/2}$	K. Desormeaux	Burt Bacharach	16.90
Tabasco Cat	Lb	126	9	$4^{1/2}$	4^1	5^1	$5^{1-1/2}$	7^2	$6^{1-1/4}$	P. Day	Overbrook Farm & D. P. Reynolds	6.10
Southern Rhythm	Lb	126	12	14	13^4	$13^{3-1/2}$	$10^{1/2}$	9^3	$7^{1-1/2}$	G. Gomez	Heiligbrodt, Keefer, New	20.00
Powis Castle	Lb	126	3	3^1	$3^{1/2}$	3^1	2^1	4^{hd}	8^2	C. Antley	Vista Stable	20.30
Mahogany Hall	L	126	6	$13^{1/2}$	14	14	$12^{1-1/2}$	$11^{1/2}$	$9^{1/2}$	W. Martinez	Robert Hoeweler	(f) 16.70
Smilin Singin Sam	Lb	126	11	11^{hd}	9^1	2nd	$3^{1-1/2}$	$8^{1/2}$	10^2	L. Melancon	Dogwood Stable	(f) 16.70
Meadow Flight	L	126	14	8^1	12^2	$11^{1/2}$	$11^{1-1/2}$	$10^{1/2}$	11^2	S. Sellers	Ben J. Aliyuee Stables	(f) 16.70
Holy Bull		126	4	$6^{1/2}$	$5^{1-1/2}$	$6^{1-1/2}$	9^2	12^4	12^2	M. Smith	Warren A. Croll Jr.	2.20
Valiant Nature		126	2	$5^{1/2}$	$7^{1/2}$	12^3	13^8	13^{16}	13^{15}	L. Pincay Jr.	Verne H. Winchell	12.00
Ulises		126	5	1^{hd}	$2^{1-1/2}$	4^{hd}	14	14	14	J. Chavez	Robert Perez	(f) 16.70

Time: :22.97, :47.21, 1:11.98, 1:37.72, 2:03.72. Track sloppy. Off at 5:34 EDT.
(f) Field.

Program #		Win	Place	Show	$2 Exacta (6-5)	$2 Trifecta (6-5-10)
6	Go for Gin	$20.20	$8.40	$5.80	$184.80	$2,351.40
5	Strodes Creek		$7.80	$6.00		
10	Blumin Affair			$8.00		

Winner: B. c. by Cormorant—Never Knock, by Stage Door Johnny. Trained by Nicholas P. Zito; bred in Kentucky by Pamela duPont Darmstadt.
$878,800—gross value and $40,000 Gold Cup. Net to winner $628,800; second $145,000; third $70,000; fourth $35,000.
Scratched—Kandaly was scratched after the fifth race because of track condition. All wagers in the straight, place, show, exacta and trifecta pools were ordered refunded. All pick-three and pick-six wagers involving Kandaly were switched to the favorite, Holy Bull.

363 nominations.
Medication: L—Lasix
Equipment: b—blinkers

Demolition Derby

THE STORY GOES THAT THE GREAT HIGH-wire walker Karl Wallenda, a man who had walked across Veteran's Stadium, the 770-foot-high Devil's Gorge in Georgia, and many other places on a three-eighth-inch strand of taut cable where a mistake meant death, once had someone suggest to him that, since he was on the small, muscular side, he should become a jockey. "Oh no," Wallenda had said, "too risky."

CAREER HIGHLIGHTS

YEAR	AGE	STS.	1ST	2ND	3RD	EARNINGS
1993	2	5	3	1	0	$174,540
1994	3	11	2	4	1	$1,178,596
1995	4	3	0	2	1	$27,730
TOTALS		**19**	**5**	**7**	**2**	**$1,380,866**

At 2 years	WON	Maiden on 3rd attempt, Remsen, Chief's Crown
At 3 years	WON	Kentucky Derby, Preview
	2ND	Preakness, Belmont, Fountain of Youth, Wood Memorial
	3RD	Forego
	UNP	Florida Derby, Woodward, Jockey Club Gold Cup, Breeders' Cup Classic
At 4 years	3RD	Churchill Downs Handicap

Wallenda was joking, but maybe not too far off the mark. On the face of it a horse race is an exercise in controlled, albeit high-speed, insanity. A dozen muscular animals with shaped rocks for feet, each weighing around a thousand pounds, fly down the track at forty miles an hour, their speeding bodies and flying hooves separated by a few feet or a few inches. And the little men astride are semi-demented, sometimes flailing whips, hell-bent on winning.

The riders, of course, are capable of reacting with split-second reflexes and consummate skill to control the animals. But sometimes someone ends up in a hospital or a wheelchair for life, or maybe the morgue. Still, most of the time races are run smoothly.

Such a race was not the 1991 Derby. Indeed, it came to be known as the "Demolition Derby."

To complicate things, heavy rain fell Derby day, changing the track to soup. The first incident occurred on the first turn, when Valiant Nature, with no place to go, clipped the heels of Holy Bull. Lafitte Pincay had to fight speed and gravity to stay aboard, but the action also drove Valiant Nature on a cockeyed path outside, derailing the straight run of Strodes Creek, who, in turn, got in the way of Meadow Flight. Then, near the three-sixteenths pole, and far back into the pack, Southern Rhythm drifted toward Meadow Flight, who proceeded to come out into Mahogany Hall's path. Mahogany Hall, who appeared to have been clipped, turned sideways, clipped another horse's heels, and, as the crowd shrieked in horror, nearly went down.

Meanwhile, one of the horses, Go for Gin, surprisingly only ridden by jockey Chris Mc-Carron for the first time six days before the Derby, kept out of trouble except for one brief whack against Tabasco Cat after the race started, and had no further interaction with other horses.

Trainer Nick Zito had yelled to previous Derby winner Strike the Gold, "Show me the way!" As Go for Gin raced along, Zito kept yelling, "We know the way!" And he did, finishing the run in 2:03 3/8.

Thunder Gulch
121st *May 6, 1995*

Gulch	*Mr. Prospector*	*Raise a Native*
		Gold Digger
THUNDER GULCH	*Jameela*	*Rambunctious*
Bay colt		*Asbury Mary*
	Storm Bird	*Northern Dancer*
Line of Thunder		*South Ocean*
	Shoot a Line	*High Line*
		Death Ray

The Winner's Pedigree

Race Day Statistics

HORSE	M/EQ.	WT.	PP	1/4	1/2	3/4	MILE	STR.	FIN.	JOCKEY	OWNER	ODDS TO $1
Thunder Gulch	b	126	16	$6^{1\text{-}1/2}$	$5^{1/2}$	$5^{1/2}$	$3^{1\text{-}1/2}$	$1^{1\text{-}1/2}$	$1^{2\text{-}1/4}$	G. Stevens	Michael Tabor	24.50
Tejano Run	L	126	14	13^{hd}	12^1	10^{hd}	6^{hd}	3^{hd}	2^{hd}	J. Bailey	Roy K. Monroe	8.60
Timber Country		126	15	$14^{1/2}$	13^{hd}	12^{hd}	11^{hd}	10^{hd}	$3^{3/4}$	P. Day	Gainesway Farm, R. & B. Lewis & Overbrook Farm	(b) 3.40
Jumron (GB)	L	126	10	8^{hd}	$9^{1\text{-}1/2}$	$9^{1\text{-}1/2}$	$4^{1/2}$	$5^{1/2}$	4^{hd}	G. Almeida	Charles W. Dunn	5.60
Mecke	Lb	126	18	$16^{1/2}$	$16^{1\text{-}1/2}$	19	$13^{1\text{-}1/2}$	$8^{1/2}$	$5^{1/2}$	R. Davis	James Lewis Jr.	(f) 11.60
Eltish		126	7	10^1	10^{hd}	11^{hd}	9^2	$6^{1/2}$	6^3	E. Delahoussaye	Juddmonte Farms	10.90
Knockadoon		126	2	19	19	18^{hd}	$14^{1/2}$	$12^{1/2}$	7^{nk}	C. McCarron	William K. Warren Jr.	(f) 11.60
Afternoon Deelites		126	12	7^{hd}	6^{hd}	$6^{1/2}$	5^{hd}	7^{hd}	8^{nk}	K. Desormeaux	Burt Bacharach	8.70
Citadeed	L	126	19	$3^{1/2}$	$7^{1/2}$	2^{hd}	$7^{1/2}$	$9^{1/2}$	$9^{3/4}$	E. Maple	Ivan Allan	(f) 11.60
In Character (GB)	L	126	9	17^1	15^{hd}	17^{hd}	$12^{1\text{-}1/2}$	13^2	$10^{1/2}$	C. Antley	Baker & Farr & Jackson	(f) 11.60
Suave Prospect	L	126	6	$9^{1\text{-}1/2}$	11^4	14^1	$8^{1/2}$	$11^{1/2}$	$11^{1/2}$	J. Krone	William Condren & M. H. Sherman	13.10
Talkin Man		126	11	$4^{1\text{-}1/2}$	3^{hd}	4^{hd}	2^{hd}	2^1	$12^{1/2}$	M. Smith	Kinghaven Farm & H. Stollery & P. Wall	4.00
Dazzling Falls	Lb	126	1	12^{hd}	$14^{1/2}$	$13^{1\text{-}1/2}$	19	15^1	13^{nk}	G. Gomez	Chateau Ridge Farm, Inc.	27.60
Ski Captain	f	126	17	$18^{1/2}$	17^{hd}	16^1	$15^{1\text{-}1/2}$	14^1	$14^{1\text{-}1/2}$	Y. Take	Shadai Racehorse Co. Ltd.	(f) 11.60
Jambalaya Jazz	Lf	126	5	$15^{1/2}$	$18^{1\text{-}1/2}$	15^{hd}	16^{hd}	16^2	15^{nk}	C. Perret	John C. Oxley	(a) 18.00
Serena's Song		121	13	1^{hd}	$1^{1\text{-}1/2}$	$1^{1/2}$	1^{hd}	4^1	$16^{1\text{-}1/2}$	C. Nakatani	Robert & Beverly Lewis	(b) 3.40
Pyramid Peak		126	3	5^1	8^{hd}	8^{hd}	17^1	17^6	17^6	W. McCauley	John C. Oxley	(a) 18.00
Lake George	L	126	8	11^1	4^1	7^1	10^{hd}	18^{12}	18^{21}	S. Sellers	William Boswell & David Lavin	(f) 11.60
Wild Syn	Lf	126	4	$2^{1/2}$	$2^{1\text{-}1/2}$	$3^{1/2}$	$18^{1/2}$	19	19	R. Romero	Jurgen K. Arnemann	18.80

Time: :22.57, :45.89, 1:10.33, 1:35.72, 2:01.27. Track fast. Off at 5:33 EDT.
Coupled: (a) Jambalaya Jazz and Pyramid Peak; (b) Timber Country and Serena's Song; (f) Field.

Program #		Win	Place	Show	$2 Exacta (11-10)	$2 Trifecta (11-10-2)
11	Thunder Gulch	$51.00	$24.20	$12.20	$480.00	$2,099.20
10	Tejano Run		$10.20	$ 6.80		
2b	Timber Country			$ 3.80		

Winner: Ch. c. by Gulch–Line of Thunder by Storm Bird. Trained by D. Wayne Lukas; bred in Kentucky by Peter M. Brant.
$957,400—gross value and $52,000 Gold Cup. Net to winner $707,400; second $145,000; third $70,000; fourth $35,000.

324 nominations.
Medication: L—Lasix.
Equipment: b—blinkers; f—front bandages

CAREER HIGHLIGHTS

YEAR	AGE	STS.	1ST	2ND	3RD	EARNINGS
1994	2	6	2	2	1	$ 271,006
1995	3	10	7	0	1	$2,644,080
TOTALS		**16**	**9**	**2**	**2**	**$2,915,086**

At 2 years	WON	Maiden on 2nd attempt; Remsen
	2ND	Cowdin, Hollywood Futurity
	UNP	Nashua
At 3 years	WON	Fountain of Youth, Florida Derby, Kentucky Derby, Belmont, Swaps, Travers, Kentucky Cup Classic
	3RD	Preakness
	UNP	Bluegrass

Last-Minute Luck

THREE WEEKS BEFORE THE DERBY, JOCKEY
Gary Stevens figured he had it made. By a quirk
of fate, he had ridden a horse in California
called The Legend of Larry and won, beating a
great jockey, Kent Desormeaux, who was on a
horse named Afternoon Deelites. Then disaster.
Legend of Larry had a damaged leg.

A couple of days later Stevens and Anderson were in their house when the phone rang.
Anderson picked up, and Stevens could tell that
Anderson was speaking to legendary trainer
D. Wayne Lukas. They spoke for a few minutes
more, and then Anderson, holding the phone in
his hand, said, "Wayne knows about The Legend of Larry. He wants you to come home and
ride Thunder Gulch."

Immediately, Stevens said no. He had ridden
Thunder Gulch, a chestnut colt, once when he
was a two-year-old, and he found him imma-
ture, uncommitted to running hard, given to
lugging—favoring a diagonal path rather than a
straight one—and tending to slow down when
he came abreast of horses.

Stevens told Anderson to tell Lukas no, which
he did, but Lukas asked to talk to Stevens.

He picked up the phone, and Lukas said,
"Ask Mike Smith about the horse."

Stevens agreed to, and he did. Smith was
positive that Thunder Gulch was capable of
winning the Derby. "I have no idea," Smith
said, "why he lost the Blue Grass, but if you
throw that race out, he fits with the rest of the
Derby horses." Stevens believed him and shortly
he was on a plane for another marathon ride to
Lexington.

When the nineteen horses were in the gate
ready to go, Stevens was astride the back of
Thunder Gulch. The colt ran a good race, but the
acid test came at the head of the stretch. Would
he go when urged to, or would he play around, or
lug, or slow down?

The answer was that he started to run
like the wind, passed everybody, and won the
race by two and a quarter lengths. Stevens
explained: "He was like a boy who that day
became a man."

Years later, Smith and Stevens were having
lunch. When the waiter presented the bill to
Mike, he said: "I ain't paying that. Stevens still
owes me."

"What the hell do I owe you for?" Stevens said.

"Thunder Gulch, asshole." And Stevens nodded and paid the bill.

Grindstone
122nd *May 4, 1996*

The Winner's Pedigree

	Fappiano	*Mr. Prospector*
		Killaloe
Unbridled	*Gana Facil*	*Le Fabuleux*
GRINDSTONE		*Charedi*
Dark bay/brown colt	*Drone*	*Sir Gaylord*
Buzz My Bell		*Cap and Bells*
		Chateaugay
	Chateaupavia	*Glenpavia*

Race Day Statistics

HORSE	M/EQ.	WT.	PP	$1/4$	$1/2$	$3/4$	MILE	STR.	FIN.	JOCKEY	OWNER	ODDS TO $1
Grindstone		126	15	15^1	$15^{1-1/2}$	14^1	$6^{1-1/2}$	$4^{1-1/2}$	1no	J. Bailey	Overbrook Farm	(x) 5.90
Cavonnier	L	126	4	$9^{1/2}$	$7^{1/2}$	$5^{1/2}$	3^1	1^{hd}	$2^{3-1/2}$	C. McCarron	Walter Family Trust	(c) 5.60
Prince of Thieves	Lb	126	10	14^2	$12^{1/2}$	$11^{2-1/2}$	4^1	$5^{2-1/2}$	3^{nk}	P. Day	Peter Mitchell	7.00
Halo Sunshine	L	126	5	7^1	$4^{1-1/2}$	4^{hd}	2^1	$3^{1-1/2}$	4no	C. Perret	Henry Pabst	28.90
Unbridled's Song		126	19	$3^{2-1/2}$	3^1	2^{hd}	1^2	$2^{1-1/2}$	$5^{3-1/2}$	M. Smith	Paraneck Stable	3.50
Editor's Note	Lb	126	17	$16^{1-1/2}$	$16^{1/2}$	16^1	11^1	7^1	6^{hd}	G. Stevens	Overbrook Farm	(x) 5.90
Blow Out	Lb	126	1	19	19	$15^{1-1/2}$	$15^{1/2}$	8^1	$7^{1-1/2}$	P. Johnson	Heiligbrodt & Keefer & New	(f) 10.80
Alyrob	Lb	126	12	13^{hd}	$13^{2-1/2}$	13^1	$7^{1-1/2}$	$6^{2-1/2}$	$8^{1-1/2}$	C. Nakatani	Four Star Stable	7.20
Diligence	L	126	3	$17^{1/2}$	17^2	$17^{1/2}$	17^2	9^2	$9^{2-1/2}$	K. Desormeaux	Kinsman Stable	(b) 13.10
Victory Speech		126	2	$10^{1-1/2}$	$9^{1/2}$	7^{hd}	9^{hd}	$10^{1-1/2}$	$10^{1-1/4}$	J. Santos	Mrs. John Magnier & Michael Tabor	(a) 24.80
Corker	b	126	9	18^2	18^2	19	18^5	18^3	$11^{2-1/2}$	C. Black	Hancock III & Kinerk & McNair	(f) 10.80
Skip Away	Lb	126	16	$5^{1-1/2}$	$6^{1/2}$	6^{hd}	10^{hd}	13^1	$12^{1/2}$	S. Sellers	Carolyn H. Hine	7.70
Zarb's Magic	L	126	7	$8^{1/2}$	$10^{1-1/2}$	$10^{2-1/2}$	$8^{1/2}$	11^3	$13^{1/2}$	R. Ardoin	Foxwood Plantation Inc.	25.70
Semoran	L	126	6	$6^{1/2}$	8^1	$8^{1-1/2}$	16^{hd}	14^4	$14^{3-1/2}$	R. Baze	Donald R. Dizney & James E. English	(c) 5.60
In Contention	Lf	126	8	$12^{1-1/2}$	14^1	18^{hd}	19	16^1	15^2	A. Black	Noreen Carpenito	19.80
Louis Quatorze	L	126	11	11^1	$11^{1/2}$	$12^{1/2}$	14^{hd}	17^3	$16^{2-1/2}$	C. Antley	Condren & Cornacchia & Hoffman	(b) 13.10
Matty G		126	18	2^1	2^1	$3^{1/2}$	13^{hd}	$15^{1/2}$	17^{nk}	A. Solis	Double J Farm	(f) 10.80
Honour and Glory	L	126	13	$1^{1-1/2}$	1^1	$1^{1/2}$	5^{hd}	12^1	$18^{2-1/2}$	A. Gryder	Michael Tabor	(a) 24.80
Built for Pleasure	Lb	126	14	4^{hd}	5^{hd}	$9^{1/2}$	12^1	19	19	J. Velazquez	Thomas H. Heard Jr.	(f) 10.80

Time: :22.34, :46.09, 1:10.15, 1:35.16, 2:01.06. Track fast. Off at 5:34 EDT.
Coupled: (a) Victory Speech and Honour and Glory; (b) Diligence and Louis Quatorze; (c) Cavonnier and Semoran; (x) Grindstone and Editor's Note; (f) Field.

Program #		Win	Place	Show	$2 Exacta (2-12)	$2 Trifecta (2-12-7)	$1 Superfecta (2-12-7-3)
4	Grindstone	$13.80	$6.00	$4.00	$61.80	$600.60	$5,844.20
3	Cavonnier		$6.20	$4.40			
8	Prince of Thieves			$4.60			

Winner - Dk.b. or br. c, by Unbridled–Buzz My Bell, by Drone. Trained by D. Wayne Lukas; bred in Kentucky by Overbrook Farm.
$1,169,800—gross value and $55,000 Gold Cup. Net to winner $869,800; second $170,000; third $85,500; fourth $45,000.
Scratched: City by Night was scratched on Friday.

361 nominations.
Medication: L- Lasix
Equipment: b- blinkers; f- front bandages

Last Race

JERRY BAILEY HAD, OF COURSE, WON HIS first Kentucky Derby on Sea Hero in 1993, and one might assume this would satiate his yearning to win. Not at all. It would only, as he said in his autobiography *Jerry Bailey, Against the Odds: Riding for My Life,* want to win another.

CAREER HIGHLIGHTS

YEAR	AGE	STS.	1ST	2ND	3RD	EARNINGS
1995	2	2	1	0	0	$ 23,510
1996	3	4	2	2	0	$1,201,000
TOTALS		**6**	**3**	**2**	**0**	**$1,224,510**

At 2 years	WON	Maiden on 1st attempt
	UNP	Bashford Manor
At 3 years	WON	Louisiana Derby, Kentucky Derby
	2ND	Arkansas Derby

In 1996 he had that chance aboard Grindstone, a dark bay D. Wayne Lukas colt who would be the smallest horse in the field. Grindstone had a reputation for being a strong closer, driving from a long way out to win. On this sunny Derby, the first Saturday in May, the track fast, that's what he would do.

When the race started Honour and Glory broke into the lead, his pace chillingly and foolishly fast, roaring through the first six furlongs in 1:10, a really impossible pace to keep up.

Bailey looked for a horse he could follow to the front. He picked Prince of Thieves, ridden by Pat Day.

Grindstone was fourteenth at the first three-quarters. Bailey was moving, though, and as he did, he flipped on clear goggles as needed. He had to work his way through a ganglia of horses to get free, but finally, going five wide, he turned into the stretch and had a clear run to the finish. Ahead of him was Chris McCarron on Cavonnier, trailed by Unbridled's Song and Halo Sunshine.

Now it was all on the table. This was the run for the roses. Bailey flipped down his next-to-last set of glasses, smacked Grindstone on the right flank, and the little horse started to give it everything he had, everything he had left.

Grindstone's mane flying, Bailey feeling the pain of the ride, his glasses clogged again but

no time to change them, the used ones interfering with his breathing, drove toward Cavonnier, and something kept screaming inside Bailey's head: Can I catch him before the wire? Can I catch him before the wire?

Pushing on Grindstone's neck, using the whip, horse and rider caught Cavonnier's flank, and then were halfway up, and then, neck and neck, with a final superhuman effort, a horse and man blasted with everything they had and crossed the wire in a photo finish.

As they slowed, Bailey asked McCarron, "Who do you think won?"

"Too close to call," McCarron responded.

But it was, of course, Bailey, and years later he would say, apologizing for sounding egotistical, that he rode the horse as well as anyone could. But he knew too, that it was that little horse with an oversize heart that had not a little to do with it. Indeed, Grindstone was so devastated by the race that he was never to race again: he had left his career on the track. Then again, when you look at the winner of the 1996 Kentucky Derby, it will always say Grindstone.

Silver Charm
123rd *May 3, 1997*

	Buckpasser	Tom Fool
Silver Buck		Busanda
SILVER CHARM	Silver True	Hail to Reason
Gray colt		Silver Tag
	Bonnie's Poker Poker	Round Table
		Glamour
	What A Surprise	Wise Margin
		Militant Miss

THE WINNER'S PEDIGREE AND CAREER HIGHLIGHTS

YEAR	AGE	STS.	1ST	2ND	3RD	EARNINGS
1996	2	3	2	1	0	$ 177,750
1997	3	7	3	4	0	$1,638,750
1998	4	9	6	2	0	$4,696,506
1999	5	5	1	0	2	$ 431,363
TOTALS		**24**	**12**	**7**	**2**	**$6,944,369**

At 2 years	WON	Maiden on 2nd attempt, Del Mar Futurity
At 3 years	WON	San Vicente, Kentucky Derby, Preakness
	2ND	San Felipe, Santa Anita Derby, Belmont, Malibu
At 4 years	WON	San Fernando Breeders' Cup, Strub, Dubai World Cup, Kentucky Cup Classic, Goodwood Breeders' Cup, Clark
	2ND	Stephen Foster, Breeders' Cup Classic
	UNP	San Diego Handicap
At 5 years	WON	San Pasqual
	3RD	Donn Handicap, Santa Anita Handicap
	UNP	Dubai World Cup, Stephen Foster

RACE DAY STATISTICS

HORSE	M/EQ.	WT.	PP	1/4	1/2	3/4	MILE	STR.	FIN.	JOCKEY	OWNER	ODDS TO $1
Silver Charm	L	126	5	6^1	4^1	3^{hd}	3^1	1^{hd}	1^{hd}	G. Stevens	Robert B. & Beverly J. Lewis	4.00
Captain Bodgit		126	4	$9^{1/2}$	7^{hd}	6^{hd}	$5^{1/2}$	3^2	$2^{3-1/2}$	A. Solis	Team Valor	3.10
Free House	L	126	13	1^{hd}	2^1	$2^{1-1/2}$	1^{hd}	$2^{1-1/2}$	3^3	D. Flores	John Toffan & Trudy McCaffery	10.60
Pulpit	L	126	7	$2^{1/2}$	$1^{1/2}$	1^{hd}	$2^{1/2}$	$4^{1-1/2}$	4no	S. Sellers	Claiborne Farm	5.70
Crypto Star		126	1	12^5	12^8	12^5	10^{hd}	6^{hd}	5^{nk}	P. Day	Evelyn & Darrell Yates	4.80
Phantom on Tour	L	126	2	$7^{1/2}$	$5^{1-1/2}$	$5^{2-1/2}$	$4^{1-1/2}$	5^2	6^{nk}	J. Bailey	Dogwood Stable	(a) 20.90
Hello (IRE)	L	126	8	$10^{2-1/2}$	10^2	$9^{1-1/2}$	8^1	8^3	$8^{5-1/2}$	M. Smith	Sandee & Al Kirkwood	9.60
Concerto	L	126	3	3^{hd}	$3^{1/2}$	4^{hd}	$6^{2-1/2}$	9^3	$9^{1-1/2}$	C. Marquez Jr.	Kinsman Stable	10.80
Celtic Warrior	Lb	126	6	13	13	13	12^1	$10^{1-1/2}$	$10^{1/2}$	F. Torres	Hutt, Quackenbush & Schaffrick	37.10
Crimson Classic	L	126	12	$4^{1/2}$	6^{hd}	$7^{1-1/2}$	9^{hd}	11^5	11^9	R. Albarado	John W. Clay	80.10
Shammy Davis	L	126	10	5^{hd}	8^1	$11^{1/2}$	13	13	12^{nk}	W. Martinez	Fox Hill Farm	(a) 20.90
Deeds Not Words		126	11	8^2	9^1	$8^{1/2}$	11^3	12^1	13	C. Nakatani	Michael Tabor & Mrs. John Magnier	32.40

Time: :23.57, :47.55, 1:12.23, 1:37.31, 2:02.44. Track fast. Off at 5:34 EDT.
Coupled: (a) Jack Flash and Shammy Davis.

Program #		Win	Place	Show	$2 Exacta (6-5)	$2 Trifecta (6-5-12)	$1 Superfecta (6-5-12-8)
6	Silver Charm	$10.00	$4.80	$4.20	$31.00	$205.40	$350.00
5	Captain Bodgit		$4.80	$3.80			
12	Free House			$5.80			

Winner: Gr./ro. c. by Silver Buck–Bonnie's Poker, by Poker. Trained by Bob Baffert. Bred in Florida by Mary L. Wootton.
$1,000,000—gross value and $55,000 Gold Cup. Net to winner $700,000; second $170,000; third $85,500; fourth $45,000.
Jack Flash and Shammy Davis raced with mud caulks in front. Crypto Star raced with mud caulks behind.

385 nominations.
Medication: L—Lasix
Equipment: b—blinkers

"Oh Lord, Don't Let It Happen Again!"

SATURDAY, MAY 3, 1997, WAS THE SECOND coldest Derby day since records were first kept in 1940. It was 51 degrees, and there was a brisk wind and overcast skies. But the line of thirteen horses waiting at the post, their colorful silks rippled by the wind, were about to heat up the track in one of the closest, most exciting Derbies ever.

Some of the greatest horsemen ever were on and off the track, including jockeys Gary Stevens, Shane Sellers, Jerry Bailey, and Pat Day, and trainers Bob Baffert, the white-haired, handsome, wisecracking man whose Cavonnier had lost the previous year's Derby by a nose, and D. Wayne Lukas, who led all other trainers in money won, then over $200 million. This year, Baffert's hopes were riding on Silver Charm, a gray colt with Gary Stevens up.

The real race started, as it so often does, at the head of the stretch, when Stevens passed the leaders for the first time. Stevens thought he was in a perfect position, but he was not the only one doing some calculating. Alex Solis, aboard Captain Bodgit, was also where he wanted to be, waiting until they had a half mile to go before making his move. And when he did, he said, "They started coming back to me," meaning the front runners, "and I hadn't asked my horse to run yet. I thought, this is great. But I wanted to be patient. With three-eighths of a mile to go I wanted to get closer, so I chirped to him and he responded. At the eighth pole, I

thought we were the winner. The leader, Silver Charm, was struggling a little bit."

And Bob Baffert, watching the unfolding drama, was worried. "When they hit the homestretch," he said, "when I saw Captain Bodgit coming up fast on the outside, I thought: Here it comes again. Oh Lord, please don't do it to me again."

Stevens was worried too. "In the stretch," he said, "I knew somebody else was going to come running. And I caught sight of Captain Bodgit coming on fast and I was afraid I'd taken the lead too soon. He got within a head of Silver Charm, who stuck his ears back and found another gear." And Captain Bodgit could not quite catch him. It took a photo to prove it, but there it was.

In the stands Bob Baffert was yelling. He knew who won. He did. And it had not been, as Yogi Berra said, déjà vu all over again.

Real Quiet
124th *May 2, 1998*

		Mr. Prospector
	Fappiano	Killaloe
Quiet American		Dr. Fager
REAL QUIET	Demure	Quiet Charm
Bay colt		In Reality
Really Blue	Believe It	Breakfast Bell
		Raise a Native
	Meadow Blue	Gay Hostess

The Winner's Pedigree

Race Day Statistics

HORSE	M/EQ.	WT.	PP	1/4	1/2	3/4	MILE	STR.	FIN.	JOCKEY	OWNER	ODDS TO $1
Real Quiet	Lb	126	3	$8^{1\text{-}1/2}$	6^1	$6^{1/2}$	1^1	$1^{1\text{-}1/2}$	$1^{1/2}$	K. Desormeaux	Mike Pegram	8.40
Victory Gallop	L	126	13	$14^{1/2}$	15	14^1	7^1	3^{hd}	$2^{2\text{-}1/4}$	A. Solis	Prestonwood Farm, Inc.	14.60
Indian Charlie	L	126	8	4^1	5^2	4^{hd}	$2^{1/2}$	2^2	3^{hd}	G. Stevens	Hal Earnhardt & John R. Gaines Racing LLC	2.70
Halory Hunter	L	126	4	15	$12^{1/2}$	12^1	6^1	5^6	4^1	C. Nakatani	Celtic Pride Stable	6.60
Cape Town	L	126	11	6^{hd}	8^{hd}	$8^{1/2}$	$4^{1\text{-}1/2}$	$4^{1/2}$	5^8	J. Bailey	Overbrook Farm	4.60
Parade Ground		126	10	$13^{1\text{-}1/2}$	$13^{1/2}$	$13^{1/2}$	10^1	6^{hd}	6^{nk}	S. Sellers	W. S. Farish & Stephen Hilbert	22.30
Hanuman Highway (IRE)	L	126	6	9^1	$9^{1/2}$	$7^{1/2}$	9^1	8^5	7^{nk}	D. Flores	Budget Stable	22.50
Favorite Trick	L	126	7	$5^{1\text{-}1/2}$	4^{hd}	$5^{1\text{-}1/2}$	$5^{1/2}$	7^{hd}	$8^{6\text{-}3/4}$	P. Day	Joseph LaCombe	4.40
Nationalore	Lb	126	1	12^{hd}	$14^{1/2}$	15	$11^{1\text{-}1/2}$	9^3	$9^{4\text{-}3/4}$	G. Almeida	Myung Kwon Cho	109.60
Old Trieste	L	126	14	$2^{1\text{-}1/2}$	1^1	$1^{3\text{-}1/2}$	3^1	10^4	$10^{3\text{-}3/4}$	R. Albarado	Cobra Farms Inc.	32.10
Chilito		126	5	3^2	3^3	$3^{1/2}$	$8^{1\text{-}1/2}$	11^5	$11^{7\text{-}1/4}$	G. Boulanger	Lazy Lane Farms, Inc.	34.80
Robinwould	Lbf	126	15	7^{hd}	7^1	$9^{1/2}$	13^5	12^2	$12^{4\text{-}1/2}$	E. Fires	Dee & William Davenport	(f) 69.80
Artax	L	126	12	10^2	10^3	10^1	12^2	13^{12}	$13^{22\text{-}3/4}$	C. McCarron	Paraneck Stable	11.50
Rock and Roll	Lb	126	9	$1^{1/2}$	2^2	2^{hd}	15	14^{15}	$14^{10\text{-}3/4}$	F. Torres	Jenny Craig & Madeleine Paulson	50.60
Basic Trainee	L	126	2	$11^{1/2}$	$11^{1\text{-}1/2}$	$11^{1/2}$	14^2	15	15	J. Velazquez	Luis A. Gambotto & Enrique Ocejo	(f) 69.80

Time: 22.75, :45.75, 1:10.62, 1:35.61, 2:02.38. Track fast. Off at 5:29 EDT.
(f) Field.

Program #		Win	Place	Show	$2 Exacta (2-12)	$2 Trifecta (2-12-7)	$1 Superfecta (2-12-7-3)
2	Real Quiet	$18.80	$ 8.80	$5.80	$291.80	$1,221.00	$3,007.40
12	Victory Gallop		$13.00	$7.60			
7	Indian Charlie			$4.20			

Winner: B. c. by Quiet American–Really Blue by Believe It. Trained by Bob Baffert; bred in Kentucky by Little Hill Farm.

$1,038,800—gross value and $65,000 Gold Cup. Net to winner $738,800; second $170,000; third $85,500; fourth $45,000.

390 nominations.
Medication: L—Lasix
Equipment: b—blinkers; f—front bandages

CAREER HIGHLIGHTS

YEAR	AGE	STS.	1ST	2ND	3RD	EARNING
1997	2	9	2	0	5	$ 381,123
1998	3	6	2	3	0	$1,788,800
1999	4	5	2	2	1	$1,101,880
TOTALS		**20**	**6**	**5**	**6**	**$3,271,803**

At 2 years	WON	Maiden on 7th attempt; Hollywood Futurity
	3RD	Futurity Trial, Indian Nations Futurity Cup, B&W Kentucky Jockey Club
At 3 years	WON	Kentucky Derby, Preakness
	2ND	San Felipe, Santa Anita Derby, Belmont
	UNP	Golden Gate Derby
At 4 years	WON	Hollywood Gold Cup, Pimlico Special
	2ND	New Orleans Handicap, Texas Mile
	3RD	Massachusetts Handicap

"A Fixer-Upper in a Run-Down Neighborhood"

SAID A WRITER FOR THE *New York Times* about the 1998 Derby winner Real Quiet: "In a sport where yearling horses often cost more than a four-bedroom house, 'Real Quiet' was a fixer-upper in a run-down neighborhood. He had a crooked right front leg, a moderate pedigree, and was sold at auction in a cattle call that finds nearly 3000 horses going through the sales ring in a week."

Indeed, Real Quiet won one for the little guys by beating horses with fancy pedigrees and high price tags—he cost only $17,000—including one who cost $525,000 as a yearling.

The race was run on a track that was fast, despite a week of clouds, chill, and rain, before a crowd of 143,215, the third largest in history at that point. And Real Quiet's competition would chill one too. Among the fourteen colts he was running against were winners of the Santa Anita Derby, the Florida Derby, the Flamingo, the Arkansas Derby, and the Blue Grass Stakes.

When the horses broke from the starting gate, a couple of long shots were leading to the turn—one at 67–1—and there were a number of early speedsters, including Old Trieste and Chilito. But after a mile they ran out of gas, and the real race began.

Included among the contenders was the great Jerry Bailey, on Cape Town, who slipped into the lead. "I thought," Bailey said, "I had a big chance turning for home."

And that turn did not go unnoticed by Bob Baffert, whose horse was Real Quiet and who the year before had won with Silver Charm. "I don't think I'll ever feel the excitement I did over Silver Charm. But when they turn for home it's unbelievably exciting. It's like a storybook."

But then the closers came running. Among them was Real Quiet, Indian Charlie on his tail, Victory Gallop coming from seventh to contention lickety-split, and it was a pell-mell blast to the wire.

Said Real Quiet's jockey, Kent Desormeaux, describing those final strides that brought him the victory—Desormeaux's first ever Derby win in seven tries—"This is one high cloud. When the posse came, I asked him to run, and he did. When I asked him for his life, he gave it."

Charismatic
125th *May 1, 1999*

		Storm Bird	Northern Dancer
			South Ocean
	Summer Squall		Secretariat
CHARISMATIC		Weekend Surprise	Lassie Dear
Chestnut colt			Sir Gaylord
	Bali Babe	Drone	Cap and Bells
			What a Pleasure
	Polynesian Charm	Grass Shack

The Winner's Pedigree

Race Day Statistics

HORSE	M/EQ.	WT.	PP	1/4	1/2	3/4	MILE	STR.	FIN.	JOCKEY	OWNER	ODDS TO $1
Charismatic	L	126	16	7^{hd}	$7^{1/2}$	$7^{1-1/2}$	$3^{1-1/2}$	2^{hd}	1^{nk}	C. Antley	Robert B. & Beverly J. Lewis	31.30
Menifee	L	126	18	14^1	$17^{1-1/2}$	$15^{1-1/2}$	12^{hd}	6^2	$2^{3/4}$	P. Day	Arthur B. Hancock III & James H. Stone	7.00
Cat Thief	Lb	126	10	$2^{1-1/2}$	$2^{1-1/2}$	$2^{1-1/2}$	1^{hd}	$1^{1/2}$	$3^{1-1/4}$	M. Smith	Overbrook Farm	7.40
Prime Timber	Lb	126	13	10^{hd}	$11^{1/2}$	11^{hd}	8^{hd}	$4^{1-1/2}$	4no	D. Flores	Marie D. & Aaron U. Jones	6.30
Excellent Meeting	L	121	5	$18^{1/2}$	$18^{1-1/2}$	$16^{1/2}$	$15^{1-1/2}$	$7^{1-1/2}$	$5^{1/2}$	K. Desormeaux	Golden Eagle Farm	(b) 4.80
Kimberlite Pipe	L	126	12	8^{hd}	$8^{1/2}$	9^{hd}	$5^{1/2}$	5^{hd}	$6^{1-1/4}$	R. Albarado	John D. Gunther & Prairie Star Racing	(f) 11.60
Worldly Manner	Lb	126	11	3^{hd}	$3^{1/2}$	$3^{1/2}$	$2^{1-1/2}$	$3^{3-1/2}$	$7^{1/2}$	J. Bailey	Godolphin Racing Inc. Lessee	14.50
K One King	L	126	9	19	19	18^1	$14^{1/2}$	$10^{1-1/2}$	8^1	A. Solis	Madeline A. & Allen E. Paulson	(f) 11.60
Lemon Drop Kid	L	126	19	$13^{1/2}$	16^{hd}	$17^{1-1/2}$	$17^{1-1/2}$	$14^{1/2}$	9^{nk}	J. Santos	Jeanne Vance	(f) 11.60
Answer Lively	L	126	7	$6^{1-1/2}$	5^{hd}	4^{hd}	$6^{1-1/2}$	8^1	$10^{1/2}$	C. Perret	John A. Franks	37.00
General Challenge	Lb	126	14	$12^{1-1/2}$	$12^{1/2}$	12^{hd}	10^{hd}	10^1	$11^{3/4}$	G. Stevens	Golden Eagle Farm	(b) 4.80
Ecton Park	Lb	126	3	16^{hd}	15^{hd}	$13^{1/2}$	$16^{1/2}$	13^1	$12^{1/2}$	R. Davis	Mark H. Stanley	(f) 11.60
Desert Hero	L	126	6	5^{hd}	$6^{1/2}$	6^{hd}	11^{hd}	11^{hd}	$13^{1-1/4}$	C. Nakatani	The Thoroughbred Corporation	19.70
Stephen Got Even	L	126	4	4^{hd}	$4^{1/2}$	8^{hd}	10^{hd}	16^4	$14^{1-1/2}$	C. McCarron	Stephen C. Hilbert	5.10
Valhol	L	126	8	$1^{1/2}$	$1^{1/2}$	1^{hd}	$4^{1/2}$	$12^{1-1/2}$	15^2	W. Martinez	James D. Jackson	(f) 11.60
First American	Lb	126	15	15^{hd}	13^1	$5^{1/2}$	13^{hd}	15^{hd}	16^2	E. Delahoussaye	TNT Stud	34.90
Adonis	Lb	126	1	$17^{1-1/2}$	14^{hd}	19	18^5	17^4	$17^{4-3/4}$	J. Chavez	Paraneck Stable	18.70
Vicar	Lf	126	17	11^{hd}	9^{hd}	$14^{1/2}$	$9^{1-1/2}$	18^5	$18^{3-1/4}$	S. Sellers	James B. Tafel	8.20
Three Ring	Lb	121	2	$9^{1/2}$	10^{hd}	$10^{1/2}$	19	19	19	J. Velazquez	B. Schwartz, E. Hauman & E. Dahlman	25.60

Time: :23.52, :47.88, 1:12.52, 1:37.58, 2:03.29. Track fast. Off at 5:29 EDT. Start good. Won driving.
Coupled: (b) Excellent Meeting and General Challenge; (f) Field.

Program #		Win	Place	Show	$2 Exacta (11-13)	$2 Trifecta (11-13-8)	$1 Superfecta (11-13-8-9)
11	Charismatic	$64.60	$27.80	$14.40	$727.80	$5,866.20	$24,015.50
13	Menifee		$ 8.40	$ 5.80			
8	Cat Thief			$ 5.80			

Winner: Ch. c by Summer Squall–Bali Babe, by Drone. Trained by D. Wayne Lukas; bred in Kentucky by William S. Farish & Parrish Hill Farm.
$1,186,200—gross value and $90,000 Gold Cup. Net to winner $886,200; second $170,000; third $85,000; fourth $45,000. 407 nominations.

Medication: L—Lasix
Equipment: b—blinkers; f—front bandages

CAREER HIGHLIGHTS

YEAR	AGE	STS.	1ST	2ND	3RD	EARNINGS
1998	2	7	1	0	3	$ 30,660
1999	3	10	4	2	1	$2,007,404
TOTALS		17	5	2	4	**$2,038,064**

At 2 years   WON   Maiden on 6th attempt
At 3 years   WON   Lexington, Kentucky Derby, Preakness
              2ND   El Camino Real Derby
              3RD   Belmont
              UNP   Santa Catalina, Santa Anita Derby

He Was Already in His Mother's Arms

As Charismatic, a beautiful red chestnut colt with white chrome on his ankles and a star, stripe, and snip down his nose, and his rider Chris Antley, clad in striped green-and-yellow silks and a little yellow bow tie, paraded past the cameras of ABC-TV on their way to the starting gate for the 125th running of the Derby, they made a striking picture. But commentators Al Michaels and Hank Goldberg were not impressed. They gave Charismatic a zero chance of winning.

Small wonder. Charismatic had not done much of anything in his career, and the thirty-two-year-old man astride him was on the comeback trail, but there was a big question mark, the question being whether he would be on drugs. Once he had been a superstar, and many still regarded him that way. Starting at Monmouth Park, a fresh-faced kid from South Carolina with striking electric blue eyes, he was a force of nature. During one record-breaking period he had won 171 races in seventy-five days, 37 more than the track record.

But in the mid-1980s Antley had started using cocaine, and over the years had been in and out of rehab and had been suspended a number of times by the racing commission both in California and on the East Coast. More, during one of his rehab stays he had been diagnosed with bipolar disorder, or manic-depressive disease. And then he found that he could no longer lose enough weight to qualify for races. In September of 1998, in disgust and despair, he gave up, retiring to his boyhood home in Columbia, South Carolina.

He rapidly ballooned—on a five-foot-three frame—to almost 150 pounds. His father suggested he open a restaurant—he had a lot of money. Do something—anything—to start to live again.

Weeks went by, and one day in late October he was in his room at his father's house when he heard a horse race being announced on the TV in the living room. He went into the room and watched, and felt the adrenaline surging in him. When the race was over, he knew that he had to get back into racing. Had to. He was a jockey,

not a restaurant owner. He told his father that he was "going back to racing."

Antley started a fierce exercise regimen, including running twenty miles a day, lifting weights, changing his diet. And he also started seeing a psychiatrist. By January of 1999 he was back at the Santa Anita racetrack, his weight problem conquered and drug-free. He started picking up mounts, and he started to win again, not 20 percent but a respectable 23 wins in 138 mounts, some trained by D. Wayne Lukas.

On April 17, 1999, following a win aboard Key to Success, which was trained by Lukas, he was in the winner's circle when Lukas approached him and told him that he wanted him, if he was interested, to take a look the next day at a colt named Charismatic, who had trained extra hard and who was running in the Coolmore Stakes in Lexington (Kentucky) the next day. Lukas also told him he had tried to get Jerry Bailey to ride the colt, but he wasn't available, and that if Antley liked him—he had to be honest—he might end up riding him in the Derby. Lukas explained that he had been remiss with Charismatic's training, and so he trained him hard, also telling jockeys not to hold him back during the first quarter mile as he had instructed, but to let him go.

What Antley didn't know was that not only Bailey but other top riders—Chris McCarron, Lafitte Pincay, and Mike Smith—had already turned Lukas down.

Antley flew to Lexington and watched Charismatic run to a two-length victory. He reminded Antley of his previous Derby winner, Strike the Gold—namely, he could blow by other horses at the end of a race. Antley telephoned Lukas and told him he was in. Antley also called his father in South Carolina and told him that he was enthusiastic about the colt he would be racing in the Derby—and just the sheer miracle of riding in the Derby again at all. His father was less impressed. He looked at the odds on Charismatic, and they were 100 to 1 against him winning.

Charismatic drew post position 16, so far outside he was almost running in the stands among spectators, but nothing seemed to bother Antley. He told one of the trainers at the Lukas farm that the night before he had had a dream, and in it he saw himself winning the Derby on Charismatic. He was sure it would happen. The trainer told him to keep it to himself.

Charismatic got off to a good start, but the pace was slow, so all the horses stayed bunched together in a thundering herd until the first turn, and Charismatic was well back in the pack.

It was a particularly rough race. There was much bumping of too-close horses this way and that, all to the music of jockeys screaming encouragement to their mounts and at each other. As they thundered onto the backstretch toward the far turn, Valhol, who had led early on, was still in the lead, followed by Cat Thief, another Lukas mount. Charismatic was seventh.

Down the backside they came, and Antley urged Charismatic on, running his knuckles down the horse's neck. If he lost a single place now, he would be out of contention.

Lukas had told him that at the half-mile point, the eighth pole, which was opposite the red-brick kitchen, he was to "lay it down," really let the horse go. So Antley urged the horse on, but he didn't move, and at the far turn he started to drop back. And now he was on the outside of the pack. Antley went to the whip, giving Charismatic a few strokes to try to ener-

gize him, get him to move, and then he stopped. He knew that he couldn't make the horse run fast.

And then Charismatic just did, Antley helping him to run even faster by pushing his neck down to lengthen his stride, driving from the outside inward.

Horses and distance started to fall away. The crowd was going wild. They passed And Lively, then Valhol, and then they were at the top of the stretch and there were just two horses ahead of him; Cat Thief and Worldly Manner were three lengths out, a long way at this point in the race.

And then, under the whip again, he felt Charismatic surge, driving, driving. Antley was to say later that though he had dreamed it, and believed he would win as he felt the horse flying beneath him, he asked himself, *Is this really happening?*"

At the sixteenth pole—just one hundred yards from the finish—this horse everyone gave up on and this jockey who had been down and out caught the leader, Valhol, and drove toward the finish line, and then Antley looked left and right and he and Charismatic were alone, and he knew that he had won the Kentucky Derby. The next day he would describe what those final few strides were like to an ABC television interviewer: "I felt the warmest feeling that I ever did. It was a feeling that if you were scared and running and crying, you went into your mother's arms and she held you. It was that feeling of comfort and that's the kind of feeling I had."

As it happened, half a heartbeat after Charismatic crossed the finish line, another horse named Menifee blasted by them. But it was half a heartbeat too late. Mother already had Antley in her arms.

Fusaichi Pegasus
126th May 6, 2000

	Mr. Prospector	Raise a Native	Native Dancer
			Raise You
FUSAICHI PEGASUS		Gold Digger	Nashua
Bay colt			Sequence
	Angel Fever	Danzig	Northern Dancer
			Pas de Nom
		Rowdy Angel	Halo
			Rambyde

THE WINNER'S PEDIGREE

RACE DAY STATISTICS

HORSE	M/EQ.	WT	PP	1/4	1/2	3/4	MILE	STR.	FIN.	JOCKEY	OWNER	ODDS TO $1
Fusaichi Pegasus	Lf	126	15	$15^{3\text{-}1/2}$	$13^{1/2}$	$11^{1/2}$	6^1	1^{hd}	$1^{1\text{-}1/2}$	K. Desormeaux	Fusao Sekiguchi	2.30
Aptitude	L	126	2	$13^{1/2}$	$14^{1\text{-}1/2}$	10^{hd}	8^1	$4^{3\text{-}1/2}$	2^4	A. Solis	Juddmonte Farms	11.80
Impeachment	L	126	14	1^9	1^9	17^{hd}	$13^{1\text{-}1/2}$	7^{hd}	$3^{1/2}$	C. Perret	Dogwood Stable et al.	(a) 6.20
More Than Ready	L	126	9	3^{hd}	3^{hd}	$3^{1/2}$	4^{hd}	2^{hd}	4^{nk}	J. Velazquez	James T. Scatuorchio	11.30
Wheelaway	Lb	126	3	6^{hd}	$8^{1/2}$	7^{hd}	5^1	$3^{1/2}$	5^3	R. Migliore	Caesar P. Kimmel & Philip J. Solondz	(f) 20.80
China Visit	L	126	11	12^5	11^{hd}	$9^{1\text{-}1/2}$	7^{hd}	6^{hd}	6^{hd}	L. Dettori	Godolphin Racing Inc.	(b) 23.70
Curule	L	126	18	14^1	15^1	16^4	$9^{1/2}$	$8^{1/2}$	$7^{4\text{-}1/2}$	M. St. Julien	Godolphin Racing Inc.	(b) 23.70
Captain Steve	L	126	7	7^{hd}	$6^{1/2}$	$6^{1\text{-}1/2}$	1^{hd}	5^1	$8^{3/4}$	R. Albarado	Michael E. Pegram	8.10
War Chant	Lb	126	8	11^1	10^1	$12^{1/2}$	14^{hd}	10^2	$9^{3\text{-}3/4}$	J. Bailey	Marjorie & Irving Cowan	9.90
Deputy Warlock	Lf	126	6	$17^{1\text{-}1/2}$	17^3	$18^{2\text{-}1/2}$	$18^{1\text{-}1/2}$	17^3	$10^{1/2}$	M. Guidry	Select Stable, Inc.	(f) 20.80
Trippi	L	126	5	$2^{2\text{-}1/2}$	2^1	$2^{1\text{-}1/2}$	2^{hd}	9^1	11^1	J. Chavez	Dogwood Stable	(a) 6.20
Exchange Rate	Lb	126	16	5^{hd}	7^{hd}	8^{hd}	$12^{1/2}$	12^{hd}	$12^{3/4}$	C. Borel	Padua Stables	59.20
Anees	Lb	126	1	16^1	16^6	$15^{1/2}$	11^{hd}	$11^{1\text{-}1/2}$	$13^{2\text{-}3/4}$	C. Nakatani	The Thoroughbred Corporation	17.10
The Deputy (IRE)	L	126	10	$9^{1/2}$	$12^{2\text{-}1/2}$	$14^{1/2}$	17^{hd}	16^{hd}	$14^{3/4}$	C. McCarron	Team Valor & Gary Barber	4.60
High Yield	Lb	126	17	$8^{1/2}$	$5^{1/2}$	$5^{1/2}$	$10^{1/2}$	15^{hd}	15^{nk}	P. Day	Robert B. & Beverly J. Lewis	(a) 6.20
Hal's Hope	L	126	4	1^{hd}	1^1	$1^{1/2}$	3^1	13^1	$16^{1\text{-}3/4}$	R. Velez	Rose Family Stables Ltd.	22.70
Commendable	Lb	126	12	10^{hd}	$9^{1/2}$	13^{hd}	$16^{1\text{-}1/2}$	18^1	$17^{3\text{-}1/2}$	E. Prado	Robert B. & Beverly J. Lewis	(a) 6.20
Ronton	L	126	19	$18^{1\text{-}1/2}$	$18^{1\text{-}1/2}$	1^9	1^9	1^9	1^8	B. Blanc	Jaltipan, LLC	(f) 20.80
Graeme Hall	Lb	126	13	4^1	4^1	4^{hd}	$15^{1/2}$	$14^{1\text{-}1/2}$	Eased	S. Sellers	Eugene & Laura Melnyk	46.30

Time: :22.47, :45.99, 1:09.99, 1:35.74, 2:01.12. Track fast. Off at 5:29 EDT. Start good. Won driving.
Coupled: (a) Impeachment, Trippi, High Yield, and Commendable; (b) China Visit and Curule; (f) Field.

Program #		Win	Place	Show
12	Fusaichi Pegasus	$6.60	$5.60	$4.00
5	Aptitude		$9.80	$5.80
1c	Impeachment			$4.00

$2 Exacta (12-5) $66.00 $2 Trifecta (12-5-1) $435.00 $1 Superfecta (12-5-1-9) $1,635.40

Winner: B. c., by Mr. Prospector–Angel Feve, by Danzig. Trained by Neil Drysdale; bred in Kentucky by Arthur B. Hancock III & Stonerside Ltd.
$1,188,400—gross value and $85,000 Gold Cup. Net to winner $888,400; second $170,000; third $85,000; fourth $45,000.
Scratched- Globalize.

400 nominations.
Medication: L—Lasix
Equipment: b—blinkers; f—front bandages

CAREER HIGHLIGHTS

YEAR	AGE	STS.	1ST	2ND	3RD	EARNINGS
1999	2	1	0	1	0	$ 6,600
2000	3	8	6	1	0	$1,987,800
TOTALS		**9**	**6**	**2**	**0**	**$1,994,400**

At 2 years	2ND	Maiden Special Weight
At 3 years	WON	Maiden on 2nd attempt, Kentucky Derby, Jerome Handicap, San Felipe, Wood Memorial
	2ND	Preakness
	UNP	Breeders' Cup Classic

A Sure Thing

WHEN SIXTY-FIVE-YEAR-OLD JAPANESE venture capitalist Fusao Sekiguchi saw this yearling, he was to say later, "When I laid eyes on this colt, I knew he was going to be a Derby winner."

Sekiguchi was right. The bay colt, who he named Fusaichi Pegasus after the flying horse of mythology, did win the 2000 run for the roses, and brought his winnings for the year to $1,987,800, immediately returning about half of the $4 million Sekiguchi had paid for him. In winning the Derby, the bay son of Mr. Prospector became the first favorite to win the Derby since Spectacular Bid did it twenty-one years earlier, in 1979.

One thing that the colt's handlers were concerned about before the race was his tendency to balk at doing certain things. But on this day he ran smoothly, professionally—and very quickly. When the race started, Fusaichi was fifteenth in a crowd of nineteen going around the first turn. Kent Desormeaux, his jockey, did not use his whip, but let the horse run his own race.

He stayed behind until the leaders turned for home, then bolted to the inside to save ground, then shot to the outside to get in the clear as 153,204 spectators—the second-largest crowd in Derby history, roared, then made his run to the wire. Said Desormeaux, "Once we straightened away and I got him in the clear, I kissed at him and asked him to run, and he accelerated. And it was over at that point. He took off like the best horse I've been involved with at this stage of the game."

Fusaichi finished in 2:01, the sixth-fastest time in Derby history.

Monarchos
127th *May 5, 2001*

		Wavering Monarch	Majestic Light
	Maria's Mon		Uncommitted
MONARCHOS		Carlotta Maria	Caro
Gray/roan colt			Water Malone
	Regal Band	Dixieland Band	Northern Dancer
			Mississippi Mud
	Regal Roberta	Roberto
		Regal Road

THE WINNER'S PEDIGREE

RACE DAY STATISTICS

HORSE	M/EQ.	WT.	PP	1/4	1/2	3/4	MILE	STR.	FIN.	JOCKEY	OWNER	ODDS TO $1
Monarchos	L	126	16	13^2	$13^{1/2}$	$10^{1-1/2}$	6^{hd}	2^3	$1^{4-3/4}$	J. Chavez	John Oxley	10.50
Invisible Ink	L	126	13	9^{hd}	$9^{2-1/2}$	$9^{2-1/2}$	5^{hd}	3^1	2no	J. Velazquez	Peachtree Stable	55.00
Congaree	Lb	126	8	$5^{2-1/2}$	$5^{1-1/2}$	$5^{1/2}$	$1^{1-1/2}$	$1^{1/2}$	3^4	V. Espinoza	Stonerside Stable	7.20
Thunder Blitz	L	126	4	11^{hd}	10^{hd}	8^{hd}	7^{hd}	6^2	$4^{2-3/4}$	E. Prado	Stronach Stable	25.40
Point Given	Lb	126	17	6^{hd}	7^{hd}	7^1	2^{hd}	$4^{1-1/2}$	$5^{1-1/4}$	G. Stevens	The Thoroughbred Corporation	1.80
Jamaican Rum	L	126	15	17	16^1	$15^{2-1/2}$	12^6	$7^{2-1/2}$	6^{nk}	E. Delahoussaye	Southern Nevada Racing Stables	20.20
A P Valentine	L	126	9	12^3	$12^{1-1/2}$	13^1	14^3	14^6	$7^{1-1/4}$	C. Nakatani	Ol Memorial Stable & Michael Tabor	19.90
Express Tour	L	126	6	8^4	$6^{1-1/2}$	6^{hd}	3^{hd}	5^{hd}	$8^{3/4}$	D. Flores	Godolphin Racing Inc.	18.10
Fifty Stars	L	126	5	$16^{1-1/2}$	17	16^3	13^2	9^{hd}	$9^{1-1/4}$	D. Meche	James Cassels & Bob Zollars	43.60
Startac	L	126	12	$10^{1-1/2}$	$11^{1-1/2}$	$11^{1/2}$	10^1	$10^{1/2}$	10^4	A. Solis	Allen E. Paulson Living Trust	102.40
Millennium Wind	L	126	2	$4^{1/2}$	$4^{1-1/2}$	$3^{1-1/2}$	8^{hd}	8^{hd}	11^{nk}	L. Pincay Jr.	David & Jill Heerensperger	9.90
Arctic Boy	L	126	7	15^4	$14^{1-1/2}$	$12^{1/2}$	11^{hd}	11^1	$12^{6-1/2}$	C. Borel	Royce G. Roberts	101.20
Songandaprayer	Lf	126	1	1^{hd}	$1^{1-1/2}$	$1^{1-1/2}$	$4^{1/2}$	$12^{2-1/2}$	13^5	A. Gryder	Devil Eleven Stable & D J Stable	35.90
Balto Star	L	126	3	2^1	2^{hd}	2^{hd}	9^1	13^{hd}	$14^{2-1/4}$	M. Guidry	Anstu Stables	8.30
Dollar Bill	L	126	10	14^{hd}	15^4	14^{hd}	16	15^4	15^{17}	P. Day	Gary & Mary West	6.60
Keats	L	126	14	$3^{1/2}$	3^{hd}	4^{hd}	$15^{1-1/2}$	16	16	L. Melancon	Henry E. Pabst	95.00
Talk Is Money	Lbf	126	11	7^{hd}	8^4	17	-	-	-	J. Bailey	Daniel M. Borislow	47.10

Time: :22.25, :44.86, 1:09.25, 1:35.00, 1:59.97. Track fast. Off at 6:11 EDT. Start good. Won driving.

Program #		Win	Place	Show	$2 Exacta (16-13)	$2 Trifecta (16-13-8)	$1 Superfecta (16-13-8-4)
16	Monarchos	$23.00	$11.80	$ 8.80	$1,229.00	$12,238.40	$62,986.90
13	Invisible Ink		$46.60	$21.20			
8	Congaree			$ 7.20			

Winner: Gr/ro c. by Maria's Mon–Regal Band, by Dixieland Band. Trained by John T. Ward Jr.; bred in Kentucky by J. D. Squires.

$1,112,000—gross value and $85,000 Gold Cup. Net to winner $812,000; second $170,000; third $85,000; fourth $45,000.

447 nominations.
Medication: L—Lasix
Equipment: b—blinkers; f—front bandages

CAREER HIGHLIGHTS

YEAR	AGE	STS.	1ST	2ND	3RD	EARNINGS
2000	2	2	0	0	1	$ 4,030
2001	3	7	4	1	1	$1,711,600
2002	4	1	0	0	1	$ 5,200
TOTALS		**10**	**4**	**1**	**3**	**$1,720,830**

At 2 years	2ND	Maiden Special
At 3 years	WON	Maiden on 3rd attempt; Florida Derby, Kentucky Derby
	2ND	Wood Memorial
	3RD	Belmont Stakes
	UNP	Preakness Stakes
At 4 years	3RD	Allowance Optional Claiming

A Real Shot

LIKE SO MANY JOCKEYS BEFORE HIM, Peruvian-born Jorge Chavez, thirty-nine, had been to the Derby before—in his case three times—without success. He had been four-teenth on Ulises in 1994, seventeenth on Adonis in 1999, and eleventh on Trippi in 2000. But Chavez said that in the 2001 Derby he felt he had a shot. "This," he said of the Derby, "is the highest you can get being a jockey. My children and grandchildren and everyone will remember. I rode three other times in the Derby but none of those horses really had a shot. I told myself this time I really had a chance, and today I was going to make it happen."

Chavez would be astride Monarchos, a big gray colt who had broken his maiden with a victory at Gulfstream the January before the Derby. Chavez, a glow in his eyes, had told trainer John Ward, "I hope this will be my Kentucky Derby horse."

Chavez then went on to win the Florida Derby, but it was not a completely smooth ride to the Derby. Three weeks before the Derby the Wood Memorial was held at the Aqueduct racetrack in New York and he was beaten by

Congaree, who was to be another contender in the Derby, though the loss did not seem to upset Ward, who regarded the race as a tune-up.

The race was run before 164,210 of the usual crazed folks.

As the race started, Chavez took the short route on the rail during the first three-quarters of a mile, then moved a bit to the outside approaching the far turn. Chavez, who is particularly good at threading his way through tight, high-speed traffic, had his work cut out for him. He found his way through the horses at the top of the stretch, then went after Congaree, now the leader and the horse who had beaten him in the Wood Memorial, caught him at the eighth pole, and won going away by four and three-quarter lengths. His time was stunning: 1:59.97. Only Secretariat was faster.

Chavez, a great jockey, was virtually unknown before the Derby, despite the fact that he had won over 3,300 races and won the 1999 Eclipse Award as America's outstanding jockey. Now, people know him a little better.

War Emblem
128th *May 4, 2002*

	Mr. Prospector	*Raise a Native*	
		Gold Digger	
Our Emblem		*Private Account*	
WAR EMBLEM	*Personal Ensign*	*Grecian Banner*	
Dark bay/brown colt		**General*	
Sweetest Lady	**Lord at War*	**Luna de Miel*	
		*The Pruner	
	Sweetest Roman	** I Also*	

THE WINNER'S PEDIGREE AND CAREER HIGHLIGHTS

YEAR	AGE	STS.	1ST	2ND	3RD	EARNINGS
2001	2	3	2	0	0	$ 36,000
2002	3	10	5	0	0	$3,455,000
TOTALS		**13**	**7**	**0**	**0**	**$3,491,000**

At 2 years	WON	Maiden on 1st attempt
	UNP	Manila
At 3 years	WON	Illinois Derby, Kentucky Derby, Preakness, Haskell
	UNP	Lecomte, Risen Star, Belmont, Pacific Classic, BC Classic

HORSE	M/EQ.	WT.	PP	1/4	1/2	3/4	MILE	STR.	FIN.	JOCKEY	OWNER	ODDS TO $1
War Emblem	L	126	5	$1^{1/2}$	$1^{1\text{-}1/2}$	$1^{1\text{-}1/2}$	$1^{1\text{-}1/2}$	$1^{1\text{-}1/2}$	1^4	V. Espinoza	The Thoroughbred Corporation	20.50
Proud Citizen	L	126	12	2^1	$2^{1/2}$	$2^{1/2}$	3^1	2nd	$2^{3/4}$	M. E. Smith	R. Baker, D. Cornstein, Wm. Mack	23.30
Perfect Drift	L	126	3	4^{hd}	3^1	$3^{1/2}$	2nd	$3^{3\text{-}1/2}$	$3^{3\text{-}1/4}$	E. Delahoussaye	Stonecrest Farm	7.90
Medaglia d'Oro	L	126	9	10^1	9^1	$7^{1/2}$	8^3	6^1	$4^{1\text{-}1/2}$	L. Pincay Jr.	Edmund A. Gann	6.90
Request for Parole	L	126	7	6^{hd}	$5^{1/2}$	5^{hd}	5^{hd}	$5^{1/2}$	$5^{3/4}$	R. Albarado	Jeri & Sam Knighton	29.80
Came Home	L	126	14	$3^{1/2}$	$4^{1/2}$	$4^{1/2}$	4^2	$4^{1/2}$	6^2	C. McCarron	Farish, Goodman, Toffan & McCaffery	8.20
Harlan's Holiday	L	126	13	$9^{1/2}$	$11^{1\text{-}1/2}$	8^{hd}	6^{hd}	7^1	$7^{3/4}$	E. S. Prado	Starlight Stable, L.P.	6.00
Johannesburg	L	126	1	$11^{1/2}$	10^1	$10^{1/2}$	$9^{1/2}$	8^1	8no	G. L. Stevens	Michael Tabor & Mrs. John Magnier	8.10
Essence of Dubai	Lb	126	8	13^2	12^{hd}	12^{hd}	$7^{1/2}$	9^3	9^1	D. R. Flores	Godolphin Racing Inc.	10.00
Saarland	L	126	15	17^2	17^2	$14^{1/2}$	16^{hd}	$13^{1/2}$	$10^{2\text{-}1/2}$	J. R. Velazquez	Cynthia Phipps	6.90
Blue Burner	Lb	126	18	5^{hd}	$8^{1/2}$	$9^{1\text{-}1/2}$	$10^{1/2}$	11^{hd}	$11^{1/2}$	P. Day	Kinsman Stable	24.20
Castle Gandolfo	L	126	11	15^{hd}	15^1	$15^{1/2}$	14^1	$12^{2\text{-}1/2}$	$12^{4\text{-}1/4}$	J. D. Bailey	Mrs. John Magnier	14.50
Easy Grades	L	126	17	12^1	14^{hd}	16^{hd}	11^{hd}	14^2	13^{nk}	J. F. Chavez	Desperado Stables	43.80
Private Emblem	L	126	10	7^1	7^{hd}	$11^{1\text{-}1/2}$	12^{hd}	10^1	$14^{4\text{-}1/2}$	D. J. Meche	James Cassels & Bob Zollars	22.40
Lusty Latin	Lb	126	4	18	18	18	18	18	$15^{2\text{-}1/4}$	G. W. Corbett	Joey & Wendy Platts	22.10
It'sallinthechase	L	126	16	$16^{2\text{-}1/2}$	16^{hd}	17^2	$13^{1\text{-}1/2}$	15^3	$16^{2\text{-}3/4}$	E.M. Martin Jr.	Darwin Olson	94.50
Ocean Sound (IRE)	L	126	6	14^{hd}	$13^{1\text{-}1/2}$	13^1	17^2	17^2	$17^{2\text{-}1/4}$	A. Solis	K.M. Stable, Jim Ford & D. Pearson	48.70
Wild Horses	L	126	2	$8^{1/2}$	6^1	6^{hd}	15^{hd}	$16^{1/2}$	18	R. Douglas	Peachtree Stable	58.50

Time: :23.25, :47.04, 1:11.75, 1:36.70, 2:01.13. Track fast. Off at 6:12 EDT. Start good. Won driving.

Program #		Win	Place	Show	$2 Exacta (5-13)	$2 Trifecta (5-13-3)	$1 Superfecta (5-13-3-9)
5	War Emblem	$43.00	$22.80	$13.60	$1,300.80	$18,373.20	$91,764.50
13	Proud Citizen		$24.60	$13.40			
3	Perfect Drift			$ 6.40			

Winner: Dk. b. or br. c, by Our Emblem–Sweetest Lady, by Lord at War (Arg). Trained by Bob Baffert; bred in Kentucky by Charles Nuckols Jr. & Sons.
$1,175,000—gross value and $85,000 Gold Cup. Net to winner $875,000; second $170,000; third $85,000; fourth $45,000.

417 nominations.
Medication: L—Lasix
Equipment: b—blinkers

*Foreign bred

Right Down the Garden Path

BOB BAFFERT, THE WISECRACKING WHITE-haired trainer who usually looks at the world through very expensive sunglasses, had a plan for the 2002 Derby. Or, more to the point, a con, a legal scam.

It revolved around his horse War Emblem, who none of the experts was much impressed with. On April 6 their assessment seemed confirmed. War Emblem had won the lightly regarded Illinois Derby, leading every step of the way, but the victory was greeted with derision by horse savants. Watching War Emblem perform in that race, they figured that Baffert was out of Derby candidates because other horses that might have been considered for the Derby had not worked out. Some proved not good enough, while others were injured.

Baffert did nothing to disabuse observers about the quality of War Emblem. When the media talked with him about the colt, he just nodded sadly, his eyes hidden behind his glasses, and predicted that War Emblem—who he was still entering in the Derby—would go to the post a 20–1 long shot. (Which proved accurate.) But mostly he kept his mouth shut, which was unusual for him.

Baffert was no beginner, and one could assume that he had to have some sort of plan for War Emblem. Baffert had three Preakness victories and a Belmont Stakes title, in addition to having captured two garlands of roses in the six years since he had given up training quarter horses.

Indeed he did have a plan, a very simple one.

And when the race started, Espinoza, War Emblem's jockey, followed the plan. Espinoza broke into the lead and stayed there, and then it was up to other jockeys to decide if the speed was cheap—he would fade after a while—and/or Victor was so inexperienced he didn't know how to slow down the fractions, and the horse would burn out. War Emblem loped along and took a length-and-a-half lead into the half-mile mark at a comfortable 47.04 seconds—and Baffert knew that he had played everyone for suckers. Before anyone realized the speed was real, War Emblem was gone.

"Nobody saw this horse developing the way I did," Baffert would say after the race. "I didn't do too much bragging, because I wanted them to leave him alone. I told Victor: 'They're probably not going to pay much attention to you.'"

They didn't. They left him alone. And he was alone at the finish, winning by four lengths.

Funny Cide
129th *May 3, 2003*

	Forty Niner	Mr. Prospector
		File
Distorted Humor		Danzig
FUNNY CIDE	Danzig's Beauty	Sweetest Chant
Chestnut gelding		Seattle Slew
Belle's	Slewacide	Evasive
Good Cide		Little Current
	Belle of Killarney	Cherished
		Moment

THE WINNER'S PEDIGREE

RACE DAY STATISTICS

HORSE	M/EQ.	WT.	PP	1/4	1/2	3/4	MILE	STR.	FIN.	JOCKEY	OWNER	ODDS TO $1
Funny Cide	L	126	5	$4^{1/2}$	$3^{1/2}$	$3^{1-1/2}$	2^{1}	1^{hd}	$1^{1-3/4}$	J. A. Santos	Sackatoga Stable (Jackson Knowlton)	12.80
Empire Maker	Lb	126	11	$8^{1/2}$	$8^{2-1/2}$	$8^{1-1/2}$	$3^{1-1/2}$	$3^{1-1/2}$	2^{hd}	J. D. Bailey	Juddmonte Farms Inc.	2.50
Peace Rules	L	126	4	$2^{1-1/2}$	$2^{1-1/2}$	$2^{1-1/2}$	$1^{1/2}$	$2^{1/2}$	3^{hd}	E. S. Prado	Edmund A. Gann	6.30
Atswhatimtalknbout	Lb	126	3	$10^{1-1/2}$	12^{2}	11^{2}	$10^{1/2}$	$5^{1/2}$	$4^{2-3/4}$	D. Flores	B. Wayne Hughes & Biscuit Stables LLC	8.90
Eye of the Tiger	L	126	12	3^{hd}	$4^{1-1/2}$	$4^{1/2}$	4^{1}	$4^{1-1/2}$	5^{1}	E. Coa	John D. Gunther	41.50
Buddy Gil	L	126	7	13^{hd}	$13^{2-1/2}$	13^{4}	11^{1}	$6^{1/2}$	$6^{3/4}$	G. L. Stevens	Desperado Stables	7.20
Outta Here	L	126	14	$15^{1-1/2}$	14^{hd}	16	15^{3}	$14^{1-1/2}$	7^{1}	K. Desormeaux	Wm. Currin & Al Eisman	39.70
Ten Cents a Shine	L	126	13	16	16	$15^{1/2}$	$14^{3-1/2}$	11^{1}	8^{nk}	C. H. Borel	Ken & Sarah Ramsey	37.20
Ten Most Wanted	L	126	15	$12^{1-1/2}$	$10^{1/2}$	$10^{1-1/2}$	$9^{1/2}$	$10^{1/2}$	$9^{1-3/4}$	P. Day	J. Chisholm, M. Jarvis & J. P. Reddam	6.60
Domestic Dispute	L	126	10	$7^{1/2}$	7^{1}	5^{hd}	7^{hd}	$7^{1/2}$	10^{1}	A. Solis	David Bienstock & Chuck Winner	44.00
Scrimshaw	Lb	126	16	$5^{1/2}$	$6^{1/2}$	7^{hd}	8^{hd}	$8^{1/2}$	11^{1}	C. Velasquez	Robert & Beverly Lewis	16.50
Offlee Wild	L	126	6	$11^{1-1/2}$	$11^{1-1/2}$	$9^{1-1/2}$	$6^{1/2}$	9^{1}	$12^{5-1/2}$	R. Albarado	Azalea Stables, LLC	29.90
Supah Blitz	Lb	126	1	$9^{2-1/2}$	$9^{1/2}$	$12^{2-1/2}$	13^{hd}	12^{1}	$13^{1-3/4}$	R. B. Homeister	Bee Bee Stables & Jacqueline Tortora	43.10
Indian Express	L	126	8	$6^{1/2}$	5^{hd}	6^{hd}	12^{hd}	$15^{2-1/2}$	$14^{1-1/4}$	T. C. Baze	Phil & Sheva Chess	10.80
Lone Star Sky	L	126	9	$14^{1-1/2}$	15^{1}	$14^{1/2}$	16	16	15^{1}	S. Sellers	Walter New	52.10
Brancusi	L	126	2	$1^{1/2}$	$1^{1/2}$	1^{hd}	5^{hd}	$13^{1-1/2}$	16	T. Farina	Michael B. Tabor	29.30

Time: :22.78, :46.23, 1:10.48, 1:35.75, 2:01.19. Track fast. Off at 6:08 EDT. Start good. Won driving.

Program #		Win	Place	Show	$2 Exacta (6-12)	$2 Trifecta (6-12-5)	$1 Superfecta (6-12-5-4)
6	Funny Cide	$27.60	$12.40	$8.20	$97.00	$664.80	$2,795.80
12	Empire Maker		$ 5.80	$4.40			
5	Peace Rules			$6.00			

Winner: Ch. g, by Distorted Humor–Belle's Good Cide, by Slewacide. Trained by Barclay Tagg; bred in New York by Win Star Farm LLC.
$1,100,200—gross value and $90,000 Gold Cup. Net to winner $800,200; second $170,000; third $85,000; fourth $45,000.

454 nominations.
Medication: L—Lasix
Equipment: b—blinkers

CAREER HIGHLIGHTS

YEAR	AGE	STS.	1ST	2ND	3RD	EARNINGS
2002	2	3	3	0	0	$ 136,185
2003	3	8	2	2	2	$1,963,200
2004	4	10	3	2	3	$
2005	5	3	0	0	0	$
TOTALS		11	5	2	2	$2,099,385

At 2 years	WON	Maiden on 1st attempt, Bertram F. Bongard, Sleepy Hollow
At 3 years	WON	Kentucky Derby, Preakness
	2ND	Louisiana Derby (elevated after DQ), Wood Memorial
	3RD	Belmont, Haskell Invitational
	UNP	Holy Bull

Ordinary Guys

ON A LOVELY POWDER-BLUE-SKY SPRING DAY
when the running of the Kentucky Derby was to
go off, most of the media attention was devoted to
the favorite, Empire Maker, a big, powerful horse
trained by the renowned Bobby Frankel, who
he predicted no one could beat; Empire Maker
was really a locomotive posing as a horse.

Only a few reporters visited the stall of Funny Cide, a small gelding. And why should they? He was a long shot, 13–1, and Empire Maker had already bested him in the Wood Memorial.

More, he didn't have Ben Jones or Sunny Jim Fitzsimmons training him. He had been trained by Barclay Tagg, who over his thirty-year career as a trainer had never qualified a horse for a race as prestigious and competitive as the Kentucky Derby. His pedigree was hardly inspiring, and his jockey was Jose Santos, a Chilean-born man who'd been riding racehorses since he was eleven years old—he was now forty-two—but who in 1992 at Belmont Park had been involved in a terrible spill. It took a dozen steel pins and two plates to reassemble him. He'd been in debt, divorced, and his career had gone into the toilet. In her biography of Funny Cide, writer Sally Jenkins said Santos was up and down so often he was seasick.

But the big thing, some said, was that the accident had broken more than bones. It had broken his courage; and after he recovered and started racing again, he demonstrated this by not getting his mounts in advantageous but dangerous situations.

But perhaps the most telling symbol of the horse's poor chances was the group of middle-aged guys who owned him. They were very ordinary guys from Sackets Harbor, New York, who had gotten into Thoroughbred horseracing on a lark and had none of the background or money of the typical horse owner at the Derby that day. Indeed, on Derby day they came to the track in a rented school bus, which one of them dubbed "our yellow stretch limo."

But inside every one of these people was a burning belief in Funny Cide. He had shown he could run like the wind, and somehow, this central fact had escaped general attention.

Like other Thoroughbreds, Funny Cide had had his share of medical problems, most particularly a lung condition that was finally diagnosed as an absence of cilia (hair) in his lungs, which caused mucus to build up in them and cut down on his ability to breathe properly, leaving him gasping for air. Treatment had cleared that up, but no one was ready for what he did on Derby day. As he headed for the paddock and entered the open track area, crowded with loud people, Funny Cide spooked, suddenly rearing up again and again, acting just plain crazy, seeming uncontrollable. His owners, watching him, were to say later that they came very close to getting him scratched.

But they kept walking him, and gradually he calmed down, and in the paddock he was fine. Jose Santos, who had been in the jockey's room during all the tumult, explained it: "Who wouldn't be nervous with all those people?"

As they broke from the gate, Funny Cide bumped into Offlee Wild, but he was able to dart forward and find an open space. At the first turn, Funny Cide was ahead of Empire Maker by six lengths, but the big favorite, Jerry Bailey up, had a clear path to the front.

At six furlongs Edgar Prado moved Peace Rules to the front, and Santos glanced back, looking for Empire Maker, knowing that the big threat would come from him. And the threat was there. Now, for the first time, he could see the big bay colt, and he was moving up.

They went past the quarter in 1:35.75 for the mile.

Then Santos saw something that gave him hope. Bailey had gone to the whip, and then Edgar Prado went to the whip. But Santos didn't have to. They turned into the stretch, and then everyone would know what ten inexperienced and uninitiated owners, a jockey, and the trainer who had never won anything knew— that Funny Cide could win, and if not having to use the whip meant anything, he would win.

Down the stretch they thundered, and Peace Rules was done, and Bailey's whip had no effect on Empire Maker. Slowly, inexorably, Funny Cide pulled away, inch by inch . . . and yes, he was going to win. And he did, and as he crossed the wire Jose Santos burst into tears, and those ten unlikely horse owners went berserk, and even the staid Barclay Tagg lost it a little.

Later, Santos described the whole experience of Funny Cide the best. "It was like a movie," he said, "just like I was in the middle of a movie."

And one, yes, with a happy ending.

Smarty Jones
130th *May 1, 2004*

		Gone West	Mr. Prospector
	Elusive Quality		Secrettame
SMARTY JONES		Touch of Greatness	Hero's Honor
Chestnut colt			Ivory Wand
	I'll Get Along	Smile	In Reality
			Sunny Smile
	Don't Worry Bout Me	Foolish Pleasure
			Stolen Base

The Winner's Pedigree

Race Day Statistics

HORSE	M/EQ.	WT.	PP	$1/4$	$1/2$	$3/4$	MILE	STR.	FIN.	JOCKEY	OWNER	ODDS TO $1
Smarty Jones	Lf	126	13	$4^{1/2}$	$4^{1\text{-}1/2}$	2hd	2^4	1hd	$1^{2\text{-}3/4}$	S. Elliott	Someday Farm	4.10
Lion Heart		126	3	$1^{1\text{-}1/2}$	1^2	$1^{1\text{-}1/2}$	1hd	$2^{3\text{-}1/2}$	$2^{3\text{-}1/4}$	M. Smith	Michael Tabor & Derrick Smith	5.40
Imperialism	Lb	126	8	$15^{1/2}$	17^3	13hd	$10^{1/2}$	$6^{1/2}$	3^2	K. Desormeaux	Steve Taub	10.90
Limehouse	L	126	1	7hd	8hd	$6^{1/2}$	$6^{1/2}$	3^2	$4^{4\text{-}1/2}$	J. Santos	Dogwood Stable	41.70
The Cliff's Edge	L	126	9	$16^{1/2}$	15hd	17^2	8^2	5^1	$5^{1/4}$	S. Sellers	Robert LaPenta	8.20
Action This Day	L	126	4	18	18	18	14^2	12hd	6^1	D. Flores	B. Wayne Hughes	43.40
Read the Footnotes	L	126	12	$5^{1/2}$	6hd	$4^{1/2}$	3^1	4hd	$7^{1/2}$	R. Albarado	Klaravich Stables Inc.	22.50
Birdstone	L	126	11	14^2	$11^{1/2}$	10hd	$9^{1/2}$	$9^{1/2}$	$8^{1/2}$	E. Prado	Marylou Whitney	21.20
Tapit	Lf	126	16	17^3	16hd	$12^{1/2}$	7^{hd}	$10^{1\text{-}1/2}$	$9^{1/2}$	R. Dominguez	Winchell Thoroughbreds LLC	6.40
Borrego	Lb	126	10	9hd	7^2	$9^{1/2}$	4hd	7hd	$10^{1\text{-}1/4}$	V. Espinoza	Foster, Kelly, Ralls, Scott, Greely	14.20
Song of the Sword	Lb	126	2	$11^{1/2}$	$13^{1/2}$	$7^{1/2}$	$12^{1\text{-}1/2}$	$11^{1\text{-}1/2}$	11^1	N. Arroyo Jr.	Paraneck Stable	55.90
Master David	L	126	7	8hd	9hd	14hd	$11^{1/2}$	13^3	$12^{1\text{-}1/2}$	A. Solis	Georgica Stable, S. Mack, Star Crown	10.60
Pro Prado	L	126	17	10^2	$10^{1\text{-}1/2}$	8hd	5hd	8hd	$13^{5\text{-}1/4}$	J. McKee	Mrs. James A. Winn	53.50
Castledale (IRE)	L	126	14	13hd	12hd	15hd	17^{20}	14^3	$14^{1\text{-}1/2}$	J. Valdivia Jr.	Frank Lyons & Greg Knee	21.90
Friends Lake	L	126	5	12hd	14^1	$16^{1\text{-}1/2}$	16hd	$15^{1/2}$	$15^{1/2}$	R. Migliore	Chester & Mary Broman Sr.	18.50
Minister Eric	L	126	6	$6^{1\text{-}1/2}$	5hd	$3^{1/2}$	$13^{1/2}$	17^{20}	$16^{3\text{-}1/2}$	P. Day	Diamond A Racing Corp.	22.50
Pollard's Vision	L	126	15	3hd	$2^{1/2}$	5^1	$15^{1\text{-}1/2}$	16hd	17	J. Velazquez Jr.	Edgewood Farm	24.00
Quintons Gold Rush	L	126	18	2^{hd}	3hd	11hd	18	18	—	C. Nakatani	Padua Stables & Jay Manoogian	51.20

Time: :22.99, :46.73, 1:11.80, 1:37.35, 2:04.06 Track sloppy. Off at 6:12 EDT. Start good. Won driving.

Program #		Win	Place	Show	$2 Exacta (15-3)	$2 Trifecta (15-3-10)	$1 Superfecta (15-3-10-1)
15	Smarty Jones	$10.20	$6.20	$4.80	$65.20	$987.60	$41,380.20
3	Lion Heart		$8.20	$5.80			
10	Imperialism			$6.20			

Winner: Ch. c. by Elusive Quality–I'll Get Along, by Smile. Trained by John Servis; bred in Pennsylvania by Someday Farm.

$1,184,800—gross value and $90,000 Gold Cup. Net to winner $884,800; second $170,000; third $85,000; fourth $45,000.

448 nominations.
Medication: L—Lasix
Equipment: b—blinkers; f—front bandages

CAREER HIGHLIGHTS

YEAR	AGE	STS.	1ST	2ND	3RD	EARNINGS
2003	2	2	2	0	0	$ 49,620
2004	3	7	6	1	0	$ 7,563,535
TOTALS		**9**	**8**	**1**	**0**	***$7,613,155**

*Includes $5 million Oaklawn Park Bonus

At 2 years	WON	Maiden on 1st attempt; Pennsylvania Nursery
At 3 years	WON	Count Fleet, Southwest, Rebel, Arkansas Derby, Kentucky Derby, Preakness
	2ND	Belmont

Just Great Good Luck

HOW COULD HE LOSE? SMARTY JONES'S pedigree was outstanding. His sire, Elusive Quality, held the world record for the mile on turf, and he is related to Triple Crown winners Funny Cide, Afleet Alex, Fusaichi Pegasus, Foolish Pleasure, Secretariat, Count Fleet, Northern Dancer, and Man o' War, who, of course, is generally considered to be the best racehorse of the twentieth century. His dam, I'll Get Along, was the winningest mare of the Someday Farm in Chester County, Pennsylvania, where he was born.

Pat and Roy Chapman, who owned Smarty Jones, almost lost him. The horse's trainer, a man named Bobby Camac, and his wife were murdered by their stepson, and this tragedy, coupled with Roy Chapman's failing health, galvanized them to close down their breeding farm, selling off all the horses except two. When buyers came calling, little Smarty Jones was in a field with his mama. The buyers never saw him, so he wasn't sold—which, Roy Chapman said, was just great good luck.

In 2003 the Chapmans hired John Servis to train Smarty Jones. In July of that year, tragedy struck again. Servis was teaching Smarty the ins and outs of the starting gate when suddenly Smarty reared up and smashed his head into the

top of the gate, which made him fall in a heap, blood pouring from his nostrils. At first Servis thought he was dead. But he wasn't, though he almost lost sight in one eye. (Ironically, in the Derby he ran in, there were two one-eyed horses.)

On Derby day, the track was not the best. It had rained, stopped, and rained again. Eighteen horses went to the post, and Smarty Jones was a 4–1 favorite because he'd won the Rebel and Arkansas Stakes. Stewart Elliott, a Canadian jockey, was up.

When the gates opened, Lion Heart, Mike Smith up, barreled to the lead with a tight cluster of horses behind him. Smarty Jones was in the middle of the pack. As he cruised along at the three-eighths pole, Elliot said later, "I knew I had a loaded gun underneath me." The question was when to fire it.

At the quarter pole Elliott caught Lion Heart, and they dueled as they went down the stretch. Elliott went to the whip, and the gun went off, Smarty grabbing the lead and drawing away to win by two and three-quarter lengths.

Smarty went on to win the Preakness by eleven lengths, but like so many great horses before him, he didn't win the Belmont.

Giacomo
131st *May 7, 2005*

			Minnesota Mac
		Great Above	Ta Wee
	Holy Bull		Al Hattab
	GIACOMO	Sharon Brown	Agathea's Dawn
	Gray/roan colt		Hail to Reason
	Set Them Free	Stop the Music	Bebopper
			Tyrant
		Valseuse	Barbarossa

THE WINNER'S PEDIGREE

RACE DAY STATISTICS

HORSE	M/EQ.	WT.	PP	1/4	1/2	3/4	MILE	STR.	FIN.	JOCKEY	OWNER	ODDS TO$1
Giacomo	L	126	10	$18^{1/2}$	$18^{2\text{-}1/2}$	$18^{1\text{-}1/2}$	11^{hd}	$6^{1/2}$	$1^{1/2}$	M. E. Smith	Mr. & Mrs. Jerome S. Moss	50.30
Closing Argument	L	126	18	5^{hd}	$6^{1/2}$	6^{hd}	4^{hd}	$1^{1/2}$	$2^{1/2}$	C. H. Velasquez	Philip and Marcia Cohen	71.60
Afleet Alex	Lf	126	12	11^{hd}	$11^{2\text{-}1/2}$	$9^{1/2}$	$6^{1\text{-}1/2}$	2^1	$3^{2\text{-}1/2}$	J. Rose	Cash is King, LLC	4.50
Don't Get Mad		126	17	19^6	$19^{3\text{-}1/2}$	$19^{3\text{-}1/2}$	10^{hd}	$7^{1/2}$	$4^{2\text{-}3/4}$	T. Baze	B. Wayne Hughes	29.20
Buzzards Bay	Lf	126	20	$10^{1/2}$	10^{hd}	$7^{1/2}$	$5^{1/2}$	5^{hd}	$5^{1/2}$	M. Guidry	Fog City Stable	46.30
Wilko	L	126	14	$13^{1/2}$	14^{hd}	$16^{2\text{-}1/2}$	$13^{1\text{-}1/2}$	$10^{1/2}$	6no	C. S. Nakatani	J. Paul Reddam & Susan Roy	21.70
Bellamy Road	L	126	16	$3^{1/2}$	5^2	5^2	2^{hd}	3^{hd}	$7^{3/4}$	J. Castellano	Kinsman Stable	2.60
Andromeda's Hero	L	126	2	16^{hd}	15^2	13^{hd}	16^2	$14^{1\text{-}1/2}$	8no	R. Bejarano	Robert V. LaPenta	57.30
Flower Alley	Lb	126	7	4^{hd}	3^{hd}	2^{hd}	$7^{1\text{-}1/2}$	8^1	9^{hd}	J. F. Chavez	Melnyk Racing Stables, Inc.	41.30
High Fly	L	126	11	6^1	4^1	3^{hd}	1^{hd}	4^1	10^{nk}	J. D. Bailey	Live Oak Plantation	7.10
Greeley's Galaxy	L	126	9	17^1	$16^{1/2}$	14^{hd}	8^{hd}	$12^{2\text{-}1/2}$	$11^{2\text{-}1/4}$	K. J. Desormeaux	B. Wayne Hughes	21.00
Coin Silver	L	126	5	$14^{1/2}$	12^{hd}	$12^{1\text{-}1/2}$	$9^{1/2}$	11^1	$12^{1\text{-}1/4}$	P. A. Valenzuela	Peachtree Stable	38.60
Greater Good	L	126	8	20	20	20	$17^{1/2}$	$15^{1/2}$	$13^{3/4}$	J. McKee	Lewis G. Lakin	58.40
Noble Causeway	L	126	4	12^2	$13^{2\text{-}1/2}$	15^{hd}	12^{hd}	$13^{1/2}$	$14^{2\text{-}1/2}$	G. L. Stevens	My Meadowview Farm	12.30
Sun King	L	126	3	$9^{1/2}$	9^{hd}	8^{hd}	$15^{1\text{-}1/2}$	16^4	15^4	E. S. Prado	Tracy Farmer	15.70
Spanish Chestnut		126	13	$1^{1/2}$	$1^{1\text{-}1/2}$	$1^{1\text{-}1/2}$	3^{hd}	9^{hd}	16^7	J. Bravo	Derrick Smith & Michael Tabor	71.00
Sort It Out	L	126	1	$15^{1/2}$	17^{hd}	17^{hd}	18^4	$17^{2\text{-}1/2}$	$17^{3\text{-}1/4}$	B. Blanc	Stonerside Stable & Preferred Pals Stable	61.90
Going Wild	Lb	126	19	2^1	2^1	$4^{1/2}$	14^{hd}	$18^{5\text{-}1/2}$	$18^{3\text{-}1/2}$	J. Valdivia Jr.	Robert & Beverly Lewis	59.50
Bandini	L	126	15	7^{hd}	8^2	$11^{1\text{-}1/2}$	20	19^3	19^{12}	J. R. Velazquez	Derrick Smith & Michael Tabor	6.80
High Limit	L	126	6	8^2	7^{hd}	$10^{3\text{-}1/2}$	19^{hd}	20	20	R. A. Dominguez	Gary L. & Mary E. West	22.50

Time: :22.28, :45.38, 1:09.59, 1:35.88, 2:02.75. Track fast. Off at 6:11 EDT. Start good. Won driving.

Program #		Win	Place	Show	$2 Exacta (10-18)	$2 Trifecta (10-18-12)	$1 Superfecta (10-18-12-17)
10	Giacomo	$102.60	$45.80	$19.80	$9,814.80	$133,134.80	$864,253.50
18	Closing Argument		$70.00	$24.80			
12	Afleet Alex			$ 4.60			

Winner: Gr/ro. c. by Holy Bull–Set Them Free, by Stop the Music. Trained by John A. Shirreffs; bred in Kentucky by Mr. & Mrs. J. S. Moss.
$2,399,600—gross value and $90,000 Gold Cup. Net to winner $1,639,600; second $400,000; third $200,000; fourth $100,000; fifth $60,000.

372 nominations.
Medication: L—Lasix
Equipment: b—blinkers; f–front bandages

CAREER HIGHLIGHTS

YEAR	AGE	STS.	1ST	2ND	3RD	EARNINGS
2004	2	4	1	1	1	$ 119,440
2005	3	6	1	1	2	$1,846,876
TOTALS		**10**	**2**	**2**	**3**	**$1,966,316**

At 2 years	WON	Maiden on 2nd attempt;
		2nd Hollywood Futurity
At 3 years	WON	Kentucky Derby
	2ND	San Felipe
	3RD	Sham, Preakness;
		UNP Santa Anita Derby, Belmont Stakes

Against Big Odds

"ALICE CHANDLER," THE *New York Times* said following the running of the 2005 Kentucky Derby, "knows a thing or two about the miracle of life. She witnesses it each January when the Thoroughbred foals start hitting the ground on her farm in Lexington, Kentucky. And two Saturdays ago it took a little over two minutes for a long-shot gray colt to remind Chandler that even the worst of times can yield something worth savoring."

As she watched the 50–1 underdog colt Giacomo thunder down the stretch inside a tornado of sound to win the 131st running of the Kentucky Derby, Chandler, seventy-nine, burst into tears.

Long before he won this race, Giacomo had another opponent called Death, but he beat that too. He was born to a mare named Set Them Free on February 16, 2002, which means that his dam was pregnant with Giacomo in March 2001, shortly before a horrific disease called mare reproductive loss syndrome hit and destroyed 2,500 horse fetuses. On Mill Ridge Farm, which Chandler owned and where Giacomo was born, one-quarter of the foal crop was either aborted or born dead.

But Giacomo survived. Said Mrs. Chandler of him growing up, "He was a tough little dude."

No one knew that better than Donnie Snellings, the farm's stallion and yearling manager. "We have a thirty-acre farm for our weanlings, and he was there with about twelve others," Snellings recalled. "He was a tiny little thing. But every time I tried to go get him, he'd take off all the way to the other fence. He was loose for three days. I saw a lot of the backside of Giacomo. I knew early he could run long."

Mike Smith, aboard Giacomo, took his time in the race.

Giacomo was jammed tight between a number of horses at the beginning, but Smith did not hurry him. He worked his way between horses six wide on the far turn, but was still behind a wall of horses entering the upper stretch. Then he steered Giacomo into position for running room. It was a barn burner to the wire, Smith urging Giacomo on in the last seventy fabulous yards—anyone who has ever seen that finish will never forget it—to cross the wire first. Surprisingly, the second-place horse, Closing Argument, was a 71–1 shot. No wonder he was only second!

Barbaro
132nd *May 6, 2006*

	Roberto	Hail to Reason
		Bramalea
Dynaformer		His Majesty
BARBARO	Andover Way	On the Trail
Dark brown colt		Mr. Prospector
La Ville Rouge	Carson City	Blushing Promise
		King Bishop
	La Reine Rouge	Silver Betsy

THE WINNER'S PEDIGREE

RACE DAY STATISTICS

HORSE	M/EQ.	WT.	PP	1/4	1/2	3/4	MILE	STR.	FIN.	JOCKEY	OWNER	ODDS TO $1
Barbaro	L	126	8	$5^{1/2}$	$4^{1-1/2}$	$4^{1/2}$	1^3	1^4	$1^{6-1/2}$	E. S. Prado	Lael Stables	6.10
Bluegrass Cat	L	126	13	$8^{1/2}$	$5^{1/2}$	$6^{1/2}$	3^1	$2^{1/2}$	2^2	R. A. Dominguez	WinStar Farm, LLC	30.00
Steppenwolfer	L	126	2	$18^{1/2}$	13^{hd}	$11^{1/2}$	6^{hd}	5^1	3^1	R. J. Albarado	Robert and Lawana Low	16.30
Jazil (dh)	L	126	1	20	20	$19^{1/2}$	17^2	6^1	4	F. Jara	Shadwell Farm, LLC	24.20
Brother Derek (dh)	L	126	18	$9^{1-1/2}$	$9^{1/2}$	$14^{1/2}$	10^{hd}	$7^{1/2}$	$4^{1/2}$	A. Solis	Cecil N. Peacock	7.70
Showing Up	L	126	6	4^{hd}	3^{hd}	3^{hd}	2^{hd}	$3^{1-1/2}$	6^3	C. Valesquez	Lael Stables	26.20
Sweetnorthernsaint	Lb	126	11	12^1	11^1	$5^{1/2}$	4^{hd}	4^{hd}	7^1	K. J. Desormeaux	Joesph J. Balsamo & Ted Theos	5.50
Deputy Glitters	L	126	14	13^1	$15^{1/2}$	$16^{1/2}$	9^1	10^1	$8^{1-1/4}$	J. Lezcano	Joseph LaCombe Stables, Inc.	60.60
Point Determined	Lb	126	5	$11^{1/2}$	10^{hd}	7^1	7^{hd}	$8^{1/2}$	9^{hd}	R. Bejarano	The Robert & Beverly Lewis Estate	9.40
Seaside Retreat	L	126	15	7^{hd}	$7^{1-1/2}$	$10^{1/2}$	15^{hd}	9^{hd}	$10^{4-1/2}$	P. Husbands	William S. Farish Jr.	52.50
Storm Treasure	L	126	19	$19^{2-1/2}$	18^2	13^{hd}	12^{hd}	$11^{1/2}$	$11^{1-3/4}$	D. R. Flores	Mike McCarty	51.90
Lawyer Ron	L	126	17	$6^{1/2}$	$8^{1/2}$	9^{hd}	$8^{1/2}$	$12^{1-1/2}$	12no	J. McKee	Estate of James T. Hines Jr.	10.20
Cause to Believe	L	126	16	$15^{1/2}$	19^2	20	18^4	17^2	13^3	R. A. Baze	Peter Redekop Ltd. & Peter Abruzzo	25.90
Flashy Bull	L	126	20	16^1	17^{hd}	17^1	$14^{1/2}$	15^1	$14^{2-1/2}$	M. E. Smith	West Point Thoroughbreds, LLC	43.00
Private Vow	L	126	12	$17^{1/2}$	$16^{1/2}$	$12^{1/2}$	$11^{1/2}$	$14^{1-1/2}$	$15^{2-3/4}$	S. X. Bridgmohan	Mike McCarty	40.50
Sinister Minister	Lb	126	4	$2^{1-1/2}$	2^2	$2^{1-1/2}$	5^1	$13^{1-1/2}$	$16^{1-1/2}$	V. Espinoza	Lanni Fam Tr & Mercedes St. & Schiappa	9.70
Bob and John	Lb	126	7	$14^{1/2}$	12^1	8^{hd}	$16^{1/2}$	$16^{1/2}$	17^{nk}	G. K. Gomez	Stonerside Stable	12.90
A. P. Warrior	L	126	10	$10^{1/2}$	14^1	$18^{1/2}$	19^5	19^5	$18^{1-1/2}$	C. S. Nakatani	Stan E. Fulton	14.10
Sharp Humor	L	126	9	$3^{1/2}$	6^{hd}	$15^{1-1/2}$	20	20	$19^{7-1/2}$	M. Guidry	Purdedel Stable	30.10
Keyed Entry	L	126	3	1^{hd}	1^2	$1^{1-1/2}$	13^{hd}	$18^{2-1/2}$	20	P. A. Valenzuela	Starlight St. & Saylor & Lucarelli	28.80

Time: :22.63, :46.07, 1:10.88, 1:37.02, 2:01.36. Track fast. Off at 6:15 EDT. Start good for all but Barbaro. Won driving.

Program #		Win	Place	Show	$2 Exacta (8-13)	$2 Trifecta (8-13-2)	$1 Superfecta (8-13-2-1)	$1 Superfecta (8-13-2-18)
8	Barbaro	$14.20	$ 8.00	$ 6.00	$587.00	$11,418.40	$84,860.40	$59,839.00
13	Bluegrass Cat		$28.40	$15.40				
2	Steppenwolfer			$ 7.80				

Winner: Dk. b or b. c. by Dynaformer–La Ville Rouge, by Carson City. Trainer Michael R. Matz Bred in Kentucky by Mr. & Mrs. M. Roy Jackson. $2,213,200—gross value and $90,000 Gold Cup. Net to winner $1,453,200; second $400,000; third $200,000.

440 nominations.
Medication: L—Lasix
Equipment: b—blinkers

Career Highlights

YEAR	AGE	STS.	1ST	2ND	3RD	EARNINGS
2005	2	2	2	0	0	$ 99,000
2006	3	5	4	0	0	$2,203,200
TOTALS		7	6	**0**	**0**	**$2,302,200**

At 2 years	WON	Laurel Futurity, Maiden on 1st attempt
At 3 years	WON	Kentucky Derby, Florida Derby, Holy Bull, Tropical Park Derby
	DNF	Preakness

Champion

ON THE NIGHT OF APRIL 29, 2003, A FOAL was born in Kentucky to a mare named La Ville Rouge. As usual, the owners and breeders, Gretchen and Roy Jackson, hoped that this colt would finally be the champion they had been trying to produce for thirty years.

They named him Barbaro.

As Barbaro grew, the Jacksons' hopes rose. They became more confident that this was a very special horse. For one thing, Barbaro could outrun anything on their property, and for another, though he was a mild-mannered and playful colt (he loved to get on his back so people could tickle his belly), he had what breeders call "the look of eagles" in his eyes: knowing, confident, fierce.

Convinced that he was special, they found the perfect trainer for him and their other horses, a man named Michael Matz, who is not only a great trainer but, like the Jacksons, loves and respects horses. And Matz liked Barbaro too. Months were spent training Barbaro, and as each day went by Matz and the Jacksons became more and more convinced: This is one great horse.

In the fall of 2005, it was time to test their assumptions. Just how good was Barbaro?

They entered him in some races on turf, and he won handily. But, they wondered, can he run on dirt? They entered him in a race on a dirt track and, watching him not run but fly, Matz says, "made me shiver."

He had won five races in a row, and everyone knew his next stop: Churchill Downs, the first Saturday in May of 2006.

It was a heady time for the Jacksons. Not only had they never entered a horse in the Kentucky Derby, they had literally never been there themselves! They arrived with Barbaro and stood on the edge of what might be the fulfillment of a dream that went beyond him being a champion, to being the winner of the Kentucky Derby.

All the stars were in place. Barbaro had been trained by a great trainer; astride him was Edgar Prado—one of only nineteen jockeys who have won more than 5,000 races—and in practice Barbaro had unleashed some astonishing times for the mile and a quarter. There was only one question. Critics said that Barbaro had not had enough tuning up in actual races before the Derby, that it had been more than a month since his last race, and he had only raced once in thirteen weeks.

Matz stood by his guns, and the Jacksons backed him. Many years ago, Matz explained, when he was a show jumper, he tuned up his horse so much that when the real competition occurred, the horse had nothing left. Matz vowed that would not happen again.

At around 5:45, twenty horses were loaded in the starting gate, ready to run in the greatest race in the world—two minutes to ignominy, or two minutes to glory.

On the sidelines, waiting, waiting, the Jacksons, people who have known each other for almost fifty years, waited again, hoping, dreaming, standing in the middle of their storybook.

The gates opened, and Barbaro stumbled, but Prado got him to recover quickly, and he was soon in fourth position behind the speedy Keyed Entry and Sinister Minister. Then he was just cruising along, just, hopefully, waiting to strike—if he could strike.

At the final turn the Jacksons knew that this was where Barbaro must move—if he could. Was Matz right? Were the Jacksons right? Just what kind of horse was turning into the stretch?

Barbaro showed the world. With nary a single whip stroke, Barbaro burst through into the clear and roared down the stretch—the announcer yelling "It's all Barbaro"—pure power, his greatness showing with every stride, and each stride taking him farther and farther away from those behind him. The crowd hammered the sky apart with noise.

And the dream came true.

And there he is, America, there he is, world. Move over for Barbaro! He blasted across the finish line six and a half lengths to the good, the largest Derby victory margin in sixty years. And someone once said, referring to the Jacksons, "It couldn't happen to nicer people."

Final Strides

If you can't make it to the Kentucky Derby, it doesn't mean that you can't be there. How? Have a Derby party. If you do it right, your friends will be galloping to it next year and for years to come.

Perhaps the key to a successful Derby party is to make it as authentic as possible.

First, send out invitations that look like Derby tickets. You'll find pictures of tickets on the Internet.

Next, dress the part. Men, wear your Sunday best, make sure you're well barbered and that your shoes are polished to a high gloss (assuming they're leather!).

Women, get hold of a dress that you know would look good strolling along the infield at Churchill Downs, and shop here, there, and everywhere for a a hat people will look at and do a double take. Almost from the beginning of the Derby women (and men) were turning the Derby walkways into fashion runways, but with the accent on flamboyant, even outlandish hats—crazed chapeaus featuring birds' nests, flowers, filled mint juleps, just about anything you could think of. But we can guarantee the overall effect: men used to having their helpmates walking around in jeans and T-shirts will look twice—or more.

Of course you will need a big-screen TV (rented, borrowed, or bought). Decorate your party room with lots of red roses, and make sure you have a copy of "My Old Kentucky Home" to play. Order traditional Kentucky Derby glasses for the event, as well as race programs. As party favors, your guests can keep their commemorative glasses. (All party items can be ordered from the Kentucky Derby Web site at the Derby Store. You can also order T-shirts for giveaways.)

Run your own betting pools: Set a price per ticket, $2.00 minimum wager. Using a slip of paper, have each of your guests write their name along with their choice of the winning horse. Guests can purchase as many tickets as they like. When the official results come in, count the total winning tickets, divide that number into the total money, and you have your payoff for each winning ticket.

Of course no Kentucky Derby party would be complete without serving mint juleps. The recipe is given in Part I of this book, but please note that this is not lemonade. Drink too many, and you'll feel like you were lying down on the first turn when the horses go by.

You should also have some traditional mouthwatering Kentucky fare (don't hold it against the state that Colonel Sanders was from there!). A traditional Kentucky Derby party brunch would consist of Benedictine dip, baked ham with maple mustard sauce, green beans with lemon, Kentucky Derby creamy cheddar grits soufflé, Kentucky country ham salad, cream biscuits, and Kentucky burgoo—and don't forget the pecan pie. Recipes for all can be found on foodnetwork.com. (Excuse us; we're going out for a snack!)

The big idea is to get yourself and your guests emotionally involved in the race. To do this, before they view the race, tell them to read as many of the race stories in the book as they can, and then they will get a much clearer sense that those horses standing in the starting gate are not just running a race. They are carrying dreams—just like us.

Also, tune in early to the TV coverage so everyone can gather facts on the horses and the people behind—and on—them this year. It will also help get guests (and you) emotionally involved, get hearts and minds pointing to one horse and rider rather than others. The more people know, the deeper the hook will go in.

Then, sit back, take a sip of mint julep, and watch the race. And when those horses thunder around the final turn into Heartbreak Lane, and what you hear makes you feel like you should have passed out complimentary earplugs, you'll know your party is a resounding success.

As horsemen say, have a good ride!

—Pam and Tom

Acknowledgments

The writing of a book of this scale, or any complete history, for that matter, requires an enormous amount of work from the writers and their sources. We would like to thank all who contributed in the making of *Two Minutes to Glory*. We could not have done it without you all, and we are truly indebted.

First, thanks to Churchill Downs Incorporated for partnering with us to make this book, and to help make it, we believe, one of the best and most complete books ever to be written on the Kentucky Derby. Without their help or various contributions to this book, we would not have been able to compile the depth of detailed expertise that makes history so much better. Special thanks to the following: Julie Koenig-Loignon, Vice President of Communications, Karl Schmitt, Senior Vice President of Special Projects, and Tony Terry, Director of Publicity.

Thanks to Tobey Roush from Licensing Partners International. You have been our main man all the way through from day one. This book wouldn't have been possible without all the work that you have put into it, and for your belief in us we are truly grateful. And we are thankful, too, to all the other behind-the-scenes folks at LPI who helped as well.

Thanks to Matthew Benjamin, our editor at HarperCollins, who has provided insight and guidance at every step of the process and whose invaluable input, we know, is going to make a good book a lot better.

Thanks to Ann Tatum, curator at the Kentucky Derby photo Archives–Kinetic Corporation. Without your help, Ann, this book wouldn't be half the book it is now. You have provided us with stirring and beautiful photos that make the heart race and help bring the Kentucky Derby experience that much closer to readers. Thanks so much.

And thanks to Chris Philbin, who helped us so much with her meticulous inputting of chart data and so much more. You, too, have added significantly to the value of this book; in any history, details count greatly.

Kentucky Derby Winners at a Glance

NO.	YEAR	WINNER	SIRE	BREEDER	OWNER	TRAINER	FAVORITE	WINNER ODDS
1	1875	Aristides, ch. c.	*Leamington	H. Price McGrath	H. Price McGrath	Ansel Williamson	Winner (entry)	2–1
2	1876	Vagrant, br. g.	Virgil	M. H. Senford	William Astor	James Williams	Winner	9–5
3	1877	Baden-Baden, ch. c.	*Australian	A. J. Alexander	Daniel Swigert	Ed Brown	Leonard (7–5)	8–1
4	1878	Day Star, ch. c.	Star Davis	J. M. Clay	T. J. Nichols	Lee Paul	Himyar (14)	3–1
5	1879	Lord Murphy, b. c.	Pat Malloy	J. T. Carter	Geo. W Darden & Co.	George Rice	Winner	11–10
6	1880	Fonso, ch. c.	King Alfonso	A. J. Alexander	J. S. Shawhan	Tice Hutsell	Kimball (3–5)	7–1
7	1881	Hindoo, b. c.	Virgil	Daniel Swigert	Dwyer Bros.	James Rowe Sr.	Winner	1–3
8	1882	Apollo, ch. g.	*Ashstead or Lever	Daniel Swigert	Morris & Patton	Green B. Morris	Runnymede (15)	10–1
9	1883	Leonatus, b. c.	Longfellow	J. Henry Miller	Chinn & Morgan	John McGinty	Winner	9–5
10	1884	Buchanan, ch. c.	*Buckden	Cottrill & Guest	Cottrill & Brown	William Bird	Audrain (2–1)	3–1
11	1885	Joe Cotton, ch. c.	King Alfonso	A. J. Alexander	J. T. Williams	Alex Perry	Winner	Even
12	1886	Ben Ali, br. c.	Virgil	Daniel Swigert	J. B. Haggin	Jim Murphy	Winner	1.72–1
13	1887	Montrose, b. c.	Duke of Montrose	Milton Young	Labold Bros.	John McGinly	Banburg (7–5)	10–1
14	1888	Macbeth II, br. g.	Macduff	Rufus Lisle	Chicago Stable	John Campbell	Gallifet/Alexandria (even)	6–1
15	1889	Spokane, ch. c.	Hyder Ali	Noah Armstrong	Noah Armstrong	John Rodegap	Proctor Knott (1–2)	6–1
16	1890	Riley, b. c.	Longfellow	C. H. Durkee	Edward Corrigan	Edward Corrigan	Robespierre (even)	4–1
17	1891	Kingman, b. c.	*Glengarry	A. C. Franklin	Jacobin Stable	Dud Allen	Winner	1–2
18	1892	Azra, b. c.	Reform	George J. Long	Bashford Manor	John H. Morris	Winner	3–2
19	1893	Lookout, ch. c.	Troubadour	Scoggan Bros.	Cushing & Orth	William McDaniel	Winner (entry)	7–10
20	1894	Chant, b. c.	Falsetto	A. J. Alexander	Leigh & Rose	Eugene Leigh	Winner	1–2
21	1895	Halma, blk. c.	Hanover	Eastin & Larrabie	Byron McClelland	Byron McClelland	Winner	1–3
22	1896	Ben Brush, b. c.	Bramble	Clay & Woodford	M. F. Dwyer	Hardy Campbell	Winner	1–2
23	1897	Typhoon II, ch. c	*Top Gallant	John B. Ewing	J. C. Cahn	J. C. Cahn	Ornament (even)	3–1
24	1898	Plaudit, br. c.	Himyar	Dr. J. D. Neet	John E. Madden	John E. Madden	Lieber Karl (1–3)	3–1
25	1899	Manuel, b. c.	Bob Miles	George J. Long	A. H. & D. H. Morris	Robert J. Walden	Winner	11–20
26	1900	Lieut. Gibson, b. c.	G. W. Johnson	Baker & Gentry	Charles H. Smith	Charles H. Hughes	Winner	7–10
27	1901	His Eminence, b. c.	Falsetto	O. H. Chenault	Frank B. Van Meter	Frank B. Van Meter	Alard Scheck (7–10)	3–1
28	1902	Alan-a-Dale, ch. c.	Halma	Thomas McDowell	Thomas McDowell	Thomas McDowell	Abe Frank (3–5)	3–2
29	1903	Judge Himes, ch. c.	*Esher	Johnson N. Camden	Charles Ellison	J. P. Mayberry	Early (3–5)	10–1
30	1904	Elwood, b. c.	Free Knight	Mrs. J. B. Prather	Mrs. Charles Durnell	Charles E. Durnell	Proceeds (even)	15–1
31	1905	Agile, b. c.	Sir Dixon	E. F. Clay	Sam S. Brown	Robert Tucker	Winner	1–3
32	1906	Sir Huon, b. c.	Falsetto	George J. Long	George J. Long	Peter Coyne	Winner	11–10

NO.	YEAR	WINNER	SIRE	BREEDER	OWNER	TRAINER	FAVORITE	WINNER ODDS
33	1907	Pink Star, b. c.	Pink Coat	J. Hal Woodford	J. Hal Woodford	W. H. Fizer	Red Gauntlet (1.50–1)	15–1
34	1908	Stone Street, b. c.	Longstreet	J. B. Higgin	C. E. & J. W. Hamilton	John W. Hall	Sir Cleges (1.74–1)	23.72-1
35	1909	Wintergreen, b. c.	Dick Welles	J. B. Respess	Jerome B. Respess	Charles Mack	Winner	1.96–1
36	1910	Donau, b. c.	*Woolsthorpe	Milton Young	William Gerst	George Ham	Winner	1.65–1
37	1911	Meridian, b. c.	Broomstick	C. L. Harrison	R. F. Carman	Albert Ewing	Governor Gray (even)	2.90–1
38	1912	Worth, br. c.	*Knight of the Thistle	R. H. McCarter Potter	H. C. Hallenbeck	Frank M. Taylor	Winner	.80–1
39	1913	Donerail, b. c.	*McGee	T. P. Hayes	T. P. Hayes	T. P. Hayes	Ten Point (1.20–1)	91.45 –1
40	1914	Old Rosebud, b. g.	Uncle	John E. Madden	Hamilton C. Applegate	Frank D. Weir	Winner	.85–1
41	1915	Regret, ch. f.	Broomstick	H. P. Whitney	H. P. Whitney	James Rowe Sr.	Winner	2.65–1
42	1916	George Smith, blk. c.	*Out of Reach	Chinn & Forsythe	John Sanford	Hollie Hughes	Thunderer/Dominant (1.05–1)	4.15–1
43	1917	*Omar Khayyam, ch. c.	Marco	Sir John Robinson	Billings & Johnson	C. T. Patterson	Ticket (1.45–1)	12.80-1
44	1918	Exterminator, ch. g.	*McGee	F. D. Knight	Willis Sharpe Kilmer	Henry McDaniel	*War Cloud (1.45–1)	29.60-1
45	1919	Sir Barton, ch. c.	*Star Shoot	Madden & Goach	J. K. L. Ross	H. Guy Bedwell	Sailor/Eternal (2.10–1)	2.60–1
46	1920	Paul Jones, br. g.	*Sea King	John E. Madden	Ral Parr	William Garth	Upset/Damask/Wildair (1.65–1)	16.20-1
47	1921	Behave Yourself, br. c.	Marathon	E. R. Bradley	E. R. Bradley	H. J. Thompson	Prudery/Tryster (1.10–1)	8.65–1
48	1922	Morvich, br. c.	Runnymede	A. B. Spreckels	Ben Block	Fred Burlew	Winner	1.20–1
49	1923	Zev, br. c.	The Finn	John E. Madden	Rancocas Stable	D. J. Leary	Enchantment/Rialto/ Picketer/Cherry Pie (2.30–1)	19.20-1
50	1924	Black Gold, blk. c.	Black Toney	Mrs. Rosa M. Hoots	Mrs. Rosa M. Hoots	Hanly Webb	Winner	1.75–1
51	1925	Flying Ebony, blk. c.	The Finn	John E. Madden	Gifford A. Cochran	William B. Duke	Quatrain (1.95–1)	3.15–1
52	1926	Bubbling Over, ch. c.	*North Star III	Idle Hour Stock Farm	Idle Hour Stock Farm	H. J. Thompson	Winner (entry)	1.90–1
53	1927	Whiskery, br. c.	Whisk Broom II	H. P. Whitney	H. P. Whitney	Fred Hopkins	Winner (entry)	2.40–1
54	1928	Reigh Count, ch. c.	*Sunreigh	Willis Sharpe Kilmer	Mrs. John D. Hertz	Bert S. Michell	Winner (entry)	2.06–1
55	1929	Clyde Van Dusen, ch. g.	Man o' War	H. P. Gardner	H. P. Gardner	Clyde Van Dusen	Blue Larkspur/ Bay Beauty (1.71–1)	3-1
56	1930	Gallant Fox, b. c.	*Sir Gallahadion	Belair Stud	Belair Stud	James Fitzsimmons	Winner	1.19–1
57	1931	Twenty Grand, b. c.	*St. Germans	Greentree Stable	Greentree Stable	James Rowe Jr.	Winner (entry)	.88–1
58	1932	Burgoo King, ch. c.	Bubbling Over	Idle Hour Stock Farm and H. N. Davis	E. R. Bradley	H. J. Thompson	Tick On (1.84–1)	5.62–1
59	1933	Brokers Tip, br. c.	Black Toney	Idle Hour Stock Farm	E. R. Bradley	H. J. Thompson	Ladysman/Pomponius (1.43–1)	8.93-1
60	1934	Cavalcade, br. c.	*Lancegaye	F. W. Armstrong	Brookmeade Stable	Robert A. Smith	Winner (entry)	1.50–1
61	1935	Omaha, ch. c.	Gallant Fox	Belair Stud	Belair Stud	James Fitzsimmons	Nellie Flag (3.80–1)	4.00–1
62	1936	Bold Venture, ch. c.	*St. Germans	Morton L. Schwartz	Morton L. Schwartz	Max Hirsch	Brevity (.80–1)	20.50-1
63	1937	War Admiral, br. c.	Man o' War	Samuel D. Riddle	Glen Riddle Farms	George Conway	Winner	1.60–1
64	1938	Lawrin, br. c.	Insco	Herbert Woolf	Woolford Farm	Ben A. Jones	Fighting Fox (1.40–1)	8.60–1
65	1939	Johnstown, b. c.	Jamestown	A. B. Hancock	Belair Stud	James Fitzsimmons	Winner	.60–1
66	1940	Gallahadion, b. c.	*Sir Gallahad III	R. A. Fairbairn	Milky Way Farms	Roy Waldron	Bimelech (.40–1)	35.20-1
67	1941	Whirlaway, ch. c.	*Blenheim II	Calumet Farm	Calumet Farm	Ben A. Jones	Winner	2.90–1
68	1942	Shut Out, ch. c.	Equipoise	Greentree Stable	Greentree Stable	John M. Gaver	Winner (entry)	1.90–1
69	1943	Count Fleet, br. c.	Reigh Count	Mrs. John D. Hertz	Mrs. John D. Hertz	G. Don Cameron	Winner	.40–1
70	1944	Pensive, ch. c.	Hyperion	Calumet Farm	Calumet Farm	Ben A. Jones	Stir Up (1.40–1)	7.10–1
71	1945	Hoop Jr., b. c.	*Sir Gallahad III	R. A Fairbairn	Fred W. Hooper	Ivan H. Parke	Pot O' Luck (3.30–1)	3.70–1
72	1946	Assault, ch. c.	Bold Venture	King Ranch	King Ranch	Max Hirsch	Lord Boswell/ Knockdown/Perfect Bahram (1.10–1)	8.20– 1

NO.	YEAR	WINNER	SIRE	BREEDER	OWNER	TRAINER	FAVORITE	WINNER ODDS
73	1947	Jet Pilot, ch. c.	*Blenheim II	A. B. Hancock and Mrs. R. A. Van Clief	Maine Chance Farm	Tom Smith	Phalanx (2.00–1)	5.40–1
74	1948	Citation, b. c.	Bull Lea	Calumet Farm	Calumet Farm	Ben A. Jones	Winner (entry)	.40–1
75	1949	Ponder, dk. b. c.	Pensive	Calumet Farm	Calumet Farm	Ben A. Jones	Olympia (.80–1)	16.00–1
76	1950	Middleground, ch. c.	Bold Venture	King Ranch	King Ranch	Max Hirsch	Your Host (1.60–1)	7.90–1
77	1951	Count Turf, b. c.	Count Fleet	Dr. & Mrs. F. P. Miller	Jack J. Amiel	Sol Rutchick	Battle Morn (2.80–I)	14.60–1
78	1952	Hill Gail, dk. b. c.	Bull Lea	Calumet Farm	Calumet Farm	Ben A. Jones	Winner	1.10–1
79	1953	Dark Star, br. c.	*Royal Gem II	Warner L. Jones Jr.	Cain Hoy Stable	Eddie Hayward	Native Dancer (.70–1)	24.90–1
80	1954	Determine, gr. c.	*Alibhai	Dr. Eslie Asbury	Andrew J. Crevolin	Willie Molter	Correlation (3.00–1)	4.30–1
81	1955	Swaps, ch. c.	*Khaled	Rex C. Ellsworth	Rex C. Ellsworth	Mesh A. Tenney	Nashua (1.30–1)	2.80–1
82	1956	Needles, b. c.	Ponder	William E. Leach	D & H Stable	Hugh L. Fontaine	Winner	1.60–1
83	1957	Iron Liege, b. c.	Bull Lea	Calumet Farm	Calumet Farm	H. A. Jones	Bold Ruler (1.20–1)	8.40–1
84	1958	Tim Tam, dk. b. c.	Tom Fool	Calumet Farm	Calumet Farm	H. A. Jones	Jewel's Reward/Ebony Pearl (2.00–1)	2.10–1
85	1959	*Tomy Lee, b. c.	*Tudor Minstrel	D. H. Wills	Mr. & Mrs. F. Turner Jr.	Frank Childs	First Landing (3.60–1)	3.70–1
86	1960	Venetian Way, ch. c.	Royal Coinage	John W. Greathouse	Sunny Blue Farm	Vic J. Sovinski	Tompion (1.10–1)	6.30–1
87	1961	Carry Back, br. c.	Saggy	Jack A. Price	Mrs. Katherine Price	Jack A. Price	Winner	2.50–1
88	1962	Decidedly, gr. c.	Determine	George A. Pope Jr.	El Peco Ranch	Horatio A. Luro	Ridan (1.10–1)	8.70–1
89	1963	Chateaugay, ch. c.	Swaps	John W. Galbrealth	Darby Dan Farm	Jimmy P. Conway	Candy Spots (1.50–1)	9.40–1
90	1964	Northern Dancer, b. c.	Nearctic	E. P. Taylor	Windfields Farm	Horatio A. Luro	Hill Rise (1.40–1)	3.40–1
91	1965	Lucky Debonair, b. c.	Vertex	Danada Farm	Mrs. Ada L. Rice	Frank Calrone	Bold Lad (2.00–1)	4.30–1
92	1966	Kauai King, dk. b./br. c.	Native Dancer	Pine Brook Farm	Ford Stable	Henry Forrest	Winner	2.40–1
93	1967	Proud Clarion, b. c.	Hail to Reason	John W. Galbreath	Darby Dan Farm	Loyd Gentry	Damascus (1.70–1)	30.10–1
94	1968	Forward Pass, b. c.	On-and-On	Calumet Farm	Calumet Farm	Henry Forrest	Winner	2.20–1
95	1969	Majestic Prince, ch. c.	Raise a Native	Leslie Combs II	Frank McMahon	John Longden	Winner	1.40–1
96	1970	Dust Commander, ch. c.	Bold Commander	Pullen Bros.	Robert E. Lehmann	Don Combs	My Dad George (2.80–1)	15.30–1
97	1971	Canonero II, b. c.	*Pretendre	Edward B. Benjamin	Edgar Caibett	Juan Arias	Unconscious (2.80–1)	8.70–1
98	1972	Riva Ridge, b. c.	First Landing	Meadow Stud, Inc.	Meadow Stable	Lucien Laurin	Winner	1.50–1
99	1973	Secretariat, ch. c.	Bold Ruler	Meadow Stud, Inc.	Meadow Stable	Lucien Laurin	Winner (entry)	1.50–1
100	1974	Cannonade, b. c.	Bold Bidder	John M. Olin	John M. Olin	Woody C. Stephens	Winner (entry)	1.50–1
101	1975	Foolish Pleasure, b. c.	What a Pleasure	Waldemar Farms, Inc.	John L. Greer	LeRoy Jolley	Winner	1.90–1
102	1976	Bold Forbes, dk. b./br. c.	Irish Castle	Eaton Farms & Red Bull Stable	E. R. Tizol	Laz Barrera	Honest Pleasure (.40–1)	3.00–1
103	1977	Seattle Slew, dk. b./br. c.	Bold Reasoning	Ben S. Castleman	Karen L. Taylor	W. H. Turner Jr.	Winner	.50–1
104	1978	Affirmed, ch. c.	Exclusive Native	Harbor View Farm	Harbor View Farm	Laz Barrera	Alydar (1.20–1)	1.80–1
105	1979	Spectacular Bid, gr. c.	Bold Bidder	Mrs. W. M. Jason & Mrs. Wm. Gilmore	Hawksworth Farm	Grover G. Delp	Winner	.60–1
106	1980	Genuine Risk, ch. f.	Exclusive Native	Mrs. G. W. Humphrey	Mrs. B. R. Firestone	LeRoy Jolley	Rockhill Native (2.10–1)	13.30–1
107	1981	Pleasant Colony, dk. b./br. c.	His Majesty	Thomas M. Evans	Buckland Farm	John Campo	Proud Appeal/Golden Derby (2.30–1)	3.50–1
108	1982	Gato Del Sol, gr. c.	*Cougar II	A. Hancock III & L. Peters	A. Hancock III & L. Peters	Edwin Gregson	Air Forbes Won (2.70–1)	21.20–1
109	1983	Sunny's Halo, ch. c.	Halo	David J. Foster Racing Stable	David Foster	David C. Cross Jr.	Marfa/Balboa Native/Total Departure (2.40–1)	2.50–1
110	1984	Swale, dk. b./br. c.	Seattle Slew	Claiborne Farm	Claiborne Farm	Woody C. Stephens	Life's Magic/Althea (2.80–1)	3.40–1
111	1985	Spend a Buck, b. c.	Buckaroo	Rowe Harper	Hunter Farm	Cam Gambolati	Chief's Crown (1.20–1)	4.10–1

NO.	YEAR	WINNER	SIRE	BREEDER	OWNER	TRAINER	FAVORITE	WINNER ODDS
112	1986	Ferdinand, ch. c.	Nijinsky II	Howard B. Keck	Mrs. Elizabeth Keck	C. Whittingham	Snow Chief (2.10–1)	17.70–1
113	1987	Alysheba, b.c.	Alydar	Preston Madden	D & P Scharbauer	Jack Van Berg	Demons Begone (2.20–1)	8.40–1
114	1988	Winning Colors, ro. f.	Caro (Ire)	Echo Valley Horse Farm, Inc.	Eugene V. Klein	D. Wayne Lukas	Private Terms (3.40–1)	3.40–1
115	1989	Sunday Silence, dk. b./br. c.	Halo	Oak Cliff Thor. Ltd.	A. Hancock III, C. Whittingham & Dr. E. Gaillard	C. Whittingham	Easy Goer/Awe Inspiring (.80–1)	3.10–1
116	1990	Unbridled, b. c.	Fappiano	Tartan Farms Corp.	Mrs. Frances A. Genter Stable Inc.	Carl Nafzger	Mister Frisky (1.90–1)	10.80–1
117	1991	Strike the Gold, ch. c.	Alydar	Calumet Farm	B. Giles Brophy, Wm. J. Condren & Jos. M. Cornacchia	Nick Zito	Hansel (.50–1)	4.80–1
118	1992	Lil E. Tee, b. c.	At the Threshold	Larry Littman	W. Cal Partee	Lynn Whiting	Arazi (.90–1)	16.80–1
119	1993	Sea Hero, b.c.	Polish Navy	Paul Mellon	Paul Mellon	MacKenzie Miller	Prairie Bayou (4.40–1)	12.90–1
120	1994	Go for Gin, b.c.	Cormorant	Pamela du Pont Darmstadt	Wm. J. Condren & Jos. M. Cornacchi	Nick Zito	Holy Bull (2.20–1)	9.10–1
121	1995	Thunder Gulch, ch.c.	Gulch	Peter M. Brant	Michael Tabor	D. Wayne Lukas	TimberCountry/ Serena's Song (3.40–1)	24.50–1
122	1996	Grindstone, dk. b./br. c.	Unbridled	Overbrook Farm	Overbrook Farm	D. Wayne Lukas	Unbridled's Song (3.50–1)	5.90–1
123	1997	Silver Charm, gr. c.	Silver Buck	Mary Lou Wooton	Robert & Beverly Lewis	Bob Baffert	Captain Bodgit (3.10–1)	4.00–1
124	1998	Real Quiet, b. c.	Quiet American	Little Hill Farm	Michael E. Pegram	Bob Baffert	Indian Charlie (2.70–1)	5.40–1
125	1999	Charismatic, ch. c.	Summer Squall	Parrish Hill Farm & W.S. Farish	Robert B. & Beverly J. Lewis	D. Wayne Lukas	General Challenge (entry) (4.80–1)	31.30–1
126	2000	Fusaichi Pegasus, b. c.	Mr. Prospector	A. B. Hancock III & Stonerside Ltd.	Fusao Sekiguchi	Neil D. Drysdale	Fusaichi Pegasus	2.30–1
127	2001	Monarchos, gr. c.	Maria's Mon	J. D. Squires	John C. Oxley	John T. Ward Jr.	Point Given (2–1)	9–1
128	2002	War Emblem, dk. b./br. c.	Our Emblem	Charles Nuckols Jr. & Sons (KY.)	The Thoroughbred Corp.	Bob Baffert	Harlan's Holiday (6.00–1)	20.50 1
129	2003	Funny Cide, ch. g.	Distorted Humor	WinStar Farm (NY)	Sackatoga Stables	Barclay Tagg	Empire Maker (2.50–1)	12.80–1
130	2004	Smarty Jones, ch. c.	Elusive Quality	Someday Farm	Someday Farm	John Servis	Smarty Jones (4.10–1)	4.10–1
131	2005	Giacomo, gr/ro. c.	Holy Bull	Mr. & Mrs. J. S. Moss	Mr. & Mrs. J .S. Moss	J. A. Shirreffs	Bellamy Road (2.60–1)	50.30–1
132	2006	Barbaro, dk. b./br. c.	Dynaformer	Mr. & Mrs. M. Roy Jackson	Lael Stables	Michael Matz	Brother Derek (3–1)	6.10–1

Race Day Statistics: 1875–2006

DATE	WINNER	JOCKEY	SECOND	THIRD	NOMINATIONS	STARTERS	NET TO WINNER	TIME	TRACK
May 17, 1875	Aristides	O. Lewis	Volcano	Verdigris	42	15	2,850	2:37¾	Fast
May 15, 1876	Vagrant	B. Swim	Creedmore	Harry Hill	34	11	2,950	2:38¼	Fast
May 22, 1877	Baden-Baden	W. Walker	Leonard	King William	41	11	3,300	2:38	Fast
May 21, 1878	Day Star	J. Carter	Himyar	Leveler	56	9	4,050	2:37¼	Dusty
May 20, 1879	Lord Murphy	C. Shauer	Falsetto	Strathmore	46	9	3,550	2:37	Fast
May 18, 1880	Fonso	G. Lewis	Kimball	Bancroft	47	5	3,800	2:37½	Dusty
May 17, 1881	Hindoo	J. McLaughlin	Lelex	Alfambra	62	6	4,410	2:40	Fast
May 16, 1882	Apollo	B. Hurd	Runnymede	Bengal	64	14	4,560	2:40¼	Good
May 23, 1883	Leonatus	W. Donohue	Drake Carter	Lord Raglan	50	7	3,760	2:43	Heavy
May 16, 1884	Buchanan	I. Murphy	Loftin	Audrain	51	9	3,990	2:40¼	Good
May 14, 1885	Joe Cotton	E. Henderson	Bersan	Ten Booker	69	10	4,630	2:37¼	Good
May 14, 1886	Ben Ali	P. Duffy	Blue Wing	Free Knight	107	10	4,890	2:36½	Fast
May 11, 1887	Montrose	I. Lewis	Jim Gore	Jacobin	86	7	4,200	2:39¼	Fast
May 14, 1888	Macbeth II	G. Covington	Gallifet	White	95	7	4,740	2:38¼	Fast
May 9, 1889	Spokane	T. Kiley	Proctor Knott	Once Again	94	8	4,880	2:34½	Fast
May 14, 1890	Riley	I. Murphy	Bill Letcher	Robespierre	115	6	5,460	2:45	Muddy
May 13, 1891	Kingman	I. Murphy	Balgowan	High Tariff	83	4	4,550	2:52¼	Slow
May 11, 1892	Azra	A. Clayton	Huron	Phil Dwyer	68	3	4,230	2:41½	Heavy
May 10, 1893	Lookout	E. Kunze	Plutus	Boundless	60	6	3,840	2:39¼	Fast
May 15, 1894	Chant	F. Goodale	Pearl Song	Sigurd	55	5	4,020	2:41	Fast
May 6, 1895	Halma	J. Perkins	Basso	Laureate	57	4	2,970	2:37½	Fast
May 6, 1896	Ben Brush	W. Simms	Ben Eder	Semper Ego	171	8	4,850	2:07¾	Dusty
May 12, 1897	Typhoon II	F. Garner	Ornament	Dr. Catlett	159	6	4,850	2:12½	Heavy
May 4, 1898	Plaudit	W. Simms	Lieber Karl	Isabey	179	4	4,850	2:09	Good
May 4, 1899	Manuel	F. Taral	Corsini	Mazo	151	5	4,850	2:12	Fast
May 3, 1900	Lieut. Gibson	J. Boland	Florizar	Thrive	131	7	4,850	2:06¼	Fast
April 29, 1901	His Eminence	J. Winkfield	Sannazarro	Driscoll	145	5	4,850	2:07¾	Fast
May 3, 1902	Alan-a-Dale	J. Winkfield	Inventor	The Rival	112	4	4,850	2:08¾	Fast
May 2, 1903	Judge Himes	H. Booker	Early	Bourbon	140	6	4,850	2:09	Fast
May 2, 1904	Elwood	F. Prior	Ed Tierney	Brancas	140	5	4,850	2:08½	Fast
May 10, 1905	Agile	J. Martin	Ram's Horn	Layson	145	3	4,850	2:10¾	Heavy
May 2, 1906	Sir Huon	R. Troxler	Lady Navarre	James Reddick	110	6	4,850	2:08⅘	Fast

DATE	WINNER	JOCKEY	SECOND	THIRD	NOMINATIONS	STARTERS	NET TO WINNER	TIME	TRACK
May 6, 1907	Pink Star	A. Minder	Zal	Ovelando	128	6	4,850	2:12³⁄₅	Heavy
May 5, 1908	Stone Street	A. Pickens	Sir Cleges	Dunvegan	114	8	4,850	2:15¹⁄₅	Heavy
May 3, 1909	Wintergreen	V. Powers	Miami	Dr. Barkley	117	10	4,850	2:08¹⁄₅	Slow
May 10, 1910	Donau	F. Herbert	Joe Morris	Fighting Bob	117	7	4,850	2:06²⁄₅	Fast
May 13, 1911	Meridian	G. Archibald	Governor Gray	Colston	117	7	4,850	2:05	Fast
May 11, 1912	Worth	C. H. Shilling	Duval	Flamma	131	7	4,850	2:09²⁄₅	Muddy
May 10, 1913	Donerail	R. Goose	Ten Point	Gowell	32	8	5,475	2:04⁴⁄₅	Fast
May 9, 1914	Old Rosebud	J. McCabe	Hodge	Bronzewing	47	7	9,125	2:03²⁄₅	Fast
May 8, 1915	Regret	J. Notter	Pebbles	Sharpshooter	68	16	11,450	2:05²⁄₅	Fast
May 13, 1916	George Smith	J. Loftus	Star Hawk	Franklin	56	9	9,750	2:04	Fast
May 12, 1917	Omar Khayyam	C. Borel	Ticket	Midway	76	15	16,600	2:04³⁄₅	Fast
May 11, 1918	Exterminator	W. Knapp	Escoba	Viva America	70	8	14,700	2:10⁴⁄₅	Muddy
May 10, 1919	Sir Barton	J. Loftus	Billy Kelly	*Under Fire	75	12	20,825	2:09⁴⁄₅	Heavy
May 8, 1920	Paul Jones	T. Rice	Upset	On Watch	107	17	30,375	2:09	Slow
May 7, 1921	Behave Yourself	C. Thompson	Black Servant	Prudery	109	12	38,450	2:04¹⁄₅	Fast
May 13, 1922	Morvich	A. Johnson	Bet Mosie	John Finn	92	10	46,775	2:04³⁄₅	Fast
May 19, 1923	Zev	E. Sande	Martingale	Vigil	145	21	53,600	2:05²⁄₅	Fast
May 17, 1924	Black Gold	J. D. Mooney	Chilhowee	Beau Butler	152	19	52,775	2:05¹⁄₅	Fast
May 16, 1925	Flying Ebony	E. Sande	Captain Hal	Son of John	139	20	52,950	2:07³⁄₅	Sloppy
May 15, 1926	Bubbling Over	A. Johnson	Bagen baggage	Rock Man	164	13	50,075	2:03⁴⁄₅	Fast
May 14, 1927	Whiskery	L. McAtee	Osmand	Jock	162	15	51,000	2:06	Slow
May 19, 1928	Reigh Count	C. Lang	Misstep	Toro	196	22	55,375	2:10²⁄₅	Heavy
May 18, 1929	Clyde Van Dusen	L. McAtee	Naishapur	Panchio	159	21	53,950	2:10⁴⁄₅	Muddy
May 17, 1930	Gallant Fox	E. Sande	Gallant Knight	Ned O.	150	15	50,725	2:07³⁄₅	Good
May 16, 1931	Twenty Grand	C. Kurtsinger	Sweep All	Mate	130	12	48,725	2:01⁴⁄₅	Fast
May 7, 1932	Burgoo King	E. James	Economic	Stepenfetchit	115	20	52,350	2:05¹⁄₅	Fast
May 6, 1933	Brokers Tip	D. Meade	Head Play	Charley O.	118	13	48,925	2:06⁴⁄₅	Good
May 5, 1934	Cavalcade	M. Garner	Discovery	Agrarian	124	13	28,175	2:04	Fast
May 4, 1935	Omaha	W. Saunders	Roman Soldier	Whiskolo	110	18	39,525	2:05	Good
May 2, 1936	Bold Venture	I. Hanford	Brevity	Indian Broom	102	14	37,725	2:03³⁄₅	Fast
May 8, 1937	War Admiral	C. Kurtsinger	Pompoon	Reaping Reward	103	20	52,050	2:03¹⁄₅	Fast
May 7, 1938	Lawrin	E. Arcaro	Dauber	Can't Wait	103	10	47,050	2:04⁴⁄₅	Fast
May 6, 1939	Johnstown	J. Stout	Challedon	Heather Broom	115	8	46,350	2:03²⁄₅	Fast
May 4, 1940	Gallahadion	C. Bierman	Bimelech	Dit	127	8	60,150	2:05	Fast
May 3, 1941	Whirlaway	E. Arcaro	Staretor	Market Wise	112	11	61,275	2:01²⁄₅	Fast
May 2, 1942	Shut Out	W. Wright	Alsab	Valdina Orphan	150	15	64,225	2:04²⁄₅	Fast
May 1, 1943	Count Fleet	J. Longden	Blue Swords	Slide Rule	110	10	60,725	2:04	Fast
May 6, 1944	Pensive	C. McCreary	Broadcloth	Stir Up	148	16	64,675	2:04¹⁄₅	Good
June 9, 1945	Hoop Jr.	E. Arcaro	Pot O' Luck	Darby Dieppe	155	16	64,850	2:07	Muddy
May 4, 1946	Assault	W. Mehrtens	Spy Song	Hampden	149	17	96,400	2:06³⁄₅	Slow
May 3, 1947	Jet Pilot	E. Guerin	Phalanx	Faultless	135	13	92,160	2:06⁴⁄₅	Slow
May 1, 1948	Citation	E. Arcaro	Coaltown	My Request	109	6	83,400	2:05²⁄₅	Sloppy
May 7, 1949	Ponder	S. Brooks	Capot	Palestinian	113	14	91,600	2:04¹⁄₅	Fast
May 6, 1950	Middleground	W. Boland	Hill Prince	Mr. Trouble	134	14	92,650	2:01³⁄₅	Fast
May 5, 1951	Count Turf	C. McCreary	Royal Mustang	Ruhe	122	20	98,050	2:02³⁄₅	Fast
May 3, 1952	Hill Gail	E. Arcaro	Sub Fleet	Blue Man	167	16	96,300	2:01³⁄₅	Fast
May 2, 1953	Dark Star	H. Moreno	Native Dancer	Invigorator	137	11	90,050	2:02	Fast
May 1, 1954	Determine	R. York	Hasty Road	Hasseyampa	137	17	102,050	2:03	Fast

DATE	WINNER	JOCKEY	SECOND	THIRD	NOMINATIONS	STARTERS	NET TO WINNER	TIME	TRACK
May 7, 1955	Swaps	W. Shoemaker	Nashua	Summer Tan	125	10	108,400	2:01⅘	Fast
May 5, 1956	Needles	D. Erb	Fabius	Come On Red	169	17	123,450	2:03⅖	Fast
May 4, 1957	Iron Liege	B. Hartack	*Gallant Man	Round Table	133	9	107,950	2:02⅕	Fast
May 3, 1958	Tim Tam	I. Valenzuela	Lincoln Road	Noureddin	140	14	116,400	2:05	Muddy
May 2, 1959	*Tomy Lee	W. Shoemaker	Sword Dancer	First Landing	130	17	119,650	2:02⅕	Fast
May 7, 1960	Venetian Way	B. Hartack	Bally Ache	Victoria Park	142	13	114,850	2:02⅖	Good
May 6, 1961	Carry Back	J. Sellers	Crozier	Bass Clef	155	15	120,500	2:04	Good
May 5, 1962	Decidedly	B. Hartack	Roman Line	Ridan	139	15	119,650	2:00⅖	Fast
May 4, 1963	Chateaugay	B. Baeza	Never Bend	Candy Spots	138	9	108,900	2:01⅘	Fast
May 2, 1964	Northern Dancer	B. Hartack	Hill Rise	The Scoundrel	138	12	114,300	2:00	Fast
May 1, 1965	Lucky Debonair	W. Shoemaker	Dapper Dan	Tom Rolfe	130	11	112,000	2:01⅕	Fast
May 7, 1966	Kauai King	D. Brumfield	Advocator	Blue Skyer	150	15	120,500	2:02	Fast
May 6, 1967	Proud Clarion	B. Ussery	Barbs Delight	Damascus	162	14	119,700	2:00⅗	Fast
May 4, 1968	Forward Pass	I. Valenzuela	Francie's Hat	T. V. Commercial	191	14	122,600	2:02⅕	Fast
May 3, 1969	Majestic Prince	B. Hartack	Arts and Letters	Dike	187	8	113,200	2:01⅘	Fast
May 2, 1970	Dust Commander	M. Manganello	My Dad George	High Echelon	193	17	127,800	2:03⅖	Good
May 1, 1971	Canonero II	G. Avila	Jim French	Bold Reason	220	20	145,500	2:03⅕	Fast
May 6, 1972	Riva Ridge	R. Turcotte	No Le Hace	Hold Your Peace	258	16	140,300	2:01⅘	Fast
May 5, 1973	Secretariat	R. Turcotte	Sham	Our Native	218	13	155,050	1:59⅖	Fast
May 4, 1974	Cannonade	A. Cordero Jr.	Hudson County	Agitate	290	23	274,000	2:04	Fast
May 3, 1975	Foolish Pleasure	J. Vasquez	Avatar	Diabolo	246	15	209,600	2:02	Fast
May 1, 1976	Bold Forbes	A. Cordero Jr.	Honest Pleasure	Elocutionist	252	9	165,200	2:01⅗	Fast
May 7, 1977	Seattle Slew	J. Cruguet	Run Dusty Run	Sanhedrin	297	15	214,700	2:02⅕	Fast
May 6, 1978	Affirmed	S. Cauthen	Alydar	Believe It	319	11	186,900	2:01⅕	Fast
May 5, 1979	Spectacular Bid	R. Franklin	General Assembly	Golden Act	299	10	228,650	2:02⅖	Fast
May 3, 1980	Genuine Risk	J. Vasquez	Rumbo	Jaklin Klugman	293	13	250,550	2:02	Fast
May 2, 1981	Pleasant Colony	J. Velasquez	Woodchopper	Partez	432	21	317,200	2:02	Fast
May 1, 1982	Gato Del Sol	E. Delahoussaye	Laser Light	Reinvested	388	19	428,850	2:02⅖	Fast
May 7, 1983	Sunny's Halo	E. Delahoussaye	Desert Wine	Caveat	405	20	426,000	2:02⅕	Fast
May 5, 1984	Swale	L. Pincay Jr.	Coax Me Chad	At the Threshold	312	20	537,400	2:02⅖	Fast
May 4, 1985	Spend a Buck	A. Cordero Jr.	Stephan's Odyssey	Chief's Crown	359	13	406,800	2:00⅕	Fast
May 3, 1986	Ferdinand	W. Shoemaker	Bold Arrangement*	Broad Brush	452	16	609,400	2:02⅘	Fast
May 2, 1987	Alysheba	C. McCarron	Bet Twice	Avies Copy	422	17	618,600	2:03⅖	Fast
May 7, 1988	Winning Colors	G. Stevens	Forty Niner	Risen Star	401	17	611,200	2:02⅕	Fast
May 6, 1989	Sunday Silence	P. Valenzuela	Easy Goer	Awe Inspiring	394	15	574,200	2:05	Muddy
May 5 1990	Unbridled	C. Perret	Summer Squall	Pleasant Tap	348	15	581,000	2:02	Good
May 4, 1991	Strike the Gold	C. Antley	Best Pal	Mane Minister	377	16	655,800	2:03	Fast
May 2, 1992	Lil E. Tee	P. Day	Casual Lies	Dance Floor	407	18	724,800	2:03	Fast
May 1, 1993	Sea Hero	J. Bailey	Prairie Bayou	Wild Gale	367	19	735,900	2:02⅖	Fast
May 7, 1994	Go for Gin	C. McCarron	Strodes Creek	Blumin Affair	363	14	628,800	2:03⅗	Sloppy
May 6, 1995	Thunder Gulch	G. Stevens	Tejano Run	Timber Country	324	19	707,400	2:01⅕	Fast
May 4, 1996	Grindstone	J. Bailey	Cavonnier	Prince of Thieves	361	19	869,800	2:01	Fast
May 3, 1997	Silver Charm	G. Stevens	Captain Bodgit	Free House	388	13	700,000	2:02⅖	Fast

DATE	WINNER	JOCKEY	SECOND	THIRD	NOMINATIONS	STARTERS	NET TO WINNER	TIME	TRACK
May 2, 1998	Real Quiet	K. Desormeaux	Victory Gallop	Indian Charlie	390	15	738,800	2:02⅕	Fast
May 1, 1999	Charismatic	C. Antley	Menifee	Cat Thief	407	19	886,200	2:03⅕	Fast
May 6, 2000	Fusaichi Pegasus	K. Desormeaux	Aptitude	Impeachment	400	19	1,038,400	2:01	Fast
May 5, 2001	Monarchos	Jorge Chavez	Invisible Ink	Congaree	447	17	812,000	1:59.97	Fast
May 4, 2002	War Emblem	Victor Espinoza	Proud Citizen	Perfect Drift	417	18	1,875,000	2:01.13	Fast
May 3, 2003	Funny Cide	Jose Santos	Empire Maker	Peace Rules	454	16	800,200	2:01.19	Fast
May 1, 2004	Smarty Jones	Stewart Elliot	Lion Heart	Imperialism	434	18	5,854,800	2:04.06	Sloppy
May 7, 2005	Giacomo	Mike Smith	Closing Argument	Afleet Alex	358	20	2,399,600	2:02.75	Fast
May 6, 2006	Barbaro	Edgar Prado	Bluegrass Cat	Steppenwolfer	440	20	1,453,200	2:01.36	Fast